THE MANAGEMENT OF
SPORT
IN SOUTH AFRICA

ENDORSEMENTS

Finally, a resource offering in-depth and current information on Sport Management for the Sport Management student and all key actors working in the South African sport domain and beyond. With this textbook, you can shape learning with a deeper understanding of Sport Management, enrich your teaching, and incorporate authentic and meaningful discourse into your programme.

Professor C.J. Roux,
Associate Professor and former Head of Department:
Department of Sport and Movement Studies, University of Johannesburg

---

The broad scope of topics these specialists cover in their respective fields epitomises the complex, multi-disciplinary and multi-dimensional nature of Sport Management. These topics form the pillars of scientific and practical discourse, which relate in one way or another to sport and the management thereof. Each chapter of this book explains the principles of Sport Management and provides information on what every student or manager in the sport industry should know and apply.

Kobus van der Walt,
Former Director of TuksSport, University of Pretoria

A fresh approach to Sport Management that addresses both theoretical and practical implications for the unique South African context. The multi-dimensional and cross-disciplinary approaches put the athlete at the centre of management within the equity and transformational agenda of South African sport. Previously neglected roles such as safeguarding athletes and their career development is reaffirmed in the management agenda.

Professor Leon van Niekerk,
Professor of Sport Psychology, University of Fort Hare

The business of sport is changing at an incredible pace, in part because it has to continually adapt to a vast range of influences.

To keep sport interesting and alive at such a demanding time for participants and businesspeople alike, a quality management approach is of the utmost importance.

Whether a participant gets involved in sport to be a weekend warrior or to become an elite athlete, if there is no system and structure in place to empower equity and fairness in the experience, it will not cultivate growth and a future for the coming generations.

Finally, here is a handbook that is written for our lived experiences by expert authors in the field of Sport Management.

Waldo van Heerden,
Biokineticist, Strength and Conditioning Specialist and Owner of Waldo Athletic

At the 1996 Olympics in Atlanta, a black South African athlete walked out on the track, in awe! The crowd of 80,000 was shouting USA...USA... cheering Carl Lewis on to another gold. The sound vibrated in our chests. His words were, "Today I come to look at them, tomorrow they will look at me". He won a medal two days later.

South Africa's raw sporting talent and pure spirit must be nurtured with cultural understanding. This monumental book can guide coaches, scientists, or managers to create our own sport launching platform with passion!! Barefoot to perfection!

Dr Philda de Jager,
Sport Medical Services

Copyright © KR Publishing and Copyright © KR Publishing and Professor Wim Hollander & Dr Louis Nolte

All reasonable steps have been taken to ensure that the contents of this book do not, directly or indirectly, infringe any existing copyright of any third person and, further, that all quotations or extracts taken from any other publication or work have been appropriately acknowledged and referenced. The publisher, editors and printers take no responsibility for any copyright infringement committed by an author of this work.

Copyright subsists in this work. No part of this work may be reproduced in any form or by any means without the written consent of the publisher or the author.

While the publisher, editors and printers have taken all reasonable steps to ensure the accuracy of the contents of this work, they take no responsibility for any loss or damage suffered by any person as a result of that person relying on the information contained in this work.

First published in 2023.

ISBN: 978-1-86922-976-4
eISBN: 978-1-86922-977-1

Published by KR Publishing
Tel: (011) 706-6009
E-mail: orders@knowres.co.za
Website: www.kr.co.za

Typesetting, layout and design: Cia Joubert, cia@knowres.co.za
Cover design: Marlene De Lorme, marlene@knowres.co.za
Editing and proofreading: Jennifer Renton, jenniferrenton@live.co.za
Project management: Cia Joubert, cia@knowres.co.za

THE MANAGEMENT OF SPORT IN SOUTH AFRICA

Edited by
**Professor Wim Hollander
& Dr Louis Nolte**

2023

ACKNOWLEDGEMENTS

We want to acknowledge and thank the following people:

- Mr Gideon Sam, for writing the foreword of this book. Your kind and unique words are seen as an extension of the commitment you have shown to sport in South Africa for longer than we can remember. We appreciate and applaud your insight into, enthusiasm for, support of and commitment to, this book. Your energy is contagious and will move sport people to learn more about managing sport.

- Knowledge Resources (KR) Publishers, particularly Wilhelm Crous, for your immediate commitment and trust in the publication of this book. We know publishers make economic and emotional decisions. Thank you for bringing these two approaches together and for understanding and guiding us through this decision.

- All the authors, for your commitment and diligence to provide unique contributions of quality in your fields of expertise. Due to their sport and other commitments, we know that sport people are challenged for time. Despite these constraints, you performed as true gold medallists, writing informative and practical chapters that will benefit current and prospective managers in the delivery of sport in South Africa and abroad. We acknowledge and appreciate your unique contributions.

- To all our friends who supported the book with recommendations. It's great to have significant people in the academic and sporting world who are willing to write recommendations for such a book. This could only be done if proper understanding and trust were evident in the editors and authors. We thank you for your support and know that your recommendations will motivate people to learn more about the management of sport.

- Cia Joubert, for your dedicated and professional conduct during the birthing process of this book. Your calm and informed approach put us at ease during a process that could have been daunting. We were always aware that you could come at any time to our rescue if necessary, which made the process much easier than expected. Thank you for being there to listen and provide guidance when required.

- Louis, for challenging me about my legacy in sport management shortly before retirement. As you know, it took little time to convince me to compile and edit this textbook. Thank you for agreeing to join me as co-editor on this journey, for taking care of the administrative function, and for the numerous discussions and decisions we made after thorough deliberation. Your commitment, communication and support are appreciated.

- Prof Wim, for playing a significant role in my PhD, my first national and international research projects, and now the first book that I have written for and co-edited. Although you are retiring, your mentorship, guidance and long hours of discussions on the management of sport are truly appreciated and ensure that your legacy continues through the knowledge you have instilled in me, and through this book.

- Our wives, Mitzi and Suzanne, for your understanding when our thinking became too book-focused and our communication less and less. Thank you for listening when we talked and for your regular input and feedback when required. Thank you for being so kind in understanding our moments of silence and sometimes frustrations. We appreciate you and know you contributed to this book through your support and comments when consulted.

TABLE OF CONTENTS

LIST OF FIGURES iii
LIST OF TABLES iii
LIST OF CASE STUDIES iv
FOREWORD by Mr Gideon Sam, Former President SASCOC v
ABOUT THE EDITORS vi
ABOUT THE CONTRIBUTORS viii
PREFACE xvii

PART I: The Managerial Context of Sport 1

    Chapter 1: A Social Perspective on Sport by *Professor Wim Hollander* 2
    Chapter 2: Social Trends and the Management of Sport by
    Professor Wim Hollander 11
    Chapter 3: The Sport Industry by *Professor Wim Hollander* 21
    Chapter 4: Governance Structures in South African Sport by *Ms Ilhaam Groenewald & Dr Nana Adom-Aboagye* 29
    Chapter 5: Sport for Development and Peace (SDP): Global and Local Perspectives and Dynamics by *Professor Cora Burnett* 41
    Chapter 6: Sport, Recreation and Leisure by *Dr Natasha Janse van Rensburg* 55
    Chapter 7: Athlete Performance Pathways by *LJ van Zyl* 67
    Chapter 8: Disability Sport by *Alison Burchell* 81

PART II: The Management of Sport 104

    Chapter 9: Strategic Management of Sport by *Dr Louis Nolte* 105
    Chapter 10: Governance in Sport by *Professor Rian Cloete & Professor Jacques Faul* 125
    Chapter 11: Sport and the Law by *Professor Steve Cornelius* 139

    Human Resource Practices in Sport 157

    Chapter 12: Volunteerism in Sport by *Professor Paul Singh* 158
    Chapter 13: Athlete Practices in Sport by *Dr Leepile Motlhaolwa* 177
    Chapter 14: Coaches' Practices by *Professor Heather Morris-Eyton* 185
    Chapter 15: Technical Officiating in Sport by *Anneline Lewies* 191
    Chapter 16: Agents and Agency in Sport by *Johan van Gaalen* 207
    Chapter 17: Leadership in Sport by *Professor Jaques Faul* 219
    Chapter 18: Motivation in Sport by *Lyndon Ferns* 231
    Chapter 19: Mentorship in Sport by *Rosemary Bartlett* 243
    Chapter 20: Sport Marketing by *Tracy Bredin* 259
    Chapter 21: Sport Finance by *Reinette van Gaalen* 277
    Chapter 22: Sport Facility Management by *Professor Marié EM Young, Phindile E Mahlalela & Dr Teneille Venter* 291

Chapter 23: Sport Event Planning and Management by *Dr Willien Fourie* 305
Chapter 24: Monitoring, Evaluation and Impact Assessment in Sport by
Professor Wim Hollander & Professor Cora Burnett 323

PART III: Contemporary Issues and The Management of Sport 335

Chapter 25: Entrepreneurship and the Management of Sport by *Dr Louis Nolte* 336
Chapter 26: Technological Innovation in Sport by *Dr Louis Nolte* 345
Chapter 27: Corridors of Uncertainty: Cricket and Managing the Race to Transform by
Professor Aswin Desai 353
Chapter 28: Safeguarding and Protection: The Management of Safe and Inclusive Sport
by *Anneline Lewies & Dr Elizabeth Smith* 363
Chapter 29: Doping in Sport by *Professor Heather Morris-Eyton & Dr Amanda Claasen-Smithers* 387
Chapter 30: The Future of Sport Governance in South Africa by *Ms Ilhaam Groenewald & Dr Nana
Adom-Aboagye* 403

ABBREVIATIONS 410
ENDNOTES 412
INDEX 447

LIST OF FIGURES

Figure 3.1: Segments and Sectors of the Sport Industry 22
Figure 5.1: Defining Sport for Development 44
Figure 6.1: The Negotiation Model 65
Figure 7.1: South African Athlete Development Support Structures 69
Figure 7.2: Long-term Athlete Development Framework 72
Figure 9.1: Internal Structure of Motorsport South Africa 110
Figure 9.2: Hypothetical structure of Advent Sport Entertainment and Media (ASEM) 111
Figure 9.3: Hypothetical Matrix Design for AFL 112
Figure 9.4: Hypothetical Network Design for SSCN 113
Figure 9.5: Strategic Sport Management Process 114
Figure 9.6: Components of Strategy 115
Figure 9.7: Power-interest Matrix 120
Figure 13.1: Human Resources and Athlete Management Process 180
Figure 14.1: The South African Coaching Framework 186
Figure 14.2: Long-term Coach Development Model – Roles and Domains within which Coaches Operate 187
Figure 14.3: South African Sport for Life Model 189
Figure 21.1: Graphical Illustration of the Operating and Cash Conversion Cycles 282
Figure 21.2: Graphical Illustration of the Cost of Capital 283
Figure 24.1. Example Results Chain – Social Cohesion and Crime Reduction Policy Rationale for Increasing Participation in Sport 326
Figure 24.2: A Continuum of Data Collection Ranging from Informal to Formal Methods 332
Figure 25.1: Entrepreneurship Ecosystem 339
Figure 28.1: Signs of Abuse 374
Figure 29.1: Role of Players in the Fight Against Doping 389
Figure 29.2: IOC Consensus Statement Regarding Dietary Supplements and High-performance Athletes 398
Figure 30.1: The IOC's Risk and Assurance Governance Model 406

LIST OF TABLES

Table 1.1: Summary of Social Theories and Value to the Manager of Sport 9
Table 8.1: Medals Won by South Africa at Paralympic Games Post 1992 94
Table 8.2: Eligible Impairment Types and Descriptions 97
Table 19.1: Identified Themes, Categories and Sub-Categories 245

Table 20.1: Commercial Rights Matrix 264
Table 20.2: A Selection of International and South African Properties and their Rights Holders 267
Table 20.3: Measuring Techbank's Sponsorship Return on Objectives 273
Table 20.4: Measuring the Outputs of Techbank's Sponsorship Leverage Tactics 274
Table 22.1: Examples of Sport Facilities 295
Table 22.2: Components of the Sports Facility Feasibility Study 298
Table 22.3: Prominent Sport Stadiums in South Africa 300
Table 29.1: Type of Non-AAF ADRV Based on The Code Articles 390

LIST OF CASE STUDIES

Case Study: Nurturing Talent in South African Athletics 79
Case Study: Cricket South Africa 134
Case Study: Netball World Cup 2023 in South Africa: A case study 168
Case Study: SAFA Suspends Referees and Clubs for Match-fixing 204

FOREWORD

Mr Gideon Sam

Former President of the South African Sports Confederation and Olympic Committee (SASCOC), Vice President of the Commonwealth Games Federation (CGF) and member of Sub-Committees of the International Olympic Committee (IOC), the Association of National Olympic Committees and the Association of National Olympic Committees of Africa.

One of the best lessons I learned as a young person during the 1960s about the business of sport is that you must learn from experienced people who gained their knowledge and expertise through long hours volunteering in sport. Although a long and tiring process, these people know not only the dimensions of sport, but also the required attitudes to be successful.

However, if you want to be somebody in sport – an athlete, coach, administrator, marketer or any other role – here is a book to help you to learn all aspects of the management of sport. Each of the chapters, well written by sport practitioners, gives the reader a sound understanding of what is required in sport to make South Africa a WINNING NATION.

The great Madiba (Nelson Mandela) drew our attention to the power of sport. He was convinced that nothing could have a socialising impact like sport. We experienced it when Francois Pienaar lifted the Webb Ellis trophy, and years later, that feat was followed by Siya Kolisi. Those of us who experienced both epochs will testify that the social fabric of South Africa was changed forever. This book, amongst others, deals with sport as a social phenomenon, with all the chapters woven into a perfect picture of South African sport. In a way, no stone has been left unturned to bring to the fore what South African sport is all about. Issues that had South Africans hot under the collar were not spared. Transformation is one of those issues dealt with comprehensively throughout this book.

When everything has been said and done, coaches, technical officials, agents, athletes and lawmakers will all feel that the book was written with them in mind. Some readers will be attracted to chapters that deal with very important components of sport, such as monitoring and evaluating the performance of sport organisations, teams and others. These themes of sport must be understood and addressed because they inform and guide strategic planning, which is crucial in sport.

Any sport enthusiast who is striving to be at the top of their game will find the answers to their questions in this contribution by well-known sport people; you will be able to learn from the volunteers and academics that share their experiences in this book. My challenge to all prospective academics, students, stakeholders and commentators in sport is to take time off and engage with the ideas shared in this book. This is a complete revelation of sport, especially in South Africa, where many debates sought to unite South African society to be ONE NATION. Those who fought on both sides of the sport struggle for non-racial sport will be proud of the ideas shared in this book. Read, and learn; it will be worth your time.

ABOUT THE EDITORS

Professor Wim Hollander

Wim Hollander has been with the Rand Afrikaans University (RAU) and University of Johannesburg for 40 years. He is currently an emeritus professor in Sport Management from the Department of Sport and Movement Studies at the University of Johannesburg (UJ). In addition to being affiliated for 10 years to the Department of Teaching Science at RAU, he chaired the Department of Sport and Movement Studies for several years and served as Executive Director of UJ Sport for 10 years. His industry-related experiences relate to playing Craven Week, Transvaal u/20 and Senior Currie Cup rugby. He further served as coach, manager and convenor of selection committees for the UJ and Transvaal u/20 and u/21 and Golden Lions Currie Cup teams, as well as South African Universities u/20 and u/21 and the South African u/21 rugby teams.

Wim holds a BSc degree, Post Graduate Teachers Diploma (PGTD), BEd Hons, Master's in Education (MEd) and two doctorates, one in Education (DEd) and the other in Sport Management (DCom). He has undertaken sport-related research for the Commonwealth Games Federation (now Commonwealth Sport), England Sport, Australian Sports Commission, Department of Sport and Recreation (South Africa), South African Rugby Union, Netball South Africa and Golden Lions Rugby Union. Wim has supervised and co-supervised 38 master's and 16 doctoral students, published 48 articles in refereed journals, and acted as moderator and external examiner for various higher education institutions in South Africa as well as abroad. He has presented more than 46 papers at national and international conferences over the years, has published 47 reports on international, national and local impact studies, and has published seven chapters in books on the management of sport.

Wim can be contacted at: wim@impactbh.com.

Dr Louis Nolte

Louis Nolte has been with the University of Edinburgh since 2020. Previously, he worked at the University of Pretoria (UP), the University of Johannesburg (UJ) and the Tshwane University of Technology (TUT). He is currently a Teaching Fellow in Sport Policy and Management at the University of Edinburgh's Moray House School of Education and Sport and is the Education Director of the Scottish Centre for Olympic Research and Education (SCORE), which is situated within this School. His industry-related experiences include, among others, winning national judo titles in South Africa and the Student Africa Games, multiple Commonwealth Judo Championships, participating at the 2006 World University Judo Championships in South Korea and attaining a 5th Dan black belt in judo. He further served as coach and manager for various South African judo teams at the national and international levels, including the 2013 Kazan Summer Universiade. He was also the head coach and owner of PMA Judo and chaired various organisations including Tshwane Judo Association and USSA Judo.

Louis holds a degree in psychology, two honours degrees (Psychology and Human Movement Sciences), a Master's in Sport Science (MPhil) and a Doctorate in Sport Management (DPhil), and recently completed a Postgraduate Certificate in Academic Practice. He has undertaken sport-related research on the

Commonwealth Youth Games and Netball South Africa, while other research projects have focused on the management of elite judo systems, schools sport and volunteers in sport. Louis has supervised numerous master's students, published seven articles in refereed journals and acted as external examiner for higher education institutions in South Africa and abroad. He has also presented multiple papers at national and international conferences and is on the Editorial Board of the International Judo Federation's *Arts and Sciences Journal*.

Louis can be contacted at: louis.nolte@ed.ac.uk.

ABOUT THE CONTRIBUTORS

Dr Nana Adom-Aboagye

Nana Adom-Aboagye is currently the Head of the Centre for Sport Leadership at Maties Sport, at Stellenbosch University. She holds a PhD in Sport Management from the University of Johannesburg. Her areas of interest/specialisation relate to women and sport; persons with disabilities; sport for development; sport policy; and gender equity.

Nana can be contacted at: nadom-aboagye@sun.ac.za.

Rosemarie Bartlett

Rosemarie Bartlett, a senior equestrian coach and administrator, has worked at every level of coaching, competition and academic training in South Africa for over 40 years. Rosemarie founded the first nationally-accredited training academy in South Africa for riding, ethology and coaching, which offers tertiary courses on a full-time basis. She also oversaw the equestrian management of Pearl Valley and Val De Vie Equestrian Estates, some 100 stables in the highest-rated residential estate in South Africa. Part of her function was to uphold best practice in all equestrian activities, including tourism, professional training, polo competitions and more. She has held several senior equestrian posts, including National Master Judge (equitation), South African Equestrian Federation (SAEF) Lead Coach and Chairperson of the National Coaching Commission. Rosemarie holds the designation of National Coach Education Advisor and Master Coach with the Professional Body for SA Sport Coaches (SASCA). She also holds the international designation of Level 2 Coach with the Federation Equestre Internationale (FEI), and is qualified through the British Horse Society. In addition, Rosemarie completed her MSc with a focus on mentorship in sport. In her free time, Rosemarie enjoys nature, her family and travelling to her mother's hometown in Northern Italy.

Rosemarie can be contacted at: recacademy@gmail.com.

Tracy Bredin

Tracy Bredin has 20 years' marketing experience, a journey which started at MTN South Africa where she spent three years in the marketing department's product development team. Following time abroad in the USA and Australia, Tracy joined Octagon Marketing, where she was the lead strategist on MTN, Coca-Cola, Standard Bank, Engen, MasterCard and the 2010 FIFA World Cup campaigns for MTN and Kia/Hyundai. Currently, Tracy is the Head of Strategy at Playmakers Sponsorship, where her 11-year tenure has seen her develop creative sponsorship strategies across a range of sports for clients including Absa, DStv, KFC, Coca-Cola, Powerade and adidas. Her expertise includes research-led strategic insights, creative ideation, strategic sponsorship evaluation, property selection, rights evaluation and measurement and reporting.

Tracy's career highlights include working on the 2010 FIFA World Cup in her home country, South Africa, and being integral to the project that led to Playmakers becoming the first South African agency to win a Clio Sports award in New York.

Tracy can be contacted at: tracyb@playmakers.co.za.

Alison Burchell

Alison Burchell gained her bachelor's degree with majors in economics and industrial sociology from UCT. She has worked in sports administration and governance for all but 10 years of her career, with much of that in disability sport in South Africa and internationally. She has worked in South Africa, Switzerland, the UK, Fiji and the Solomon Islands, where she is currently the Chief Executive Officer of the Solomon Islands National Sports Council.

Alison cut her teeth in disability sport working for the National Paralympic Committee of SA, where she managed numerous disability sport teams, helped organise various events and led the establishment of Disability Sport SA as an inclusive disability sport organisation. This led to improved awareness of disability and sport and increased cooperation with disabled people's organisations. She also led the input on sport and recreation from South Africa into the UN Declaration on the Rights of Persons with Disabilities.

Alison has received awards in administration in squash from the former National Sports Council in SA, and has published an article in *The Commonwealth Health Ministers Reference Book 2006* titled, "The importance of sport to the disabled". She also co-authored an article in *Palaestra* on "The Athletic Ability Debate: Have we reached a tipping point?"

Alison can be contacted at: alison.burchell@outlook.com.

Professor Cora Burnett

Cora Burnett is a professor at the University of Johannesburg and Acting Director of the UJ Olympic Studies Centre. She holds doctorates in Human Movement Studies and Social Anthropology. She has published 170 peer-reviewed articles in research journals, and has written multiple chapters and books, including *Sport in Society: Issues and Controversies*, which she co-authored with Jay Coakley. She also co-designed the Sport in Development Impact Assessment Tool (SDIAT), which received international recognition and is used for impact assessments for multiple projects. Over the years she has undertaken collaborative research in 15 African countries, engaged in policy evaluation and development, and lectured internationally on SDP. She recently completed a regional research project for the African Union Sports Council (AUSC) Region 5 on gender equity. Currently she is engaged in a WADA-funded project with universities in the UK, Russia and Austria regarding effective interventions in anti-doping education. She co-developed the UN SDP toolkit and is currently assisting with the roll-out.

Cora can be contacted at: corab@uj.ac.za.

Dr Amanda Claassen-Smithers

Amanda Claassen-Smithers started her academic and professional journey with a BSc and BSc Honours in Dietetics (North-West University, South Africa), followed by a PhD in Sport Science and PG-Dip in Health Economics (University of Cape Town). After her PhD, she spent time doing sports nutrition consulting with recreational to elite-level athletes, as well as working in the public, government and private sectors, where applying the latest research and innovation within a real-life environment was a key feature of her roles. Amanda spent eight years as Education & Research Manager at the South African Institute for Drug-Free Sport (SAIDS, the National Anti-Doping Agency), and represented SAIDS as a member of the UNESCO Inter-Governmental Committee for Physical Education & Sport, South Africa. In 2021 she was invited to join the World Anti-Doping Agency (WADA) Global Learning & Development Framework Technical Working Group for Education, which was tasked with developing professional standards and training content for various audiences within the industry. She is also a member of the Africa Zone VI Regional Anti-Doping Organisation Technical Working Group for Education, where she assists with education strategy and programme development within the Zone VI region. Throughout her career she has remained involved with academic research and lecturing, and is always seeking opportunities for the co-creation of projects between industry and academia, ranging from health, nutrition and physical activity interventions, to anti-doping education and research projects. A member of the South African Sports Medicine Association EXCO, Amanda also recently joined the UCT Researcher Development Academy, where she is providing professional training to African researchers at all stages of their careers, whilst continuing her academic involvement at the UCT Health through Physical Activity, Lifestyle & Sport Research Unit.

Amanda can be contacted at: Amanda.Claassen-Smithers@uct.ac.za.

Professor Rian Cloete

Rian Cloete obtained BLC and LLB degrees from the University of Pretoria, while the University of South Africa (UNISA) conferred a doctoral degree on him in 2001. In 2014, Rian obtained his Master's Degree in International Sports Law and Practice from De Montfort University (DMU) in the United Kingdom. Rian was admitted as an attorney of the High Court of South Africa in 1992, after which he joined the Department of Procedural Law at the University of Pretoria. He rose to the rank of Professor in 2004 and has been the Head of the Department of Procedural Law since 2012.

Rian established the Centre for Sports and Entertainment Law at the University of Pretoria in 2002 and serves as Director. The mission of the Centre is to provide a centre of excellence in providing high quality services, research and programming to the sporting world at large. As a sports lawyer, he has advised and represented most sporting bodies in South Africa such as Cricket South Africa (CSA), Athletics South Africa (ASA), South African Rugby Union (SARU), Basketball SA, Boxing SA, Netball SA and the South African Institute for Drug-Free Sport (SAIDS).

Rian can be contacted at: Rian.Cloete@up.ac.za.

Professor Steve Cornelius

Steve Cornelius is a professor at the University of Pretoria, where he is Head of the Department of Private Law and Co-director of the Centre for Sports and Entertainment Law. Steve holds BJuris and LLB degrees from the University of South Africa and an LLD degree on the interpretation of contracts from the University of Pretoria. He is an Advocate of the High Court of South Africa, fellow of the Southern African Association of Arbitrators and member of the South African Academy of Science and Art. His fields of research focus on sports law and the law of obligations. Steve is also a member of the Independent Anti-Doping Hearing Panel, which was established in terms of the South African Institute for Drug-free Sport Act, and is part of a task team that is reviewing the current South African legislation and rules relating to doping in sport. Steve also serves on the independent hearing panel of Badminton World Federation and the Council on Anti-illegal Betting and Related Financial Crime of the Asian Racing Federation, as well as the Panel of Experts of the Canadian Sports Law and Governance Association.

Steve can be contacted at: steve.cornelius@up.ac.za.

Professor Ashwin Desai

Ashwin Desai is Professor of Sociology and the SARCHI Chair in Social Change at the University of Johannesburg. Among his latest books are *Wentworth*: *The Beautiful Game and the Making of Place* (winner of NIHSS for the best single authored book, 2021); *Reverse Sweep: A Story of South African Cricket Since Apartheid*; and most recently, the co-authored *Durban's Casbah: Bunny Chows, Bolsheviks and Bioscopes*. Ashwin's work is internationally celebrated for its courage and clarity of vision, and for its focus on the lived experience of oppression and resistance. Ashwin holds a MA Sociology (Rhodes University) and a PhD (Michigan State University), and was awarded with the USAF-NIHSS gold medal in the established researcher category.

Ashwin can be contacted at: agdesai@uj.ac.za.

Professor Jacques Faul

Jacques Faul is a well-known cricket administrator and has been a CEO in cricket for 20 years. During this time, he has consulted on behalf of the Cricket Council with members of the Council to provide strategic direction. Jacques is regarded as a turnaround specialist in sports and is credited with various successful turnaround strategies. His field of study includes stakeholder management, law and mega and major sporting events.

Jacques can be contacted at: jacquesf@cricket.co.za.

Lyndon Ferns

Lyndon Ferns is a retired Olympic gold medallist and former world record holder who swam for South Africa at the 2004 and 2008 Olympic Games. Lyndon holds a BSc Accounting degree from the University of Arizona and currently works as Divisional Chief Executive for CFAO Mobility, where he oversees multiple motor dealerships with a staff complement of around 400 employees. Lyndon has worked in the motor industry for numerous years, following his career as a professional athlete, while accumulating numerous OEM performance awards. Lyndon still serves on the board of directors for a number of sporting entities, and hosts motivational talks from time to time.

Lyndon can be contacted at: lferns@cfaomotors.co.za.

Dr Willien Fourie

Willien Fourie taught at the school level for six years before moving on to higher education, then left academia to become the Senior Sport Manager at the Higher Education Institution. In 2001, she returned to higher education as Programme Head: Sport Management at the Central University of Technology (CUT) until 2016, before lecturing in Tourism Management until her retirement in 2019. Willien represented the Western Province in Athletics on both the junior and senior levels, and obtained Senior GW Colours for Hockey. Her knowledge regarding event management developed in her roles as Manager of the Rest of South Africa, Junior Springbok and Springbok Athletics teams. She also managed the first SA Athletics team that went abroad in 1992 to Senegal. From 1992 to 2001, Willien managed the SA and SA Student teams to African Championships and Universiades, and was the media liaison officer for South Africa at the Beijing Universiade in 2011.

Willien holds a BA in Physical Education from the University of Stellenbosch, as well as a Higher Education Diploma, BA Hons from Free State University and a master's degree from Vista/CUT. She is completing her PhD in Education with the topic: The development of a track and field management manual for local organising committees in South Africa. She has delivered several papers locally and abroad, has written and reviewed numerous articles, and has written a book for event managers on planning. Willien has also received several awards, including Honorary Colours in Track and Field from the University of Stellenbosch, Springbok Colours, the Free State Sport Writers Award, the Durbanville Hills Trophy for Sport Administrator of the year and the Faculty of Management Sciences Teaching award.

Willien can be contacted at: ironlady@mweb.co.za.

Ilhaam Groenewald

Ilhaam Groenewald is currently the Maties Sport Chief Director and serves on a few representative boards and committees. Ilhaam joined Stellenbosch University in 2014 from the University of the Western Cape, where she held the position of Director of Sport Administration for more than a decade. Ilhaam is qualified with an Honours degree in Business Administration and a Master's Degree in Sports Management. At Stellenbosch University she is a representative on several committees, such as the Employment Equity Forum, Institutional Transformation Committee and Senate. She is currently enrolled for her PhD at Stellenbosch University. During 2016, Ilhaam became the first female Executive Council member for SA Rugby and has occupied various representative roles within the higher education sport environment. These have included, among others, Chairperson of the Heads of Sport Forum of South Africa, First Vice President and President of University Sport South Africa (USSA), Varsity Cup board member and a board member of the University Sports Company. She was also recently appointed to serve as a South African Sport Confederation & Olympic Committee (SASCOC) board member. She also acted as a judge for the Discovery Sport Industry awards from 2017 to 2020. She recently joined the United Coalition for Sport & Community-based Organisations (UCSCBO), which supports federations in highlighting key issues impacting the development of sport in the Western Cape.

Several special recognitions have included the University of the Western Cape Chancellor's Award in 2017, Stellenbosch University Chancellor's Award in 2022, and in 2019 she received the Ministerial Award by Sport & Recreation South Africa for her contribution towards sport in South Africa and breaking the boundaries with her leadership involvement in rugby.

Ilhaam can be contacted at: ilhaamgr@gmail.com.

Dr Natasha Janse van Rensburg

Natasha Janse van Rensburg is a lecturer at the University of Johannesburg's Department of Sport and Movement Studies. She is a specialist in sport and recreation, with a Master's Degree and PhD in Recreation Sciences. She also obtained an MBA from the NWU Business School in Potchefstroom. Natasha supervises postgraduate students, focusing on multi-disciplinary research in sport, recreation and other health-related fields. She loves the outdoors and enjoys spending time with her family.

Natasha can be contacted at: natashajvr@uj.ac.za.

Anneline Lewies

Anneline Lewies has a Master of Science in the Management of Technology and Innovation from the Da Vinci Institute for Technology Management. A part-time lecturer in Sport and Movement Studies in the Faculty of Health Sciences at the University of Johannesburg, she is also a facilitator, assessor and moderator for SASCOC, a National Coach Education Advisor for the South African Sports Coaching Association (SASCA), and an Education Officer for the South African Institute for Drug-free Sport (SAIDS). She also serves on the SASCA Board as Vice-Chairperson, is a member of SASCA's Education Panel for RPL and Designations, and assists several national federations, such as Lifesaving SA, as a consultant for coach education.

Anneline's primary research interests are focused on organisational behaviour, specifically women and children in sport and sport coach education. In 2022 she received the Top Achiever Award for Management of Technology in the Master of Science in Management of Technology and Innovations Degree from the The Da Vinci Institute for Technology Management

Anneline can be contacted at: anneline@wol.co.za.

Phindile Mahlalela

Phindile Engel Mahlalela is a HSRC-DSI Research Intern at the University of the Western Cape where she works as a research assistant providing administrative and academic support to both staff members and students within the Department of Sport, Recreation and Exercise Sciences. Phindile completed an Honours degree in Recreation and Leisure Studies and graduated cum laude with an Advanced Diploma in Sport Management from the University of Venda. She is a powerful force in the workplace and uses her positive attitude and tireless energy to bring out the best in others. Phindile is inspired to further her studies and explore more on sport, recreation, leisure and wellness. In her free time, Phindile likes to engage in volunteer work related to community development, hiking and learning coding languages.

Engel can be contacted at: nkosiengel@gmail.com.

Professor Heather Morris-Eyton

Heather Morris-Eyton is an associate professor in the Department of Sport and Movement Studies in the Faculty of Health Sciences at the University of Johannesburg. She has a DPhil (Sport Science) and lectures on both undergraduate and honours programmes. Her research focus is on sports coaching, anti-doping education as well as safeguarding in sport. She has been in academia for the past 20 years. Heather is also an anti-doping education officer for the South African Institute for Drug-Free Sport, where she conducts workshops and outreach programmes for schools and sports federations. She has been a national coach and team manager for various Lifesaving South Africa international competitions.

Heather can be contacted at: heatherm@uj.ac.za.

Dr Leepile Motlhaolwa

Leepile Motlhaolwa is a Programme Coordinator and Lecturer in the Higher Certificate in Sports Sciences and Bachelor of Education qualification in the Faculty of Education at the University of Pretoria. He holds a Bachelor of Sports Sciences degree, a Master's Degree in Human Movement Sciences from the University of Pretoria and a CIES-FIFA in Sports Management qualification from the International Centre for Sports Studies (CIES). Leepile also holds a PhD in Education; his research interests centre around physical education, rurality, youth development through sport and community development.

Leepile co-authored the toolkit: *Let's Get Moving Together! Empowering Future Leaders in International Grassroots Sport.* In his academic career, he has published in accredited scientific journals, contributed to book chapters, acted as a reviewer of scientific articles and books, and supervised postgraduate students at the University of Pretoria.

Leepile can be contacted at: Leepile.motlhaolwa@up.ac.za.

Professor Paul Singh

Paul Singh has had a 45-year-long involvement in the sport industry in South Africa and continues to engage in various regional, national and local sport initiatives, projects and research. He was the Chief Director of Sport at the National Department of Sport and Recreation from 2010 until 2017, and is a master facilitator and designer of learning programmes in sport and recreation. He has lectured on Sport Management and Recreation Management at the University of KwaZulu-Natal, the University of Pretoria, Rand Afrikaaans University, University of Johannesburg, University of Venda and Da Vinci Business School. Paul is an NRF-rated researcher who has published over 50 scientific articles in accredited journals. He also serves on the editorial boards of several scientific research journals, and is a member of several professional bodies. He has vast consulting and learning facilitation experience in the field of sport regarding team management, risk management, sports law, coaching, governance and ethics. He has supervised several master's and doctoral studies and is currently the head of the postgraduate programme at the Da Vinci Business School.

Paul can be contacted at: psby.singh@gmail.com.

Dr Elizabeth Smith

Elizabeth Smith is a specialist in Prior Learning Assessment and completed her D Litt et Phil at the University of Johannesburg in 2004. She also holds a Post Graduate Diploma in Industrial Education and Training from RMIT University (Australia), and a Certificate of Mastery in Prior Learning Assessment from the Council for Adult and Experiential Learning (CAEL) and De Paul University (USA). Between 2004 and 2014, Elizabeth held the position of RPL Specialist: Policies and Special Projects at the University of South Africa (UNISA), creating an RPL department and establishing UNISA as a leader at the forefront of RPL in South African higher education institutions. Elizabeth currently works as an RPL consultant, which has included creating an RPL infrastructure for SASCOC and developing policies, procedures, assessment tools, training sessions and training materials for 56 National Sports Federations.

Elizabeth has facilitated Prior Learning Assessment training workshops for a variety of target audiences across a spectrum of qualifications, including in Kenya, Swaziland, Botswana and Seychelles. She has developed RPL policy documents; conducted theoretical, practical and vocational assessments; examined two doctoral dissertations; and has served on nine national RPL committees, including: CTP, SAQA, Higher Education South Africa, the DoE RPL Task Team and SASCOC.

Elizabeth can be contact at: priorlearning@outlook.com.

Johan van Gaalen

Johan van Gaalen is an admitted attorney in South Africa who studied for a BCom LLB at the Rand Afrikaanse University (presently known as the University of Johannesburg) and an International Law Certificate at the University of Antwerp, Belgium. Johan has been a member of the FIFA Dispute Resolution Chamber since 2009 and is also a previous member of the FIFA Players Status Committee. Johan has been elected to the list of International Who's Who of Sport & Entertainment Lawyers since 2013 for being among the world's leading sport and entertainment lawyers.

Johan has published and presented on various topics and articles relating to sport over the years, including: *Who owns Sport Broadcasting Rights* (presented at the 10th International Congress of the International Association of Sports Law in Athens); *South Africa: Government interference in Sports Governance* (article published in the World Sports Law Reports); *Legal aspects in African football* (presented at the FIFPRO Lawyers Network Congress in Amsterdam); *Retrenchments of footballers* (the African Sports Law Journal); *Financial Unfair Play* (presented at the FIFPRO Lawyers Network Congress in Lisbon); and *The impact of Covid 19 on Football* (in a chapter on South African football).

Johan can be contacted at: johan@vangaalenlaw.co.za.

Reinette van Gaalen

Reinette van Gaalen is a lecturer at the Department of Accountancy at the University of Johannesburg. Reinette holds a M.Com Financial Management degree from the University of Johannesburg. Reinette lectures on Financial Management and Sport Finance and has played an active role in developing finance modules for the BCom International Accounting online qualification. She has supervised a number of master's students in the field of Financial Management and Sport Finance, and has been a reviewer for the *International Journal of Sport Finance* and the *Journal of Economic and Financial Sciences*. Reinette has also published and presented on various topics and articles relating to sport finance, including: *Factors affecting the value of South African rugby players* (presented at the FIFPRO Lawyers Network Congress in Amsterdam) and *The announcement impact of hosting the FIFA World Cup on host country stock markets* (presented and published in the conference proceedings of the 4th Economics & Finance Conference in London). Reinette is one of the authors of *Fundamentals of Finance: A practical guide to the world of finance* (LexisNexis). Reinette loves spending time with her family, especially on the tennis court.

Reinette can be contacted at: rvangaalen@uj.ac.za.

LJ van Zyl

It took LJ van Zyl nine years before he won his first major senior event and many more to be recognised as an elite athlete, which is why he understands the numerous challenges elite athletes encounter. As a three-time Olympian who also represented South Africa at various prestigious events from 2001, it became increasingly apparent to him that only some of the athletes with whom he had competed at a junior level had successfully transitioned to senior and elite sport. LJ is a lecturer and sports practical coordinator at the University of Pretoria in the Faculty of Education and completed a second master's degree in Olympic Studies at the German Sports University. He is currently busy with his PhD on career pathways of Olympic and Paralympic athletes beyond sport participation.

LJ can be contacted at: lj.vanzyl@up.ac.za.

Dr Teneille Venter

Teneille Venter is a lecturer and researcher at Cape Peninsula University of Technology (CPUT), Cape Town. Teneille graduated with her PhD (Doctorate of Philosophy), specialising in Sport and Exercise Science in 2022 at the University of the Western Cape (UWC). Teneille, as an emerging researcher, has published articles and working papers on sport and exercise science, physical education in schools and management in higher education institutions. She has an active role in dynamic international collaborative projects, both past and present. She believes much is gained from these projects globally for both academics and students. Teneille also focuses on community engagement projects, passionately serving communities through CPUT and in her private capacity. She is particularly focused on how students can interact, gain knowledge and experience, and improve local organisations. Teneille is active in her area of expertise as a registered biokineticist of the HPCSA and AIESEP member as a Young Researcher. Teneille is on her faculty Scientific review committee board and is also on the committees of community engagement, Teaching and Learning and Health and Safety. Teneille has a passion for encouraging active and healthy living for all.

Teneille can be contacted at: ventert@cput.ac.za.

Professor Marié Young

Marié Young is an Associate Professor in the Department of Sport, Recreation and Exercise Science at the University of the Western Cape. She has a D.Phil in Human Movement Science and lecturing experience of more than 20 years in the field of sport and recreation management. Marié holds several leadership roles at the University and is deemed an expert in her field. Her research interests, publications and conference presentations lie within sport, leisure, recreation and therapeutic recreation, promoting health and quality of life. She has published 29 peer-reviewed articles and three book chapters and policy briefs. She participates in interdepartmental and inter-institutional projects nationally and internationally, for which she has received grants and served as project leader. Marié serves on the Board and Executive Board of Directors for the World Leisure Organisation, and was recently appointed the Regional Editor for Africa for the *World Leisure Journal*. She has served as visiting professor at the University of Northern Iowa, Winston Salem State University and East Carolina University in the United States, as well as the LAB University of Applied Sciences, Finland.

Marié can be contacted at: myoung@uwc.ac.za.

PREFACE

The *Management of Sport in South Africa* is the first textbook written by multiple practitioners and academics with substantial sport management experience in South Africa. This provided the opportunity to publish a book that offers a variety of theoretical and practical insights into managing different sport environments within the South African context. A historical, transformational and futuristic perspective is woven throughout the book, providing a golden thread related to the uniqueness of the South African sport context. Discussions and examples mainly provide South African cases that further add to the value of this publication.

The book comprises three parts: **Part 1** focuses on the Managerial Context of Sport; **Part 2** on the Management of Sport; and **Part 3** on Contemporary Issues in the Management of Sport. Each chapter contributes to, and elaborates on, the focus of the Part under discussion. In **Part 1**, the first three chapters (A Social Perspective on Sport; Social Trends and the Management of Sport; The Sport Industry) are dedicated to understanding sport from a social theory perspective, sport-related trends established in society, and the sport industry as a social construct in society.

This is followed by a chapter that provides an understanding of the governance structures in South African sport. These structures play a pivotal role in regulating and managing various aspects of sport. Furthermore, the environments for sport participation encompass Sport for Development and Peace, Recreation and Leisure, Competitive and High-Performance Sports (through Performance Pathways), and Disability Sport.

Part 2 includes introductory chapters on Strategic Management, Governance, and the Legal Aspects of Sport in South Africa. These chapters set the scene for the operational aspects of the management of sport. Eight chapters are dedicated to human resource practices, including Volunteerism in Sport; Athlete, Coach and Technical Official practices; Agents and Agency; and Leadership, Motivation and Mentorship.

This part concludes with four further operational management chapters: Sport Marketing, Sport Finance, Sport Facility Management and Event Management, as well as a chapter that discusses Monitoring, Evaluation and Impact Assessment.

Part 3 addresses select issues related to the management of sport, such as Entrepreneurship, Technological Innovation, Transformation, Safeguarding and Protection, Doping, and Future Governance. These topics are contemporary given that the South African sport industry, as in the case of other countries, is challenged with these in the daily management of sport and recreation participation and therefore must be addressed.

PART I

THE MANAGERIAL CONTEXT OF SPORT

A SOCIAL PERSPECTIVE ON SPORT

Professor Wim Hollander

LEARNING OUTCOMES

At the end of this chapter, you should be able to:

1. Distinguish between the different social theories in describing society.
2. Discuss examples of sport-related events and/or processes that provide evidence of social theories in sport.
3. Explain the social theories in describing sport in South Africa.
4. Argue the value of social theories in describing sport in society.
5. Debate why the figurative or process theory could be seen as a culmination of all other social theories.

1.1 INTRODUCTION

The focus of this chapter is to provide managers with an understanding of the context of sport from a social perspective. The first question that comes to mind is: What is a social perspective? The second question is: Why is a social perspective relevant for the managers of sport? Gammelseater[1] described a social perspective as an approach to understanding human behaviour within its broader context; it is a way to know why people act in specific ways, as individuals, in a community, or in a society. Why do people do what they do? As sport participation is directly related to human behaviour, the study of sport from a social perspective could provide managers of sport with relevant information on people's behaviour in sport. This information could impact the planning, decision-making and implementation of sport programmes during management.

A social perspective on sport, therefore, creates an opportunity for the managers of sport to understand sport within the context of the manifestations of behaviours in society. To do this, it is imperative to understand different social theories that provide sport-related perspectives on the behaviour of society.

For this reason, some social theories will be discussed with specific reference to their interpretation within the context of sport and their implications for managers of sport.

1.2 SOCIAL THEORIES AND SPORT

During the 1970s, several sociologists, amongst them Max Weber, used the functional theory to research various questions in sport and society.[2] In reaction to this, the conflict theory of Karl Marx and others was formulated to describe the conflict in society.[3] Sociologists also use several forms of the critical theory to describe and understand the everyday realities of individuals, groups and communities in sport. Supporters of Eric Dunning study sport in light of the figurative theory that originated in the thoughts of Norbert Elias, a German sociologist, who claimed that life consists of a complex network of interdependent social structures.[4]

Each theory possesses unique characteristics that offer insights into the multi-dimensional image of sport in society. They further include the possibility that the complexity of sport could be described as a societal-related phenomenon. Within this context, it is necessary to investigate the following social theories to establish their value and impact on sport, and therefore, the management of sport.

1.2.1 Functional Theory

The functional theory presupposes that society is an organised system of interdependent parts constructed through people's communal values and processes of consensus. According to this theory, society's underlying motive is to balance the social system to be effective and functional. This balance is naturally achieved when groups unite, strive for communal values and command functional societal structures.[5] Two groups of researchers and approaches to the functional theory appear in the theoretical frameworks, known as the hard and soft forms. Whereas the hard theory allocates specific roles to people to benefit society, the soft approach focuses on the entirety of society. Both these theories postulate that order is a natural phenomenon in society brought about by both action and forms of behaviour. For example, Frey and Eitzen suggested that when action or forms of behaviour contribute to order in society, it is seen as functional. In contrast, it is seen as dysfunctional when it influences the social order negatively.[6] This approach presupposes that the functional theory negates conflict as a societal phenomenon.

According to Coakley, the functional theory requires four societal functions before it can be functional. First, there should be methods through which people could be educated in the social system's basic life rules and values.[7] As forced conformation to these rules and regulations could lead to frustration, opportunities should be developed for members of society to release stressful experiences.

According to this theory, sport could be utilised as a form of escapism for members of society from those frustrations experienced. For example, Roman festivals utilised 'participants' or 'outcasts' in battle-to-death events with lions and tigers while spectators were relieved from stress.[8] Today, members of society utilise gymnasiums, health programmes, fanatical spectatorship and participation in social and recreational sport and events to relieve the pressures of their work situations. The functional theory presupposes then that the social order of society could be repaired through sport and related activities, and that it could also create social control.

The second prerequisite for the effective functioning of a social system is that it should have mechanisms at its disposal to bring and bind people together and to establish integrated social relationships.[9] An example of this is that the achievements of the South African women's national soccer team (Banyana Banyana), the women's national cricket team and the Springbok rugby teams in the sporting arena are experienced by supporters as a personal victory or triumph. After capturing the 1995 Rugby World Cup trophy, late President Nelson Mandela thanked Francois Pienaar (rugby captain) by saying, *"Thank you for what you have done for South Africa".*[10] Through his words, the President wanted to show that the victory brought South African society together and united it, i.e., sport can bring about the conformation of communal norms and values.

Thirdly, methods should be used to educate people about society's political goals and ideologies to maintain the status quo.[11] With this, they must also be educated on how these goals could be obtained. For example, in English public schools, Physical Education was used during the previous century to develop an understanding of the body and character of learners, in line with the ideology of the particular community and society. This is evident where 'sport schools' in South Africa utilise sport to educate learners in sport spectatorship, positive ways to support their team, and acknowledging their opponent during and after game time. However, given the downscaling of Physical Education to a component of Life Orientation in public schools in South Africa during the 1990s, this subject now has a different purpose in society, i.e., the main focus is now on the development of self in society, social and environmental responsibility, democracy and human rights, careers and career choices and some physical education.

Lastly, the social system must have at its disposal mechanisms that can adapt to changes that may occur in society without disturbing the internal order of the system.[12] This, in turn, is related to the necessity that changes should take place progressively and evolutionarily. This requirement is in direct contrast with the conflict theory, which indicates that change occurs through revolution, and the figurative theory, which explains change from a historical perspective.

When the required processes for the effective functioning of the social system are studied, it is evident that the functional theory see them as the building blocks based on which the social order in the community is brought to pass and maintained. In this case, the role of sport and, in particular, the management of sport, is to use sport as an agent to bring about good order and the optimal functioning of society.[13] This should be done by ensuring that a positive relationship between participation in sport and the development of good character is made evident. With this, it is accepted that sport can, among other things, integrate groups, communities and societies socially; motivate participation and accomplishment; and serve as a medium to communicate ideology and values.

Within this context, the managers of sport should understand the essence and principles of the functional theory, its implications (both positive and negative), and the contribution that sport could make within the context of the requirements and needs of society. For example, sport could be managed as a vehicle towards character building, social hierarchy and communal values. The Sport Manager should also determine whether sport can contribute to the personal development of people, families and households, through which the preservation of the social order on all levels of society may be accomplished. Further examples are managing sport in such a way that it confirms the value of sport to relieve stress, contribute to educational goal accomplishment, create joyous social togetherness, and sustain health and fitness. The functional theory, therefore, contributes to the statements on the purpose of education and governments in various societies, in this case, through sport.

1.2.2 Conflict Theory

Unlike the functional theory, Coakley argued that the conflict theory does not assume that society is a stable system with interdependent parts, but rather that it comprises a continually changing set of relationships that exist because of inherent differences over economic interests.[14] Social order exists because certain people do not have equal access to resources, and they are subtly manipulated into accepting the ideologies and values (work and sport ethic) of the economically strong groups.[15] Winning and persistence are core ideologies of the conflict theory, focussing on indoctrination and the implementation of economic principles. This view of society presupposes that class relationships, systems or social stratification are the departure points.

Class relationships refer to the social process concerning power and how economic power is applied to favour the economically prosperous at the expense of the less privileged.[16] Research on class relationships focuses on change. For example, social stratification, based on ethnic groupings in society, focuses on maintaining stability and order in society.[17] This theory addresses a gap that exposes the functional theory, namely that societal inequalities cannot be the focus. The conflict theory creates the possibility that negative trends that form the essence of sport in society may be exposed.

The conflict theory is based on the Marxist theory of Karl Marx, who described his theory of change in the 19th century through conflict and economic power.[18] His theory is used as a departure point to describe events as they occur in the social lives of countries with capitalist economies. According to the conflict theory, sport is understood and formed through the structures of the economic community. This furthers the interests of the economically prosperous members of the community and is used as a medium to keep the working class focused and to avoid bringing about change in the social environment.

According to Coakley, workers in the industrial bureaucracy often do sophisticated and highly specialised work, which means that there are few challenges for these workers in the workplace.[19] The result is that they continuously search for activities that offer a combination of challenge and thrill-producing enjoyment. The result is that the workers in the market economy are subtly manipulated through effective marketing to satisfy their desire through the mass promotion of sports-related spectacles and the purchase of equipment, clothing and other goods.[20] Under these social circumstances, sport is seen as a popular commodity that could allow economically influential people to ensure and cement their societal position.[21] An example of this was Rupert Murdoch, who was called the world's most economically influential man in the 1990s, given his ownership of 29% of the global film and television industry, including the broadcasting rights for the Olympic Games.[22] Similarly, the owners of Coca-Cola and Visa have benefitted economically as transnational sponsors of the modern Olympic Games, while Budweiser, the sponsor of the FIFA World Cup, has the pouring rights in stadiums during matches. The reason for this is to increase their worldwide sales figures.

Similar examples exist in South Africa, with FNB as the title sponsor for the South African Rugby Union and Varsity Cup SA (a student rugby competition), and SPAR for Netball South Africa. Some brands in South

Africa are also involved through individual athlete sport sponsorships, such as adidas, Puma, Pepsi, Coca-Cola and Red Bull. An example is the South African athlete and world record holder in the 400 metres, Wade van Niekerk, who had a sponsorship with Audi cars and a net worth of R3 million in 2023.

Following the 'Packer Revolution' in the 1970s, cricket became professional in Britain, and post the 1995 Rugby World Cup, rugby professionalised in South Africa. South African rugby players, in particular, displayed power during their negotiations for exceptional contracts, with a players union being established to take care of the players' interests after South Africa won the World Cup.

The focus of the conflict theory in sport is, therefore, mainly on how sport could be used as a medium to bring about the power and favouring of elite groups in society. Themes that are commonly adhered to focus on how athletes see their bodies as objects to reach results and how sport can be used to manipulate people. The relationship between sport, nationalism and militarism, and the connection between sport, racism and sexism, are well known. Examples of this include the development of professional sport, globally and in South Africa, where participants (athletes/players/coaches/administrators/umpires/referees/sport scientists) are compensated for their 'work' and achievements. Similarly, corporate health programmes are utilising gymnasiums to increase the productivity of their employees.

The conflict theory points out stratification and power relationships, unequal access to sources in society, and that sport is seen as a way to maintain this imbalance. This demystifies the fundamental ideology of people with power in society. This results in the negative aspects of sport being pointed out and that radical change in the community and sport is propagated. In most cases, the conflict theory is used to further sport as a source of expression, physical health and creative energy. The conflict theory is thus used to highlight and condemn the exploitation of the have-nots in society.

Several related aspects can be identified in this theory. One of these is that sport and physical activity have become increasingly professional. In turn, this has contributed to a more scientific approach to sport, which has led to chasing achievements and records related to funding and sponsorships. As organised business has become increasingly involved in professional sport through sponsorships and broadcasting rights, the stratification of society in and through sport has become more evident.

In conclusion, the conflict theory is mainly used as an agent of transformation and change against the economic exploitation of participants and other parties interested in sport. Through this, the economic favouring and inequalities of sport in society are described and an attempt is made to expose the underlying ideologies that exploit workers. The conflict theory, therefore, offers managers of sport the opportunity to study and analyse sport from a market economy perspective. In this way, the ideologies underlying the economic systems in sport can be learned and considered by managers in sport.

1.2.3 Critical Theory

The critical theory deals with power within the context of people's social relationships. It comprises various approaches designed to discuss the source of power, functioning and movement in different situations and aspects of society.[23] The theory originates in humanity's involvement with reality to make people's lives more just and open to diversity. This supposes a focus on practical programmes such as transformation in the seeding and selection of teams to further equality, justice and openness in sport and society. The theory is implemented in order to oppose the political goals pursued to favour those with power.

Most researchers who use the critical theory as a point of departure attempt to describe the social order of society according to political conflict against economic power. Through this, people struggle for freedom in all sectors of society. Critical questions asked concern the rights of employees, women, people infected with HIV/Aids, people with disabilities and children.[24] In South Africa, the foci of the fundamental questions in sport include equal opportunities for participation for all groups in society, the role of women in sport management structures, the detrimental consequences of professional participation in sport, and many more.

The critical theory is increasingly used in the sociological study of sport as it offers the possibility of acknowledging the role of power in structuring sport. The trend that emerges from this should be seen in the context of a changing society. The basis of this theory presupposes that sport cannot be studied outside the context of historical and cultural existence, but that it is constantly structured by people to cope with the realities of everyday life. The result is that the position and role of sport will differ from society to society because the structures of societies differ.

Williams noted that hegemonic relationships could be seen as unequal power relationships in society and that people have the power to use sport as an agent of change in the structures of society.[25] A typical example is the role sport played in the isolation of the National Party (the governing party during the Apartheid period) to bring about political change in South Africa. Morgan argued that the theory of hegemony does not contribute to initiating change in society, but rather describes it.[26] However, it may be that the social construction of sport is continuous, regardless of whether it occurs naturally or because of manipulation. As society changes, the social relationships of sport within the community will change. It is, therefore, necessary to analyse the role of sport within the context of the historical and social development of communities.

Sport-related research based on the critical theory focuses on "why" certain forms of sport are practiced in communities and societies. For example, a specific research focus in the United States of America could be to identify the excellence of dominant forms of sport. Does this excellence relate to world records, financial income or ways of participation? In South Africa, meanwhile, questions on the meaning and source of "transformation" in sport could be explained using the critical theory. Answers could describe the manner of participation and management of sport in South Africa. The critical theory thus provides a framework to question and explain the characteristics of modern and postmodern elite sport.

The critical theory was designed as an instrument to study the functioning of society critically; it aims to understand, explain and initiate change in society. It presupposes answering questions about the role of sport in different communities, how sport opportunities differ from one community to another, and how sport could be changed to further the interests of all participants. The essence of the critical theory is that sport acts as an agent for change and other social relationships in communities.

A combination of the functional, conflict and critical theories may expose three different perspectives on trends of sport in society. For this reason, managers of sport should contextually understand trends, individually and in combination, to define, describe and consider their impact during the management process. First, however, in order to describe these trends according to their origins and nature, it is necessary to study the figurations in society as they have gradually developed.

1.2.4 Figurative or Process Theory

The figurative theory focuses on people's relationships in a social and historical context within society. People are, according to Dunning, part of a dynamic relationship or social network of structures in society.[27] Social networks are complex figurations or processes with interdependent links of power relationships in a community. Ten processes appear in society as an explanation of the process diagram of complex societies. Examples of these in the development of sport are globalisation, secularisation, bureaucratisation and industrialisation.[28] People create these processes or figurations, which can be distinguished but not separated.

The exposure of the complex processes or figurations as they appear in the historical world of people could be described as the figurative or technique approach in sociology. By describing the figurations of society, as they seemed historically and at present, managers of sport can understand the social structures that appear in society. A figurative theoretical framework offers the possibility to describe various complex processes and figurations of people in their interdependence within society. Only people can create these figurations, both consciously and unconsciously, to order their world. Through this, the world's complexity is structured in figurations that can be understood, living the reality of life. An example is that sport was created as a social construct or figuration, given that sport is understood as a phenomenon. Therefore, the study of sport as figuration, as it developed historically, could contribute to understanding sport's complexity and provide significant insight into the management of sport.

Where people create sport-related figurations in society, they will necessarily be connected with, and dependent upon, other figurations of society, such as globalisation, market segmentation, social stratification and commercialisation. Therefore, these figurations should also be described as societal trends that manifest in sport, which will, in turn, expose sport-related management approaches as they developed historically and will develop in the future.

The study of society, given the figurative theory, offers the manager of sport the opportunity to understand the figurations that judge the functioning of society. Through this, the figurations are described, and the development of the figurations is historically set, so that future figurations may be inferred and anticipated.

The figurative theory has at its disposal the possibility to study sport as a figuration from a historical perspective. In doing so, sports trends as they have developed historically could be exposed. By using the figurative theory in conjunction with the functional, conflict and critical theories to identify and describe sport-related trends, managers of sport could understand the development of sport and its management. This opens up the possibility that a combination of the theories could explain the complexity of the reality of sport in its essence and scope, and provide an opportunity to identify and describe sports trends as they manifested and still manifest.

The nature of the figurative theory is that it creates the possibility that the origin, soul and development of sport over time could be described phenomenally. The theory offers the opportunity to explain the current appearance of sport in its multitude of forms. This, in turn, provides a phenomenological view of sport's current and future appearances in its complexity. This presupposes that the figurative theory could be seen as a possible tool to expose the trends in sport as they have appeared in the past, as they appear now, and as they may appear in the future, thus providing the manager of sport with a tool to develop strategies to manage sport not only now, but also in the future.

Table 1.1: Summary of social theories and value to the manager of sport

	Functional Theory	**Conflict Theory**	**Critical Theory**	**Figurative Theory**
Suppositions in respect of the social order	Social order is based on consensus and social values, as well as interdependent systems.	Social order is based on coercion, exploitation and the subtle manipulation of individuals.	Social order is negotiated by people in the framework of historical powers, cultural ideologies and material circumstances of social life.	Social order consists of figurations that have been created and maintained historically by people.
Focus on the study of society	What are the essential parts of the structures of social systems? How do social systems function smoothly?	How is society divided and used? How do societies change and what can be done to bring about change?	How is social life created and recreated through social relationships and cultural practices? How could people become agents to change society to reach its full potential?	How have or are figurations being developed in society? How could figurations be used to structure and restructure society?
Conclusions about the sport-society relationship	Sport is a valuable social institution for the individual and society. Sport is seen as a source of inspiration on personal and social levels.	Sport is a distorted form of physical exercise that was developed through the needs of a capitalistic economic system.	Sport is a social construct that is created by social power and relationships. Sport is a cultural practice that can control, highlight and empower.	Sport is a historical development from figurations of human existence. Through understanding figurations, the development of sport can be anticipated.

	Functional Theory	**Conflict Theory**	**Critical Theory**	**Figurative Theory**
Value for the manager of sport	To what extent should sport contribute to the basic social needs of the community, such as recovering from stress, adaptation to new situations, fitness and health, time-out opportunities, social cohesion, etc.?	To what extent should sport delivery counter and/or mitigate control, estrangement, commercialism, sexism, racism and other social ills?	What should be included in sport in the community?

How should sport be defined and organised in society?

How should sport be related to the development of, and change in, society? | Which figurations of sport exist in society and what future figurations could develop?

To what extent could sport create, explain and develop figurations in society? |

1.3 CONCLUSION

In conclusion, it could be stated that the figurative theory, in combination with the functional, conflict and critical theories, offers managers of sport the opportunity to study sport and physical activity as they have been practiced and managed historically, as they are currently practiced and managed, and as they will possibly be practiced and managed in the future. This could describe historical, current and future sports trends.

An approach to viewing sport as it manifests in society opens up the possibility that managers of sport could identify and describe trends in sport in society that could influence sport as a phenomenon. This presupposes that sport could be understood as a figuration of society. In addition, sport could be analysed in combination with the functional, conflict, critical and figurative theories, utilising the phenomenological method to identify sports trends that could, directly and indirectly, impact how sport is managed in society. A sociological and context-sensitive management approach will influence how sport can and should be addressed.

SELF-ASSESSMENT

1. Distinguish between the different social theories in the understanding of society.
2. Discuss examples of sport-related events and/or processes linked to the different social theories.
3. Argue the value of social theories in describing sport in society.
4. Explain the social theories in describing sport in South Africa.
5. Debate why the figurative or process theory could be seen as a culmination of all the other social theories.

SOCIAL TRENDS AND THE MANAGEMENT OF SPORT

Professor Wim Hollander

LEARNING OUTCOMES

At the end of this chapter, you should be able to:

1. Describe social trends in society that relate to sport.
2. Provide a historical perspective on the trends in sport in society.
3. Explain sport in society utilising historical and trend perspectives.
4. Debate how trends in society impact the management of sport.

2.1 INTRODUCTION

The previous chapter provided a social perspective on sport. This chapter will focus on trends as they manifest in society, particularly those that have impacted, and are still impacting, sport. These trends derive from the various social theories discussed in the previous chapter, however society brings about these trends, not the formally structured sport industry. Several trends such as demystification, institutionalisation, globalisation, professionalisation, commercialisation, market segmentation and embodiment appear in society and are also evident in sport. Some of these will be discussed in the following paragraphs.

2.2 TRENDS IMPACTING THE MANAGEMENT OF SPORT

The identification and description of trends impacting the management of sport require questions to be answered regarding the nature, character and application of sport management as a field of study as it developed historically and may develop in the future. For example, one trend that has appeared in sport from the earliest times and still appears today is that sport was, and still is, manipulated for political, commercial and other reasons. Identifying and understanding these reasons will provide a Sport Manager with a broader perspective of sport as a phenomenon.

Trends in sport should be studied in relation to the theories discussed in the previous chapter, for example, the professionalisation of sport could be seen as linked to the conflict theory perspective, as commercial opportunities are provided to those who own, participate in and utilise sport for commercial reasons to the detriment of others. Another example is that institutionalisation and globalisation could be studied from the perspective of the figurative theory, which presupposes that society is a compilation of figurations. It is argued that where sport appears as an integrated figuration of society, trends that occur in society will also be found in sport. When sports trends are collectively exposed according to the theories, it offers the possibility that sport could be studied in its complex entirety, including the management of sport as it developed over time.[1]

2.2.1 Manipulation

Since the earliest times, people have used and manipulated sport and related activities to reach specific goals. Although the conflict and critical theories are used in the study of manipulation as a trend, in most cases, they directly relate to the functional value of sport, regardless of its nature. In this way, sport was utilised during the years of Apartheid in South Africa by the government (National Party) to keep Black citizens out of White social structures, while the African National Congress (ANC) used sport to regain the rightful place of Black people in society. In this context, sport structures, such as the South African Council of Sports (SACOS) and the South African Sports Association (SASA), used sport to force the government of the day to grant the Black population in South Africa their rightful, equal and democratic place in the political, social, religious and economic systems of society. This was pursued by establishing a sport moratorium, where the international sporting community prohibited the predominantly White South African sportspeople and teams from competing abroad.

After the ANC came to power as the ruling party in 1994, sport and physical activity were seen as a 'vehicle' to address the inequalities of the past through the initial use of the Reconstruction and Development Programme (RDP). Solomon Morewa of the South African Soccer Football Association (SAFA) was quoted by Miller in the *London Times* as saying: *"We in sport see ourselves as transforming society; we are what society is. Soccer in South Africa is the most cross-cultural activity in the country, embracing everybody."*[2]

To address inequalities, sport in South Africa was initially divided into three umbrella structures: the Department of Sport and Recreation, the National Council for Sport and the Olympic Committee of South Africa, each of which had their own unique goals.[3] These structures were seen as vehicles to take participation in sport to the masses, to identify and develop potential elite athletes, and to win medals for South Africa.

Sport is, therefore, amongst others, manipulated by politicians to promote their ideologies. An example of this in South Africa is transformation in sport (participation, technical officiating, administration), where the composition of sport teams at the school, local, national and international levels must contain a specified number of participants from the previously disadvantaged population. The obligation placed on coaches to have players from this group in national sport teams is a further example of how people who were historically disadvantaged could take their rightful place in the local, national and global sport world. Here it is expected that 'chance-poor learners' and community members are included in sport teams to address the past's inequalities and injustices, which could build unity and cohesion in a diverse population.[4]

In South Africa, sport organisations and the general public are convinced that sport can serve as a medium to bring diverse groups together, in particular when winning global competitions such as World Cups and other sport events.[5] The triumphs of the 1995, 2007 and 2019 Rugby World Cups, as well as the 1996 Men's Soccer Africa Cup of Nations, the 2022 Women's Soccer Africa Cup of Nations, and reaching the semi-finals of the 2023 International Cricket Council (ICC) Women's T20 World Cup, amongst others, are examples where it is believed that sport is uniting South Africa as a nation. Winning is seen as a joint accomplishment of the South African population, uniting all diverse groups into one nation as winners.

Another example of the manipulation of sport lies within education and training. Historically, Physical Education was seen by governments, and in particular the South African government during the Apartheid period, as an essential component of the school curriculum. It was and is still believed that developing the physical ability of learners and educating them to understand their bodies will positively impact their learning processes. In South Africa, Physical Education was incorporated in 2002 as a component of the Life Orientation programme, which placed less emphasis on the physical development of learners and more focus on equipping learners with the *"knowledge, skills and values necessary for self-fulfilment and meaningful participation in society as citizens in a free country".*[6] This resulted in a decline in physical activity as part of the South African school curriculum as well as sport participation at schools. Schools that recognise the opportunity to develop their marketing strategy through sport (known as sport schools) manipulate sport differently. They use school sport not only as a marketing instrument, but also believe that sport participation and the support of fellow athletes contribute to learners' motivational levels and education.

From the above, it is clear that sport has been manipulated throughout the centuries to reach various societal objectives. Sport in ancient times was, and still is, used by political groups and economically prosperous individuals for their benefit. However, this phenomenon could be debated from the conflict theory perspective as it manifests in different forms in South Africa.

Manipulation is a trend in society when sport forms part of the political world, as it is accepted that sport always plays a political role in society. This political role of sport should be determined and understood by all participants of sport, in particular the managers of sport. The manipulation of sport could be emphasised politically, where governments believe that athletes and teams winning gold medals at the Olympics and World Cups epitomises good governance of governments. They also believe this may influence nation-building, so sport is manipulated to benefit politicians and their ideologies.

Lastly, entrepreneurship as a trend established itself in sport due to it being used for economic purposes. Examples are the manufacturing and sales of sport goods and the marketing and presentation of health and well-being as a product of gymnasiums to attract members and professional sport teams that participate nationally and internationally. This phenomenon has resulted in business people increasingly reaching the fore in the sports world to promote their economic interests.

Sport managers should be aware that people can manipulate sport for several reasons, which could simultaneously be positive and negative. For example, when sport and physical activity are used to enhance the health of people through gymnasiums, trail runs, cycling and other sporting events (functional theory), the managers of sport should always be aware that the underlying reason for these could be harmful (conflict theory) if they manipulate the situation to generate exorbitant sums of money from people and exclude those who cannot afford such events. Therefore, Sport Managers should understand the context of sport and physical activity in order to distinguish between the actual value of programmes and events from the perspective of manipulating sport.

The manipulation of sport is a precursor for institutionalisation as a trend. As sport is manipulated for one reason or another, it is placed in structures to control activities more efficiently. This is because the goal of manipulation determines the structure in which sport is manipulated.

2.2.2 Institutionalisation

Organised, competitive sport, as it is known today, has its direct origin in industrialisation and the social constructs of people that arose during the industrial revolution.[7] Although it is difficult to link the start of the industrial revolution to one specific event, it was characterised by the development of factories, the mass production of consumer goods, and increased dependency on technology. This phenomenon resulted in people increasingly having time at their disposal to take part in leisure activities. As a result, sport became more popular and competitions began.

During the late 19th and early 20th centuries, a growing focus on the governance and control of sport in American communities was observed. As a result, sport and other activities were placed in a communally organised structure in the form of clubs.[8] Sport club membership was restricted to reasonably prosperous people and after-school learners, while external funding was used to develop and deliver competitions. These competitions drew spectators from all social classes, benefiting the presenters financially. This trend was also seen in South Africa and Europe (especially England), with England regarded as the birthplace of modern sport.

As sport began to be used to contribute to economies and communities, it increasingly received support for participation across all levels of diversified societies. This resulted in sport being practiced on the assumption that it was a societal need requiring control on a more organised and structured basis.[9] Sport clubs were created to allow participants to participate for recreational purposes or with a focus on achievement (winning). As sport was being managed on a more structured basis, economically prosperous citizens increasingly focused on achievement, which led to the development of amateur sport. Middle- and lower-class citizens, meanwhile, continued participating in sport mainly for financial gain. This led to an increase in the number of participants in sport, as people saw an opportunity to earn an income from it. However, it should be evident that sport participation was not limited to elite athletes, but was also practiced for recreation and relaxation.

As participation in sport gained enhanced status and became more globalised with a growing field for competitive events, its rules were standardised internationally.[10] International sport bodies were created to coordinate the international structures of the sport by setting out specific requirements for affiliation and participation.

The structuring and institutionalisation of sport brought about the need for the general public to control sport facilities, meetings and clubs. As products of that era, various potential occupational fields and occupationally-oriented tasks came to the fore. Participants were trained, facilities were built and maintained, meetings and recreational activities were institutionalised, and sport and recreational activities were reported on by the media, while equipment was manufactured and sold. Not all of these tasks were performed on a formal basis within specific occupations, thus many were done during people's spare time as volunteers.

2.2.3 Professionalisation

As sport activities became more structured, they cemented the class systems in Europe, the United States of America (USA) and Canada.[11] Elite clubs emphasised attaining performance achievements in sport, an orientation that later led to amateurism. The concept of 'amateur' was finally applied as a medium through which the working class was prevented from participating in sport meetings with the elite. This aspect brings critical and conflict theories to the fore. Through this, there was an attempt to maintain social stratification in the community to protect the participation interests of elite citizens in sport.[12] The sporting activities of the working class thus focused more on sport-related religious meetings and commercialised sport. This combination eventually led to the professionalisation of sport because the working class could get additional benefits, apart from wages, from their participation in sport.

By 1920, sport in the USA had developed to the extent that the desire to generate money had led to tertiary educational institutions marketing spectator sports professionally. The more prominent forms of sport demonstrated unique characteristics of aggression and dominance to generate maximum profits, promote patriotism and establish national loyalties. Emphasis was placed on competition, winning and setting records to promote the commercial interests of sport. Control structures for professional sport were formed, and an association for sport at tertiary educational institutions was founded.[13] Several other national sport associations were founded, such as Olympic Committees, mainly due to the potential economic value for financially prosperous people and the political advantages for politicians of the participating countries.

At this stage, large stadiums and clubhouses began to be built at universities in the USA with taxpayers' money. Sport became seen as a means of marketing universities, and cultural imperialism came to the fore. Countries supported each other financially to ensure that competition in sport could occur so that the ideology of politicians could be promoted through it. Examples include the Union of Soviet Socialist Republics (USSR), the USA and England, which promoted imperialism as a global ideology. In addition, private ownership of sports, such as baseball in the USA and soccer in South Africa in later years, followed, with professional sport clubs being established that provided job opportunities to athletes, coaches and managers. At the same time, the newspapers reported on sensational sport happenings to increase their circulation figures. The radio, and in the 1970s, television, also brought sport into the houses of South African spectators.[14]

Athletes became the primary focus of interest in many schools and training institutions such as universities and colleges, as they were recruited to form part of institutions' sports programmes to contribute to their marketing plans. This trend led to students' bodies being seen as a commodity. In this regard, Donnelly referred to the ethical dilemma of recruiting so-called 'sport workers' to market institutions and their programmes.[15] To what extent is it ethical to expose children to sport employment in professional sport?

In addition, coaching became a specialised technical profession, and coaches were employed to maintain the winning records of teams and individuals.[16] In this way, the management of teams moved away from the players to the coaches, managers, owners and administrative staff. Principles of scientific management were used to teach coaching strategies, and athletes were trained professionally and used physicians and training specialists to improve their results. Following the debate on 'genetic engineering' in the 1990s, medicine became more institutionalised due to professionalisation. This trend became a requirement in the early 20th century to push sportspeople to their limits. Sport physicians, physiotherapists, biokineticists, psychologists and coaches started to play an increasingly important role in professional sport in the 1980s,[17] as they were created to promote sports participation and achievement.

Coakley pointed out that the rules of various kinds of sport were standardised nationally and internationally, making sport a global commodity.[18] This ensured that international competitions could be held, particularly as air travel became an everyday event. Television and other media, such as the Internet, email and social media, changed sport into a product that was accessible to all. The result was that Sport Managers could offer greater exposure to athletes and potential sponsors, eventually leading to the commercialisation of sport.[19]

The development of sport as an industry stimulated by commercialisation resulted in the growth of related occupations. For example, spectators who undertake trips abroad to attend international sporting events or meetings give the tourism industry an opportunity to compile sport-related travel packages. De Knop and Standeven specifically indicated that sport tourism is a direct result of the professionalisation of sport.[20] Several occupations have their origins in this domain, for example, sport tour leaders, sport tourism marketers, sport tourism consultants and sport holiday programme and facilities managers. Within the context of the development of the sport tourism sector, several cities compete with each other to host mega events such as the Olympic Games, the Rugby World Cup, the FIFA World Cup and the Commonwealth Games because of the economic advantages offered. As infrastructure is created, cities are marketed and the tourism industry attracts more clients. Additionally, spectator-related occupations flourish, such as radio commentators, television presenters, bookies and reporters.

Apart from the developments mentioned above in the sport industry, professionalisation and the development of occupations have contributed to the scientification of sport. Furthermore, as competition and sports achievements demanded more from participants, research increasingly undertook to further achievements scientifically. The scientification of sport has also contributed to the creation of scientific fields such as Sport Psychology, Sport Sociology, Sport Management, Sport Science, Biokinetics, Sport Communication, Sport Law and Facilities and Event Management.[21] In the 1960s, the first academic journals in Sport Sociology and Sport Management were published, proving that sport became increasingly scientific at this time.

It is clear that as the practice of sport became increasingly formalised and professional, various occupational fields developed during the early 20th century. Examples of this include professional participants such as athletes, coaches, team managers and administrators; sport media workers such as reporters and commentators; sport-related medical workers such as training specialists, biokineticists, optometrists, orthopaedic surgeons, physiotherapists and sport psychologists; sporting goods manufacturers and salespeople; marketers of sport and sport-related products; as well as educational and training specialists who present education and training in the field of sport.

In conclusion, sport became increasingly diversified in the 1920s due to the needs of various groupings in society.

2.2.4 Segmentation

After the Second World War (post-1945), society diversified even further as more effective production technologies and marketing techniques allowed the business community to develop products for a more sophisticated target market. This situation enabled products to be designed for specific users in their unique circumstances, known as the segmentation of products.

Two trends interacted with segmentation: a move towards an information-driven society (demystification) and decentralisation. Consumers became increasingly informed through different mediums available on the market (marketing communication), while the production and distribution of products were decentralised. This also meant that transnational companies could not only distribute products worldwide, but that sport could obtain transnational sponsors to finance participation, while companies could do their marketing simultaneously. When information is readily available, it influences the production of goods and services as consumers increasingly demand them, eventually leading to a trend of personification.[22]

The trend of segmentation in sport mainly has its origins in the ideological orientation of modern society, namely equal opportunities and fair competition for all, which can be related to the critical theory. Segmentation in sport can be described in numerous ways. Primarily, it presupposes that different kinds or forms of sports are offered to multiple societal participants. Examples of this are that the rules for the same type of sport are adapted for different age groups and sexes to fulfil the specific needs of the participants, e.g., mini-soccer in the Netherlands accommodates a smaller number of players.[23] The rules for school rugby also differ from those for adults, while older players use an adapted form of school rugby. Similarly, Rugby 7s was developed as another form of rugby that draws different kinds of players and spectators. There are also four international forms of rugby, namely "Rugby Union", "Rugby League", "Australian Rules" and the American "Gridiron". The rules of each are not only adapted to accommodate the needs of the participants, but also to attract large crowds to the matches.[24]

Spectators and supporters are divided into market segments: those who watch games at a stadium, those who watch television, and those who read about players and matches in papers and journals. Market segmentation has contributed to the increasing emergence of marketers and merchants in sport and sport-related products.[25] This trend implies that new sport products are continuously designed, manufactured and marketed. Apart from the contribution of the industrial revolution to the structuring, professionalisation and segmentation of sport, another direct result of the technological development of society has been demystification.

2.2.5 Demystification

Demystification and scientification as trends in society are related to the information revolution. The capacity to spread and gather information in greater volume and in an easily understood format in the community presupposes that information is more accessible to more people.

The phenomenon of demystification could be attributed to three related developments in society. In the first instance, reductions in the price of computers made personal computer technology affordable for many,[26] although home computers are still less common in developing countries. Secondly, sufficient computer programmes became available for use in most workplace and sport situations such as administrative, financial and governance packages. Finally, the value of telecommunication as a carrier and distributor of information had exceptional possibilities.

These advances meant that people who had traditionally been the only ones to have access to professional information found themselves increasingly in a position where their clients could easily access the same information, as well as use the opinions of experienced people as a sounding board for decision-making. This trend also had an impact on the practice of sport. In the first instance, the role of the trainer changed, as participants, especially at the professional level, could easily access relevant information. Training also increasingly became a process of consultation, culminating in a consensus decision. The role of the trainer thus changed from being the person with the required knowledge and expertise to coach, to one who has to manage people. Readily available information also led to a trend in which individuals could increasingly manage their training through distance education and telematic training.

Demystification also led to the scientification of sport. Information could be gathered from electronic media, books and magazines, leading to an increased number of people studying sport. In this situation, sport users became increasingly informed about the practice of sport. Demystification further influenced the role of journalists, television commentators, web managers and web commentators in sport reporting, not only in terms of changing technology, but also in terms of their technical knowledge of sport. This trend directly impacted higher education, the medical profession and many other professions where a learner should ideally be trained before they access information and analyse and interpret data. As information becomes more available and obtainable, the more people self-medicate, self-educate and self-train.

2.3 CONCLUSION

Identifying and describing sports trends as figurations of society is possible; examples include demystification, market segmentation and embodiment, institutionalisation, globalisation, professionalisation and commercialisation, all of which developed over time. These trends, and many others not discussed in this chapter, such as the global migration of athletes, coaches and administrators, provide managers of sport with an understanding of contextual information in light of the continuous development of sport in society. Sport managers should thus be sensitive to existing and developing global and local trends to manage societal sports environments effectively.

SELF-ASSESSMENT

1. Argue the value of a historical perspective to describe global societal trends.
2. Provide a historical perspective on the trends in global society.
3. Explain sport in society utilising historical and trend perspectives.
4. Debate how trends in society impact the management of sport.

THE SPORT INDUSTRY

Professor Wim Hollander

LEARNING OUTCOMES

At the end of this chapter, you should be able to:

1. Define the different segments and sectors of the sport industry.
2. Relate the segments and sectors of the sport industry to societal trends.
3. Debate the social theories about the segments and sectors of the sport industry.
4. Describe the South African sport industry by using relevant examples.
5. Describe the roles and responsibilities of Sport Managers in the sectors of the sport industry.

3.1 INTRODUCTION

To describe the structure of sport in an industry, it is necessary to relate the social theories discussed in Chapter 1 with the trends and related jobs in sport addressed in Chapter 2. This provides an opportunity to identify and describe the segments and sectors of the sport industry. The question arises: What are segments and sectors, and how are they linked to define the sport industry?

Segments refer to the larger sections of the sport industry that distinguish themselves from each other by providing a unique set of products and services to consumers. Sectors refer to subdivisions of segments that can be grouped based on providing related products to consumers as defined by the segment. Segments can be constituted by multiple sectors, depending on the economically viable associated groups of products and services delivered to consumers. Sectors, therefore, suppose related products and services that are clustered scientifically as segments, while at the same time significantly distinguishing one from the other.

3.2 SEGMENTS AND SECTORS OF THE SPORT INDUSTRY

During the late 1980s and early 1990s, researchers tried to define the structure of sport in society.[1] Some identified five areas of sport, namely state-based sport, regional and local sport associations, commercial organisers of sport, public sector sport and sport agencies.[2] De Sensi, Kelly, Blanton and Beitel, meanwhile, identified six sectors of the sport industry as post-school sport, private sport clubs, university sport clubs, professional sport, and state and volunteer sport agencies.[3] Kjeldsen concluded that students studying sport management access jobs in six sectors of the sport industry: higher education institutions, professional sport, facility management, marketing, school sport and sport agencies.[4]

The similarities among these sectors are higher education institutions, professional sport, sport agencies and sport in the public sector. Professional sport in this context is defined as full-time participation in sport and related activities as a professional, i.e., earning an income through sport participation. On the other hand, public and state sport refers to sport and related activities on an amateur basis, with the objectives of enjoyment, leisure, health and well-being, and competition. In this case, the participants do not earn any money from a sport or its related activities.

Hollander described the sectors of the sport industry from a social perspective, grouping sport-related occupations separately from discussions on sport as a social phenomenon and related trends in society.[5] These occupation groups imply structuring segments and related sectors in the sport industry. In Figure 3.1 below, the segments and sectors of the sports industry are indicated. The purpose is to provide a total view of the industry as it exists in society, and in this case, globally and within the South African context.

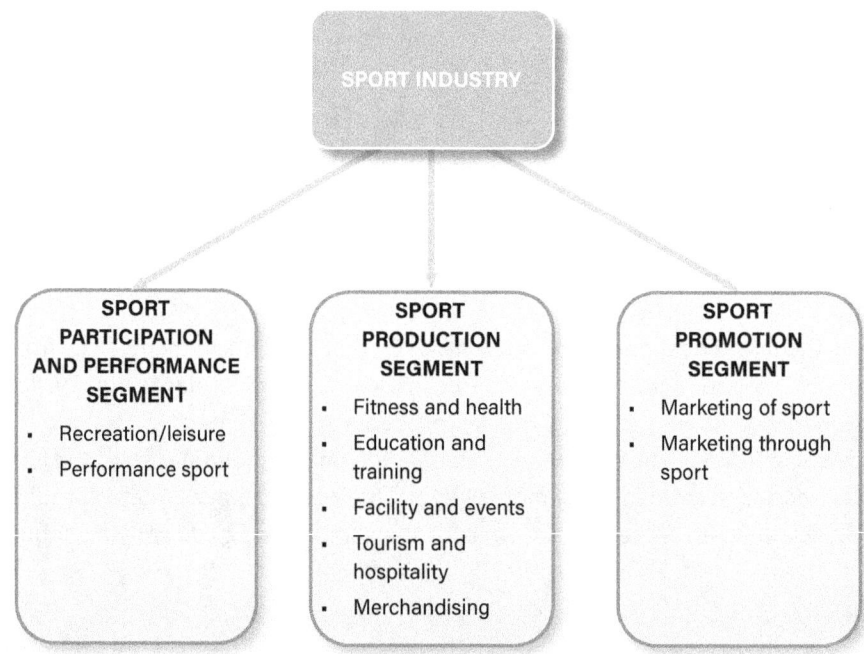

Figure 3.1: Segments and sectors of the sport industry

Parks, Zanger and Quarterman argued that the sport industry could be divided into three broad segments utilising the concepts of the type of products, services and consumers.[6] These are sport participation and performance, sport production and sport promotion segments. The sport participation and performance segment implies that professional or amateur participants are involved in sport and physical activity directly or indirectly. Such participants include athletes, coaches, sport scientists, officials, referees, umpires, volunteers, supporters, spectators, the media and sponsors.[7]

The sport production segment relates to the products required to influence, create and present sport and recreation participation opportunities.[8] Five sectors shape the sport production segment: sporting goods, education and training, recreation and tourism, event and facilities, and fitness and health.

The third segment of the sport industry is the sport promotion segment. This segment is seen as the processes utilised to market sport as a product or where companies market their products through sport.[9] When products are marketed through sport, companies are involved in sports sponsorships, promotional products, activation events, etc.

3.2.1 Sport Participation and Performance Segment

The sport participation segment of the sport industry constitutes all sport and recreational participation designed and delivered by people and organisations, such as sport and recreational clubs. Participation could be on different levels: club, regional, provincial, national and international. Participation could also be for social, recreational and leisure purposes, at competitive and elite levels, and on an amateur or professional basis. In South Africa, amateur and professional sport participation after 1994 was positioned under the management of the National Sports Council (NSC), the National Olympic Committee of South Africa (NOCSA) and the Department of Sport and Recreation (DSR). All sport clubs and National Sport Federations, amateur and professional, were obliged to affiliate with the NSC. This was done to merge the separate sport federations (Black, White, Indian and Coloured) developed during Apartheid into one structure. Amongst others, this enhanced the development of sport in South Africa and contributed to identifying elite athletes who could win medals in various international sporting competitions.[10] These sport structures were replaced by the Department of Arts, Culture and Sport (governmental structure) and the South African Sport Confederation and Olympic Committee (SASCOC), which oversee sport delivery in South Africa (see Chapter 4).

The sport participation and performance segment of the sport industry further constitutes primary, secondary and tertiary consumers. For example, athletes are seen as primary consumers as they participate in sport-related activities or events. Referees, umpires, supporters, spectators and administrators are secondary consumers as they provide an enabling environment for the primary consumer to participate. Tertiary consumers consist of the media, sponsors and others that report on and support primary and secondary consumers in one way or another. Primary consumers either participate as amateurs or sports professionals to achieve specific goals. Amateur participants mainly focus on the enjoyment of sport and physical activity at a cost, while professionals participate for remuneration.[11]

Members of the management committees of sports clubs or enterprises are defined as secondary consumers of sport and recreation as they manage the environment to deliver sport participation services.[12] Members of the management plan, develop and deliver sport and related activities to primary consumers in a structured and formal way.[13] This implies, amongst others, the recruitment of members for a sport club, as well as managing the finances, facilities, equipment, events, competitions, coaches and players of a club. Through management, sport organisations develop opportunities for primary consumers to consume sport and related services. This function of sport clubs is undertaken jointly with regional, national and international sport federations.

Similarly, sport medical services are seen as secondary consumers of the sport participation and performance segment. This category of consumers is linked to a broad spectrum of clinical and scientific knowledge and sports-related competencies. Examples are the physical and psychological preparation and rehabilitation of athletes. This includes exercise scientists, biokineticists, sport psychologists, optometrists and orthopaedic surgeons. As sport adopts a more scientific approach, the increased involvement of sport medical support is utilised to improve and sustain sport performance.

Besides those providing sport medical services to athletes, coaches, referees and umpires are also considered secondary sport consumers. Coaches are secondary consumers whose primary function is to ensure the consistent performances of athletes and sports teams. As coaches become more professional, the coaching function becomes more scientific.[14] In addition to their coaching knowledge and experience, coaches are increasingly required to gain scientific knowledge through educational programmes. Furthermore, they use specialised support, such as sports medicine practitioners, exercise scientists, sport psychologists, dieticians and others, to prepare athletes and teams (see scientification in Chapter 2). This approach to coaching is increasingly being researched as managing multiple experts in the coaching setup requires people to manage and coordinate this highly scientific environment.

Lastly, referees and umpires are also seen as secondary consumers of sport. With them, it is easier to stage sport matches and competitions. Moreover, referees and umpires are knowledgeable people who are central to the production of games as they have the knowledge and competence to interpret rules and manage risks of injury during play, as well as indirectly influencing the experiences of supporters and spectators at competitions and events. It is therefore required that umpires and referees continuously do in-service training on the development of rules and regulations in sport, as well as the application of such knowledge.

Media officials such as reporters, commentators and announcers are seen as tertiary consumers of the sport participation and performance segment of the sport industry. They contribute to the publicity of sport through their reporting and commentary, as well as add value to the globalisation of sport through broadcasting sport events and competitions (see Chapter 2). Because the media has a significant interest in sport, information is distributed locally, regionally, nationally and globally through electronic and printed media. Sport organisations use the media to market sport and enhance publicity, and utilise exposure to television to motivate sponsors to get involved in sponsoring competitions, events and sport organisations. In this context, local, regional, national and international sponsors such as Coca-Cola, Visa, Panasonic, Samsung and other international organisations sponsor the Olympic Games. Spar, Discovery and Vitality are sponsoring Netball South Africa (NSA) and the 2023 Netball World Cup hosted by NSA in Cape Town, while Nike is the apparel sponsor of the South African Rugby Union (SARU).

Over time, sport media became an integral part of the sport industry as it developed public interest in professional sport with global sport competitions. This resulted in increased circulation figures of papers and sport journals. The symbiotic relationship between the media and sport provides benefits to both.

For sport organisations, media exposure provides them with access to sponsorships, while television broadcasters increase their viewer numbers.

In conclusion, the sport participation and performance segment of the sport industry includes all sport structures, such as clubs and confederations, which deliver sport to communities on different levels (club, regional, provincial, national and international) to primary, secondary and tertiary consumers. Each of these consumer groups presupposes they are involved in one way or another in consuming sport products and services. For example, athletes participate as primary consumers, while coaches, sport medical staff, referees and umpires, and events and competition managers participate as secondary consumers. In turn, the sport media and sponsors participate as tertiary consumers.

The second segment of the sport industry is the sport production segment. This segment presupposes that sporting goods or participation opportunities and activities, as discussed above, are structured for the members of communities to utilise during their free time.

3.2.2 Sport Production Segment

The sport production segment is comprised of five sectors: sporting goods, events and facilities, education and training, recreation and tourism, and fitness and health. These sectors deliver sports clothing and equipment, as well as the production of sport and recreational participation opportunities.[15] For example, utilising sport facilities and equipment could contribute to the structuring of sport events that provide participation opportunities to consumers. For example, a local athletics club without an athletic track and equipment, such as hurdles and high jump equipment, must rent or agree with owners on the use of facilities and equipment to deliver their athletics programme. This could be the local municipality or a facility owner of a private organisation. Similarly, the Rugby World Cup is offered in a host country, understanding that the host will provide all required facilities for the event. Within this context, education and training as a sector of the sport industry could provide sport communities with educated and qualified coaches, managers of sport, umpires, referees and sport scientists, who could provide unique services to communities and society as a whole.

3.2.2.1 Sporting goods sector

The sporting goods sector of the sport industry focuses on the design, manufacturing, marketing and sale of sport clothing and equipment. Design and manufacturing are highly technical and expensive, so the sporting goods sector is a significant component of the sports industry. Examples of sport brands that design and manufacture sporting goods are Nike, adidas, Puma, Asics, New Balance and Reebok. At the same time, various companies distribute these in South Africa, such as Fitness Solutions, Decathlon, Sportsmans Warehouse, Totalsports and SportSA. During the development and manufacturing of sporting goods, traders add to the performance levels of athletes and teams and gain economic benefits through this initiative.

With required entrepreneurship, traders and sport organisations could gain financial benefits as registered logos of sport clubs and organisations could be printed or embroidered on clothing for which royalties could be accrued.[16] Through this, branding of sport organisations becomes not only a financial benefit but also a marketing tool to establish the brands of these organisations. For example, the logos of Kaizer

Chiefs, Sundowns, Pirates, Blue Bulls, Lions and Stormers, as well as universities such as the University of Pretoria (UP), the University of Johannesburg (UJ), and Stellenbosch University (US), are well-established in South Africa through branded clothing.

3.2.2.2 *Events and facility sector*

According to Hollander, the events and facility sector focuses on effectively managing and delivering sport events and facilities for primary, secondary and tertiary consumers.[17] The management of facilities relates to the design, construction, maintenance and utilisation of facilities to provide safe and secure participation environments for sport. Facilities such as sport stadiums, indoor sport centres and multi-sport facilities provide opportunities to stage sport events. Event management, on the other hand, includes the design, development and presentation of sport participation opportunities to athletes in the form of events and competitions according to the requirements of the particular sport. As an example, in order to provide a hockey event, numerous activities would constitute the delivery of such an event such as the marketing of the event, sales of tickets, and the provision of security, parking, ablution facilities, food and beverages and others.

3.2.2.3 *Recreation and sport tourism sector*

The combination of recreation and sport tourism as a sector implies the availability and consumption of recreational programmes, such as golf, being part of a supporters group to attend sport competitions and events abroad, or attending the Netball World Cup in 2023 in Cape Town while hiking around Table Mountain. These and other activities could be described as sports tourism. In this case, sport tourism refers to activities such as outdoor adventure camps, walking trails and attending environmental health programmes, primarily providing supporters of touring sports teams with positive or recreational experiences. Recreation managers typically manage these programmes and activities.

The recreation and tourism sector supposes that participation in sport and other physical activity results in positive tourism and sport experiences. Here, consumers use tourism-related recreational sports such as golfing tours and supporters tours for sports teams touring distant venues.

3.2.2.4 *Education and training sector*

The education and training sector of the sport industry relates to all sport and recreation-related education and training. For example, it could be teachers educating learners at school about the theoretical and practical aspects of sport and recreation and the value of continuous sport participation to ensure lifelong sport and recreational participation. It could also be seen as sport coaches acquiring the finer nuances of coaching different age groups according to their developmental needs. In addition, it could be a student completing a formal qualification in sport management, exercise and coaching science, physiotherapy, or any sport-related qualification at a higher education institution.

South Africa's education and training sector is divided into formal and informal structures. Where schools, universities, Technikons and colleges form the formal educational component, education and training are sometimes provided through informal structures and programmes. Examples are national sport federations that offer training such as coaching and administration programmes. These are seen as informal as they are not registered with the South African Qualifications Authority on the National Qualifications Framework

(NQF), a national education and training requirement in South Africa. This poses a problem in establishing the quality of such training programmes. In addition, the competence and expertise within and amongst sport federations differ, which could impact the consistency and quality of training in the South African sport industry.

This situation has changed as the South African Qualifications Authority (SAQA) requires that all education and training programmes are registered to ensure quality curricula and effective delivery.[18] For this purpose, sport structures such as the South African Sport Confederation and Olympic Committee (SASCOC) formed an essential component in structuring a professional board for sport coaches, providing a qualification structure for coaches aligned with the requirements and accreditation by SAQA. In addition, universities use the developed required standards for curricula in structuring coaches' training programmes on behalf of SASCOC.

3.2.2.5 *Fitness and health sector*

Fitness and health in today's context focus on raising awareness and activating the community to embrace a healthy lifestyle. This sector's origin lies in people's self-motivation to live healthily and secure a longer life expectancy.[19] As work environments changed from being active to more passive with longer working hours, a need developed amongst the population for after-work and weekend physical activity. As these needs increased, gymnasiums were built, health clubs were developed and after-work-hours exercise programmes were developed. This was done to ensure the increased availability of facilities and opportunities to live healthier lives in changed working environments. Examples of health programmes in South Africa are the Integrated School Health Programme, which contributes to the health and well-being of learners in schools, as well as Run Walk For Life, FitSlim 2022, Virgin Active, Brasilfeit South Africa, Pro Active Imports cc and Crossfit CFM.

In conclusion, the sport promotion segment of the sport industry can be described as the segment that mainly focuses on the enabling of sport and recreation participation through the education and training of consumers of sport, the production of sport events and activities utilising facilities, the manufacture and distribution of sport clothing and equipment, and the development and presentation of fitness and health as well as recreational programmes.

3.2.3 Sport Promotion Segment

The sport promotion segment originated in demystification and globalisation as societal trends (see Chapter 2). This segment refers to all activities related to the marketing of sport services such as events, facilities and programmes, and the marketing of products such as sports equipment, clothing and shoes through sport. These two activities form the core of this segment. As sport organisations become more professional due to access to funding through television rights, sport has increasingly become more visible to supporters and spectators. In turn, brands such as Nike, adidas, Asics and others utilised the sport environment to market their products through sport sponsorships, naming rights, athlete sponsors and others. From this, the sport marketing sector is identifiable when analysing sport promotion as a segment.

3.2.3.1 *Sport marketing sector*

The trend of segmentation (see Chapter 2) in sport shows a close link to marketing. This sector presupposes that consumers of sport are introduced to sport products and services in various ways. Hence, sports managers continuously market sports events, competitions and activities to consumers through utilising marketing agencies or television, papers, journals and electronic media as marketing mediums. This is known as the marketing of sport.

A second significant and beneficial marketing instrument in sport is organisations utilising sport as a medium for marketing their products and brands. Examples include organisations marketing single and multiple sport events, leagues or competitions through shared sponsorship. Another is high-profile players being sponsored to endorse clothing manufacturers or products for companies such as Nike, adidas and Puma. Sometimes, motor vehicle companies (e.g., Toyota or Mercedes Benz) sponsor teams or sports personalities. Further, organisations market their brands or products through organisational and team endorsement and nonspecific sport use. Finally, examples of corporate endorsements include sport organisations endorsing brands through naming rights negotiations, such as DHL Stormers and Toyota Cheetahs, or sports facilities, such as the FNB stadium and Coca-Cola Park. In addition, these sponsorships and endorsements offer an opportunity to sport organisations and leagues to negotiate broadcasting rights from television companies.

Irrespective of the product that is being marketed, various marketing activities are required. Examples are that market research should be undertaken, a marketing plan should be developed, the sport product or service should be developed, and promotion opportunities should be planned and implemented. After the planning and implementation processes have been concluded, the marketer should implement and monitor the impact of the marketing plan.

3.3 CONCLUSION

In conclusion, three segments constitute the sport industry: sport participation and performance, production and promotion. Each segment includes one or more sectors. For example, the sport participation and performance segment constitutes the sport consumers sector, consisting of primary, secondary and tertiary consumers. The sport production segment includes the sporting goods, events and facilities, education and training, recreation and tourism, and fitness and health sectors. Finally, the sport promotion segment constitutes the sport marketing sector that includes the marketing of sport and products related to sport.

SELF-ASSESSMENT

1. Define the different segments and sectors of the sport industry.
2. Relate the segments and sectors of the sport industry to societal trends.
3. Debate the social theories concerning the segments and sectors of the sport industry.
4. Describe the South African sport industry by using relevant examples.
5. Describe the roles and responsibilities of Sport Managers in the sectors of the sport industry.

GOVERNANCE STRUCTURES IN SOUTH AFRICAN SPORT

Ilhaam Groenewald & Dr Nana Adom-Aboagye

LEARNING OUTCOMES

At the end of this chapter, you should be able to:

1. Discuss South Africa's complicated sport history.
2. Debate how and why South African sport bodies are structured the way that they are at present.
3. Explain the need for transformation in South African sport.
4. Argue the need for governance structures in South African sport.

4.1 INTRODUCTION

South Africans are passionate about, and avidly participate in, sport and recreational activities. However, due to Apartheid, the history of governance structures in South African sport became closely intertwined with the country's complex socio-political landscape. This segregation had a profound impact on the way that sport in South Africa was structured post-democracy. Following the end of Apartheid in the 1990s, efforts were made to transform the country's governance structures and promote inclusivity. Transformation and equity remained focal points in developing governance structures in South African sport, aiming to address historical imbalances and foster a more inclusive sporting landscape. This chapter provides a concise overview of how and why South African sport was restructured.

4.2 HISTORICAL OVERVIEW

This section provides an insight into Apartheid's effect on sport, specifically its political influence and impact on South African sport. Following Apartheid, South Africa transitioned to a democracy, leading to the restructuring of sport bodies and a new way of governance for local sport, which is still experienced today.

4.2.1 South African Sport – A Brief History

Apartheid policies and the racial segregation of sporting facilities and leagues profoundly impacted sport in South Africa, especially between 1948 and 1979. This meant that Black (non-White) athletes, coaches, technical officials and administrators were excluded from participating in many sports domestically, and were denied opportunities to compete at the highest levels. As a result, many talented Black athletes could not reach their full potential and missed out on opportunities to represent South Africa. On the other hand, Whites could freely participate in any sport of their choosing and enjoyed the use of world-class facilities. This, whilst Blacks were restricted to specific sports such as football, boxing and athletics (track and field), with no or limited access to inadequate and often ill-equipped facilities.[1] Due to the advantages afforded to White South African athletes, South Africa collected more than 50 Olympic medals before its suspension from the Olympic Games in 1964. This suspension was due to the continued discrimination and racial segregation brought about by the Apartheid government.

The 1960s signified an era of well-organised domestic and international political resistance, led by the Supreme Council for Sport in Africa. South Africa's exclusion from major international competitions was led by political pressure from anti-Apartheid activists within South Africa and abroad, which led to a moratorium on rebel sport tours.[2] Despite South Africa's exclusion from international competition, groups of sporting individuals (usually cricket and rugby players) often attempted to compete in South Africa and vice versa. This often led to the proposed tours (when found out) being cancelled and, at times, individuals receiving bans within their home nations and internationally.[3;4] At the time, the organisations involved in the sports-based protest saw sport as a vehicle with several possible uses, aiming to eradicate Apartheid. What was required to harness sport-based protest into an effective force was a central force (unified action) that would act as a point of reference for the different forms of action against South Africa – international economic, financial and cultural sanctions.[5] The role of Dr Sam Ramsamy, executive chairperson of the South African Non-Racial Olympic Committee (SAN-ROC) from 1976 to 1991, can be argued as being the most active and effective in the development and expansion of the profile of sport-based protest, after the establishment of SAN-ROC in 1962 as a domestic pressure group. SAN-ROC's original mandate was to force the International Olympic Committee (IOC) to recognise that the all-White South African National Olympic Committee (SANOC) was unrepresentative of the South African population.[6]

Political leadership continued to play an essential role in supporting economic boycotts (such as bans on imports, travel and investments) against South Africa,[7] impacting sport and leading to punitive measures against sporting codes such as rugby and cricket – mainly due to their representation only including Whites.[8] On the other hand, sport stakeholders such as the IOC, the Commonwealth Games Federation (CGF) and the International Amateur Athletics Federation (IAAF) (now World Athletics) were all mobilised to support the boycotts to demonstrate their support against Apartheid.[9]

In the early 1970s, the political pressure and boycotts were considered superficial. In 1973, however, the South African Council on Sport (SACOS) was established with the slogan, *'No normal sport in an abnormal society'.* SACOS continued challenging the ongoing racial segregation, refused to separate sport from society, and unconditionally rejected the ruling National Party's (NP) sports policy. In declaring solidarity with the Supreme Council for Sport in Africa, SACOS rejected all forms of racism in sport and called for a complete moratorium on all sports tours to and from South Africa until all the restrictions and exclusions of Apartheid were removed from South African sport. A well-known South African activist in sport, Dennis Brutus, who led SAN-ROC, facilitated anti-Apartheid unity under the already established SACOS slogan *'No normal sport in an abnormal society'*. However, SACOS' principal weapon against Apartheid in sport was the international boycott of South African sport, as this influenced widespread resistance against Apartheid worldwide.[10]

Towards the late 1980s, internal sport reforms were effected under the NP's regime due to international political pressure and isolation.[11] SACOS also maintained its uncompromising ideology during the 1980s, establishing a pro-collaboration group named the National Sports Congress in 1989 to establish a non-racial sport order. The removal of political bans on the African National Congress (ANC), the Communist Party (CP) and the Pan African Congress (PAC) in February 1990 fundamentally changed the South African political dispensation. This led to a transitional period from Apartheid to democracy (1990-1994) and allowed for the establishment of a new non-racial umbrella to control bodies for Olympic and non-Olympic sports. The additional support of the ANC leadership led to most international federations lifting their boycotts on South Africa by 1992.[12] The national reforms by the NP also contributed towards South Africa's readmittance to the Olympic Movement, and a small, racially mixed Olympic team competed in the 1992 Summer Games in Barcelona.

The influence of sport's contribution to the end of Apartheid is unquestionably significant in South African society. South Africa's sporting isolation in the 1970s and 1980s coincided with, and contributed to, the erosion of Apartheid, particularly in the move away from social segregation.[13] This contribution provides the context to understand the significant impact of Apartheid on sport in South Africa. The far-reaching effects led to the exclusion of Black athletes, coaches, technical officials and administrators, and damaged the country's international reputation and relationships with other nations.

4.2.2 Democratic Elections and Impact on Sport Governance

It was only after the end of Apartheid in the early 1990s that sport in South Africa started to become more integrated, allowing all athletes, regardless of their race, to compete at the highest level. South African sport entered a new era when the first democratic elections were held in 1994, with the formation of a new Constitution and Bill of Rights that provided the basis for sporting unity and solidarity.[14] The first democratically elected President, Nelson Mandela, publicly advocated for national unity by supporting the national rugby team at the 1995 Rugby World Cup held in South Africa. He wore the (White) captain's jersey to symbolise reconciliation between White and Black South Africans.[15]

South Africa winning the 1995 Rugby World Cup was used as an opportunity to gain support for the team among South Africans of all races, to provide them (citizens) with a common goal of using sport to change the racial divisions left by Apartheid. Other post-Apartheid sports teams started participating and performing well on the international stage. South Africa's presence began to take a positive turn when South Africa's national football team, affectionately nicknamed Bafana Bafana (Zulu for 'The Boys'), returned to international competition and won the 1996 African Cup of Nations at home, followed by inaugurally qualifying for the 1998 FIFA World Cup in France.[16] These events contributed towards building global sport leadership confidence. This pinnacle led South Africa to host the 2010 FIFA World Cup, the first time an

African country was selected. At the time, the then FIFA President, Sepp Blatter, hailed South Africa as one of the most successful hosts.

4.2.3 Governance of Sport in South Africa post-1994

Apartheid officially ended in South Africa in 1994, ushering in a new era of democracy and governance for the country, with sport governance also undergoing significant changes. The institutionalism of sport has also developed in many other countries over the past few years, with sport policies being incorporated into governmental responsibilities.[17;18;19] National sport departments started developing specific policies and organisations to govern sports, and South Africa took a similar approach. In 1996, the first consolidated attempt at sports governance was introduced when the then Ministry for Sports and Recreation released a White Paper on Sports and Recreation. After that, in 1998, the *National Sports and Recreation Act* was promulgated into law, along with the *South African Sports Commission Act*.[20;21]

4.3 NATIONAL AND PROVINCIAL LEGISLATIVE GOVERNANCE

Following its first democratic elections in 1994, South African sport entered a new era with a new Constitution and Bill of Rights, which provided the basis for a sport environment that would work towards unity and inclusivity. This followed the implementation of the White Paper on Sports and Recreation and the promulgation of the *National Sport and Recreation Act* into law, along with the *South Africa Sports Commission Act*. These led to the absorption of the South African Sports Commission (SASC) into the then national sport ministry – Sport and Recreation South Africa (SRSA) – and the creation of the South African Sports Confederation and Olympic Committee (SASCOC).

SASCOC was tasked with delivering elite sport development and facilitating international competitions for Team South Africa's participation, such as the Olympic Games, Commonwealth Games and All-Africa Games. SASCOC's role was also to create enabling environments for sport participation and to contribute to policy formulation, international cooperation and social development.[22] SRSA's role was to develop policy and oversee mass participation in sport nationwide.

4.3.1 The Legislative Governance Framework (National and Provincial)

A Ministerial Task Team (MTT) on sport was established following the country's dismal performance at the 2000 Sydney Olympic Games. The recommendations of the MTT influenced the current delivery of sport and recreation in South Africa.[23] The MTT's report represented a comprehensive analysis of key stakeholders in the high-performance sport sector in South Africa. As a result, the MTT developed a blueprint for this sector to streamline and professionalise service delivery to elite athletes to advance the country's high-performance programme. This blueprint also included recommendations for a clear pathway for talent development at the school level, through coaching and scientific support provided by the national sport federations in collaboration with provincial academies.[24] The report by the MTT led to the revision of the

White Paper on Sport and Recreation, which was considered ground-breaking in terms of advancing sport governance in South Africa.

Despite adopting the country's first official legislation on sport, the MTT also discovered inefficiencies within sport governance structures in the country. This led the government to the slow but eventual redefinition of sports governance in the country by introducing the *Road Map to Optimal Performance and Functional Excellence* (Road Map) in 2011. The White Paper and the Road Map constituted the more comprehensive *National Sports and Recreation Development Plan* (NSRP), which represented a concrete implementation plan for policy framework development in the country. The NSRP was founded on three core pillars of implementation, namely: (1) an active nation using increasing citizens' access to sport and recreational activities; (2) a winning nation able to support athletes in achieving international sporting success; and (3) an environment that would enable achievement of both pillars.[25] In addition, it serves as the implementation plan of the policy framework for sport and recreation, as captured in the revised White Paper for elite and mass participation sport.[26]

Over the years, the National Department of Sports, Arts, and Culture (DSAC) (formerly SRSA before June 2019) implemented multiple initiatives utilising sport for socio-political reform and nation-building. This was guided by the implementation of the Transformation Charter for South African Sport (Transformation Charter) in 2012. The Transformation Charter addressed the inequality in South African sport associated with historically institutionalised and exclusionary practices that targeted segments of the population, particularly Black Africans, which had resulted in discrepancies in resource distribution and discrimination across all levels of sport in South Africa.[27]

DSAC and SASCOC oversee mass participation and high-performance sport, respectively, across the country, whilst provincially, the mandate for the delivery and implementation of policy frameworks is governed by the NSRP.[28]

4.3.2 Sport Governance Changes

A study by Ferkins and Shilbury,[29] which focused on the governance of sport organisations on the African continent, suggested that governance in the sport management domain is one of the most significant elements to ensure the success of any non-profit organisation. The study emphasised the strategic management function of boards and is still considered relevant, considering that in South Africa, poor governance within sport federations often requires political intervention. The most well-known intervention was the Zulman Commission of Inquiry.

In 2017, the then Minister of Sport and Recreation appointed a Commission (Zulman Commission) to investigate allegations of poor governance in sport, specifically targeting the national Olympic body, SASCOC. The Commission was tasked with investigating allegations of maladministration and financial irregularities at SASCOC. The final report strongly recommended implementing a structural and strategic review, including change management processes.[30] Considering the submissions made by the then SASCOC board during the hearings, the inquiry found that there was no compliance within the organisation concerning the basic principles of ethics, transparency, accountability and good governance, nor with policies and procedures for managing the affairs of SASCOC, including its financial affairs. In addition, the

Commission discovered that factionalism hampered the performance of the SASCOC board, manifesting in the non-delivery of its sole mandate, which was the delivery of Team South Africa.[31]

The recommendations in the report mainly focused on strengthening SASCOC's governance going forward. These changes were included in SASCOC's amended Constitution, which was adopted in November 2022.[32] Overall, the changes in sport governance in South Africa aimed to promote greater inclusivity and access to sport for all South Africans, as well as to boost the country's profile on the international sporting stage.

DSAC (formerly SRSA) released the draft National Sport and Recreation Amendment Bill 2020 to impede further national sports sector governance issues. The Bill aimed, *"To amend the National Sport and Recreation Act, 1998, to delete, amend and insert certain definitions".*[33] The amendments clearly outlined the national minister's purview concerning the protocol of governance expectations, matters arising, and issues. However, the Bill was yet to be formally adopted into legislation at the time of writing.

4.4 SPORT GOVERNANCE STRUCTURES IN SOUTH AFRICA

Sport in South Africa is governed by several organisations and bodies, both at the national and international levels. However, sport governance in South Africa is primarily overseen by the Department of Sport, Arts and Culture (DSAC) and the South African Sports Confederation and Olympic Committee (SASCOC). Both these structures have specific processes that guide and inform their respective governance responsibilities, such as developing and implementing policies that promote participation in sport and overseeing the administration and regulation of sport bodies in the country.

Setting the agenda for political reform in sport, the then National Sports Council (NSC) hosted a national sport conference in 1993 entitled, 'Vision for Sport'. The aim was to create a framework for unifying democratic sport structures and to advance equitable access to sport in a newly democratic South Africa. This conference shaped the design and policies of the first unified post-Apartheid Department of Sport and Recreation, established in 1994. The conference laid the foundations for mass participation and the development of elite sport, including identifying four focus areas for South African sport: 'foundation', 'participation', 'performance' and 'excellence'. Therefore, the NSC conference agreed that the post-Apartheid government should 'Get the Nation to Play'.[34]

Nearly two decades after the NSC conference, the *National Sport and Recreation Plan* (NSRP) was developed in 2011. The NSRP is the main policy document guiding sport governance in South Africa, which sets out a vision for developing sport and recreation in the country and outlines a range of strategic objectives designed to achieve this vision.[35] At the national level, DSAC is responsible for developing and promoting sport in the country and provides funding and support to various sporting organisations, including SASCOC and the National Sports Federations (NSFs), which oversee and regulate specific sports in the country.

Overall, the policy governance structures of sport in South Africa are designed to promote participation in sport and recreation, develop high-performance athletes, and ensure that sports bodies are governed, accountable and transparent.

4.4.1 Macro, Meso and Micro Levels of Sport Governance

Sport governance in South Africa is managed across three levels – macro (national), meso (provincial) and micro (local) – and shall be discussed below.

4.4.1.1 Macro level

Sport and recreation in South Africa are represented in three of the five government clusters (each cluster consists of several different government departments), namely the Social Cluster; the International Relations, Peace and Security Cluster; and the Governance and Administration Cluster. In addition, the National Department of Sport (formerly SRSA, now DSAC) supports hosting significant events, aiming to leave a legacy that ensures a better life for all South Africans.[36] An example of collaboration amongst the clusters is with the South African Police Services, Department of Basic Education, and other international stakeholders such as the British High Commission and British Airways on the 'Sport for Safety' project.[37]

SRSA's 2012 National Sport and Recreation Plan included the importance of international diplomacy, led by the then Deputy Minister of SRSA, focusing on peacebuilding and collaboration. This speaks to the signing of the Millennium Development Goals (and now the Sustainable Development Goals). South Africa increasingly views sport as a vehicle to address political objectives. This is usually in terms of contributing to social cohesion; enhancing health for all; improving international relations; enhancing peace, development, tourism and human empowerment; developing infrastructure; and hosting successful international competitions, like the 2010 FIFA World Cup.[38] The Minister of Sport and Recreation has the legislative powers, as reflected in the *National Sport and Recreation Amendment Act* (Act No. 18 of 2007), to oversee the development and management of sport and recreation in South Africa at the macro level. Transformation, inclusion and equality were the main thrusts for the five-year *Strategic Plan of SRSA*, in line with the *Constitution of the Republic of South Africa, Act 108 of 1996*.[39] This directive was supported by five programme areas, of which critical deliverables included delivery on the guarantees signed with FIFA (e.g., training of volunteers and mobilising South African support that would leave a lasting legacy) and delivering mass participation programmes in impoverished communities (*Siyadlala*) and schools (School Sport Mass Participation Programme).[40] This international footprint allowed the then SRSA to forge strategic partnerships with global stakeholders such as UNICEF, South Africa and the European Union.

State intervention in sport is imperative, as it is viewed as an effective vehicle for nation-building, forming a national identity, and helping to address national priorities such as community regeneration and racial transformation.[41] Hosting high-profile international sporting events and developing sport and recreation infrastructure, especially in previously disadvantaged communities, are some interventions used in post-Apartheid South Africa to address racial and class inequalities. International relations, national unity and prestige on the global sport stage are essential signifiers of good governance and political validation to be recognised at all levels of engagement. The state has a central role to play in the development of 'enabling' policies, representative structures and adequate resourcing for the different agencies and role players in a mutually beneficial partnership to deliver on national targets for elite performance and increased mass participation.[42]

4.4.1.2 Meso-level of sport governance

At the meso-level, several organisations, as defined by SASCOC's constitution, are responsible for the delivery of sport in South Africa. These include NSFs and associate members such as universities and sport confederations.

a)   National Sport Federations (NSFs)

The NSFs govern and develop specific sports in South Africa, such as athletics, cricket, rugby, soccer and swimming. Furthermore, they are responsible for selecting athletes to represent the country at international competitions, organising domestic competitions, and developing grassroots programmes to promote their respective sports. In addition to these national bodies, various international sporting organisations guide the governance of specific sports globally, including the International Olympic Committee (IOC), the International Cricket Council (ICC), FIFA (the international soccer governing body) and World Rugby, among others. Furthermore, all NSFs in South Africa are affiliated with an International Sport Federation (ISF). They utilise their governance structures and recommendations to guide their operations, aligning with SASCOC and DSAC recommendations.

b)   Universities

The governing body for university sport in South Africa is University Sport South Africa (USSA), which was established in 1992. The significance of establishing the South African Student Sports Union (SASSU) was to unify two historically separate groupings within South African society, i.e., students from historically Black and traditionally White institutions. The intention was to harness the experience and expertise of both groups to establish a structure that reflects the aspirations of all student sports. SASSU was founded to promote sporting values and encourage sporting practice in harmony with, and complementary to, the academic character of tertiary education institutions.[43]

USSA is responsible for coordinating and developing sport at the country's universities. It oversees various sporting codes, including athletics, basketball, cricket, football, hockey, netball, rugby, swimming and volleyball. Each year, USSA hosts several national championships in various sports, bringing together teams from universities across the country to compete against one another. In addition, Varsity Cup and Varsity Sports competitions were introduced just over a decade ago to provide high-performance competitions within university sport, focusing on the country's most popular sport codes (by numbers), such as athletics, netball, football and rugby. Governed as a commercial entity, Varsity Sports operates separately from, but engages with, USSA, and as an amateur sport environment, provides a platform for semi-professional sport opportunities.

In 2003, a Ministerial Task Team (MTT) was formed by the then-national Department of Sport – Sport and Recreation South Africa (SRSA) – that included the then South African Student Sport Union (SASSU), now University Sport South Africa (USSA). The MTT acknowledged that South Africa had made gains in transforming sport development in a post-Apartheid society, but it was evident that the legacy of Apartheid remained a central feature. Following the recommendations of the MTT, several sport structures, including the then SASSU, had to develop policies and strategies to advance the delivery of sport at Higher Education

Institutions (HEIs). These policies and procedures addressed past inequities for mass participation and elite performance.[44]

In South Africa, essential policy documents, such as the White Paper for Sport and Recreation in South Africa,[45] are meant to guide HEIs concerning sport. However, very few mentions are made about the importance of specific guidelines regarding what happens at a Higher Education (HE) level and how this can be articulated with the country's competitive sporting systems.[46] The latter refers to the systemic articulation and alignment between universities and broader systems that became crucial given resource identification in the aftermath of Apartheid and institutional reform – including that of HE.[47]

As an associate member of SASCOC, USSA considers the level of participation (recreation, competitive and high performance) to form an essential part of the country's sporting culture. The country has a long history of successful sporting achievements; in particular, South African universities have a rich sports tradition, with many offering a wide range of sports and recreational activities and facilities that contribute to the overall sporting experience of students in South Africa. The HEIs, as members of USSA, provide students with a relatively well-resourced and specialised environment for recreation and high-performance sport participation.

USSA's governance is mainly informed by its business plan, constitution, regulations and other related documents. The constitution acknowledges its annual general meeting (AGM) and general counsel (GC) as its highest decision-making structures.

With a strong history of good corporate governance and with most of its member universities offering, on average, about 20 or more sports, it is evident that university sport in South Africa plays a vital role in promoting physical fitness, social interaction and healthy competition among students.

c) Sport confederations

Sport confederations in South Africa are governed by various bodies, including the South African Sports Confederation and Olympic Committee (SASCOC), national federations and provincial sport confederations. Sport confederations administrate, promote and monitor sport within provinces and are an umbrella body for all sport federations, including local and district sport councils. Provincial sport confederations are responsible for the administration of sport at the provincial level and the development of their respective sports in their regions, including organising provincial competitions, talent identification and development. Sport confederations work closely with their regional and local sports councils to develop sport at the community level. They work closely with schools and local clubs to promote sport participation and are responsible for organising local competitions and events.[48] The South African Local Government Association (SALGA) works with confederations, federations and local and district sport councils to deliver sport to communities by effectively managing available resources.[49]

4.4.1.3 *Micro-level of sport governance*

South Africa has a vibrant and diverse sports culture, with a wide range of sport clubs catering to sport participation by both amateur and professional athletes. These sport clubs have set governance structures and are managed by volunteers. The following is an overview of the amateur, semi-professional and professional sport clubs in South Africa:

a)   Amateur sport clubs

Sport clubs are organisations created to provide a place for individuals to participate in sport and recreational activities. Volunteers generally run these clubs and are often focused on a particular sport or activity, such as athletics, cricket, hockey, netball, rugby and soccer.

b)   Semi-professional sport structures and clubs

Semi-professional clubs are those that operate at a level below professional sport. These clubs may pay their players a small stipend or provide them with other benefits, but the players typically also have other jobs or sources of income. Examples of semi-professional sport clubs in South Africa include the South African Rugby Union (SARU) Provincial Rugby Teams (e.g., Western Province Rugby and Blue Bulls Rugby), South African Football Association (SAFA) Regional Leagues (e.g., Paarl United and the University of Pretoria) and National First Division clubs (e.g., Stellenbosch University/Maties FC and University of Witwatersrand (WITS) FC). Depending on the level of competitiveness and benefits provided, university sport clubs fall within the scope of amateur and/or semi-professional sport clubs.

c)   Professional sport clubs

Professional sport clubs pay their athletes to play and compete in a particular sport. These clubs are typically associated with major national leagues and are at the highest level of competition. Examples of professional sport clubs in South Africa include Cape Town City, Kaizer Chiefs, Mamelodi Sundowns and Orlando Pirates football clubs, and the Lions, Bulls, Sharks and Stormers professional rugby unions.

The variety of sport clubs, semi-professional and professional, cater to the diverse interests and talents of the country's athletes. Whether it is mass participation endeavours for recreation or the support necessary for high-performance competition, sport clubs across the country can offer options and solutions to citizens.

4.4.1.4   School sport

The National Education Policy Act further governs school sport, with the School Sport Policy positioned under the Department of Basic Education (DBE) and the various provincial education departments. The DBE is responsible for setting policies and guidelines for school sports. At the same time, the provincial departments of education are responsible for implementing these policies and procedures at the provincial and local levels. The main objectives of school sports in South Africa are to promote physical fitness, healthy competition and teamwork, as well as to foster social and emotional development among students. To achieve these objectives, the DBE and provincial departments of education have established several regulations and guidelines for school sports, which include the following:

1.   Code of conduct: All students, coaches and officials involved in school sports must adhere to a code of conduct that promotes fair play, respect for opponents and adherence to the game's rules.

2. Safety: Schools must ensure that all sports activities are conducted in a safe environment, with appropriate equipment and facilities, and with proper supervision and medical support.
3. Age restrictions: Students must compete in sport according to their age group, as determined by the DBE and the provincial education departments.
4. Selection criteria: Schools must have clear and transparent standards for selecting students to participate in school sports activities, emphasising fairness and inclusivity.
5. Competitive levels: Schools are grouped into different competitive levels based on the size and resources of the school, as well as the level of competition in the region.
6. Sports curriculum: Schools are encouraged to incorporate sports into their curriculum, focusing on developing fundamental movement skills and physical literacy among students.[50]

The *National Sport and Recreation Plan*[51] and Memorandum of Understanding (MoU),[52] which were signed between the Department of Basic Education (DBE) and the Ministry of Sport, Arts and Culture (then known as Sport and Recreation South Africa or SRSA) informed a policy framework for operationalisation. In addition, this document provided further guidance to national sport federations and provincial departments of education to promote school sport as an essential part of the education system in South Africa and to improve access, participation and quality in school sports programmes.

In addition, Burnett[53] identified the vital governance structures and practices needed in school sport through a study that involved 55 schools, namely:

1. active and engaged school sport committees at the circuit, district and school levels (reported by schools in several provinces);
2. regular meetings, good communication and mentorship at the school level, led by a Sport Manager or Sport Coordinator to ensure regular competitions and active engagement, teacher-coach empowerment and training, and effective collaboration with external agencies;
3. a functioning school-sport system within schools and articulation with the circuit and district levels to channel talent identification and development, as well as facilitate inclusive (mass) participation;
4. active leadership and policy initiatives driven by teachers in collaboration with School Governing Bodies (SGBs); and
5. representative school, cluster and district committees or structures that ensure regular competitions, timely communication and optimal school participation.

This research was mandated by the DBE, which noted multiple governance challenges for implementing school sport nationally for lower quintile schools. Roles and responsibilities, particularly considering the involvement of two entities in the partnership, needed to be clarified in practice, and these principles provided that clarity.

4.5 CONCLUSION

This chapter demonstrates that South Africa has a decentralised sport governance structure, with different bodies responsible for different sport codes. The Department of Sport, Arts and Culture oversees the implementation of government policies and programmes in sports. There are also national governing bodies for each sport, such as Cricket South Africa, the South African Rugby Union and Netball South Africa, which are responsible for the administration, regulation and development of their respective sports. To address these issues, the South African government has introduced several measures, such as the National Sport and Recreation Amendment Act in 2007, to improve national sport bodies' governance and accountability, as well as to promote diversity and inclusion in sports. The government has also established bodies such as the South African Sports Confederation and Olympic Committee (SASCOC) to oversee sport administration at a national level.

Despite these efforts, sport governance in South Africa remains a complex issue that requires ongoing attention and action. The country has a rich sporting history, but governance has challenged the sports sector, despite having improved since the segregationist policies of Apartheid. Given the local need for change as well as the world's demand for innovation, the governance of sport at the national and international levels requires a different, scientific and context-specific response guided by sound governance principles and policies. Like any institution that experiences change, it will take time to ensure that governance is wholly adhered to in South African sport. To do that, an understanding of how things were once structured, then reordered to be more inclusive, is needed – which is what this chapter aims to provide.

SELF-ASSESSMENT

1. Discuss South Africa's sport history.
2. Debate what you know about sport governance in South Africa that you did not know before.
3. Explain the various levels of sport governance in South Africa.
4. Argue the need for the changes that happened in South African sport governance.

SPORT FOR DEVELOPMENT AND PEACE (SDP): GLOBAL AND LOCAL PERSPECTIVES AND DYNAMICS

Professor Cora Burnett

LEARNING OUTCOMES

At the end of this chapter, you should be able to:

1. Discuss Sport for Development and SDP as a philosophy and practice globally and in South Africa.
2. Define Sport for Development and related concepts.
3. Explain Sport for Development and Peace (SDP) as a movement concerning different stakeholders.
4. Discuss the role of United Nations agencies in different phases of SDP and the relevance thereof for South Africa.
5. Critically reflect on the central issues in SDP for developing nations in the Global South.
6. Describe the introduction of SDP into South African sport.
7. Reflect on the role of prominent stakeholders in SDP in South Africa.
8. Discuss selected case studies of SDP work in South Africa in line with global and regional trends.
9. Discuss possible future trends of SDP based on the knowledge and insights from the chapter.

5.1 INTRODUCTION

Sport for Development (SfD) as a philosophy and Sport for Development and Peace (SDP) as a social movement both acknowledge sport as a cost-effective tool for development constructed under the leadership of the United Nations. In this regard, the global influence found traction in the establishment of the United Nations Inter-Agency Task Force on Sport for Development and Peace (SDP), which is amongst several structural arrangements focused on delivering on the outcomes of the eight Millennium Development Goals (2000-2015) and the 17 Sustainable Development Goals (2015-2030).[1;2]

The Sport for Development and Peace International Working Group (SDP IWG) was established in 2004 with South Africa's Deputy Sports Minister as one of the rotating Chairs with Russia.[3] The SDP IWG became the leading organisational arm for SDP, hosted by the United Nations Office for Sport for Development and Peace (UNOSDP) as per the General Assembly's Resolution A/RES/63/135. The organisation was mandated *"to promote and support the adoption of policies and programmes by national governments to harness the potential of sport to contribute to the achievements of development objectives."*[4]

Many resolutions and developments followed, and over time, the value of sport became prominent through advocacy, policy development, programme implementation and scientific evidence. As a global force, the United Nations, in partnership with international organisations such as the International Olympic Committee (IOC) (which has had observer status in the UN General Assembly since 2009) and the Commonwealth Games Federation, has announced a philosophy to guide social transformation. Leading sport organisations identified several sustainable development goals for endorsement and alignment with mega sport event legacy projects.[5] The current Olympism 365 IOC strategy bears witness to such a global initiative.[6] A recent development was to roll out of the UN SDP Toolkit by invitation from June 2023 as per national governments' requests to advance development work through and in sport and other related sectors.[7]

5.1.1 Sport for Development in South Africa

SDP had made inroads in South Africa through the leadership position of South Africa's then Deputy Minister of Sport and Recreation in the SDP IWG and to drive nation-building through sport. The Ministry of Sport and Recreation (SRSA, now the Department of Sport Arts and Culture, or DSAC) focused on redressing the systemic disenfranchisement caused by the Apartheid dispensation, guided by a human rights framework. That led to the inclusion of sport for development perspectives in the first National Sport and Recreation Plan, which was drafted in 2011 in articulation with the principles enshrined in the South African Constitution that awards the Minister with legislative powers, guided by various prominent Acts.[8]

With South Africa's Vision 2030 guiding elite sport development and sport for development to ensure *An Active and Winning Nation*, the National Sport and Recreation Plan identified 31 strategic objectives. Six objectives focus on non-elite sport by referring to health, physical education, recreation and sport-for-development initiatives.[9]

The government (SRSA, now DSAC) funded and implemented a community-based mass sport participation programme called *Siyadlala* (a Zulu word meaning, *Let us play*). Four main categories of organised sport, games and physical activities were included: aerobics, ball games (e.g., handball, basketball and baseball), athletics (big walks/fun runs) and indigenous games. The latter entailed nine games associated with the cultural background and history of different racial groups in South Africa.[10] This programme was followed by the launch of a School Mass Participation Programme for Sport in 2008. The vision was to link "no-fee" schools to community sports structures for optimal participation and the revival of sports (including girls' participation) in sports like rugby, cricket, netball and football. In this way, opportunities for involvement afforded children and youth from impoverished communities to benefit by addressing the many social ills they face in their daily lives through sport and life skill training, as well as the offering of mentorship and support.[11]

At that stage, international agencies like the Australian Sports Commission (ASC) and the German Development Agency (GIZ) also entered the national sport for development space to spread an SfD philosophy and offer programmes in partnership with the government and other agencies. GIZ rolled out the GIZ/YDF (Youth Development through Football) programme as part of their international diplomacy and support for the 2010 FIFA World Cup hosted by South Africa, following the 2006 FIFA World Cup in Germany. They rolled out various initiatives across 10 African countries and co-founded (with Nike South Africa) the Sport for Social Change Network (SSCN). The GIZ/YDF programme developed several toolkits and capacitated life skills trainers to offer training as part of the License D Football coach qualifications in South Africa.[12]

Currently, the SSCN, renamed the SSCNA (Sport for Social Change Network Africa), is the official network for recognised non-governmental organisations that are funded by the government (DSAC). Schools remain preferred institutions for delivering SfD initiatives, which are often integrated or packaged as sport and physical activities linked to life skills training relevant to physical education (PE) and school sport. In 2011, SRSA and the Ministry of Basic Education signed a Memorandum of Understanding (MOU) to ensure that all learners in public schools would benefit from participation in school sports or structured physical activities as part of Life Orientation, in which PE is situated. Life Orientation as a school subject fosters life skills development, including social, health and sport-for-development paradigms. This MOU was revised in 2017 to clarify the roles and responsibilities of the different ministries, as well as for the DSAC to take responsibility for the latter phases in developing sporting talent in collaboration with the competitive sport sector, whilst acknowledging the role of education within existing school sport practices.[13]

The 2013 White Paper, produced by SRSA, recognised the UN's stance on sport and recreation as a fundamental human right and a tool for development and peacebuilding. This has special meaning for the peaceful co-existence of diverse populations that stem from deeply rooted racial, class and gender divides.[14] In addition, the sport ministry's bilateral partnership with an international non-government organisation, LoveLife,[14] is combating health pandemics such as the relatively high infection rate of HIV/Aids amongst South African youth. A similar scenario was seen in the aftermath of the Covid-19 pandemic, where physical education, physical activity and sport (PEPAS) played a crucial role in schools and communities to counter the negative health-related impacts caused by national lockdown periods.[15;16]

However, stakeholder buy-in, resource provision and local circumstances still need to be improved. Two national studies report that multiple barriers are preventing a functional and integrated system for competitive sport and using sport to bring about social change.[17]

5.2 DEFINITIONS AND CONCEPTS

Since its inception, sport for development (SfD) has been defined based on sport lying along a continuum. The one end features sport as a formal competitive activity, inclusive of social, recreational and physical performances associated with modern sports like rugby, netball and cricket, or with traditional sports such as stick fighting. When used for developmental outcomes, the conventional forms of sport may serve various educational and competitive purposes. On the other end of the spectrum, sport can be used to intentionally address a societal problem, for example addressing deviant behaviours such as drug abuse, and deliver on non-sport results ("plus sport").[18;19]

Figure 5.1 provides a continuum for explaining the categorisation and placement of the Plus-Sport, Sport-Model adapted from Fred Coalter.[20] This definition draws insights from various documents.[21]

Sport	Sport Plus	Plus Sport	No Sport
Sport Development	**Sport for Development**		**Development (without sport)**
Focusing solely on sport objectives, such as the development of sport specific competencies (techniques, tactics), competition, etc.	Using sport as a core activity, adapted in various ways to achieve certain development objectives, e.g., healthy lifestyles.	Using sport as an entry point, means or additional component for development objectives, e.g., employability.	Other development activities and approaches that do NOT involve sport (e.g., specific education, peace building, social cohesion programmes).
	Sport for Development (S4D) refers to the intentional use of sport, physical activity and play to attain specific development objectives, including, most notably, the UN Sustainable Development Goals (SDGs).		

Figure 5.1: Positioning sport for development[22]

Sport in development focuses on its inclusion within the scope of 'other' development work, such as a value-add to international diplomacy, related infrastructure development and socio-economic empowerment projects. More recently, the competitive forms of sport (e.g., leagues) have also been used for delivering broader social outcomes, as in the case where sport structures and competitions have been established in relatively poorly resourced environments. In this regard, Australian stakeholders in the Pacific Islands have established rugby and netball leagues to create meaningful sport and non-sport (specific or SfD) outcomes.[23]

The boundaries are sometimes blurred, but the definitions may help a level of differentiation and the understanding of different phenomena. Sport for development thus represents an approach where development outcomes are the priority, such as health and employability, or other outcomes, such as gender inclusion, as opposed to the practice of sport, where sport participation and performance are prioritised.

Sport for Development and Peace (SDP) is the intentional organisation and implementation of sport-based programmes to meet broadly defined non-sport goals of development and peace. In the SDP framework, sport participation is essential, but the goal is to support and facilitate external development and peace outcomes. In this sense, 'peace' refers to peaceful coexistence, particularly in contexts where different groups or populations conflict. For example, the Football4Peace organisation used sport to bring Jewish and Palestinian communities together to facilitate understanding, acceptance and tolerance among communities in the Middle East.[24] In South Africa, SDP initiatives may integrate immigrants or refugees into host communities, combat emerging animosities and prevent xenophobic attitudes. Sport and peace thus have a bearing on protecting human rights, conflict resolution and transformation that enables social inclusion.[25;26]

Another concept to be understood is 'development' – what does it mean and what would the positive outcomes be? Coalter[27] rightly asked, whose 'development' and on what terms should this development take place? For this reason, multiple opinions and voices need to be captured to determine what development means for real people in real-life settings.

5.2.1 Development Phases of SDP at the Global Level

5.2.1.1 Sport as inspiration for development (2000 and ongoing)

Since the inception of SDP, the United Nations agencies have provided leadership and created heightened levels of awareness and advocacy for the potential role of sport in achieving non-sport outcomes. In 2001, the then UN Secretary General Kofi Annan appointed Mr Adolf Ogi as the Special Adviser on SDP, who was followed by Mr Wilfried Lemke in 2008. According to the next UN Secretary General, Ban Ki-moon:

> *"Sport is increasingly recognised as an important tool in helping the United Nations achieve its objectives, particularly the Millennium Development Goals. By systematically including sport in development and peace programmes, the United Nations can use this cost-efficient tool to help us create a better world."*[28;29]

This message found global acceptance amongst governments and other stakeholders. Nelson Mandela, the first democratically elected South African president, shared similar inspirational views at the 2000 Laureus World Sports Awards Ceremony:

> *"Sport has the power to change the world. It has the power to inspire. It has the power to unite people in a way that little else can. Sport can awaken hope where there was previously only despair."*[30]

In 2005, the UN declared it the International Year of Sport and Physical Education (IYSPE) and integrated SDP in the first UN Action Plan on SDP (A/61/373), followed by actions that created an enabling environment for stakeholders to collaborate with each other.[31] This was the era where such advocacy inspired many stakeholders and convinced sport-leading organisations to engage in development work around the sport for the greater good of humanity, for instance, the African Union launched the International Year of African Football in 2006.[32] The IOC, FIFA and many other international sport federations also selected specific global goals through which sport could contribute to societal change.

More than two decades later, Mandela's quote inspired the use of sport to address broader societal outcomes. One of the most recent developments include TAFISA's Mission 2030, which focuses on bringing about social change and the "power of sport" to achieve development.[33]

5.2.1.2 Sport as a tool and social movement (2008 and ongoing)

As SDP spread globally, it attracted funding and began to be used in the fight against HIV/Aids, as well as other development priorities. In this way it created a community of practice recognised as a social movement.[34] Bruce Kidd remarked:

> "During the last two decades, national and international corporations, foundations, non-governmental organisations (NGOs), sports organisations and professional and Olympic athletes have responded to the inadequacy of public schools and recreation centres that once provided accessible opportunities for sport and physical activity by creating their organisations and programmes."[35]

In 2011, the second International Forum on Sport for Peace and Development was co-hosted by UNOSDP and the IOC in Geneva. This resulted in a renewed partnership around development issues between the UN and the sporting world. By 2014, such engagement led to the proclamation of 6 April as the International Day of Sport for Development and Peace (IDSDP).[36] Efforts were coordinated to deliver on global and national development priorities through sport, but in a more streamlined and integrated way following the system integration of SDP across UN agencies.

5.2.1.3 Sport as a catalyst in/for development (post-2015, SDGs)

In 2015, the UN Human Rights Council recommended using sport and the Olympic ideal to promote human rights and strengthen universal respect (A/HRC/30/50). At the same time, the 2030 UN Agenda for Sustainable Development (A/RES/70/1) and the International Charter of Physical Education, Physical Activity and Sport, which included principles of equality, non-discrimination and social inclusion, propagated development in and through sport (UNESCO). At UNESCO's MINEPS VI conference in 2017, the Kazan Action Plan (KAP) was adopted to move from "intent to action",[37] which was followed by the closing of the UNOSDP and direct partnership with the Olympic Movement. The KAP serves as:

> "...a voluntary, overarching reference for fostering international convergence amongst policy-makers in physical education, physical activity and sport, as well as a tool for aligning international and national policy in these fields with the United Nations 2030 Agenda. (UNESCO 2017 as referenced in United Nations 2018, Resolution 71/160 – A.4)."[38]

At the core of this resolution and based on member states' input, the UN system identified 10 of the 17 Sustainable Development Goals and 36 associated targets to be addressed through sport, physical activity and physical education. It also directed internal changes in UN agencies to create a more coherent and aligned approach towards SDP by transferring UNOSDP to the Department of Economic and Social Affairs, thereby accelerating the process of mainstreaming SDP initiatives.[39]

In 2018, the World Health Organisation (WHO) launched its Global Action Plan on Physical Activity (2018-2030), which became highly relevant to the health risks brought about by the Covid-19 pandemic. The Commonwealth Sport & SDG Toolkit (V4.0) was published at the same time, while the Fit4Life global initiative of UNESCO was launched to accelerate the recovery from the pandemic and prioritise healthy living, inclusion and equality.[40;41]

Like other countries, South Africa responded to these initiatives and served as a pilot to adopt Quality Physical Education (QPE). In addition, the South African country offices of UNICEF and UNESCO launched initiatives such as GBEM (Girls and Boys Educational Movement) in partnership with DBE and the Fit4Life initiative.[42] At the country level, development outcomes related to the use of sport for improving academic performance, enhancing mental and physical health, delivering on gender and disability justice and addressing a myriad of "social ills" relevant to different environments.[43] More recently, sport for specific outcomes translated into more specialised approaches, such as using "sport for employment", where initiatives focused on using sport to enhance the employability status of youth and to lead to employment opportunities through entrepreneurship or formal working environments.

5.3 MAIN ISSUES RELATING TO SDP IN THE GLOBAL SOUTH

5.3.1 Unequal Power Relations

The international and foreign flow of funding and ownership of SDP projects are rooted in the politics of 'development' and the construction of neo-colonial spaces evident by European domination. There is still a significant Western ideological bias toward programmes implemented by the developed environments or Global North holding ownership and power over projects implemented in the Global South, also known as the "two-thirds world."[44] Funding and developing agencies in Europe and the UK (Global North) tend to dictate terms to often resource-poor implementing agencies in developing nations, which must comply to continue receiving funding and resources. This has led to a mismatch of what is delivered and what is needed, and an over-emphasis on positive outcomes by implementers. Coalter referred to an evangelical approach to feature life-changing experiences ascribed to a particular intervention that is not substantiated by real impact that may be less profound.[45]

A similar trend has been observed in the domination of first-world scholars undertaking short-term research in Africa and producing knowledge underpinned by Western paradigms. Local researchers only sometimes have the access, adequate funding or institutional support to publish in open-access, high-impact international journals. This means that knowledge production and reproduction are continually underpinned by Western thought, whereas local voices are often silenced or filtered.

5.3.2 The Issue of Sustainability

Without challenging the seat of power, masked notions of equal partnership arrangements still dominate development work, enshrined by exit strategies that entail the handing over of ownership for sustainable programme delivery. There is a significant difference between community-based and community-driven programmes, where 'empowerment' entails much more than providing resources and training.

Sustainable service delivery has become the key to safeguarding donor investment and ensuring an exit strategy is possible within multiple local stakeholder arrangements. However, ownership is seldom transferred timeously or shared in a meaningful way. Top-down planning often overrides possible multi-directional and complex community-level stakeholder collaboration and long-term reciprocal benefits for all involved.[46]

Stakeholders do not always fit into clear-cut categories and may transcend expected operational arrangements. For instance, systemic barriers are difficult to overcome, as evidenced by the Pacific Netball Partnership (PNP), where the national Australian Netball Federation and its partners assisted with implementing netball in five Pacific Island Nations.[47] The latter study identified multi-levelled implementation barriers ranging from culture to patriarchal ideology, infrastructure, health awareness, development priorities and the lack of local stakeholder collaboration. Women in southern Africa encounter similar systemic barriers to accessing leadership roles and closing the gender inequality gap in terms of taking up positions of influence.[48;49] Without a well-structured and supported pathway to development, women and girls will remain marginalised and drop-out rates high, particularly during early adulthood. In addition, complex social issues (such as gender inequality) are often simplified and channelled to represent achievable outcomes, without tackling the root causes or recognising that behaviour changes take time and systemic barriers require political engagement.

Chasing numbers to demonstrate impressive reach often trumps the real and lasting change that mostly matters to local populations. Without continued resourcing and capacity to attract multi-year funding, implementing organisations (e.g., non-governmental agencies) may close down as funding agencies are often reluctant to invest in organisational growth and capacity.

5.3.3 The Notion of Volunteering and The 'Youth Trap'

Most SfD work is implemented by the NGO sector that engages peer leaders or educators. In some cases, international volunteers will engage in such work. Still, their circumstances differ vastly from local 'volunteers', who are dependent on a stipend and are mainly recruited from employability training. In many cases, these youth leaders are acknowledged as role models, even though they are under-employed or partially employed depending on the number of contracts held by their employers, who rely on external funding for programme implementation.[50] This creates tension as organisations that upskill youth workers without offering them career pathways constantly lose some should they find formal employment or more lucrative contractual work.

In many cases, a worker's youth status stretches for over a decade, and you may find 40-year-old 'youth leaders' still working for minimal wages within the informal SDP sector. The over-simplification of 'fixing lives' through life skill education for youth, who "volunteered" as coaches in an Olympic grassroots outreach programme, has led to high levels of frustration and resistance as the latter expect to be paid for their effort.[51]

5.3.4 The Deficit Perspective

The manifestation of poverty is multi-faceted and interwoven into the real-life circumstances of individuals and collectives identified as 'vulnerable' and earmarked for development work. Risk-taking and anti-social behaviour do not rest with poor or uninformed decision-making only, and hold different expressions and interpretations. It is a broader social issue entrenched in socialisation practices, ideology, culture and survival strategies, with a reach far beyond bio-power and individual choice. It is also questionable if sport-related interventions alone can address entrenched societal issues on the premise that it is anti-social behaviours that can be corrected through SfD interventions.

Coalter argued against the deficit approach, explaining that impoverished populations are not inherently 'deviant', but shaped by multiple influences in their respective social worlds.[52] Inherent in this critique is the reality that Eurocentric views prioritise foreign insights of 'othering', framed by (Western) ways of knowing and doing, rather than having contextual relevance and transferring agency to people earmarked for development.

5.3.5 Lack of Evidence and Knowledge Production

The lack of evidence discourse in SDP research speaks to inadequate scientific rigour and the limitations of small-scale projects for extrapolated learning. Researchers increasingly utilise the Participatory Action Research (PAR) methodology to counter dominant neo-colonial and Western paradigms.[53] Participatory Action Research entails a participatory process and reciprocal agency between researcher and research participant, focusing on capturing indigenous ways of knowing and local understanding of how social phenomena affect them. Without theory generation to describe contextual sport-for-development manifestations and create conceptual clarity, the phenomenon will be constructed within the plurality of paradigms to serve the hegemonic discourses of the scholars making the argument.

It is also not an issue of positionality alone of researchers or evaluators (local or not). Rather, it is about understanding local realities and producing scholarly work that would enrich the existing sport-for-development diverse bodies of knowledge. The challenge exists that not all evaluation studies are robust enough to deliver scientific knowledge or a more comprehensive understanding of complex issues underpinned by sound theoretical and conceptual insights.[54] Many mapping studies provide summaries and thematic analyses rather than insightful analyses. Regarding Africa, Laurenz Langer critically reflected on the depth of impact assessment SDP research and argued for scientific inquiry to reach beyond indicator-directed investigations.[55] He discussed multiple layers of analysis, including indigenous ways of interpreting data that articulate real-life experiences and constructions. Such a robust approach is evident in the stakeholder mapping in the SDP field as a comparative analysis between Africa and Europe, where the findings demonstrate a relative need for inter-stakeholder collaboration within the African context.[56]

5.4 STAKEHOLDERS AND SDP CASE STUDIES IN SOUTH AFRICA

5.4.1 Stakeholder Types

Giulianotti identified key agencies and institutions within the SDP sector such as non-governmental, non-profit organisations *like Right to Play and Streetfootballworld (renamed as Common Goal)* that bring development projects to local communities.[57] A second category includes intergovernmental and governmental organisations, in which the United Nations and associated agencies (e.g., UNICEF) and agencies linked to national governments. Global sport organisations like FIFA use sport-for-development projects as their Corporate Social Responsibility/Investment/Strategy (CSI) platform. Then there are partners in the private sector, e.g., Vodafone, Mercedes-Benz or Nike, which work in partnership with sport federations or non-government organisations. Lastly, there are radical NGOs or social movements with politicised approaches and often-radical agendas supported by activist social movements or agencies.

For countries hosting sport events, sport legacy projects attract multiple agencies from the private (e.g., corporate sponsors), public (e.g., government agencies), sport (e.g., sport federations), and non-governmental sectors (e.g., NGOs). Lindsey et al. reflected on the role of government in six main configurations of partnerships, i.e., state-centred, complementary implementation, co-produced, non-state-centred, state-led regulation and non-state-led adversarial advocacy.[58]

Different stakeholders may provide complementary resources (e.g., government and the sport sector) and leadership (e.g., UN agencies) for service delivery and penetration into marginal communities earmarked for development (e.g., NGOs). Such partnerships are often directed by a neoliberal agenda, guided by Western hegemonic policies and good practices dissemination within a market-driven environment. As a result, corporates emerge as influential players in creating their sport for social change policies and programmes, whilst national governments often withdraw their resources and depend on (other) stakeholder support for the delivery of sport as social aid.[59]

In South Africa's SfD space, the government sector provides the policies and often controls access to impoverished public spaces and school populations. For this reason, partnerships with various ministries or governmental entities at different levels (e.g., local municipalities) are forged to enable especially civil society agencies to deliver SfD programmes at schools, community centres and health clinics. In partnership with government entities, civil society agencies form the backbone of community-level delivery. The private sector operates differently. For instance, the corporate sector often favours competitive sport that would enhance their public profile and ensure media interest, attracting more consumers in a competitive market. The higher education sector represents a somewhat untapped source where academics and post-graduate students can undertake policy work, impact assessments, and assist in education, training, and capacity building.

5.4.2 Key South African Players in the SfD Field

Hundreds of organisations deliver SDP programmes across South Africa, thus choosing only a few does not do justice to the significant impact all have at the local level. For the sake of brevity, only two network organisations are presented in this chapter: Laureus Sport for Good and a national project led by SSCNA. Their partnerships with community-based organisations and the latter's work tell a collective story of SDP at local levels of engagement.

5.4.2.1 Laureus

Background: Laureus is comprised of the Laureus World Sports Academy, the Laureus Sport for Good Foundation and the Laureus Sports Awards, which *"collectively harness the power of sport to produce social change (and celebrate sporting excellence)"*.[60] The organisation was founded under the patronage of Nelson Mandela.

Laureus Sport for Good uses sport as a cost-effective tool to help children and young people overcome violence, discrimination and disadvantage in their lives in 50 countries globally, including South Africa.[61] They support their partners and fund more than 275 programmes, of which 28 partners and their diverse programmes are in South Africa, including martial arts, boxing, performing arts (circus), surfing, canoeing, surfing, rugby, soccer, netball, basketball, rope skipping and physical education.

Mission: The Laureus Sport for Good Foundation believes that sport can change how people view the world. For them, the values of sport can bring together families, friends, nations – and on occasion, the whole world – in a way that no other human activity can.

Aims: The following aims linked to different SDGs guide the funding, support, leadership and advocacy offered by Laureus Sport for Good:

- Health and well-being: enhance mental well-being and increase access to healthy living (SDG 3).
- Education: access to, and support for, individuals to complete formal education programmes (SDG 4).
- Women and girls: promote equality, empowerment and safety (SDG 5).
- Employability: develop skills and create pathways to employment (SDG 8).
- Inclusive society: create communities where people embrace ethnic, cultural and physical differences (SDG 11).
- Peaceful society: reresolvesolving conflict, promote community peace-making and create safe spaces (SDG 16).

5.4.2.2 Sport for Social Change Network Africa (SSCNA) – Youth employment project

Background: In South Africa, the SSCNA is the leading SDP network.[62] A recent focus in on a nationwide programme, for which it partnered with the Presidential Youth Employment Intervention (PYEI) as part of the Presidential Employment Stimulus (PES), that can be identified as a sport-for-employment initiative.[63] Six of the SSCNA member organisations became implementing partners. Five non-government agencies (NGOs) appointed an initial 215 youths as interns, whilst Special Olympics South Africa (SOSA) recruited 4,000 Persons with Intellectual Disabilities (PWID) among their athlete population.

Aim: To enhance employability and access to employment opportunities for youth placed with Altus Sport, Children of the Dawn (COTD), SCORE, Tidimalong and Hout Bay United FC (HBUFC). In addition to the NGOs, Special Olympics South Africa (SOSA) made history and set a gold standard for the employment of their athletes, offering the *So Fit* programme at schools and skill centres across South Africa.

Programme: All the organisations received training and support and adhered to a rigorous monitoring system of online reporting and evaluation through scientific investigation, following a theory of change approach and participatory action research through online and on-site multi-method data collection. All stakeholders implemented the programme as part of their current offerings, focusing on building capacity and providing pathways to improved employability and employment (in some cases).

Outcomes: The programme enhanced entrepreneurship (20% of respondents), provided access to further education and training (ranging from 30% to 100% in different settings), improved employability and personal development, and developed vocational and soft skills related to self-efficacy, social skills and resilience. In addition, it provided access to employment (an average of 65%) in teacher assistant, coach, administrative and retail roles.

Households benefited by having income generation (poverty relief with 40% acting as temporary breadwinners), whilst the youth received acceptance and recognition (especially those with Special Olympics). The community benefited through safeguarding children, providing access to sport, employment opportunities and community integration. The programme increased its capacity and reach, added to the diversification of offerings and stakeholder engagement, and produced various good practices for the organisation.

5.5 CONCLUSION

The field of SDP in which SfD work is situated is a highly complex and interlinked ecosystem where multiple and diverse stakeholders across different sectors deliver on development and peace initiatives associated with sport and/or non-sport outcomes. UN leadership has created policy directives, frameworks and tools for government and other sectors to align their policies and programmes to ensure coherence and collaboration in order to bring about societal change. However, contextual realities and needs still inform local agendas for SfD projects, and tensions are created when international agencies create unequal partnerships and continue to dominate approaches and resource allocation.

The three phases show recognisable characteristics and transitions, although these may differ within different local settings and run concurrently as advocacy links to using sport as a tool for development within and across sectors. At the same time, collaboration between similar and different stakeholder types informs partnership dynamics for reciprocal benefits. For example, ministries of sport, government departments at different levels and non-government sectors have had long-standing partnerships in the SDP field. However, there is still a lack of meaningful integration at the policy level and meaningful collaboration (including the sharing of ownership and resources) between different government departments (e.g., sport, education, health, youth, arts and culture) and external stakeholders (e.g., corporates, the competitive sport sector, the media and civil society agencies). The shadow from within relates to power-sharing, sustainability, volunteerism and youth employment, the deficit perspective, and the co-creation of knowledge. Learning from good practices and finding innovative ways to harness the power of sport need to go beyond the rhetoric of language of inspiration to produce action and find ways to make a difference within and through sport.

As we are just a few years from the 2030 global and national visions for change, the time for action in clear and pragmatic ways is most urgent. We cannot wait for international inspiration, but must bring about the change we want wherever we may find ourselves.

SELF-ASSESSMENT

1. Differentiate between Sport for Development (SfD) and Sport in Development.
2. Provide examples to explain the difference and links between Sport Plus (sport for good) and Plus Sport (development of and through sport).
3. Describe SDP as a social movement as discussed by Bruce Kidd in his 2008 publication.
4. Identify three main developmental phases in SDP and provide examples of being inspirational as a tool for development and as a catalyst for change in an integrated way.
5. Describe the timeline of global developments regarding SDP globally and discuss how it influenced SDP in southern Africa.
6. How did SDP take root in South Africa in the aftermath of the dismantling of Apartheid?
7. Reflect on the role of prominent stakeholders in SDP in South Africa.
8. How did the Covid-19 pandemic influence the role of civic society as a stakeholder in SDP in South Africa?
9. Discuss some case studies of SDP work in South Africa and reflect on how you would implement the SDP initiatives of your choice.

SPORT, RECREATION AND LEISURE

Dr Natasha Janse van Rensburg

LEARNING OUTCOMES

At the end of this chapter, you should be able to:

1. Define the concept of leisure.
2. Describe the various elements of leisure.
3. Differentiate between recreation and sport by using examples of activities.
4. List the activity areas and formats commonly used in leisure programme classification.
5. Describe the three categories of benefits as they relate to leisure participation.
6. Define leisure constraints.
7. Illustrate the stages of the leisure constraints negotiation process diagrammatically.
8. Explain how a Sport Manager could assist in negotiating strategies to increase leisure participation.

6.1 INTRODUCTION

An essential part of the management of sport is understanding the terminology underpinning various customer behaviours. While many people participate in organised sport events in South Africa, the country also supports multiple leisure activities. Many people may not realise that a Sport Manager should have a broad understanding of people's leisure behaviours and preferences. The successful management of sport programmes relies on a proper knowledge of sport and recreation and how these concepts relate to leisure. This chapter will discuss the concepts of leisure, recreation and sport. Additional topics central to working with people in the sport and recreation professions and understanding their needs include reasons for participation and leisure constraints.

6.2 DEFINING CONCEPTS

When considering the definition of sport, *The White Paper on Sport and Recreation for the Republic of South Africa* states that people could participate in sport within a structured or unstructured environment for various reasons, including relaxation, physical health or emotional growth, to name a few. To better understand the definition of sport, a sport management professional should consider the theoretical foundation upon which sport is constructed. The way we think about sport, its benefits and its constructs is based on the leisure theory.[1;2] Because leisure may be conceptualised in a variety of ways, the personal meaning leisure has for an individual will guide, in a way, how much time and effort they will spend on activities during their leisure time. People's perceptions of the value of leisure will influence their motivation to seek activities, as well as their motivation to participate in those activities. The same can be said for a Sport Manager. Their perception and knowledge about leisure will influence their actions, for example, the reasons for choosing certain activities, the benefits they foresee and how they will choose to market their programmes.

For the Sport Manager to become more aware of the various leisure theories, it is essential to understand the various terminologies. Terms such as sport, recreation and leisure are interchangeable, but are not synonyms. A professional part of our work is to use the correct concepts in the right context, therefore a thorough knowledge of the concepts (sport, recreation and leisure) is needed. While all three concepts are used in the sport management profession, the idea of sport and recreation activities and their benefits stems from leisure, i.e., sport and recreation are born from leisure. Leisure is not only an activity but rather a viewpoint or concept; it is overarching and includes sport and recreation as activity choices based on people's preferences. Typically, when people make time in their busy lives (leisure time), they feel motivated to spend it on certain activities (sport or recreation), which will give them specific benefits. In the next section, it will become evident that leisure has more to do with time, activity choice and reasons for participation and benefits. Without leisure, both sport and recreation would not exist. Consequently, discussing each concept and describing how they relate is necessary.

6.2.1 Leisure

The definitions of leisure vary.[3;4;5;6;7] Many researchers agree that leisure can be viewed based on specific activities, free time and state of mind. All three of these concepts can be perceived differently, for example, the concept of activity is contested in terms of its appropriateness to the theory of leisure. An activity should be well organised, essentially being *built* for a specific purpose or benefit to be obtained from it, like participating in a hiking trail with the guidance of an instructor. Therefore, merely walking in the park would not be considered as organised compared to a hiking trip. For this reason, more organised activities would be needed to meet the rigour of the leisure theories. What is free time? While most think it is time set aside for relaxation or forgetting about work or other obligations, many people do not have time available or even options for activities to participate in during their free time. For this reason, we see many people experiencing boredom during free time or even anxiety. Differences in definitions could even be based on those who work in the field of leisure (professionals) and those who do not work in the area (non-professionals). When asked, some professionals will have a deeper and more differentiated understanding of leisure.[8] Like many businesses, when Sport Managers work with clients daily, they learn how their clients behave, which programmes are more successful, and which outcomes or benefits can be obtained. In essence, it is about understanding the clients in a real-life situation, which is the context of their population.

While those who work with leisure daily might explain leisure based on their observations of their clients, we (as scholars) can define leisure from what is written in academic work such as textbooks and journal articles. Conceptualising leisure purely from literature might be problematic since much of the published work is from Western countries, with very few publications on leisure research based on the South African population. Adopting a Western description of leisure in South Africa could be challenging, however. The sport management professional should consider that a Western definition might not agree with the cultural consensus of the leisure concept within their population, i.e., a definition may be based on the influence of demographic characteristics such as gender, ethnicity and race, which research has shown influence leisure preferences and behaviour.[9] It is reasonable to assume that given your race or gender, certain activities might be inappropriate, less attractive or even unreasonable, which will change how leisure is defined. While it is important to recognise that not all people would define leisure in the same way, Sport Managers should beware of typical stereotypes and their association with leisure preference (e.g., gender- or age-specific activities). When working with a diverse population, such as in South Africa, the sport management professional should always consider the effects of gender, ethnicity and race on leisure behaviour and deploy efforts to understand their clients' needs.[10;11;12;13;14] By undertaking a needs assessment, a professional could build a clear picture of the leisure preference of a population, rather than relying on predetermined ideas.

While needs assessments help determine a communities' leisure perceptions, the definition of leisure could be problematic. Considering if a Western-defined concept is appropriate for non-Western countries (e.g., South Africa) or non-English-speaking cultures shows how difficult it is to determine one specific definition of leisure which everyone would agree on. The translation of leisure to Afrikaans or Sotho, or any other official language spoken in South Africa, is not easy since many of the 11 official languages in South Africa do not include a word for leisure. The professionals should thus ask themselves how they would be able to determine what people would like to participate in (needs assessment) if the word for leisure is not available in someone's home language. While some languages do not include a word for leisure, research has found that language and how leisure is translated do not influence how leisure is experienced or perceived. Yet even if there is no evidence that language and how leisure is translated influence how leisure is experienced, explaining what it means is essential if you provide a professional service in that domain.[15] To provide the best possible sport service to all South Africans, how individuals will relate to leisure activities and how they will explain their leisure needs will depend on the person and context in which leisure is perceived.

For the purposes of this chapter, the general description or definition of leisure used is: 'Being intrinsically motivated to participate in a freely chosen activity during a person's free time.'[16;17] To unpack the concept of leisure, it is best to take each part of its description as a point of discussion:

1. Free time or non-obligated time.
2. Chosen activity.
3. State of mind.
4. Intrinsically motivated.

6.2.1.1   Free time or non-obligated time

One of the common elements included in the various definitions of leisure is the inclusion of the phrases 'free time' or 'non-obligated time'. According to some researchers, the time a person has available can be divided into three key area, namely existence, subsistence and discretionary time.[18] A person's time on fulfilling basic needs, such as working or eating, refers to the existence and subsistence times. In contrast, the time people have not allocated to obligations (non-obligated time) refers to discretionary time.

As Sport Managers, it is essential to think of people's personal preferences and how every person can increase the amount of money and time spent between these different times in their daily lives. For example, depending on your client's preference and circumstances, they may spend more time on household duties and have less free or non-obligated time to spend on activities. Separating what constitutes existence, subsistence and discretionary time can be difficult. An example might be eating – for many people eating is part of existence, while others might use baking or cooking to fill their free time. Yet others might enjoy trying new recipes or restaurants, whereas some make it their job to prepare food, write about it or own such a business.

When considering sport, the same problem of identifying obligated vs. non-obligated time arises. Researchers have explained that when looking at the physical nature of sport activities, they can be seen as healthy or fun, or even both.[19] Therefore, participating in sport may be done in existence and discretionary time. People who try to live healthy lives balance their existence, subsistence and discretionary time, and how they choose to balance their time is based on personal preference. Environmental changes, such as economic factors, might increase the likelihood of people working longer than decades ago. On the other hand, the trend in careers such as social media influencers and bloggers has allowed society to incorporate their interests with paying jobs.[20] Even famous athletes tend to participate in other sporting codes during their free time. Another prominent researcher in the field of leisure, Professor Karla Henderson, includes another way to look at the difference between obligated and non-obligated time by referring to cyclical or linear time. She explained that linear time is structured using diaries or calendars and is planned around obligations such as work hours. Cyclical time is not scheduled or fixed, however, but is rather designed around a recurring cycle which repeats itself endlessly.[21] For example, a person participating in a specific sport or recreation activity will experience something new (stimulus) while participating, and will move onto a new or more challenging activity level as they adapt or learn from the stimulus.

6.2.1.2   The activity

The second key element in the definition of leisure is 'activity'. Considering that leisure occurs when a person has non-obligated time, it is easy to understand that something must occupy that time. This is more challenging than one might think, as activity is difficult to define.[22] Some leisure scholars describe an activity as something a person chooses to participate in during their free time, like swimming.[23] Some disagree, however, arguing that an activity should be official to add to the definition of leisure. They say that for any activity to be officially called leisure, there needs to be some research to test if it is officially leisure or not.[24] Testing activities for this research require an assessment of how often the activity is participated in (frequency), the benefits derived from participation, and the money spent. Marking activities as official leisure activities or not is essential for Sport Managers since some people participate in leisure as a time-filler, like watching television, which is different from what we (as leisure scholars) would define as leisure. Sport managers should, however, be careful to look at context, motivation (covered later in this chapter) and personal perceptions before determining what official leisure or time-fillers are.

One way to think about these views (context, motivation and personal perceptions) in a practical example is gardening. Many people would say that gardening is a hobby, explaining that it provides relaxation during their free time. They invest primarily in buying plants and equipment, with some visiting gardening shows or exhibitions. Others may say gardening is merely maintenance and service, however, which they would rather contract out than do themselves. Another vital message Sport Managers can take from the gardening example is that leisure activities should be seen as non-work, meaning activities that hold no relation to work duties or the feeling of *working*.[25] All scholars agree that the list of leisure activities is endless, subjective and forever evolving.

6.2.1.3 State of mind

A third element of the definition of leisure relates to one's 'state of mind'. Leisure scholars explain that for leisure to be experienced, a specific state of mind must be present.[26] Four forms of state of mind are frequently found during leisure participation: perceived freedom, positive affect, intrinsic motivation and perceived competence.

For this chapter, perceived freedom refers to a person's feeling of freely choosing the activities they wish to participate in. In contrast, positive affect refers to how much people feel they can influence their leisure experience. Perceived competency is the self-perception of a person that they have the required skills to participate in the activity they have chosen. The last state of mind refers to intrinsic motivation, also known as self-determined behaviour, meaning a person is in complete control of participating in the selected activity. This state of mind (intrinsic motivation) has been a focus of many leisure scholars' research and will be discussed in the following section.

If leisure cannot be forced on someone and requires a specific state of mind, how would it be possible to forget all other responsibilities during participation? For example, someone who jogs or gardens for relaxation might still feel anxious about work or meetings ahead. Then the activity does not serve a purpose under the concept of leisure. Instead, what is needed is the feeling of being absorbed into the activity at such a level that the participant *forgets*. Some leisure researchers refer to this absorbing experience as flow.[27] Csikszentmihalyi's theory of flow (1975) proposes that for a person to have a positive experience while participating in an activity, there should be a balance between their skill level and the level of challenge.[28] When there is a balance between the two, the person will experience flow. When will participants feel happy, have no distractions and optimally engage in the activity by acting spontaneously? For this balance to occur, it takes knowledge on behalf of the professional to match the clients' abilities (skills) with the correct activity level (challenge). When any activity poses too big of a challenge to a participant, the participant will become anxious, or if the activity is not a challenge, boredom is experienced. Therefore, balance is essential.

6.2.1.4   Intrinsically motivated

The last element of leisure is derived from the previous section, which spoke about a person's state of mind, and includes participation that was not forced and was undertaken for personal reasons (intrinsically motivated). Sport managers must understand why people participate in leisure activities, whether sport or recreation, as their ability to participate is what will determine the success of programmes. For scholars in sport and recreation, the question "What motivates people to participate?" is always present and the focus of many research studies. While motivation research transcends the sport and recreation field, this standard psychological process helps Sport Managers to understand what initiates and sustains sport and recreation participation. To cover this element, it is best to look at motivation as one part.

Motivation is defined as *"an interaction of internal factors (unconscious and conscious psychological compulsions) and external factors (social and familial gratification and recognition), which are combined with a variety of drives (basic drives, self-image, experience) that can evolve and change over time".*[29] For this chapter, Sport Managers should know that motivation consists of various hidden forces that influence a participant's behaviour. While it is essential to understand that specific forces could assist Sport Managers in increasing participation, the opposite might also happen, i.e., these forces might cause non-participation or single participation. For example, objectively viewing a participant who goes to the gymnasium seven days a week, one might think they are highly motivated, yet there is no way to accurately measure motivation just by viewing behavioural aspects. For example, this person might gain multiple points from their healthcare insurer and work out to get a certain percentage of their monthly premium deducted. Based on the previous information on leisure participation, does the same level of 'being highly motivated' still apply for the benefit of health and wellness, or is it personal gain?

While there are many theories of understanding or determining motivation, it is essential to recognise the interaction between internal and external factors when determining motivation for sport and recreation activities. An example of this interaction would be how a sport competition will motivate participation for the prize money or the need to achieve something like social standing. As an element of leisure, being intrinsically motivated to participate is essential.

There must be something like being non-intrinsically motivated if there is intrinsic motivation. This type of behaviour refers to extrinsic motivation and amotivation. According to the motivation researchers Ryan and Deci, the opposite of intrinsic motivation is extrinsic motivation, for example, when a person does an activity for external rewards or to avoid punishment.[30] When a person has no feeling of being competent to participate in an activity, and they might not see any benefit from participating, it may cause them to feel unmotivated. Research has found that boredom, nonattendance or decreasing participation is linked with amotivation.[31] A person who experiences amotivation has no control over their participation, nor can they understand their participation (what is the benefit of this?). Therefore, these participants will drop out or not return as customers or frequent participants. For many sport and recreation programmes, regular participation or sustainability is essential. The need for participants to be intrinsically motivated is thus evident, yet participation is sometimes sparked by the hope of winning a prize or getting recognition. Therefore, it is unlikely that all motivation is intrinsically regulated. While some people might start participating for the award or recognition, they might find internal benefits from participation and need to remember it is a competition.

Although motivational factors may differ from one person to the next, or even from one activity to the next, understanding this behaviour gives valuable insight for any Sport Manager into their potential client's behaviour. In addition, this behavioural information provides the basis for other managerial plans, like segmentation for marketing efforts and the provision of additional services. These services may include both sport and recreation activities.

6.2.2 Recreation

Now that it has been established that leisure is more about what a person's free time is, what a person chooses to do in that time is where recreation and sport concepts come into play. While society uses the concepts of leisure and recreation interchangeably, it is essential to realise that they are not synonymous.

Recreation can be defined as different activities people participate in during their leisure time.[32] The number of recreational activities is impossible to determine as the activity areas and formats are broad and ever-increasing as society evolves. Recreational activities could be as physical and adventurous as rock climbing or shark diving, or as mentally stimulating as playing chess or gardening. A Sport Manager must thus have extensive knowledge of various recreation activities and connect each with their customers' preferences or needs. Some researchers have found that client satisfaction is directly linked to how recreation activities are structured, an activity that the Sport Managers have direct control over.[33;34] Because there are many different recreation activities to choose from, these activities are commonly grouped in activity areas or sets.[35] These areas or sets include aquatics (e.g., swimming, boating or other water sports), adventure (e.g., rock climbing, surfing or hiking), dance (e.g., ballroom, tap or ballet), drama (e.g., plays, puppetry or films), fine arts (e.g., painting, photography or sculpture), crafts (e.g., needling, pottery or cooking), music (e.g., instrumental, vocal or listening), hobbies (e.g., collecting, educational classes or shows), outdoor or nature (e.g., camping, backpacking or stargazing), intellectual or literary (e.g., reading, writing or puzzles), travel (e.g., tours, cruises or eco-tourism), social recreation (e.g., parties, picnics or dances), volunteer services (e.g., coaching, fundraising or youth mentorship) and sports (e.g., physical games, extreme sports or team athletics). The list is endless, and as technology advances, more activities are moving online or becoming virtually available.

While it might be difficult to decide if activities, for example, hiking, are outdoor or adventure, the activity areas are guidelines for the Sport Manager or programmer to choose from a large variety of activities or similar activities when needed. The recreational experience of the activities presented in the activity areas can be organised by deciding on certain structures, which are referred to as programme formats.[36] Programme formats may include competitions, leagues, drop-ins, clubs, and instructional or class formats. Other elements such as intensity levels, frequency and participation styles are aspects the Sport Manager can control, which depend on the customer's age, race, gender, ability and competitiveness. The Sport Manager must thus match the correct activity with their customers' needs to experience leisure. But this is no small task. Leisure scholars have stated that determining which format is the best for all customers is complex, and no consistent formula is available.[37] Therefore, this function could be seen more as an art than a management function. Due to the importance of this function within the field of leisure research, this function has its speciality and is referred to as leisure programming.

Another reason why matching a client's need with the correct format is a function on its own is the need to adjust, modify, swap and tailor formats for clients. Like a suit, many recreational activities and how they are participated in cannot fit all people in society as is. The Sport Manager, as the programmer, needs to have the ability to reprogramme recreational activity formats to meet specific clients' needs if the occasion calls for it. An example of adapting designs could be due to participants' abilities, like easing rules for children or adjusting the equipment for disabled clients. Some clients prefer less competitive formats, like participating for fun, while others would like to test their skills in competition formats. While competing against an opponent is one way of participating in a sport like basketball, a client must have been instructed in the sport before. Many clients need instruction, and giving them exposure to new activities is as important as organising tournaments or competitions. Sport managers also need to recognise that some clients are more experienced in a particular sport, even working with athletes who are well known in specific sport codes, and thus might need to participate in recreational activities for relaxation and fun during their leisure time. The challenge Sport Managers face is to understand clients' needs, be informed on trends like online activities, or be able to adapt to circumstances like the recent Covid-19 pandemic.

Additionally, a Sport Manager must consider their client's additional needs, such as socialisation, and choose the format according to this need. For example, while a client participates in many recreational activities (such as reading), meaning there is no need for a companion to execute the activity, others need additional participants (such as football). Clients might want the benefits, like meeting new people, from leisure participation to increase their satisfaction. Others might participate with friends and family, like going on a hike during the weekend with their loved ones. Subsequently, the selected format by a Sport Manager may affect a client's satisfaction, either positively or negatively. Sport managers' ability to be more creative and think of ways to alter traditional formats of recreation activities is the only way to become competitive in the market.[38] Being knowledgeable about the population and individual needs, as well as supplying well-thought-out recreation activities (with adaptable formats), is a critical skill for Sport Managers. Even though it is not part of this chapter, the topic of inclusiveness and its relationship with adopting activities for special needs adds to the Sport Managers' catalogue of programming skills.

6.2.3 Sport

It is essential to distinguish between sport and recreation, i.e., the definition of sport relates to an established, competitive and physical activity using certain or specialised facilities and equipment and having specific rules stipulated.[39] While not all sport activities are physical, for example, chess, it is because of the activity's competitive nature that it is classified as a sport. In the context of this chapter, the connection between leisure and sport is the motivational part. Motivation for sport is intrinsic and extrinsic,[40] yet as per the previous section, we know that for any activity to be considered leisure, participation should be due to intrinsic motivation.

For this reason, when athletes become highly competitive, they move outside the parameters of leisure and their extrinsic motivation is money or acknowledgement. Therefore, participation for cash contradicts the fundamentals of leisure. For this reason (within the leisure perspective), the Sport Manager can look at sport activities as an option within clients' needs to fill their leisure time rather than as recreation activities.

Sport within leisure time can also be divided between active participation and spectating. Both these forms use sport within the client's leisure time, yet in one, the client is directly involved (participation), and in the other, they are indirectly involved (spectating). People enjoy both, and both have benefits. Educating a client in a sport is more successful when the Sport Manager provides them with direct involvement, meaning the opportunity to participate. Although not everybody can play for a national sports team, many people are satisfied to fill their leisure time by observing them play. The same kind of satisfaction might not be obtained from watching an amateur team play and refers once again to understanding the client and their needs.

6.3 BENEFITS OF LEISURE

There are many benefits obtained from participation in well-thought-out and structured activities during leisure time.[41] However, it is said that the activity (recreation or sport) is only the vehicle through which the benefits are carried. Therefore, the activity can be designed like a vehicle to do a specific job. In this case, the job refers to a particular benefit or benefits.

In the literature on leisure, many benefits are mentioned, ranging from physical and cognitive, to emotional, social and spiritual.[42;43] Many of these benefits overlap, which is why researchers have organised them into three categories: 1) improving condition; 2) prevention or maintaining condition; and 3) satisfying recreation experiences.[44]

The first category refers to how leisure tends to improve conditions. For example, how active participation in physical activities will have the natural tendency to increase fitness and assist with weight loss. Global issues with obesity show a need for more participation in physical leisure activities to prevent health issues and assist with balancing a healthy lifestyle. While many people do not have access to gymnasiums or structured weight loss programmes, re-engineering sport and leisure activities to be fun while activating is one way of increasing physical activity levels. Research has shown that an early introduction to physical activity assists with lifelong participation.[45] Introducing more types of sport and recreation activities to young children will thus assist in creating a habit of participation. In addition, participation in leisure activities (sport or recreation) reduces stress levels, and has even shown an increase in students' academic performance.[46;47]

The second category refers to leisure's ability to maintain a stable condition. While no physical change needs to happen, participation in leisure will keep the participant's current state (or community) from becoming problematic. An example of this is the saying: "Those who play together, stay together." In leisure terms, this saying can be explained as how activities can help people deal with stress or learn to take breaks in their busy life by taking the time to participate in constructive leisure activities (sport or recreation).[48] There is also a sense of a protective factor in activities embedded in our heritage, which are practiced to keep them as traditions. Many traditional or indigenous activities need to provide platforms in which participation is planned, not only to show or educate new generations, but also to keep them from being lost. Providing communities with opportunities to showcase their heritage assists in them feeling socially accepted. Consistent participation in leisure activities will make a person feel more competent, self-sufficient and self-determined.[49] These are essential skills as they will help people deal with issues they might face in their everyday lives and teach them how to persist during difficult times.

Participation in group activities has also shown an increase in social interactions, promoting friendship and support. Social support has numerous benefits, but having a sense of belonging is an essential stabiliser for many people to exist. Research has shown that social support can decrease depression, which is a significant societal issue.[50] Group activities also provide the opportunity for unity when rules must be respected and followed. This encourages the same feeling in society and helps maintain community peace. Through participation, many people get a break from their everyday lives as it allows them to escape their responsibilities and restore their mental health. Although the hope is that all leisure activities are fun, they also provide some time for introspection and thinking of ways to deal with situations by transferring lessons from the activity to real life.[51] Some leisure activities are complex and need those who choose to participate in them to have endurance and resilience, which are valuable skills to cope with life.

The third and final category refers to the intrinsic value gained through participation in leisure activities. Participation in activities will be experienced differently for each person, like the differences in their reasons for participation. For example, if a client would like to learn more about a specific sport code, their reason for participation in the activity is purely for education. While participating, they may meet other people at the programme and gain friendships as a benefit they did not plan on (neither did the Sport Manager when they started the planning). In the same programme, some people might not make any friends, however. Some benefits, like instructional benefits or learning something new, can be controlled by the Sport Manager, but others cannot be controlled or planned. This can be referred to as how leisure creates opportunities for the programmer or Sport Manager (in this case) to plan certain physical, social and natural elements to activities so that people can gain optimal benefits through their participation.[52]

When characterising leisure from a business perspective, it should be seen as a service rather than a product, since specific benefits are expected from participation. As per the previous section, benefits can be unpredictable, however. Like a business, leisure participation should be sustainable. Importantly, when certain predetermined benefits are not obtained, the client will feel disappointed. At this point in the post-participation evaluation, frequency declines or stops altogether. Other factors could also cause a client to refrain from participating or stopping their participation. These are what leisure scholars refer to as leisure constraints.

6.4 LEISURE CONSTRAINTS

Leisure constraints are defined as factors that prevent participation in leisure activities.[53] There are three types or dimensions to constraints: structural, intra-, and interpersonal. Structural constraints refer to resources that affect leisure participation, such as transportation, access to or lack of facilities, and lack of finances. Intrapersonal constraints refer to personal characteristics that affect leisure preferences, such as abilities, while interpersonal constraints are obtained from a person's immediate environment (like family and friends). Each of the constraints plays a significant role and will be present. The ability to negotiation through constraints determines participation or nonparticipation. Based on this information, the negation model (Figure 6.1) was proposed.[54;55]

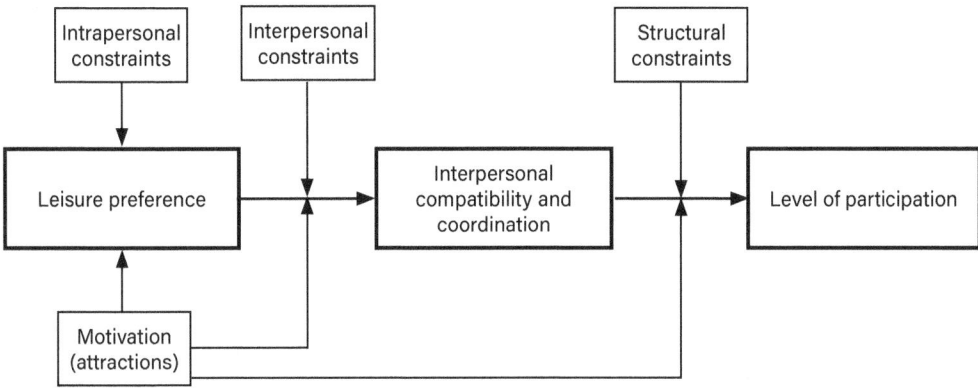

Figure 6.1: The negotiation model[56]

The model proposes that the three constraints are sequenced in the following manner and will affect a person in the same order, starting with intrapersonal, then interpersonal and lastly, structural constraints. For the Sport Manager to see participation in a leisure activity, the clients would have been able to negotiate the various leisure constraints successfully, starting with intrapersonal constraints. Intrapersonal constraints need to be dealt with first because this includes personality factors. An example of this kind of constraint would be a shy person or someone who struggles to meet people. While the person is mainly responsible for learning negotiation strategies and assisting themselves with negotiating past these constraints, the Sport Manager or programmer could also have a role to play. The wrong conclusion is that these people should only participate in activities meant to be experienced independently and avoid team or social activities. The role of a programmer could be to assist by allowing people to participate in group activities with friends and family. Therefore, the objective of programming leisure activities is to modify the behaviour, rather than for the behaviour to lead to non-participation. In the model, motivation is included because it can influence a person's capability of negotiating intra- and interpersonal constraints. An example would be someone who does not want to participate, therefore their motivation and willingness to negotiate the rules will be low.

The second constraint refers to interpersonal feelings, such as being bored with the activity or that close family and friends would not agree with someone's participation. In society, interpersonal constraints often relate to stereotypes, especially in sport and recreation, where many activities are gender biased. One strategy to assist with the negotiation would be encouraging friends and family to come along or encouraging new activity formats to try out. Education regarding sport and recreation in terms of breaking the stereotypes that some activities can only be participated in by a particular race or gender, starts with support from the programmer's side. The last constraint that needs to be negotiated is structural constraints. This might refer to not having the proper equipment or clothing, or not having enough time to participate. This last constraint is seen as a barrier that can directly affect participation and should be actively managed by the Sport Manager or programmer. One way to assist would be to include equipment or clothing hire as an option, to get more sponsors involved to reduce participation prices, or to shorten the time needed to complete the activity.

Many researchers have studied the factors causing leisure constraints, such as demographic variables, and even tried to find other conditions to become better at increasing participation. From a business perspective, it is essential to understand your client's behaviour; removing as much resistance to using your service would mean better business. Whether it is a non-profit organisation's community project, such as learn how to swim programmes or community football clubs, the local park or the private country club in the community, each programme needs to be sustainable. Sustainability, in this sense, means continuously meeting the client's needs by understanding their leisure behaviour.

6.5 CONCLUSION

In this chapter, the concept of leisure was discussed. While the definition of leisure is not readily agreed upon, various elements are common among leisure scholars. To understand leisure, it is necessary to look at each of these elements separately and how they relate to leisure. It was also required to define recreation and sport, since these concepts are used interchangeably in South African communities. The Sport Manager must understand why people participate and what might stop or reduce their participation. The last part of the chapter presented a model on leisure constraint negotiation, represented in Figure 6.1. This provided ideas on negotiation strategies that Sport Managers could consider to assist in the participation of leisure activities.

SELF-ASSESSMENT

1. By using your language, translate the word 'leisure'. Name the translated word to a close family or friend and ask them to explain it to you. Does this sound close to the definition of leisure?
2. Using your own words, define the term 'leisure'.
3. There are some aspects of the concept of leisure. Explain each and provide relevant examples of how they relate to leisure.
4. Search the internet for pictures of one recreation and one sport activity. Use your image to explain the difference between recreation and sport activities.
5. Participation in leisure provides several benefits, which can be categorised into three areas. Describe each of the categories and provide examples of each.
6. Discuss the relevance of leisure constraints in the context of sport management.
7. Create a figure to demonstrate how a person will negotiate leisure constraints to participate in leisure activities. In the discussion of the figure, including negotiation strategies for each condition and how the Sport Manager could assist at that stage.

ATHLETE PERFORMANCE PATHWAYS

LJ van Zyl

LEARNING OUTCOMES

At the end of this chapter, you should be able to:

1. Describe the significance of performance pathways in South Africa.
2. Differentiate between the "pillars of performance" for all sport.
3. Discuss the early discontinuation of sport.
4. Argue how challenges in the high-performance phase can be addressed.

7.1 INTRODUCTION

National sport systems typically operate within the broader policy frameworks of governments and sport ministries. While variations across countries may exist, national sport systems generally align with government-level guidance and policies. The extent to which these systems follow government-level guidance can vary depending on the specific country's governance structures. Ministries of sport or equivalent government bodies are responsible for developing and implementing policies that govern sport at the national level. These policies often address athlete development, sport infrastructure, funding, governance, anti-doping and sport education. National Sport Federations' (NSFs) sport systems typically align their strategies, programmes and operations with these policies. Government-level guidance provides national sport systems' overarching visions, goals and strategic directions. It sets the policy agenda, outlines funding priorities and establishes regulations and standards for sport organisations and stakeholders. NSFs, in turn, interpret and operationalise these policies within their specific contexts. They design programmes, initiatives and pathways that align with the government's priorities and contribute to achieving the stated objectives. The partnership and alignment between NSFs and government bodies are essential for the effective and coordinated development of sports at the national level.

In the past two decades, we have witnessed increased participation in professional and amateur sport, restricting the long-term athlete development pathway (LTAD). LTAD has been described as the structured and progressive growth of athletes through different stages of development, resulting in some athletes achieving elite sport status.[1] The interest in the athletic performance pathway from a holistic perspective has contributed to management approaches underscoring sustainable talent development and participation in sport. Internationally, early talent identification and development has become increasingly important within youth sport structures and programmes. To achieve international and elite levels of competition, national sport systems provide a blueprint for youth athlete development.[2] Burnett[3] noted that national policy frameworks and guidance advise and align stakeholders in a delivering system or pipeline to foster athlete development. In addition, provincial and national development programmes focus on managing practices that influence athletes' holistic development to position them on a path of elite sport performance from an early age.[4]

In South Africa, NSFs are given priority by the government based on their historical significance, popularity and international success. The priority NSFs in South Africa typically include rugby, cricket, soccer, athletics, netball and swimming. These sports receive more funding, resources and attention from NSFs and government bodies than other sports. The emphasis on priority NSFs can have implications for implementing performance pathways. Firstly, it may lead to a concentration of resources and support within these sports, creating a disparity in opportunities for athletes in less-prioritised sports. Athletes in sports with limited resources may need help accessing quality coaching, training facilities and competitions, hindering their development and progression within performance pathways. Secondly, prioritising NSFs can influence talent identification and selection processes. NSFs and talent scouts may primarily target athletes in priority sports, potentially overlooking talent in others. This can result in a narrow talent pool and limit the diversity and breadth of athletes within performance pathways.

Furthermore, prioritising certain sports may impact specialised support services and infrastructure availability, for example, sport science, medicine and high-performance training facilities may be more readily available for priority sports. In contrast, athletes in other sports may need more access to these resources, affecting their overall development and performance.

7.2 PERFORMANCE PATHWAY THEORETICAL FRAMEWORK

A theoretical framework provides a lens through which understanding can be gained of a phenomenon through an in-depth discussion of relevant concepts, assumptions, discourses and theories related to the field.[5] The transition theory, in this case, can underpin a performance pathway.[6] This theory argues that individuals move in, through and out of life situations in an integrated way. To assist an individual in navigating through a transition, resources in a 4S System (situation, self, support, strategies) are regarded as assets to successful transitions. Individuals must be aware of their current situation and the reality of potential transitions, with that self-awareness including an understanding of one's coping assets and liabilities to manage transitions. Available support systems and strategies to cognitively approach, respond to and manage a change's positive and negative realities round out the 4S System of the transition theory. In a sport context, elements of the transition theory are applied and reflected in the career transition of the LTAD model of Balyi (1998) and different approaches to dual sport career development.

The career pathway model of Balyi[7] presents sport career development pathways that articulate progressive human growth and development. The differential layering of development phases relates to the socialisation process (into and through sport), which underpins the Olympic sport participation trajectory. Career development models will be selected because they represent Olympians' careers as an ongoing sequence rather than a single event. This supports the idea that athletes should be treated and viewed holistically by considering more than only athletic performance.

7.3 ATHLETE PERFORMANCE PATHWAYS IN SPORT

In discussing athlete performance pathways in South African sport, a combination of elements of the 4S System of the transition theory and the career pathway model of Balyi will be followed. These will include the athlete development support structures, long-term athlete development (LTAD) framework and resourcing of LTAD in South Africa.

7.3.1 Athlete Development Support Structures in South Africa

The National Department of Sport, Arts and Culture (DSAC), which oversees sport in South Africa, has charged the South African Sport Confederation and Olympic Committee (SASCOC) and the NSFs with providing high-performance sport to everyone in South Africa. The pathway for elite athletes to achieve high-performance status in sport includes tertiary institutions, sport academies and professional sport clubs. The South African system of supporting high-performance sport is shown in Figure 7.1.[8]

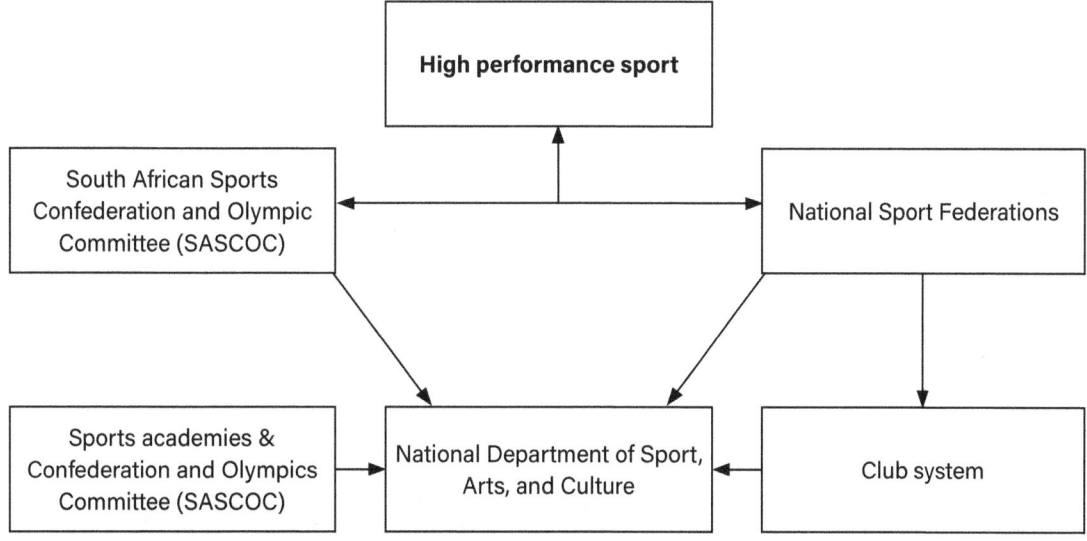

Figure 7.1: South African athlete development support structures

Performance pathways in South Africa provide a road map that brings an athlete through the stages of Long-Term Athlete Development (LTAD), while breaking down the levels of competition or events that fall within each stage. This helps to provide age- and developmentally-appropriate opportunities to participate in sport.[9]

7.3.1.1 Athletics South Africa athlete development support structures

Athletics South Africa (ASA), the national governing body for athletics in South Africa, has a structure that aligns with the principles of LTAD. LTAD provides a framework for the progressive development of athletes from grassroots levels to elite performance, taking into account age-appropriate training, skill acquisition and overall athlete well-being.

From a community to an elite level, the, ASA's structure can be outlined as follows:

1. Grassroots/Community Level: At the grassroots level, ASA encourages participation and introduces young athletes to the sport. This stage promotes physical literacy, fundamental movement skills and a love for athletics. Local clubs, schools and community-based initiatives are vital in providing entry-level opportunities for children to engage in basic running, jumping and throwing activities. ASA may provide resources, coaching guidance and support to clubs and schools to foster development at this stage.
2. Development Level: The development level aims to nurture young athletes' potential and enhance their athletic skills. This stage's essential components are talent identification programmes, school championships and provincial competitions. Athletes showing potential are identified with opportunities for specialised coaching, technical development and participation in higher-level competitions. ASA's development programmes may include training camps, talent identification initiatives and support services to assist athletes in reaching their full potential.
3. Provincial/National Level: At the provincial and national levels, athletes who demonstrate talent, dedication and performance potential progress further. Provincial athletics associations allow athletes to compete at a higher level in their regions, and successful performances at provincial championships and trials may lead to selection for national teams and competitions. ASA coordinates national championships, trials and high-performance training camps for athletes who have reached this stage.
4. High-Performance/Elite Level: The high-performance level encompasses athletes who have achieved a significant level of performance and represent South Africa at international competitions, such as the Olympic Games and World Championships. At this stage, ASA works closely with elite athletes, providing specialised coaching, access to sport science and medical support, and opportunities for international exposure and competition. National training centres and institutes may be utilised to provide state-of-the-art facilities and resources for elite athletes.

The LTAD framework informs the overall progression of athletes within ASA's structure, ensuring a systematic and progressive pathway for athlete development from community to elite levels.

7.3.2 The South African Long-Term Athlete Development Framework

From a management perspective, Sport Managers must recognise whether their sport is an early or late specialisation sport. This understanding helps develop appropriate training programmes, talent identification strategies and competition structures. Here are some examples of South African NSFs representing early and late specialisation sports, along with an overview of how the different phases of LTAD apply to them:

Early Specialisation Sport:

1. Gymnastics is an early specialisation sport where athletes train young to develop specific technical skills and flexibility. The different phases of LTAD focus on introducing fundamental movement skills and basic gymnastics techniques in the Active Start and FUNdamentals phases. As athletes progress to the Learn to Train and Train-to-Train phases, they receive more specialised training in apparatus-specific skills, strength, conditioning and competition readiness.
2. Diving is another example of an early specialisation sport. Athletes in diving require specific skills and techniques from a young age. In the early phases, emphasis is placed on developing fundamental movement skills, body awareness and basic diving techniques. As athletes move through the LTAD stages, the focus shifts towards more advanced diving skills, technical refinement, physical conditioning, mental skills training and competitive performance.

Late Specialisation Sport:

1. Athletics includes various track and field events and is a late specialisation sport. In the early phases of LTAD, athletes engage in various activities, developing fundamental movement skills, coordination and overall athleticism. As they progress through the LTAD model, athletes may specialise in specific events based on their abilities and interests. The training focus becomes more event-specific, including technical skill development, event-specific strength and conditioning, competition preparation and performance optimisation.
2. Basketball is a late specialisation sport where athletes can benefit from participating in multiple sports and developing a broad range of physical skills. In the early stages of LTAD, athletes engage in general physical preparation, skill development and exposure to different game formats. As athletes advance through the LTAD phases, the focus shifts towards position-specific skills, tactical understanding, strength and conditioning, competitive play and performance enhancement.

Understanding whether a sport is an early or late specialisation sport allows managers to tailor their strategies accordingly. They can provide diverse participation and skill development opportunities in early specialisation sports. In contrast, in late specialisation sports, they can emphasise multi-sport participation, overall athleticism and gradual specialisation as athletes progress through the LTAD stages. This approach supports long-term athlete development, maximises potential and helps create a sustainable talent pipeline in each sport.

The seven-stage LTAD framework is used in South Africa as a performance pathway that guides participation, training, competition and recovery pathways in sport and physical activity over time. These stages are Active Start, FUNdamentals, Learning to Train, Training to Train, Training to Compete, Training to Win, and Active for Life (see Figure 7.2).

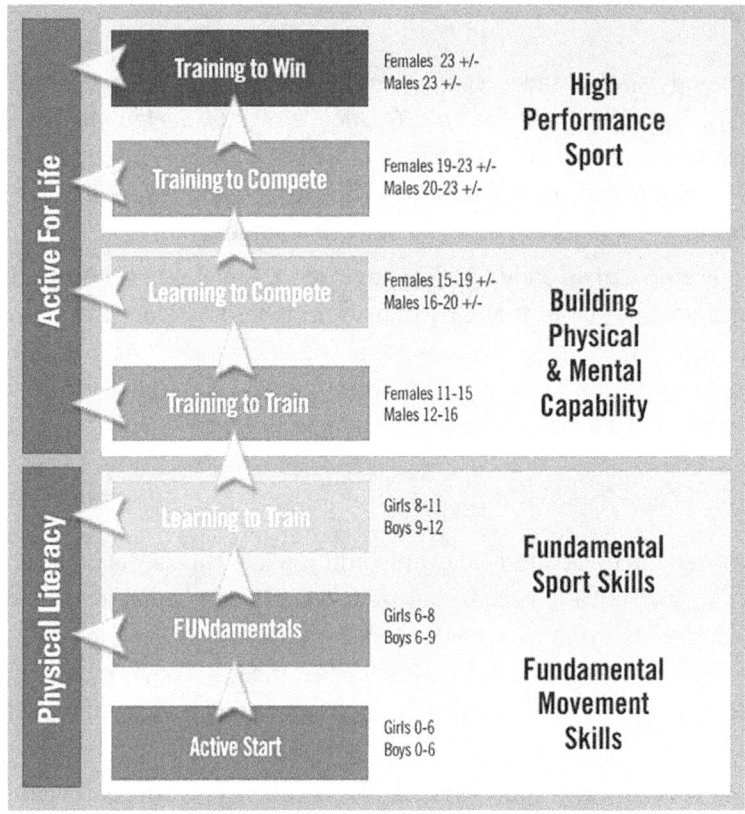

Figure 7.2: Long-term athlete development framework[10]

7.3.2.1 *Active start*

As the first stage of the LTAD model, the goal of Active Start is to make physical activity an essential and enjoyable component of everyday life. It introduces physical activity into a child's daily routine through casual play. From birth to six years for both males and females, this stage is the kickstart to nurturing a healthy attitude towards physical activity and nutrition throughout a child's life.

7.3.2.2 *FUNdamentals*

This stage introduces fine-tuning motor skills through agility, balance and coordination ABCs. It continues to instil the fun of everyday play and sport, emphasising structured movement such as running, jumping, kicking, catching and twisting. This stage typically occurs from ages six to nine for boys and six to eight for girls. It encourages experiences in sport while remaining fun and safe.

7.3.2.3 *Learning to train*

This stage improves upon the ABCs while monitoring physical, mental and emotional components. The performance of motor skills is evident in this stage as individual characteristics continue to develop. Gender differences become increasingly apparent during this stage and training guidelines become more individualised. Boys aged nine to 12 are included, while girls are between 8 and 11.

7.3.2.4 *Training to train*

This is the most challenging transition of all stages in the LTAD model. As individuals develop sport-specific skills, physicality changes rapidly and needs to be monitored for mental and physical health. This stage reflects ages 12 to 16 for males and 11 to 15 for females. Skills development involves endurance, strength and speed. Rapid growth can lead to poor habits, therefore flexibility, posture and technique should be closely encouraged and monitored.

7.3.2.5 *Training to compete*

This stage focuses on the introduction of competition into athlete development. Competition should be integrated to encourage physical, mental, emotional and cognitive preparedness. With competition comes specialisation as the athlete implements specific protocols to identify areas of strength and weakness. Advanced motor skills become more necessary between the ages of 16 to 18 for males and 15 to 17 for females. Skills such as speed, strength, endurance and power are optimised.

7.3.2.6 *Training to win*

At this stage, performance excellence is prioritised. During this time, mental, emotional, cognitive and physical development are monitored to support an athlete's elite career. For male and female athletes between the ages of 20 and 23, skills are challenged while they learn the importance of healthy competition.

7.3.2.7 *Active for life*

This final stage is critical to the long-term well-being of athletes. After athletes have fully retired from their competitive careers, this stage helps them to integrate into an unfamiliar way of life. This occurs at any age for both sexes, providing a structure and focus to post-sport athletes' everyday lives.

In the application of the LTAD framework, it is essential to identify which athletes have entered the "Learn to Train" or "Train-to-Train" stages in their respective sports and guide programming accordingly (see Figure 7.2). These stages pave the way for both the Podium Pathway and the Active for Life stages of LTAD. Typically, once an athlete reaches the onset of their growth spurt or menarche, or around ages 11-15 for females and ages 12-16 for males, they have reached the biological markers of athletes entering the Train-to-Train stage. This stage is critical for participants to develop into high-performance athletes. After that, they usually either begin their journey on the Podium Pathway within their sport, become competitive or Fit for Life in their chosen sport, or they drop out altogether. It is important to note that the specific age ranges and competition levels may vary slightly between different sports and NSFs, however this example illustrates how Athletics South Africa's performance pathway aligns with the LTAD stages, providing age- and developmentally-appropriate opportunities for athletes to progress in their athletic journeys, while catering to elite and recreational pathways.[11]

7.3.3 Resourcing of Athlete Performance Pathways

7.3.3.1 Coach education and development

effective coach education and development programmes are crucial components of athlete performance pathways. This involves providing coaches with the necessary knowledge, skills and qualifications to identify and nurture talented athletes. ASA invests in coach education programmes, offering certifications, workshops and ongoing professional development opportunities. Well-trained coaches contribute to implementing effective training methodologies, talent identification and athlete development strategies.

7.3.3.2 Priority access to facilities for elite athletes

Ensuring elite athletes have priority access to high-quality training facilities is vital for their development within performance pathways. ASA works closely with relevant stakeholders, including government bodies and facility managers, to secure dedicated training venues and resources for elite athletes. These facilities may include tracks, strength and conditioning centres, medical and sport science facilities and rehabilitation centres.

7.3.3.3 Partnerships and collaboration with international training centres

Building partnerships and collaborations with international training centres can enhance athlete development within performance pathways. ASA thus seeks opportunities to send athletes and coaches to train and learn from world-class training environments abroad. These partnerships facilitate exposure to international expertise, training methodologies and competition structures, broadening athletes' horizons and raising the overall level of performance in South Africa.

7.3.3.4 Financial support to build the right infrastructure

Sufficient financial support is necessary to establish and maintain the infrastructure that supports performance pathways. In collaboration with South African bodies, ASA seeks funding to develop and upgrade facilities, provide equipment and support talent development programmes. Financial resources are also allocated to support athlete scholarships, coaching salaries and the overall administration of performance pathways.

7.3.3.5 Needs analysis for different sports codes

Conducting thorough needs analyses specific to different sporting codes is essential to tailor performance pathways to meet the unique requirements of each discipline. ASA conducts regular assessments to understand the specific needs of various athletic events, such as sprints, jumps, throws and endurance events. This analysis helps allocate resources, design training programmes and provide sport-specific support services to athletes.

7.3.3.6 *Talent identification structures*

Effective talent identification structures are the foundation of performance pathways. ASA collaborates with schools, clubs and provinces to implement talent identification programmes and initiatives. These structures may include school championships, development squads, talent identification camps and performance monitoring systems. Clear criteria and evaluation processes are established to identify athletes with potential and provide them with appropriate development opportunities.

7.3.3.7 *Sport sciences support*

Sport science plays a vital role in supporting athlete development within performance pathways. ASA employs sport scientists, physiotherapists, nutritionists and other experts to provide comprehensive support services to athletes. These services encompass performance analysis, injury prevention and rehabilitation, strength and conditioning programmes, sport-specific training strategies and sport psychology support to optimise athletes' physical and mental preparation.

7.3.3.8 *Anti-doping structures*

Maintaining clean and fair competition is crucial within athlete performance pathways. ASA adheres to international anti-doping regulations and collaborates with anti-doping agencies to implement robust anti-doping structures. This includes conducting education and awareness programmes, implementing testing protocols and enforcing sanctions for athletes guilty of doping offences. Anti-doping measures ensure the integrity and credibility of performance pathways.

7.3.3.9 *Role of agencies in communication and administration*

Clear communication and efficient administration are essential for the smooth operation of athlete performance pathways. As the governing body, ASA is crucial in maintaining effective communication channels between stakeholders, including coaches, athletes, parents, schools and clubs. This involves disseminating information, coordinating competitions and events, and ensuring transparent administration and governance within political boundaries.

Factors influencing athlete performance pathways that control talent development over an extended period are professional coaches' availability, coach development, training facilities, financial aid, athletic support and opportunity to compete.

7.4 CHALLENGES WITH PERFORMANCE PATHWAYS IN SOUTH AFRICA

The performance pathway from school to senior level presents various challenges for athletes in South Africa. This section explores athletes' experiences navigating the path and highlights critical challenges such as inadequate support systems, diverse coaching and training plans, the risk of injuries, and demanding qualification standards and expectations. Addressing these challenges is crucial to optimise the development of elite athletes and create a more conducive environment for their success. This section will discuss these challenges within the context of the LTAD model in South Africa.

7.4.1 Inadequate Support System

One of the biggest challenges athletes face in South Africa is insufficient support systems. Athletes require a comprehensive support structure encompassing financial assistance, sports science expertise, access to quality training facilities and mental health support, however in many cases, athletes face limited financial resources, inadequate access to sports science services and a lack of mental health support. These deficiencies hinder their progress along the performance pathway and impede their overall development.

7.4.2 Diverse Coaching and Training Plans

Athletes transitioning through the performance pathway often need more consistency in their coaching and training plans, as different coaches may have varied approaches, methodologies and philosophies, resulting in athletes receiving conflicting guidance. This inconsistency can hinder their development, as they may need help to adapt to new coaching styles and training methods when transitioning to different levels or teams.

7.4.3 Risk of Injuries

Injuries pose a significant challenge for athletes progressing along the performance pathway. The demanding nature of training, competition schedules and the pressure to perform at a high level increases the risk of injuries. Limited access to proper injury prevention strategies, rehabilitation facilities and sports medicine expertise further exacerbates this challenge. Athletes must balance their pursuit of excellence with injury prevention and recovery to sustain their long-term athletic careers.[12]

7.4.4 Demanding Qualification Standards and Expectations

The qualification standards and expectations placed on athletes can be demanding and sometimes unrealistic. High-performance targets and rigid selection criteria may put undue pressure on athletes, affecting their mental well-being and performance. Additionally, the narrow focus on achieving specific performance outcomes may hinder the holistic development of athletes, neglecting other important aspects such as education and personal growth.

The challenges athletes face in South Africa's performance pathway require attention and proactive measures to create a more supportive and conducive environment. Adequate financial support, consistent coaching and training plans, injury prevention strategies and realistic qualification standards are crucial aspects that must be addressed. By addressing these challenges, South Africa can foster the development of elite athletes and enhance their chances of success on the national and international stages. Collaborative efforts between sports organisations, government bodies, coaches and stakeholders are essential in overcoming these challenges and ensuring athletes' sustained growth and success along the performance pathway.

7.4.5 Challenges in the High-Performance Phase

It is noteworthy that although the reasons for athletes dropping out are closely related to the challenges they face and are presented as reasons in some cases, the causes and challenges are not necessarily the same. For example, an athlete may encounter the challenge of competing against stronger competition, yet they stopped the sport because they did not have the psychological support to deal with the challenge.

According to a study by Sabato, Walch and Caine, some athletes experience a lack of familial support, inadequate motivation, low social mobility, a critical attitude toward competitive sport and injuries.[13] Further, some participants revealed that they no longer competed in track and field not because of their challenges, but rather because they needed more means to overcome those challenges. Some participants singled out challenges such as a lack of motivation caused by qualifying standards, training programme changes, stricter competition and physiological changes as reasons for dropping out. In addition, they noted a lack of financial support as a reason for quitting. Only one of the participants received external financial assistance immediately after school. Even in cases where the athletes identified injuries or a lack of time because of studies as the reasons for dropping out, it is possible that those reasons may not have existed if they had adequate financial support to compete full-time with timely medical assistance.[14]

The participants rarely stated missing free time, enduring conflicts in their athletic environments and lacking family support. The athletes who had dropped out would only have ended their careers with inadequate financial support. Athletes in South Africa receive different financial support than athletes in other countries, thus financial constraints and a lack of sponsorships are why elite athletes fail to continue seemingly successful athletic careers at the training-to-win phase.

7.4.6 Support Systems

A consideration of the literature reveals that policies and systems are in place to support, for example, track and field athletes. Internationally, these support systems make specific provisions for the challenges athletes face when transitioning between different phases of their careers, however in South Africa, the support systems are aimed at elite athletes and need to make specific provisions for developing athletes or athletes transitioning between stages. Unfortunately, literature is scarce on the effectiveness and sustainability of these systems from the perspective of local athletes.

Although the inadequate support governing bodies provide to athletes throughout their school careers, most athletes require additional financial assistance from these bodies. This assistance is particularly crucial in covering expenses related to medical needs, coaching, travel, and other performance-related costs.

Although there are cases of occasional financial assistance, this support is normally minimal and does not last for extended periods. More specifically, a consideration of the reason for dropping out needs to be provided with the means to overcome challenges. It is suggested that the necessary support performance pathway systems need to be in place or are being implemented successfully.

The availability of intermediate competitions to support athletes' transition to senior-level athletics should be provided to compete at the highest level eventually. This would enable them to deal with the psychological difficulty of competing at a higher level. In addition, support in finding people to talk to about their challenges should be considered in an LTAD programme. In essence, governing bodies should put systems into place to provide athletes access to people who have experience with their situation and, accordingly, could mentor or counsel them. Concerning guidance, athletes need help finding coaches or seeking support with their training programmes. Furthermore, there needs to be more clarity between what is stated in policy documents concerning the support supposedly provided to South African athletes and the actual type and amount of support athletes receive.

Literature in the international context has suggested parental support, talent identification, structured programmes and introducing the 'fun factor' in athletics are ways to increase support for track and field athletes. It is also recommended that athletes are educated on the transition process, including developing a positive balance and creating a support network. Literature on enhancing support for South African athletes is scarce, however,[15] and there is an urgent need for improved support systems from Athletics South Africa. Better training programme guidance, more robust moral support from past athletes and aligning the local qualifying standards to the World Athletics' qualifying standards are initial recommendations. Furthermore, increased financial assistance is imperative. This issue was the golden thread and is the one variable with which athletes abroad do not struggle. Local athletes cannot afford good training gear, facilities, medical assistance, supplements or high-quality coaches without money. By implication, without sufficient funding, athletes are unable to address other, relatively minor challenges, which can ultimately lead to them dropping out. Therefore, conducting thorough research within the South African context is crucial to understand how the allocated funding can effectively reach its intended recipients.

Furthermore, the development of athletes in all sports is based on three primary pillars of performance: technical skills (hands), physical skills (feet), and mental skills (head). Each of these pillars develops at a different pace and holds varying significance during different stages of the athlete's progress.

7.5 CONCLUSION

This chapter focussed on long-term athlete development in South African sport. It covered the structures supporting LTAD, the LTAD framework and resourcing of LTAD in South African sport. Examples from ASA were provided that clarified the propositions of LTAD and implementation in sport, before concluding with a discussion of the current challenges when it comes to implementing LTAD in ASA and the broader South African sport environment.

Sport managers should take cognisance of the processes and procedures of LTAD, as well as its role, aims and objectives, in order to engage with coaches and administrators in the planning and implementation of LTAD programmes towards sport excellence and lifelong participation.

SELF-ASSESSMENT

1. Describe the significance of performance pathways in South Africa.
2. Differentiate between the "pillars of performance" for all sport.
3. Discuss the early discontinuation of sport.
4. Argue how challenges in the high-performance phase can be addressed.
5. Read the case study below and answer the accompanied questions.

Case Study: Nurturing Talent in South African Athletics

This case study explores the athlete performance pathways in South African athletics and focuses on the journey of a young track and field athlete, Thabo, who aspires to compete at the highest level. Thabo's story illustrates the challenges, opportunities and critical decisions that athletes face in navigating the performance pathway in South Africa. Thabo, a talented sprinter, grew up in a township with limited resources for athletics. Despite the challenges, he displayed exceptional speed and determination from an early age, catching the attention of his physical education teacher, Coach Nomsa. Recognising Thabo's potential, Coach Nomsa encouraged him to pursue athletics seriously and introduced him to the local athletics club, where he joined the development programme and participated in regular training sessions, focusing on building his fundamental movement skills and athletic abilities. Thabo's journey thus began with talent identification at the grassroots level.

1. How can talent identification programmes be improved to ensure talented athletes like Thabo are not overlooked, especially in underprivileged areas?
2. How can the availability of training facilities and qualified coaches be increased in underprivileged areas to support the development of talented athletes?
3. What strategies can be implemented to ensure a smooth progression for athletes like Thabo from regional to national and international levels of competition?
4. How can the availability of financial support and sponsorships be increased to provide equal opportunities for athletes from all backgrounds?
5. What factors contributed to Thabo's success despite the challenges he faced? How can similar success stories be replicated for other aspiring athletes?

DISABILITY SPORT

Alison Burchell

LEARNING OUTCOMES

At the end of this chapter, you should be able to:

1. Explain the origin and genesis of different international organisations catering for disability sport.
2. Discuss the origin and development of the national organisations catering for disability sport.
3. Argue the context and impact of sports independence as part of mainstreaming disability sport.
4. Debate the basic principles of classification and eligibility for athletes with disabilities.

8.1 INTRODUCTION

The development of disability organisations at an international level and the impact on the framework of disability organisations at a national level are explored in this chapter. Further, the similarities, alignment and differences between sport for those with and without disabilities and those who are Deaf and hearing are set out to enable a better understanding for those involved in and interested in sport. The bottom line is that sport is sport, whether for a person with a disability or for one without. In the same way that there is diversity in the general population, there is diversity in the arena of disability sport.

8.2 PERSPECTIVES ON DISABILITY

There are several definitions of disability, depending on the sector and country of application, however the World Health Organisation (WHO) set out a generally used definition in the *International Classification of Functioning, Disability and Health* (ICF) after it was adopted in May 2001 by the 54th World Health Assembly. As per the below, the ICF is the WHO's framework for health disability:

> "It is the conceptual basis for the definition, measurement and policy formulations for health and disability. It is a universal classification of disability and health for use in health and health-related sectors. ICF, therefore, looks like a simple health classification, but it can be used for several purposes. The most important is as a planning and policy tool for decision-makers."[1]

The ICF defines disability as: *"...an umbrella term for impairments, activity limitations and participation restrictions. It denotes the negative aspects of the interaction between an individual (with a health condition) and that individual's contextual factors (environmental and personal factors)."*[2]

The WHO indicates that disability is part of being human and that everyone is likely to experience some limitation on their activity – a temporary disability – during their life, for example, from an ankle sprain or a broken arm. In the case of a person with a disability, this will likely be permanent, however there are degenerative conditions such as multiple sclerosis where the person's ability to move reduces over time. In some instances, a disability could be ameliorated through an operation, for example, through eye surgery. This is a factor in the classification of athletes with disabilities.

Traditionally, the medical model of disability was used, which *"views disability as a feature of the person, directly caused by disease, trauma or other health condition, which requires medical care provided in the form of individual treatment by professionals"*.[3] However, in later years, the social model of disability was developed, which *"sees disability as a socially created problem and not an individual attribute. On the social model, disability demands a political response, since the problem is created by an unaccommodating physical environment brought about by attitudes and other features of the social environment"*.[4]

The ICF continues that, *"three levels of human functioning are classified by ICF: functioning at the level of body or body part, the whole person, and the whole person in a social context. Disability, therefore, involves dysfunctioning at one or more of these same levels: impairments, activity limitations and participation restrictions. The formal definitions of these components of ICF are provided in the box below"*.[5]

Body Functions are physiological functions of body systems (including psychological functions).

Body Structures are anatomical parts of the body such as organs, limbs and their components.

Impairments are problems in body function or structure such as a significant deviation or loss.

Activity is the execution of a task or action by an individual.

Participation is involvement in a life situation.

Activity Limitations are difficulties an individual may have in executing activities.

Participation Restrictions are problems an individual may experience in involvement in life situations.

Environmental Factors make up the physical, social and attitudinal environment in which people live and conduct their lives.

While the ICF moves the dial on the issue of physical and intellectual disability from the medical to the social model, it is essential to understand the inclusion of people who are Deaf as disabled.

The first recorded reference to disability is from 1552 BC.[6] There are several origins or causes of disability, including but not limited to:

1. Meningitis leading to Deafness.
2. A lack of oxygen to the foetus leading to cerebral palsy.
3. Alcohol foetal syndrome leading to intellectual impairment.
4. Congenital disorders leading to Down Syndrome and an intellectual impairment.
5. Trauma through war, car accidents or falling off a roof leading to a physical disability.

There are many, including Deaf people, who do not believe that they are disabled, as the impact of Deafness is predominantly in language and communication. In South Africa, the Deaf have long been involved in the disability rights movement. In addition, since the inception of democracy in South Africa, there was a lobby to include Sign Language as the nation's 12th official language. As a result, Sign Language has been gradually accepted into the everyday lives of people, with interpreters on the television news and at most extensive public occasions. It was approved as an official language by Parliament in May 2023, however Deafness does lead to a need to adapt to the rules of the sport, and could affect a person's balance as the ear is critical to balance.

In South Africa, the Integrated National Disability Strategy[7] (INDS), published as a White Paper in 1997, began to place disability in the context of human rights and based it squarely on the terrain of the social model of disability. The INDS outlined the probability that people with a disability are more likely to live in poverty, however this is changing as people with a disability can now access education, transport and other essential opportunities based on the human rights approach. Indeed, the South African Human Rights Commission has included disability as one of its seven focus areas.[8] Chapter 2 of the South African Constitution specifically mentions disability as a form of discrimination, along with several other types of discrimination which continue to exist. The INDS[9] identified a policy objective of developing and extending *"sporting activities for people with disabilities in both mainstream and special facilities so that they can participate in sport for both recreational and competitive purposes"*, as persons with disabilities have the same desire to participate in sport and recreation as their non-disabled peers. With the origin of disability sport being rooted in rehabilitation, this is an essential aspect of improving access to sport and recreation.

The INDS sets out the background of the language used:

> *"Harmful attitudes are one of the biggest barriers disabled people face when accessing mainstream programmes. Negative attitudes are reinforced whenever disability is portrayed as a 'problem', where disabled people are regarded as helpless, dependent, sick, or tragic victims. In addition, cultural beliefs play an important role in how we relate to people with disabilities, as do images and language."*[10]

Finding a balance between being sensitive and patronising is the best way forward. Questions are often asked about the correct terminology to use, as there is a slight difference between the sport and the civil society sector. The table below sets out a summary of such, with descriptions, including "handicapped", "cripple" and "differently abled", not being used.

Sport in SA	Civil society in SA
Disabled	Impaired
Disability	Impairment
Able-bodied	Non-disabled
Deaf	Deaf
Intellectually disabled OR impaired	Intellectually impaired
Multiple disabilities	Multi-impairments

At the time of the 1996 Paralympic Games, the South African Paralympic team decided to give themselves the nickname of the "Amakrokokroko",[11] While it was meant in good faith, the name caused controversy, mainly as disabled people's organisations were working to move away from the concept of being "crocks". This was also linked with the desire to move towards athletes being regarded as athletes, first and foremost, who may happen to have a disability.

Some people have more than one disability, e.g. Deaf and blind, blind and paraplegic. In the context of sport, however, the disability which has the most significant impact on an athlete's ability to move is likely to be the disability by which the athlete is classified.

8.3 A HISTORICAL PERSPECTIVE ON DISABILITY IN SPORT

As a large part of disability is a result of trauma, war and complications associated with birth, it could be that disability sport has been organised for centuries. While this may be true in an informal context, the organisation of disability sport is a relatively recent phenomenon. The International Olympic Committee (IOC) was established in Paris in June 1894 to organise the Olympic Games, reviving the ancient Olympics that were first held in Olympia in Greece in 776 BC as part of a festival to honour the Greek God Zeus.[12] Following the establishment of the IOC, several sports organised themselves into international federations.

There is a perception that athletes with disabilities only really started to compete in later years, however the first known athlete with a disability who competed in the Olympic Games was George Eyser, a leg amputee, in gymnastics in 1904, who won six medals. Others followed him in archery, athletics, baseball, equestrian, shooting, swimming, table tennis and water polo.[13]

The first disability sport organisation was established as the International Committee of Sport for the Deaf (ISCD) in 1924,[14] when the first International Silent Games were organised in Paris. The ICSD was, at that time, also known as *le Comité International des Sports Silencieux* (the International Committee of Silent Sports), which then became the *Comité International des Sports des Sourds*. The ICSD organises winter and summer Deaflympics along the same lines as the Olympic Games, under the motto, "Equal through sport". Although recognised by the IOC in 1955,[15] in 2001, the ICSD received recognition from the IOC to use 'Deaflympics' as the name for the Deaflympic Games.[16]

Sir Ludwig Guttman CBE FRS is generally regarded as the father of the Paralympic Movement. A German (now part of Poland) by birth, he qualified as a medical doctor and practiced until 1933, when the Nazis forced all Jews to stop working at 'Aryan' hospitals.[17] He became a neurologist at the Jewish hospital in Breslau until he emigrated to the United Kingdom in 1939. In 1943, the Government asked him to become the Director of a new National Spinal Injuries Centre at Stoke Mandeville, treating mainly soldiers injured during the Second World War, and so began the Paralympic Movement. Guttman used sports activities as rehabilitation, including wheelchair basketball and archery. The latter was the primary sport at the inaugural Stoke Mandeville Games held in 1948, which opened on the same day as the Opening Ceremony of the 1948 Olympic Games hosted in London. In 1952, some Dutch competitors joined, and the International Stoke Mandeville Games were established.[18] This led to the establishment of the International Stoke Mandeville Games Committee, which became a Federation (ISMGF) in 1972 to help coordinate the increasing number of competitions for persons with a disability. In 1991, it became the International Stoke Mandeville Wheelchair Sports Federation (ISMWSF), as different disability sports organisations established themselves and the International Paralympic Committee (IPC) was created.

The Stoke Mandeville Games were the precursor of the Paralympic Games (meaning parallel to the Olympics and not Paraplegic Games, as is often believed). The first Summer Games described under the banner of 'Paralympic' were held in 1960 in Rome, Italy, and the winter version in 1976 in Örnsköldsvik, Sweden. The Winter and Summer Games now occur every four years, predominantly in the same city that hosts the Olympic Games for both winter and summer editions.

In 1960, the International Working Group on Sport for the Disabled, operating under the auspices of the World Federation of Veterans, helped to establish the International Sports Organisation of Disabled (ISOD) in 1964.[19] ISOD catered for those who could not affiliate with the ISMGF, specifically athletes who were blind or visually impaired, amputees and later athletes with cerebral palsy.

In 1968, the Special Olympics[20] was formed, building on the first summer camp held in 1962 in Washington, USA, which was known as the "Shriver camp". The driving force behind the Special Olympics movement was Eunice Kennedy Shriver, whose sister, Rosemary, had an intellectual disability. When this was made public in 1962, the attitude to what was then regarded as "mental retardation" changed significantly.

Special Olympics International (SOI) focuses on the participation of athletes with intellectual impairment in both the Summer and Winter Special Olympics World Games. A strong worldwide identity is promoted by SOI, together with guidance for national Special Olympics organisations. In 1988, SOI gained recognition from the IOC for using the word "Olympics"[21] and promoting sport for individuals with an intellectual disability.

Due to the special interests of some disability groups, other international organisations were established, including the Cerebral Palsy International Sports and Recreation Association[22] (CP-ISRA) in 1978 and the International Blind Sports Association[23] (IBSA) in 1981. In addition, another organisation catering specifically for athletes with an intellectual disability, International Sports Federation for Persons with an Intellectual

Disability[24] (INAS-FID), was established in 1986 (now called Virtus). INIS-FID was considered the European response to the establishment of SOI and promoted competition through the Virtus and Paralympic Games.

ISOD, ISMGF, CP-ISRA, IBSA, and later INAS-FID, organised their games independently, but over time, they came together to form the forerunner of the IPC in 1982. The International Coordinating Committee for Sports for the Disabled in the World (ICC) began coordinating their activities and the Paralympic Games. Two other disability sports organisations joined in 1986: the ICSD and the newly established INAS-FID.

In 1989, these six organisations formed the IPC in Germany as the worldwide governing body of the Paralympic Movement, which is also responsible for the Paralympic Games. The six organisations continued to operate with some realignment as the Paralympic Movement and Games operations moved to the IPC. In 1995, the ICSD withdrew from the IPC as it became clear that Deaf athletes could not easily be included in the Paralympic Games.[25] In 2004, the ISMWSF and ISOD merged to form the International Wheelchair and Amputee Sports Federation (IWAS). Following discussions over recent years, IWAS merged with CP-ISRA on 6 April 2023[26] to form World Abilitysport.

The first Paralympic Games organised under the umbrella of the IPC were in Barcelona in 1992. Since the Games held in Seoul, Korea, in 1988 and in Albertville, France, in 1992, the Summer and Winter Paralympic Games have been held in the same city as the Olympic Games.

8.3.1 Sport Independence

The IPC has been the governing body for the Paralympic Games and several sports for many years. This initially caused a perception of a conflict of interest, as it manages the Games for both sports for which it is responsible, as well as those that are the responsibility of international sport federations, either focused on disability sport or under an international sports federation. This led to the concept of "sports independence", where the governance of a particular sport is transferred from the IPC, CP-ISRA, IBSA, IWASF or Virtus to an international sports federation, or the sport is allowed to become independent in its own right.

While there are international sports organisations that cater for specific disability groups, there are some organisations for athletes with disabilities that have developed independently of these international organisations. For example, the International Wheelchair Tennis Association[27] was founded in the USA in 1988 and ran the organisation until 1998, when it was incorporated into the International Tennis Federation. This is a trend followed by several other sports which belonged to the IPC, which then agreed, following a resolution at its 2003 General Assembly, to promote sports independence:[28]

- *Para Archery:* governance responsibility was transferred from IPC to World Archery in 2009.[29]
- *Para Cycling:* became part of the Union Cycliste Internationale in 2007.[30]
- *Para-Equestrian:* the Fédération Équestre Internationale took on governance responsibility in 2006.[31]
- *Para Table Tennis:* became part of the International Table Tennis Federation when the governance was transferred from the IPC in 2007.

In another development, with the growth of the Paralympic Games and an increasing commitment to inclusion from international sports federations, several Para sport equivalents were established within the respective international federations:

- *Para Canoe:* was initiated by the International Canoe Federation[32] in 2008.
- *Para Rowing:* started in the 1920s,[33] but World Rowing established an Adaptive Rowing Commission in 2001 and the Para sport was included in the Paralympic Games in 2008 for the first time.
- *Para-Taekwondo:* in 2005, World Taekwondo established the Para-Taekwondo Committee.[34]
- *Para Triathlon:* began to work on developing this discipline in the early 2000s[35] and it made its debut on the Paralympic Games programme in 2016.
- *Wheelchair Curling:* began in Europe in the 1990s and expanded to North America in 2002. The first world championships, held under the World Curling Federation, was held in 2002 leading to inclusion in the 2006 Winter Paralympic Games.

Another model exists where sport-specific international federations have been established, including:

- *Boccia International Sports Federation (BISFed):* became independent of CP-ISRA in 2013[36] and is now known as World Boccia.
- *International Federation of Cerebral Palsy Football (IFCPF):* became independent of CP-ISRA in 2015.[37]
- *International Wheelchair Basketball Federation:* was initially established as a part of ISMGF in 1973, became independent in 1993, and now works more closely with the Fédération Internationale de Basketball[38] (FIBA), although it remains independent.
- *International Wheelchair Rugby Federation:* was established as part of ISMWSF in 1993 and became independent of its successor organisation, IWASF, in 2010. Now known as World Wheelchair Rugby.
- *Para-Badminton:* operated independently since the 1990s but was integrated into the Badminton World Federation in 2011.[39]
- *World Para Volley:* established as the World Organisation of Volleyball for the Disabled in 1981 as part of ISOD, but became independent in 1992.

Several sports will remain part of the IPC until it transfers governance responsibilities to an international federation or supports them to become independent by 2028.[40] These 10 Para sports are alpine skiing, athletics, biathlon, cross-country, dance sport, ice hockey, powerlifting, shooting, snowboarding and swimming.

Other sports on the Paralympic programme that belong to the International Federations of Sport for Persons with Disabilities, are:

- *Blind football:* part of IBSA.
- *Goalball:* part of IBSA.

- *Para Judo:* part of IBSA which cooperates with the International Judo Federation.
- *Wheelchair fencing:* part of IWASF.

8.4 DISABILITY SPORT IN SOUTH AFRICA

There are four leading organisations for sports for persons with disabilities in South Africa and a few sports-specific national federations. The South African Deaf Sports Federation (SADSF) was established in 1981, with their first international competition being held in Sofia, Bulgaria, at the 1993 World Games for the Deaf.[41] The SADSF has regular national championships involving its nine provincial associations and caters for individual sport national championships. The sports operating under SADSF are athletics, badminton, basketball, bowls, cricket, cycling, football, golf, netball, rugby, swimming, squash, table tennis and volleyball.

The SADSF has subcommittees dealing with each sport, which organise the national championship for that particular sport. The SADSF hosts the annual National Deaf Development Games for athletics, chess, football, netball, table tennis and volleyball. In 2020, it revived the SA School Sports Association for the Deaf, initially established in 2004.

The SADSF is also affiliated with the Confederation of African Deaf Sports (CADS) and the ICSD. The ICSD constitution states that the Executive Board must consist of Deaf persons who understand international sign language.[42] The CADS was established in 1997 and currently has 27 members. With the use of international sign language, the ICSD and CADS, as well as other members of the ICSD, are genuinely able to communicate in a universal language. In South Africa, sign language has dialects, which has led to the development of South African Sign Language as the universal South African language for the Deaf.

Perhaps the best-known Deaf athlete is Terence Parkin, who not only won the silver medal in the 200m breaststroke at the 2000 Olympic Games, but also 29 gold and three silver medals in swimming in the Deaflympics from 1997 to 2009. He won one bronze medal in cycling in 2009, after which he switched to cycling full-time. Parkin now looks forward to winning more awards in Masters swimming and hopes to compete in the 2025 Deaflympics.

The South African Paraplegic Games Association was established in 1962.[43] It became the SA Sports Association for Physically Disabled (SASAPD) in 1976 after the 1976 Paralympic Games, reflecting the inclusion of more disability groups. However, much of its history is within the Apartheid era when the development of sport was based on "separate development", i.e., a team could generally be an all-White or all-non-White team, they had separate travelling arrangements, and White and non-White team members could not compete against one another at international events.

The Rotary Club of Orange Grove initiated a national association to support the sporting needs of persons with paraplegia following Neville Cohen's rehabilitation experience at Stoke Mandeville Hospital with Sir Ludwig Guttman in 1955.[44] The inaugural meeting on 12 November 1962 at the Old Edwardian Club, a multi-racial club in Johannesburg, accepted the Constitution and elected an interim Executive Committee. All four provinces were represented and the South African Paraplegic Games Association was established.

In 1967, the name was changed to the South African Sports Association for Paraplegics and Other Physically Disabled, which enabled the inclusion of persons with amputations and those with cerebral palsy. However, as the International Federations were established and developed, the Association had to accommodate these and another name change was required. In 1976, the name changed to SASAPD, which included persons with visual impairments and *Les Autres* (French for *the others*). This category is for athletes whose disability does not fit the other categories.

In 1974, the Constitution of the Association was amended to include non-discriminatory clauses, with membership of all senior clubs open to all disabled persons. However, on 20 April 1975, the National Council determined that the SA Team to the 24th ISMG would be selected on merit only. As a result, a multi-racial team was sent to the International Stoke Mandeville Games, apparently with approval from the then Government.[45]

Over the years, SASAPD endeavoured to administer and develop sport at junior and senior levels for persons with disabilities. A Junior Advisory Committee was established to ensure opportunities to play sport for clubs operating within the school system developed. Annual National Championships were organised, classification was done and updated yearly, and sports tournaments and the development of new sports (boccia, wheelchair rugby, CP soccer) were organised. A Medical and Classification Committee was also established to manage the classification process and classifiers' training nationwide.

The policy of inviting selected international athletes to compete at national championships ensured the opportunity of providing international sporting competition continued. From 1987, SASAPD hosted individual athletes from Israel, Germany and the USA, while South West Africa (Namibia), Lesotho and Swaziland (eSwatini) regularly participated at national championships.

Yet SASAPD's and its predecessor's participation in international sport conflicted with the sports boycott and contravened the Gleneagles agreement.[46] Through this agreement, the Commonwealth heads of government resolved in 1977 to halt their participation in events in which South Africa competed to increase pressure on the Apartheid government. Thus, international participation was sporadic:

1. In the International Stoke Mandeville Games from 1962 to 1985, "White" teams went to the ISMG in 1966, 1968, 1970 and 1974, and "Black" teams went in 1965, 1967, 1971 and 1973. In 1975, the first multi-racial team participated in the Games following the first integrated national competition. In 1977, a multi-racial team competed causing two countries to withdraw, while in 1979, a multi-racial team finished third of 30 participating teams, with medals won by both White and Black athletes.
2. The 1962 Paralympic Games had an 'all White' team.
3. In the 1976 Paralympic Games, South Africa's participation resulted in the withdrawal of eight nations.
4. The 1980 Paralympic Games were closed to the South African team following a resolution of the Dutch Parliament in 1979.

The first Paralympic Games in which South Africa officially participated was in 1992. South Africa has continued to do so since 1996 under the banner of the National Paralympic Committee of South Africa (NAPCOSA), then Disability Sport South Africa (DISSA), the South African Sports Confederation and the

Olympic Committee (SASCOC), now the South African Sports Confederation, Olympic and Paralympic Committee (Sport SA).

SASAPD now caters to the following disability groups: amputees, blind and visually impaired, cerebral palsied, spinal cord injuries, and *Les Autres*, including polio, osteogenesis imperfecta and people of short stature.

The SASAPD offers eight sports across nine provinces and 13 regions, and is responsible for preparing and sending teams to various international competitions: Athletics – via Sport SA, Boccia directly to World Boccia events, CP Football directly to IFCPF events, Goalball directly to IBSA events, Judo directly to IBSA events, Powerlifting and Swimming via Sport SA.

Over the years, a similar trend has been seen internationally and in South Africa. Wheelchair Basketball SA remains an independent NF, and Wheelchair Tennis SA joined Tennis South Africa in July 2019,[47] having been independent since 2005.

The South African Sports Association for Intellectually Impaired (SASA-II), previously established under the SA Sports Association for Severely Mentally Handicapped in 1990, caters for sport in all nine provinces. It aims to promote, encourage and advance sport for the intellectually disabled, irrespective of race, colour, creed, gender, language, religion or political dispensation.

SASA-II recognises the rights of persons with an intellectual disability to enjoy and participate in sport, and works through partnerships with other stakeholders to change attitudes, create opportunities and develop pathways in sport, ensuring that athletes with an intellectual disability can compete at the highest possible level.

SASA-II depends on schools for development programmes and talent identification. Schools participate on a district level and select athletes to compete on a provincial and national level. Approximately 200 schools, training centres, workshops and clubs are affiliated, with around 23,000 athletes participating from the grassroots to the international level. Cooperation and support from the provincial departments responsible for sport and education are crucial to SASA-II's operations. SASA-II also cooperates closely with the NFs responsible for athletics (including cross country and half marathon), basketball, blackball pool, cricket, cycling, football (including futsal), gymnastics, netball, rowing, swimming and table tennis to develop their sports, often being an associate member of the national federation.

SASA-II holds national championships annually for the following sports in the SA Summer Games, usually in February or March: blackball, cricket, indoor rowing, swimming and table tennis. After that, SASA-II organises SA Age Group or SA Open Games in the following sports in September or October: athletics, basketball, cross country, football, futsal, hokker (Hokker is a hybrid sport for intellectually impaired participants[48]) and netball.

The Executive Committee of SASA-II appoints a national sports convenor to coordinate sports convenors for each sport, who work with the provinces and schools, as SASA-II is predominantly a schools-based organisation. It prepares and sends teams to the Global Games, now the Virtus Global Games, and individual sport world winter and summer championships. It is affiliated with both Virtus and Virtus Africa.

Special Olympics South Africa (SOSA) was founded in 1981 and offers between 13 and 18 sports to 45,000 athletes.[49] SOI accredits SOSA, which is run similarly to a franchise and is part of SOI. As an organisation, SOSA encourages participation at several levels across various initiatives promoted by SOI, including games and competition, inclusive health, youth and schools, and leadership, which all SOI nationally accredited organisations follow.

SOSA has a Board of Directors, which SOI often approves. These high-profile directors marshal corporates, celebrities and sports people to support its operations, such as the "Polar Plunge" and health screenings for athletes using a mobile clinic. In addition, recognising the likelihood that many athletes with an intellectual disability will not attain a matric, SOSA has worked to develop a National Qualifications Framework 5 qualification for group exercise instructors.

The sports offered[50] are aquatics, athletics, basketball, bocce, bowling, equestrian, figure skating, floor hockey, football/soccer, golf, netball, open water swimming, table tennis and volleyball. In addition, SOSA offers unified sports where athletes with intellectual impairments compete with those without. Their national games happen annually in different parts of the country.

In 2020, the SOSA team participated in the first Pan African Games,[51] which were held in Egypt. In addition, the athletics, basketball, bocce and football competitions were part of other initiatives, including Healthy Athletes medical screenings, a Middle East and North Africa Regional Youth Summit, and the Young Athletes and Motor Activity Training Programme.

SOSA has been able to participate in the summer and winter versions of the Special Olympics World Games since 1993. The Special Olympics World Summer Games happen every four years, with the winter version taking place in the intervening years on a four-year cycle. The last Special Olympics World Summer Games took place in Germany in 2023 (delayed due to Covid-19).[52]

Due to the overlap in athletes' eligibility to compete in SASA-II and SOSA, in 2003 Disability Sport South Africa (DISSA) initiated cooperation between the two organisations. This led to an agreement to form a new organisation, called Sport for the Intellectually Disabled South Africa (SIDSA).[53] SIDSA was envisaged as a coordinating structure, with SASA-II and SOSA under its umbrella. As it is more focused on participation than competition, SOSA was to take the primary responsibility for mass participation and development, while SASA-II would take responsibility for developing athletes who could compete at an elite level at the Paralympic Games. Every athlete could compete in the Special Olympics World Games or the Virtus Global Games, as several competed in both. Unfortunately, while there was agreement locally, SOI did not support the initiative and it fell by the wayside. However, both SASA-II and SOSA come together to represent the sport for the intellectually disabled at meetings of Sport SA.

8.5 THE NATIONAL PARALYMPIC COMMITTEE OF SOUTH AFRICA

Following the participation of SASAPD in the 1992 Paralympic Games, the need to establish a National Paralympic Committee (NPC) was promoted by the IPC, bringing together the disability sport organisations which form part of the IPC under one national umbrella. This led to the formation of NAPCOSA in 1994.

This was supported by the Department of Sport and Recreation (DSR), which indicated that it only wanted to work with one disability sports structure. As a result, the three affiliates of NAPCOSA were SASAPD, SADSF and the South African Sports Association for Severely Mentally Handicapped (SASASMH), now known as SASAII.[54]

NAPCOSA took on the role of preparing, selecting and sending teams to IPC world championships and qualification events for the Paralympic Games. It sent teams to the 1996, 2000 and 2004 Paralympic Games, and also sent Africa's first Winter Paralympian, Bruce Warner, to the 1998, 2002, 2006 and 2010 Winter Paralympic Games. In 1999, NAPCOSA partnered with the Sports Information and Science Agency (under the DSR) to provide athletes with a focused sports science and medical support programme. This programme continued with the University of Stellenbosch being the lead service provider. At the same time, the structure of South African sport changed as SISA became part of the South African Sports Commission's High-Performance Programme (2000 to 2005), which then became the National Academy programme under Sport and Recreation SA's high-performance unit. This had a significant impact on focusing athletes to improve their performances and introduced disability sport to a number of universities involved in the High-Performance Programme. This was supported by an athlete support programme which helped to fund specific activities, equipment and other needs for the athletes in the selected squad. NAPCOSA also had a vibrant sponsorship programme built off the back of the 2004 Cape Town Olympic and Paralympic bid, where a representative of NAPCOSA was a director on the Board. As a result, the bid presented a separate Paralympic bid book outlining the proposals for hosting the Paralympic Games should Cape Town have won – unfortunately, that opportunity went to Athens. Sponsors of the Paralympic team from 1996 to 2008 included blue chip companies Daimler-Chrysler, Dimension Data, Nedbank, Nike, Pick 'n Pay, SAA, SASOL, Sun International, Telkom, Vodacom and the National Lottery.

NAPCOSA also established a development trust that was primarily funded by Transnet, Nedbank Corporate and Nomads. Grants were provided to the three affiliates to implement development programmes, purchase equipment and train coaches at a grassroots level. An appointment was also made to develop a talent screening, identification and development manual using expertise from an Australian who was involved in the early days of TID at the Australian Institute of Sport. This manual was made available for other developing countries to use.

Despite being an NPC, NAPCOSA also incorporated the SADSF. As the Deaf were not included in the Paralympic Games, the support given to the SADSF was minimal and led to the formation of DISSA, which also acted as an NPC to be inclusive and increase support to the SADSF.

As a Section 21 Company with the same three affiliates, DISSA replaced NAPCOSA in 2001, and the functions of NAPCOSA were incorporated into the High-Performance Programme of DISSA. The transformation of NAPCOSA to DISSA had three focus areas:

1. High-performance programming preparing elite athletes for various World Championships and Paralympic, Deaflympic and Global Games.
2. Talent identification and development across athletes, coaches, administrators and technical officials.
3. Development and administration.

In 2001, DISSA fully funded the South African team for the Deaflympics in Rome with a grant from the South African National Lottery. The South African team was one of a handful of fully funded teams. Unfortunately, this initiative did not continue beyond 2005, so SADSF and Deaf athletes must raise funds for development. Similarly, when INAS-FID was suspended from participating in the Paralympic Games as a result of a journalist revealing that several basketball players without an intellectual impairment competed in the 2000 Paralympic Games,[55] INAS-FID created the Global Games. These Games took place in 2004 in Sweden, and similarly, the South African team was largely funded by DISSA.

The sponsors from NAPCOSA held faith with DISSA during its transition to support a consistent high-performance programme aimed primarily at Paralympic athletes, but also increasingly included the intellectually disabled and Deaf. This enabled DISSA to host the 2006 IPC Swimming World Championships[56] in Durban in cooperation with Swimming South Africa. This was the first IPC world championship to be hosted in South Africa and Africa, with 549 swimmers competing over seven days.

One of the key focus areas for DISSA was that of inclusion premised on the adage, *"We may not be able to compete against you, but we can compete with you".* In several countries, the National Sport Federation (NSF) is responsible for preparing all athletes, with and without disabilities, hearing and Deaf, to perform exceptionally well in international competitions. Given the background of the INDS, including persons with disability in the mainstream of sport made sense. It could rationalise the number of sports structures, increase resources, improve standards and results, ensure that NSFs are the governing bodies for sport in the country, and ensure that all athletes are treated equally as athletes first and foremost, regardless of whether they have a disability or are Deaf. As a result of agreement between the three affiliates, discussions began with several NSFs that were open to the idea of taking on the responsibility for all athletes within their sport. Cycling SA, Swimming SA and the SA Table Tennis Board were the first to sign the inclusion agreements based on a mutual understanding of the benefits of inclusion. The other NSFs did not get the opportunity to do so as DISSA dissolved in favour of the South African Sports Confederation and Olympic Committee (SASCOC), which adopted a disability sport policy in 2022. This was shared with NSFs in January 2023.[57] For a genuinely inclusive NSF, however, there needs to be a commitment from the disability sport organisations and the NSF.

From the days of NAPCOSA through DISSA to SASCOC, South Africa has been a member of the African Sports Confederation of Disabled (ASCOD), which was established in 1987 in Algeria and formalised in 1990.[58] The Africa Sports Confederation of Disabled was the first continental organisation for Paralympic committees within the IPC umbrella, even preceding the establishment of the IPC in 1989. The African Sports Confederation of Disabled initiated the inclusion of athletes with disabilities in the All Africa Games and athletics and swimming debuted on the programme in 1999.[59] However, the continued inclusion of sports for disabled athletes has been inconsistent within the All-Africa Games, perhaps due to a lack of political and organisational support. In 2023, the African Para Games will be held separately in Ghana. The Africa Sports Confederation of Disabled, which is headquartered in Egypt, also transformed to become the African Paralympic Committee (APC) in 2009, and is headquartered in Angola.

Following the perceived poor performance of the South African Olympic Team in the 2000 Sydney Olympic Games, then Minister Ngconde Balfour instituted a task team to assess ways in which South African sport could produce better results. The Ministerial Task Team Report[60] was submitted in 2002, which led to a further review, including organisational mandates and a desired simplification of the sports system. As a result, there was a consensus decision to dissolve all multi-sports organisations and form SASCOC in 2004. Organisations that dissolved following this decision were the National Olympic Committee of SA, the SA Commonwealth Games Association, the SA Sports Commission and DISSA. The United Schools Sports Association of SA was also effectively dissolved, with Sport and Recreation SA and the Department of Education taking on greater responsibility for school sport. However, the South African Students' Sport Union, now University Sport South Africa, continues to operate. As a result, SASCOC became the NPC and a member of the APC and IPC. Despite a resolution of the IPC in 2005 that all NPCs must include "Paralympic" in their registered name, which should be the name in daily use, SASCOC only complied with this IPC membership requirement in 2022.

When DISSA and the other multi-sport organisations were dissolved, it became clear that the three affiliates of DISSA, plus Special Olympics SA, continued as multi-sport organisations. Accordingly, the three disability sport organisations became associate members of SASCOC, now Sport SA (the short version of the SA Sports Confederation, Olympic and Paralympic Committee), and now come together in the Disability Sport and Classification Commission re-established in 2021. However, Sport SA has a clear mandate with its Paralympic function because it is the country's NPC and is not a member of the ICSD or Virtus.

Sport SA is responsible for delivering Team South Africa to all multi-sport events, including the Olympic and Youth Olympic Games, Paralympic Games, African Games, African Para Games, African Union Sports Council Zone V Games, Commonwealth and Commonwealth Youth Games, World Games and International School Sports Federation Gymnasiade. Furthermore, being the NPC, Sport SA is responsible for preparing, selecting and sending teams to the IPC World Para sports world and African championships, specifically athletics, powerlifting, shooting and swimming.

South Africa's performance peaked in 2008 following the rankings on the medals' tables (a better measure than medal numbers):

Table 8.1: Medals won by South Africa at Paralympic Games post 1992[61]

Games	Place on table	Gold	Silver	Bronze	Total
1992	27	4	1	3	8
1996	15	10	8	10	28
2000	13	13	12	13	38
2004	13	15	13	7	35
2008	6	21	3	6	30
2012	18	8	12	9	29
2016	20	7	6	4	17
2020/1	32	4	1	2	7

The best South African performer in the Paralympic Games was Natalie du Toit, who won 13 gold and 2 silver medals between 2004 and 2012. She set 10 world records for Para swimming in various events, including freestyle, butterfly and individual medley. In addition to her medals, du Toit received several important awards for her achievements:

1. In 2002, the David Dixon Award for the most outstanding athlete at the Commonwealth Games.
2. The Whang Youn Dai Achievement Award at the 2008 Paralympic Games.
3. In 2009, the Order of Ikhamanga in Gold.
4. In 2010, she was named the Laureus World Sportsperson of the Year with a Disability.
5. An honorary Order of the British Empire in 2013.

The first African female athlete to win a gold medal in the post-Apartheid era was Zanele Situ, who won in her favourite event, the javelin, with a throw of 14,45m at the 2000 Sydney Paralympic Games. She received the Order of Ikhamanga (silver) in 2003 for her achievements at the 2000 Paralympic Games and for serving as a role model to South Africans.[62] In the 2004 Paralympic Games, while not winning a medal, Zanele was awarded the Whang Youn Dai Achievement Award for the female athlete who best embodied the spirit of the Games.

The longest career in the Paralympic Games is a record held by Ernst van Dyk, whose career spanned from 1992 to 2021. He has competed in three different sports, namely athletics, swimming and cycling. Van Dyk is a prolific marathon racer who has won the Boston Marathon 10 times,[63] but announced his retirement in 2023. In 2010, Ernst was awarded the Order of Ikhamanga in silver for his sport achievements.[64]

Perhaps the best-known Paralympic athlete, both on and unfortunately off the track, is Oscar Pistorius. He was nicknamed "Blade Runner" and "the fastest man on no legs"[65] after he burst onto the Paralympic scene at the 2004 Paralympic Games. He was not afraid to take on the might of the International Association of Athletics Federations, now World Athletics, to be able to compete in the 2012 Olympic Games.

8.6 CLASSIFICATION AND ELIGIBILITY – THE KEY DIFFERENCES IN SPORT FOR PERSONS WITH DISABILITY

Classification is not a new concept; it has been used in sport for persons without a disability for decades. Classification can be weight divisions in strength and combat sports, a golf handicap, or differentiation between men's and women's events. It is a way in which, as far as possible, competition can be made fair and unpredictable. However, there are always natural physical differences that lead to a competitive advantage. For example, the current tallest basketball player is Tacko Fall, a Senegalese player who is 2,26m tall and plays for the Cleveland Cavaliers,[66] or a very light cox in rowing eights.

8.6.1 A Short History of Classification

For about 20 years, at the beginning of what has become known as Para sport, the classification system consisted of only four classes for participants in athletics events and table tennis. For example, in swimming, participants were divided into two groups, namely those with complete spinal cord lesions and those with incomplete spinal cord lesions.[67]

After the 1968 Paralympiad in Israel, the ISMGF medical subcommittee started investigating the possibilities of using a fairer system to categorise athletes. In July 1974, a revised classification system was finally accepted by the ISMGF Committee that was still based on athletes' medical diagnoses and used for all sports. Eight classes, based on spinal cord lesions, were divided into two groups, namely cervical lesion: P1a, P1b, P1c (quadriplegia – all four limbs affected) and thoracic lesion: P2 – P6 (paraplegia – lower limbs affected). In 1964, ISOD also followed the principle of medical classification for athletes with amputations using classes:[68] A1 – A4: Amputation above or through the elbow joint; A5 – A8; Amputation above or through the knee joint; and A9: Amputation of upper and lower limbs.

In 1978 CP-ISRA set their competition criteria, perhaps being the first to consider movement ability as a criterion for classification.[69] They identified eight classes: CP1 – CP 8, with CP1 as the most severely affected in movement ability.

In 1980, athletes with spinal cord impairments, visual impairments, amputations and CP competed at the International Games in Arnhem, Netherlands. This, as the relevant international organisation for sport for people with disabilities, created its criteria for eligibility and grouping of competitors.[70] As the Paralympic movement matured, the focus switched away from rehabilitation and began to focus on the sport's specific requirements, the beginning of sport-specific classification systems.

As the initial classification process in the Paralympic movement was based on a medical approach, classification along functional lines was formalised in time for the Paralympic Games in Barcelona in 1992, where appropriate groups for competition based on movement profiles were organised. For example, swimming used an integrated, functional classification system where swimmers with CP, amputations, spinal cord injuries and the *Les Autres* group competed against one another in the same class according to the movement ability assessed during classification by qualified swimming classifiers. This sport-specific process continued independently until the IPC established its classification code in 2007,[71] modelled on the World Anti-Doping Code. While classification is the major difference in sport for those with and without disabilities, it is also a significant risk as athletes have abused it. Therefore the IPC has been very focused on ensuring that the sports classes allocated are based on objective evidence of the extent of the disability and that the process followed is consistent and fair.[72]

As with challenges faced in sports at all levels, cheating could happen through taking a performance-enhancing substance or as a result of illegal betting and match manipulation. Cheating in classification is another challenge specifically faced by sport for those with disabilities.

8.6.2 Classification in Para Sport

Classification in Para sport is essential to ensure fair competition. It assures the public that winning an event is determined by athletes' skill, fitness, power, endurance, tactical ability, mental preparation, nutrition and other skills. It is the process by which athletes are grouped to compete against each other in both team and individual sports.[73] Each International Sport Federation (ISF) handles the classification process and trains classifiers. There has been recognition that classification needs to be sport specific, for example, classification will be different for a visually impaired athlete competing in the 100m on an athletics track compared to a tandem cyclist or an alpine skier.

The first step in the classification process for a Para athlete is to assess if he or she has an eligible disability, which is done based on a medical report. The list of eligible impairment types is set out below.

Table 8.2: Eligible impairment types and description[74]

Impairment type	Description
Impaired Muscle Power	Athletes with Impaired Muscle Power have a health condition that either reduces or eliminates their ability to voluntarily contract their muscles to move or to generate force.
	Examples of an underlying health condition that may lead to Impaired Muscle Power include spinal cord injury (complete or incomplete, tetra-or paraplegia, or paraparesis), muscular dystrophy, post-polio syndrome and spina bifida.
Impaired Passive Range of Movement	Athletes with Impaired Passive Range of Movement have a restriction or a lack of passive movement in one or more joints.
	Examples of an underlying health condition that may lead to Impaired Passive Range of Movement include arthrogryposis and contracture resulting from chronic joint immobilisation or trauma affecting a joint.
Limb Deficiency	Athletes with Limb Deficiency have total or partial absence of bones or joints because of trauma (for example traumatic amputation), illness (for example amputation due to bone cancer) or congenital limb deficiency (for example dysmelia).
Leg Length Difference	Athletes with Leg Length Difference have a difference in the length of their legs because of a disturbance of limb growth or because of trauma.
Short Stature	Athletes with Short Stature have a reduced length in the bones of the upper limbs, lower limbs and/or trunk.
	Examples of an underlying health condition that may lead to Short Stature include achondroplasia, growth hormone dysfunction and osteogenesis imperfecta.
Hypertonia	Athletes with Hypertonia have an increase in muscle tension and a reduced ability of a muscle to stretch caused by damage to the central nervous system.
	Examples of an underlying health condition that may lead to Hypertonia include cerebral palsy, traumatic brain injury and stroke.

Impairment type	Description
Ataxia	Athletes with Ataxia have uncoordinated movements caused by damage to the central nervous system.
	Examples of an underlying health condition that may lead to Ataxia include cerebral palsy, traumatic brain injury, stroke and multiple sclerosis.
Athetosis	Athletes with Athetosis have continual slow involuntary movements.
	Examples of an underlying health condition that may lead to Athetosis include cerebral palsy, traumatic brain injury and stroke.
Vision Impairment	Athletes with Vision Impairment have reduced, or no, vision caused by damage to the eye structure, optical nerves or optical pathways, or visual cortex of the brain.
	Examples of an underlying health condition that may lead to Vision Impairment include retinitis pigmentosa and diabetic retinopathy.

The second step is for an assessment to be made of whether the athlete's disability meets the minimum impairment criteria. For example, an athlete may have had part of their foot amputated, but this is insufficient to be deemed eligible for swimming. Likewise, it is possible that an athlete may meet the minimum impairment criteria in one sport but not in another.

Assuming that the steps above are affirmative, classifiers allocate a sports class based on athletes' ability to execute specific tasks and movements associated with the sport. Classifiers assess athletes in bench tests and action, testing their physical and technical abilities. This is why an athlete who has both legs amputated may be eligible to compete against another who is paraplegic in athletics, or why a swimmer who has cerebral palsy can compete against an athlete with amputations. Classification is therefore based on the functions athletes can perform, hence the description of functional classification.

Once a sports class has been allocated, athletes are observed by a classification team in a competition. This is based on the assumption that athletes are unlikely to cheat in competition as they are motivated by a desire to win. When all else fails, classification could be done at the final stage of an event. This is not the only way that classifiers and other athletes review an athlete's classification now, however, as the rise of videos and selfies on social media has provided other avenues.

Athletes can request a review of their sport class and also request a review of another athlete's sports class. A classification panel could also recommend that athletes' classes be reviewed. A completely new panel will be required to do such a review in all cases.

The classification process requires a mix of people with medical, para-medical and sports technical knowledge, who then make up a classification panel. Medical classifiers could be medical doctors, physiotherapists or occupational therapists. For the visually impaired, the classifier must be an ophthalmologist or, in some instances, an optometrist. A technical classifier is usually a coach, former athlete or someone with a deep understanding of movement abilities. International Sport Federations are responsible for ensuring that a consistent classification system exists, while this is the responsibility of

NSFs at a national level. The large body of expertise in South Africa rests with SASAPD until the NSFs take on the responsibility for athletes with disabilities.

8.6.3 Classification of Athletes With Intellectual Impairment

The classification process followed for athletes with an intellectual impairment is similar to that for athletes with physical and visual impairments, however there are some differences. Virtus (formerly INAS-FID) requires that all minimum eligibility impairment documents are submitted for assessment via SASA-II to confirm that the intellectual disability is characterised by significant limitations, both in intellectual functioning and in adaptive behaviour, as expressed in conceptual, social and practical adaptive skills.[75]

Based upon the above, the Virtus Eligibility Criteria for athletes with an intellectual disability are:

1. Significant impairment in intellectual functioning, which is defined as a full-scale IQ score of 75 or lower.
2. Significant limitations in adaptive behaviour as expressed in conceptual, social, and practical adaptive skills.

    These significant limitations are defined as performance that is at least two standard deviations below the mean of either:

    a. one of the following three types of adaptive behaviour: conceptual, social, or practical skills; or
    b. an overall score on a standardised measure of conceptual, social and practical skills.
3. The intellectual disability must be evident during the developmental period, which is from conception to 22 years of age.

Virtus uses these three elements to assess athletes' intellectual impairment and if they are eligible for Virtus sport. Further sport-specific assessments are undertaken if an athlete wishes to compete in Para sport, leading to participation in the Paralympic Games. International Sport Federations (ISFs) undertake physical and technical sport-specific assessments, followed by allocating a sports class. Generally, there is only one sports class for athletes with intellectual disabilities due to the higher functioning ability of athletes in the Para sport stream.

The IPC definition is, *"Athletes with an Intellectual Impairment have a restriction in intellectual functioning and adaptive behaviour which affects conceptual, social and practical adaptive skills required for everyday life. This Impairment must be present before age 18".*[76] This differs from the Virtus requirement of the developmental period being up to 22 years of age.

In addition to the Virtus eligibility criteria being met, most ISFs will require a Training History and Sport Limitation Questionnaire to be submitted before a sport cognition test battery and a technical assessment assess the minimum impairment criteria.[77] Tests often do the cognition test battery on a touchscreen computer covering the following components, tests, tasks, scoring and cut-off scores:

Component	Tests	Task	Scoring	Cut-off Score
Processing Speed and Attention-Concentration Skills	Flanker Test	To react as fast as possible to four different stimuli, with the corresponding arrow key, while ignoring the distractors.	Number of correct responses in 30 seconds	41
Memory and Learning	Corsi	To remember a sequence of blocks and repeat the sequence in the same order.	Average length of a sequence	6.69
Visual-motor Skills	Finger Tapping	To tap the spacebar 10 seconds as fast as possible with the dominant and non-dominant hand.	/	/
Executive Functioning	Tower of London	To copy the frame structure by moving balls in the least number of moves possible.	Number of items solved correctly	12.43
Visual Perception and Fluid Intelligence	Block	To copy patterns with white/red.	Raw total performance	58.31
	Design	Cubes	Score	
	Matrix Reasoning	To indicate out of five pictures which one belongs at the place of the question mark in the matrix.	Number of items solved correctly	28.91

Thereafter, athletes are assessed from a technical and in-competition perspective and allocated a sport class. The initial Virtus assessment is undertaken by a psychologist who acts as the national eligibility officer and is sent to Virtus. When the ISF takes on the next steps, they will use their regular classification panels of medical and technical classifiers.

In the Special Olympics movement, sports competitions are based on the idea that athletes of all abilities should be given an equal chance of succeeding, whether a personal best or a gold medal, with the primary factor being athlete's ability. Special Olympics International also has a form of classification called divisioning[78] to ensure an equal chance to compete.

The first step is where a coach completes a player's rating or skills assessment form. This is easier where the achievement of events is measurable in distance or time. In a racket or team sport, coaches' assessment of athletes' ability is critical. Athletes' ability is assessed in competition, preferably at Special Olympics events. Finally, a committee will place each athlete in a division where there are no less than three and no more than eight athletes or teams in a competition. For example, if a competition has 20 entries, the Committee will assess the results to ensure that the number of athletes is between three and eight, based on a difference in results of athletes of no more than 15%. There is also a provision to include age and gender as variables to group athletes, however a division could consist of an age range of 22 to 30, combining genders, so grouping is flexible. The bottom line is the ability and ensuring that athletes compete against others of similar ability – similar to the Para sports process.

As there are several events, such as the 100m, which are based on divisions, each athlete who wins a division will receive a medal. This has led to the perception that the Special Olympics ethos is more about participation than elite competition. That may be true to a large extent, but it allows more athletes to participate and win medals. It should, however, be reiterated that the key personnel who manage the divisioning process are coaches and members of the sports technical committee.

Again, there is a minimum eligibility requirement for sports events involving the Deaf. For ISCD events, Deafness is defined as a hearing loss of at least 55dB pure tone average (PTA) in the better ear (three-tone pure tone average at 500, 1000 and 2000 Hertz, air conduction, ISO 1969 Standard)[79] where the athlete is required to take an audiology test without any hearing aids and to compete without any hearing aids. After that, no other sport-specific process is needed, and athletes can participate in their chosen sport. If athletes have less hearing loss, they are deemed to be hard of hearing and are not eligible to compete in Deaf sports.

A critical commonality between all sports for athletes with disabilities is that the rules are often adapted. For example, in Para sport, there is usually provision for assistive devices such as wheelchairs, prosthetic devices, handcycles, reins and strapping. In other sports, such as for the visually impaired, guide runners are permitted for athletics, tappers for swimming and assistants for boccia. For the Deaf, starting guns and whistles are of no use, therefore flags are used to replace them, while in swimming, strobe lights are used to start a race. In the case of the intellectually disabled, there are no changes to on-field competition rules, but rather changes in the system of draws (divisions) or the eligibility process are followed.

8.7 THE FUTURE

Much of what happens in South Africa regarding disability sport will be influenced by developments in international sport. Since the first cooperation agreement between the IOC and IPC was signed in 2000,[80] this has been extended at various points to bring the Olympic and Paralympic movements closer. The latest agreement takes the cooperation up to 2032.[81] In addition, as part of the IOC's reforms after the Salt Lake City scandal, where some IOC members were removed from office for taking bribes,[82] the president of the IPC is also an ex officio member of the IOC, which has helped bring the two organisations closer together. Indeed, some of the Olympic Programme sponsors have also elected to sponsor the IPC and Paralympic Games.

In time, the relationship between the IPC and IOC should filter down to the national level. In South Africa, that has already happened, putting South Africa on the map as one of a handful of countries where the NOC and NPC are one organisation. Other countries are the USA, Norway, Netherlands and Saudi Arabia.[83] In many countries there is increasing cooperation between the NPC and NOC, however the economies of scale will not be realised and the equitable treatment of Olympic and Paralympic athletes is often only achieved once one organisation catering for all athletes is in place.

Special Olympics International has a programme of partnerships with ISFs.[84] The aim is to demonstrate the unique ability of sports to transcend barriers and serve as a vehicle for social inclusion for children and adults with intellectual disabilities. However, there needs to be an indication of transferring governance responsibility from SOI to ISFs for those athletes participating in a sport.

Concerning the Olympic and Paralympic Games joining into one, this is unlikely due to the size and length of time necessary for both Games to take place. For example, the Olympic Games in 2020 hosted 11,420 athletes competing in 339 events over 18 days[85] and the Paralympic Games 4,403 in 539 events over 13 days. However, one organising committee for the Olympic and Paralympic Games has been the model for organising both Games since 2002.

A similar approach is likely to be followed with SOI, Virtus, ICSD, IBSA and IWASF continuing to manage their world games or championships separately to promote their development initiatives, on the basis that without high-profile international events, their sports will not develop new talent. Without these events, these organisations may not continue to exist, however as demonstrated by several athletes with disabilities, in addition to the 18 Deaf athletes who have competed in the Olympic Games over the years, athletes would likely elect to compete in the Olympic Games and continue participating in the Paralympic Games and Deaflympics.

The Commonwealth Games included athletes with disabilities in Vancouver in 1994[86] for the first time. While athletes with disabilities did not compete in 1998, since 2002, the programme for disabled athletes has steadily increased. The Commonwealth Games are thus the only genuinely integrated Games, but do not include a complete Para sport programme. However, with elite athletes with a disability included in one Commonwealth team, it does encourage closer cooperation between NPCs and National Olympic Committee (NOC), as most Commonwealth Games Associations (CGAs) are also NOCs.

Internationally, an increasing number of ISFs aspire to be included in the Paralympic programme and automatically incorporate Para sport into their operations to encourage their NSFs to do the same. The IPC has indicated that it will transfer governance of its 10 Para sports either to an existing ISF or to allow the Para sport to establish itself as its own ISF by 2028. What will be interesting to watch is if and how World AbilitySport, IBSA and Virtus follow suit.

Nationally, Sport SA shared its Sport for Persons with Disabilities policy in January 2023 with the NSFs that showed an interest in the policy, the concept of disability sport and inclusion. With an increasing number of ISFs responsible for Para sport (mainly physically and visually impaired), combined with the IPC's sports independence process, NSFs will, of necessity, follow suit. This implies that national disability sport organisations may need to transform from being self-governed to being governed by NSFs. As per the policy, this will require NSFs to take on not only the governance, but also the classification, of athletes and funding responsibilities. There will also need to be a realignment of the support services for NSFs from the sports science, medical and technology sectors, predominantly through tertiary institutions. Funding from the national department responsible for sport, the National Lottery and sponsors will also help to encourage the inclusion of disabled and Deaf athletes into the NSFs, provided that such funding is available and ring-fenced.

Several Deaf athletes are trained by hearing coaches, which implies that coaches are part of NSFs. However, there is a relatively easy step that NSFs could take to include Deaf athletes. Terence Parkin's performance in the Deaflympics and the Olympics, where he won a silver medal, demonstrates that Deaf athletes can compete with hearing athletes, leading to improved standards and competition locally and internationally.

There is fear of athletes with disabilities getting "lost" in an NSF, thus a monitoring system should be instituted by the governmental departments responsible for sport and disability with Sport SA and other stakeholders to ensure this does not happen and that funding is available.

Another aspect to consider is the gradual improvement of medical and health standards, particularly in developed countries. For example, some impairments leading to vision loss can be corrected. This will be interesting to follow because the number of disabled people should reduce as the numbers of athletes with disabilities who have corrections increase, particularly in the developed world.

8.8 CONCLUSION

Disability is a fact of life; it could happen to anyone, and disabled people's rights are human rights. Society should be inclusive and encourage all citizens to achieve their full potential in academia, business or sport. To do this, full inclusion should be demonstrated, and all barriers addressed that prevent some people from achieving their potential.

"We may not be able to compete against you, but we can compete with you."

SELF-ASSESSMENT

1. Explain the origin and genesis of different international organisations catering for disability sport.
2. Discuss the origin and development of the national organisations catering for disability sport.
3. Argue the context and impact of sports independence as part of mainstreaming disability sport.
4. Debate the basic principles of classification and eligibility for athletes with disabilities.

PART II

THE MANAGEMENT OF SPORT

STRATEGIC MANAGEMENT OF SPORT

Dr Louis Nolte

LEARNING OUTCOMES

At the end of this chapter, you should be able to:

1. Define strategy in the context of the strategic management of sport in South Africa.
2. Apply theoretical frameworks to the strategic management of sport in South Africa.
3. Identify prominent organisational structures in sport organisations and relate them to strategy.
4. Describe the environment and process of the strategic management of sport organisations and apply this process to the management of sport in a South African setting.
5. Identify and apply performance measures to demonstrate how sports organisations monitor, evaluate and adjust their strategies.

9.1 INTRODUCTION

Strategy in the management of sport is about positioning sport organisations to be sustainable and attain a competitive advantage over their peers. A unique aspect of this process is that sport organisations work with their competitors to structure leagues and competitions while competing for resources such as sponsors, facilities, players/athletes and staff.

Developing a strategy in sport involves choosing what products and services to offer. These considerations include opportunities to compete at junior, intermediate, senior and elite levels; hosting and participating in clinics, camps and leagues; establishing supporter groups; and resourcing such activities. For example, Gymnastics South Africa (GSA) is a National Sport Federation (NSF) in South Africa that offers opportunities to participate in training and other events, from grassroots to elite level participation, supported by trained coaches and judges.

Therefore, a strategy's primary goal is to create a value proposition for shareholders and stakeholders, such as supporters, sponsors and the broader public, by providing customer value. Continuing the previous example, Gymnastics SA partners with various organisations, such as the National Lotteries Commission, for funding, while the International Gymnastics Federation enables event participation. In doing so, they have produced multiple world class gymnasts who serve as an inspiration (value proposition) for future gymnasts. Competitive strategies should deliver a unique mix of value to stakeholders that represent the long-term direction of organisations.

Whilst the strategic management process in sport organisations represents strategy as practice, the reality is that it is often subject to changes in the environment that are seldom linear and often unpredictable. Sport organisations in other sectors operate in a dynamic environment of constant change. One such example is the immediate and long-term impact of the Covid-19 pandemic and the associated lockdowns on both on-field and off-field sport-related activities, such as cancelling sport events and changing financial conditions that directly and indirectly impacted sport organisations. Other examples include the increasing use of, and reliance on, technology (such as Video Assistant Referee technology in football) and the ever-increasing social media footprint of sport organisations globally to engage with their fans and supporters more effectively. Cricket South Africa (CSA) is one such organisation, which has more than four million Facebook followers. Within this context, managers of sport need to formulate and implement strategies that enable their organisations to survive in their environments and achieve a sustainable competitive advantage. To do this, sport organisations are structured to pursue these strategies effectively and efficiently; hence they are informed by their strategy. Navigating this dynamic, open environment effectively requires sound theoretical frameworks to inform Sport Managers.

9.2 THEORETICAL FRAMEWORKS IN THE MANAGEMENT OF SPORT

Theoretical frameworks contribute to explaining, understanding and controlling critical aspects in practice, and advance learning, understanding and research.[1] Therefore, incorporating theoretical frameworks in the management of sport is essential as it informs aspects such as service delivery and the practical application of work conducted in the sport industry. Various reductionist theories have attempted to simplify the understanding of management phenomena. According to Chelladurai,[2] the most prominent include the goals model (the extent to which an organisation achieves its goals), the systems resources model (the extent to which organisations are successful at identifying and gaining access to scarce resources), the process model (the extent to which the organisation's processes are aligned with its desired outputs), and the multiple constituency model (the integration of various perspectives of effectiveness from a variety of constituencies). In line with Chelladurai, the following section discusses prominent theories that provide frameworks to analyse the management of sport organisations from the perspective of systems, processes, structures and designs. These include the systems theory, Resource Dependence Theory and organisation theory, with applied examples in the South African context.

9.2.1 Systems Theory

The systems theory attempts to explain organisational effectiveness from a unified perspective that corporate systems cannot be studied in isolation, but as their dynamic nature forms them. This is because of their constant interaction with the external environment. The theory postulates that a system is a collection of elements or sub-systems in an organisation that are unified by regular interaction and interdependence. Sub-systems collectively perform various nonlinear functions at different times and scales of magnitude towards the equilibrium or performance that are constantly influenced and shaped by the dynamic interactions from the external macro environments. Examples of factors in the macro environment include the economy, technological developments, social changes, legal implications and political decisions, which require organisational systems and sub-systems to change constantly as open systems. Trenberth and Hassan[3] indicated that it is essential to approach the development of multi-faceted contextual sport systems from a dynamic, open systems point of view. From a systems theory perspective, environmental factors impact the extent to which sport organisations gain access to resources (input) and are strategically managed to deliver programmes such as talent development pathways (output) and, ultimately, sustainable performance (outcome). These resources could be human (e.g., athletes, coaches, administrators and technical officials), physical (e.g., facilities and equipment), financial (e.g., sponsorships, broadcasting rights and lottery funding) and information (e.g., research, communication and marketing).

NSFs in the public sector in South Africa, such as Cricket South Africa (CSA), strategically manage various resources (such as coaches, players and staff, facilities, funding and information databases) to develop and implement pathways that enable the systematic development of athletes and teams to High Performance (HP) level. For example, the success of its national teams could measure CSA's outcomes. However, some sport organisations and clubs operating in the private sector (such as those that offer personal coaching) could measure their performance based on profit margins. In contrast, others in the non-profit sector (such as Altus Sport) could measure their performance based on various outcomes related to the social change initiatives they are engaged with.

9.2.2 Resource Dependence Theory

Fundamentally, the Resource Dependence Theory (RDT) postulates that dependence on essential resources influences the way that organisations act and that these could be explained by specific dependency situations that arise.[4]

Governments have increasingly invested in sport since the advent of professionalisation, triggered by the commercial success of the 1984 Los Angeles Olympic Games. These investments recognise sports' potential political and socio-economic benefits, such as nation-building, improving national health and comparing positions on the global sport stage with government success. There are numerous instances where governments engage in targeted investment, whereby vast amounts of resources are allocated to a limited number of National Sport Federations (NSFs) based on their potential to deliver successful performances on the world stage. In South Africa, these sports include, among others, cricket, rugby and soccer.

Targeted investment implies that strategies to deliver sustainable performance outcomes are highly dependent on allocating resources effectively. In the public sector, NSFs compete for greater access to these resources. This is even more relevant in South Africa, where resource access is often severely constrained. For example, Operation Excellence (OpEx), an elite athlete programme of the South African Sport Confederation and Olympic Committee (SASCOC), was designed to provide financial and athlete support to the most talented athletes in South Africa to varying extents based on three tiers. However, due to financial constraints, athletes received little support for the period preceding the Tokyo 2020 Summer Olympic and Paralympic Games. Other funding was sourced from organisations such as the National Lotteries Commission (NLC), with approximately ZAR 56 million and ZAR 20 million allocated to preparation for the Tokyo Summer and Paralympic Games, respectively.[5] By comparison, Great Britain's support package for these Games amounted to £342 million, emphasising the need for strategically utilising available resources to ensure the competitiveness of South African athletes at the international level.

A wicked problem also arises, whereby policies are put in place that expect sport organisations to perform on higher levels to gain access to financial resources. However, these sport organisations are simultaneously deprived of resources due to a lack of performance, whilst other more successful sport organisations are supported and strengthened.[6] These scenarios lead to significant power imbalances and dependencies on external providers for resources. This results in organisations that control vital resources that having the power to influence the strategies and behaviour of sport organisations.

In South Africa, NSFs are also under scrutiny for their on-field performances. They could be penalised in various ways, including the withdrawal of funding and the right to host significant events should they not meet agreed-upon transformation criteria. These criteria are set out in a memorandum of understanding with the Department of Sports, Arts and Culture and the South African Sports Confederation and Olympic Committee (SASCOC). From an RDT perspective, these dependencies create power imbalances between NSFs and government organisations such as SRSA and SASCOC. Therefore, managers of sport in South Africa should be capable of analysing, interpreting and implementing structures and processes that align sport organisations strategically to pursue these targets.

9.2.3 Organisation Theory

One of the critical questions that organisation theorists attempt to address is how organisations are structured. Understanding the structures of organisations could provide insight into organisational aspects, ranging from how these organisations gain access to resources, to how and to what extent teams and individuals communicate with each other. However, analysing these aspects in isolation does not provide a holistic understanding of organisations. One theory that enables organisations to understand the organisational structure in this context is the organisation theory. Parent and O'Brien[7] defined organisation theory as the scientific study of organisational structure, processes and design, while advocating the use of this theory as a lens to understand sport organisations.

9.3 ORGANISATIONAL STRUCTURES IN SPORT

Organisational structures are critical levers for the effective implementation of strategies and relate to the hierarchical arrangements within sport organisations, and the structural dimensions of complexity, formalisation and centralisation.[8]

Complexity is the extent to which sport organisations are differentiated horizontally, with larger sport organisations in South Africa often grouping similar jobs together, such as technical, events and finance committees. This makes functional units more manageable, unlike local sport clubs with limited resources that often have small committees that perform multiple functions. Vertically, larger sport organisations in South Africa could have a CEO, Board of Directors, portfolio managers and others, whereas local sport clubs could have an owner and coach that performs multiple functions. Spatially, South African NSFs are geographically dispersed to ensure national reach, compared to local sport clubs that only serve their surrounding communities.

Formalisation refers to how sport organisations have written and codified rules, regulations, policies, processes and procedures that guide individuals' actions, positions, roles and relationships. In South Africa, the situation often arises that local sport clubs have limited access to resources and, as a result, rely on the policies of their provincial and national federations for guidance.

Centralisation is the extent to which decisions are made at the top leadership of sport organisations. In decentralised organisations, decision-making is typically delegated to lower levels, however it is often the case that sport organisations display decentralised and centralised decision-making characteristics. For example, Executive Boards of NSFs in South Africa might make strategic decisions that impact the long-term direction of organisations, with provincial federations and local sport clubs taking responsibility for the contextual adaptation and implementation of plans to achieve strategic outcomes.

Besides the generic characteristics of organisational structure, O'Brien and Gowthorp[9] pointed out unique features related to the structural design of sport organisations, i.e., functional, divisional, matrix and network designs.

9.3.1 Functional Design

Functional, structural designs of sport organisations are typical of international and national federations such as Motorsport South Africa (MSA) (Figure 9.1), where specific functions or specialisations are grouped to represent inputs to organisations. This type of design reflects a relatively centralised decision-making structure, which could prove challenging during rapid environmental change when swift decisions are required. This structural design also requires effective communication to ensure that all units pursue the same strategic direction and outcomes. In MSA, all their business and affairs have been vested in the Management Committee, however it can only act within the scope of policies the Board of Directors sets out. From a strategic perspective, MSA's Board of Directors is responsible for setting a medium-to long-term vision, controlling the company and the strategic direction (which ultimately influences its performance). The CEO is accountable to the Board of Directors for implementing various policies, strategies, business plans and other decisions that could be made occasionally (resolutions). Any other committees act within a specific scope set out and approved by the Board of Directors on the recommendation of the Management Committee. These committees report directly to the CEO.

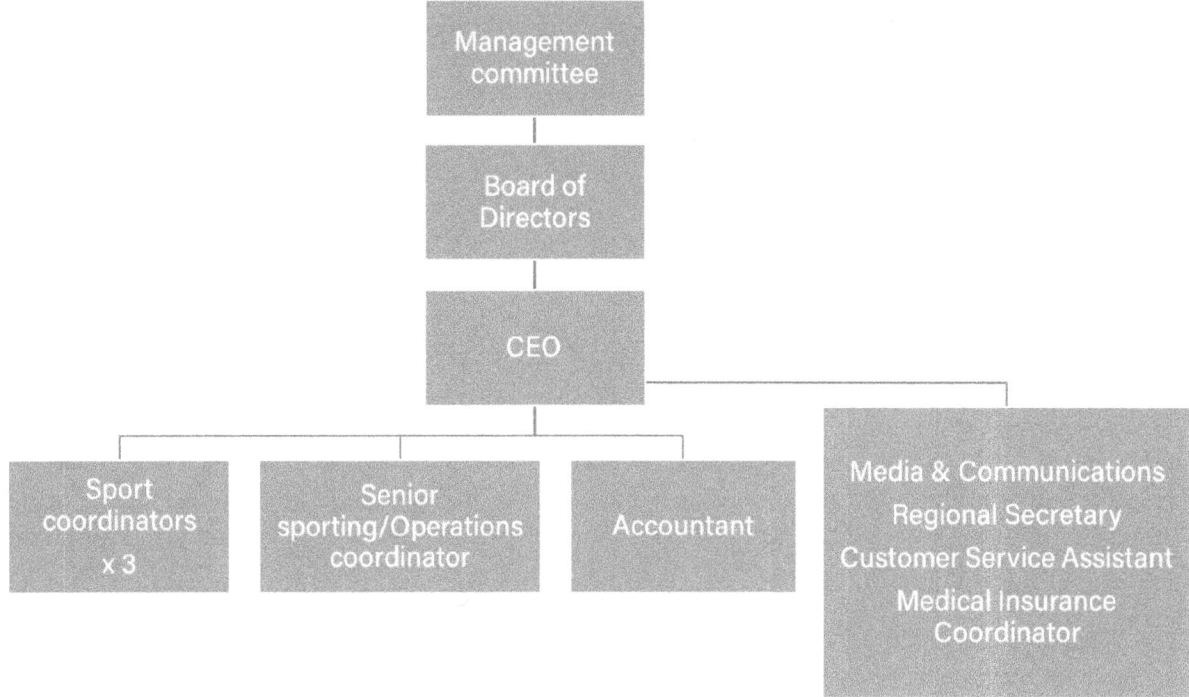

Figure 9.1: Internal structure of Motorsport South Africa[10]

9.3.2 Divisional Design

In contrast, the divisional structure is segmented according to outputs such as services and products. This design is appropriate for larger organisations that need to react to environmental change quickly through a decentralised decision-making structure. For example, this structure could be suited to Advent Sport Entertainment and Media (ASEM), a media rights house that manages, among others, Varsity Sport (see Figure 9.2). ASEM is the full-service agency for managing the Varsity Sports league on behalf of the University Sports Company. The context and responsibilities are significantly different to ASEM Schools Sport, which focuses on managing media and sponsorship rights for interschool rugby sevens and netball events. This is as opposed to ASEM Engage, which advises on aspects such as community engagement, public relations, social media strategies and content production. The functions of each of these companies are different and the services they offer vary depending on the organisation's type and context. In addition, each company has their unique blend of human resources, requiring a decentralised approach to management.

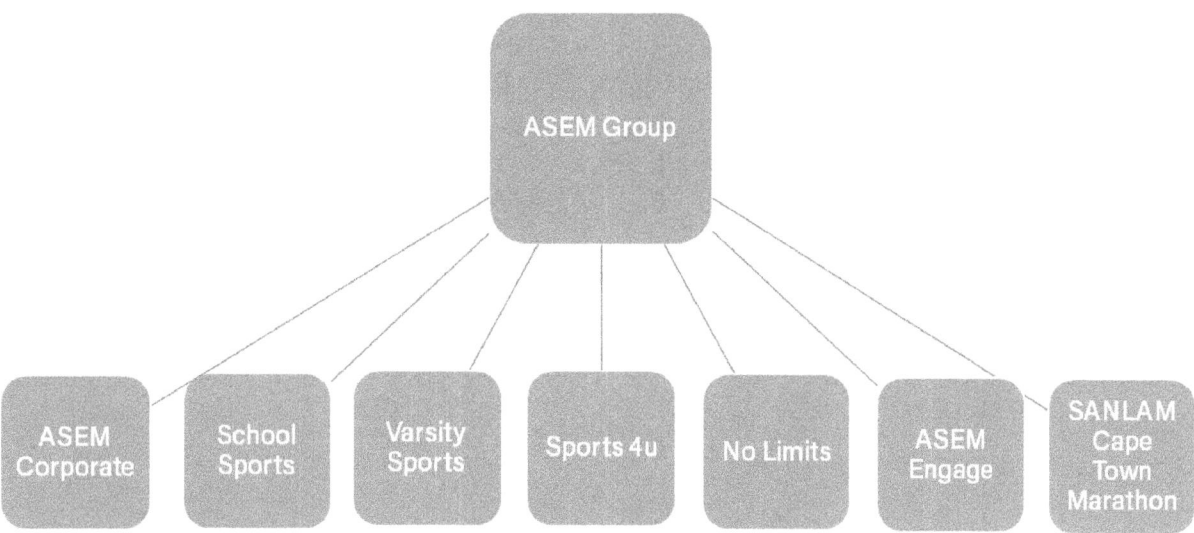

Figure 9.2: Hypothetical structure of Advent Sport Entertainment and Media (ASEM)

9.3.3 Matrix Design

Matrix structures are most appropriate when knowledge and expertise are shared across different operations and where resources are constrained; a balance is required between in-depth technical knowledge (functional design) and innovation (divisional design), and multi-directional coordination and information processing ensure certainty in unstable environments. For example,[11] AFL Architects designed the Peter Mokaba Stadium for the 2010 FIFA World Cup in South Africa, thus the matrix design could be appropriate for such an organisation (see Figure 9.3). In this case, the Director for Sport and Leisure's projects might provide specific instructions on what the sport project requires (such as constructing a stadium large enough for a World Cup). At the same time, the architect and Director of Sustainability might use this information to share their knowledge and expertise to construct the stadium appropriately, functionally and sustainably. However, the horizontal and vertical interaction places demands on the adequate training of the organisation's human resources, and identifying individuals to communicate with about specific issues could become a challenge.

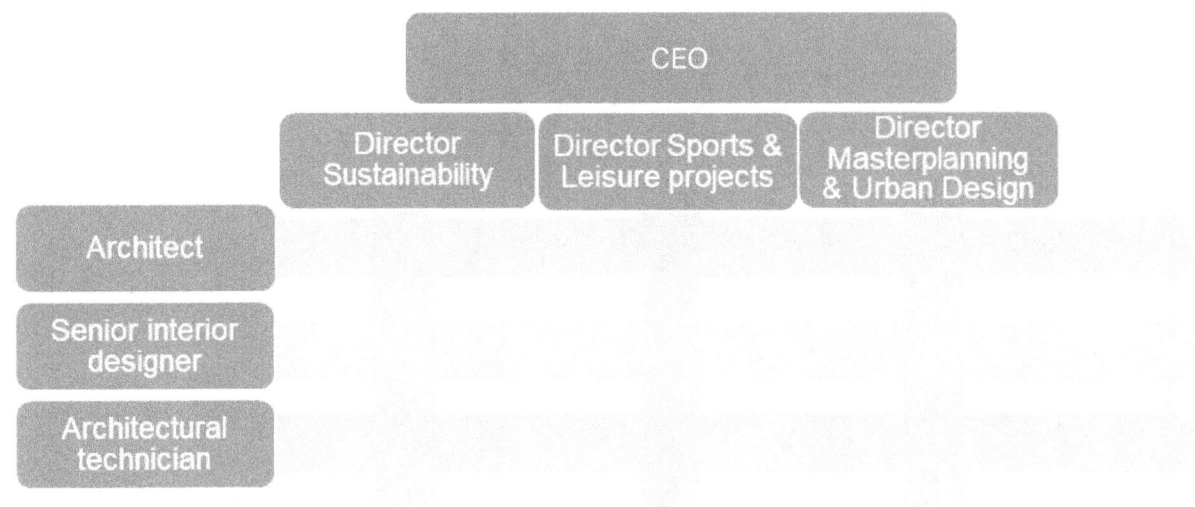

Figure 9.3: Hypothetical matrix design for AFL

9.3.4 Network Design

Numerous partnerships between private, public and non-profit organisations combine to deliver sport events, leagues, tourism, sport-for-all, elite sport and others, making network designs in the sport sector familiar. The Sport for Social Change Network (SSCN) in South Africa is an example where characteristics of the network design are evident. While remaining a relatively small team, SSCN mobilises resources, shares knowledge and provides opportunities for the development of youth in and through sport by establishing partnerships with multiple non-profit and community-based organisations that are geographically dispersed (see Figure 9.4) for a hypothetical network design with SSCN at the core and numerous partner organisations in the South African provinces and the rest of Africa represented by the surrounding bubbles. The 2003 Men's Cricket World Cup also displayed several network design characteristics, with South Africa, Zimbabwe and Kenya co-hosting the event. The media rights firm Octagon CSI selected Gravity Media to supply the high-end technical facilities required to broadcast the event, while ensuring technical coordination between Octagon CSI and other suppliers at all the venues. The responsible South African Sport and Recreation Portfolio Committee appointed various suppliers to host a successful event, such as international tour operators, wine suppliers, travel agents, a hotel group to provide official accommodation, and emergency medical services.[12]

Figure 9.4: Hypothetical network design for SSCN

One of the significant benefits of network design is that the coordinating organisation can focus on managing the process and outsource activities to specialists. In contrast, this design could also result in a lack of scrutiny and quality control. This was evident when the Kaizer Chiefs hosted a 2018 semi-final cup match against the Free State Stars. To ensure safety and security at such an event, significant coordination and clear communication are required between the hosts, stadium management and the South African Police Services. However, despite a pitch invasion being flagged as a possible outcome during the event, a communication breakdown led to ill-prepared police services and the inadequate training of stewards, resulting in violent protests and a pitch invasion that left 18 people injured, despite the presence of police and private security forces.[13]

The strategic competitive advantage that sport organisations achieve is highly dependent upon a structured approach to dividing and coordinating tasks, and to what extent these structures are appropriately aligned with their context. This process of strategic management is discussed in the following section.

9.4 THE PROCESS OF STRATEGIC MANAGEMENT IN SPORT

Effective strategies require sport organisations to engage in the strategic analysis of the internal and external environments, formulation and implementation of strategy, and evaluation. These environmental analyses are essential in understanding the organisation's position and inform the overall strategic management of a sport organisation (see Figure 9.5).

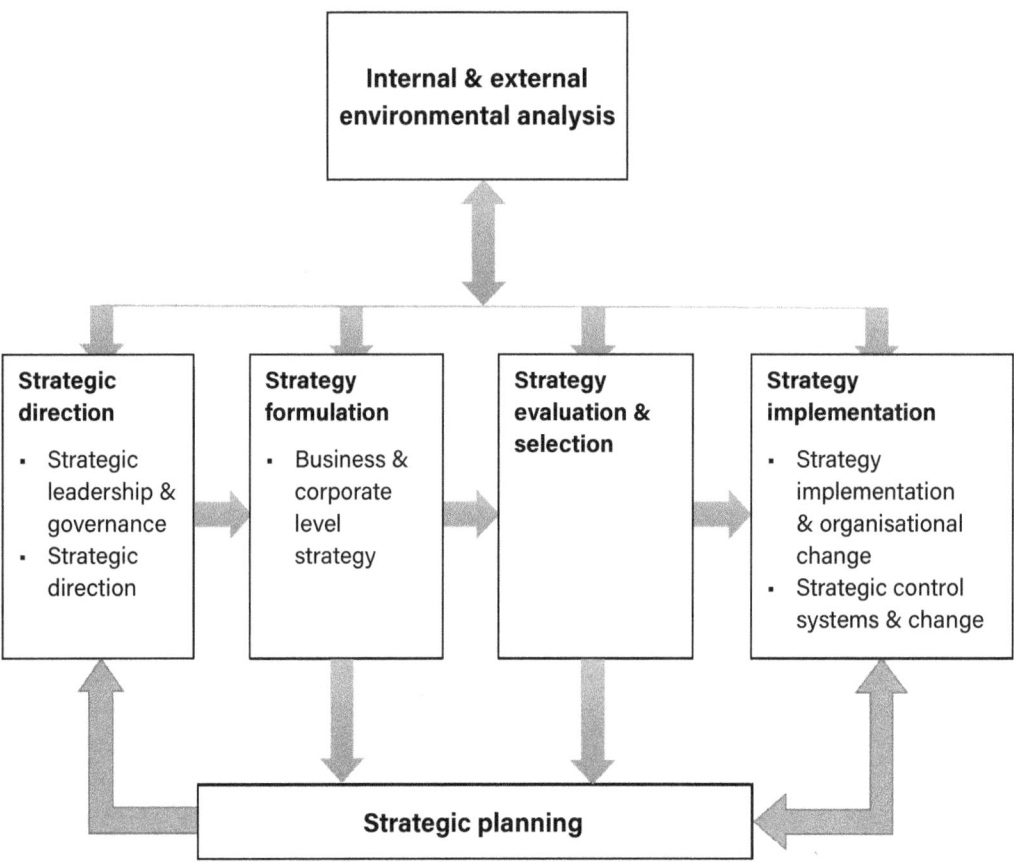

Figure 9.5: Strategic sport management process[14]

The strategic management process, therefore, emphasises a range of essential components, such as analysing and interpreting data from their internal and external environments and establishing a strategic direction that informs the formulation and implementation of strategies to achieve goals and objectives and satisfy organisational stakeholders.

9.5 KEY COMPONENTS OF STRATEGY

Clegg et al.[15] described strategy as consisting of knowledge and capabilities. Knowledge represents the skills required and concepts to imagine the future, while capabilities are the power to accomplish things by implementing visions, ideas and plans. These components inform one another, as is represented in Figure 9.6.

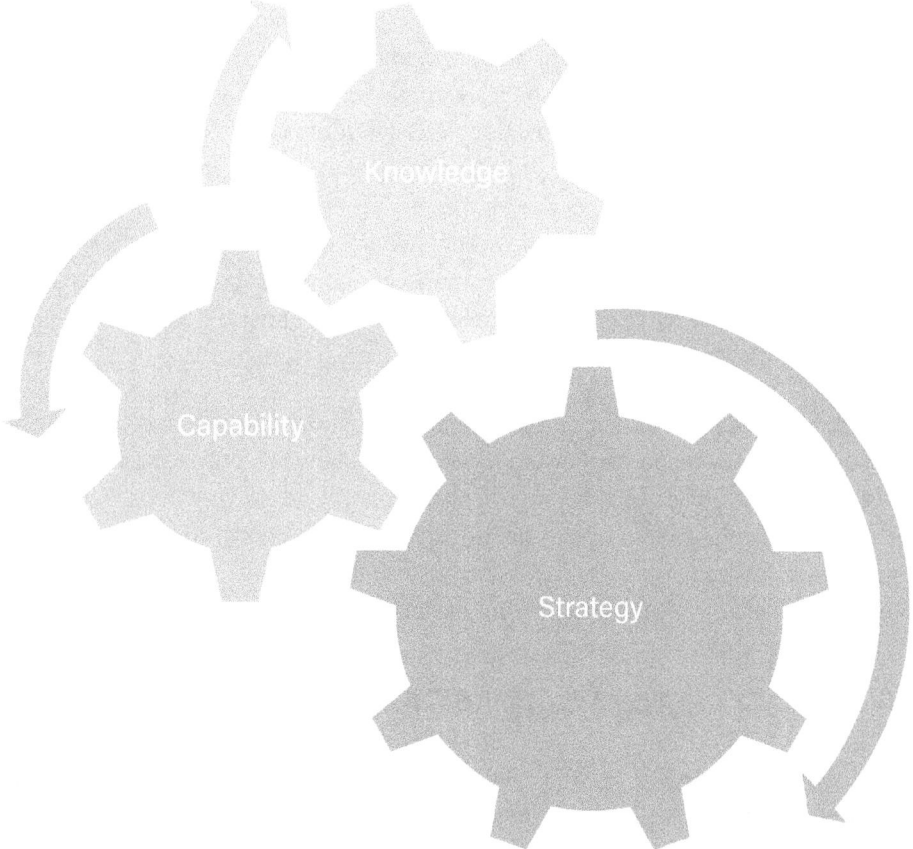

Figure 9.6: Components of strategy

9.5.1 Strategic Purpose: Vision, Mission and Objectives

Sport managers must consider whether strategies are conceivable and doable. In this regard, the purpose of strategy does not serve to reach an end, but contributes to making a vision reality. Vision statements refer to aspirational views of what organisations want to achieve or become in the long term, guided by core values. Therefore, the purpose of visions is to guide organisations to establish a form of control that enables them to achieve desirable states. Furthermore, visions of organisations and associated strategies are often rooted in history and informed by past practices that could provide insight into the position of sport organisations in their environments. In this regard, the purpose of organisations is defined by a mission statement.

Objectives are targets that set out what organisations aspire to achieve in a specified period. Sport managers should also adopt values that define their beliefs, principles and rules that regulate how they manage organisations. This will often be displayed as corporate values that inspire organisations to achieve their goals.

An excellent example of strategic purpose can be found in one of South Africa's most successful NSFs, the South African Rugby Union (SARU). The Strategic Transformation Development Plan 2030[16] states that SARU's vision is to *"be the leading Rugby Nation, inspiring all South Africans"*. The mission statement emphasises the desire to be the leading rugby nation by maintaining good governance and the development of rugby as a form of entertainment and sustainable performance, by stating that: *"To be the leading rugby nation by providing well governed, world-class innovative sporting entertainment and sustainable high-performance systems, processes and people."* Referring to the strategy components in Figure 9.5, knowledge and capabilities should contribute to achieving their desired outcomes. A range of values, including excellence, inclusivity, innovation, ethics and collaboration, guide the organisation's strategic management process. As previously indicated, these components depend upon strategic planning (Figure 9.5) that is informed by internal and external analyses of the environment.

It is evident from the preceding discussions that the effective functioning of sport organisations is highly dependent on their access to resources and to what extent they can utilise these effectively, especially when they have limited capacities, cooperation, collaboration and partnerships with stakeholders that could support processes and address potential shortcomings. Globally, there is a convergence of the systems that manage resources in sport organisations, yet the contextual adaptation of these to align with their environments most effectively determines their success.

9.6 THE SPORT MANAGEMENT ENVIRONMENTS

One of the most vexing features of sport is the investment of resources in unpredictable outcomes. Recently, this was evident when the South African women's cricket team unexpectedly beat second-ranked England in the semi-final of the 2023 Women's T20 Cricket World Cup, which was hosted in South Africa. To counteract this unpredictability, sport organisations increasingly invest in auxiliary services such as hospitality and merchandise. The quality of such supplementary products and services is essential, considering the potential for drop-offs in on-field performance in all forms of competitive sport.

Like organisations globally, sport organisations in South Africa, such as Cricket South Africa (CSA), Netball South Africa (NSA), South African Rugby Union (SARU) and Judo South Africa (JSA), to name a few, are not static and isolated, but constantly interact and react to broader pressures that could be political (e.g., transformation targets), social (e.g., change in demographics) and economic (e.g., depreciation of the South African Rand) in nature. In this context, the sport environment in South Africa consists of a micro-environment, the market (meso) environment and the remote (macro) environment. Therefore, Sport Managers should be capable of analysing the dynamics of these environments by applying tools such as the SWOT and PESTEL frameworks.

9.6.1 Macro-Environment of Sport

The macro-environment consists of political, economic, social, legal and environmental environments outside the organisation's control. In HP sport, smaller nations such as the Netherlands and New Zealand increasingly adopt systematic, strategic and in-depth, long-term plans to succeed. This reduces the impact of macro-level factors such as population, indicating that strategically managed public investments under the direct influence of policies are increasingly the determinants of success. However, in the case of nations with developing economies such as South Africa, macro-level factors such as the economy's strength significantly impact the available financial resources and the money available to expose HP athletes to international events.

One of the most significant political factors in managing South African sport is meeting transformation targets. Transformation in South Africa has often been perceived, almost exclusively, as an attempt to achieve representative targets in national sport teams based on racial demographics. This is in response to racial segregation in the country during Apartheid. However, the Transformation Charter of Sport in South Africa also emphasises achieving equality, diversity and inclusion regarding considerations such as gender, disability and geographic location. Although NSFs in South Africa are expected to pursue broad national transformation targets, they also have self-selected targets. A good example is SARU's Strategic Transformation Development Plan 2030,[17] which sets out a clear plan with transformation targets from age-level rugby onwards, supported by a range of resources. In an environment where the extent of access to resources is already constrained, this requires careful strategic planning and allocation of resources to ensure that transformation and performance targets are met.

9.6.2 Market (Meso-level) Environment of Sport

The market (meso) environment is comprised of role players such as customers, suppliers of capital and materials, the labour force such as volunteers and unions (players and coaches), competitors (other sport clubs or NSFs), and intermediaries such as wholesalers, agents, brokers and retailers. The role of policies and politics at this level should also be considered as these could be directly influenced by, and influence, sport organisations. The meso-level thus consists of institutions and processes that influence and shape social and environmental outcomes.

Meso-level policies related to athlete support, for example, could enhance the provision of sport science support to athletes at the micro-level. Procedures at the meso-level govern athlete development pathways. The extent to which these pathways and policies align with their vision, mission, goals and objectives impacts the quality of the development of coaches, athletes, administrators and technical officials over the long term. Ultimately, the success of these pathways will determine the extent to which they can produce sustainable sport performances.

Sponsors are among the most significant stakeholders that could impact sport at this level. From a systems theory perspective, organisations require financial resources to perform certain functions, while sponsors could aid organisations. For example, consider sponsors' significant role in empowering women's sport in South Africa, such as Sasol's sponsorship of women's football, Momentum's sponsorship of the

Proteas women's cricket team, and Telkom's partnership with Netball South Africa. However, when taking a resource-dependency perspective, the (over-) reliance on sponsors could place sport organisations in a potentially vulnerable financial position that leads to power imbalances. There is also the potential for reputational damage, such as in the cases of Standard Bank and PUMA. In 2020, Standard Bank withdrew its longstanding sponsorship deal worth approximately ZAR 100 million a year from Cricket South Africa (CSA) because of reputational damage suffered by governance issues in CSA. Similarly, PUMA withdrew from a sponsorship deal with SAFA in 2013 that was due to last until 2018. This deal was terminated due to match-fixing allegations, with PUMA indicating that they were withdrawing for ethical reasons.[18]

9.6.3 Micro-Environment in Sport

Sport organisations, with their resources, functions, strategies, policies, processes and procedures, standards and conduct, structure and strategic components, represent the micro-environment. UK Sport[19] also emphasises the importance of these components in achieving and maintaining standards of good governance. The micro-environment shapes the processes, operations and methodologies to develop athletes in an HP environment. When appropriately managed, these factors, such as the timing of athlete selection, could support the meso-level implementation of talent identification and development policies.

At NSA, the micro-environment consists of an amateur foundation of coaches, players, administrators and technical officials. This forms the basis of a trajectory culminating in semi-professional and professional pathways. At these levels, athlete support, national and international experience, scientific support, contracting, development pathways, talent identification and recruitment form part of the micro-environment.

To make sense of a sport organisation's internal and external environments, managers of sport in South Africa can use several tools that serve as frameworks to analyse these environments and inform their decision-making.

9.7 FRAMEWORKS OF ANALYSIS

9.7.1 Strengths, Weaknesses, Opportunities and Threats (SWOT) analysis

Analysing organisations' strengths, weaknesses, opportunities and threats (SWOT) is a tool used as part of the strategic planning and management process that could enable managers to analyse the internal and external environments of sport organisations. The SWOT components consist of organisational strengths and weaknesses that could place organisations at an advantage or disadvantage over other organisations in the industry. Similarly, environmental threats and opportunities that are external to organisations could be identified and taken notice of, and could be to the benefit or detriment of organisations.

Whilst numerous factors could be considered, highly commercialised sport organisations in South Africa such as SARU, CSA and SAFA have, among others, access to financial and physical resources (e.g., facilities and equipment), which could represent organisational strengths. These organisations can host significant sport events regularly, among others, due to the extent of their access to physical resources. This places these sport organisations at a competitive advantage over smaller, lesser-known organisations that often rely on external providers to gain access to venues to host events at a high cost (organisational weakness).

Environmental opportunities and threats could present in the form of societal changes. In line with global trends, NSFs in South Africa have increasingly and successfully focused on promoting female participation in sports such as rugby, cricket and soccer.

While the SWOT analysis provides an opportunity to analyse the internal and external environment of organisations, a further tool for managers of sport to understand the impact of macro-environmental factors is the Political, Economic, Social, Technological, Environmental and Legal (PESTEL) framework of analysis.

9.7.2 Political, Economic, Social, Technological, Environmental and Legal (PESTEL) Analysis

Political, economic, social, technological, environmental (natural) and legal (PESTEL) dimensions form the core of the macro-environment of sport organisations. For example, in South Africa, political decisions to segregate sport and society based on racial demographics resulted in South Africa being banned from the Olympic Games (from 1964), only to return in 1992. More recently, the 2010 FIFA World Cup in South Africa was branded as 'Africa Rising' to promote unity across the continent. However, many questioned whether the significant resource investments were justifiable following the completion of the event. Some of the doubts related to, among others, the fact that fewer tourists visited the country than expected; the maintenance costs of stadiums over the long term; and the development of infrastructure to transport tourists around airports and to areas where crime was less prevalent, thus reinforcing wealthier, more developed areas.[20]

Although there are numerous potential advantages of sport in the context of poverty, high poverty levels are associated with lower participation in sport. South Africa is predicted to have the highest level of unemployment globally in 2023 at more than 35%, which will inevitably impact sport participation. Therefore, social issues such as social inequality caused by high unemployment are also reflected in sport participation rates. In terms of technological factors, digital technology could contribute to reducing poverty. The United Nations (UN) recognises that companies such as Jumping Kids in South Africa are already enhancing access to sport by developing assistive technologies. In addition, South Africa's National Sport and Recreation Plan (NSRP)[21] highlights that sport should be used to promote environmental messages and be practiced in an environmentally appropriate manner. Finally, the NSRP emphasises that the nonracial, nonsexist and democratic values enshrined in the South African Constitution should be pursued in and through sport.

9.7.3 Stakeholder Analysis

Stakeholders are *"groups and individuals who can affect, or are affected by, the strategic outcomes of a firm"*.[22] External stakeholders of sport organisations are individuals, groups and organisations that are not part of the strategic direction of sport organisations, such as the government, sponsors, media, athletes, members and coaches. In contrast, internal stakeholders are staff and volunteers (the operational team) or individuals and groups that ensure strategic direction (such as executive boards and senior management). Internal stakeholders ensure that organisations' missions are pursued in practice. The highly regarded Australian sport system serves as an example of how engagement with stakeholders and intra-organisational cooperation could contribute to the resilience of sport systems and to gaining access to alternative sources of income. This system incorporated government support and funding to improve the functioning of NSFs, leading to the professionalisation and commercialisation of Australian sport. Ultimately, this resulted in, for example, the diversification of funding sources, such as the government and multiple sponsors, and the involvement of various stakeholders to formulate and implement strategies, policies and programmes.[23]

To gain a strategic competitive advantage over their competitors, managers of sport organisations in South Africa should be aware of the environment that their organisations operate in to ensure that their vision and mission statements align with the interests of external stakeholders. Especially in non-profit sport organisations, external stakeholders could provide vital access to financial and non-financial resources (such as access to facilities, sport equipment and technical expertise). The power-interest stakeholder matrix is an effective tool for identifying key stakeholders in the industry (Figure 9.7).

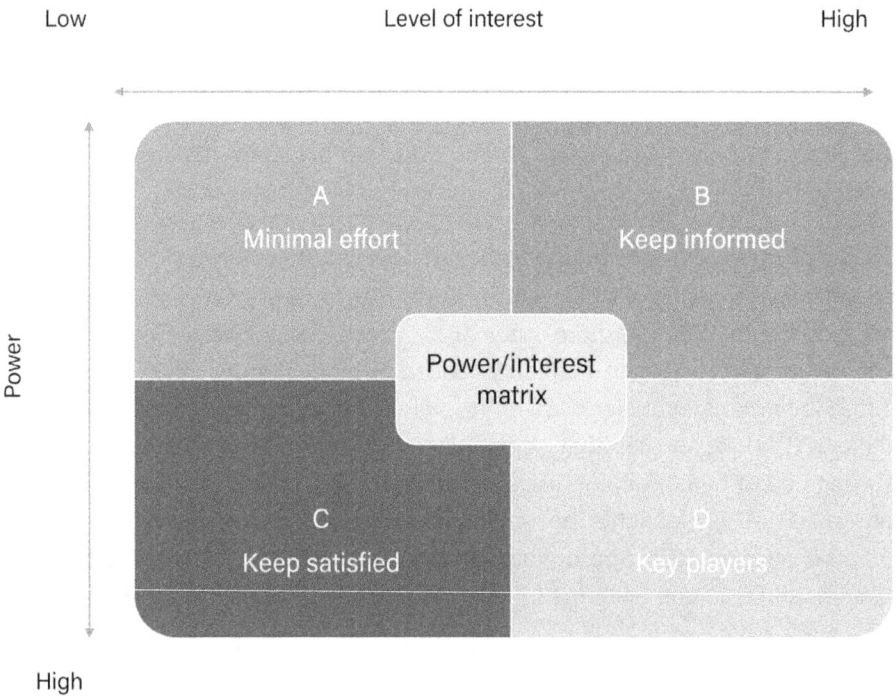

Figure 9.7: Power-interest matrix

In the context of NSFs such as SARU, SAFA and ASA, key players (D) could be members and spectators as they directly impact the level of support at events, as well as the status and income that these organisations generate. In some cases, the relevant International Sport Federation (ISF), such as World Rugby, can also be regarded as a critical player. The extent to which these NSFs are required to comply with policies, such as those related to transformation in South Africa, to gain access to resources would imply that the government could occupy both, or shift between, Keep satisfied (C) and Keep informed (B). Sponsors could be in a similar position as they could make strategic decisions to support sport organisations in the immediate and long term, based on the extent to which these organisations demonstrate that they satisfy key criteria in their agreements. In terms of Minimal effort (A), these could be other sport organisations that are not involved in rugby and, as a result, do not directly impact their ability to offer their products and services.

Sport managers in South Africa should thus thoroughly analyse the stakeholders in their internal and external environments to ensure their buy-in. This support is necessary to access essential resources when formulating and implementing strategy, and contributes to achieving sustainable performance outcomes in the organisation's context.

9.8 PERFORMANCE MEASUREMENT

The preceding discussions in this chapter indicate that the strategic management of sport organisations is multi-faceted, and Sport Managers require a thorough understanding of the role of the external environment (e.g., political, social and financial factors and policies) in shaping strategies. Furthermore, for sport organisations to successfully implement their strategies, their overall targets must be pursued rather than emphasising the priorities of individuals and teams in the organisation (also see Chapter 24). To do this, managers of sport should identify Critical Success Factors (CSFs) that represent the characteristics (e.g., price advantage), conditions (e.g., good customer mix) or variables (e.g., structural elements) that could significantly impact the success of the organisation.[24] Appropriate performance indicators should accompany these CSFs.

Parmenter[25] identified four types of performance measures, including:

9.8.1 Key Result Indicators (KRIs)

KRIs provide the board of an organisation with an overall summary of how it is performing. KRIs should be reported at, for example, board meetings, representing a past performance measure. This implies that organisations cannot react to KRIs to change direction or improve performance, but provide insight into the impact of these measures on an organisation's governance and management. For example, KRIs for an organisation in the private sector might include net profit and employee satisfaction, whilst sport organisations in the public and non-profit sectors might be interested in reporting on the availability of their services and membership numbers.

9.8.2 Result Indicators (RIs)

Result indicators provide less of an overall view of the organisation's activities than KRIs and, as a result, fall under KRIs. RIs give the management of an organisation insight into how different teams combine to produce results on a daily, weekly and monthly basis. For example, a sport organisation in the private sector could report on the number of sales made on a particular day and how this contributes to the organisation's overall financial performance. These results depend on a combination of multiple teams, such as marketing and sales, working together. Public and non-profit sport organisations could adopt RIs such as utilising their facilities every week, or the extent to which grants from the National Lottery have been implemented concerning the agreements.

9.8.3 Key Performance Indicators (KPIs)

Key performance indicators provide management with feedback on the daily or weekly progress that the organisation is making concerning its CSFs. According to Parmenter,[26] there are seven characteristics of KPIs: 1) KPIs should be **non-financial**, failing which they become RIs; 2) KPIs should be tracked constantly to ensure that the organisation can adjust and make changes that ensure success, i.e., they should be **timely**; 3) there should be a **CEO focus**, which implies that CEOs, or managers of sport organisations, speak to staff daily about progress made to achieve KPIs; 4) KPIs should be **simple** and indicate what needs to be adjusted to ensure that targets are met; 5) KPIs should be **team-based**, meaning that teams in an organisation should be able to take responsibility for taking corrective action; 6) KPIs have a **significant impact** on the organisation's CSFs; and 7) KPIs that are tested to ensure that they do not result in unnecessary and damaging unintended consequences result in a **limited dark side**. An example of a KPI for sport organisations in the private sector could be reporting the number of complaints received from key customers that have not been resolved to the CEO within a specified time. In the public and non-profit sport sector, managers of sport might expect daily feedback on the number of volunteers registered to assist, over a set number of weeks, before hosting a sports event.

9.8.4 Performance Indicators (PIs)

Performance indicators provide feedback on the output teams deliver and could be captured using team scorecards. Whereas KPIs are indicators of the overall performance of an organisation, PIs offer insight into the alignment of the performance of individuals and teams in the organisation with KPIs. Examples could include the number of late deliveries in the private sector and the number and date of research projects into customer/athlete needs in the public and non-profit sectors.

Sport managers can use various tools to monitor performance, such as Board Dashboards and Balanced Scorecards (BSCs). Regarding strategy, BSCs provide a management system that enables managers of sport to translate the strategic goals of sport organisations into a set of performance objectives. These objectives are constantly measured, monitored and adjusted to meet the organisation's strategic goals.

9.9 CONCLUSION

This chapter demonstrated the importance of a strategic approach to managing sport organisations in South Africa, by defining and positioning strategy within the strategic management process of sport in the country. In addition, it explained how the systems, resource dependence and organisation theories relate to the context of the sport environment in South Africa. Managers of sport in South Africa should incorporate, for example, transformation from a South African perspective into a strategic plan that ensures success over the short, medium and long term. Four prominent structures in sport organisations (functional, divisional, matrix and network) were described and applied to a South African context. Appropriate frameworks of analysis (SWOT, PESTEL and the power-interest stakeholder matrix) were applied to the South African sports environment, and the importance of performance measurement to ensure the effective implementation of the strategy was discussed in the context of sport organisations in the private, public, and non-profit sectors.

SELF-ASSESSMENT

1. Define strategy in the context of the strategic management of sport in South Africa.
2. Apply the systems, resource dependence and organisation theories to the strategic management of sport in South Africa.
3. Identify prominent organisational structures in South African sport organisations and relate them to strategy.
4. Describe the environment and process of the strategic management of sport organisations in the South African context.
5. Identify and apply performance measures to sport organisations in South Africa and demonstrate how strategy is monitored, evaluated and adjusted.

GOVERNANCE IN SPORT

Professor Rian Cloete & Professor Jacques Faul

LEARNING OUTCOMES

At the end of this chapter, you should be able to:

1. Describe the fundamental principles and concepts of governance in sport.
2. Argue various sport governance structures, including national and international sport governing bodies.
3. Identify and analyse governance challenges faced by sport governing bodies.
4. Critically evaluate best governance practices in the sport industry.

10.1 INTRODUCTION

10.1.1 Objectives of the Chapter

The objectives of this chapter on governance in sport are to provide students with an understanding of the importance of good governance in sport. Students will be introduced to the key concepts and principles that underpin effective governance in the sports industry. This chapter will discuss the principles and characteristics of good governance in sport, explore concepts such as transparency, accountability, integrity, inclusivity, fairness and athlete welfare, and explain their importance in promoting effective governance.

The various governance structures that exist in sport at different levels, such as international governing bodies (Fédération Internationale de Football Association (FIFA), World Rugby, International Cricket Council (ICC), World Athletics, World Netball) and National Sports Federations (South African Football Association (SAFA), South African Rugby Union (SARU), Cricket South Africa (CSA), Athletics South Africa (ASA), Netball South Africa (NSA)), will be explored. Their roles and responsibilities are examined against the specific challenges they face that impact sports governance, including corruption, doping, ethical dilemmas, financial management, decision-making processes and balancing interests among stakeholders.

Overall, this chapter on governance in sport aims to educate students about the fundamental principles, challenges and best practices related to sport, empowering students to contribute to developing and improving governance in South African sport.

10.1.2 Definition of Governance in Sport

There is no exact definition of "corporate governance",[1] however it can be defined as a system by which companies and other entities are directed and controlled. Governance in sport refers to the system, processes and structures through which governing bodies are managed, regulated and directed. This involves establishing and enforcing policies, rules and procedures that guide the conduct and operation of sports at various levels, including international federations, National Sports Federations and local sports organisations or clubs. Corporate governance systems must be adopted for the benefit of all stakeholders in sport.[2]

10.1.3 Importance and Values of Good Governance in Sport

Governance in sport plays a crucial role in ensuring the proper functioning and development of a particular sporting code. Good corporate governance makes business sense because well-managed and transparent sports bodies attract and retain sponsorship. This ensures the continued financial sustainability of the sports body and gives stakeholders comfort that the sport is properly managed.[3] But good governance is about more than rules and regulations; it is an attitude of mind and about a governing body's ethical culture and people's behaviour.

10.1.4 Transparency, Accountability and Responsibility

Effective governance in sport ensures transparency, accountability, responsibility, fairness, integrity and the protection of the rights and welfare of athletes and stakeholders.[4] It promotes transparency in decision-making processes, financial management, and the overall management of governing bodies in sport. It further ensures that stakeholders have access to information that enables them to make informed decisions. This empowers them to hold governing bodies accountable for their actions, promoting trust and confidence in sport.[5] Governing bodies in sport must assume responsibility for the assets and actions of the sports body and be willing to take corrective actions.

10.1.5 Sustainability

Good governance facilitates sustainable sports development by implementing long-term financial strategies, promoting grassroots participation and creating opportunities for talent development in the community. It takes resource management, strategic planning and financial stability to support the growth and longevity of a sport.

10.1.6 Inclusivity and Diversity

Good sports governance promotes inclusivity and diversity by creating equal opportunities for participation and representation. It encourages the involvement of underrepresented groups, such as women, minorities and individuals with disabilities, in decision-making processes and leadership positions on the boards of governing bodies.

10.1.7 Stakeholder Management

Governance ensures the active involvement of stakeholders, including athletes, coaches, officials, fans, broadcasters, sponsors, player representative bodies and the wider community.[6; 7] It also encourages dialogue, consultation and collaboration, which enables a more democratic and inclusive decision-making process within the governing body.

In summary, effective sports governance is essential for maintaining sports' integrity, fairness and sustainability. It ensures transparency and accountability, promotes inclusivity and diversity, protects athletes' rights, and enables the sports industry's positive development and growth.

10.2 CORPORATE GOVERNANCE IN SOUTH AFRICA

Most governing bodies[8] in professional sport are managed through incorporated entities, similar to private companies. Unfortunately, most of these governing bodies have a poor corporate governance record.[9] Corruption, fraud, bribery, nepotism, mismanagement and other integrity-related scandals have tainted the image of sport in South Africa, which keeps hitting the headlines for all the wrong reasons.[10] This has necessitated the implementation of corporate governance principles and practices among governing bodies. It is important to note that all sporting bodies should comply with corporate governance, even if they operate through unincorporated entities such as voluntary associations.[11; 12]

10.2.1 The King IV™ Report on Corporate Governance

The first King Report on Corporate Governance (King I) was released in 1994 by the Institute of Directors in response to growing concern about corporate failures in South Africa. The purpose of King I was to promote the highest standards of corporate governance.[13] The King II report was finalised in March 2002 and emphasised aspects such as accountability, responsibility and transparency,[14] with the King III Report[15] following in 2009. This was replaced with the King IV Report in 2016.

The King IV™ Report on Corporate Governance[16] is a comprehensive document that provides guidelines for good governance practices. The legal status of King IV is that of a set of voluntary principles and leading practices. In South Africa, a hybrid corporate governance system has developed over time. Some good governance practices have been legislated (for example, in the Companies Act 71 of 2008)[17] in parallel with the voluntary King Code of Governance. The law prevails if there is a conflict between legislation and the King Code. Company directors have always been required to adhere to their accountability, transparency and fiduciary duties under the common law and the Companies Act. Common law fiduciary duties include, for example, acting in the company's best interest; exercising reasonable care, skill and diligence; acting in good faith; and avoiding conflicts of interest.

King IV builds on its predecessors' positioning of sound corporate governance as an essential element of good corporate citizenship, with a clear emphasis on transparency. Good corporate governance is integral to society and has accountability towards all stakeholders.[18] With the introduction of an 'apply and explain' regime, King IV asks governing bodies to be transparent in applying their corporate governance practices by 'applying' the principles and 'explaining' how they are being effected.[19] King IV outlines the following 17 principles that are fundamental to good governance:[20]

Principle 1	The governing body should lead ethically and effectively.
Principle 2	The governing body should govern the ethics of the organisation in a way that supports the establishment of an ethical culture.
Principle 3	The governing body should ensure that the organisation is and is seen to be a responsible corporate citizen.
Principle 4	The governing body should appreciate that the organisation's core purpose, its risks and opportunities, strategy, business model, performance and sustainable development are all inseparable elements of the value creation process.
Principle 5	The governing body should ensure that reports issued by the organisation enable stakeholders to make informed assessments of the organisation's performance and its short-, medium- and long-term prospects.
Principle 6	The governing body should serve as the focal point and custodian of corporate governance in the organisation.
Principle 7	The governing body should comprise the appropriate balance of knowledge, skills, experience, diversity and independence for it to discharge its governance role and responsibilities objectively and effectively.
Principle 8	The governing body should ensure that its arrangements for delegation within its own structures promote independent judgement and assist with balance of power and the effective discharge of its duties.
Principle 9	The governing body should ensure that the evaluation of its own performance and that of its committees, its chair and its individual members, support continued improvement in its performance and effectiveness.
Principle 10	The governing body should ensure that the appointment of, and delegation to, management contribute to role clarity and the effective exercise of authority and responsibilities.
Principle 11	The governing body should govern risk in a way that supports the organisation in setting and achieving strategic objectives.
Principle 12	The governing body should govern technology and information in a way that supports the organisation setting and achieving its strategic objectives.
Principle 13	The governing body should govern compliance with applicable laws and adopted non-binding rules, codes and standards in a way that supports the organisation to be ethical and a good corporate citizen.

Principle 14	The governing body should ensure that the organisation remunerates fairly, responsibly and transparently to promote the achievement of strategic objectives and positive outcomes in the short, medium and long term.
Principle 15	The governing body should ensure that assurance services and functions enable an effective control environment, and that these support the integrity of information for internal decision-making and of the organisation's external reports.
Principle 16	In the execution of its governance roles and responsibilities, the governing body should adopt a stakeholder-inclusive approach that balances the needs, interests and expectations of material stakeholders in the best interests of the organisation over time.
Principle 17	The governing body of an institutional investor organisation should ensure that responsible investment is practiced by the organisation to promote good governance and the creation of value by the companies in which it invests.

These principles aim to guide governing bodies in achieving effective, responsible and ethical governance practices that benefit all stakeholders, contributing not only to the long-term success of the governing body, but also the sport and its athletes.

10.3 SPORTS GOVERNING BODIES

10.3.1 National Sport Federations (NSFs)

National sport federations are the governing and regulatory bodies for specific sports within a country. NSFs play a crucial role in governance within their respective sporting landscapes and are affiliated with the South African Sport Confederation and Olympic Committee (SASCOC).[21] SASCOC is South Africa's national multi-coded sporting body, which is responsible for the preparation, presentation and performance of teams to all multi-coded events, namely the Olympic Games, Paralympic Games, Commonwealth Games, World Games, All Africa Games, Olympic Youth Games, Commonwealth Youth Games and Zone VI Games. SASCOC is also responsible for awarding National Protea Colours to athletes/officials who have met the criteria for representing South Africa in different sporting codes and arenas, as well as endorsing the applications for bidding on and hosting international events.

NSFs today face management and governance challenges that were unheard of in the past. Public scrutiny is more intense than ever, and sports funding is under increasing pressure. It is, therefore, essential for NSFs to ensure that they are operating as effectively and efficiently as possible; they must be held accountable for their internal governance and administration. To oversee an NSF's operations, federations must establish proper governance structures, including boards and committees. NSFs should develop strategic plans, manage finances, implement policies and ensure compliance with legal and ethical standards, as well as establish and enforce rules, regulations, technical standards and policies to govern their sport nationally. These rules and regulations must be aligned with the rules and regulations of the International Sport Federation (ISF). NSFs are also responsible for organising and managing national-level competitions, championships and other events within their sport.[22] In this regard, they handle event planning, logistics, venue arrangements, officiating and ensuring compliance with relevant regulations.

NSFs play a vital role in stakeholder management, as they engage with various stakeholders, including athletes, coaches, officials, clubs, sponsors and government entities. NSFs promote the interests of their sport and its stakeholders at the national and provincial levels, and represent their sport in discussions and negotiations with government bodies[23] (e.g., Department of Sports, Arts and Culture), SASCOC and funding agencies (e.g., National Lotteries Commission)[24] to seek support and resources to advance the sport's development and create an enabling environment for athletes and participants.

NSFs also select and manage national teams and athletes for international competitions, including establishing criteria and processes for athlete selection, managing team logistics and providing support services for athletes. Finally, NSFs represent their country's interests in ISFs (such as FIFA, World Rugby, World Athletics and World Netball) and facilitate athlete representation in decision-making processes.

10.3.2 International Sport Federations (ISFs)

International sport federations are international non-governmental organisations that are responsible for the integrity of their sport at the international level. ISFs are responsible for managing the world's various sporting codes, including monitoring the everyday administration of their sport, coordinating with NSFs from various countries, establishing criteria for NSF recognition and membership, and guiding NSFs in governance and administration. NSFs must abide by the decisions of an ISF,[25] which represents their sport internationally and maintains relationships with other international organisations, such as the International Olympic Committee (IOC).

ISFs organise and oversee international competitions, such as the Olympic Games, World Cups, World Championships and Continental Championships. They further establish qualification criteria, coordinate event schedules and manage the overall organisation of these events. They are also responsible for the rules and regulations for their respective sports and must ensure fair play and integrity.

Overall, ISFs act as the governing bodies for their respective sports, ensuring their growth, development and global representation. They undertake a wide range of responsibilities to regulate, promote and advance their sports at the international level.

10.3.3 Influence of Global Sporting Events on Governance

Global sporting events have a significant influence on governance in various ways. Some of the key aspects of how global sporting events have an impact on governance include:

10.3.3.1 Increased scrutiny and accountability

Global sporting events, such as the Olympic Games or FIFA World Cup, attract substantial media attention and public scrutiny,[26] therefore the sports organisations that host these events face increased pressure to uphold governance standards, transparency and accountability. The spotlight on governance practices during major events often leads to enhanced scrutiny and measures to protect fundamental human rights. The controversy surrounding the 2022 Qatar World Cup concerning the country's alleged human rights violations, specifically migrant worker rights, women's rights and the rights of the LGBTQ community, became the most prominent issues, leading to demands for reforms from Western countries.

10.3.3.2 Infrastructure development and governance reforms

Hosting major sporting events (such as the 2010 FIFA World Cup in South Africa) requires significant investment in infrastructure, including stadiums, transportation systems and accommodation facilities.[27] This infrastructure development goes hand in hand with governance reforms, as host countries or cities must comply with specific governance standards and human rights. FIFA has been accused of failing its human rights responsibilities by refusing to compensate migrant workers for abuses while preparing and delivering the 2022 Qatar World Cup.

10.3.3.3 Legacy and sustainability

Mega sporting events, such as the Olympic Games and FIFA World Cup, impact host cities and countries over the long term; the financial impact of hosting these events has been devastating for some. Governance considerations are therefore crucial in legacy planning, which involves establishing governance structures (such as legacy committees) that facilitate the effective management of legacy funds and the repurposing of event infrastructure, stadiums and resources.

10.3.3.4 Policy and regulatory reforms

Hosting global sporting events often necessitates introducing or revising legislation, policies and regulations. Adopting the Safety at Sports and Recreational Events, Act 2 of 2010,[28] directly resulted in South Africa being granted hosting rights for the 2010 FIFA World Cup. Other reforms may encompass human rights such as gender equality, freedom of expression, right to education and the right to non-discrimination based on race, ethnicity, religion and disability. Global sporting events catalyse policy changes as host countries or cities align their governance practices with international standards and expectations. For instance, FIFA has implemented a strong anti-discrimination framework, acting against racism, sexism and other forms of discrimination in football.

10.3.3.5 Broadcasting rights and commercialisation

Global sporting events attract substantial broadcasting rights deals, sponsorship agreements and commercial interests. Managing these revenue streams and the associated contracts require robust governance mechanisms to ensure transparency, fairness and the avoidance of conflicts of interest. The broadcasting rights for the 2023 FIFA Women's World Cup in Australia and New Zealand are valued at between $1m and $10m, compared to the $100m to $200m paid for the men's 2022 FIFA World Cup. FIFA considers this morally and legally unfair.

10.3.3.6 International reputation

Hosting global sporting events can significantly impact a nation's or organisation's international perception and reputation. Effective governance is critical in managing the event's organisation, delivery and legacy to ensure a positive and credible image; it requires transparency, integrity and adherence to ethical principles, which can contribute to building trust and attracting future events, investments and partnerships. The

2022 FIFA World Cup in Qatar was overshadowed by corruption and bribery allegations, which tarnished the reputation of FIFA and Qatar.

In summary, global sporting events profoundly influence governance by driving reforms, enhancing accountability, fostering collaboration, and shaping the policies and practices of sports governing bodies. The requirements and demands of hosting such events necessitate effective governance to ensure successful delivery and leave a lasting positive impact.

10.4 ETHICAL ISSUES AND CHALLENGES IN SPORT GOVERNANCE

Ethical issues and challenges in sport governance encompass a range of complex and multi-faceted concerns that can arise in the management and administration of sports governing bodies. Here are some key ethical issues and challenges:

10.4.1 Corruption and Bribery

The Prevention and Combating of Corrupt Activities Act 12 of 2004 is the primary law governing corruption prevention in South Africa. Corruption can be defined as the abuse of entrusted power for private gain. Sport governing bodies worldwide have faced challenges related to corruption, bribery and financial irregularities, including issues such as secret commissions, embezzlement, kickbacks and the misuse of funds. Effective governance must address these issues through robust financial controls, transparency and accountability mechanisms. Governing bodies should thus have an effective internal audit system, with an audit committee that consists of mostly independent directors with a financial background to ensure compliance with the King IV principles.

10.4.2 Match-Fixing and Betting

Any person who undermines the integrity of any sporting event is guilty of a criminal offence in terms of section 15 of the Prevention and Combating of Corrupt Activities Act. This includes any form of match-fixing or spot-fixing. Illegal betting poses a significant ethical challenge, undermines the integrity and fairness of competitions, erodes public trust and has financial implications. Effective governance must therefore include preventive measures, strict regulations and education programmes to combat match-fixing and protect the integrity of sport.[29] Governing bodies should establish an anti-corruption unit to monitor and investigate match-fixing offences.

10.4.3 Conflict of Interest

Governing bodies and board members have a fiduciary duty to act in good faith and must always act in the best interests of the federation. A conflict of interest occurs when individuals in positions of power or influence have personal or financial interests that may compromise their objectivity or decision-making. This can include situations where administrators, officials or board members have affiliations with commercial entities, sponsors, suppliers or agents that may influence their actions. Robust governance frameworks should address and manage conflicts of interest to ensure fair and impartial decision-making.

10.4.4 Emerging Sports Technologies

Rapid technological advancements, such as wearable devices, performance-enhancing equipment and data analytics, raise ethical questions in sport governance. Issues include using prohibited technologies, data privacy concerns and the potential for unfair advantages. In 2009, World Aquatics, formerly known as the Fédération Internationale de Natation (FINA), banned Speedo's LZR Racer swimsuit after 23 out of the 25 swimming records at the 2008 Beijing Olympics were broken by athletes wearing it. In 2020, World Athletics banned the Nike Vaporfly running shoe after the Kenyan runner Eliud Kipchoge became the first person to run a marathon distance in under two hours. The governing bodies are responsible for navigating these challenges by establishing clear guidelines, monitoring technologies and ensuring a level playing field.

10.4.5 Athlete Exploitation and Abuse

Protecting athletes' rights and well-being is a critical ethical responsibility in sport governance, as physical and emotional abuse, harassment, discrimination and inadequate support systems are possible. Strong governance should prioritise athlete welfare, enforce strict codes of conduct and provide safe reporting mechanisms, such as whistleblowing, to address and prevent athlete exploitation.

10.4.6 Drug Use and Anti-Doping

The South African government is a signatory to the World Anti-Doping Code and formally recognised the role of the World Anti-Doping Agency (WADA) through the Copenhagen Declaration of Anti-Doping in Sport (2003). WADA provided the framework for the Anti-Doping Rules of the South African Institute for Drug-Free Sport (SAIDS), which governs the conditions under which sport is played in South Africa. SAIDS is a public entity established by an Act of Parliament (Act 14 of 1997).[30]

The core focus of SAIDS is to tackle doping in sport and ensure clean and fair competition. Anti-doping governance faces challenges in terms of performance-enhancing substances, testing procedures, sanctions and the evolving landscape of doping practices. SAIDS collaborates with other national anti-doping agencies worldwide to achieve international harmonisation and the improvement of standards and practices in anti-doping. Governing bodies are responsible for complying with the WADA Code and the Anti-Doping Rules of SAIDS through effective governance, rigorous anti-doping measures and the education of athletes.

Addressing these ethical issues and challenges requires a comprehensive approach that includes robust governance frameworks, clear policies, ethical codes of conduct, education and awareness programmes, and mechanisms for reporting and investigating misconduct. These require the commitment and collaboration of stakeholders, including the sport's governing bodies, athletes, officials and regulatory bodies, to uphold the sport's ethical values and integrity.

10.5 CASE STUDY: CRICKET SOUTH AFRICA

Cricket South Africa (CSA) was one of the first national federations to embrace the 'rainbow nation' and transform the game on all levels, with the intention of developing the game of cricket in all communities. The Proteas men's team has failed to win the World Cup, but they have always been very competitive and are loved worldwide. The administration was however excellent with a good governance structure. The historic governance structure included mostly union presidents, however this was a challenge in terms of vested interests as one president may have put their union first rather than cricket as a whole. This is not to say that these individuals did not act in the best interest of the national sport; the initial period of administration was groundbreaking and united many South Africans. In 2003 South Africa hosted a successful World Cup, showcasing our ability to host a world-class sporting event.

All sports governing bodies will face challenges, including governance issues. CSA is no exception and has had its fair share of governance failures:

10.5.1 Bonus Scandal

Until around 2009, Cricket South Africa (CSA) was the poster boy of sports administration in South Africa, however this all changed with a bonus scandal in 2010, when the CEO was rewarded for hosting the Indian Premier League (IPL) in South Africa. At the time, the President of CSA questioned the CEO, and in a public disagreement, the two attacked each other. The President was removed after a vote of no confidence, however this decision was overturned in court due to procedural irregularities. The process was subsequently rectified and the President was removed. At this time, CSA lost most of their sponsors and there was an outcry in the media, with people insisting that the Minister of Sport should intervene and that the board and CEO resign. In reaction to the outcry, the Minister ordered the Nicholson Commission of Enquiry to investigate the affairs of CSA in 2011. This enquiry recommended that the CSA board be reduced in size and comprise a majority of independent, professionally skilled, non-executive directors with an independent board chairperson.

However, it was impossible for CSA to fully implement the Nicholson Commission's recommendations as SASCOC threatened to suspend CSA as it contradicted their constitution, which requires a majority representation of union presidents on a board and that a union president must be the board's chairperson. An independent nominations committee subsequently appointed the independent directors, which was a drastic departure from the past.

10.5.2 Global T20

Post 2012, the new CSA board of 12 members consisted of five independent directors and CSA had stabilised and signed lucrative sponsorship agreements. In September 2017, the CEO and CSA board parted ways after a breakdown in their relationship, however. This was related to a global T20 competition, when CSA announced a new series with eight private team owners in London and presented it to the world. After the resignation of the CEO, it was decided not to continue with the series. This ended a period of relative stability as negative sentiment flared up again, with questions about governance failures re-emerging.

10.5.3 Revoking of Media Accreditation

The CSA board again came under attack from the media, making headlines for all the wrong reasons. These included a legal battle with the South African Cricketers Association (SACA), the suspension of three senior officials for alleged dereliction of duty, debt in the region of R650 million and struggles in turning the Mzansi Super League (MSL) into a lucrative product. This resulted in a significant sponsor withdrawing their sponsorship and another insisted that the CSA board resign. The last straw was when the CSA management revoked the accreditation of journalists that had been critical of the CSA. In 2019 the CEO was suspended and Fundudzi Forensic Services were appointed to conduct an audit of allegations of financial mismanagement. There was an outcry when CSA announced that only a summary of the Fundudzi report would be released, leaving CSA once again to reassure players and stakeholders (including spectators) that the sport was being run fairly and properly.

10.5.4 Social Justice and Nation Building

The Black Lives Matter campaign and allegations of racism against CSA led to the establishment of the Social Justice and Nation Building (SJN) project. This was a sad period in the history of CSA and the SJN hearings laid bare the demons of discrimination. There was a request for the Minister to intervene once again and for the CSA board to resign. The board remained under pressure and eventually resigned to be replaced by an interim board appointed by the Minister of Sports, Arts and Culture.

The interim board proposed a new Memorandum of Incorporation (MOI), which suggested a majority of independent directors and an independent chairperson. This resulted in a standoff between the Members Council (MC) and the interim board, as the Member's Council consisted of the union presidents. The Minister of Sport threatened the Members Council with withdrawing recognition of CSA as the official federation for cricket, however the Council eventually conceded and a historic new MOI was adopted. This occurred despite the fact that the MOI contradicts the SASCOC constitution, leaving CSA as the only federation with a majority of independent directors and an independent chairperson.

10.5.5 Summary

The last decade has seen CSA challenged as a governing body on various levels. Their compliance, or lack thereof, with corporate governance principles has been under scrutiny, and the mere fact that there are more independent directors is only sometimes effective. It does add to the independence and skillset needed to be successful, but it is essential to ensure that the right people – who do not have a toxic agenda – are elected.

The above case study has shown that CSA can survive and recover after a governance crisis. Regrettably, their dirty washing is continuously aired in the public domain, but that is true for all sporting codes. This leads to a negative perception that may result in losing sponsorship and fan support. This highlights the need for a sporting body to have a sound governance structure.

10.6 BEST PRACTICES IN SPORT GOVERNANCE

10.6.1 Lessons Learned

Governing bodies have learnt that sound sports governance requires strong leadership and clear governance structures. Federations should thus implement best practices in sport governance, which encompass a range of principles and strategies to promote effective and transparent management.

Governing bodies must strive for independence and diversity in board and committee compositions, and board members should possess the necessary skills, knowledge and experience to fulfil their roles effectively. An independent director should chair all board committees, and independent directors should also play important oversight roles in these committees, especially the audit and remuneration committees.[31]

Governing bodies should further establish transparent processes for decision-making and financial management, including providing all stakeholders with access to relevant information and mechanisms to hold governing bodies accountable. Actively involving athletes, coaches, officials, fans, broadcasters, sponsors, player unions and the broader community in decision-making processes is key, as is seeking input, feedback and stakeholder collaboration to ensure inclusivity and diversity in governance, and fostering a culture of ethical conduct and integrity.

Governing bodies must also adopt sound financial policies and practices regarding budgeting, financial reporting and internal controls, including the maintenance of financial sustainability through diversified revenue streams, responsible expenditure and long-term planning. Sustainability requires robust risk management processes to identify, assess and mitigate potential risks and ensure compliance with applicable laws, regulations and ethical standards.[32]

Governing bodies should tailor their governance practices to suit their unique circumstances while aligning with the fundamental principles of transparency, responsibility, accountability, fairness and integrity. Governance is not a tick-box exercise, thus governance policies must be treated as living documents and be revisited regularly.

10.6.2 The Use of Technology

Lessons were also learned during the Covid-19 pandemic, for example most constitutions of national federations did not provide virtual meetings, electronic voting or round-robin decision-making processes. Hopefully, these constitutions have now been amended to allow technology to improve governance, as these tools enhance accessibility and participation in decision-making processes by reducing logistical constraints and costs. Online platforms also enable direct engagement and feedback from fans, allowing their voices to be heard in governance matters. Social media, online surveys and interactive platforms also foster dialogue, enable public consultation and allow fans to make decisions.

Governing bodies should use technology to enhance governance compliance, as technology enables the collection, storage and analysis of vast amounts of data related to governance processes and financial management. Advanced data analytics tools can provide valuable insights into governance practices, identify trends and support evidence-based decision-making. Technology can also reduce the risk of financial irregularities, for example, digital platforms and tools can facilitate transparent financial management and reporting. Online financial systems and electronic payment methods can further enhance revenue generation and expenditure tracking transparency, as well as assist in monitoring compliance with governance standards, regulations and ethical codes; automate compliance checks; track governance policy adherence; and provide real-time alerts on potential risks or breaches.

Technology can also provide an anonymous platform for whistleblowers, with whistleblowing becoming the most effective governance tool of late.[33;34] Financial irregularities, corruption, doping offences and match-fixing have all been exposed by whistleblowers recently.

While technology offers numerous benefits, addressing potential challenges such as data privacy,[35] cybersecurity and the digital divide, is essential to ensure equitable access and the responsible use of technology in sport governance. Collaborative efforts among sport's governing bodies, technology providers and regulatory bodies can harness the power of technology to enhance governance practices and uphold the integrity and values of sport.

10.7 CONCLUSION

Good governance requires board members and governing bodies to act with integrity; promote ethical behaviour and a culture of honesty, trust and openness; and fulfil their fiduciary duties diligently and responsibly. Board members and governing bodies should act independently of any conflicting interests, must promote transparency and should avoid situations that may compromise their independence. Governing bodies should further create a code of conduct and ensure compliance.

Fairness should be promoted in all aspects of governance, with all stakeholders being treated fairly, provided equal opportunities, and not being subjected to discrimination. Fair remuneration practices should also be implemented, along with transparent reporting and communication. Governing bodies should disclose all relevant information promptly and accurately, ensuring that stakeholders and members have access to the information necessary to make informed decisions.

Those responsible for governance should be accountable for their actions and decisions, provide all stakeholders with a clear understanding of how their governing body is managed and perform regular assessments of their effectiveness. Board members should also take responsibility for their decisions and the performance of their governing body, including considering the interests of all stakeholders and acting in a manner that balances the needs of these stakeholders.

If governing bodies in sport are perceived to be transparent, accountable and responsible, it will undoubtedly result in improved broadcasting revenues, sponsorships, fan support and performances by national teams. In addition, if governing bodies learn from their mistakes and adhere to best practices in sport governance, it will allow players to focus on their performances on the field, rather than concern themselves with boardroom battles.[36]

SELF-ASSESSMENT

1. Describe the fundamental principles and concepts of governance in sport.
2. Describe the various sport governance structures, including national and international sport governing bodies.
3. Identify and analyse governance challenges faced by sport governing bodies.
4. Critically evaluate best governance practices in the sport industry.

SPORT AND THE LAW

Professor Steve Cornelius

LEARNING OUTCOMES

At the end of this chapter, you should be able to:

1. Name the most important pieces of legislation that apply to sport and briefly explain what each one provides.
2. Understand the concept of integrity in sport and explain how match-fixing and unlawful gambling undermines integrity.
3. Explain when a sport federation or club will have jurisdiction to take disciplinary action against someone.
4. Explain how the law regulates and protects the various sources from which a sport federation can derive an income.
5. Explain how a sport federation can incur civil liability for loss, damage or injury which occurs in the context of sport.

11.1 INTRODUCTION

Like any other human conduct, sport is subject to the law. Participation in any form of an organised sport occurs in complex contractual relationships between the National Sport Federation (NSF), sport league, sport club, organisers and players.[i] These contractual relationships are expressed, among others, in the rules or laws of the sport. Clubs and players are, therefore, subject to these rules or laws because they submit to the authority of the NSFs and agree to play under those rules or laws. This is why a professional footballer in South Africa may be subject to the rules of the Professional Soccer League, but the league does not concern itself with friends kicking around a football in their backyard.[ii]

---

i   Rowles v Jockey Club of South Africa 1954 1 SA 363 (A) 364D; Jockey Club of South Africa v Transvaal Racing Club 1959 1 SA 441 (A) 446F, 450A; Turner v Jockey Club of South Africa 1974 3 SA 633 (A); Jockey Club of South Africa v Forbes 1993 1 SA 649 (A) 645B, 654D; Natal Rugby Union v Gould 1999 1 SA 432 (SCA) 440F; Johannesburg Country Club v Stott 2004 5 SA 511 (SCA).

ii   *Cronje v United Cricket Board of South Africa* 2001 (4) SA 1361 (T).

In *Cronje v United Cricket Board of South Africa*,[iii] the Supreme Court of Appeal explained that, for a sports federation to have jurisdiction over a person or club, the *"contractual basis must exist when the decision is made"*.[iv] This is known as the privity of contract. The doctrine of privity of contract is arguably one of the most fundamental principles of the law of contract.[v] Hutchinson and Pretorius[1] referred to the privity of contract as one of the cornerstones of the law of contract. Although parties enjoy substantial autonomy to regulate their relationship most appropriately, the doctrine of privity of contract implies that the terms of their agreement would only have an effect among themselves and not typically affect anyone else who is not a party to that contract.[vi] The parties cannot bind third parties to comply with the terms of their agreement unless they agree otherwise.

However, the relationships in sport are not solely based on contracts. There are also applicable legislation and common law rules that apply where someone participates in sport.

11.2 REGULATORY MATTERS

11.2.1 National Sport and Recreation Act

The National Sport and Recreation Act (NSRA)[vii] is the primary legislation dealing with sport in South Africa. The NSRA was adopted to promote and develop sport and recreation and co-ordination of the relationships between the government, the various sport and recreation federations and other agencies involved in sport. The NSRA established Sport and Recreation South Africa (SRSA) as the government department responsible for sport and recreation at the national government level.[viii]

In section 2(1) of the NSRA, the national minister responsible for sport and recreation must recognise in writing a sports confederation which will be the national co-ordinating macro body for promoting and developing high-performance sport in South Africa. The Minister thus recognised the South African Sports Confederation and Olympic Committee (SASCOC).[ix] All National Sport Federations (NSFs) must be recognised by and affiliated with SASCOC.[x]

To be recognised by SASCOC, an NSF must be properly constituted and operate on democratic principles; have a formal written constitution and an acceptable democratically elected committee that works in a transparent, accountable and responsible manner; demonstrate management and financial accountability and stability; have affiliates or members within at least five provinces functioning within the principles of good governance; provide a development programme and an equity plan; and be recognised by the relevant international controlling body for the sport concerned.[xi] Office bearers of the NSF must be elected

---

iii   2001 4 SA 1361 (T).
iv   See also *Johannesburg Country Club v Stott* 2004 5 SA 511 (SCA).
v   *Cullinan v Noordkaaplandse Aartappelkernmoerkwekers Koöperasie Bpk* 1972 1 SA 761 (A) 770D-H.
vi   *RMB Private Bank v Kaydeez Therapies CC* 2013 6 SA 308 (GSJ); *First National Bank v Clear Creek Trading 12 (Pty) Ltd* 2014 1 SA 23 (GNP).
vii Act 119 of 1998.
viii Section 1.
ix   *White Paper* 2011:6.
x   Recognition of Sport and Recreation Bodies Regulations, 2011.
xi   Regulation 3(1).

at least every four years by the members or in terms of its constitution.[xii] The NSF must also comply with existing anti-doping legislation.[xiii] Participation must be open to all community sections and not be restricted for reasons of cost, gender, disability or any other reason that may constitute any form of direct or indirect discrimination.[xiv]

In section 13 of the NSRA, every sport federation must provide for its dispute resolution procedure in its constitution.[xv] If the dispute cannot be resolved in terms of the internal procedure, the matter may be submitted to SASCOC, which may institute an enquiry into the dispute and decide on the resolution of that dispute.[xvi] If SASCOC cannot resolve the dispute, the Minister may intervene by referring the matter for mediation or issuing a directive.[xvii]

Section 13A of the NSRA provides that the Minister must provide guidelines or policies to promote equity, representativity and redress in sport and recreation. SRSA thus established a Transformation Charter, which SASCOC and National Sports Federations adopted. An Eminent Persons Group was appointed to audit compliance with the Transformation Charter and monitor the transformation of sport in South Africa.

11.2.2 South African Institute for Drug-free Sport Act

The South African Institute for Drug-free Sport Act[xviii] (SAIDS Act) was promulgated to promote participation in sport free from the use of prohibited substances or methods intended to artificially enhance performance, as well as to prohibit doping practices which are contrary to the principles of fair play and medical ethics, in the interest of the health and well-being of athletes.

The SAIDS Act established[xix] the South African Institute for Drug-free Sport (SAIDS), consisting of a chairperson and nine members appointed by the Minister based on their unique knowledge of doping in sport.[xx] SAIDS is independent but may cooperate with SRSA and SASCOC to achieve its objectives.[xxi]

SAIDS must promote participation in sport, free from the use of prohibited substances or methods intended to artificially enhance performance; encourage the development of programmes for the education of the community in general, and the sporting community in particular, in respect of the dangers of doping in sport; provide leadership in the development of a national strategy concerning doping in sport; promote and ensure the adoption of a centralised doping control programme, which may subject any athlete to testing, with or without advance notice, both in and out of competition; ensure that National Sports Federations and other sports organisations adopt and implement anti-doping policies and rules which conform with the Code and with the requirements set out in the anti-doping policy and rules of the Institute; and promote the establishment and maintenance of an accredited anti-doping laboratory in South Africa.[xxii]

xii	Regulation 3(4).
xiii	Regulation 3(2).
xiv	Regulation 3(3).
xv	Section 13(1).
xvi	Section 13(2).
xvii	Section 13(3).
xviii	Act 14 of 1997.
xix	Section 2.
xx	Section 3.
xxi	Section 10(2).
xxii	Section 10(3).

11.2.3 Safety at Sports and Recreation Events Act

The Safety at Sports and Recreation Events Act[xxiii] (SASREA) provides minimum safety and security standards that sports events must enforce. An NSF, event organiser, or stadium or venue owner must implement measures to ensure the physical safety and security of persons and their property at an event.[xxiv]

A stadium or venue owner must apply annually to the relevant local authority for a safety certificate for that stadium or venue. The safety certificate must be accompanied by a grading certificate in which the local authority indicates the safe spectator capacity of the stadium or venue, as well as the level of risk of any event that may be hosted at the stadium or venue.[xxv] Where a new stadium or venue will be constructed, the owner must apply for a certificate in respect of the safety of the design of the new stadium or venue at least three months before construction commences.[xxvi] The same applies where alterations or extensions are made to an existing stadium or venue.[xxvii]

Event organisers must submit an annual schedule of events at least six months before any calendar year or the start of a new season to the National Commissioner of the South African Police Service.[xxviii] The National Commissioner must then categorise each event as low-, medium- or high-risk, based, among other considerations, on the popularity or reputation of any team or person participating in that event; the expected attendance at that event and, where available, a historical record of attendance at similar events; the location where the event is to be held; and the level of intensity of the rivalry between competing sports teams or athletes participating in that event and any tensions which may exist between the supporters of those sports teams or athletes.[xxix] Other factors, such as the sale and consumption of alcohol at the event and the age profile of expected attendees, are also considered.[xxx]

There must be an event safety and security planning committee that is chaired by a police officer with the rank of at least captain, which is designated by the National Commissioner and consists of representatives of the local authority disaster management department or centre; the controlling body in respect of high-risk events only; the stadium or venue owner; the event organiser; an emergency service provider; a health and medical service provider acting in terms of the National Health Act[xxxi]; a security service of the State; a provincial health department; a security service provider; and any other person whom the designated police officer deems necessary.[xxxii] There must also be a Venue Operations Centre (VOC) where the safety and security operation at the stadium, venue or along a route is coordinated.[xxxiii]

---

xxiii	Act 2 of 2010.
xxiv	Section 4(1).
xxv	SASREA section 8.
xxvi	SASREA section 9.
xxvii	SASREA section 10.
xxviii	Section 6(1).
xxix	Section 6(7).
xxx	Ibid.
xxxi	Act 61 of 2003.
xxxii	SASREA section 15.
xxxiii	SASREA section 17.

11.2.4 South African Boxing Act

The South African Boxing Act[xxxiv] was promulgated to provide a structure for professional boxing in South Africa and create synergy between professional and amateur boxing. This Act established an independent[xxxv] commission, known as Boxing SA,[xxxvi] to oversee the sport of boxing in South Africa. All boxers, event officials, trainers, managers and promoters must be registered with Boxing SA.[xxxvii]

11.2.5 Other Legislation

Apart from the legislation mentioned above, other legislative provisions may also apply to NSFs and sport events.

Paragraph 10 of the Schedule to the Promotion of Equality and Prevention of Unfair Discrimination Act[xxxviii] states that sports clubs and associations may not unfairly refuse to consider a person's application for association or club membership on any prohibited grounds. Furthermore, a club or association may not unfairly deny a member access to, or limit a member's access to, any benefit provided by the association or club. Lastly, failure to promote diversity in selecting representative teams also constitutes an unfair practice.

Regulation 317 of the National Road Traffic Regulations[xxxix] provides that racing or sports events may only occur on a public road if the relevant Member of the Executive Council for the province concerned has obtained prior written consent. Where the event takes place wholly within the jurisdiction of a local authority, the prior written consent of that authority must be obtained.

11.3 INTEGRITY IN SPORT

11.3.1 Gambling and Match-Fixing

Sports betting has become commonplace in South Africa, however only licensed gambling is legal. The Constitution[xl] contemplates two forms of lawful gambling:[xli] Firstly, casinos, racing, gambling and wagering are regulated concurrently at the national and provincial levels. Secondly, lotteries and sport pools are expressly excluded from regulation at the provincial level.

---

xxxiv Act 11 of 2001.
xxxv SABA section 5.
xxxvi SABA section 4.
xxxvii SABA section 19.
xxxviii Act 4 of 2000.
xxxix Government Notice R.225 of 17 March 2000.
xl Constitution of the Republic of South Africa, 1996
xli S 104(1)(b)(i) read with schedule 4 part A.

At the national level, the National Gambling Act[xlii] provides that the National Gambling Board[xliii] is the regulatory body to monitor and control gambling in terms of that Act. Each of the nine provinces also has a provincial gambling board that acts in terms of the relevant provincial legislation.[xliv]

Lotteries and sport pools are regulated nationally in the Lotteries Act[xlv] by the National Lotteries Board. A sport pool is any scheme under which a person is invited or undertakes to forecast the result of any series or combination of sporting events in competition with other participants, and a prize is to be awarded to the competitor who predicts the result correctly or whose forecast is more correct than the forecasts of other competitors, or several prizes are to be awarded on that basis. The forecast of a result includes the forecast of the person, animal, thing or team that will be victorious or otherwise, and any forecast relating to scoring in a match or the person responsible for the score.[xlvi]

Only the licensee of the National Lottery may be awarded an additional licence to conduct a national sports pool.[xlvii] No other sports pool could be licensed under the Lotteries Act[xlviii] or any other Act. However, this does not allow the licensee to conduct any sports pool as it wishes. For example, in the *National Soccer League trading as Premier Soccer League v Gidani (Pty) Ltd*,[xlix] the court ruled that the licensee must also have the consent of the sport federation or league and clubs concerned.

The current regulation of sports betting is mainly made through provincial legislation, although the National Gambling Act[l] sets out specific national standards that must be complied with.[li] These uniform standards aim to safeguard people participating in gambling and their communities against the adverse effect of gambling. To achieve this aim, gambling activities are effectively regulated, licensed, controlled and policed; members of the public who participate in any licensed gambling activity are protected; society and the economy are protected against over-stimulation of the latent demand for gambling; and the licensing of gambling activities is transparent, fair and equitable.

Unfortunately, gambling also brings the risk that gamblers or players may attempt to manipulate the outcomes of events. The Prevention and Combatting of Corrupt Activities Act[lii] (PreCCA) expressly provides

---

xlii	Act 7 of 2004.
xliii	The National Gambling Board was established by section 2 of the National Gambling Act 33 of 1996. This Act was repealed by the National Gambling Act 7 of 2004. Section 64 of the 2004 Act provides that the National Gambling Board is retained under the 2004 act.
xliv	Eastern Cape Gambling and Betting Act 5 of 1997; Free State Gambling and Racing Act 6 of 1996 (soon to be replaced by the Free State Gambling and Liquor Act 6 of 2010); Gauteng Gambling Act 4 of 1995; KwaZulu-Natal Gambling Act 10 of 1996 (possibly soon to be replaced by the KwaZulu-Natal Gaming and Betting Bill, 2010); Mpumalanga Gaming Act 5 of 1995; Northern Cape Gambling and Racing Act 5 of 1996; Northern Province Casino and Gaming Act 4 of 1996; North West Gambling Act 2 of 2001 and the Western Cape Casino and Racing Law 4 of 1996.
xlv	Act 57 of 1997.
xlvi	However, this definition does not include any scheme or competition in respect of horse racing which is authorised by the board, or which is conducted in the same format and manner and under the same circumstances as a scheme or competition in respect of horse racing that existed prior to 18 June 1997. A 'sporting event' in turn is defined to mean any football, rugby, cricket, golf or tennis match, any boxing, wrestling, shooting or swimming contest, any foot, cycle, motor, boat or horse race and any other lawful sporting contest, competition, tournament or game usually attended by the public (Lotteries Act section 1).
xlvii	s 55(1) of the Lotteries Act 57 of 1997.
xlviii	57 of 1997.
xlix	[2014] 2 All SA 461 (GJ).
l	Act 7 of 2004.
li	Section 44 of the National Gambling Act 7 of 2004.
lii	12 of 2004.

for the offence of corrupt activities relating to sporting events.[liii] Section 1 of PreCCA defines a "sporting event" as any event or contest in any sport, between individuals or teams, or in which an animal competes, which is usually attended by the public and is governed by rules that include the constitution, rules or code of conduct of any sporting body which stages any sporting event or of any regulatory body under whose constitution, rules or code of conduct the sporting event is conducted. This definition is wide enough to include all organised sports, including horse racing.

In terms of s 15 of PreCCA, the offence of corrupt activities relating to sporting events can be committed in various ways. In the first instance, it is committed where a person is induced to perform any act that threatens or undermines the integrity of any sporting event, including, in any way, influencing the run of play or the outcome of a sporting event.[liv] This provision is aimed at match-fixing. It acknowledges that match-fixing occurs not only when the result is rigged. Punters often bet on the occurrence of events which may seem innocuous in the greater scheme of a match, such as when the first free kick will be awarded or how many yellow cards will be awarded in a particular match, etc.

The offence in section 15 is further committed if a person carries into effect any scheme that threatens or undermines the integrity of any sporting event, including, in any way, influencing the run of play or the outcome of a sporting event.[lv] At first glance, this provision also deals with match-fixing in the sense discussed above. However, on closer analysis, the scope of this provision is vast and could include conduct that one would not ordinarily have counted under the general heading of "match-fixing".

Thirdly, the offence of corruption in sporting events is also committed if a person is induced to frustrate the reporting of a corrupt act contemplated in section 15 to the managing director, chief executive officer or any other person holding a similar post in the sporting body or regulatory authority concerned, or at their nearest police station.

Section 16 of PreCCA provides for offences concerning corrupt activities relating to gambling or games of chance. Any person who induces someone or who is induced to engage in any conduct which constitutes a threat to, or undermines the integrity of, any gambling game or a game of chance, including in any way influencing the outcome of a gambling game, commits an offence in terms of section 16 (a) and (b). Section 16 (c) provides that a person who carries into effect any scheme which constitutes a threat to, or undermines the integrity of, any gambling game or a game of chance, including in any way influencing the outcome of a gambling game, commits an offence.

In terms of section 34 (1), any person who holds a position of authority and who knows or ought reasonably to have known or suspected that any other person has committed an offence under PreCCA, must report such knowledge or suspicion or cause such knowledge or suspicion to be reported to any police official. Any person who fails to comply with this duty is guilty of an offence.

For section 34 (1), a person holds a position of authority if they are the manager, secretary or director of a company or a member of a close corporation, a chief executive officer or an equivalent officer of

---

liii   s 15.
liv   s 15 (i) (aa) PreCCA.
lv   s 15 (c) PreCCA.

any organisation, or the person responsible for the overall management and control of the business of an employer. This also includes any person appointed in an acting or temporary capacity.

Section 35 of PreCCA provides for extraterritorial jurisdiction. Even if the act alleged to constitute an offence under PreCCA occurred outside South Africa, a South African court shall, regardless of whether or not the act constitutes an offence at the place of its commission, have jurisdiction in respect of that offence if the person to be charged is a South African citizen or resident, was arrested in South Africa, or is a company or other body of persons, incorporated or unincorporated, in South Africa.

A South African court will also have jurisdiction over an offence committed outside South Africa if the act affects or is intended to affect a public body, business or any other person in South Africa, and the wrongdoer is found in South Africa and is not extradited.

In terms of section 26 of PreCCA, any person convicted of an offence under PreCCA is liable in the case of a sentence imposed by a High Court to whatever fine the court deems appropriate, or to imprisonment up to a period of imprisonment for life. In the case of a sentence to be imposed by a regional court, such person is liable to a fine not exceeding R720,000 or to imprisonment for a period not exceeding 18 years.[lvi] Finally, in the case of a sentence to be imposed by a magistrate's court, such person is liable to a fine not exceeding R200,000 or to imprisonment for a period not exceeding five years.[lvii] In addition to any fine a court may impose in terms of section 26, the court may also impose a further fine equal to five times the value of the gratification involved in the offence.

11.3.2 Disciplinary Hearings

Since participation in sport is primarily based on contract, the jurisdiction of NSFs or clubs to take disciplinary action against athletes, officials or others must also be determined from that contractual relationship. In the English case of *Modahl v British Athletic Federation Ltd*,[lviii] three grounds for the establishment of regulatory and disciplinary authority were explained:

11.3.2.1 *Club or other affiliation*

Membership of a club, association or league can provide the basis for a federation's regulatory and disciplinary authority if the rules or constitution of the club, association or league provides that its members are subject to the rules and discipline of a particular international federation.[lix]

11.3.2.2 *Participation*

Where an athlete or club participates in an event hosted by the federation, the athlete or club can be taken to have submitted to the rules and discipline of the federation through its participation.

---

lvi In terms of s 1 (1) (a) of the Adjustment of Fines Act 101 of 1991, read with GN 217 of 27 March 2014 and s 92 (1) (b) of the Magistrates' Courts Act 32 of 1944.
lvii Ibid.
lviii [2002] 1 WLR 1192.
lix See also *Malan v Ardconnel Investments (Pty) Ltd* 1988 2 SA 12 (A).

11.3.2.3 Submission

Where an athlete or club faces a federation's regulatory or disciplinary authority, the athlete or club can submit to such authority. The athlete or club will then be bound as if the athlete or club had been a federation member all along. Care should, however, be taken in this regard. As the court has shown in *Herbex (Pty) Ltd v Advertising Standards Authority*,[lx] there may need to be more than mere participation in disciplinary proceedings to establish submission to a federation's regulatory and disciplinary authority.

The case of *Cronje v United Cricket Board of South Africa*[lxi] added another option which can be applied in appropriate circumstances.

11.3.2.4 Party autonomy

The doctrine of privity of contract and party autonomy also means that a party, in general, is free to decide with whom it contracts. A party can resolve that it and its members will not contract with a particular athlete or club in the future, effectively imposing a ban on such athlete or club.[lxii]

And lastly, in the US case of *NCAA v Tarkanian*,[lxiii] the court provided a fifth option in which an NSF can impose its authority and disciplinary authority on an athlete or club.

11.3.2.5 Indirect enforcement

An NSF can secure indirect enforcement of its rules and disciplinary measures by leaving it up to its member, to which the athlete or club is affiliated, to act. Suppose such a member fails to act. In that case, the federation can then impose its regulatory and disciplinary authority on its member and sanction it for failing to address the compliance and discipline of an athlete or club affiliated with that member.

When taking disciplinary action, a sports federation or club must act under its own constitution, rules, regulations and disciplinary code.[lxiv] Any disciplinary committee or tribunal established by an NSF or club must act strictly under the constitution, rules, regulations and disciplinary code.[lxv] If this is not done, the disciplinary proceedings are unlawful and any decision a disciplinary tribunal takes in such circumstances is invalid.[lxvi]

A disciplinary tribunal must also observe the rules of natural justice when it performs its disciplinary hearings. This means that the adjudicator must be disinterested and unbiased. The disciplinary tribunal must act under its rules and constitution, discharge its duties honestly and impartially, give the person charged a proper hearing and the opportunity to present evidence and to contradict or correct adverse statements or allegations made against such person, listen fairly to both sides and observe the principles

---

lx   2016 5 SA 557 (GJ). See also *Medical Nutritional Institute (Pty) Limited v Advertisings Standard Authority* (15/30142) [2015] ZAGPJHC 317 (18 Sept 2015).
lxi   2001 4 SA 1361 (T).
lxii   See also *Advertising Standards Authority v Herbex (Pty) Ltd* 2017 6 SA 354 (SCA).
lxiii 488 US 179 196.
lxiv   *Jockey Club of South Africa v Forbes* 1993 1 SA 649 A 654G.
lxv   *Constantinides v Jockey Club of South Africa* 1954 3 SA 35 C 44E.
lxvi   *Jockey Club of South Africa v Forbes* 1993 1 SA 649 A 667C

of fair play and natural justice, make fair and honest findings on the facts presented to it, and conduct an active investigation into the truth of allegations made against the person charged.[lxvii]

The right to procedural fairness is also protected in section 33 of the Constitution,[lxviii] which provides that all administrative action must be lawful, reasonable and procedurally fair. Everyone whose rights have been adversely affected by administrative action has the right to be given written reasons for such actions.

11.4 COMMERCIAL ASPECTS OF SPORT

Sports federations primarily have six sources of income from which sports can be financed and from which athletes can derive income: government subsidies, gate fees, commercial sponsorships, image rights of athletes, merchandising and media rights. If sports bodies cannot protect these resources, professional sport and many amateur sports will not be possible. Government subsidies generally contribute very little to the total revenue of sports federations,[2] therefore other sources must be sought. The general principles of property law protect gate fees according to which the right of admission can be reserved,[lxix] merchandise is protected in terms of trademark law,[lxx] the common law prohibits passing off[3] and assimilation[lxxi] and statutory measures aimed at counterfeit goods.[lxxii] In contrast, commercial sponsorships can be protected against illicit advertising by implementing statutory measures against ambush marketing.[lxxiii]

11.4.1 Ticketing

National sport federations make use of tickets to control access to sport events. This is firstly done to secure some income from the event and defray the costs of hosting that event. Secondly, it is also done to manage the number of spectators who can safely attend the event.[4] Ticket prices are often set below the actual market value for a particular event. This is done to attract more spectators and to keep tickets affordable for less affluent fans.[5] However, sometimes, when the demand for a particular event, such as a cup final, is very high, tickets that have already been bought get resold, often at a price that is much higher than the original selling price. This is known as ticket scalping or ticket touting.[6] With the development of new technology, some ticket touts also set up complex bots to buy up large numbers of tickets for events likely to attract large numbers of spectators. These tickets are then resold at higher prices to eager fans who need help to obtain a ticket.[7]

Section 5(2) of the SASREA prohibits ticket touting. No person may, without the prior written consent of the event organiser or venue owner, for a commercial purpose, obtain an event ticket to resell or use such ticket or any right about such ticket, whether it is done for a profit or not.[lxxiv] It is also impermissible to directly or indirectly sell, dispose of or promote event tickets, or any right to such tickets, or to use a ticket for advertising, sales or promotional purposes, or as part of a hospitality or travel package, or make it available

---

lxvii   *Turner v Jockey Club of South Africa* 1974 3 SA 633 A 646F, 652H; *Jockey Club of South Africa v Forbes* 1993 1 SA 649 A 654G.
lxviii   Constitution of the Republic of South Africa, 1996
lxix   *Kingsway Caravan Park (Pty) Ltd v Rudman* [1999] JOL 4884 (SE).
lxx   Trade Marks Act 194 of 1993
lxxi   *Idem* 2012:122 ff.
lxxii   Counterfeit Goods Act (Act No. 37 of 1997).
lxxiii   a 15A Merchandise Marks Act (Act No.17 of 1941).
lxxiv   SASREA section 5(2)(a).

or advertise it for any such purpose, unless the prior written consent of the event organiser or venue owner has been obtained.[lxxv] In addition, it is unlawful to use a ticket obtained in contravention of section 5 of the SASREA.[lxxvi]

11.4.2 Branding and Merchandising

Sport clubs, leagues and federations operate within a highly competitive environment in which success and sustainability ultimately depend on their ability to generate an income from their activities. With the necessary income, sport clubs can secure the services of professional athletes, managers, coaches, trainers and other staff. Similarly, with income, leagues and federations can organise and host events, competitions and tournaments. Sport, like any other industry, relies heavily on consumers to generate that income.

National sports federations can also leverage the need of sport consumers to socialise with the NSF and each other by providing the means to associate more directly with a particular club or team. This is done through merchandising. Marketers have long since realised that one can take two identical shirts and sell one for a substantially inflated price if it is adorned with the logo or other identifying marks of a particular sport star or sport team.

Any successful merchandising programme is invariably based on two essential elements. Firstly, a corporate identity is required,[8] and secondly, merchandising requires the existence of intellectual property and related rights which can be exploited, protected and enforced.[9]

Identity includes the attributes that differentiate one individual or enterprise from another.[10] Corporate identity is defined by corporate behaviour, culture, communication and design. In the case of an NSF, it firstly entails the registered and common law trademarks of that NSF,[lxxvii] but it entails much more. Identity also involves the specific product the NSF offers and its packaging. In the case of an NSF, the "product" is the sport event. The NSF's identity is reflected in the tournaments and matches presented by that NSF and sets it apart from other NSFs.

Licensing is the contractual relationship that grants permission for one party, the licensee, to use the intellectual property that belongs to another party (the licensor).[11] Licensing and merchandising rights concerning sports events are in demand, commanding high returns for the rights owners (licensors) and concessionaires (licensees). Licensing allows producers of various products to place the trademarks, logos or other identifying features of sport clubs on their products or to manufacture replica sport gear.[12]

11.4.3 Ambush Marketing

Ambush marketing in sport is defined as marketing that enables a business enterprise to insinuate a relationship between specific goods or services and a sport event without the marketer making any financial contribution to the sport event, whether by sponsorship or any other method.[13] The aim here is to use the goodwill of the sport event to secure exposure for the goods or services of the advertiser.[14] According to

---

lxxv   SASREA section 5(2)(b) - (c).
lxxvi   SASREA section 5(2)(d).
lxxvii   Trade Marks Act 194 of 1993.

Epstein,[15] ambush marketing consists of any marketing activity relating to a sport event involving a party without them being an official sponsor. This occurs when an enterprise, with no direct involvement with, or interest in, a sports event, presents its trademarks, trade names, goods or services in such a way that it creates the impression that a relationship exists between the sport event and that enterprise when in reality there is no such connection.

The interest that a sport event generates with the public bestows an inherent goodwill or marketing value on that event. A sponsor effectively "purchases" the NSF's permission to use that goodwill or marketing value to its advantage. Ambush marketing means that a third party, often a direct competitor of the sponsor, unlawfully tries to gain an advantage from the marketing value of the sport event without the permission of the NSF, diverting the focus from the sponsor and diminishing the impact of the sponsor's advertising.

A business enterprise resorts to ambush marketing with one aim: to associate the enterprise's goodwill so closely with the goodwill or marketing value of the sport event that the goodwill of the event enhances the enterprise's goodwill.[16] This is also an important characteristic distinguishing ambush marketing from parallel marketing.

Ambush marketing can also create uncertainty among consumers so that they identify the goods or services in the advertisement with the specific sport event. The goal is to create the impression that the enterprise is associated with the sport event. The objective is two-fold: to advance the enterprise's goods or services and simultaneously to undermine the impact of the advertisements of the official sponsors.[17]

Section 15A of the Merchandise Marks Act[lxxviii] deals with ambush marketing in South Africa; it applies to any exhibition, show or competition of a sporting nature which is held in public that is likely to attract the attention of the public or to be newsworthy and is financed by commercial sponsorship. This also includes any broadcast of such an event. In terms of section 15A, the National Minister of Trade and Industry in South Africa may, by notice in the official *Government Gazette*, designate an event as a protected event if the staging of the event is in the public interest and the Minister is satisfied that the organisers of the event have created sufficient opportunities for small businesses. In the notice, the Minister must indicate the exact period before, during and up to one month after the event, during which it will be a protected event.

While an event is protected under section 15A, no person may use a mark or trademark concerning the event in a manner calculated to achieve publicity for that mark or trademark or to derive benefit from the event, unless the prior authority of the event organiser has been obtained. Using a mark or trademark includes any visual or audible representation of the mark or trademark intended to be brought directly or indirectly into association with an event or to allude to the event.

Any person who contravenes the provisions of section 15A commits a criminal offence and may be liable to a fine or up to three years imprisonment for a first offence, and a fine or up to five years imprisonment for a subsequent offence. In addition, if a person is convicted of an offence in this regard, the court may order the confiscation of all the goods in respect of which the offence has been committed.

Apart from the express criminal provisions which the legislation, as mentioned earlier, introduced in the fight against ambush marketing, it should also have an indirect impact on the remedies that may be

---
lxxviii Act 17 of 1941.

available to sports federations, event organisers or sponsors who may be affected by ambush marketing. The legislation should clear one of the main obstacles that has in the past prevented civil claims in delict against ambush marketers.

11.4.4 Media Rights

By far the greatest single source of income for NSFs is the fees that sport federations impose on media networks for sport broadcasts.[lxxix] It used to be reasonably easy to control the broadcasts of sport events, as until only recently, it was very expensive to broadcast sport – live or otherwise. Such broadcasts were only possible using expensive, bulky equipment that was transported to sports meetings in large trucks. If a television network or radio station had obtained the so-called broadcasting rights for a specific sport event, the only infringement that could have occurred was if another network or station had also tried to broadcast the event. On the whole, television networks and radio stations honoured the exclusivity of broadcasting rights and cases where competitors tried to infringe on the rights of others were few.[lxxx]

The technology of the 21st century has, however, greatly changed things. This has given rise to new media, which has substantially changed the sport broadcasting landscape over the past two decades.

New media is dispersed and pervasive. The audience has become fragmented and differentiated, and there is a proliferation of media offerings that can be accessed in various ways. Sophisticated camera equipment and remote-controlled drones have become reasonably compact and inexpensive, and anyone with a mobile phone can nowadays virtually immediately distribute images from various angles or commentary of a game over the internet. The internet also provides a node that removes the need for expensive transmission stations and masts. In addition, equipment capable of intercepting television signals is also generally available, with the result that it is relatively easy to distribute images on the internet without the knowledge of the broadcaster. Hence, the protection of intellectual property has become much more complex.[lxxxi] NSFs and networks that have obtained the rights to broadcast sport events must therefore guard against efforts that threaten to prejudice the exclusivity of their rights.[lxxxii]

Media rights in sport can be derived from recognising and protecting goodwill, reputation and identity. The next logical question would be to whom the rights belong. The answer is obvious – the sport body whose goodwill, reputation and identity are at stake – but in most sport there is not necessarily a single interested party. In a Premier League football match, for instance, the goodwill, reputation and identity of the home and visiting teams are involved, but it also involves the goodwill, reputation and identity of the Football Association, which organises the competition.

It is important to note that media rights in sport are not unlimited. When unauthorised sports broadcasts occur, the goodwill, reputation, right to identity and right to freedom of association of the sport federation is often weighed against the broadcaster's right to freedom of expression. Any unauthorised sport broadcast must be wrongful before a sport federation can succeed with a civil action against a broadcaster. Consequently, some grounds of justification could result in the unauthorised sport broadcast not being

---

lxxix Act 17 of 1941. *Ibid*.
lxxx   For a few examples see eg *Rudolph Mayer Pictures Inc v Pathe News Inc* 255 NYS 1018; *National Exhibition Co v Teleflash Inc* 24 F Supp 488; *Twentieth Century Sporting Club v Transradio Press Service* 300 NYS 159.
lxxxi WIPO 2014.
lxxxii Lister 2009:31 *et seq*.

wrongful. These grounds include, among others, consent,[18] truth and public interest (such as news reports)[lxxxiii], fair comments[lxxxiv] and parody.[lxxxv]

11.4.5 Image Rights

A common law approach is followed to protect an individual where the attribute of that person is used without consent for commercial purposes in South Africa. In *Grütter v Lombard*,[lxxxvi] the Supreme Court of Appeal held that privacy is merely one of a variety of interests that enjoy recognition in the concept of personality rights in the context of a delictual claim. The interest that a person has to protect his or her image and identity against exploitation is also part of those personality rights.

In this context, the right to identity can be violated in one of two ways. Firstly, a person's right to identity is violated if the attributes of that person are used without permission in a way that cannot be reconciled with the actual image of that person. Apart from the unauthorised use of a person's image, this kind of infringement also entails some misrepresentation concerning the individual, such as that the individual approves of or endorses a particular product or service, or that a player has joined a club, when this is not the case. The unlawfulness in this kind of case is found in the misrepresentation concerning the individual and, consequently, in violation of the right to human dignity.

Secondly, the right to identity is violated if the attributes of a person are used without authorisation by another person for commercial gain. Apart from the unauthorised use of the individual's image, such use also primarily entails a commercial motive exclusively to promote a service or product, or to solicit clients or customers. The mere fact that the user may benefit or profit from any product or service in respect of which the individual's attributes have incidentally been used is not in itself sufficient.[lxxxvii] This violation of the right to identity, therefore, also entails unauthorised use of the individual's attributes with a commercial purpose, whether done through advertisement or the manufacture and distribution of merchandise covered with the characteristics of the individual. The unlawfulness, in this case, is mainly found in the infringement of the right to freedom of association and commercial exploitation of the individual.

As a personality right, the right to identity attaches to the individual and cannot devolve or be traded. As a proprietary right, the right to identity is distinct from the individual and forms an immaterial asset in the individual's estate. It can be inherited, and the individual can trade the right, for instance, by authorising a particular company to use their name or image for marketing.

Image rights are not absolute. Using a person's attributes must be unlawful before a plaintiff succeeds with any delictual claim. With any action due to infringement of a subjective right, various conflicting interests must be weighed against each other. Using a person's image, the rights to identity, human dignity

---

lxxxiii *Idem* 313.
lxxxiv *Idem* 315.
lxxxv *Idem* 317.
lxxxvi 2007 4 S.A. 89 (SCA).
lxxxvii In *Wells v Atoll Media (Pty) Ltd and another* (11961/2006) [2009] ZAWCHC 173 par. 49 Judge Davis explained that "the appropriation of a person's image or likeness for the commercial benefit or advantage of another may well call for legal intervention in order to protect the individual concerned. That may not apply to the kinds of photographs or television images of crowd scenes which contain images of individuals therein. However, when the photograph is employed, as in this case, for the benefit of a magazine sold to make profit, it constitutes an unjustifiable invasion of the personal rights of the individual, including the person's dignity and privacy".

and freedom of association of the individual must often be weighed against the user's right to freedom of expression. Neethling[19] also correctly stated that public policy can justify an apparent violation of the right to identity, for instance, using someone's image in news reports on sports events or off-field incidents.

11.4.6 Civil Liability

There used to be a general acceptance that athletes who participate in sport and spectators who attend sport events cannot hold sports federations or event organisers liable if they should get injured.[lxxxviii] However, in recent years, this has changed significantly, and sports federations should be aware of potential civil liability which can occur.

As explained above, in cases where claims are brought based on sports injuries, courts generally submit to the rules or laws of the sport concerned. This is because participation in any form of organised sport, whether as a beginner, amateur or professional player, occurs in terms of a contractual relationship between the sports federation, sports league, sports club, organiser and players.[lxxxix] This contractual relationship is expressed, among other things, in the rules or laws of the particular sport, and players, therefore, agree to play by those rules. In this regard, it is essential to note that in the law of contract, there is a presumption that parties intend to conclude a lawful contract and that the parties have contracted according to existing law.[xc] This means that in the context of sport, it is also presumed that the rules or laws of the sport, as contractual terms to which the parties have agreed through their participation, complies with existing law. Accordingly, it is also assumed that the rules or laws of sport are valid and lawful unless the party alleges otherwise and can convince a court that a particular rule is unlawful, and therefore unenforceable or void. The onus rests on the party disputing the validity of a specific rule to provide the necessary proof on which a court can legitimately hold that a particular rule is unlawful.

Although the contractual relationship between the parties often does not feature as such in claims based on sports injuries, it is essential to remember that the legal relationship in organised sport is contractual. In the case of social participation, such as where friends or relatives play with each other for mere entertainment or recreation, the position will likely be different. With social participation in sport, one does not find the contractual relationship present in organised sports and social players only sometimes adhere to a particular sport's rules. This can have significant consequences when a court considers a sports injuries case.

It is against this background that consent as a defence to a claim for a sports injury should be considered. Neethling, Potgieter and Knobel[20] explained that:

> "[c]onsent takes two forms: consent to injury and consent to (or acceptance of) the risk of injury. Since both are forms of the same ground of justification, the same principles apply to each.

---

lxxxviii *Boshoff v Boshoff* 1987 2 SA 695 (O).
lxxxix *Rowles v Jockey Club of South Africa* 1954 1 SA 363 (A) 364D; *Jockey Club of South Africa v Transvaal Racing Club* 1959 1 SA 441 (A) 446F, 450A; *Turner v Jockey Club of South Africa* 1974 3 SA 633 (A); *Jockey Club of South Africa v Forbes* 1993 1 SA 649 (A) 645B, 654D; *Natal Rugby Union v Gould* 1999 1 SA 432 (SCA) 440F; *Johannesburg Country Club v Stott* 2004 5 SA 511 (SCA).
xc *Kotze v Frenkel & Co* 1929 AD 418; *Claasen v African Batignolles Construction (Pty) Ltd* 1954 1 SA 552 (O); *Douglas v Tromp & Sons (Tvl) (Pty) Ltd* 1959 4 SA 752 (T); *Cape Town Municipality v F Robb & Co Ltd* 1966 4 SA 329 (A); *Lesotho Diamond Works v Lurie* 1975 2 SA 142 (O); *Karstein v Moribe* 1982 2 SA 282 (T); *Nuwe Suid-Afrikaanse Prinsipale Beleggings (Edms) Bpk v Saambou Holdings Ltd* 1992 4 SA 387 (W); *Kirsten v Bankorp Ltd* 1993 4 SA 649 (C).

In the case of consent to injury, the injured party consents to specific harm... e.g.,... the rugby prop-forward consents that his opponent may scrum against him...

In the case of consent to the risk of injury, the injured party consents to the risk of harm caused by the defendant's conduct."[xci]

If the abovementioned cases are considered, both consent forms can be relevant to sports injuries. An athlete agrees to play by specific rules and agrees to any harm that occurs strictly by the rules, but the athlete also assumes the risk that other harm, such as physical injury, can occur during the game. For example, a rugby player agrees that, during a match, he may be tackled if he has the ball because the rules provide as much. But the player also assumes the risk that he may fall badly and injure his knee or shoulder when tackled. Similarly, a judoka agrees that her opponent might throw her on her back for an ippon or pin her to the ground because the rules of judo provide for that. However, the judoka also accepts the risk of sustaining an injury if she lands or lies awkwardly.

It is, however, essential to note that participation in sport does not establish consent as a comprehensive defence against all claims for sports injuries. Claims for sports injuries have thus far failed substantially because conduct that would otherwise have been unlawful can be excused. After all, the participants in a particular sport consented to the risks generally associated with that sport.

Consent is a unilateral act, so it is not necessary to determine whether there is any agreement between the injured player and the player who caused the injury.[21] As a German court correctly remarked, consent is determined objectively so that any subjective reservations a player may have, are irrelevant.[xcii] This means that consent cannot merely exist in the player's mind but must, in one way or another, be made visible to the outside world. Consent can often be inferred from the behaviour of the consenting player and is, therefore, usually given tacitly. The mere fact that a player participates in sport can justify the conclusion that the player consents to the dangers and risks inherent in the sport. In other words, the question is whether a reasonable person can infer from the player's conduct that the player should have foreseen the risks and dangers inherent in the sport[xciii] and therefore has assumed the risks and dangers associated with the sport.

But since consent is granted unilaterally, it can also be withdrawn unilaterally, with the result that any harm that may then occur would indeed be unlawful.[22] Since the existence of consent is determined objectively, the revocation of consent must also be determined objectively. A boxer, for example, consents to assume the risks and dangers inherent in boxing, but if the boxer should throw in the towel during a bout, this consent is withdrawn and the opponent may not deliver any further blows to that boxer.

Consent is a juristic act that limits the rights of the consenting player.[23] This means that consent only serves as a defence against a claim by the consenting player and does not apply to claims by third parties. Here it is important to note that the same act (or omission) may cause harm to more than one person and could therefore constitute multiple wrongs committed against multiple parties. If a player is injured while participating in a sport, it is not only the player who may potentially have a claim against the offender who caused the injury. Other parties who suffer harm or prejudice due to the injury may also have potential

---

xci Italics as per the original text.
xcii *Schadensersatzanspruch eines Fußballspielers* 1975 NJW 109. See also the Canadian case of *R v Ciccarelli* 54 CCC 3d 121.
xciii *Maartens v Pope* 1992 4 SA 883 (N) 888B.

claims against the perpetrator. Here one can think of the dependents of the injured player, the club that employs a professional player, or the player's support staff, to name a few. The player, however, cannot exclude the separate claims of all third parties when he consents to the risks associated with them.[xciv]

However, the position regarding consent where children are involved has yet to be clearly defined.[xcv] Where a child cannot legally grant consent, the parent or guardian may consent on behalf of the child[xcvi] but it should be remembered that in every matter that affects a child, the overarching principle is the child's best interest.[xcvii] It is by no means inconceivable that a court may find that the decision, whether by the child himself or by a parent or guardian, to participate in a particular sport, like boxing or rugby, and the apparent consent to injury associated with that, is not in the best interest of the child and therefore does not provide valid consent to injury. Consequently, consent as a defence where children are involved is questionable.

Secondly, consent must be given freely. This means that a party can consent only if that party is aware of the risk, understands the risk and voluntarily agrees to accept the risk. In *Union National South British Insurance Co Ltd v South African Railways and Harbours*[xcviii] the court[xcix] suggested that an employee or contractor who is required by the employment contract to take the risks associated with their work and workplace cannot consent freely to the risk concerned. Such an approach makes sense because to hold differently would be in direct conflict with international treaties and local legislation on occupational health and safety.[c] Since professional players, at least as far as team sports are concerned, are generally regarded as employees of the various sports clubs or federations,[24] this would mean that consent to injury in the context of professional sport cannot justify otherwise unlawful conduct.

Thirdly, the permission must be granted with full knowledge of the extent of any possible harm or risk.[25] Fourth, the player must fully appreciate the nature and extent of any obtrusion.[ci] In other words, a player participating in sports must be aware of the risks usually associated with the sport and understand the consequences if the risk is realised. This aspect formed the basis for a claim that several retired football players instituted in the United States against the National Football League (NFL).[26] The players claimed that the NFL was aware of the dangers and long-term side-effects of concussions in football at all levels and that the NFL sought to downplay or conceal those risks.[27] There could not be any suggestion that those football players would have consented to the risks of concussion when playing football. It is, therefore, little wonder that the NFL settled the case for $675 million.[28] More and more studies are also starting to shed light on the extent of sport injuries; the problem may be worse than initially thought. This means that participants may need help understanding the risks generally associated with the sport or what consequences, in particular long-term consequences, can occur if the risk is actual.

---

xciv	*Johannesburg Country Club v Stott* 2004 5 SA 511 (SCA) 516I-517A.
xcv	Ibid.
xcvi	*Ibid.*
xcvii	*Fraser v Fraser* 1945 WLD 112 119; *Blume v Van Zyl and Farrell* 1945 CPD 48 49; s 28(2) Constitution of the Republic of South Africa, 1996; Children's Act 38 of 2005. For a discussion of this principle in the United States, see Kopelman, LM "The Best-Interests Standard as Threshold, Ideal, and Standard of Reasonableness" 1997 *J Med Philos* 271; Child Welfare Information Gateway *Determining the best interests of the child* (2013).
xcviii	1979 1 SA 1 (A).
xcix	9A-H.
c	See for example the Convention concerning Occupational Safety and Health and the Working Environment of 22 June 1981 which, in terms of Article 1 "applies to all branches of economic activity".
ci	*Idem* 113.

Fifth, the party concerned must indeed agree to the risk of harm or injury. As mentioned above, consent can be inferred from the facts and is usually found to exist if a party understands the nature and extent of the risk and the consequences if harm may befall him.[29]

Finally, the consent must be lawful.[30] This means that the relevant consent must be acceptable according to the legal convictions of society. Regarding sports, consent to even relatively serious injuries is admissible if the player causing the injury plays according to the sport's rules.[cii]

Where a player knowingly violates the rules and, in the process, an opponent is injured, that amounts to assault, and such a player cannot raise consent as a defence. That is why a rugby player was held liable in *Roux v Hattingh*[ciii] for an injury to an opponent when the player wilfully performed an unlawful manoeuvre in a scrum.

11.5 CONCLUSION

Sport administrators and athletes must know the legal aspects that impact their sport. That is the only way in which they can ensure that they practice all aspects of sport, including administration, marketing, participation and spectating, in an ethical, safe and responsible manner. The law serves to protect the integrity of sport, but also to ensure that participation is free, fair and sustainable.

SELF-ASSESSMENT

1. What is the legal basis for participation in sport?
2. Name the legislation that regulates sport in South Africa and briefly explain what each regulates.
3. Is match-fixing a crime in South Africa? Explain with reference to applicable legislation.
4. Is ticket touting lawful in South Africa? Explain with reference to applicable legislation.
5. What is ambush marketing and how is it regulated in South Africa?
6. Can a player claim damages or compensation from an NSF for injuries that they sustained while participating in sport?

---

cii *Roux v Hattingh* 2012 6 SA 428 (HHA).
ciii 2012 6 SA 428 (SCA).

HUMAN RESOURCE PRACTICES IN SPORT

VOLUNTEERISM IN SPORT

Professor Paul Singh

LEARNING OUTCOMES

At the end of this chapter, you should be able to:

1. Clarify the meaning of volunteerism.
2. Explain the roles that volunteers play.
3. Distinguish between different categories of volunteers.
4. Discuss the reasons why people may volunteer.
5. Draw up a job description for a volunteer.
6. Recruit volunteers.
7. Identify where to find volunteers.
8. Discuss how volunteers can function as part of a team.
9. Recognise and reward work done by volunteers.
10. Develop guidelines for the management of volunteers.
11. Create and use guidelines for the protection and safety of volunteers.

12.1 INTRODUCTION

This chapter is designed for volunteers associated with sport and recreation and those administrators who must manage them. The phenomenon of volunteering, which is universal, is presented from the perspectives of the volunteer and the Sport Manager. The chapter is designed to improve volunteers' skills during volunteer work. Volunteers have, to a large extent, contributed to the development of sport and recreation activities globally and in South Africa,[1;2;3] which is an aspiring developing country with numerous socio-economic challenges and wicked problems.[4;5] The best example of volunteering in South Africa is Mandela Day, which is a day of community service held annually on Nelson Mandela's birthday on the 18th of July. It is worth remembering that Nelson Mandela called for participatory democracy in South Africa. Volunteers locally respond to this clarion call to participate positively in the affairs and activities of their communities.

Volunteers play a huge role in promoting the successful delivery of major sport events and tournaments; they are among the most valuable and necessary human resources in the events and festivals sector as they provide both organisational and economic efficiency, and introduce innovation into organisations by suggesting new and fresh ideas. Furthermore, volunteers minimise the costs involved with the staging of events through their free labour. Several significant events' operational and financial successes (e.g., the Cape Cycle Challenge, Two Oceans Marathon, Comrades Marathon, 947 Cycle Challenge, Netball World Cup, etc.) have become highly dependent on their contribution.[6;7] In addition, several globally recognised sports events are held annually in the Western Cape, the most prominent of which are the Cape Town Cycle Tour, the biggest timed bicycle race in the world with an estimated 35,000 participants,[8] the Absa Cape Epic, the most televised mountain bike race in the world,[9] and the Two Oceans Marathon, which is Africa's biggest running event by economic impact.[10]

The importance of volunteers in sports events is commonly known.[11] They are central to the service delivery of sport and are an essential element of sport event management, as they provide Sport Managers with the ability to offer, sustain or even expand the quantity, quality and diversity of sport organisations' services. Furthermore, an evident and critical positive effect of volunteer engagement is reduced costs for the organisation. It is thus incumbent upon Sport Managers and event organisers to recruit, train and sustain their volunteers.[12;13]

Approximately 950,000 volunteers offered much-needed services to the organisers of 530 major multi-sport games and world championships, held in 556 cities in 84 countries from 2007-2014, with around 88 million spectator attendees in total. In the case of the 2016 Olympic Games in Rio de Janeiro, 240,000 people applied for 70,000 volunteer positions, while approximately 240,000 applied for 90,000 volunteer positions for the 2020 Tokyo Olympic Games.[14] For the 2010 Football World Cup held in South Africa, 15,000 volunteers applied and underwent training in different metropoles.

Volunteers provide considerable human capital for sports events, which are primarily dependent on educators, parents, former athletes and others who offer their services to governing bodies.[15;16]

At the Mandela Day events in 2018, volunteers offered their services with a focus on social welfare and assistance (56%), sports (38%), the physical environment (29%), education (25%), vulnerable populations (15%) and a range of other purposes.[17] These survey findings indicate the diverse areas in which South African volunteers focus beyond sport activities.

12.2 WHAT IS A VOLUNTEER?

There are many definitions of volunteers, but essentially volunteers are people who:

1. do work willingly for other people;
2. provide their time and skills at no cost to the organisation; and
3. have a love for sharing with others.

Voluntary service encompasses a wide range of activities. The one common thing amongst volunteers is that they all want to experience the rewards of serving others, which are so great that they are best understood only by those who have volunteered. Volunteers voluntarily donate their time, energy and capabilities to support sport and recreation events and programmes in South Africa. Some volunteers may be novices, while others could be episodic or regular.[18;19;20] Let us delve into the motivations for people volunteering in sport and recreation activities and events.

12.3 WHY PEOPLE VOLUNTEER

People offer their services for a variety of reasons. Their motivations can be grouped into altruistic, instrumental and social/egoistic.[21;22;23] According to Compion et al.,[24] altruistic or value-driven motives refer to the desire to help support others, to fulfil a civic duty, or to set an example for children and others. Utilitarian or instrumental reasons refer to volunteering to gain new functional skills and experiences, to impress a boss, because it is a school/university/work requirement, or for personal emotional and spiritual fulfilment. Finally, social or ego-defensive motives include volunteering to make new friends, to expand one's social network, to find a fun activity, or because friends/family offered an invitation to volunteer.

Often, people volunteer not just for a single reason but for many reasons.[25] Most volunteers want to give something back to their community and contribute to making it a better place. In contrast, others do it for their advancement. Generally, volunteers also enjoy getting along with people and enjoy helping. Sometimes people volunteer to meet new people, to fill up spare time rather than waste it, and to gain additional experience.[26] Sport curriculum students also volunteer to gain work-integrated learning.

Many people volunteer without calling themselves volunteers. For example, if you belong to a women's club, attend meetings regularly and organise events for women in your community, but you're not getting paid, you are a volunteer. Likewise, you volunteer if you are a sports team member and give up your free time to train, play, attend club meetings and help fundraise for a new kit without getting paid.

In South Africa, we are all busy trying to rebuild our communities, improve our own lives and the lives of those around us, and empower others and ourselves. Volunteers are essential in this process; they are the foundation for community development,[27] nation-building and social cohesion.[28] In the context of South Africa, this form of social behaviour and commitment to community and a greater good is related to the concept of *'Ubuntu',* which is a *Nguni'* word that translates to human kindness and a broad communitarian approach to life.[29]

Volunteers thus place the welfare and image of their community before their own interests. As they have a strong sense of association and belonging to their community and its multiple organisations, they may be urged to give back to organisations that have benefitted them directly or indirectly.[30] However, many do not belong to these organisations and are not required to.[31]

Compion et al.[32] found that when volunteers find the experience fun and socially meaningful, they begin volunteering more often and regularly because their motives change, i.e., they become more altruistic. Sport and recreation activities are indeed fun, not only for the active participants, but also for others like volunteers who are involved in such activities. However, altruistic people volunteer more frequently because they have a different ethos.

Some of the more common reasons why volunteers offer their services[33] are to:

1. improve the quality of life of others;
2. do something useful or enjoyable;
3. contribute to a worthy cause;
4. explore new career options;
5. gain professional experience or training;
6. maintain skills while unemployed;
7. acquire new skills to enhance their marketability;
8. fulfil the service requirements of a church or club;
9. complete mandatory community service;
10. be creative, solve problems and do challenging work;
11. make new friends and work with peers;
12. belong to a group or community;
13. explore their strengths;
14. relieve boredom and monotony;
15. feel needed;
16. repay what they have received; and
17. develop and grow personally.

12.4 DO YOU HAVE WHAT IT TAKES TO BE A VOLUNTEER?

Source: Volunteering Barnet (VB).[34]

You do not need to be an educator or professional or have any other formal qualifications to volunteer. But, on the other hand, volunteering does require a special kind of person. All you need is a love for your community and a positive, can-do attitude.

People volunteer for many reasons, but most volunteers share certain ideals; they want to make a difference in the world and they don't expect financial rewards in return, but they wish to receive personal and spiritual fulfilment from their labour and the satisfaction of helping others or completing a difficult task.

> **Activity 1:** Answer the following questions:
>
> 1. Write down at least one time that you have volunteered.
>   ....
> 2. List some of the tasks you performed.
>   ....
> 3. What did you enjoy about volunteering?
>   ....
> 4. What did you not enjoy about volunteering?
>   ....

12.4.1 What are The Qualities of a Successful Volunteer?

Volunteers are some of the best role models in society. The most effective means of recruiting new volunteers is the positive conduct of existing volunteers. It is not only WHAT you do, but also HOW you do it. If you want to be a respected volunteer, you should always strive to:

1. be **flexible**;
2. willingly serve others and be **sensitive** to their needs;
3. show **initiative**;
4. have a sense of **humour**;
5. be prepared to **learn and accept feedback**;
6. be sensitive to **cultural differences**;
7. be willing to accept **different opinions**;
8. work as a member of a **team**;
9. be **realistic** about your limitations; and
10. be **honest, fair, and trustworthy** in all you do.

Being an effective volunteer also means that you have to **accept responsibility**. People will come to think of you and recognise you as a member of a volunteer group, and this means that you will have to act responsibly and be the role model your community expects you to be. This is particularly important for those volunteers who want to gain experience and use it to further their chances of gainful employment:[35]

1. **Assist** wherever you can.
2. Be **polite** at all times.
3. Be **honest** about your expectations and limitations.
4. Be **dependable** – do what you say you will do and do not let others down.

5. Be **loyal** to your organisation and offer positive suggestions.
6. Be **enthusiastic**.
7. Be a **team player**; don't force your views onto others and respect the views of your fellow volunteers.
8. Give **honest feedback** about your work.
9. Always be **willing to learn** and acquire new skills.
10. **Don't criticise** what you do not understand – first, learn the ropes and ask questions.

> **Activity 2:** Think of an outstanding volunteer in your community. List some of the qualities that make this person special.
>
> ....
> ....
> ....
> ....
> ....

12.5 WHAT TASKS CAN VOLUNTEERS PERFORM?

Volunteers can perform various services and tasks and can become involved in almost any part of community life. Volunteers function in three areas: administrators, delivering programme activities, and support services.

12.6 VOLUNTEERING FUNCTIONS

Volunteers could do any job where extensive training for professional registration is not required. This could be anything from administrative to support services and programme activities.

12.6.1 Administration

Administration refers to any administrative functions volunteers could do, based on their skills and competencies. Examples are:

1. acting as a committee or subcommittee member, such as a chairperson, secretary, club leader, treasurer, planner etc.;
2. being a fundraiser or doing marketing and promotion for a club, event or programme;
3. doing typing or administration such as filing, sending emails, answering telephone calls etc.;
4. capturing data of events and programmes; and
5. doing any other required administrative tasks.

12.6.2 Programmes and Activities

Volunteer work related to programmes and activities takes place when those programmes are planned and delivered. Examples include:

1. programme leaders;
2. coaches, umpires, referees, judges and managers;
3. tournament directors;
4. coaches, teachers and instructors;
5. record keepers;
6. organisers of club functions;
7. crowd control assistant;
8. ticketing stewards; and
9. play leaders.

This Photo by Unknown Author is licensed under CC BY.

12.6.3 Support Services

Volunteers also deliver support services to other units in organisations, such as cleaning sport facilities. Further examples include the below:

1. Facility and equipment management:
    a. building maintenance
    b. caretakers of equipment/uniforms

    c. venue/ground preparation steward
    d. housekeeping
2. Professional skills, e.g., doctors, first-aiders, accountants and dieticians:
3. Translators, drivers and guides
4. Public relations and marketing
5. Publicity officers
6. Team managers and organisers
7. Counsellors

Activity 3: If you were to volunteer in your community or a major sport or recreation event, list the possible tasks that you would be able to perform.

1. ....
2. ....
3. ....
4. ....
5. ....
6. ....
7. ....
8. ....

12.7 WHEN WILL VOLUNTEERS BE NEEDED?

Volunteers need to always be active in their communities; they have the specific task to "Get our Nation to Play". Only by volunteering regularly to promote this goal will we succeed. In this way, the **spirit** of volunteering will grow and our communities will increasingly benefit through more activities, more positive role models and more community involvement, more often.

However, volunteers will occasionally be called upon to assist with specific events or activities. The need for volunteers will depend on the organisation's requirements and the event's nature. Examples could include:

1. before, during and after big sports or recreational events, e.g., African Games, Comrades Marathon, Midmar Mile, Cape Cycle Challenge, Netball League, Varsity Cup, Community Sports Festivals, etc.;
2. fundraising drives;
3. training sessions or programmes;
4. for specialised skills such as bookkeeping, first-aid, transport, social media, etc.;
5. to recruit other volunteers;

6. to get more people involved in sports and recreational activities more often; and
7. others:

   a ....

   b ....

   c ....

   d ....

   e ....

> **Activity 4:** Write down at least five organisations/institutions in your community that would benefit from your services as a volunteer. Next to each, write down one task that you would be able to perform.
>
> **Organisation/Institution   Task**
>
> 1. ....
> 2. ....
> 3. ....
> 4. ....
> 5. ....

12.8 HOW DO VOLUNTEERS ORGANISE THEMSELVES AT A COMMUNITY LEVEL?

It is possible to work informally as a community volunteer. You will, however, serve your community far more effectively if you assist in forming a community-based Sports and Recreation structure and work as part of a team. In many communities, this is called the Community Sports and Recreation Council. In this way, sport and recreation activities and the work of volunteers can be well coordinated in the community.

> **Activity 5:** How would you go about establishing a sport and recreation council in your community? Write down at least six simple steps. *(Don't look below this activity box!!!)*
>
> 1. ....
> 2. ....
> 3. ....
> 4. ....
> 5. ....
> 6. ....

If your suggestions included some of the following, then you're on the right track:

1. Try to informally recruit a few enthusiastic people who see the need for a sport and recreation structure in your area.
2. Call a formal meeting of interested persons, clubs, schools and religious/social organisations in your area, i.e., anybody who may be interested in promoting sport and recreation.
3. At the meeting, explain the need to develop sport and recreation, record names and addresses, and have a general discussion (appoint a temporary secretary to take minutes).
4. Vote on whether to form a structure or not. It would be best if you got majority support.
5. Elect an interim committee to set up the structure further.
6. Call the first general meeting of the structure at which a draft constitution is presented.

12.9 WHAT ARE THE BENEFITS OF BEING A VOLUNTEER?

Although volunteering can be hard work without financial benefits, there can be many other rewards:[36]

1. You have an opportunity to learn new skills.
2. You gain self-confidence.
3. You could explore possible new career opportunities.
4. You could make new friends by meeting other people.
5. You will improve your standing in the community.
6. You could get a new direction and purpose in life and discover things about yourself you never knew before.

Not everyone may recognise these benefits or understand why you want to volunteer. Some may secretly think you are receiving financial help because they cannot understand why you want to work for free. Others may think you have a hidden agenda of some kind. Incorrect perceptions are generally the result of people needing to learn or understand what volunteerism is all about. This can be challenging, but it is part of being a communal South African volunteer to inform people about what it means to be a volunteer and even to get them to become volunteers themselves, with the knowledge that they may all have certain constraints and challenges in life.[37]

Activity 6: Suggest a few things which can be done to better recognise the role that volunteers play in the community.	
1	2
3	4
5	6

12.9.1 Volunteer Awards

An attempt was made to create a national system that would recognise and reward volunteers in sport and recreation following the dawn of democracy in South Africa. In the 1990s, the then National Department of Sport and Recreation initiated a South African Volunteer Involvement Programme, however this was not sustained for various reasons. The Local Organising Committee created a volunteer policy in 2007 to prepare for the 2010 FIFA Football World Cup.

In 2012, Sport and Recreation South Africa (SRSA) established a national policy called the National Sports Volunteer Corps, which focused on volunteer recruitment, development and retention.[38] The National Sports and Recreation Plan has an objective that focuses on the importance of sport volunteers:[39] "Strategic objective 19: To empower volunteers to support the South African sports system adequately." However, none of these policy initiatives has been sustained. Perhaps it is for the best that voluntary activities should not be over-regulated. Nonetheless, when the time comes for significant events, volunteers show up in greater numbers than can be accommodated, as was the case of the Netball World Cup in 2023.

Case study: Netball World Cup 2023 in South Africa

What are the main reasons for utilising volunteers in this event?

The Volunteer Program plays a critical role in any significant event. Volunteering means providing a spark and helping to create experiences like no other, filled with unforgettable memories that will last a lifetime for both the volunteers and event attendees, not to mention all the World Netball Family fans around the world. But "amazing" does not just happen on its own – it happens because of people like volunteers, who bring us together in ways we never imagined possible, creating memories that people will never forget – creating a legacy to be proud of. The Volunteer Program is the heartbeat of the event.

In what roles will they serve, and what will they be responsible for?

Volunteers are deployed in various positions that we normally refer to as 'Functional Areas'. These FAs vary in requirements and the numbers needed per FA. Our Vitality Netball World Cup here in South Africa is divided into the following FAs (these can vary from event to event):

1. Welcome Desk - Airport
2. Welcome Desk - Venue
3. Help Desk - Official Hotels
4. Main Venue
5. Training Venues
6. Change Rooms
7. Doping Control Room
8. Recovery Room
9. Media
10. Volunteer Centre

11. Public Area
12. Hospitality
13. Special events, e.g., World Netball Congress
14. Technical Officials' Space
15. Accreditation
16. Security and Marshalls
17. Marketing

The responsibilities of volunteers vary from one FA to the other. However, the primary responsibility of any volunteer is to uphold the event's image and always be a perfect example.

How many volunteers will you have, and if possible, can you give a gender breakdown?

The Vitality Netball World Cup here in Cape Town will have 300 volunteers; 70% will be female and 30% male. The criteria for choosing volunteers were based on 70% South Africans, 20% Africans and 10% from the rest of the world.

What challenges do you encounter in managing volunteers for this event?

Diversity management! Like in any other big event, volunteers come from different backgrounds and volunteer for various reasons. Therefore, challenges differ in that regard. However, the most common challenge would be to adhere to the code of conduct.

Is any other exciting/novel information on volunteers being used for this event?

This being the first-ever Netball World Cup on African soil, we have seen a tremendous interest in volunteering from all over. As a result, the number of applicants came up to close to 10k versus the 300 required when the closing date of 15 February 2023 arrived.[i]

SRSA hosts the National Sports Awards annually, presenting various awards to deserving sports sector recipients. One relevant award presented is for an outstanding sports volunteer. Locally, all organisations and events managers should give due recognition and awards to such deserving volunteers.

12.9.2 Rewarding Volunteers

Some ideas for rewarding volunteers and making them feel appreciated include:

1. letter or postcards of thanks;
2. informal certificates;
3. recognition in local newspapers, notice boards and newsletters;
4. recognition at meetings;
5. special awards at functions;
6. naming an event after a volunteer;

---

i   Personal communication via email from NWC Tournament Director, 23 April 2023.

7. a social event to thank volunteers;
8. thank you notes from teams;
9. ensuring that all expenses are reimbursed;
10. annual volunteer days to honour all volunteers; and
11. nominating local volunteers for local and national awards.

These ideas can be used to retain volunteers.

12.10 HOW DO YOU RECRUIT VOLUNTEERS?

The more you play an active role in your community, the more you will realise that you need plenty of volunteers. By learning and sharing the benefits of volunteering, you will encourage others to join. When you decide to start a recruitment campaign, take some time to plan your recruitment activities. Here are a few helpful hints:

1. Decide how many volunteers you need and what tasks they will be expected to perform.
2. Have a "bring-a-friend" event. Reward existing volunteers for recruiting their friends.
3. Use the local community notice boards, newspapers and radio stations, your club newsletter, or social media. You can even arrange for announcements at churches, mosques, school assemblies, etc.
4. Produce leaflets for distribution at local schools, shops and businesses. These can also be distributed among local senior citizens, who usually possess many attributes and skills gained in their youth and life journey.
5. Visit the local tertiary institutions.
6. Set up an Open Day at your club for potential volunteers to come and meet the committee, the teams and other volunteers.
7. Involve community organisations such as civic associations, women's organisations, youth organisations and social clubs.
8. Approach the parents of club members, ex-players and the unemployed.
9. Use libraries, doctors' rooms, clinics and similar gathering spaces as points to recruit volunteers.

12.10.1 Where to Look (Search) for Volunteers

Some of the most appropriate places to find volunteers include:

1. business and professional organisations;
2. chambers of commerce;
3. churches and other religious groups;
4. community service restitution programmes;
5. conferences/special events;
6. employment assistance programmes;

7. families;
8. job seekers;
9. military units and retired military personnel;
10. new residents of the community;
11. parents' groups;
12. public agencies and retired personnel;
13. rehabilitation agencies/programmes;
14. retired executives and teachers;
15. schools, especially service-learning programmes;
16. Scout troops or youth groups;
17. senior citizen groups;
18. service organisations, e.g. Rotary clubs;
19. unions and trade associations; and
20. university and community organisations.

12.10.2 Inviting Volunteers

Pointers for effective invitations include:

1. be prepared;
2. be sure that you are the right person to extend the invitation;
3. personalise your invitation;
4. think about how the invitation will sound to the prospective volunteer;
5. be enthusiastic;
6. be realistic with your expectations;
7. remember the courtesy factor;
8. bring closure to the conversation;
9. follow up quickly; and
10. accept "no" graciously.

12.10.3 Here is a Pre-Recruitment Checklist:

1. Management has supported the recruitment of volunteers.
2. Staff are prepared to interview, screen, train and supervise volunteers.
3. Everyone is knowledgeable and trained in volunteers.
4. Volunteer materials are prepared.
5. There is a place for volunteers to work.
6. Policies, procedures and record-keeping systems are in place.

7. Legal and liability issues of volunteers are resolved.
8. Staff are ready to respond to enquiries by potential volunteers.
9. Volunteer recruiters can speak knowledgeably and enthusiastically about the mission and work of the organisation.
10. All staff know how to handle direct calls from potential volunteers.

12.10.4 Job Description Components

It is best to have a clear job description for all volunteers. The following are some of the primary considerations:

1. A job title.
2. Main purpose or reason.
3. Immediate supervisor and channels of reporting.
4. Place and time requirements.
5. Duties and responsibilities.
6. Expenses, budgets and allowances.
7. Basic qualifications needed.
8. Special skills or training required.

Activity 7: Think about your community. Think of any other ways that you could recruit volunteers.

1. ....
2. ....
3. ....
4. ....
5. ....

12.10.5 How Does One Become a Volunteer?

You can become a volunteer by simply offering your services at any club, school or institution in the community. Better still, start your own club or community organisation! This will create volunteering opportunities for yourself and other interested persons.

12.11 HOW DOES ONE MANAGE VOLUNTEERS?

Event organisers and relevant stakeholders expect sports managers to implement sound management principles and practices if they are to remain financially viable. At the same time, they must retain community support from their multiple stakeholders.[40] Davies, Krajňáková, Šimkus, Pilinkiene and

Grabowska[41;42] highlighted an important issue, which is that the apparent lack of adequate planning of volunteer programmes invariably impacts the success of an event. They pointed out that the potential adverse outcomes for an event can be attributed to limited knowledge about volunteers' backgrounds, contexts and motivations, as well as an inadequate understanding of their lived experiences, which in turn have implications for the processes of volunteering and the actual volunteer management practices.

Additional considerations could include a lack of suitable mechanisms (e.g., political will and financial and organisational resources) in place before and throughout the event lifecycle; the absence of these factors can also widen the gap between the effective management of volunteers and the overall event success and sustainability.[43] Krajňáková et al.[44] advised that Sport Managers should consider the barriers to successfully using volunteers in order to make events sustainable. Additionally, Maralack and Jurgens[45] found that volunteers are dwindling, insufficient younger people are volunteering, and health, safety and security policies are becoming increasingly onerous on sports organisations.

An effective way for Sport Managers to approach their volunteer responsibility requires developing a volunteer management system. This involves, among others, the following activities:

1. Orientate staff towards volunteers.
2. Teach staff to train, recruit, evaluate and supervise volunteers.
3. Respond to issues that prevent people from volunteering.
4. Collect and disseminate success stories.
5. Advertise volunteer activities that are easily accessible to people.
6. Visit volunteers – check what they are doing and whether they are satisfied with their brief.
7. Place volunteers in high-status positions.
8. Give important assignments that make the volunteers visible to the public.

12.11.1 Addressing a Community Imperative Through Volunteerism

Unemployment in South Africa and globally is at an all-time high. While this paints a grim picture of poverty and other related socio-economic realities, one can also consider the opportunities that arise from this.[46] Additional and specific consideration should be given to working with unemployed volunteers, as their contexts differ and they could be gainfully utilised with special attention.[47;48] These could include the following:

1. Short term or episodic volunteering.
2. Family volunteering.
3. University volunteers.
4. Virtual volunteering.
5. Volunteers with disabilities.
6. Potential volunteers who are unemployed.

In South Africa, many companies support their employees' participation in the annual Mandela Day of Service activities. Colleges, universities, schools, businesses and corporations often do not just promote volunteering, but they actively facilitate volunteering opportunities. This is primarily episodic volunteering at significant events, like the ones mentioned in this chapter. This opportunity highlights the inequality inherent in some volunteer work: volunteering is more accessible and available to those with time, skills, education and resources – and can have positive outcomes for the volunteer.[49]

Davies[50] found that sport and festival events, on average, used similar numbers of volunteers in the Western Cape, but volunteer-supported sport events created twice the number of temporary jobs and around four times more permanent jobs than festival events. Sport events also attracted extra private sponsorship, achieved more significant income flows and generated more profit.

12.11.2 Safeguarding Volunteers

An earlier chapter discussed the phenomenon of safeguarding in sport. As sport is a microcosm of society, behaviours we find in the community also occur in the world of sport. Sport is not immune from the unsavoury and unwelcome conduct of those few who prey upon unsuspecting participants. In the context of volunteerism, it is, therefore, crucial that all volunteers are made aware of the rights and obligations of participants and volunteers.[51] It is advisable to heed the relevance of the ancient proverb, "Prevention is better than cure".

12.11.3 Why are Sport And Recreation Activities Vulnerable Environments?

There are various reasons why sport and recreation activities could be seen as vulnerable environments:

1. They involve children of all ages.
2. Sports are often gender specific.
3. Children are taught to obey adults, even those who are strangers to them.
4. Parents do not always question what leaders do, especially in competitive sports.
5. A high percentage of volunteers are not screened properly.
6. Parents are trusted automatically and unconditionally.
7. The close relationship between leaders and participants.
8. Children are required to dress in common bathroom areas.
9. Leaders touch children to show techniques.
10. Players spend a great deal of time with leaders.
11. Overnight trips and stayovers are common.
12. Coaches wield enormous power over children.

12.11.3.1 *Formal preventative measures*

Some of the legal measures that are essential to adopt include the following:

1. Learn about harassment and sexual abuse.
2. Commit the organisation to act against them.
3. Involve all stakeholders in the fight against abuse.
4. Understand your moral, ethical and legal obligations to protect children.
5. Make formal statements of principle.
6. Make standard policies and procedures for the prevention of abuse.
7. Conduct a risk assessment.
8. Address the risks identified in clear terms that are openly communicated and understood.

12.12 CONCLUSION

In an era where the world is characterised by disruptions encapsulated by acronyms such as VUCA, RUPT and TUNA, tensions, stress and pressures are widespread and pose severe threats to human wellness.[52] Sport addresses these negative influences and contributes to universal understanding, peace and harmony. Volunteerism in the sport sector plays a major role in facilitating the diverse and significant benefits that all stakeholders in the sporting arena expect to enjoy, and volunteerism in and of itself is a fun activity. One can only appeal to more people to volunteer more often and open the doors to the fantastic opportunities that come your way through healthy sport participation for all.

SELF-ASSESSMENT

1. Clarify the meaning of volunteerism.
2. Explain the roles that volunteers play.
3. Distinguish between different categories of volunteers.
4. Discuss the reasons why people may volunteer.
5. Draw up a job description for a volunteer.
6. Recruit volunteers.
7. Identify where to find volunteers.
8. Discuss how volunteers can function as part of a team.
9. Recognise and reward work done by volunteers.
10. Develop guidelines for the management of volunteers.
11. Create and use guidelines for the protection and safety of volunteers.

ATHLETE PRACTICES IN SPORT

Dr Leepile Motlhaolwa

LEARNING OUTCOMES

At the end of this chapter, you should be able to:

1. Describe what human resource athlete practices in sport organisations entail.
2. Identify and apply the human resource management process phases to a sport organisation.
3. Describe an enabling environment and identify factors contributing to high athlete turnover rates in a sports organisation.
4. Discuss the importance of human resource development to achieve success in sports organisations.

13.1 INTRODUCTION

The development of athletes is an integral part of sports organisations. Worldwide, sport organisations, such as clubs and National Sport Federations (NSFs), are key institutions for developing athletes. Sports organisations are essential for nurturing athletes' talent and providing support that leads to excellence and an increased likelihood of success. In South Africa, NSFs identify and develop athletes' talent in their respective sport codes. This is achieved through the delivery of programmes and the development of strategic plans embedded in athletes' continuous learning and improvement.

Sport organisations vary, ranging from non-profit sport organisations, such as community sport clubs competing in local leagues, to professional sport organisations, such as the South African Football Association (SAFA) and South African Rugby Union (SARU), which organise highly competitive and professional sports leagues in South Africa.[1] Whether big or small, every sport organisation requires a good human resource management process to identify and attract the best talent. Sport organisations rely on recruiting the best athletes and having appropriate personnel in place to meet the needs of the athletes.[2] The athlete is presumably a sport participant and the most valuable asset within the sport organisation. The responsibility of the sport organisation is to create plans and strategies for managing and supporting athletes. There needs to be more certainty in the current sport environment, and social, technological and environmental changes are always taking place in sport organisations. Therefore, organisations compete for the best athletes, and athletes compete for the best employment opportunities.

The human resource athlete practices in a sport organisation involve long-term decision-making about the organisation's strategies, policies and procedures used to support and retain athletes. Sound athlete management systems are designed to provide athletes with sufficient support and resources. The core concepts that underpin athlete management, especially elite athletes, are based on strategies to improve the well-being of athletes by providing financial support, effective coaching, access to high-quality training facilities, and proper nutrition to enhance athletes' performance.

13.2 ELITE ATHLETE DEVELOPMENT, RESOURCES AND SUPPORT

In South Africa, the South African Sports Confederation and Olympic Committee (SASCOC) is the statutory sporting body responsible for developing high-performance sport and implementing elite sport programmes for South African national athletes.[3] Through funding provided by the Department of Sports Arts and Culture (DSAC), the SASCOC mandate by the DSAC is two-fold: (1) develop and support elite athletes to achieve their potential and excellence in sport performance; and (2) ensure elite athletes' success at major international sport competitions, such as the Olympic Games. This mandate is realised by providing funding support, scientific services, and coaching and training support to ensure that athletes reach optimal performance and excellence.

Funding support for elite athletes is among the fundamental resources necessary for their development. This support allows athletes to access quality facilities and coaching. Furthermore, financial support enables athletes to focus on their training and performance. A lack of adequate funding and financial support from NSFs, the government and sport governing bodies may hinder athletes' development pathway.[4] Hence, it is crucial for sport organisations and government institutions to develop policies and financial resources to contribute to athletes' development and enhance their performance.

Different factors influence the funding support for elite athletes, for example, it depends on the athletes' performances, national policy agenda and NSFs' strategic approach to developing athletes.[5] In South Africa, the funding support systems are linked to the DSAC's strategic objectives to support high-performance athletes. The DSAC has developed an integrated funding model and support plan to ensure that elite athletes and sport organisations can access funding resources and increase the number of athletes in high-performance sport programmes.[6] The funding of elite athletes in South Africa is derived from the following sources:

1. Government funding: High-performance sport programmes are funded mainly by the Department of Sports, Arts and Culture (DSAC). The funds and grants provided by the DSAC cover training expenses and competition-related costs.
2. National Lotteries Commission: Provides financial support to sports organisations and NSFs in South Africa.
3. South African Sports Confederation and Olympic Committee: SASCOC allocates funding to elite athletes through their Operation Excellence Programme (OPEX). The OPEX is developed to provide funding support to athletes based on their performance level and potential to qualify for, and win medals at, international competitions.[7]

4. Personal sponsorship: In some instances, elite athletes are supported financially by private companies and organisations. Personal sponsorship is mostly commercially motivated and based on a sponsor's interest in an athlete or a sport.

Elite athletes must compete at the highest level (i.e., national and international competitions), therefore funding support helps to cover the costs associated with travelling to the competitions, quality training and ensuring that they experience quality coaching. In essence, adequate funding support can contribute to athletes' success and enhance sports excellence.

Sport can also impact the health and well-being of athletes, thus nutritional support is one of the most crucial factors in high-performing sports and elite athletes' well-being. Elite athletes are exposed to high-intensity training, hence a balanced diet is vital for overall performance. Furthermore, elite athletes require regular fuelling before, during and after training, so healthy and sufficient meals will help to ensure that they perform optimally. The NSFs and sport organisations should provide a conducive environment that is cognisant of athletes' unique nutritional needs and supplementation, according to the various sports codes. Qualified nutritionists and experts in sports nutrition should work closely with athletes to provide nutritional guidance.

Another crucial aspect of elite athletes' support includes scientific research and sport sciences support. Sport sciences support is important to enhance the development and performance of athletes and helps them with issues related to sports medicine, sport psychology, performance analysis and advanced training methods. For example, sport scientists with expertise in exercise physiology could assist in developing training programmes that improve athletes' physiological capacity, such as endurance and muscular strength. In turn, a performance analyst could help to evaluate some critical aspects of individual performance and make recommendations to improve performance and enhance the training approach.

The support and resources allocated to elite athletes and collaboration between stakeholders (e.g., government, NSFs and sport organisations) are crucial to nurture talented athletes and enable them to perform at their best. Apart from the support and resources provided to elite athletes, government policies and strategies developed by NSFs, quality coaching, and access to sports facilities can influence the development and success of elite athletes.

13.3 THE HUMAN RESOURCE MANAGEMENT PROCESS IN SPORT ORGANISATIONS

Sport is highly commercialised and increasingly professional due to the money secured through sponsorships and broadcast rights.[8] In this context, the financial success of sport organisations is reliant on the team performance of athletes and staff.[9] For example, if the Lions Rugby Union team keeps losing matches, their fans might lose interest, which could decrease the income generated from ticketing and thus profitability. It is argued that talent, if managed well, can lead to an organisation's success and generate income. The following figure (Figure 13.1) displays the human resources and athlete management process in a sport organisation, consisting of phases including human resources planning, attracting athletes, retaining athletes and developing athletes. These phases are discussed accordingly.

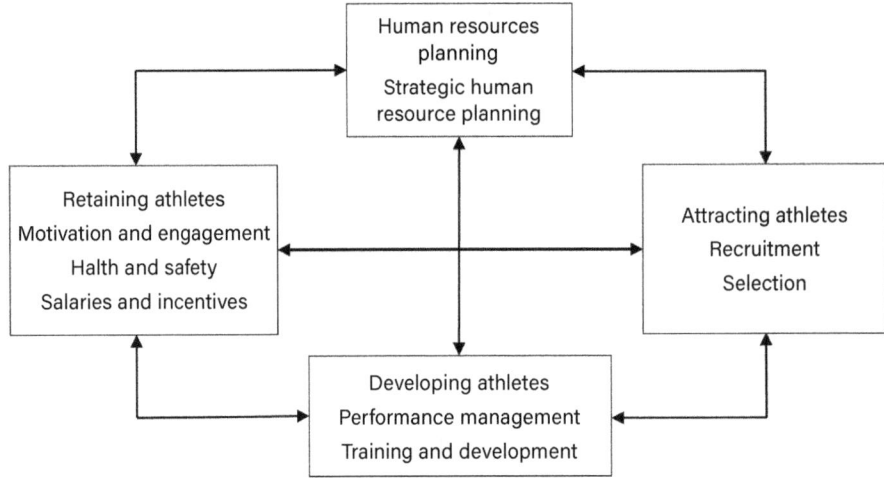

Figure 13.1: Human resources and athlete management process

13.3.1 Human Resources Planning Phase

The human resources planning phase involves assessing and predicting a sport organisation's needs, and developing strategies to meet those needs.[10] The planning phase of human resources has three significant benefits: 1) assessing whether current athletes and players within the sport organisation are adequate to contribute to the success of the organisation; 2) attracting and recruiting the best talent for the organisation; and 3) assessing the skills and performance of the current athletes and identifying the gaps in the capabilities of the athletes in relation to the future demands of the sport organisation. It is essential for sport organisations to ensure that they have talented athletes if they are to achieve their strategic goals.

An internal and external analysis of the labour force should thus be undertaken to determine the human resource needs related to the athletes and players.[11] An internal analysis involves assessing the skills and performance of the current athletes/players and an assessment of how the organisation's current workforce will change, while an external analysis examines the extent to which the organisation can find athletes/players with the necessary skills to address any gaps in the team. For instance, in a rugby club, some players might leave or retire at the end of the league season, and the organisation must recruit appropriate replacement players. Effective human resources planning should enable sport organisations to develop a recruitment and selection plan to address their needs and achieve current and future goals.

13.3.2 Attracting Athletes

Sport organisations are responsible for identifying and attracting the best talent for a team or organisation. Recruitment and selection represent an essential human resource in athlete practices, and it is critical for sport organisations to develop recruitment and selection strategies that can contribute to the organisation's competitive advantages and enable the organisation to attract talented athletes and players.[12]

Recruitment is the process that the sport organisation uses to attract skilled athletes and players to strengthen and address the gaps within the team or sport organisation.[13] Recruitment of highly skilled athletes and players is integral to most professional sport organisations. Sport organisations recruit and select athletes and players through talent identification programmes, while sport agents and sport scouts can contribute to identifying suitable players for the organisation. For example, sport scouts could observe players during a netball match and gather information to determine whether a player's skills and talents represent what the sport organisation needs. Once suitable players are selected and recruited, sport organisations need to manage athletes strategically to motivate and enhance their performance. In rugby, the most scouted players are often recruited at a young age to join youth development programmes so that they can develop the skills required to be promoted to the first team. In this context, youth development programmes (youth academies) are the primary source of nurturing talent and recruitment for the first team.

Should the players in youth development programmes not meet the requirements for promotion, or experienced players are required, then players can be bought from other clubs, including amateur clubs. Thus, coaches and managers need to ensure that athletes and players fit into the culture and philosophy of the sports organisation. In this regard, the essence of sport organisations is to empower athletes and players through effective communication, recognition and incentives.

13.3.3 Developing Athletes

After the sport organisation has recruited and selected its players, it must introduce the athletes to the culture and philosophy of the organisation. Furthermore, the sport organisation must develop the athletes and players by training them and monitoring their performance.[14] Professional sport clubs, such as Sundowns Football Club, conduct an orientation with new players to highlight the club's culture, policies and philosophy. Training and development are critical aspects of player development, and in essence, the organisation's success depends on the continual growth and improvement of the athletes and players. Training and development in a sports organisation is a process through which athletes' skills are enhanced and nurtured to be effective in their roles.[15] The process will involve evaluating the players to identify the necessary skills to perform optimally, assess their current skills, identify weaknesses, and develop specific training programmes to enhance their skills. In principle, training and development is a continuous process to help players and athletes improve their performance. After athletes are trained, sport organisations need to monitor and assess the performance of the athletes. It is, therefore, critical for coaches and managers to observe and note athletes' performances to determine if it is adequate. This extent of performance management enables the sports organisation to develop and retain the best talent.

13.3.4 Retaining Athletes

Sport organisations must understand the needs of their athletes and keep them satisfied; managers and coaches can help to motivate athletes through incentives and recognition. A sport organisation that is perceived to be supportive, compensates athletes with bonuses and pays competitive salaries tends to attract talented athletes. Some sport organisations have developed compensation systems linked to the team or individual performances. It is essential that these sport organisations formulate appropriate policies that contribute to an environment where athletes are incentivised appropriately to retain them. In the process of establishing such supportive environments, Sport Managers should consider the following factors that contribute to the high turnover rates of athletes:

1. Lack of opportunity for development.
2. Breakdown in coach-athlete relationship.
3. Athletes who do not align with the sport organisation's culture and philosophy.
4. The perceived unfairness of outcomes or processes.
5. The perceived need for recognition and appreciation.
6. The perceived unfairness of personal treatment.

To mitigate athlete turnover and ensure that they are committed to the organisation, Sport Managers should consider providing ongoing performance feedback, offer competitive compensation, recognise hard work by letting athletes know that they are appreciated, provide fair and equitable treatment, and consider the health and safety of athletes by ensuring proper safety measures are in place (including injury management). The incentives and compensation can motivate and encourage the athletes to remain with the sport organisation and should be incorporated into organisational practices.

13.4 ORGANISATIONAL PRACTICES THAT CONTRIBUTE TOWARDS ATHLETE SUCCESS

Several organisational practices could contribute to an athlete's success, although they might vary based on the sport organisation and individual needs:[16]

1. Sport organisations must develop clear goals to enable athletes to evaluate their performance. Successful athletes are renowned for their excellent work ethic and sports commitment. They frequently adhere to strict schedules and make sacrifices to achieve their goals.
2. A safe and encouraging environment is essential for an athlete's performance. This includes the level of encouragement and the extent of appropriate resources the sport organisation provides.
3. Access to competitive opportunities, such as tournaments and leagues, allows athletes to demonstrate their abilities, gain experience and evaluate their performance against competitors.
4. Compensation and funding support are essential in attracting and retaining athletes in the organisation.

It is important to remember that various elements influence an athlete's success in a sports organisation. While some athletes may thrive in some areas more than others, human resource practices are essential for managing athletes in sport organisations. Therefore, a sport organisation should support and monitor their athletes' progress. Athletes who are not supported and empowered may lose interest and lack commitment.

13.5 CONCLUSION

Human resource athlete practices in sport refer to organisations' policies and procedures to manage athletes. These practices are designed to support, recruit, develop and retain talented athletes. The aim is to promote a positive work environment and support athletes' success. This can be achieved by providing resources (funds, scientific research and nutritional support) and incorporating effective management practices to ensure that athletes can perform at their best, ultimately contributing to the success of the sport organisation. In addition, effective human resource practices can assist the sport organisation to attract and retain the best athletes.

SELF-ASSESSMENT

1. Describe what human resource athlete practices in sport organisation entail.
2. Identify and apply the human resource management process phases to a sport organisation in South Africa.
3. Describe an enabling environment and identify factors contributing to high athlete turnover rates in a South African sport organisation.
4. Discuss human resource development's importance to success in South African sport organisations.

COACHES' PRACTICES

Professor Heather Morris-Eyton

LEARNING OUTCOMES

At the end of this chapter, you should be able to:

1. Identify the basic requirements for a coach education framework.
2. Explain the role of the Sport Manager in supporting coaches on their coach education journey.
3. Categorise the primary functions for each coaching role.
4. Explain the synergies between the long-term coach education framework and long-term participant development.

14.1 INTRODUCTION

Coaching sport in South Africa is widely volunteer-based and driven. Coaches permeate all sectors of sport and are fundamental to the delivery of sport programmes at the club, district, provincial and national levels of participation and competition. A 2010 South African Sport Confederation and Olympic Committee (SASCOC) national federation audit found that most national coaches were volunteers without formal contracts.[1]

The South African National Development Plan (2030)[2] has a clear transformation vision for sport in South Africa. This plan includes participation in the various sporting codes to reflect South Africa's demographics, expanding opportunities for representative participation in sport, and expecting the countries' sporting results to reflect that of a middle-income country with a population of 50 million people. To deliver on this plan, National Sport Federations (NSFs), sports administrators and coaches will all need to play an active role within the sport sector to educate coaches, provide an enabling coaching environment, and ensure that women and girls in sport are specifically targeted within transformation planning.

This chapter will examine sport coaching in light of the current South African coaching framework, identify challenges that coaches are currently facing within the sport system, and examine the role of Sport Managers in addressing some of the issues that will be highlighted.

14.1.1 What is a Good Coach?

Coaching sport comes with judgments that parents, athletes, employers, sponsors and supporters make regarding how good the coach is, based on performance outcomes set according to the context within which the coach operates. At a school level, the performance of a coach may be linked to how teams perform in league competitions or at school sport festivals. At the international level, coaches may have performance contracts linked to specific outcomes, such as qualifying for a global event (a World Cup or the Olympic Games) or the win/loss record of the team. These judgements, irrespective of performance outcomes, determine the perception of whether a coach is good.[3]

Global technology and the importance of quality education have impacted sport coaching, where quality coaching is a sought-after commodity. This could be linked to the judgements made regarding a good coach, where the performance of teams or individuals is an important factor. It also aligns with the education and qualifications a coach must have to operate at all levels of participation. Quality could also be seen in a coach's pragmatic and holistic approach towards their athletes and from a management perspective, ensuring quality control and effective management of the coaches within a National Sport Federation (NSF), province, district, school, club or sport academy. The focus on quality and its impact on performance outcomes directly influence the success of the athlete or team.

Professional standards linked to coach education are becoming the norm across NSFs globally, including in South Africa. These standards could be well designed, such as the South African Football Association's (SAFA) coach education programme, whose main objective is coach development for advancing football players,[4] or absent, where NSFs implement their coaching standards based on contextual needs.

14.2 THE SOUTH AFRICAN COACHING FRAMEWORK

Figure 14.1: The South African Coaching Framework[6]

SASCOC is the "national sporting body responsible for preparing, presenting and performing teams to all multi-coded events".[5] They are also responsible for the awarding of national Protea colours and the endorsement of applications for bidding and hosting international events. As a major role player within the South African sports sector, SASCOC designed and implemented the South African Coaching Framework in 2011 (see Figure 14.1).

The Coaching Framework set out to provide reference points to guide coaching development, recognising the needs of coaches at all stages of their development. The detailed framework includes pillars (system, coaches and impact), actionable building blocks and keystones (long-term participant development and coach development models).[7] Coaches are a central part of the framework, where their recruitment and education are seen as a driving force in creating a workforce of coaches in sport clubs, provinces and nationally. Coach education and qualifications, considering the recognition of prior learning (RPL), are fundamental in accessing a system for education and development at all levels of coaching.

The long-term coach development model recognises all coaching roles and domains (children, participation, talent development and high performance) where coaches could be coaching (see Figure 14.2). The roles include the apprentice coach, who supports assistant coaches and is usually the parents or young adults helping with coaching without a formal commitment to a specific coaching role.[8] Volunteer coaches form the bulk of the South African coaching workforce and receive no remuneration for services rendered. These coaching roles include assistant coaches and coaches. Professional coaches are those who receive some payment in any coaching capacity.

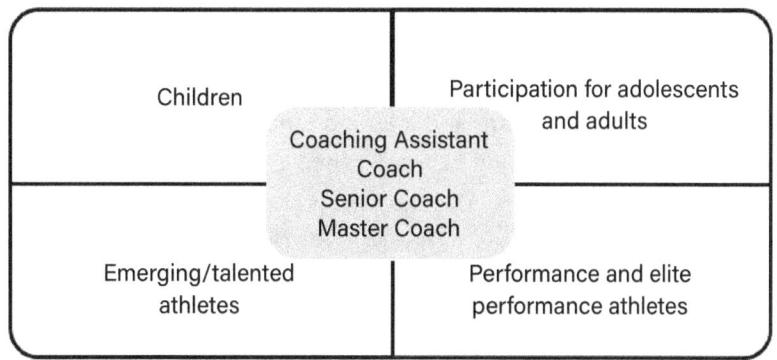

Figure 14.2: Long-term coach development model – roles and domains within which coaches operate[9]

14.2.1 Long-Term Coach Development

The South African Model for Long-Term Coach Development (LTCD) emanated from the coaching framework and provides details of formal learning requirements, functions, competencies, knowledge and assessment. It also details formal coach education learning, the requirements for accumulation of hours in the field as well as cumulative experiences for coaching. The assistant coach, coach, senior coach and master coach (see Figure 14.2) may be applied to any of the four coaching domains and were foreseen as being contextualised within each sport.[10] The primary functions, competencies and knowledge requirements for each coaching role act as a reference points for NSFs to benchmark their existing coach education programmes, or where they have no education system in place, to provide a framework for developing the coaches' education system.

The primary functions for all coaching roles included the following:[11]

1. Set the vision – the coach is require to create a vision and strategy based on the contextual needs of the coaching programme and athlete development, and consider the organisation (club, school, federation) within which the coaching is being conducted.
2. Shape the environment – the coach commits to working with a group of athletes and takes responsibility for developing and implementing training plans. This includes managing the environment in which training occurs.

3. Build relationships – communication and building relationships are vital in successful coaching. Positive and effective relationships with athletes, sponsors, employers, parents, schools, managers and administrators form part of the coaching environment, where the coach is responsible for engaging with stakeholders and making a positive contribution.
4. Conducting practices and structuring competitions – the coach needs to organise and implement suitable training sessions and target appropriate competitions for continuous development and improvement.
5. Read and react to the field – the coach observes and appropriately responds to situations occurring on and off the field. Effective decision-making is key in the implementation of this function.
6. Learn and reflect – the coach reflects and evaluates the training programme, which is a continuous learning and self-development process. Coaches should also be available for the development of other coaches.

Each coaching role has specified knowledge and learning outcomes, prescribed competencies and core knowledge requirements. Sport-specific and domain-specific knowledge and outcomes were included to allow NSFs to contextualise their coach education programmes within the four domains of coaching (children, participation, emerging talent and performance). The process of assessment, as well as the recognition of prior learning, was incorporated to validate and recognise all learning outcomes for all coaching roles.[12]

Whilst the coaching framework and long-term coach development model provided a base from which NSFs could benchmark and/or implement their own coach education pathways, the standardisation of coach education certification has been fraught with issues around governance and implementation. Both documents are under review as coach education seeks relevance and recognition within the sport coaching sector. Depending on their scope of operation, Sport Managers should be able to interrogate and insist on coaching documentation that identifies competencies and outcomes before a coach takes up a position either as a volunteer or paid professional. This would ensure the legitimacy of the coach and provide some safeguarding in the knowledge that core competencies and sport-specific knowledge outcomes have been ascertained.

14.2.2 Long-Term Participant Development (LTPD)

The second keystone of the coaching framework is the long-term participant development (LTPD) model that all NSFs were required to have developed and implemented during the framework's implementation (2011 - 2018). It was expected that by 2018, the sport system within South Africa would show signs of transformation within the coaching system.[13] A skilled volunteer and paid workforce of coaches would meet the demands of mass participation in sport, enhance athlete performance at the high-performance level and expand opportunities for improving South Africa's results in the global sporting arena. The key factor that sets the South African model apart from the internationally-recognised LTAD is the inclusive nature suggested in the word 'participant'. Here, the focus is drawn away from developing athletes to rather emphasise the role of life-long sport participation. This was the core pillar of the South African Sport for Life model (see Figure 14.3).

The stages for long-term participant development are embedded within the South African Sport for Life model. These stages are identified within two key factors – physical literacy (stages 1-3) and excellence (stages 4-6). The age groups for each stage are recognised, considering the differences in maturation between males and females. Physical literacy can be seen as the development of fundamental movement and sport skills, which enable a child to move confidently and with control in a wide range of movements and sport situations.[14]

There are seven stages of long-term athlete development (see Figure 14.3):

1. Active start: 0-6 years of age
2. FUNdamentals: girls 6-8 years, boys 6-9 years
3. Learn to train: girls 8-11 years, boys 9-12 years
4. Train-to-Train: females 11-15 years, males 12-16 years
5. Train to compete: females 15-21 years, males 16-23 years
6. Train to win: females 18 years and older, males 19 years and older
7. Active for life: males and females can enter at any stage of their life

The LTPD model recommends sport fitness and skill development for life-long participation in physical activity and a pathway for athlete excellence within the high-performance domain. Sequential stages are based on the maturation and development of the individual and recognise the importance of physical literacy in providing a solid foundation for skill development and participation in sport.

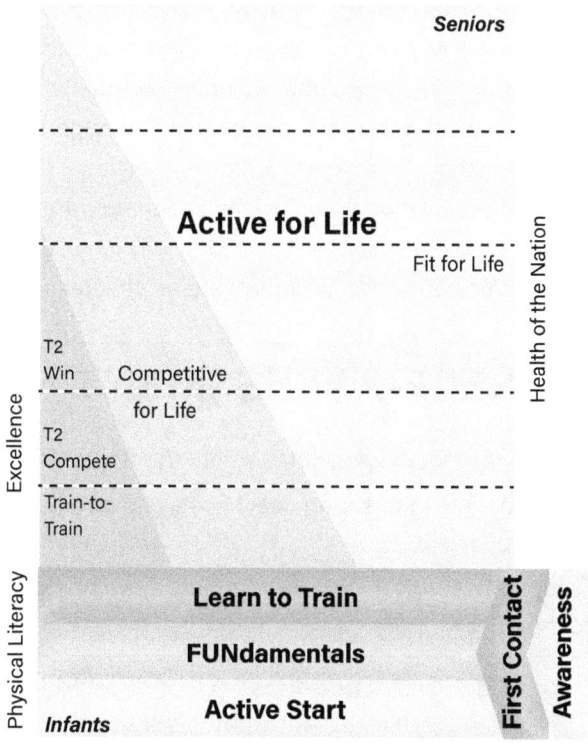

Figure 14.3: South African Sport for Life Model[15]

14.2.3 Challenges Coaches Face Within The South African Sport System

Coaching sport poses various challenges for coaches as they are required to perform a variety of roles which go beyond the implantation of training programmes and preparation for competition. Specific barriers that have been identified within the South African context include a lack of support, especially for female coaches; difficulty in gaining entry to coaching positions; job insecurity; difficulties in working with parents; insufficient compensation for coaching services; interference from management in the coaching domain; pressure to win, including from parents who involve themselves in the coach's domain; and a lack of resources.[16;17;18] Research examining the barriers to holistic coaching for positive youth development in South Africa[19] identified concerns regarding the quality of coach education programmes; winning being rewarded and recognised with an over-emphasis on high-performance excellence; and a lack of coaching knowledge and education. Sport managers who manage coaching programmes and coaches should take cognisance of these challenges and implement plans to effectively create supportive coaching environments. Not only will this allow for better coaching practice, but it will also enhance the performance-related outcomes set for each sporting context.

14.3 CONCLUSION

Coaching sport within the South African context has a mandate for transformation in reaching the goals set out by the National Development Plan (2030). To be an active role player in achieving transformation within the sport sector, Sport Managers need to have an inherent understanding of coaching and the mandate given to coaches through federations, clubs, schools and academies, which operate at different levels and within different domains. Sport managers may be team managers who will need to work closely with coaches to ensure that the logistics of managing teams or individual athletes are executed to ensure the best possible outcomes for success. Understanding the coaching framework, the ambit within which coaches operate and the challenges coaches face will go a long way in ensuring a coaching workforce that can concentrate on maximising participation in a way that retains athletes to be active for life.

SELF-ASSESSMENT

1. Discuss some of the challenges faced by coaches within the South African sport system.
2. Explain the role of Sport Managers in ensuring coaches have the required competencies to execute their duties within a sports federation.
3. Summarise the difference between the long-term athlete development model and the long-term participant development model.

TECHNICAL OFFICIATING IN SPORT

Anneline Lewies

LEARNING OUTCOMES

At the end of this chapter, you should be able to:

1. Explain the categories of technical officiating.
2. Distinguish between the organisational policies or guidelines for the various categories of technical officiating.
3. Describe the legal duties of the various technical officials for maintaining the standard of care and risk and safety management strategies, including specific technical skills.
4. Reflect on the roles and responsibilities of technical officials within the South African context.
5. Debate what information is needed and how to go about the recruitment, selection, promotion and self-management of technical officials.

15.1 INTRODUCTION

Within the sporting arena, the appointment of technical officials is imperative. In defining a technical official, a person controls the participation and play of a competition by applying the sport-specific rules and regulations to judge rule infringements, performance, time or ranking.[1] Technical officiating is one of the core drivers of matches, events and sport competitions. Technical officials should thus understand and apply fairness, encourage the spirit of true sportsmanship, control the playing environment through game rules and regulations, and promote safety. In addition, they must perform with integrity and character, as in the instance of a police officer, lawyer, judge or any person with authority.

Technical officials, such as directors, juries, referees, umpires, judges, touch judges, chief marshals, assistant marshals, timekeepers, scorers, competition secretaries, weigh-in officials and doctors on duty, are involved in the competition. This chapter aims to provide an overview of the developments in the management of games and competitions as applicable to technical officials within the South African sporting context.

15.2 CATEGORIES OF TECHNICAL OFFICIALS

In South Africa, 85 National Sport Federations (NSFs), as the custodians of sport, are registered with SASCOC. Each of these NSFs has technical officials operating in different roles with varying responsibilities. Sport competitions in South Africa and globally are only able to function as technical officials bring control to chaos, promote safety in sport, and provide the necessary management required of their roles and responsibilities. Considering the importance of the technical officiating roles in sport, it is relevant to discuss the various categories of technical officials in sport.

15.2.1 Competition Director

A competition director is appointed to oversee and manage the running of a sanctioned competition programme, which includes registering and approving the event. The competition or tournament director would be appointed for sport events where teams participate annually at national competitions such as wrestling. In sport, a volunteer takes a leadership role by organising a sport competition and is often called the tournament director, as found in national netball championships played annually, chess competitions or rugby competitions. World Rugby has had a full-time appointed 'Competitions Director' since 2020. The functions of this individual often include enforcing rules and regulations, arbitrating disputes and officiating awards ceremonies. Various sports have different titles depending on the sport, for instance, in motor racing, the title is 'Race Director'.

15.2.2 Judges, Referees, Umpires and Arbiters

It is often debated what the correct word is when referring to officiating in sport. In sport, where a score is assigned to an individual athlete, such as gymnastics, diving, figure skating, ski jumping, and to an extent, boxing and wrestling, the judges use a form of a rating scale for performance to determine the winner. A study conducted in rhythmic gymnastics to assess how the attention, emotion, recognition and expertise of judges influence accuracy of performance assessment, indicated that the outcome of performance does not exclusively rely on objective measurements, but on more subjective cues. The results of this study were considered for practical purposes and implications to enhance the relationships between attention and emotion, recognition and knowledge and the accuracy of sports performance evaluation.[2] A prior study of judging the judges' performance in rhythmic gymnastics already indicated that international-level judges outperformed judges with less experience and training.[3] It was suggested that experienced judges on probability use different cognitive strategies, increasing error detection efficiency and the capability of their peripheral vision. They do not only rely on visual fixation to detect errors (correct visual fixation allows carrying out "simple" actions such as reading, and complex actions such as detecting stimuli easily in a complicated visual scene), where novice judges tend to mostly consult their score sheets. However, international judges still scored far below the expected optimum.[4] The expected optimum is determined by a Judge Evaluation Program, where the intrinsic judging error variability is periodically recalibrated.

The officiating of referees is considered in terms of three basic knowledge categories: strategic, declarative and procedural knowledge. Strategic knowledge is the continuous overview between the declarative and procedural knowledge and consists of interlinking strategic planning based on monitoring and regulation (declarative rules and judgements) and process (procedural progress and likely outcomes of complexity of the process). Declarative knowledge is the knowledge that pertains to the rules and facts of a specific event in action, while procedural knowledge refers to implementing such regulations in actual performance and tasks.[5]

Umpires and referees oversee and control competitive sport; umpires are responsible for inspecting the environment, players and equipment, and are also vital in ensuring the safety of participants through game management, which is very similar to referees. Referees are part of the game on the field of play, making sure that rules and regulations are followed on field whilst the game is in progress. In controlling the game, umpires are responsible for making decisions, which are final and cannot be contested by the players or coaches. Communication is an essential skill in umpiring to communicate decisions and confirm with scorers and timekeepers.

Judges, referees, umpires and arbiters must have excellent decision-making, visual, emotional intelligence, attention and recognition skills. In addition, their communication with athletes and other technical officials is a tremendous benefit to communicating verbal and non-verbal (signals) to athletes, coaching staff, technical officials (timekeepers, touch judges, support staff) and spectators.[6]

In a sport such as chess, the arbiter is the technical official responsible for decision-making and dispute resolution. The arbiter oversees matches and must ensure that the rules of chess are followed.[7]

In motorsports, race officials are appointed and are required to know the rules of the sport and ensure that they are followed to provide fair competition to all competitors.

15.2.3 Touch Judges and Assistant Referees

In a sport such as rugby, the 'team of officials' are the referee – with, touch judges or assistant referees. The word 'referee' may be used interchangeably for the on-field referee, touch judges or assistant referee. The touch judge has become a vital part of the game of rugby and contributes to the game to benefit the players, officials and spectators. The referee, assisted by capable touch judges, is in a better position to perform his/her duties in the game of rugby due to the size of the field and varying components of the game to be monitored and adjudicated.[8] The touch judge, raising the flag, informs the referee that the ball is in touch, allowing the referee to prepare for the next phase of play.

In football, often referred to as soccer, reference is made to the assistant referee, who calls for offside or directs a throw-in using the flag. The most basic signal is the 'flag up', which informs the referee that play must be stopped for some reason, including a foul. Should the referee not see the signal, the second assistant referee will 'mirror' the signal to attract the referee's attention. The assistant referees have two important jobs, i.e., indicating when the ball is out and how the game should proceed. For a throw-in, the flag is raised at a 45-degree angle and pointed horizontally in the direction of the attacking team. Should the assistant referee be near the goal line, they are signaling for a goal kick, but should they be near the goal line and point at a downward 45-degree angle toward the corner flag, they are signaling for a corner kick. The assistant referees also indicate offside by a flag straight up in the air. The referee calls the offside with a whistle or can give a waving gesture, indicating no advantage, and play continues. In the event of an offside being called, the flag will be held at a 45-degree for an offside on the far side of the field, a straight horizontal flag signals an offside in the middle of the field, and a downward 45-degree signal is for the near side of the field.

Assistant referees also watch for substitutions by holding the flag with both hands above their head. When the assistant referees think a goal has been scored, they will lower the flag and may point to the centre with their hand or sprint back to the centre line. Disputing a goal, the assistant referee will stay in position and put the flag up. The penalty kick signal raises the flag, flicks it and lowers it. The assistant referee will move towards the corner flag if a foul is called. When the assistant referee keeps the flag straight up, he/she indicates the need to engage with the referee. When a yellow or red card is considered, the assistant referee will place their hand over their chest badge.

15.2.4 Timekeepers

Timekeepers operate the timing clock following all competition rules. They start, stop and restart the timing clock following the specific practical implementation of any given sport, game or competition. Operating the timing clock requires the ability to remain focused all the time and collaborate cooperatively with the judge, referee or umpire and the competition director. The timekeeper should have excellent communication and administrative skills, as duties to complete sheets for injury, suspension and extra time, as per the instructions of the referee, umpire or judge, need to be communicated. A strong work ethic and working under pressure are added skills for timekeepers.

15.2.5 Scorers

Many National Sport Federations (NSFs) appoint official scorers to keep accurate match, game or event scores. Electronic scoring systems are widely used to ensure that athletes, team officials and spectators are kept abreast of the scores. In some sports, such as golf, bowls and tennis, the athletes keep scoring and completing the necessary result forms, however technology has changed the outcome of certain calls through specific systems. In tennis, the Cyclops and Hawkeye tracking systems have changed professional tennis, giving precise calls and eliminating arguments. In golf, the television made its mark regarding a travelling call, a sport considered to stick to its traditions. Through electronic timers, photo finishes in Olympic and animal races assist with over 3,000 frames per second to determine who should be crowned.[9] Scoring in cricket is very technical, as scorers must be alert at every point in a match; they need to watch every ball and coordinate with the umpire constantly. A ball missed could affect the whole score's accuracy, thus even in international matches, manual scoring is a must. Manual scoring is done with utmost accuracy, and umpires will consider the manual score rather than the television scoring for accuracy. The scorer will record all runs scored, all wickets taken, and the number of overs bowled for each team.[10]

15.2.6 Video Assistant Referee and Digital Technology

Television or video assistant referees in rugby and cricket are very popular as they allow for referees to reassess decisive situations, determining the outcome of a try scored or whether a player or team is punished. In cricket, they determine various aspects of the game regarding extras runs or whether a player is dismissed through a catch or leg before wicket (LBW), or other ways. Television has also effectively spotted unfair competition or poor sportsmanship by players, for example, when the Australian cricket team tampered with the ball during a test series against South Africa in 2019.

Technology in officiating is considered a tool to assist decision-making in American football, tennis, rugby and basketball. Professional soccer also introduced video assistance referees (VAR) in 2018. A research project indicated that VAR interventions were significantly better at making correct decisions than initial referee decisions, with accuracy increasing from 92.1% to 98.3%.[11]

15.2.7 Smart Fabric and Costumes

In a dynamic sport such as fencing, florets and swords are developed with intelligent sensors that are capable of detecting the impact of each hit on the opponent. The costumes are designed to allow an electrical current to travel its length, and special clothing can also analyse the movement of athletes through connection to sensors.[12]

15.3 GOVERNANCE OF TECHNICAL OFFICIALS IN SPORT

In sport, technical officiating is a system where the rules or laws to control discipline and order are implemented. In team sports, referees or umpires apply the laws or rules of the sport through sport-specific interventions. Similarly, in other sporting codes, the competition/tournament directors, judges, arbiters, marshals and other technical officials are responsible for the authoritative command (order) and event decision-making. Occasionally, athletes such as golfers or tennis players can score themselves, checking with opponents. However, even in these sports, tournament directors or appointed technical officials can render decisions where a dispute arises.

ISFs and National Sport Federations (NSFs) guide the governance of a specific sport, with ISFs overseeing the requirements for technical officials globally. In the South African context, NSFs are guided by the Sport and Recreation Act, 110 of 1989, as amended by Act 18 of 2017 under the auspices of the Department of Sport, Arts and Culture. National Sport Federations are also registered to the South African Sports Confederation and Olympic Committee (SASCOC). The member NSFs, depending on the specific sport, are represented at the provincial level and governed by Provincial sport organisations. In South Africa, each province is divided into districts, with clubs affiliated to these districts. The districts are responsible for a league system for clubs and their teams or individuals to participate. In South Africa, the school sport system is active in sports such as athletics, rugby, netball, football, hockey, cricket and tennis. Some schools may offer other sports such as swimming, rowing, chess and water polo. Most NSFs accommodate young athletes in their clubs, but do not form part of the school system. Affiliation as a member to an NSF is a requirement for technical officials, similar to registration and affiliation of athletes, coaches and administrators. The constitution of each of the NSFs guides the membership and has specific requirements for technical officials in various capacities, as outlined in Section 2 of this chapter.

Technical officials can enrol for courses to obtain a qualification in an NSF's specific sport that is recognised by the various levels of sport governance. As a technical official in netball, for example, there are various courses for which umpires, scorers and timekeepers can register. People do accreditation or grading with the necessary qualification and experience, and are mostly appointed by official technical panels or umpires' associations. This is the norm for all NSFs, although educational institutions will occasionally offer technical officiating courses. However, membership to the mother body of a sport is a requirement to officiate at any relevant event, from club to national level. To qualify for international recognition as a technical official, the individual must follow a pathway of education, grading or accreditation to be considered for selection to officiate at elite and international events, such as Commonwealth Games and World Cups.

The National Sport and Recreation Act, 110 of 1998, as amended by Act 18 of 2007, was promulgated to: provide for the promotion and development of sport and recreation and the coordination of the relationships between the South African Sports Confederation and Olympic Committee (SASCOC), national and entertainment federations and other agencies; provide measures aimed at correcting imbalances in sport and recreation; promote equity and democracy in sport and recreation; provide for dispute resolution mechanisms in sport and recreation; empower the Minister to make regulations; and provide for matters connected in addition to these.[13] Closely related to the Sport and Recreation Act is the Safety at Sports and Recreational Events Act, 2 of 2010, which recognises the physical well-being and safety of persons attending sport, recreational, religious, cultural, exhibition, organisational or similar events, as well as the safety of their property.[14] This legislation and national and international regulations and guidelines form the framework relevant to South African safeguarding protocols for sport.

Risk management is a tool by which sportspeople can seek to meet their duties and thus avoid liability. Risk management is a governance obligation and thus includes legal risks – losses and costs arising from legal actions for breach of common law or statutory duty of care. Technical officials, umpires and referees must understand that they oversee a sport involving physical contact and inherent dangers. Technical officials must determine a participant's age and officiate games with the necessary sympathy. Technical officials should also use their position to officiate with authority to ensure the game or competition takes place within the rules/laws of the game or competition as safely as possible.

Every person involved in sport has a legal duty of care to ensure that they manage risks appropriately and that the safety protocols are adhered to within the South African sporting context. Officials may be liable for an injured player if they fail to properly carry out their duty of care. Negligence is a failure to comply with the standard of care to be exercised by a reasonable person in particular circumstances. The test used in labour law is to determine whether a reasonable person/official placed in a similar situation would have acted in the same manner to avoid harm, such as illegal scrummaging in rugby. It is important to note that officials do not necessarily risk liability due to a player being injured, as there needs to be probable cause that the official's conduct fell below standard. However, common sense should always prevail in risk and safety management. Common sense is unwritten and unspoken, but it is the knowledge that every person must sensibly make sound decisions and judgements. A very practical example of common sense is that your biological mother cannot be younger than you are!

>
> **Critical Note:**
>
> Risk management plans must be in place to indicate negligence and consequences thereof and officials need to be appropriately trained and educated.

As the custodians of the various sporting codes, NSFs must have policies concerning safeguarding and protection, coaching, technical officiating, disciplinary measures, and a code of behaviour for athletes, coaches, technical officials, staff, executive members and spectators (parents, specifically). The responsibility for policies and the provision and delivery of sport and recreation is vested in the Department of Sports, Arts and Culture, previously known as the Department of Sport and Recreation.[15]

15.4 ROLES AND RESPONSIBILITIES OF TECHNICAL OFFICIALS

Technical officials play an essential role in preparing and delivering safe sport events, therefore they must attain appropriate levels of competence within the ambit of the sport they are officiating. In addition, officials need to meet the legal and moral obligations of the sport and abide by the safeguarding policies of the sport and NSF. One of these requirements is to attend a safeguarding course and obtain a police check or police clearance.

Certain individual tasks are required for each technical official position, however all technical officials must comply with the following requirements:

1. Ensure that the field of play (the competition area, including the warm-up area) is safe for athletes, team officials (coaches, managers, team doctors, etc.), technical officials and sport-specific volunteers/staff.
2. Know the technical and competition rules and regulations.
3. Apply (not interpret) the technical rules without fear or favour.
4. Use a degree of 'common sense' when confronted with non-technical issues. The official will need to make a judgement call on the probable outcome, e.g., a golf ball landing on a crocodile lazing in the sun, and the crocodile decides to enter the water. Was the ball grounded on the side of the water or in the water?

Technical officials must JUDGE WHAT THEY SEE, NOT WHAT THEY THOUGHT THEY SAW!

Before a game, technical officials must:

1. attend an obligatory meeting for the appointed technical officials;
2. be present at their respective working locations or assigned positions at least 30 minutes before commencing their duties; and
3. ensure that all facilities, equipment and documents meet the relevant sport-specific technical and competition rules and regulations. It is recommended that a checklist of all items that may be required

be kept by the officials, such as the law/rule book, NSF information handbook with competition rules, duration of matches and conditions of play for different teams such as age groups, etc.

During a game, a technical official must:

1. be present at the introduction of the technical officials;
2. make the correct decision about when to act or not act. They should be well educated, appropriately qualified, and graded according to the level of officiating for the specific competition;
3. act immediately once an infringement is realised, with fairness, impartiality and consistency;
4. remain in their assigned position/working location until the completion of all ceremonies, such as games, races, events and awards of medals directly after an event;
5. conduct themselves professionally and present a good image. Personal presentation is critical in how players view the umpire/referee, and "looking the part" will impact players and spectators alike;
6. be and remain attentive;
7. be friendly and courteous;
8. be aware of and sensitive to language, cultural and religious differences;
9. promote a safe and harassment-free environment where participants are treated with respect;
10. be firm and decisive;
11. respect the work/position of other technical officials and sport-specific volunteers/staff;
12. respect accreditation levels and areas of access privileges;
13. disaffiliate from team responsibilities; and
14. assist whenever possible in any area, such as peer support and providing positive and developmental feedback.[16]

Within the sport ambit, participants and spectators often judge officials. This judgement is often related to the official's behaviour, as they are expected to be professional and responsible throughout. For this reason, officials must approach their officiating in line with the aims of the competition, as it impacts the participants' experience – whether for enjoyment or winning.

The expectations of technical officials' conduct are related to their leadership and guidance of participants in staging competitions. The essential qualities of a technical official are respect, integrity, honesty and trustworthiness; they are responsible for their attitudes and actions. Every participant views the competition they participate in as the most important, and therefore the officials are expected to be:

1. trustworthy – honest and impartial;
2. responsible – have integrity and take the role seriously;
3. prepared – physically and mentally; and
4. competent – have and are further developing skills for the job.[17;18]

All technical officials must remain until the end of a match, game or event as required by the specific sport. The technical officials start and stop the event; their decision at the end of the event is final to signal the outcome of the match, game or event. When a technical official cannot finish a game, match or event due to injury or being rendered unable, or where there are extenuating circumstances, the competition or tournament director would have prepared for such an instance. A third umpire, replacement referee or stand-in technical official should be available to proceed with the duties during a match, game or event and finish the said competition. This would be under the rules or laws of the specific sport, such as in netball, a third umpire is appointed to each game.[19]

15.4.1 Game Management

The fast-changing environment of sport across the globe requires that technical officiating adapts to the pace of change and ensures that emphasis is placed on encouraging and training technical officials to "manage" games rather than "control" them. Modern thinking and knowledgeable athletes and coaching staff appreciate this change in attitude. It has also improved communication between all parties, leading to a more professional approach and deeper enjoyment of sports.[20]

In technical officiating, a concise checklist for officials can enhance the game or competition for the athlete, coaches, spectators and other technical officials. This may include:

1. how to manage adjudication;
2. creating a relaxed and positive environment for all;
3. watching and discussing games at all levels to learn to understand the game better;
4. evaluating their performance by watching and discussing videos of their officiating performance at games with a mentor or technical official coach;
5. knowing when to manage minor technical infringements by talking to the offender initially before penalising on the second occasion;
6. being prepared for new tactics by players;
7. being firm and decisive, and making decisions quickly;
8. giving brief and concise explanations of decisions;
9. avoiding debating decisions with captains, other players, coaches and spectators;
10. involving the captains positively to help manage the game or competition where applicable; and
11. using signals, advantages and sanctions as per the laws/rules of the sport and the competition.[21]

Technical officials should apply the coaching effectiveness concepts for technical officiating. Integrated knowledge is required for role-related competencies, i.e., professional knowledge (specialised knowledge to officiate); interpersonal knowledge (connection with the participants considering different ages and competitive levels to relate differently in the specific social context); and intrapersonal knowledge (openness to continued learning and self-reflection for clarity). The 4 Cs of athlete outcomes refer to the athlete's competence, confidence, connection and character, however a technical official can internalise these outcomes in performing their own duties to further develop their technical officiating capability.[22]

Further to the 4 Cs, the IRB (2002) focuses on the three Cs for technical officials, i.e., concentration, consistency and control. The technical official, even when relaxed, should be engaged throughout a game/competition, focussing on control, consistency and concentration. It is important not to be distracted by anyone disagreeing with a decision. Being consistent in decisions creates a positive environment for athletes, support staff and spectators, and sets the mood for the duration of the game/competition. Lastly, control is an integrated part of game/competition management. It is necessary to be firm but not authoritarian, and where necessary, to be cautious to ensure the safety of all participants through managing problems or vigorous athletes.

The technical officials can enhance their roles and responsibilities by demonstrating the following attributes:

1. Know the laws/rules of the game/sport.
2. Update knowledge regularly by attending courses, clinics, meetings, seminars and conferences.
3. Keep physically and mentally fit.
4. Concentrate.
5. Be consistent.
6. Control and manage appropriately.
7. Be firm, polite and keep calm.
8. Look and behave professionally as expected from a technical official.

15.5 RECRUITMENT, SELECTION AND PROMOTION OF TECHNICAL OFFICIALS

The recruitment of technical officials in sports depends on a person's interest and ability to become a technical official. There are no entry requirements for technical officials in sport, however a basic knowledge of the sport, game or event, as well as an understanding of the game or event, is an advantage. It is also beneficial if the person has played or participated in the sport. The decision to become a technical official rests on the choice of the individual to form part of the game, race or event in another capacity than that of an athlete. In all technical officiating roles, the person must enter a formal course to acquire the knowledge of basic skills to officiate, using principles of safety, equity and the laws or rules to ensure enjoyable competitions for all participants and spectators.

Practical activity in competitive situations allows apprentice referees, umpires, judges, scorers, timekeepers, touch-line judges and other technical officials to practice their techniques to become skilled. The laws or rules not only pertain to techniques, but also involve decision-making as a management skill. Planning is an important tool for an official to get the best results possible and to succeed on the playing field or in the competition arena.

Specifications and skills for those interested in officiating include the following:

1. Excellent knowledge of the latest rules or laws relevant to the competition regulations.
2. Continuous professional development of the sport.
3. Teamwork on and off the field, court, pitch or arena.
4. A good understanding of English, both verbal and written, as briefings are done in English for most sporting organisations.
5. Event fit, both physically and mentally.
6. Support for colleagues and participants.
7. Act with integrity and be trustworthy and impartial.
8. Have good people and communication skills, including good listening skills.

The various NSFs and ISFs have different principles for the selection of technical officials for local and global events:

1. Gender equity, using the International Olympic Committee (IOC) principles as a guideline.[23]
2. Continental representation/balance.
3. Participating member federation competing at the event.

Conditions before being nominated:

1. Adequate qualification.
2. Valid licence.
3. Availability for the duration of the event.
4. Responsibilities/skill set (having the correct qualification and experience).

When requested by an NSF or ISF, member federations can propose technical officials to officiate at national and world championships. The technical committee selects from a list of technical officials in consultation with the President and Technical Committee Chairperson for the final appointment. The NSF or ISF determines the number of technical officials to be selected based on the exact programme of the championships. Member federations that submit official technical nominations are advised of the appointment or non-appointment of their technical officials. The national or international federation reserves the right to appoint technical officials outside of those nominated from any member federation. The appointed technical officials and their respective member federations will be duly advised.

The national or international federation Technical Committee Chairperson, in conjunction with the Competition Director, assigns the selected/appointed technical officials to the specific categories or groups before the start of the competition.

For the Olympic Games, technical officials are selected six months before the Games start by the International Executive Board from the candidates submitted by the member federations, upon recommendation from the International Technical Committee.

Appointed technical officials may not be members of their national (Olympic) team.

Referees, umpires and judges from the same member federation/National Olympic Committee (NOC) must be selected to adjudicate in a different group.

Appointed technical officials who do not show up, without valid reason and notification to the International Secretariat and Technical Committee Chairperson, for the event may be excluded from selection to other events for a period decided upon by the international federation.

Technical official group allocations/assignments are made by the Competition Director, in cooperation with the national or international federation Technical Committee Chairperson, before the technical officials meeting. The objective is to achieve 50% female representation within each group of technical officials selected and appointed. Upon being advised of their appointment, selected technical officials must confirm their acceptance and participation. Technical officials must attend the event from the start to the end of the competition, including technical officials' meetings before and mid-competition.[24]

15.6 SELF-MANAGEMENT

Within the sporting environment, officiating is a varied yet exciting activity. Individuals striving to be technical officials will be successful when they demonstrate leadership skills and are flexible and adaptable. In addition, they need to accept constructive and often negative criticism, evaluate their performance (actions and decisions) and be able to assess others.

Personal requirements for technical officials include:

1. knowledge of the rules/laws of their preferred sport;
2. proficiency in their sport;
3. ability to manage themselves;
4. patience and dedication;
5. good communication skills;
6. good interpersonal and conflict resolution skills;
7. enthusiasm, confidence, dedication and discipline;
8. ability to encourage, inspire and motivate; and
9. professional presentation and pride in personal appearance.

It is important to note that experience as a competitor does not guarantee success as a technical official.

Learner Tip/Truths:

A useful tip regarding the concept under discussion is for technical officials to demonstrate leadership and be flexible and adaptable.

15.7 TIPS FOR TECHNICAL OFFICIATING

1. Officials must learn to manage their behaviour.
2. Good officials have integrity and the courage to do the right thing at the right time.
3. Officials do not get flustered or harassed.
4. Officials must be lifelong learners.
5. Officials must check themselves in the mirror or use video footage to help see how they look when officiating.
6. Officials must be their own most severe critic, writing down any errors immediately after officiating and finding solutions to correct mistakes.
7. Officiating is a practical 'doing' operation.

15.8 CONCLUSION

This chapter focused on the technical officiating of games and competitions, which is, without doubt, an integral part of managing sport; without technical officials, games and competitions could not proceed. The legal implications for technical officials are set out in the relevant policies, codes of conduct, and the appointed technical official's duty of care and accountability measures. Decision-making and leadership are fundamental aspects of implementing technical officiating, thus VAR is a valuable tool to ensure a suitable platform for competition and can improve decision-making. It is also beneficial to spectators who often criticise the decisions of technical officials.

Self-management is essential for technical officials, as this is the basis of evaluating and reflecting on one's performance and setting actions in motion to learn and grow through continuous professional development or lifelong learning.

Case Study: SAFA suspend referees and clubs for match-fixing[25]

The purpose of a case study is to learn as much as possible about an individual or group so that the information can be generalized to many others, where possible.

The South African Football Association (SAFA) Vhembe region in Limpopo has suspended referees, clubs and a match official after allegations of misconduct. The allegations include, amongst others, match-fixing, unethical conduct and soliciting bribery before and during games. The match officials are both from the LFA Leagues as well as the ABC Motsepe League in the province.

The clubs implicated are Tshikhwani Stone Breakers, Phylimak Football Club and Muchipisi Happy Fighters, which play within the SAFA Vhembe Leagues.

In a statement released by the regional secretary, SAFA Vhembe said they stand for integrity in football, for a Football Association that soccer-loving people can trust, and having clean competition is their greatest asset.

"Our football matches should not be decided on the gambling market, but on the football fields. It is for this reason that SAFA Vhembe has decided to tackle match-fixing, unethical conduct and/or any corrupt activity head-on, by imposing a zero-tolerance policy. "We have opted for a combined repressive and preventive approach consisting of a wide range of actions and measures," read the statement. We once more make an appeal to all our teams to report any sign of attempted match fixing and unethical conduct by our referees immediately and therefore, discourage any club official and referee from involving themselves in corrupt activities during our games."

Referees' shenanigans

Match-fixing shenanigans are rife in the ABC Motsepe League and other SAFA lower leagues, specifically in the Limpopo province.

In 2018, the owner of Ndengeza FC, Akani Siweya, was expelled from football after physically attacking a referee whom he accused of taking a bribe from an opposition club.

He was later reinstated but sold his status.

Last season, Phinnet City owner Makgaba Letsoalo stormed inside the pitch and ordered his players to leave the field in the middle of an ABC Motsepe League match.

Letsoalo had accused match referees of taking bribes as well.

SELF-ASSESSMENT

1. Identify all categories of technical officials and write a short description of each technical official.
2. Describe the legal duties of the various technical officials for maintaining a high standard of care, as well as risk and safety management strategies, including specific technical skills.
3. Technical officials have specific roles and responsibilities. Why is it necessary for technical officials to meet the legal and moral obligations of a sport and always adhere to a code of conduct?
4. Read the case study and describe the actions of SAFA towards the appointed technical officials and what you would have concluded regarding the sanctions.
5. What information is necessary for the organisational recruitment, selection, promotion and self-management of technical officials in various sports?

AGENTS AND AGENCY IN SPORT

Johan van Gaalen

> ## LEARNING OUTCOMES
>
> At the end of this chapter, you should be able to:
>
> 1. Explain the responsibilities and duties of sport agents.
> 2. Describe how the profession is regulated.
> 3. Debate the importance of regulating the profession.

16.1 INTRODUCTION

"*Show Me the Money!*" is a well-known saying from the hit movie *Jerry Maguire*, which is about an agent acting on behalf of his client, an American football player. The sport industry is all about money, and the various role players or stakeholders are in competition to access it.

The regulation of sports agents and agencies varies across different sporting codes and countries. While there are many similarities in agents' regulations across the various sporting codes, some key differences are unique to each sport. There is further a place and purpose for agents in all sports. Agents can be vital stakeholders in sporting codes if they are recognised in the sport and the relationship between the agent and clients is appropriately regulated.

Depending on the industry, the conduct of certain people in the industry acting as sport agents and the nature of a sport agent, sports agents can sometimes be referred to as "the opportunists" in sports. However, if sport agents are correctly regulated and creatively business-minded, they can be the kingmakers of sport. Just as an entertainer needs a talent manager to strengthen their possibility of success, athletes need an agent to help them grow and earn the most out of their sporting career.

This chapter will summarise what a sport agent is, what the role of a sport agent entails, and the sport agent's role in making a specific sporting code a thriving industry.

16.2 AGENCY AND SPORT AGENTS

The fundamental principles for being an agent are representation and mandate; without a mandate, agents cannot act on behalf of someone or represent them.

16.2.1 Agency: The Principal and Agent Relationship

An agency relationship is a relationship where one person appoints someone else to carry out duties for them. It is a relationship based on trust and therefore a relationship of a fiduciary nature.

Agency is a relationship whereby one party expressly or impliedly authorises another to act under his or her control and on his or her behalf. The parties to this type of relationship are known as the "principal" and the "agent". The principal and agent theory emerged in the 1970s from the combined disciplines of economics and institutional theory. There is some contention as to who originated the theory, with theorists Stephen Ross and Barry Mitnick both claiming authorship.

The law of agency in South Africa regulates the performance of an act on behalf or in the name of one person ("the principal"), e.g., an athlete/client, by another ("the agent"), whom the principal authorises to act. This mandate given by the athlete/client to the sports agent to work on their behalf provides the sports agent with the authority to establish a legal tie between the athlete/client and a third party (e.g., a sponsor, club etc.), which creates, alters or discharges legal relations between the athlete/client and a third party. In other words, if the athlete gives the sports agent a mandate to act on their behalf, the sports agent may bind the athlete to third parties.

The principal is the person or entity who gives the authority to another person or entity to act on his/her/its behalf. Therefore, the agent is the one who acts for and represents the principal – the person or entity being authorised/instructed by the principal. In other words, the agent steps into the shoes of the principal, represents them and acts for and instead of them in matters so authorised.

For example, an agent may not, without the consent/authorisation of their principal, use information acquired through the principal/agent relationship to make a secret profit. More obviously, an agent may not benefit from breaching their duties to their principal. This agency relationship is guided by a specific mandate.

16.2.2 What is a Sport Agent and What Do They Do?

A sport agent is a person who searches for talented athletes and who manages and assists the athlete to achieve the most from their playing career. The role of sports agents is different from that of coaches or scouts; sport agents can represent sporting institutions, sport clubs and athletes. Sports agents play a specific role in contract negotiations and sponsorship/endorsement deals, and must be cautious not to act on behalf of two or more parties in contractual negotiations because it may result in a conflict of interest. Sport agents were once predominantly men, however there are now more women working as sport agents due to the increasing number of women playing professional sport and the great focus on equality in sport.

Although sport agents are mainly associated with professional sporting codes (due to the financial interest and benefits), some sport agents assist amateur athletes in the hope that their clients will become professional.

Sport agents can be natural persons or a group operating outside a legal entity, however some sporting codes allow only natural persons to register as agents as they have to obtain the necessary agent licence for that particular sporting code.

16.2.3 Characteristics of a Sport Agent

The ideal person for this type of profession is a person who is passionate about sport, has excellent communication skills, and is a social person who enjoys working with people and creating opportunities to maximise their client's potential. A sport agent must have a great work ethic and plenty of patience. On top of that, sport agents need to be confident, have an assertive personality and have excellent negotiation skills to secure good deals. A sport agent must also understand the industry and know what is best for their client, for example playing for a lower division team rather than not playing at all, or getting a small endorsement deal rather than none.

The good thing about becoming a sport agent is that you do not have to have played organised amateur or professional sport. Likewise, a sport agent can become a sport agent without any athletic skills. Despite this, it may be to their advantage if they have some experience playing organised sport and an understanding of how the sporting world operates, the industry operations and the politics behind the scenes. This personal experience of a sport will give the sport agent a sense of what athletes go through to achieve the highest sport accolades, e.g., the tennis agent who used to be a tennis player understands which tournaments you need to play to obtain better rankings points in order to be accepted for the bigger tournaments. With this knowledge of the game, such an agent's client will receive better advice and inside knowledge of how to achieve the highest accolades in the sport.

An athlete's career gets placed in the hands of sport agents, thus sport agents must be creative with high professionalism. In addition, sport agents must understand how to form relationships that are established on honesty and trust.

Sport agents must enjoy travelling and be prepared to travel a lot, as they will have to meet with athletes all over the country or the world to recruit them. Although modern communication technology makes communicating with athletes or potential clients easier, the sport agent must travel to build the relationship. The value of physical meetings has been undermined since Covid-19, however working from anywhere has become possible.

Long work hours are synonymous with sport agents, and their time is never their own; it is always the athlete's time. Working as a sport agent is a highly fulfilling career. Most sport agents enter the industry because they have a true passion for everything related to a sport. Like any profession, the output will be a direct result of the input, therefore to be successful, a sport agent needs to work hard. After concluding a deal for a client after months of negotiations, the sport agent will receive compensation, making their effort worthwhile.

Trust can be regarded as the most fundamental characteristic and element of a sport agency to guarantee success. Trust is necessary for building strong cohesion between the athlete and sport agent in order for the relationship to reach its full potential. Without trust there will not be a quality relationship. Trust will result in loyalty, each party knowing their roles and responsibilities, proper communication, confidence and a relationship with great rewards for both the athlete and the sports agent. The following elements and core principles will contribute to a healthy and successful sport agent and athlete relationship:

1. Trust
2. Competence
3. Loyalty
4. Ethics
5. Communication

Sport agents with the characteristics stipulated above will be regarded as a competent sport agent, who will be able to successfully look after his/her client in order for the relationship to work for both parties.

16.2.4 Essential Skills for Sport Agents

Sport agents must wear many hats; their job does not finish after the signing of a contract and the athlete taking the field. Sport agents must advocate for their clients in many facets of everyday life. The most successful sport agents work endlessly to ensure the health and safety of their athletes. A successful sports agent will possess incredible negotiation skills and an in-depth understanding of every line of a standard contract. Not only does this mean sport agents must get an education in contract negotiation and similar topics, but they must also develop and learn contractual negotiating skills for the contract negotiation process.

Another critical skill for successful sport agents is a deep understanding of their athletes' sport. For example, a sports agent for a professional football (soccer) player must understand things about the average player, such as:

1. If employed, do you need to be registered?
2. Are you employed if not registered?
3. The exact remuneration for the duration of the contract.
4. When will the remuneration be payable?
5. The rules and regulations of the industry.
6. What is the professional league?
7. Are there any rules and regulations to which the player and the sports agent are subject?
8. How long does the average career last?
9. Common injuries that might occur.
10. How does player insurance work?
11. How can a player's contract help when the player is forced to retire early or take a break from competitive play, or becomes injured during the scope of employment?

The difference between a good sport agent and an exceptional sport agent is a person:

1. who knows the sport inside and out;
2. who is a lawyer or someone who surrounds themself with qualified lawyers who understand the profession;
3. with some formal education;
4. with experience in the sport;
5. who always seeks new opportunities;
6. who is capable of mediating any dispute;
7. with exceptional negotiating skills;
8. with dedication;
9. with critical thinking skills;
10. with persistence;
11. who listens; and
12. who is an organised communicator.

Sport agents must present their athletes positively to potential sponsors and the public. Some sport agents work just as hard on public relations for their clients as they do in contract negotiations. After all, some of the most impressive earnings for a professional athlete may come from the partnerships the athlete has with sponsors and advertisers.

16.2.5 Qualifications of Sport Agents

There are no formal qualifications for a sport agent, however obtaining some commercial and legal qualifications may be advisable so that the agent can provide the best possible advice to the athlete. The core of the sports agent's business relates to contract law; the better their knowledge of contracts, the better they can negotiate on behalf of their client and ensure that both parties are adequately protected.

Some sport agents pursue professional degrees or advanced degrees in targeted areas like law, business and sport management. For some sport agents, knowledge and applying the law are vital skills they can build. In addition, a law degree can offer exceptional benefits during contract negotiations and other legal wranglings in sport.

Similarly, business skills may help a sport agent to assist their client reach the pinnacle of the sport world with sponsorships worth millions of dollars. It is relatively rare for sport agents to enter the profession without the benefit of some formal training. That training may come in the form of an internship or obtaining some formal kind of qualification, such as:

1. a certificate and/or diploma in contract negotiations;
2. legal courses and/or a legal degree, with the law of contracts and/or employment law being part of the course or degree;
3. a sport management course; and/or
4. a certificate and/or diploma in business law and management.

In order to become a registered agent for a specific sporting code, the sporting code may require the person to complete certain internal examinations or have a minimum qualification.

Formal training in these areas can help sport agents master every facet of the average sports agent's responsibilities and give them an edge over other sports agents.

16.2.6 Duties and Responsibilities of Sport Agents

The primary responsibilities of sport agents may include any or all of the following:

1. Negotiating contracts, bonuses and salaries.
2. Promoting athletes to potential sponsors.
3. Understanding the nuances and details of their athlete's sport.
4. Creating a professional network for their athlete.
5. Accumulating data on their athlete's professional career.
6. Setting up and conducting promotions on their athlete's behalf.
7. Maintaining their athlete's financial wealth.
8. Public relations.
9. Giving the athlete legal advice.
10. Negotiating on behalf of a client with teams or sponsors.
11. Communicating with coaches and other professionals.
12. Organising training.
13. Building the athlete's brand.

The essential duties of sport agents are related to acting according to, and not exceeding, the express or implied authority given by the athlete, while using all proper skills and care to avoid conflicts of interest.

16.2.7 Regulating Sport Agents

Whether sport agents require a licence to trade in a specific sporting code will depend on that code. No standardised, worldwide or nationwide licencing organisation exists for sport agents, however some requirements exist for agents who work in certain sporting codes or have clients who play for specific sport organisations.

Regulations for sport agents are designed to protect the interests of athletes and the stakeholders in the sport, as well as to ensure that agents act professionally and ethically. Regulating agents in a sporting code ensures that specific standards are set and that the flow of money stays within the code. While there are differences in the regulations across sport, the core principles of licencing, code of conduct and regulation of player transfers are present in most sport.

The Fédération Internationale de Football Association (FIFA) made the crucial mistake of de-regulating football agents in 2014 when it excluded agents from its regulations and passed down the power of regulating agents in football to its member associations. The result was that football agents were not adequately regulated and abused the system to the detriment of their clients. As a result, the players and FIFA lost control and power over the activities of agents, which led to more illegal activities in the sport of football. Therefore, when FIFA introduced the new FIFA Football Agents Regulations[1] in 2023, it aimed to clean up the "Wild West", get control back over the agents in its jurisdiction, and protect all stakeholders in the sport against the illegal and corrupt activities of persons acting as football agents.

As regulating sport agents in a sporting code protects the stakeholders and ensures the sporting code maintains a good reputation, it also results in greater interest from third parties in the sport and more financial assistance and support from commercially interested parties.

Regulating entails setting specific standards and providing rules regarding how agents must operate in the sporting code. The regulations stipulate the requirements for agents to obtain licences or certifications, which may involve passing background checks, demonstrating knowledge of the sport, and meeting education or experience requirements. Part of regulating agents is that the sporting code will require sport agents to carry professional liability insurance and pay annual fees to maintain their licences or certifications.

In addition to sport agents' rules, regulations and licencing requirements, sporting codes often establish codes of conduct to which its licenced agents must adhere. These codes of conduct outline the agent's responsibilities to their clients, the teams they represent and the sport.

Overall, regulating sport agents is essential for maintaining integrity and protecting the interests of the athletes and other stakeholders. By establishing clear rules and regulations and enforcing them effectively, the sporting codes can ensure that agents in the sporting code act professionally and ethically and that the athletes they represent receive the best possible representation and guidance.

It is important to note that even in a sport where there is no specific regulatory body for agents, there may still be legal principles, laws and regulations in place that indirectly govern the activities and relationships of sport agents.

The regulation of sport agents in a few South African sporting codes will be discussed in the following paragraphs.

16.2.7.1 *Football/Soccer*

Sport agents who want to represent players in football must be accredited and licenced by FIFA for international matters and accredited and licenced for South African-related issues by the South African Football Association (SAFA). Regarding the FIFA Football Regulations, only natural persons can register as football agents. Each member association, e.g., SAFA, must implement the new agent regulations by 30 September 2023. Furthermore, as of 2023, all football agents must adhere to a strict code of conduct.

In terms of the FIFA Football Regulations,[2] those registered as a football agent are entitled to render football-related services on behalf of a client, including any negotiation, communication relating or preparatory to the same, or other related activity with the purpose, objective and intention of concluding a transaction.

Before rendering any football-related services, a football agent must have a written representation agreement with their client.

The football agent representation agreement's minimum requirements are that it must be in writing; it must include the names of the parties; it can only be for a maximum of two years; it must include the fee due to the agent; it must stipulate the services to be provided; and it must be signed.

There are no period restrictions if an agreement is concluded with clubs, associations or a single-entity league, however. The term of the representation agreement with a player may be extended by completing a new representation agreement. Any automatic renewal clause in a representation agreement, or any other provision that purports to extend any term beyond the two years or the agreed period (for a representation agreement with players), will be null and void.

Under the FIFA Football Regulations, agents must disclose any conflicts of interest to their clients and obtain written consent from their clients before taking any action on their behalf. For example, when an agent acts on behalf of a player and the football club where the player plays or did play, they must obtain written consent from both stakeholders. In addition, the agent must disclose whether they are acting on behalf of both parties. FIFA-licenced agents are also subject to transfer regulations that limit the commission (the service cap) they can earn on player transfers.

16.2.7.2 Basketball

In basketball, the regulatory body for agents is the International Basketball Federation (FIBA). Basketball South Africa (BSA) is the governing body for men's and women's basketball in South Africa and is responsible for the administration of the South African national basketball teams. BSA is an affiliate of FIBA Africa.

Basketball agents are also strictly regulated; like FIFA, FIBA requires agents to be licenced and registered. A person must complete an interview and written test to be granted a FIBA agent's licence. In addition, FIBA agents are required to complete an ethics course and pay annual fees. To become a FIBA agent, the person must have a formal qualification in the sport, e.g., a degree. However, there are exceptions for former players with some experience in the NBA.

Once certified, agents must abide by a strict code of conduct that governs their interactions with players and teams. For example, agents are prohibited from offering or accepting compensation from players or their families before the player signs a contract. They are also prohibited from making any false or misleading statements or engaging in any conduct that could be seen as harmful to the interests of their clients.

As with football agents under the FIFA Football Regulations, FIBA agents must disclose any conflicts of interest to their clients and obtain written consent before acting. This includes negotiating contracts, endorsing products or services, and arranging for appearances or other opportunities.

The objectives of regulating basketball agents are to protect players' interests and ensure that the game remains fair and transparent.

16.2.7.3 Tennis

In tennis, agents are not regulated on either the national or international level. A tennis agent preliminarily procures and negotiates endorsement contracts for the tennis player. Entry to any tournament mostly depends on the player's rankings and performance, therefore the tennis agent is limited to more specific sponsorship and endorsement contract negotiations.

16.2.7.4 Rugby

In rugby, the respective countries' rugby unions (e.g., the South African Rugby Union - SARU) are responsible for authorising, licencing and regulating agents acting on behalf of their members (or persons within their jurisdictions).

The difficulty with this regulations model is in respect of international disputes; which rugby union has the jurisdiction to deal with the dispute and how would any sanction be imposed and enforced?

World Rugby only sets out guidelines and minimum standards for regulations for agents, which need to be implemented by rugby unions on national levels. Save for rugby unions' obligations to include the minimum requirements in their agents' regulations, unions are free to regulate the licenced agents within their jurisdictions in any manner they see fit.

Regarding South African rugby players' agent regulations, a player themself, an immediate family member of the player and employees of the South African Rugby Players Association (SARPA) are exempt from registering as a rugby player agent. It is expressly stipulated that legal practitioners, without being registered rugby agents, may provide advice, counselling or assistance to players concerning the interpretation or application of a player's contract or any other related agreements. Rugby agents must be natural persons.

In rugby, an agent means an agent or adviser acting on behalf of a person, union, rugby body or club about that person's, union's, rugby body's or club's activity in the game of rugby, limited to the jurisdiction of such rugby union's country.[3]

To obtain a South African agent's licence, agents must meet various requirements, complete an examination and pay an annual fee. Rugby agents are also obliged to attend workshops and complete online tests annually.

The rugby agent representation agreement's minimum requirements are that:

1. it must be in writing;
2. the duration may not be for a period of more than two years;
3. it may not automatically be renewable or extendable for a further period;
4. it must stipulate who is responsible for paying the agent, how much and when;
5. the names of the parties to the agreement must be included;
6. there must be dates and signatures on the agreement; and
7. the date of commencement of the agreement must be included.

Any party may terminate the representation agreement by giving four months' notice. During this notice period, the player may not be represented by any other agent. If an agent's licence is cancelled, any representation agreement becomes null and void.

16.2.7.5 Cycling

A rider's agent is regarded as a powerbroker who is very influential. They are the person who dictates for whom the rider may ride and where they may ride for the team, and has therefore an essential role in the career of a professional cyclist and in how much a rider will get paid.

The International Cycling Union (UCI) is the main regulatory body overseeing agents' work in cycling. For legal representatives or riders' relatives, all natural persons who want to represent a rider from a team in the first or second division (UCI World Team or UCI ProTeam) must obtain a rider's agent's licence from their National Federation.[4] The National Federation, i.e., the representing authority for cycling in a specific country, is a member of the UCI, however National Federations may set further rules and regulations for rider agents.

A rider agent is responsible for negotiating a contract on behalf of the rider, ensuring the rider gets a top team and ensuring all insurance is in place.

One of the primary requirements for rider agents is that the UCI must licence them. To obtain a licence, rider agents must meet various requirements, including passing a background check, providing evidence of insurance coverage and paying an annual fee. They must also have a certain level of education or experience in cycling.

Once licenced, riders' agents must follow the strict code of conduct set out by the UCI. This code of conduct outlines a rider's agent's responsibilities to their client, the team they represent and the sport.

16.3 CONCLUSION

The regulation of sport agents varies across different sporting codes and countries. While there are many similarities in the rules across sport, there are also some key differences. Some of these differences are apparent in individual sport compared to team sport.

Sport agents are expected to operate within the rules and regulations designed to protect athletes' interests. By adhering to strict standards of conduct and ethical behaviour, agents can help their clients succeed both on and off the field, while also upholding the integrity of the sport.

An agent needs more than talent to build a sterling career. Star athletes need star agents behind them to act as promoters, negotiators, counsellors, friends and advisors. A sport agent is there to build the athlete's brand, i.e., a sport agent is a brand manager.

A sport agent career is fascinating, challenging, fast-paced, high-pressure and immensely rewarding. Although sports agents have been active in the sporting field since the late 1800s, the sport agents' activities and profession have grown in prominence in more recent years. Due to the significant role sport agents now play in the economics of sports, they need to be strictly regulated. For this reason, the athlete and the sport agent contribute significantly to sport's societal impact and economic value.

SELF-ASSESSMENT

1. Explain the agency relationship with specific reference to the terms "principal" and "agent".
2. Explain the responsibilities and duties of sports agents.
3. Describe how the profession is regulated.
4. Debate the importance of regulating the profession.

LEADERSHIP IN SPORT

Professor Jacques Faul

> ## LEARNING OUTCOMES
>
> At the end of this chapter, you should be able to:
>
> 1. Describe the sports leadership framework in South Africa.
> 2. Identify leadership styles and comprehend leadership theories.
> 3. Explain the concepts of ethical and toxic leadership.
> 4. Identify and map stakeholders in sport.
> 5. Discuss racial information in sport.
> 6. Debate crisis management in sport.
> 7. Discuss the difference between crisis and brand management.

17.1 INTRODUCTION

Every industry requires good leaders, and sport is no different. Good leaders provide direction and inspire, but most of all, leadership is about action rather than position. Sport leadership is in the public domain as it is visible to all, and leaders' actions are scrutinised more than in other industries. This is because sport is seen as 'owned' by the public as supporters follow their famous brands (teams). The analogy of a man on a stage with his every move being watched by the crowd is a fair comparison. However, in sport, the leaders on an administrative and governance level are only some of the actors. The players and athletes are the true actors, on and off the field. It is common for the CEOs of sport organisations to not be the highest-paid employee. This honour is reserved for those players with exceptional sport talent who are the stars entertaining the spectators. This is an indication of the quiet but important role that needs to be played by sport leaders in governance and administration, as the limelight belongs to the athletes.

The CEO's leadership is like the roles related to team captaincy and coaching, which the public closely follows. This is also valid for the CEOs of the National Sport Federations (NSFs) of prominent sporting codes and even large sport clubs. There is an understanding that a good sport leader on an administrative level is like a referee in sport; you should not notice them while they are working, but they are an integral part of the game. Understanding the leadership framework in sport and the related principles for implementation is essential. Further to this are the duties and responsibilities of sport leaders.

17.2 LEADERSHIP POSITIONS/STRUCTURES IN SPORT

Leadership positions, roles and responsibilities in sport vary from the Minister of Sport to leaders of NSFs to the captains of school sport teams. There are thus many layers of leadership positions within sport, which are political and strategic within the government, NSFs, provincial sport structures and sport clubs.

17.2.1 Political Leadership in Sport

Parliament's leadership influence is via the Minister of the Department of Arts, Sport and Culture, as regulated by the Sports Act;[1] they are essential for setting policy and implementing it. The implementation of government leadership is often criticised as it is argued that they do not deliver on sport infrastructure to support transformation in sport (see Chapter 27), as was set out in the White Paper on Sport and Recreation.

Another significant sport body is the South African Sport Confederation and Olympic Committee (SASCOC), which oversees the management of elite sport in South Africa. The duties of this body are to be an overarching umbrella body for all affiliated NSFs.[2] SASCOC has been criticised for its leadership role, especially involving planning for the performance of athletes at the Olympics, for supporting athletes to compete at the highest levels, and for winning medals at the Olympic Games and other international competitions. The President of SASCOC and the elected SASCOC board play a significant role as leaders in the South African sporting landscape to provide and support joint initiatives with NSFs towards the excellence of South African sport teams and individual athletes.

17.2.2 Leadership in National Sport Federations (NSFs)

Some NSFs have boards and other management committees that oversee the leadership role of sport organisations. These bodies usually manage domestic and international competitions, matches and recreational games. Leaders on the management committees of NSFs are elected from the provincial sport or club structures, whilst national CEOs and staff are appointed. Not all national bodies have many employees in their administrative offices, however larger NSFs that manage rugby, cricket and soccer in South Africa, do. These leadership positions receive media, and thus public, attention.

17.2.3 Provincial and Club Leadership

Provincial sport organisations have boards and administrative managers who sometimes manage these organisations' recreational and professional sport divisions. This may also extend to working at a sport facility that manages these facilities on behalf of municipalities and/or facility owners.

17.2.4 Leadership in Other Sporting Structures

Educational institutions such as schools and universities are essential within the sporting pipeline, as they develop young, talented athletes. This requires dedicated management regarding talent identification, development of this talent, academic and scientific support, provisioning of sport facilities and equipment, and administering all activities.

Sport is critical to some schools and most universities as they tend to utilise it as a marketing tool. They thus invest in dedicated sport staff, including administrative and managerial support for sport programmes.

17.2.5 Team and Athlete Leadership

As might be expected, different leadership roles are evident in sport teams. These include team managers who oversee all aspects of a team, such as managing kit, transport, food and medical support. The leadership roles of coaches and captains are different in that coaches oversee all aspects related to team or individual coaching, such as individual athlete and team skills, physical conditioning, motivation and others. The team captain takes on the position of leading individuals or team members on and off the playing field. Finally, individual athletes are responsible for leading themselves regarding discipline, motivation, conduct and others.

17.3 LEADERSHIP POWER AND STYLES

Power is seen as the ability to influence the actions of others, while leadership is seen as the process of influencing others. Two sources of power exist in sport organisations: the positions in organisations and the individuals holding those positions. For example, the positions of president of an NSF, head coach and team manager have vested powers that are guided and positioned within the structures and policies of the organisation. Similarly, the people in these positions have certain powers that are inherent as capabilities such as knowledge, skills and attitudes. Utilising both these sources of power enables managers in sport to provide leadership. Approaches towards providing leadership are referred to as leadership styles. Leaders have unique leadership styles that culminate from a combination of their positions and personal traits.

17.3.1 Leadership Power

Leaders in sport are, by their position, influential people. Hellriegel et al.[3] noted that leadership is the ability to influence others and power is the possibility to lead. There are five power types: legitimate, reward, coercive, referent and expert power.

Legitimate power is the power that is vested within positions in organisations. Positions such as the CEO of Cricket South Africa (CSA) or Director of Sport at the University of Pretoria (UP) have power and require the incumbent to utilise that power to obtain agreed-upon objectives in the organisation.

Reward power is where leaders use a reward system to obtain organisational objectives. Examples are that coaches and athletes of national teams are rewarded for winning major competitions. Examples include the Banyana soccer team receiving money for winning the 2022 Women's Africa Cup of Nations competition and the national men's soccer team (Bafana Bafana) being motivated with remuneration if they qualify for the FIFA Football World Cup. Rewards could also be in the form of promotions to individuals, such as a coach being promoted to head coach from being assistant coach.

Coercive power is the form of power where people's compliance is negotiated through fear and punishment, for example, SASCOC only recognises an NSF if it complies with specific governance and other requirements. Another is that when an NSF does not comply with transformational targets, the Minister of Sport, Arts and Culture could suspend the board or management committee, or withdraw their recognition as a South African NSF.

Referent power is based on followers' respect and personal identification with their leader. Followers acknowledge referent power and perceive the leader as trustworthy, informed and knowledgeable. One of the best examples was the leadership of Nelson Mandela, former President of South Africa, who was a humble and respected leader with referent power.

Expert power is when leaders have specialised knowledge and are known for this. In sport, some coaches are known for being experts in coaching. One such coach was Kitch Christie, coach of the 1995 Rugby World Cup-winning Springbok team.

Where power is seen as the ability to influence the actions of others, leadership can be explained as the way in which leaders utilise power to influence others. This could be done in various ways.

17.3.2 Leadership Styles

Kurt Lewin, a psychologist (1939), categorised three main leadership styles, namely the authoritarian/autocratic or dictating style, the democratic or participative style, and the laissez-faire or delegation style.

The **authoritarian/autocratic or dictating** leadership style is where leaders utilise power to tell subordinates what is required from them and the way to obtain objectives. There is no room for subordinates to take initiative and/or devise different solutions to obtain these objectives. For example, a coach who tells players of a team exactly what they should do on the sport field, without letting them take any initiative during matches, is an authoritarian who wants to dictate how players should always play.

Democratic or participative leaders let everyone participate in planning and decision-making to come to a joint solution to obtain objectives. We do not have many examples in sport related to this, however someone like the Blue Bulls Rugby President, Willem Straus, seems to include many stakeholders in his leadership. The same can be said of the former SA Cricket President, Joseph Pamensky, who involved a broad spectrum of people when devising strategic solutions to challenges.

The **laissez-faire or delegating** leadership style is where leaders refrain from interfering with processes and procedures to obtain organisational objectives. Sometimes organisations are highly effective because of a delegating leadership style, while others need more guidance. The laissez-faire leadership style would, in its most extreme form, make it seem that the leader is not interested in how objectives are obtained or whether objectives are obtained at all.

There are arguments and motivations for all three styles. The autocratic style allows for swift decision-making, which is helpful in a crisis; the democratic style has apparent advantages as it allows for input from everyone; while the delegation style works well with experienced, mature followers.

17.4 LEADERSHIP THEORIES

It is of value to have at least a basic understanding of leadership theories to help understand the different approaches to leadership and identify the advantages and disadvantages of these theories. Three main categories of leadership theories and styles are described by Demirtas and Karaca:[4] the trait theory, the behavioural leadership theory and situational leadership theories. The trait theory recognises the importance of personal characteristics in leadership; it argues that leaders are born and not 'made'. It further claims that these leaders have exceptional talent to lead.

The behavioural leadership theory mainly describes the behaviour of leaders to provide a framework, which serves as a guideline to understand leadership from a behavioural perspective. This can be utilised as a guideline for required behaviour in leadership situations.

The situational leadership theory presupposes that leaders lead within the requirement of situations. In other words, different situations require different leadership styles. In one situation, the leader is expected to be autocratic, while in another, to be democratic. This theory, therefore, supports multiple styles of leadership.

Every leader has a unique leadership style with positive and negative characteristics, thus understanding your own style and possible shortcomings will help you evolve and grow by indicating growth and leadership development areas. None of the great leaders in the world, including sport leaders, started off being great. They may have had early leadership roles, but they improved their leadership skills over the years.

The following summarises the mainstream leadership theories:[5]

Ohio	Behavioural leadership theories suggest that specific behaviours differentiate leaders from non-leaders. Hellriegel et al. note that Ohio State University asked employees to describe the behaviours of their supervisors, leading to the identification of two leadership styles: 1. Considering leadership (concern for employees' well-being) 2. Initiating leadership (planning, controlling, coordinating)
Great man theory	Great people are influential leaders and leadership is generic
Trait theory	Leaders have traits that make them effective
Behavioural approach	Leadership can be learned, thus the effectiveness of leaders depends on their learned behaviour
Hersey Blanchard's model	The leadership style depends on the maturity of the followers; the more mature the followers, the more they will appreciate and value the leadership of leaders

Fiedler's theory	This relates to the leader/follower relationship; it varies from a good relationship when tasks are planned and structured with high leadership power, to a moderate to bad relationship between the leader and follower
Path-Goal theory	Different approaches of leadership should be utilised, depending on the certainty, complexity level and stressfulness of tasks
Iowa	A democratic leader is the most effective in the long run
Michigan	Employee-orientated leadership style is the most effective
Blake Mouton	Team leadership with consideration for results and people is the most effective

Source: Uslo[6]

All theories refer in some way or another to a leader and their followers and their relationship to the task or results. A different focus is required taking into account the maturity of the followers or the prevailing circumstances. Sport leaders such as Dr Ali Bacher, Dr Danie Craven, Patrice Motsepe and Dr Irwin Khosa are hailed as great sport leaders who have different leadership styles. Sport leaders embrace a leadership theory and style based on their behaviour and characteristics, or a learned method, because they believe it is the most effective. Knowledge and awareness of their views make it possible to categorise sports leaders. It is also true that, in many instances, sports leaders need to analyse their own styles and approaches.

17.5 EFFECTIVE SPORT LEADERSHIP

Hollander[7] noted that sport leaders require leadership attributes, including a good and strong character and the will and commitment to be a sport leader. In addition, personal aspects such as being self-driven, disciplined and a person with a vision make for a good sport leader. Joe Pamensky, the previous chairperson of SA Cricket and a Cricket South Africa honorary life member, famously said that sport leaders are temporary custodians of the game and must be servants of sport.

Hollander also noted that leadership competencies include leading people, being result-driven and building effective coalitions.[8] South African sport leaders must understand South African sport's divided history and racial transformation, which requires balancing multiple goals, from development to winning on the field, to uniting people. This requires an astute sport politician, as sport provides an opportunity to transform and unite people.

There needs to be a clear understanding for a leader of the boundaries between oversight and overreach. In essence, the abuse of power or undue influence is counterproductive to finding amicable solutions to managerial challenges. Sport leaders require moral fibre and a 'north star' that requires them to always act in the game's best interest.

17.5.1 Toxic Leadership

Robbins et al. stated that toxic leadership is a pattern of repeated, deliberate, destructive behaviour and mistreatment of subordinates. Being exposed to this type of leadership influences the victim's health and productivity, creating a fearful environment where attaining constructive goals is sometimes impossible. It is tough to deal with this as the leader intimidates their subordinates, and subordinates fear repercussions. In contrast, non-performers may sometimes lay claims against toxic leadership as a survival strategy.

An *Indian Express*[9] news article published on 6 March 2023 reported that: *ICC (International Cricket Council) CEO Manu Sawhney resigns amid inquiry over conduct.* It is alleged that Sawhney's "authoritarian style of functioning" was far removed from the inclusive approach of the previous CEO, which had not gone down well with the employees. The article further suggested that he had an abrasive attitude towards his colleagues. These allegations were taken so seriously that the ICC investigated his behaviour. Similar claims were made against a high-ranking official of Cricket South Africa (CSA) involving the unfair dismissal of Clive Eksteen in 2020.

Leaders, including sport leaders, are influential, thus processes must be established to track and address bad behaviour. Anonymous staff questionnaires are of great value in identifying such behaviour against staff, while mentorship programmes for young leaders can educate and make them aware of challenges related to toxic leadership. Everyone must buy into a code of conduct based on respect and understanding, including the leaders of sporting organisations.

17.5.2 Ethical Leadership

The essential characteristic of any sport leader is that they are ethical. This is a crucial requirement that will set the tone for the rest of the organisation.

17.5.2.1 Ethics and morality

Two recent definitions of ethical leadership include the following by Javed:[10] *"The leadership that ensures that leaders act by rules and that depicts confidence in their attitude and advocates honesty and serves as a source of knowledge for their followers"*, and this by Ko, Ma, Bartnik, Haney and Kang:[11] *"The leader whose attitude is ethical and reliable is a source of motivation for his followers."*

Ethical leadership is essential for any sport organisation as it will lead to an ethical culture. The tone at the top sets the mood for the entire organisation, however unfortunately there have been many examples of unethical behaviour by sport leaders. These include the use of drugs, bribery of referees and umpires, intimidation and violence amongst players on and off the field, spot match fixing and gambling, and non-compliance to media rights and sponsorships.

17.5.3 Stakeholder Management

Brenner[12] defined stakeholders as those who: *"are or which could impact or be impacted by the firm/organisation"*, while Donaldson and Preston defined them as, *"persons or groups with legitimate interests in procedural and substantive aspects of corporate activity"*. Sport has many diverse stakeholders, including players, coaches, officials, sponsors and clubs. Stakeholders who are not directly related to the organisation include the media, fans, government and local authorities. Stakeholders could even include lobbying groups and political parties, depending on the circumstances.

The process of understanding the roles and positions of stakeholders in organisations is known as mapping the power interest grid of organisations. Sport leaders must understand and manage their stakeholders effectively with the golden key, i.e., the early and frequent engagement of critical stakeholders.

Stakeholders must first be categorised according to their level of power and interest according to one of four main categories: high interest, regular engagement, keep informed and low priority.

Key stakeholders have a **high interest** in an organisation and have significant power. The primary sponsor of a sport organisation is a good example. The main sponsors of the Springbok and Protea teams, Standard Bank and MTN respectively, are good examples, as they are primary sponsors that contribute a vast amount of money to the respective NSFs and require ethical conduct, transformation and other aspects from their sponsorships. These stakeholders must be engaged regularly and before the sport organisation makes any strategic decisions that could impact sponsorship agreements.

Stakeholders that require **regular engagement** need to be engaged well in advance of any decisions that could impact possible legislation and other changes. City and local authorities will likely fall into these categories as they serve a larger constituency than the sport organisations, and changes could impact the larger community.

Keep informed stakeholders need to be informed about changes in the policy and direction of sport organisations. Clubs and supporters of sport organisations could be considered 'keep informed stakeholders' of NSFs. Although they do not directly influence the strategic direction of the professional component of NSFs, these stakeholders need to be informed as decisions could impact them to a certain extent.

Low priority stakeholders normally have relatively low power and interest in the strategic direction and operational aspects of sport organisations such as NSFs. These may include charities related to the NSF.

17.5.4 Transformation

South Africa has a sad, divided past, which includes the history of our sport, thus all NSFs are required to implement and track transformation on all levels. This is a complex task and sport leaders must do so with sincerity and act responsibly. This may be very challenging to some, however true leaders will unite racial groups and strive towards creating opportunities for all. If transformation is done correctly, it does not have to compromise excellence; the South African Rugby Union (SARU) has proven that there is talent across all the racial groups. A strong pipeline of athletes, technical officials and administrators that creates opportunities for all is vital for transformation to be successful. Transformation is not the end goal, but the normalisation of society is. This is a point where the demographics of South Africa (race, gender, ability) are reflected in all structures on merit.

17.5.5 Event and Facilities Management

Sports leaders usually oversee a sporting event – a match or race showcasing the players or athletes. Getz[13] defined events as temporary occurrences, planned or unplanned, with a finite timespan. He added that a principle underlying all events is that they are quick and that *"every such event is unique, stemming from the blend of management, program, setting, and people"*.[14] Event management is an essential activity for any sport leader. This requires a sound understanding of project management, including the legislation that regulates sport events. Permission needs to be provided for most events by the local authority, and insurance is needed for public liability. A stadium rarely uses more than 30 event days per calendar year, and most stadiums aim to multi-use their facilities, which may include concerts.

The success of a sport event is usually judged on in-stadium support, for example, the South African T20 cricket tournament was launched in January 2023 to unprecedented in-stadium support. Because of this and factors such as the competition level and television coverage, the competition was quickly declared a success.

Facilities are owned, and in some cases maintained, by the local government. Sadly, the provincial government is losing the ability to maintain these stadiums, in part due to the ongoing energy crisis. Sport leaders must thus have a maintenance plan in place in order to refrain from falling into the trap of underspending on maintenance and repairs.

17.5.6 Crisis Management

Crises share six characteristics: rarity, significance, high impact, ambiguousness, urgency and high stakes. A crisis creates a period of discontinuity or a situation where the organisation's core values are threatened, requiring critical decision-making. In addition, there is a destabilising effect on the organisation and its stakeholders.

Koehn[15] stated that real leaders are forged in crisis, concluding that courageous leaders are not born; their ability to help others triumph over adversity is not written into their genetic code; and they are shaped as leaders during a crisis. During an emergency, leadership is most needed. Think of a leader as someone standing on a stage with their followers looking at them; they see his/her every move. The South African business icon Johann Rupert once said that nobody wants to get on a plane with a nervous pilot. A leader needs to provide direction and guidance during a crisis. Many South African sporting NSFs have been embroiled in crises and their poor leadership only increased the negative impact on them. There is a proven methodology for dealing with a crisis:

1. Calm down all involved as much as possible.
2. Analyse and assess whether the crisis is factually correct.
3. Obtain the best expert advice possible.
4. Appoint a crisis team.
5. Draft a response plan.
6. Communicate proactively with stakeholders.
7. Action your plan, review and adjust.

17.5.7 Brand and Communication

Sport leaders should not seek the limelight and attention; this should be reserved for athletes and players. However, sport leaders are public figures and will have their brands, especially if they are ex-players or athletes. They, along with the team, are the face of the sport organisation. In an era of active social media, it is essential to note that the leader's brand will be scrutinised daily.

Teams and sport organisations are brands, as are sponsors; the latter will not associate with sport brands that do not reflect their values. The Proteas men's team struggled to secure a sponsor after the national body was embroiled in a Black Lives Matter crisis, when the national players were told they had to go on their knees before matches to acknowledge the movement.

Sport leaders' communication ability is vital, as they operate in the public domain; they are required to address crowds, meetings and the media. They should be strongly encouraged to receive formal training to help them master this.

17.5.8 Professional Team Management

Managing professional sport is challenging as there is only one champion. Supporters and fans emotionally connect with teams, whose performance influences their psyche. Unfortunately, management and sport leaders are regularly blamed if the unit is not doing well, while the players and coaches receive credit when the unit is winning. This is a reality that is part of the burden of command. Sport leaders thus need good insight into the factors that will make teams and athletes compete, and ultimately win. This includes the application of science and technology to provide support to the coaching staff. Leaders are cautioned not to micromanage coaching staff, but to allow them the freedom to operate without undue influence. When results are not going their way, leaders should not have an emotional overreaction.

17.5.9 Recreational Sport

Recreational sport is also referred to as amateur or grassroots sport. Recreational sport is needed to sustain the professional arm of a sport, i.e., a programme to induct young children into a sport ensures that the code grows, or at least stays relevant. Leaders operating on this level are foot soldiers of sport, and it is essential to acknowledge their contribution. Sports that are actively played in schools have a distinct advantage, e.g., rugby, cricket, athletics, swimming and tennis. However, not all communities have access to schools that cater for sport. Where possible, therefore, sport organisations need to develop structures that provide access to their sport to as many people as possible.

17.6 CONCLUSION

Sports leaders are unique as they may not be their organisation's highest paid or highest profile member. The leadership framework in South African sport is also unique as it includes political leaders, NSF leaders, PSF or affiliate leaders, and club and team leaders.

Leaders are individuals who influence organisations and people, and have a unique management style. This may focus more on the task or the follower. It is important for leaders to understand their leadership styles in order to understand their strengths and weaknesses.

Influential leaders guide and inspire their followers, which is critical during a crisis. Being ethical is also key, as a leader sets the tone for the organisation. Sport leaders are temporary custodians of the game and must serve and protect their sport organisation; they are representatives of the sport.

The modern sport leader must manage a complex environment with diverse stakeholders, therefore a good understanding of stakeholder management is a necessity. Further to this, facilities management knowledge is needed to administer sport. Finally, South Africa has a divided past, thus leaders must understand the challenges involved in racial transformation.

SELF-ASSESSMENT

1. Describe the different levels of leadership roles within the South African framework.
2. How would you describe your leadership style?
3. Distinguish between ethical and toxic leadership.
4. Identify the stakeholders of a soccer club and map them according to their level of power and interest.
5. Why is it important to understand the history of South Africa when you are a manager in sports?
6. How would you deal with the crisis if your club was accused of racism? How would you protect the club's brand?
7. Name the essential similarities and differences between recreational and professional sport.

MOTIVATION IN SPORT

Lyndon Ferns

> **LEARNING OUTCOMES**
>
> At the end of this chapter, you should be able to:
>
> 1. Outline the fundamentals of motivation.
> 2. Differentiate between motivators.
> 3. Better grasp aspects of remaining motivated.
> 4. Address setbacks and obstacles while pursuing goals.

18.1 INTRODUCTION

Motivation is a driving force that propels individuals to achieve greatness. The flame burns within, pushing one to overcome challenges, persevere through obstacles, and ultimately achieve success. As an Olympic gold medalist, I have experienced firsthand the power of motivation in my journey to the top of the podium. With this, I will share my perspective on motivation, drawing on my experiences as an elite athlete. I will explore the different facets of motivation, including intrinsic and extrinsic motivation, and delve into the various factors influencing motivation, such as goal setting, self-belief, resilience and passion.[1] I will also discuss how motivation can be nurtured and maintained, and the role of setbacks and failures in the motivational process. Finally, I will highlight the significance of motivation beyond sports and its relevance in various aspects of life, including education, career and personal growth.

As an Olympic gold medalist, I have had the privilege of competing at the highest level of sports and experiencing the thrill of the ultimate victory. My journey to the top was not without its share of challenges, setbacks and moments of self-doubt, yet what kept me going – what fueled my unwavering determination – was my motivation. The fire within me burned intensely, driving me to push my limits, strive for excellence and ultimately achieve my goal of winning a gold medal.

The Olympic Games is one of the most prestigious sporting events in the world, and athletes who participate in this competition are often seen as role models for people from all walks of life. The motivation of these athletes is crucial to their success, and is a topic that has been extensively researched in sports psychology. Motivation is a multi-faceted construct influenced by various internal and external factors.

18.2 UNDERSTANDING MOTIVATION

Motivation is a fundamental aspect of sports psychology that is critical to an individual's success; it is a complex psychological construct that plays a pivotal role in human behaviour.[2] It is the force that initiates, guides and sustains our actions towards achieving specific goals or outcomes.[3] Motivation is the catalyst that ignites the passion, drive and discipline required to excel in a highly competitive and demanding environment.

Motivation was critical in my journey to achieving the ultimate prize in sport. Winning an Olympic gold medal is about physical ability and having the right mindset and motivation. The concept helped me and other Olympic gold medalists achieve our goals; it is a critical factor to achieve success in any sport. Athletes must be highly motivated to overcome training and competition's physical and mental challenges. Motivation is a complex concept influenced by various factors, including intrinsic and extrinsic motivators,[4] personal values, goals and environmental factors. Identifying the different types of motivation that drive an athlete to achieve the highest level of success in sport is critical, as motivation can influence their behaviour, thoughts and emotions, and determine their commitment and persistence towards their goals.[5] Highly motivated athletes are more likely to engage in intense training, set challenging goals and persist in facing setbacks and challenges.

As a mental state that energises and directs behaviour towards a particular goal, motivation can determine how much athletes invest of their time, effort and resources to achieve their desired outcomes.[6] Motivation can be influenced by a range of factors, including personality traits, social environment and past experiences, but it is generally viewed as a dynamic construct that fluctuates over time. Therefore, understanding the nature and determinants of motivation is crucial for coaches and athletes seeking to optimise performance.

Motivation is a multi-dimensional concept that is studied extensively in psychology, education and sport science. In sport science, motivation has been identified as a critical factor in achieving success in athletes' respective fields. It can be seen as the force that drives us to act in a certain way to achieve our goals and gives us the energy and focus to pursue our dreams and overcome obstacles. Different theories of motivation help us understand the other factors that drive us to act in a particular way.

One of the most popular theories of motivation is Maslow's hierarchy of needs. Maslow's theory suggests that our needs are arranged in an order, with basic physiological needs at the bottom, followed by safety, love and belonging, esteem, and self-actualisation needs at the top. According to Maslow, we must satisfy our lower-level needs before we can move up to our higher-level needs.[7;8]

Another theory of motivation is the self-determination theory (SDT), which suggests that humans have three basic psychological needs: autonomy, competence and relatedness. Autonomy refers to the need for control over our lives; competence refers to the need to feel capable of achieving our goals; and relatedness refers to the need for social interaction and connection.[9]

18.3 INTRINSIC MOTIVATORS

Intrinsic motivators are internal factors that drive a person's behaviour or actions without needing external rewards or punishments. These motivators are based on a person's interests, passions, values and desires, and they typically lead to feelings of enjoyment, satisfaction and fulfilment. Intrinsic motivation is a more robust and long-lasting motivator.

The experience of intrinsic motivation can be profound and influential in achieving excellence in one's sport. Intrinsic motivation in this context is often driven by a deep passion for the sport, the desire to push oneself to the limits of physical and mental endurance, and the satisfaction of achieving personal goals and breaking records.

An athlete may be intrinsically motivated by a desire to achieve mastery of the sport. This could mean setting personal records, improving technique and training to compete at the highest level. This desire for knowledge can be fueled by a love for the sport and the satisfaction of seeing incremental improvements over time.

Another intrinsic motivator for an athlete could be the sense of purpose that comes from representing their country on the world stage. The desire to perform well and make their country proud can motivate athletes and contribute to a sense of fulfilment and purpose in their sport.

Curiosity and creativity can also be intrinsic motivators for high-level athletes. For example, an Olympic gold medalist in gymnastics may be intrinsically motivated to develop new routines, moves and skills that are innovative and unique, leading to a new level of creativity and self-expression in the sport.

Overall, intrinsic motivation for a high-level athlete is often fueled by a deep passion for the sport, a desire for mastery, a sense of purpose and a drive for creativity and self-expression. These motivators can lead to a sense of fulfilment and achievement that is difficult to replicate through external rewards alone.

Intrinsic motivators are often seen as more powerful and sustainable than extrinsic motivators[10;11] because they come from within and align with a person's values and goals. For example, these goals could be attaining one's ambition to achieve something meaningful. When intrinsically motivated, people feel more engaged, productive and fulfilled in their work or activities.

Pure examples of intrinsic motivators include:

1. Autonomy: The desire to have control over one's work and decisions.
2. Mastery: The desire to improve one's skills and abilities in a particular area.
3. Purpose: The desire to contribute to something meaningful or important.
4. Curiosity: The desire to learn and explore new ideas and concepts.
5. Creativity: The desire to express oneself uniquely and innovatively.

18.4 **EXTRINSIC MOTIVATORS**

Extrinsic motivators are external factors that drive a person's behaviour or actions,[12] typically in response to the promise of a reward or the threat of punishment. These motivators are often based on external incentives, such as money, recognition, or tangible or intangible rewards.

Extrinsic motivators can also play a significant role in an elite athlete's experience, particularly when it comes to the rewards and recognition that come with success in their sport, such as winning a gold medal at the Olympic Games.

For example, an elite athlete may be extrinsically motivated by the prospect of receiving significant financial rewards, sponsorships and endorsements for their performance.[13] These external rewards can be a powerful motivator for athletes, mainly as they often come with significant financial benefits that can support an athlete's training and future career opportunities.

Another extrinsic motivator for an elite athlete could be the recognition and admiration of being a champion. Being the best can bring fame, prestige and social status, motivating athletes who desire recognition and validation for their achievements.

The desire to compete against other athletes and win at the highest level can also be an extrinsic motivator for competitors such as Olympic athletes. In addition, the competitive nature of sports can lead athletes to seek external rewards, such as beating a rival athlete or winning a championship title, to validate their skills and abilities.

While intrinsic motivation may be the driving force behind success, extrinsic motivators such as financial rewards, recognition and the desire to win can also play an essential role in motivating athletes to perform at their best.

Extrinsic motivators can effectively drive behaviour and achieve desired outcomes, particularly in the short term. For example, employees may work harder to achieve performance targets if promised a bonus, or students may study more diligently if they know they will receive a good grade or reward.

However, extrinsic motivators are often less effective than intrinsic ones in sustaining long-term motivation, particularly if the reward or incentive does not align with a person's internal values and goals, which can lead to feelings of disengagement or dissatisfaction with the task or activity.

Extrinsic motivators can effectively drive behaviour and result in the achievement of desired outcomes in the short term. Still, they may not be sustainable or aligned with a person's internal values.

Examples of purely extrinsic motivators are:

1. Financial rewards: bonuses, commissions or other incentives for achieving specific goals or performance targets.
2. Recognition: awards, certificates or public recognition for a job well done.

3. Punishments: fines, demotions or other penalties for failing to meet performance standards or expectations.
4. Competition: the desire to beat others or to win a prize or award.

18.5 SELF-DETERMINATION THEORY (SDT)

The SDT is a theory that consists of multiple components, including autonomy, competence and relatedness, which are discussed below.

18.5.1 Autonomy

Autonomy is one of the three innate psychological needs proposed by the self-determination theory, which refers to the need to control one's own life and decisions. Freedom is about feeling a sense of ownership and volition over one's actions and experiences; a fundamental human need arises from the desire for self-direction and the ability to make choices that align with one's values and interests.[14]

In the context of SDT, autonomy is essential because it supports intrinsic motivation and personal growth. When individuals feel they can choose their path, they are more likely to engage in meaningful and enjoyable activities. This, in turn, can lead to a sense of competence and fulfilment, which contributes to overall well-being.[15]

On the other hand, when individuals feel that their choices and actions are being controlled or dictated by external forces, such as rewards or punishment, their motivation is more likely to be extrinsic. This can lead to feelings of resentment or disengagement, which can undermine personal growth and well-being.

Autonomy is essential to SDT because it supports intrinsic motivation, personal growth and well-being by giving individuals control over their lives and decisions.

18.5.2 Competence

Competence is the second innate psychological need proposed by the self-determination theory and refers to the need to feel effective and capable in one's pursuits. Competence is about feeling a sense of mastery over challenges and using one's skills and abilities to achieve desired outcomes.[16]

In the context of SDT, competence is essential because it supports intrinsic motivation and personal growth. When individuals feel they have the skills and abilities to handle challenges and achieve their goals, they are more likely to be motivated to pursue them. This, in turn, can lead to a sense of accomplishment and self-efficacy, which contributes to overall well-being.

On the other hand, when individuals feel that they lack the skills or abilities to handle challenges, their motivation is more likely to be extrinsic or even result in demotivation. This can lead to feelings of frustration or inadequacy, which can undermine personal growth and well-being.

In summary, competence is an essential component of SDT. It supports intrinsic motivation, personal growth and well-being by providing individuals with mastery and self-efficacy over challenges and goals.

18.5.3 Relatedness

As the third of the innate psychological needs proposed by the SDT, relatedness refers to the need to feel connected and cared for by others.[17] Relatedness is about feeling a sense of belonging, attachment and social support in one's relationships.

In the context of SDT, relatedness is essential because it supports intrinsic motivation and personal growth. When individuals feel they have meaningful relationships and social connections, they are more likely to be motivated to engage in activities and pursue essential goals. This, in turn, can lead to a sense of belonging and emotional well-being, which contributes to overall well-being.

On the other hand, when individuals feel isolated or disconnected from others, their motivation is more likely to be extrinsic or even demotivating. This can lead to feelings of loneliness or depression, undermining personal growth and well-being.

In summary, relatedness is an essential component of SDT because it supports intrinsic motivation, personal growth and well-being by providing individuals with a sense of social connection and support in their relationships. For instance, when an individual feels a sense of relatedness, it means they perceive their relationships as supportive, caring or meaningful, and this feeling of connection satisfies their need for social interaction and belongingness. This sense of well-being could assist in maintaining motivation.

18.6 NURTURING AND MAINTAINING MOTIVATION

Nurturing and maintaining motivation involves establishing a basis in the first place and sustaining it over time. Maintaining motivation is difficult, thus individuals must develop strategies to stay focused and driven while implementing them to stay on track and ultimately achieve their goals.

Strategies that have proven successful include the following:[18]

1. Goal setting: setting specific, measurable, achievable, relevant and time-bound goals helps athletes stay motivated by providing a clear target to aim for.
2. Visualisation: visualisation involves mentally rehearsing a performance or a scenario in one's mind. This technique helps athletes build confidence and focus by mentally rehearsing success.
3. Self-talk: self-talk is another strategy used by athletes to stay motivated. Positive self-talk involves using positive affirmations and statements to reinforce self-belief and confidence. Negative self-talk, on the other hand, can lead to self-doubt and a lack of motivation.
4. Set clear goals: define your goals and be specific about your plans. Setting clear and achievable goals can give you direction and help you stay motivated.
5. Break tasks into smaller steps: large jobs can seem overwhelming, so break them down into smaller, more manageable steps. This can help you feel more accomplished as you complete each step, leading to a sense of progress and motivation.

6. Find inspiration: surround yourself with things that inspire you, whether it's quotes, images, music or people. Motivation can help you stay focused and motivated on your goals.
7. Reward yourself: set up a reward system for when you reach milestones or complete tasks. A reward can be small, such as taking a break or treating yourself to a favourite snack, or more significant, such as taking a day off or going on holiday.
8. Practice self-care: taking care of yourself can help you maintain your motivation. Make sure to get enough rest, eat well, exercise regularly and take time for relaxation and self-reflection.
9. Stay accountable: find someone who can hold you responsible for your goals, such as a friend, mentor or coach. Accountability can help keep you motivated and on track.
10. Celebrate successes: celebrate your successes, no matter how small. Recognising and celebrating your progress can help boost your motivation and keep you moving forward.

Being and staying motivated doesn't always guarantee a smooth journey without setbacks and failures. As an elite athlete, I've experienced my fair share of disappointments and obstacles to Olympic gold.

18.7 SETBACKS AND FAILURES IN THE MOTIVATIONAL PROCESS

While motivation can lead to successful outcomes, setbacks and failures can occur throughout the process. Overcoming setbacks is the ultimate paved road to success. Still, individuals must understand motivational strategies, setbacks and losses, as well as how to address and overcome them.

Setbacks and failures are common in the motivation process and can be discouraging – not achieving the desired outcome, failing to reach a target or even sustaining an injury. However, they can also provide valuable learning experiences and opportunities for growth. Overcoming a failure is mainly achieved by knowing your capabilities.

In my experience of setting and pursuing my individual goals, some vital aspects assisted me in regrouping and resetting when I wasn't achieving my desired outcomes:

1. Reframe your mindset: instead of seeing setbacks and failures as roadblocks, view them as opportunities to learn and grow. Adopting a growth mindset can help you maintain motivation in facing challenges.
2. Revisit your goals: take some time to revisit them and make sure they are still relevant and meaningful, then, if necessary, adjust them based on new information or changing circumstances. One of the primary reasons for motivational setbacks is the need for more clarity in goal setting.[19] If the goals are not specific, measurable and achievable, it can turn to frustration, demotivation and disengagement. For example, setting a vague goal such as "I want to lose weight" is less effective than setting a specific purpose such as: "I want to lose 10 kilograms in two months by exercising for 30 minutes a day and eating a balanced diet."
3. Break goals into smaller steps: if you're feeling overwhelmed, break your goals into smaller, more manageable steps. This can help you feel less discouraged and maintain motivation. Setting intelligent, specific, measurable, achievable, relevant and time-bound goals is essential. Additionally, it's vital to break down plans into smaller, possible tasks to build momentum and track progress.[20]

4. Seek feedback: seek feedback from others who can provide constructive criticism and help you improve, such as input from a valued mentor or coach. Use this feedback to adjust your approach and stay on track. Trusted feedback is essential in the motivational process as it gives individuals information about their progress and helps them change their behaviour. Conversely, the absence of feedback from a mentor or coach can lead to uncertainty, lack of direction and disengagement. To overcome this, seek regular and constructive feedback to help you stay motivated and adjust your behaviour. Feedback should be specific, timely and focused on behaviour rather than personality.

5. Stay positive: focus on your progress rather than on setbacks or failures – condemnation kills! Celebrate your successes, no matter how small, and use them as motivation to keep going.

6. Practice self-compassion: treat yourself with kindness and compassion, even when things are unplanned. Recognise that setbacks and failures are a natural part of the learning process and do not define your worth or abilities.

7. Reach out for support: seek support and a supportive environment from friends, family or a professional who can provide resources and training while fostering a culture of collaboration and teamwork when you feel overwhelmed or discouraged. Talking to someone can help you gain perspective and renew your motivation. Support can come in various forms, such as emotional, informational and instrumental support; this can help individuals stay motivated and overcome challenges.

It is, therefore, essential to understand yourself and tailor your motivational strategies accordingly. For example, an individual with a fixed mindset may benefit from feedback that emphasises effort rather than ability. In contrast, individuals with a growth mindset may benefit from challenges and opportunities to learn and develop. Setbacks and failures are a natural part of the motivation process, however by reframing your mindset, revisiting your goals and breaking them into smaller steps, seeking feedback, staying positive, practicing self-compassion and reaching out for support, you can overcome obstacles and maintain motivation in the face of challenges.

18.8 MY JOURNEY TO AN OLYMPIC GOLD MEDAL

This section provides an overview of my journey to winning an Olympic gold medal in the context of motivation. The section discusses where the dream of winning a gold medal at the Olympic Games originated; how I overcame challenges and mental barriers and embraced failures; and the role that setting goals and staying focused played in staying motivated. The discussion concludes with a section on how these experiences have contributed to my career following my success at the Olympic Games.

18.8.1 Beginning of a Dream

As a child coming from a determined, sport-loving family, I was always captivated by the Olympic Games. The stories of athletes pushing their limits, defying the odds and achieving greatness inspired me. I would spend hours watching the competitions on television, imagining myself standing on that podium with a gold medal around my neck. It was a dream that burned within me with an unquenchable fire that would shape my life in unimaginable ways.

I was just seven years old when I started swimming competitively. My parents enrolled me in a local swimming club, and from the moment I dived into that pool, I knew I had found my passion. I spent countless hours in the water, pushing my body to the limits, driven by an insatiable hunger to excel. Despite the early mornings, the gruelling workouts and the sacrifices, I knew deep in my heart that I was meant for something greater.

The dream of participating in the Olympic Games and representing my country internationally soon consumed my mind, fueling my motivation while constantly driving me to success.

Being unbeaten for four consecutive years, it seemed that the dream would soon become a reality, but my blessing of being a genuinely talented swimmer would quickly become my curse. While others were spending more and more hours training to beat me, I would spend less and less in the pool, all while pursuing greatness in team sports. However, I soon realised that talent alone was merely part of the recipe to becoming an Olympic champion, and at the mere age of 15, I learned the most valuable life lesson – hard work beats talent when talent does not work hard.

18.8.2 Overcoming Challenges

As I progressed in my swimming career, I faced numerous challenges. Sometimes, I doubted myself and faced setbacks and failures that made me question if I was on the right path. But every time I encountered an obstacle, I drew strength from my unwavering motivation to become an Olympic champion.

One of my biggest challenges was a severe shoulder injury that threatened to derail my dreams. The pain was excruciating and doctors told me that I might never be able to swim again, let alone compete at the highest level. It was a devastating blow and my world crumbled around me. Deep down, however, I refused to give up. I underwent a month of grueling physical therapy, could not lift my arm for 16 weeks and endured setbacks and disappointments, but I never lost sight of my goal. While the pain and agony of being unable to compete were real, my unwavering motivation fueled my determination to overcome the odds.

Month after month, I would push the boundaries while trying to increase the strength and mobility in my shoulder. Finally, the pain subsided daily and the test results showed that not only was my shoulder now stronger than my other, dominant shoulder, but it tested stronger than ever before.

18.8.3 Setting Goals and Staying Focused

I learned the importance of setting goals and staying focused to achieve success. I had a clear vision of what I wanted to achieve, and I put both short-term and long-term goals in place to keep me on track. For example, I broke down my goal of winning an Olympic gold medal into smaller, more manageable steps, such as improving my times daily, mastering new techniques and maintaining a strict training regimen.

Staying focused took work. There were distractions along the way, temptations to veer off course, and moments when I felt overwhelmed by the pressure. However, as a student-athlete on scholarship in the United States, I not only had to ensure top performance in the pool, but at all times, I had to maintain a minimum of 75% academically.

But I learned to stay disciplined and true to my purpose. I surrounded myself with a supportive team of coaches, trainers and fellow athletes who helped me stay focused and motivated, even during the most challenging times.

18.8.4 Embracing Failure as a Stepping stone

Failure was an inevitable part of my journey. There were races I lost, times I fell short and moments when I doubted my abilities, but I learned to embrace failure as a stepping stone to success. I realised that failure was not a sign of weakness but a chance to learn, grow and improve.

After a disappointing performance at the 2004 Olympic trials, I could have given up, but I chose to use it as motivation to work harder – the team needed me more than ever. I analysed my mistakes, adjusted my training and used the experience to fuel my determination to improve. I learnt that failure was not the end of the road but an opportunity to reset, refocus and come back stronger.

18.8.5 Overcoming Mental Barriers

While physical training was crucial to my success as an athlete, I also knew that mental strength was equally important. I faced moments of self-doubt and fear of failure, with recent poor performances always in the back of my mind. Anxiety before major races began to affect my ability to focus and perform at my best; fear quickly set in and self-doubt got the better of me.

With an Olympic gold medalist as a coach and a secure team environment, we all worked together to regain the confidence and drive to achieve the goal lingering in me for a grueling 13 years. While practicing new techniques and exposing myself to situations that made me feel uncomfortable in the water, the fear soon subsided to be replaced by feelings of confidence that enabled me to focus on my strengths rather than my weaknesses.

Physical breaks became more regular while I focused on visualisation, which would relieve a feeling of pressure, all while minimising distractions. I soon overcame all mental barriers by practicing these techniques and concentrating on my performance, rather than external factors.

Soon I was performing at my best and achieving my goals once again.

18.8.6 The Power of Motivation

For me, the road to Olympic gold was long and arduous, filled with countless hours of training, sacrifices and setbacks. The journey required unwavering dedication, discipline and passion. At the heart of it all lay motivation – the inner fire that kept me going, even when the going got tough.

Motivation was the catalyst that fueled my desire to excel and reach my full potential. The multi-faceted concept encompassed both intrinsic and extrinsic factors; my intrinsic motivation came from within and was driven by a genuine love and passion for the sport. It was the pure joy of competing, the thrill of pushing myself to new heights, and the satisfaction of achieving my personal goals. On the other hand, my extrinsic motivation came from external sources such as rewards and possible financial incentives and endorsements, but mostly the desire to make my country, coach and family proud.

18.8.7 Olympic gold

The day of competing at the Olympic Games was the culmination of years of hard work, dedication and sacrifice; I was realising a lifelong dream and the pinnacle of my career. The day was filled with excitement, nerves and anticipation as I prepared to compete with my relay team against the best in the world.

My pre-race routines, which included visualisation, stretching and warm-up exercises, were in the morning's order. My race strategy and goal were reviewed, and I mentally prepared myself for the challenge that lay ahead.

I felt nervous and excited, all while staying calm and relaxed to conserve my energy and focus on the task at hand. As I walked into the arena, adrenaline flushed through my veins; a 13-year dream was within my grasp.

My intrinsic motivation took over subconsciously, while at the same time I was physically experiencing the extrinsic motivation of my coach, family and country. The apparent motivation was on the line: Olympic gold.

As I hit the water, the years and years of training and visualisation took over and I was operating on autopilot. Three minutes and 13 seconds later, we did it, a world record and Olympic gold! Years in the making and finally a reality!

18.8.8 Post-Olympic gold

I can attest that motivation played a pivotal role in enabling me to achieve my goal of standing atop the Olympic podium and proudly wearing that coveted gold medal. Motivation is the ultimate driving force that propels athletes to push beyond their limits, overcome challenges and strive for sports excellence. It was critical in my journey to achieving the ultimate prize in sports. I have since used these strategies to stay motivated and focused throughout my career post-swimming.

The post-Olympic gold period was a particularly difficult time for me as I transitioned from the intense focus and training of competition to the challenges of navigating the business world. With the unique skills and attributes of becoming an Olympic gold medalist, such as discipline, perseverance and mental toughness, I strove to drive my success in business. At the same time, I had to recognise the new challenges that I faced in transitioning to the business world, such as the need to adapt to new environments and manage the expectations of others, all while staying motivated in different areas.

As a post-graduate in BSc Accounting from the University of Arizona, I now lead a multi-million Rand business where these critical aspects of motivation occur daily. New challenges arise where individuality is substituted with leading and motivating a team.

While self-motivation is essential, motivating a team is crucial for the success of any group project or business venture. While encouraging a team requires different skills and strategies than motivating oneself, the core remains the same. Compelling team motivation involves setting clear goals and expectations, like motivating oneself, fostering a positive and inclusive culture, leading by example, providing feedback and support, and encouraging teamwork and collaboration. By investing in these areas, leaders can create an environment where team members are motivated,[21] engaged and committed to achieving shared goals, leading to increased productivity and success. Motivating a team requires leadership skills, clear communication and a positive and inclusive culture.

18.9 CONCLUSION

In closing, motivation is critical beyond sports because it is a driving force that can help individuals achieve their goals and aspirations in all aspects of life. Motivation refers to the inner desire or incentive that pushes people to act or behave in a certain way; it is a powerful force that can impact all aspects of life, from Olympic golds to career success, personal growth, health and wellness, and relationships. It is a fundamental aspect of human behaviour and has significant implications in various areas of life. By understanding the importance of motivation, individuals can cultivate this inner drive and achieve their goals and aspirations, whatever they might be.

SELF-ASSESSMENT

1. Identify the fundamentals of motivation.
2. Differentiate between motivators.
3. Describe the aspects of remaining motivated.
4. How should one address setbacks and obstacles while pursuing goals?

MENTORSHIP IN SPORT

Rosemary Bartlett

> **LEARNING OUTCOMES**
>
> At the end of this chapter, you should be able to:
>
> 1. Explain empowering mentorship with its role in coach development.
> 2. Debate the critical qualities of a successful mentor and mentee relationship and recognise how to build trust and maintain communication in a mentorship relationship.
> 3. Discuss ethical considerations concerning the power dynamic, conflicts of interest and confidentiality in sports mentorship.
> 4. Argue the importance of facilitated mentoring programmes for future generations of athletes and coaches.

19.1 INTRODUCTION

Mentorship, as researched in our early history of some 3,000 years ago, has its roots in Greek mythology in the character of Mentor in Homer's *Odyssey*. This ancient Greek poem describes how Ulysses entrusted his young son, Telemachus, to the care of Mentor, his trusted companion. Today, mentorship shapes attitudes and values, enabling people to cope with present and future challenges and possibilities. Whether as a mentor or a mentee, the cornerstones of mentorship are a personal vision, specific goals and a good grasp of reality, Mentorship is a powerful tool in sport for athletes and coaches, as is described in this chapter.

The chapter will also explore the requirements for a successful mentor-and-mentee relationship and outline practical mentorship goals and strategies for success, both on and off the field. A recent South African study undertaken in the equestrian coaching industry highlights the importance of mentorship.

The benefits and challenges of sport mentorship include ethical considerations related to power dynamics, conflicts of interest and confidentiality. Lastly, the need for facilitated mentorship programmes in the broader sport community and the importance of giving back as a mentor to future generations of athletes and coaches will be discussed.

19.2 THE IMPORTANCE AND ROLE OF MENTORSHIP IN COACH DEVELOPMENT

The benefits of mentorship for athletes and coaches in the sport industry are well documented. A recent study in South Africa on a target group of high-performance (HP) coaches with between 30 and 40 years of coaching expertise in three Olympic equestrian disciplines, as well as less experienced coaches with less than five years of experience, revealed some of the most significant benefits of mentorship. These professional coaches brought richness to the research as they explored their mentorship journey through the research questions, which explored the impact of mentorship on each coach's professional development as a HP coach.

The research questions also explored how each coach viewed mentorship as valuable for further developing non-professional or less experienced coaches. It is worth noting that the less experienced coach mentees in the study were also competing athletes. Furthermore, while this study focused on the mentorship of equestrian coaches and the equine athlete, the author believes the outcomes can be applied comparatively to other sporting codes within the trio of mentor, coach and athlete.

The coaches were selected because they had lived experiences relevant to the study's focus and thus would be motivated to talk about those experiences.[1] A closely defined group for whom the research question was significant was selected through purposive sampling.[2] Purposive sampling assisted the researcher in choosing coaches with consideration to the sample criteria based on experience, qualifications and position held.

Sixteen coaches were initially selected for this study. The sample with the characteristics described above included eight professional coaches from different equestrian disciplines and eight non-professional coaches who could give complementary and comparative input on mentorship in their equestrian field. While the sample size in this study initially comprised 16 coaches, as qualitative research is data-dense, the point of diminishing returns became apparent and the study reached saturation point after 13 interviews.[3]

Semi-structured interviews are in-depth, provide thick descriptions[4] and allow the researcher to collect relevant data from appropriately selected coaches, focusing on 'how' things are understood rather than 'what' happened regarding the phenomena being studied.[5] Asking open-ended questions enabled the researcher to explore nonapparent issues and build rapport and trust with the coaches.[6] To refine the questions that coaches may have found too general, prompts encouraged them to explore individual interpretations of mental phenomena.[7] Semi-structured interviews allowed the interviewer to cover the desired topics while providing the coaches with room to tell their stories. These formal interviews took place in person on a one-to-one basis, lasting between 30 to 45 minutes.

Clear themes evolved from the data coding process, with four main themes emerging that are set out in Table 19.1 with categories and sub-categories. These themes are learner outcomes for this chapter and will be explored in the following themes and subcategories.

Table 19.1: Identified themes, categories and sub-categories

Themes	Categories	Subcategories
Theme 1: Ineffective mentorship	1. Communication	Mistakes Problem identification Accessibility
	2. Confidence	Stress Adaptable Guilt
	3. Knowledge	Holistic Interaction Impact
	4. Mentorship	Focus Reflection Inclusive Empathy
Theme 2: Mentorship in advancing coaching	1. Exposure	Holistic Interactive Understanding
	2. Intrapersonal skills	Development Self-confidence Responsibility Advancement
	3. Improve horse and rider	Connectivity Interpersonal skills
	4. Knowledge transference	Professional knowledge Adaptability Structure Connection
Theme 3: Mentorship influence on coaching	1. Independence	Development Principles Motivation
	2. Differences	Recognition Adaptable Open minded Encouraging Understanding

Themes	Categories	Subcategories
Theme 3: Mentorship influence on coaching (continued)	3. Life-long learning	Patience Adaptable Reflection Foundational knowledge
	4. Find own path	Individuality Bigger picture Perspectives Well rounded
Theme 4: Need for mentorship programmes	1. Career	Knowledge Technique Guidance Support Accessible
	2. Better coach	Merge 'how' with 'what' Professional knowledge transfer Intrapersonal knowledge mastery Interpersonal knowledge skills Life-long learning

19.2.1 Theme One: Empowering mentorship

It is well-accepted that mentorship is a crucial aspect of the professional development of the athlete and the coach in the sports industry. This relationship provides unique opportunities for athletes and less experienced coaches to learn from the experience, knowledge and wisdom of those who have excelled in their field.

The impact of a lack of mentorship reflected in the sub-themes communication, confidence, knowledge and mentorship below speaks to the coaches' reflections related to their interpretations of the lack of progress in coach development without exposure to a mentoring process. These various aspects were expressed as a sense of what they would have missed if they did not have the opportunity of mentorship in their coaching development.

19.2.1.1 Communication

Communication is described as having the skill to communicate with mentors in transferring important professional knowledge and interpersonal abilities.

It was evident from the coaches' perspectives that they needed the skills to communicate with their athletes while transferring essential skills and knowledge with the guidance of a mentor. Coaches indicated that communication in the mentoring process gave them the confidence in not always having the right answer and to make mistakes while still providing a way to empower their athletes by building on what is good.

Further extracts clearly show mentorship's crucial role in providing individuals with diverse perspectives and alternative solutions. In turn, this serves as a reminder for coaches to tailor their coaching approaches to the athletes' personalities and learning styles, reinforcing effective coaching practices. Coaches noted how mentorship provided them with skills in reframing problems, making them easier to solve, adding that mentoring often occurs unconsciously, further emphasising its inherent value. These interviews revealed that **communication** is essential in knowledge transfer and **building trust** in coaching relationships. Mistakes during learning are embraced, as communication offers alternative answers, boosting the coach's confidence.

19.2.1.2 Confidence

Confidence is described as having the support of mentors in applying important knowledge and abilities to become learner-centred, which builds trust in the relationship. Knowledge reduces stress, develops adaptability and grows confidence.

The coaches indicated the value of being exposed to their respective mentors in developing the **confidence** they currently possess. In addition, the fact that mentorship allows space for error and a community of some sort to share errors or concerns, allowed them to be better coaches. Interview extracts illustrate some confidence-related responses and highlight how the absence of a mentor can significantly negatively impact one's confidence and lead to an increase in mistakes. This was particularly true in coach mentorship, where mentors play a crucial role in helping less experienced coaches understand their athletes better. Improved confidence empowers coaches to share knowledge and interact effectively to benefit their athletes.

19.2.1.3 Knowledge systems

Knowledge is described as the transfer of knowledge through mentorship of systems and business processes that are part of the coaching business.

This category highlights the importance of mentorship in the coaching industry, offering valuable insights for knowledge transfer and enabling coaches to make informed decisions and reflect on their experiences. Mentorship support goes beyond sports achievements, providing a safe environment for reflection and support in assisting coaches to separate their personal and professional lives. Mentors can offer emotional support, guidance and problem-solving skills by drawing from their own experiences off the field and the achievement of successful athletes they have mentored. Thus, choosing the right mentor is crucial due to their significant impact on coaches' careers.

19.2.1.4 Need for mentorship

The importance of mentorship is described as the achievement of learner outcomes in recognising different ways of learning and using reflection to focus on various answers for decision-making.

Coaches recognised the need for mentoring in SA equestrian sport. They compared it to other sports where mentors are essential for success, providing the opportunity to learn from mistakes and transfer knowledge to their athletes. The interview responses also highlighted the reluctance of older coaches to share their expertise with younger coaches. Therefore, more coaches must volunteer as mentors and participate in formal mentorship programmes to promote continuous development and knowledge sharing. Coaches strongly supported integrating mentorship into coach education.

19.2.2 Theme Two: Mentorship in Advancing Coaching

This theme expressed indicators of various learning skills that the coaches felt had assisted them in advancing their coaching careers due to their exposure to the mentoring process. This theme further expressed the positive influences that mentoring had on them as professional coaches and the ripple effect mentoring experiences had on their personal lives.

19.2.2.1 Experiential learning

Experiential learning is described as learning by doing and exposure to various learning approaches and skills as a result of mentorship by a more experienced person.

This category examined the coaches' reflections on different coaching approaches and the role of mentorship. It highlighted skills that are only accessible through mentorship and the first-hand perspective of coaches who had experienced it. These insights demonstrate the positive and negative effects of informal methods on coaches and athletes. Older coaches often need more openness to new approaches, while formal mentorship programmes promote confidence and the value of seeking guidance. The coaching approach has evolved to include empathy, with many coaches relying on mentorship for developing empathy, self-awareness and adaptability. The absence of a mentor can lead to more mistakes and the formation of bad habits, supporting the idea that coaching without a recognised system increases stress. The coaches agreed that mentorship revealed empowerment by showing the value of experiential learning and that having all the answers is not essential.

19.2.2.2 Self-confidence and improvement in coaching

Self-confidence is described as understanding the principles of interpersonal skills and how people learn differently through interaction.

This category focuses on coaching and mentoring for interpersonal skills development, which is the relationship between the coach and athletes and the interrelationship of athletes within the team. Coaches found that having a mentor in the coaching process improved their interpersonal skills and self-confidence, guiding knowledge transfer and implementation in coaching. Coaches emphasised the role of mentorship in building self-confidence and improved coaching, especially for individuals who learn at different speeds. Thus mentorship developed interpersonal skills, reflective abilities and the confidence to apply different approaches to achieve coaching goals.

19.2.2.3 Improving the horse and rider

Improvement of the athlete is described as the guidance of an experienced expert in knowledge transfer to develop skills in the coach to enhance the athlete's relationship within the team.

The mentorship role in equestrian coach advancement and success is like the bond between the horse and rider. This bond allows access to valuable information and develops skills that benefit both. Interview responses show that equestrian mentorship goes beyond technical aspects, focusing on timing, understanding cues and effective coaching. Mentorship promotes adaptability and holistic athlete development, highlighting the importance of communication skills and the learning barriers of a coach-centred approach.

19.2.2.4 Knowledge transfer

Mentorship is the conduit for transferring professional, interpersonal knowledge skills from an older, more experienced coach to a younger, less experienced coach.

Mentorship transfers knowledge from experienced individuals to less experienced ones in a sport. The right coach is important, especially for those with a successful track record. Older mentors help coaches develop structure, impart accurate knowledge and improve their business skills. Mentorships provide valuable insights into elite sports, benefiting athletes and coaches. A good mentor allows exploring different approaches and fosters self-awareness in coaches to establish a solid foundation based on tested methods, while encouraging openness to new information and coaching styles. Overall, mentorship develops well-rounded coaches through knowledge transfer.

19.2.3 Theme Three: Mentorship Influence on Coaching

This theme refers to the impact that the mentorship approach tends to have on the coaching and training perspectives of the coaches. Within this process, the mentees expressed that life-long learning and being viewed as mentors at some stage gave them some double-bound visualisation where they could reflect as mentees and mentors at the same point in their careers. In this way, not only are they developing as mentees and coaches, but they are also beginning to take on the mentor role.

19.2.3.1 Independence (Find my path)

Independence is described as using the knowledge skills provided by mentorship to build on and acknowledge one's approach to coaching.

This category examines the impact of mentoring on the mentee coaching process. It focuses on a learner-centred approach, incorporating technical knowledge and intrapersonal and interpersonal skills. Interviews highlight the importance of finding independence, distinguishing teaching from coaching and guiding others. Mentors contribute unique qualities, aiming to instil confidence, discipline, commitment and resilience in their mentees. Intrapersonal skill development shows how mentorship empowers individuals to learn in their own time and style. Mentorship encourages coaches to pass on this philosophy to younger peers.

19.2.3.2 Identifying differences

Differences are described as building foundational principles whilst being adaptable to technology, innovation and the management of people.

This category highlights coaches recognising diverse approaches in coaching and learning sports. Exposure to mentoring emphasises the value of mentorship in identifying differences. Coaches stressed the importance of combining established methods, openness to new information and adaptable coaching styles. Individual needs and empathy are promoted. Mentorship offers a broader perspective and acknowledges multiple paths to success. Mentors should encourage embracing differences and leveraging unique strengths rather than fixating on weaknesses.

The coaches noted that knowledge transfer varies across individuals and timeframes, which was lacking in the past. This view was shared by older professional and younger non-professional coaches.

19.2.3.3 Lifelong learning process

Lifelong learning is the time needed to perfect the three foundational knowledge skills: professional, intrapersonal and interpersonal knowledge.

This category emphasises the importance of mentorship in the lifelong learning process. The interviews showed that continuous personal and professional development is crucial, whilst knowledge exchange among individuals is highlighted, indicating the value of everyone's experiences. Thus the value of mentorship is significant, as skills acquired from mentors can be shared with others. Formal and informal mentoring arrangements are distinguished within this sharing, occurring in various settings.

Coaches should regularly assess themselves, identifying areas for improvement. Young coaches often need more interpersonal skills despite strong technical abilities gained over time. Coaches may unknowingly receive mentoring from those around them, emphasising the need for formal programmes to guide their professional growth, as mentorship serves as a transformative source of inspiration for coaches to strive for improvement.

19.2.4 Theme Four: Need for Mentorship Programmes

The value of formal mentorship for career advancement is described as providing skills in knowledge transfer through mentoring to become more professional.

This theme refers to the coaches indicating a need for a mentoring process in the South African context. Through their personal experience regarding the mentorship process, coaches expressed the need for mentoring from an equestrian perspective. This might be due to the process they were exposed to and the fact that they had realised that mentoring is crucial to become a better equestrian coach.

19.2.4.1 Career advancement

Mentorship plays a crucial role in guiding mentees, as it goes beyond simply teaching them what to coach and focuses on showing them how to coach. Coaches felt this process should be formalised to allow experienced individuals to influence and guide others effectively. By engaging in mentorship, coaches can enhance their abilities and gain valuable experience.

Mentorship is a source of inspiration and vision, encouraging individuals to think critically and develop coherent coaching philosophies. It also plays a crucial role in helping coaches and athletes progress to the next level, providing the guidance needed to overcome challenges and reach new heights. Mentoring can also contribute to a coach's reputation, establishing them as someone dedicated to teaching and improving others. Moreover, mentorship extends beyond coaching, playing a significant role in life. When recognising people's different learning styles, mentorship becomes valuable in addressing diverse challenges and finding effective solutions. Additionally, mentorship can reaffirm a coach's strengths, reinforcing their confidence and competence in their chosen field. Mentorship is vital to the coaching journey, enabling continuous growth and development.

19.2.4.2 Better coaching

Better coaching is described as attributes learnt through mentoring to develop a good coach into a great one.

This category refers to the processes provided for the mentee, by the mentor, for development within their career. The coaches reflected on needing their mentors' assistance to become better coaches. This process allowed them to develop confidence and certain skill sets transferred by the mentors as part of the skills that these mentors were once exposed to in the knowledge development processes of their professional development. In the world of mentorship, mentors must have certainty in the knowledge they impart, as mentees tend to believe it as true. When faced with new scenarios or challenges, mentees rely heavily on their mentors for guidance and support. Mentorship not only instils confidence and aids in better planning, but also cultivates discipline in coaches and athletes.

One of the significant outcomes of mentorship is the development of well-rounded coaches who approach their athletes with an open mind rather than being dominant or rigid. This shift in coaching style allows for a more adaptable approach to different athletes, resulting in a more inclusive and effective coaching environment. Being better equipped to adapt to the needs of their athletes, coaches can foster a more positive, progressive coaching relationship.

For coaches, building a solid foundation is essential and mentorship is a valuable resource for improvement. Without a mentor, coaches may struggle with the lack of structure or a system to follow, leading to increased stress. Unfortunately, this stress can be transferred to the athletes, creating an unfavourable environment for growth and performance.

The summarised contributions from the study demonstrate the value of an empowering mentoring relationship and contextual interaction between the coach, the athlete and the team. With the attributes learnt through the mentoring process, one can develop from a good coach into a great coach.

19.3 KEY QUALITIES OF A SUCCESSFUL MENTOR AND MENTEE RELATIONSHIP

Developing a mentorship relationship in sports requires effort and dedication from the mentor and the mentee. Key qualities such as trustworthiness, dedication, patience, open communication, supportiveness, expert knowledge and a learner-centred approach are needed to establish a successful mentorship relationship. These qualities and attributes build trust in the relationship when guidance and advice are needed during challenging times. Active listening builds strong relationships and is an invaluable communication skill. Strong and effective communication skills are essential when emotions often reach critical mass.

19.3.1 Identify Potential Mentors/Mentees

Identifying potential mentors and mentees is crucial in establishing a successful mentorship relationship. A mentor should possess a set of qualities and skills that can contribute to the growth and development of their mentee. Similarly, mentees should be willing to learn and grow to fully benefit from the mentorship relationship.

Experience and expertise in their respective fields, with a deep understanding of the industry, will empower mentors to offer practical advice and guidance to their mentees. The willingness of the mentor to invest time and effort into their mentee's development is the cornerstone of successful mentoring. Providing constructive feedback throughout the mentoring process can motivate the mentee to identify areas for improvement.

When identifying potential mentees, looking for motivated individuals who are committed to their growth and development is important. Additionally, mentees should have a clear idea of their goals and be able to articulate them to their mentor. This will help ensure that the mentorship relationship is focused and productive.

One strategy to identify potential mentors and mentees is to network within the industry and seek recommendations from colleagues and peers. Professional associations and organisations may also provide mentorship programmes or resources to help match mentors with mentees. Social media platforms and professional networking sites can provide a valuable tool to identify and connect with potential coaches with similar interests and goals.

19.3.2 Establish Clear Goals

Establishing clear goals is a critical aspect of a successful mentorship relationship. When the mentor and mentee clearly understand what they hope to achieve, they can work together in an open and honest dialogue to establish and effectively attain those goals.

This dialogue should involve identifying the strengths and weaknesses of the mentee and outlining the areas in which they want to improve. The mentor should also be clear about their expectations and goals for the relationship and how they can help the mentee reach their desired outcomes. Once the goals have been established, the mentor and mentee should work together to develop a plan for achieving them. This will include specific action items, timelines and milestones that can be used to track progress. The mentor should also be clear about the resources and support they can offer to help the mentee reach their goals.

It is important to note that the goals established in a mentorship relationship should be realistic and achievable. Unrealistic goals can be discouraging and demotivating and may ultimately hinder the relationship's success. Goals should be regularly revisited and revised to remain relevant and attainable. Ultimately, this will lead to a more productive and rewarding mentorship relationship.

19.3.3 Set Expectations

Setting expectations is an essential aspect of establishing a successful mentorship relationship. Both the mentor and mentee should clearly understand what they hope to achieve from the mentorship relationship and what each person's responsibilities and commitments are. This can include discussing the frequency and duration of meetings, the topics to be covered and the timeline for achieving specific goals.

One strategy for setting expectations is to establish a mentorship agreement or contract. This can outline the mentorship goals, each party's specific roles and responsibilities, and the timeline for achieving these goals. A written agreement can help the mentor and mentee stay on track and provide a clear roadmap for the mentorship.

Another strategy for setting expectations is establishing regular check-ins to evaluate progress and adjust goals if necessary. This can help ensure that the mentorship remains focused and effective, and allow the mentor and mentee to address any concerns or challenges that arise during the mentorship.

Ultimately, setting clear expectations is important because it can help prevent misunderstandings and ensure the mentor and mentee are fully invested in the mentorship relationship. The mentorship is more likely to succeed when expectations are aligned and benefit both parties.

19.3.4 Trustworthiness

Building trust is vital in establishing a successful mentorship relationship. Trust is particularly important in a mentor-mentee relationship where the mentee is expected to be open and honest about their weaknesses and challenges.

A key strategy for building trust is establishing clear and open communication. The mentor and mentee should be encouraged to share their expectations and goals for the relationship and any concerns and potential challenges. This can help to establish mutual understanding and ensure that both parties are on the same page.

It is important in the trust relationship to maintain confidentiality. The mentor must respect the mentee's privacy by not sharing their personal information or issues with others. This will create a safe space for the mentee to share their thoughts and feelings.

Consistency is also important in building trust between mentee and mentor and promotes a sense of reliability and dependability. The mentor should try to be available and responsive to the mentee's needs and maintain regular communication and meetings.

Finally, the mentor should model ethical and professional behaviour. The mentor should act as a role model for the mentee by exhibiting honesty, integrity and a strong work ethic. This strengthens feelings of respect and trust, as the mentee will be more likely to emulate these qualities and behaviours.

19.3.5 Open Communication

Effective communication is a key strategy to establish a successful mentorship relationship. Good communication can help establish mutual trust and understanding, facilitate the exchange of ideas and feedback, and help the mentor and mentee achieve their goals. Effective communication involves conveying ideas and information clearly, actively listening and being open to feedback.

During their communication, the mentor and mentee should be honest, transparent and respectful of each other. The mentee should feel comfortable sharing their thoughts, concerns and questions. At the same time, the mentor should provide constructive feedback, guidance and support, as well as praise and recognition when the mentee progresses or achieves their goals. As a mentee progresses in their development, they may need different types of guidance and support, which the mentor can provide by adapting their communication approach and strategies. Maintaining effective communication is crucial for building a successful mentorship relationship. Clear communication channels, actively listening and being open to feedback allows both mentor and mentee to build mutual trust and understanding, facilitate the exchange of ideas and feedback and achieve appropriate goals.

19.3.6 Flexibility and Adaptability

Flexibility and adaptability are essential attributes and strategies to establish a successful mentorship relationship. The mentor and mentee need to be flexible and adaptable to changes in the relationship, goals and circumstances, and both parties should be open to making adjustments as needed, making the relationship more productive and effective.

19.3.7 Lifelong Learning

Lifelong learning is the commitment to continuous learning and improvement throughout one's life. Mentoring is essential because it ensures that both the mentor and the mentee remain up-to-date with the latest trends, developments and best practices in their field.

For the mentor, the commitment to lifelong learning means continually seeking new knowledge and skills to share with the mentee. This commitment demonstrates to the mentee that the mentor is invested in their growth and development, which can motivate them to follow suit.

For the mentee, the commitment to lifelong learning means they are open to receiving new information and feedback from their mentor. They are willing to try to develop their skills and knowledge and will remain motivated to learn from their mentor's experiences. This strategy ensures that the mentorship relationship remains dynamic and relevant, as both parties are constantly working towards improvement and growth.

19.3.8 Summary

Developing a successful mentorship relationship requires certain essential qualities and strategies based on clear goals and expectations. These strategies result in building trust, rapport, effective communication, flexibility and adaptability, and enable the mentor and mentee to establish a supportive and productive relationship that promotes personal and professional growth.

Mentorship is a valuable tool for sports professionals seeking to achieve their goals – investing in a mentorship relationship can be a game-changer in their careers.

19.4 ETHICAL CONSIDERATIONS IN MENTORSHIP

Mentorship in sports is a critical aspect of athlete and coach development and is a relationship that requires a great deal of responsibility and ethical considerations. The mentoring relationship can be complex, and both parties must know the ethical implications of their actions and interactions. Ethical considerations are related to power dynamics, conflicts of interest and confidentiality in sports mentorship.

19.4.1 Power Dynamic

Power dynamics are significant in mentorship, especially in sports. Mentors influence their mentees' development and lives, particularly if they are high profile. Mentors must be aware of their power and use it responsibly, empowering mentees. This includes providing growth opportunities, valuable connections and advocating for success. Mentors should consider how actions are perceived, as accepting gifts may damage the mentorship relationship. Mentees have autonomy and mentors must respect their decisions, even if they disagree.

19.4.2 Conflict of Interest

Conflicts of interest in sports mentorship may occur when the mentor has a financial or personal stake in their mentee's success. For instance, a coach who doubles as an agent for an athlete may be driven to secure lucrative contracts or endorsement deals that benefit both parties. While it's not inherently unethical for mentors to have such interests, they must handle potential conflicts of interest responsibly. Transparency and refraining from decisions that appear self-serving over their mentees' well-being are crucial.

19.4.3 Confidentiality

Ethical sports mentorship requires respecting mentees' privacy and maintaining confidentiality. Mentors should not disclose personal information without consent and must store sensitive data securely. However, mentors may share relevant health information with medical professionals or coaches to ensure appropriate care while protecting the athlete's privacy and maintaining trust.

While mentoring can be incredibly rewarding, it can also be challenging. Some of the challenges associated with mentoring athletes are discussed in the next paragraph.

Firstly, time constraints can be a significant hurdle as mentors juggle their careers and personal lives alongside their mentoring responsibilities. Secondly, mentors need to strike a delicate balance between offering valuable advice and allowing their mentees to make their own decisions and learn from their mistakes without stifling their independence and creativity. Moreover, mentors must be cautious of creating a dependent relationship where mentees rely on them for all decisions and actions, instead fostering a sense of empowerment and encouraging mentees to take responsibility for their personal and professional growth.

Lastly, potential personality clashes between mentors and mentees can pose challenges, necessitating early recognition and proactive resolution to maintain a harmonious and productive mentorship dynamic.

19.5 THE IMPORTANCE OF FACILITATED MENTORING FOR FUTURE GENERATION ATHLETES AND COACHES

At a programmatic level, the mentoring activity must be embedded in a focused and purposeful model. The mentoring programme must allow for the specialised knowledge skills for technical knowledge transference to be effective. Studies underpinning this evidence for facilitated learning opportunities through mentoring have been recommended by Cushion.[8] Mentoring that takes place only once off or without direction risks loss of confidence in the process.

In the words of a Coach: *"I would like to see more formal mentorship for the experienced coaches especially to grow, and I would like to have a programme and subject matter and a choice of mentor and for a sustained period so that I can call on that mentor."*

Mentorship programmes help to foster a culture of support and collaboration within the sports community. By providing guidance and support to mentees, mentors demonstrate the importance of supporting and lifting others in pursuing their goals. This inspires mentees to pay it forward and become mentors, thus continuing the cycle of support and collaboration within the sports community. This can lead to a more cohesive and supportive sports community, with athletes and coaches working together to achieve their goals.

Mentorship programmes may provide opportunities for underrepresented groups to gain access to knowledge and experience that may otherwise be out of reach. This helps to level the playing field through a more inclusive and diverse sports community. Additionally, mentorship programmes can help to break down barriers and stereotypes by creating opportunities for individuals from different backgrounds to work together and learn from one another.

19.6 CONCLUSION

Developing a successful mentorship relationship requires certain essential qualities and strategies. These qualities and procedures are based on clear goals and expectations, building trust and rapport, effective communication, flexibility, adaptability, continual learning and development.

These strategies enable the mentor and mentee to establish a supportive and productive relationship that promotes personal and professional growth. Mentorship is a valuable tool for sports professionals seeking to achieve their goals, and investing in a mentorship relationship can be a game-changer for them.

Mentorship, as a critical aspect of athlete and coach development, is a relationship that requires a great deal of responsibility and ethical considerations. Mentoring relationships can be complex, and both parties must know the ethical implications of their actions and interactions.

In this chapter, empowering mentorship highlighted a specific focus on the personal relationship between a mentor and a coach concerning knowledge transference and trustworthiness. In addition, the availability and accessibility of the mentor were also seen as crucial characteristics that needed to be created in this relationship.

Concerning the relational context between the horse and rider unique to this study, a comparative insight can be drawn in the context of other sporting codes. A mentorship relationship between a mentor and a mentee recognises individual learning as a critical characteristic underpinned by the Social Learning Theory. Thus the main inference drawn from this comparison is that *any* mentorship programme must take cognisance of individual learning styles and pace of learning.

As a structured process, facilitated mentoring programmes are crucial to achieving effective mentoring, allowing mentees reasonable access to their mentor for at least one or two years. Within this time frame, informal mentorship could be included as an appropriate approach, with opportunities to meet to discuss areas of mutual benefit.

When considering the impact of mentorship on the broader sports community, it is essential to recognise the importance of giving back. As athletes and coaches reach the pinnacle of their careers, they can use their experience and knowledge to give back to the sports community by becoming mentors.

In sharing their experiences and providing guidance to future generations of athletes and coaches, mentors can contribute to the continued growth and success of the sports community. This benefits the mentees and helps create a legacy for the mentor, as they can pass on their knowledge and experience to future generations.

SELF-ASSESSMENT

1. Explain empowering mentorship and the importance of its role in coach development.
2. Debate the critical qualities of a successful mentor and mentee relationship and recognise how to build trust and maintain communication in a mentorship relationship.
3. Discuss ethical considerations concerning the power dynamic, conflicts of interest and confidentiality in sports mentorship.
4. Argue the importance of facilitated mentoring programmes for future generations of athletes and coaches.

SPORT MARKETING

Tracy Bredin

LEARNING OUTCOMES

At the end of this Chapter, you should be able to:

1. Explain the distinction between the marketing of sport and marketing through sport.
2. Describe the relationship between rights holders, properties and sponsors.
3. Debate the steps undertaken by a rights holder in the marketing of sport.
4. Argue why brands sponsor sport and what sport sponsorship offers brands as a marketing tool (marketing through sport).
5. Defend strategic sports sponsorship selection criteria.
6. Discuss sponsorship measurement principles.

20.1 INTRODUCTION

As Nelson Mandela, former president of South Africa, said at the inaugural Laureus World Sports Awards in 2000: *"Sport has the power to change the world. It has the power to inspire. It has the power to unite people in a way that little else does. It speaks to youth in a language they understand."*[1]

Sport has a breadth and appeal that can span geographies, languages and cultures. It is a unifier, a means of escapism, a source of inspiration and, without doubt, a cause for passion. With its ability to reach and resonate, it's unsurprising that organisations and businesses have come to realise the power of sport and seek to harness it to drive their commercial agendas. Sponsors across the globe pay top dollar to align their brands with sport – be it shirt sponsorship of a Premier League football team or airing an advertisement during America's biggest annual sporting showdown, the National Football League (NFL) Super Bowl.

However, because of its importance to fans and its profile, any endeavour to market sport or use sport as part of a marketing mix should be thoroughly considered. As Mullin, Hardy and Sutton wrote: *"Humans view sport as a special experience or as having a special place in their lives, and marketers must approach sport differently than they do used cars, doughnuts, or tax advice."*[2]

This chapter outlines sport marketing in its two different roles: **marketing through sport**, or the use of sport as a marketing tool to promote the commercial interests of an entity or entities within the sports marketing ecosystem, and the **marketing of sport as a product**, or promoting a sport organisation, event or team.

20.2 WHAT IS SPORT MARKETING?

Different entities within the sports marketing ecosystem have different goals. As a result, sports marketing has various applications. For example, a company wishing to build awareness of its brand within a particular target market could consider using sport as a marketing communications tool, or marketing through sport, to achieve this. This could entail sponsoring a national team: in exchange for an agreed-upon rights fee, the brand would receive exposure on the team's shirt and television coverage of team matches.

Conversely, a commercial entity that owns, administers or runs an event, such as the Fédération Internationale de Football Association (FIFA), the Premier Soccer League (PSL) or the Comrades Marathon Association, ultimately aims to maximise revenue from the event. To achieve this, they need to employ the marketing of sport, making their event appealing to participants, spectators, broadcasters and sponsors. Inherent to both instances of sports marketing is sports sponsorship.

20.3 WHAT IS SPORT SPONSORSHIP?

Sport sponsorship can be defined as *"the acquisition of rights to affiliate or directly associate with a sports property to derive benefits related to that affiliation or association"*.[3]

Sponsorship is a relationship between three entities: a sponsor, a property (or sponsee) and a rights holder.

In sport sponsorship, the property is an athlete, team, sport event, league, competition, sport development initiative or sport broadcast. The sponsor is typically an entity (business, organisation or brand) that pays a fee for the right to associate with the property. This fee is paid to the rights holder, the entity that owns and controls the rights to the property. For example, the rights to sponsor the 2010 FIFA World Cup (the property) were bought by the sponsor, Mobile Telephone Networks (MTN), from the rights holder, FIFA.

While there are several other role players within the sports marketing ecosystem, including agents, sports marketing agencies, broadcasters and fans, this chapter will focus on three: **the rights holder**, i.e., the party concerned with the marketing of sport; **the sponsor**, which is concerned with marketing through sport; and **the property**, which is the underlying asset in both instances.

20.4 RIGHTS HOLDERS

The term 'rights holder' refers to the governing body, federation or association that administers a sport. It is the entity that holds and controls the rights of a sports property.

Rights holders have a variety of roles:

20.4.1 Operational

The operational role of a rights holder varies depending on the property type. For example, in the case of a team, the operational or administrative role of a rights holder includes activities related to the selection, development, performance and remuneration of a team. In the case of an event, league or competition, the operational role of a rights holder includes activities related to event planning, event execution and reporting. For individual professional athletes, administrative activities such as managing an athlete's engagements with sponsors and media are typically performed by the athlete's agent.

20.4.2 Grassroots Sports Development

The responsibility of introducing youth to a sport, fostering the development of a sport amongst young players and ensuring participation in a sport often rests with the rights holder. Rights holders of national teams such as Cricket South Africa (CSA), the South African Football Association (SAFA) and the South African Rugby Union (SARU) are generally accountable for producing a pipeline of players to feed national teams. See Table 20.2 for additional South African and international rights holders and their associated properties.

20.4.3 Commercial

The commercial role of the rights holder includes activities related to the marketing of the sport property as a product, such as building the brand equity of the property, building the property's fan or participant base, maximising revenue (from the sale of tickets or entries, broadcast and sponsorship rights and merchandise) and ensuring that sponsors' rights are delivered (for example, ensuring that a sponsor's branding is set up for an event as agreed, without any competitor branding visible). This function is most relevant in the context of marketing of sport and will be considered in the most detail in the following sections.

The same principles will apply if the rights holder is a national team appealing to a broad cross-section of the public and major corporate sponsors, or a smaller club aiming to grow membership and receive financial support through sponsorship. Of course, the objectives and detail/execution of the plan may vary depending on the rights holders' goals and budget. Still, in both instances, the rights holder would benefit from developing a clear marketing plan for their property.

20.4.3.1 *Development of a property's strategic marketing plan*

The first phase in marketing a sport to fans and potential sponsors is for rights holders to develop a strategic marketing plan, including the following:

a) Set objectives or goals for the property

To set the marketing objectives of the property, consider what stage of the product lifecycle the property is at. For example, a new event might set a goal to build awareness and credibility before entering a ticket sales phase, while an established property with dwindling attendance might aim to reach new markets or find new ways to engage new and existing fans at events to make itself more appealing.

b)   Understand the property's fan base

As with any strategic marketing plan, the rights holder must identify the target audience of their product,[4] that is, whom the property reaches (spectators, participants or both), and define the size of the audience or fan base. This data can be obtained from the property's databases (ticket sales and race registrations for attendees and participants) and television audience data (viewership of live matches, highlights and repeat shows).

Understanding the demographic and psychographic profile of the fan base and the buyer behaviours of different segments within the fan base is also essential.[5] For example:

1. Can demographics segment the fan base? For example, is the fan base skewed towards a particular gender, age group, income group or geography?
2. How do different segments consume the property? For example, do they attend live events or prefer to watch them on television? Do they consume property-related content on social media?
3. What attracts each segment to live games and televised products? Equally, what barriers or inhibitors are there to each segment's ticket purchase or event entry? For example, are ticket prices to live games affordable? Is the stadium experience safe and pleasant? Is the stadium easy to access? For televised games, are live games broadcast on pay television or free-to-air? What language is commentary delivered in?

Rights holder databases, television audience data, social media data and market research are all valuable sources of fan insights. For example, an audience analysis of a televised broadcast may provide an overview of how many fans watched a particular game on each channel and their demographic profiles. This is valuable information for a rights holder to share with potential sponsors; it provides sponsors with data to support that the property reaches the fan base or audience the sponsor is targeting.

c)   The property's positioning

To achieve its objectives and offer value to the fan base and sponsors, the property must define its position in the minds of the consumer,[6] including:

1. the property's offering;
2. how the property differs from other competitor properties;
3. its unique selling point (USP); and
4. its visual identity (logo, typeface, tagline, style guide).

Competitor analyses and a strengths, weaknesses, opportunities and threats (SWOT) analysis are valuable tools to determine a property's positioning for fans and sponsors.

d)   Identify leverage opportunities

Rights holders must consider all the different options prospective sponsors will have to engage with the audience pre-event, at-event and post-event. These could include: the use of sponsor content in event newsletters distributed to race participants by the rights holder, the opportunity for sponsors to have stands or run brand engagements at events to display or sell their products, venue branding, branding of team kit, event activation such as entertainment by the sponsor at half-time, competitions and promotions encouraging fans to buy sponsor products to stand a chance to win tickets, mentions in social media posts, access to team merchandise, access to players for use in advertising and promotional campaigns, and ticketing and hospitality.

e) Develop ticket or entry pricing

Target audience demographics and the ticket or entry prices of competitor properties should be considered when determining the cost of tickets. Some of these considerations should include:

1. *Considering the target audience segmentation:* do different segments warrant having different categories of tickets, such as season tickets, student tickets, family bundles and early bird specials? Again, analysing a database of existing fans will help inform this segmentation and ticket pricing strategy.
2. *Affordability:* is the ticket price affordable for the fan base? What are similar events charging and how do their offerings compare?

A balance must be found between setting a price that is attractive to fans and maximising the rights holder's ticket sales revenue stream.

f) Determine sales channels

Considering how tickets or entries will be made available to fans is essential. This could be through a ticket sales platform (such as Ticketmaster, Ticketpro or Computicket), at the event, or both.

g) Develop a promotional plan

The rights holder must develop and implement a promotional plan to communicate the product and its positioning to the target audience to influence ticket sales and grow its fan base. The following should be taken into consideration when developing a promotional plan:

1. *Messaging:* what does the content of any communication aim to achieve? Is it to create hype and excitement around an upcoming event, using images of hero-worshipped players? Or is it more functional, such as an emailer communicating early bird ticket specials?
2. *Timing:* rights holders must consider the best time for ticket sales. Are there other significant events targeting the same audience and taking place simultaneously? When do fans typically buy tickets for the event? Does the event sell out quickly, or do fans wait until the last minute to buy tickets?
3. *The media plan:* a plan should detail how the property positioning, ticket sales or entries will be communicated to different segments. In addition, rights holders should consider what media channels will be most effective and efficient to reach each segment. For example, the rights holder of a university sports festival aiming to get a young, digitally savvy audience might choose to market the event and tickets to the event through a partnership with a social media influencer whose posts will reach and resonate with this audience.

Once a strategic marketing plan has been prepared, the rights holder is ready for the sponsorship sales phase.

20.4.4 Sponsorship Sales

This includes developing a sponsorship proposal or sales pack that provides prospective sponsors with the following:

1. An overview of the sponsorship property and its fans, using insights gleaned from the strategic marketing plan phase to motivate why the property offers a fit for prospective sponsors. This can be determined in terms of brand positioning, target audience and ability to deliver on the brand's marketing objectives.
2. A commercial rights package detailing the rights the sponsor will receive in exchange for the requested rights fee for a specified sponsorship level. (See Table 20.1 for an example of a commercial rights matrix.)
3. The requested rights fee, or the financial cost or 'in-kind' service, that the sponsor must provide in exchange for the rights set out in the rights package.

20.4.4.1 Commercial rights packages

Having identified various leverage opportunities available to sponsors, the rights holder should consider how to package these as commercial rights, with different rights available for varying levels of sponsors. The commercial rights package needs to be structured to maximise revenue from sponsorship sales for the rights holder while providing maximum benefit to the sponsors at each level. For example, a title sponsorship commanding the highest rights fee should, in return, offer the most valuable rights package (with higher media exposure from the sponsorship, more valuable ticketing and hospitality packages, and more frequent access to players). A rights matrix is a helpful way to define the different levels or tiers of sponsorship and the rights on offer for each tier. See Table 20.1 for a hypothetical example of a rights matrix for a football team.

Table 20.1: Commercial rights matrix

Right	Tier 1	Tier 2	Tier 3
Designation (what the sponsor can refer to itself as in its marketing activities)	Title or shirt sponsor	Associate sponsor	Official supplier
Category exclusivity (no competitor brands from the same category)	Yes	Yes	Yes
Kit branding	Front of shirt	Shirt sleeve	None
Stadium branding (Note: this assumes the event sponsor would receive 20% of stadium branding inventory)	• 30% of static and LED perimeter boards in home stadium	• 10% of static and LED perimeter boards in home stadium	• 40% of perimeter boards in home stadium divided equally between all official suppliers

Right	Tier 1	Tier 2	Tier 3
Use of marks and images	- Use of team logo - Use of player imagery. Generally, a three or four player rule applies: the sponsor may not include only one player in their marketing collateral, as this could be interpreted as an association with the player, rather than the team. To mitigate this, the rights contract will stipulate the number of players that must be included in an image.	- Use of team logo - Use of player imagery	- Use of team logo - Use of player imagery
Activation and promotional rights	- Right to run promotions and activations featuring the team logos, merchandise and imagery outside the stadium - Right to half time promotion - Stadium activations	- Right to run promotions and activations featuring the team logos, merchandise and imagery outside the stadium - Stadium activations	- Right to run promotions and activations featuring the team logos, merchandise and imagery outside the stadium - Stadium activations
Player appearances (subject to team availability)	- Six player appearances - One team appearance	- Three player appearances - One team appearance	- One player appearance
Broadcast elements	- On-screen logo - One squeeze back per half - 30 second insert - Full page advertisement in match programme - Right to include sponsor logo on rights holder website - Right to two posts per month on rights holder's social media platforms	- On-screen logo - One squeeze back per innings - Half page advertisement in match programme - Right to include sponsor logo on rights holder website - Right to one post per month on rights holder's social media platforms	- One lower third strap per match - Third page advertisement in match programme - Right to include sponsor logo on rights holder website - Right to one post per month on rights holder's social media platforms

Right	Tier 1	Tier 2	Tier 3
Hospitality	- 100 general access tickets per game - Right to buy 50 additional general access tickets - Two suites per game - 10 parking tickets	- 50 general access tickets per game - Right to buy 25 additional general access tickets - One suite per game	- 25 general access tickets per game - Right to buy 10 additional general access tickets - One suite per game

Identifying potential sponsors for each sponsorship tier and approaching them with a proposal or prospectus tailored to their brand and marketing objectives will significantly increase the proposal's relevance and chance of a successful sponsorship sale. Researching the potential sponsor's market challenges, marketing objectives, brand positioning, target audience and current sponsorship portfolio, and demonstrating how the property can align with and address these, will make for a more compelling proposal.

Likewise, a rights package designed or negotiated to suit a sponsor will be far more attractive to a potential sponsor than an off-the-shelf rights package, including rights that a sponsor pays for but doesn't need.

Once a sponsorship agreement has been concluded, the rights holder must focus on implementing or delivering the contractual rights to sponsors.

20.4.4.2 *Delivery of contractual rights*

Once the sponsorship rights sales process has been concluded, a legally binding contract is signed by the two entities (rights holder and sponsor) outlining the following:

1. The rights fee and payment terms.
2. The term or duration of the contract.
3. The sponsor's rights.
4. Renewal terms.
5. The obligations of the sponsor (such as payment of the rights fees as stipulated in the contract, not infringing on the rights of other sponsors, and not breaching the terms of the agreement or the regulations of the sport).
6. The obligations of the rights holder.

The rights holder's obligations are primarily concerned with ensuring that the sponsor's rights are upheld or delivered, including ensuring:

1. exposure for the sponsor in relevant media, as stipulated in the contract;
2. exclusivity; while there may be several sponsors per property, there is generally one sponsor per category or industry (telecommunications, banking, quick service restaurants, soft drinks, alcoholic beverages, etc.);

3. that non-sponsors do not gain exposure from or association with the property. The Olympic Games strictly enforces this with its 'clean venue' principle, which requires host venues to remove all non-Olympic branding for the duration of the Olympic Games; and
4. protection from ambush, including monitoring event venues and brand campaigns to ensure that non-sponsors do not promote themselves in association with the property and seek legal action against brands that engage in ambush marketing. A notable case of ambush marketing was carried out in South Africa during the 2010 FIFA World Cup at the Netherlands versus Denmark match, where 36 female supporters in orange dresses were ejected from the stadium by FIFA officials because the stunt, coordinated by non-sponsor Bavaria, constituted ambush marketing and infringed on the rights of official beer sponsor Budweiser. As a result, FIFA sought legal action against Bavaria and some participants but dropped the charges after reaching an out-of-court settlement.

20.5 PROPERTIES

The property lies at the heart of sports marketing. It is the consumer-facing event, team or league that fans watch, participate in and are passionate about; or the venue that is home to a favourite team, rich with history and traditions.

The rights holder administers the property, i.e., it is the entity that holds and sells rights to sponsors and broadcasters so that they can reach fans of the property. Some international and South African properties and their respective rights holders are listed in Table 20.2.

Table 20.2: A selection of international and South African properties and their rights holders

Properties	Rights holder
Olympic Games Paralympic Games	International Olympic Committee (IOC)
FIFA World Cup FIFA Women's World Cup	Fédération Internationale de Football Association (FIFA)
Rugby World Cup Rugby World Cup Sevens HSBC Sevens Series	World Rugby
ICC Men's Cricket World Cup, ICC Women's Cricket World Cup	International Cricket Council (ICC)
Men's and women's South African national football teams (Bafana Bafana, Banyana Banyana)	South African Football Association (SAFA)
Men's and women's national rugby teams (Springboks)	South African Rugby Union (SARU)
Men's and women's South African national cricket teams (Proteas) KFC Mini-Cricket	Cricket South Africa (CSA)

Properties	Rights holder
DStv Premiership MTN 8 Cup Nedbank Cup Carling Knockout Cup	Premier Soccer League (PSL)
Spar Proteas Telkom Netball League	Netball South Africa (NSA)
Comrades Marathon	Comrades Marathon Association (CMA)

A property may also be the television broadcast of a match or event. A broadcast sponsorship would entail a brand purchasing a package of sponsorship elements such as on-screen logos, squeeze backs (the process of reducing the size of the image on a television display to allow other items such as logos or sponsor graphics to be seen in the display area) and the right to flight 30 second advertisements. Typically, this is treated as a media buy, with the package purchased from the broadcaster instead of the rights holder. The broadcaster must ensure that the broadcast sponsor does not conflict with property sponsors or that property sponsors have the first right of refusal to buy sponsorship packages.

20.6 SPONSORS

20.6.1 Why Do Brands Sponsor Sport?

While rights holders are concerned with marketing their sport property to maximise revenue or growth, a sponsor will undertake sports marketing with a different agenda. This could include promoting and selling its products or services to a target audience through the property. According to IEG, "*Sponsorship is a cash or in-kind fee paid to a property (typically in sports, arts, entertainment or causes) in return for access to the exploitable commercial potential associated with the property*".[7] Sponsors market themselves through sport sponsorship, using a sport sponsorship as a marketing medium.

One of the significant benefits of sports sponsorship over other forms of marketing is its ability to enable brands to connect to people through something they are deeply passionate about. As Bill Shankly, former Liverpool FC Manager, said: "*Some people believe football is a matter of life and death. I am very disappointed with that attitude. I can assure you it is much more important than that.*"[8]

This passion gives marketers the advantage of an audience that is receptive. Sports fans who are actively tuned into a game, actively seeking out content related to their sporting passion point, are attentive and in an emotionally-rich environment. As Skildum-Reid notes, "*Sponsorship is the most emotional and personally relevant of all marketing media*".[9]

20.6.1.1 The role of sponsorship

Sport sponsorship has evolved since the 1970s and 1980s when the end goal was to drive awareness by applying a corporate logo to as much inventory as possible. Today's approach to sport sponsorship is more sophisticated and strategic. Rather than tactical logo placement to garner exposure and brand awareness, sport sponsorship is a strategic marketing tool to help brands deliver on their broader marketing objectives or market themselves through sport.

A sponsor may embark on marketing itself through sport to achieve the following objectives:[10]

1. Build brand awareness and visibility through at-event reach and media exposure.
2. Build brand stature, salience and image using sponsorship to change or reinforce a perception around the brand, differentiate the brand and shape consumer preference.
3. Acquire new customers through lead generation, sales promotions and on-site sampling linked to the sponsorship.
4. Drive brand loyalty by enhancing relationships through emotional engagement with key customers and stakeholders through access to sought-after events and sponsorship-related experiences.

20.6.1.2 Build brand awareness and visibility

Sponsorship can be used to build awareness and reach new markets. Typically, brands using sponsorship for this reason would be brands that are new to a market or brands with low levels of awareness in a market.

Sunfoil Pure Sunflower Cooking Oil's sponsorship of South African test cricket in 2011/12 illustrates how a brand with low levels of awareness within a particular audience effectively used sponsorship to address this.

While the Sunfoil brand was powerful in KwaZulu-Natal, it was relatively unknown in other regions. Sunfoil subsequently took naming rights sponsorship of Proteas test cricket and implemented a through-the-line campaign to leverage the sponsorship, with the following elements:

1. *In-store promotions:* purchases of Sunfoil oil in retail stores were rewarded with complimentary match tickets.
2. *In-stadium branding:* this generated exposure in the stadium and the television broadcasts.
3. *In-stadium activation:* Sunfoil branded caps and autograph cards were given to fans at the game. In addition, fans spotted wearing the Sunfoil branded cap were featured on camera and stood a chance to win product-related vouchers.
4. *Online:* fan photographs taken on the day were posted on the brand's website, where consumers could access educational product information.

The campaign delivered notable results for Sunfoil:

1. The brand received exposure on SABC3 and SuperSport, with an average viewership of 2,498,014 viewers at any given time and a total available audience of 17,625,523 viewers.
2. Product sales doubled in targeted regions.
3. The brand was rated the top South African cricket brand for the season.[11]

20.6.1.3 Build brand stature, salience and image

Over and above its ability to generate exposure that aids in building brand awareness, associating with a property provides the sponsor with borrowed brand equity. The positive attributes of the property are also associated with the sponsor. This can positively impact brand stature and trust.

Borrowing equity through sponsorship can also build brand salience or relevance by helping a sponsor to craft a particular brand image or support its positioning. For example, if a property is perceived as a wholesome, family-friendly event, these qualities may also be attributed to the brand sponsoring the property.

Brands should carefully evaluate properties, especially individual athletes, before entering into sponsorship agreements. For example, brands could suffer reputational damage should an athlete they sponsor behave in an unethical or undesirable manner. Thus it is advisable to consider the property's history and track record with prior sponsors if possible.

20.6.1.4 Acquire new customers

By leveraging sponsorship rights that the target audience perceives as valuable, such as exclusive tickets, experiences and merchandise, sponsorship can drive sales, product sampling at events and lead generation.[12]

Carling Black Label's "Be The Coach" campaign is an award-winning South African sponsorship market case study. Developed around the insight that South African football fans wanted their football expertise to be acknowledged, Carling Black Label gave fans the ultimate opportunity to "be the coach" and select players for the starting line-up of Kaizer Chiefs and Orlando Pirates teams in a new cup competition, the Carling Black Label Cup, played by the country's two biggest teams. The simple entry mechanic required fans to submit a code from the cap of a Carling Black Label bottle via a custom-built mobile platform, which generated significant sales. Ruud Gullit, former manager and international player, was the ambassador of the inaugural campaign, encouraging fans to vote for their team. Content communicating the campaign and fostering debate amongst fans delivered notable increases in traffic to the brand's social media sites (the Carling Black Label Facebook page grew by 450% and its Twitter following grew by 600%). Over R83 million worth of public relations exposure was generated for Carling Black Label.[13]

Since the inaugural event in 2011, the Carling Black Label Cup has continued to evolve and drive results for the brand. The 2019 edition recorded a 7% increase in product sales, the highest volume growth for the brand in 10 years for the same period. It also saw a 29% increase in reach among the target 18-to-30-year-old audience.[14]

20.6.1.5 Drive brand loyalty

Loyal customers are a valuable asset to a business. According to IEG, emotional engagement with customers is an effective way to differentiate a brand and influence sales and customer retention. Using sponsorship to link a brand to a property that customers care about provides an opportunity to leverage this emotion.[15]

Through exclusive and sought-after rights such as tickets and hospitality, sponsorship can offer money-can't-buy experiences to a brand's customers. This, in turn, gives a brand something valuable and meaningful to leverage to build emotional engagements with key customers and incentivise retention.

Once a sponsor has defined what marketing goals they would like to achieve through sponsorship, the sponsor should select the sponsorship that best suits their needs and budget.

20.6.2 Strategic sponsorship selection criteria

Having defined its sponsorship objectives, a brand must consider the following criteria when selecting a property to sponsor, giving consideration to which standards are essential and how the property scores on each:

1. *Exclusivity:* how cluttered is the property? Will the brand be one of a few or many sponsors? Are there competing brands already sponsoring the property? Are there opportunities for ambush?
2. *Brand fit:* do the property's values align with the brand's importance? Are the attributes of the property desirable to the brand? Is the brand happy being associated with the property's co-sponsors?
3. *Audience fit:* does the property give the brand access to its desired target audience at live events, on television or both? Consider the demographic and geographic makeup of the property's audience. For the sponsorship to be effective for the brand, the property must reach an audience sought-after by the brand.
4. *The prestige of the property:* how prestigious is the property? Is it known and sought-after by the target audience? Is the property's prestige commensurate with the requested rights fee?
5. *Ability to leverage:* what is the property's promotional time frame? Is it once-off or year-round? Does this fit strategically with the brand's marketing calendar? Can the brand leverage the property with the rights on offer, or must the brand negotiate additional rights? For example, in Table 20.1, a brand signing an 'official supplier' agreement may wish to develop a campaign with multiple pieces of content featuring players. However, since the rights contract only gives official suppliers access to one player appearance, the brand would need to negotiate a preferential rate for additional appearances or forgo other rights of equal value in exchange for further player appearances.
6. *Media exposure:* what media exposure is the rights holder guaranteeing? Will the sponsor allocate a significant additional budget to amplify the sponsorship?
7. *Ability to integrate product or drive sales:* for a beer brand, will the sponsorship include pouring rights to ensure the exclusive sale of the brand's product at event venues? Can the rights be negotiated for a banking brand to allow discounts on ticket purchases made with the brand's credit card?
8. *Ability to incentivise retailers:* for retail brands such as Coca-Cola, stocked in multiple retail outlets, a vital consideration is whether the property can incentivise sales through promotions. Also, if various retailers stock the brand, can exclusive promotions be offered to each?
9. *Track record:* does the rights holder have a good form in dealing with sponsors and delivering on rights as promised?
10. *Continuity/ability to extend:* can the sponsorship become a long-term partnership if the sponsor desires? Can it be expanded into other markets if this is a focus for the sponsor?

20.6.3 Sponsorship leverage

The term 'leverage' is often used in the context of sports marketing and sponsorship. It refers to the financial spend by a sponsor over and above the rights fee to exploit or unlock the sponsorship rights. Sponsors must make provisions for leverage spend to get the best results from their sponsorship. By analogy, a brand spending all its budget on sponsorship rights without allocating money to leverage these rights is like buying an expensive toy without the batteries to run it.[16]

Leverage is also often and incorrectly used interchangeably with 'activation'. Activation refers to face-to-face activities, generally conducted on-site (at an event related to the sponsorship) or off-site (at a venue not necessarily associated with the sponsorship, such as a shopping mall or a sponsor's head office). Activation is one of many ways or tactics to leverage sponsorship.[17]

Leverage, on the other hand, refers to a broad range of tactics that a sponsor may implement in the build-up to an event, at the event and post-event. Leverage thus extends beyond the event itself, enabling a sponsor to engage with a broader audience over a longer timeframe to deliver on its objectives ultimately. Leverage opportunities include:[18;19]

1. *Above-the-line:* television, radio, print and out-of-home campaigns or content that communicate the brand's narrative through the sponsorship and extend the reach of the sponsorship beyond the live event.
2. *Social media and digital campaigns:* organic and paid content that communicates the brand's narrative through the sponsorship and extends the reach of the sponsorship beyond the live event.
3. *Public relations:* growing the reach of the sponsorship and the brand's role through media relations.
4. *Ambassador and influencer marketing:* using influential personalities to amplify the brand's sponsorship and give it relevance.
5. *In-store:* promotional activities related to the sponsorship at a point of sale or transaction.
6. *Customer Relationship Management (CRM) or retention programmes:* using sponsorship rights (such as tickets or merchandise) to incentivise lead generation or reward loyal customers.
7. *Brand activation:* in-person fan engagements or experiences, on-site or off-site. These may include product sampling, discounts or giveaways.
8. *Hospitality:* a form of brand activation where the sponsor hosts key customers, staff or fans in an exclusive environment such as a suite or area with limited seating.

Since sport is highly emotional to fans, leverage tactics should be carefully considered. Leverage activities most likely to resonate with fans and have an impact are those that add value to the fan experience rather than disrupt it. To resonate with fans, sponsors need to place fans at the heart of their leverage campaigns, fully understanding their needs, likes and dislikes to improve their experience related to the sponsored property. As Skildum-Reid suggests, successful sponsorship leverage puts fans – not brands – at the heart.[20]

Sponsors should also be mindful of integrating their brands authentically, offering an experience that is true to their brand, rather than simply relying on applying their logo to sponsorship collateral to deliver on their objectives.

Between rights fees and leverage spending, sponsorship investment can be significant. Sponsors should thus measure the performance of a sponsorship to assess its effectiveness and return on objectives.

20.6.4 Sponsorship measurement

Sponsorship measurement should be carried out in two streams. Firstly and most importantly, sponsors should measure outcomes or return on objectives. Secondly, sponsors should track outputs to assess which leverage tactics or campaign elements have been effective in delivering on the overall outcome.

To illustrate, assume the fictitious TechBank is a digital-only financial services provider new to the South African market. TechBank wants to build awareness and relevance in the youth market to grow its market share. To achieve this, it sponsors a national university rugby tournament.

In addition to the field branding TechBank receives at rugby games, fixtures are also broadcast on television. The rights include broadcast sponsorship elements like squeeze backs and corner logos. For example, TechBank inserts a QR code on squeeze backs that directs viewers to the brand's mobile banking application, where they see a message that TechBank offers zero student banking fees.

At games, TechBank has an augmented reality kicking activation where fans can win prizes if they beat the scores of top university players. To play the game, fans need to provide contact details and have an opportunity to opt into marketing communications from the bank.

TechBank also creates a campaign on social media to leverage the sponsorship, featuring game highlights and interviews with players hosted by a well-known rugby legend. The campaign is promoted with paid media spending. It encourages fans to vote for their favourite player to stand a chance to win vouchers from the tournament's co-sponsor, a leading activewear brand. In addition, the content gathers leads for TechBank: fans who engage with content are served other content communicating TechBank offerings tailored for students. TechBank's measurement of the sponsorship should comprise two streams. First, TechBank should clearly define the sponsorship objectives and metrics, as illustrated in Table 20.3.

Table 20.3: Measuring TechBank's sponsorship return on objectives

Objective	Metric
Build awareness of TechBank in the youth market (18-25)	Percentage of youth market (18-25) who are aware of TechBank
Build TechBank's relevance in the youth market (18-25)	• TechBank is a brand for me • TechBank is a 'cool' brand • TechBank brand understands me
Grow TechBank's share of the 18-25 year old market	Increase in market share

TechBank should measure each of the metrics in Table 20.3 after leveraging the sponsorship and compare these scores to a benchmark (before sponsorship leverage started or year-on-year scores). Comparing scores of those aware of or exposed to the sponsorship with those not familiar or exposed can also indicate the sponsorship's effectiveness.

Secondly, TechBank should measure outputs associated with various tactics or campaign elements to assess their effectiveness. Finally, every tactic should be linked to one of the over-arching sponsorship objectives. (See Table 20.4 for an example.)

Table 20.4: Measuring the outputs of TechBank's sponsorship leverage tactics

Objective	Tactic	Output metric
Build awareness of TechBank in the youth market (18-25)	On-field branding	- Reach of on-field branding at the event and through broadcast - Exposure value of on-field and television branding elements (this can be supplied by a third party specialist)
Build TechBank's relevance in the youth market (18-25)	Social media campaign	- Content views and engagement - AR activation engagement
Grow TechBank's share of the 18-25 year old market	QR code directing viewers to TechBank's mobile application	- App downloads and visits via QR code featured in - Television squeeze backs - Leads gathered at AR activations

While the outputs listed in Table 20.4 should not be considered outcomes, they provide TechBank with guidance regarding which tactics within the leverage plan were effective and how the brand should allocate its leverage spending going forward. For example, if only ten fans participated in the AR activation at events, and of these, only two opted in to further communication, TechBank should consider whether the activation was worth the cost compared to the cost of other lead generation tactics such as the social media content or lead generation campaigns not related to the sponsorship.

20.7 CONCLUSION

This chapter has provided an overview of the power of sport and its appeal as a marketing medium. It has illustrated the relationship between the rights holder, property and sponsor, and demonstrated the application of sports marketing by a rights holder (marketing of sport) and a sponsor (marketing through sport). The different types of properties have been covered, as have the fundamental steps that a rights holder undertakes to market their sport (development of a property's strategic marketing plan, the sponsorship sales process and delivery of contractual rights). From a sponsor's perspective, this chapter has provided an overview of sponsorship rationale (why brands sponsor sport), strategic sponsorship selection criteria (how brands strategically select the best property to sponsor), sponsorship leverage principles (what to do with a sponsorship once rights have been acquired) and a sponsorship measurement framework (how to measure the return of the sponsorship against objectives and the effectiveness of leverage activity).

SELF-ASSESSMENT

1. In February 2023, South African Tourism's proposal to sponsor the English Premier League team Tottenham Hotspur was the subject of much debate and controversy. What, according to SA Tourism, was the rationale for the sponsorship? In your view, would the sponsorship have been a sound strategic choice to accomplish this objective? Consider the property's target audience and the rights offered to SA Tourism.

2. The launch of the inaugural Betway SA20, a T20 cricket tournament hosted across South Africa featuring South African and international players in teams owned by Indian Premier League (IPL) franchises, took place in 2023. How was the brand-new property positioned? How was it promoted and communicated? Given the positioning and style of communication, who was the target audience? What were the property's objectives?

3. Your client is an established medical aid provider in South Africa that wants to grow its market share by increasing the number of women it insures. In addition, the client has just signed on as the title sponsor of the 2023 Netball World Cup in South Africa. Based on the rights below, develop a leverage plan to help your client achieve its objective assuming a generous budget:

   a. Naming rights
   b. Right to use tournament logo and marks
   c. Rights to match footage
   d. Match tickets to all games
   e. On-site branding at matches
   f. On-site activations
   g. Right to run marketing promotions
   h. Broadcast sponsorship package including two squeeze backs per game, corner logo and a thirty-second television commercial

4. Design a measurement framework for the Sunfoil Proteas sponsorship, identifying objectives, tactics and possible metrics for each. Show the two 'streams' of metrics as outlined in Section 20.6.3.

SPORT FINANCE

Reinette van Gaalen

LEARNING OUTCOMES

At the end of this chapter, you should be able to:

1. Explain the evolution of sport finance.
2. Debate the role of financial management in a sport organisation.
3. Describe the primary financial objective of a company.
4. Explain the agency problem and agency cost.
5. Argue the decisions faced by the financial manager.
6. Describe the importance of working capital management in a company.
7. Compare and interpret the cash conversion cycle and operating cycle.
8. Discuss why organisations budget and prepare budgets.
9. Explain why budgets are helpful to a company.
10. Distinguish between the different financial records kept by a company.
11. Explain the various categories of financial ratio analysis.

21.1 INTRODUCTION

This chapter will consider the role of finance with regard to sport organisations, teams and players. Sport finance is defined as *"the study of effective management of cash flows by sports organisations in pursuit of their objectives"*.[1]

In the past, sport was practiced as a recreational activity or on an amateur level. The progression from amateur to professional status has increased sport's popularity and drawn attention to the business potential. Businesses can only survive with finance. The saying, '*Money makes the world go round*', is true.

The evolution of the sport industry necessitates the need to manage and control financial operations like any other profit-seeking industry. Although sport finance is unique to the sporting industry, it imitates all other businesses' financial issues.[2]

Sport finance analyses where the money comes from, where the money goes and how to utilise any remaining funds to help foster future growth effectively. It provides an essential input in the decision-making process within sport organisations, helping to identify the most appropriate course of action in any decision-making situation.

Some of the fundamentals of financial management will be discussed in this chapter in order to understand concepts such as revenue generation, budgeting and financial planning in sport finance.[3]

21.2 FINANCIAL MANAGEMENT

What would be the motive to start up any business?

To create job opportunities? To produce a product or deliver a service where there is a demand for it?

The motivation and reason for starting any business is to make money.

This leads to the next question; how do we determine if a company is making money? Looking at a profit is a starting point, but not the correct measure. Profit maximisation focuses on the short term only as it is primarily the result of increased sales and lower costs. Instead, a company should focus on maximising shareholders' wealth.

A business or company can only be started or operated with sufficient funding. Owners or investors in a business could finance the operations through savings or loans. Alternatively, the public (shareholders) could issue shares to raise funds. All the shareholders are effectively the owners of the company.

21.2.1 The Goal of Financial Management

Maximising shareholders' wealth will increase the wealth of the shareholders (owners) of the company over the long term. Maximising shareholders' wealth is preferred to maximising profits for the following reasons:

a) Cash flows

Cash flows are specific, whereas accounting profits are merely an accounting entry. Accounting records are prepared on an accrual basis and reflect transactions as they are recorded. Cash flow reflects the actual in- and outflow of money from a bank account. Cash is king from a financial management point of view. This is one of the most significant differences between accounting and financial management, and one of the reasons why shareholders' wealth maximisation is preferred over profit maximisation.

b) The timing of cash flows

The actual timing of cash flow, as opposed to the time of recording a transaction, is another reason profit maximisation is not preferred. As time passes by, money loses value. A product sold a year from today will have a higher cost than today because of the time value of money principle. In addition, money has an opportunity cost in the form of interest. This implies that money invested today must earn interest to compensate the owner for insufficient money for productive use.

c) Risk

Every decision in life and business has some risk attached to it. The more risk, the higher the reward required to compensate for taking the risk. Profit calculations do not take risk into account. Risk is fundamental in financial management and is typically considered in the required return or interest rate attached to an investment.

Therefore, a company's main objective should be to maximise shareholders' wealth by maximising cash inflows as soon as possible with the lowest potential risk on a sustainable basis.

21.3 THE ROLE OF THE FINANCIAL MANAGER IN THE ORGANISATION

Today most companies are not managed by the owners (shareholders) of the company but by the employees, management team or board of directors on their behalf. This creates an agency problem.

21.3.1 Agency Problem

The agency problem is a conflict of interest in a relationship where one party is expected to act in the other's best interest. The agency problem exists when the employees and management of a company are not the company's owners and, as a result, may not act in the best interests of the owners or shareholders of the company. When decisions are made that are not in the best interest of the owners (or shareholders), shareholders' wealth will no longer be maximised.

It is, therefore, essential to ensure that the goals of the shareholders and the employees and management of a company are aligned. Shareholders' wealth is maximised when the company's shares' value increases or dividends on the shares owned are received.

Decisions by the employees and management (agents) should create value for the company and more wealth for the shareholders. Value is made over the long term and not the short term, therefore it is essential to incentivise management in line with the shareholders' goals.

The manager's performance is measured based on short-term profit.

21.3.2 Agency Cost

Agency costs are incurred as a result of the agency problem. For example, initiatives to resolve the agency problem lead to agency costs. These costs are incurred to align management goals with shareholders' goals, namely maximising shareholders' wealth.

Financial incentives are given to management to encourage them to act in the best interests of the company, e.g., by:

- linking a performance bonus to the share price of the company; and
- giving management ownership in the form of shares.

21.4 THE ROLE OF THE FINANCIAL MANAGER IN DECISION-MAKING

Financial management includes all the activities in a company that involves money. The role of the financial manager is decision-making, keeping the goal of maximising shareholders' wealth in mind.

Suppose a business is considering manufacturing a new product or delivering a service. Careful consideration should be given to the following:

1. What product or service should be invested in?
2. Where will the business get long-term funds to fund the operations?
3. Where will the business get short-term funds to support the day-to-day operations? This includes collecting short-term funds and paying short-term obligations that are due.

These decisions can be divided into two categories:

21.4.1 Investment Decisions

The assets and projects the company should invest in are determined when making investment decisions.

21.4.2 Finance Decisions

The finance options available and how the company will finance its operations are determined when making financing decisions. For example, consider how the short-term, day-to-day operations will be funded and how longer-term operations that require a more extended period will be financed.

Short-term funding refers to up to 12 months, and longer-term financing refers to more than 12 months.

In addition to the shareholders, the various stakeholders must be considered in all decisions. Stakeholders include all the people involved in the business, like employees, suppliers, the general public and local government. Decisions are made to create value for the company and wealth for the shareholders.

Therefore, financial management focuses on creating value for *all* stakeholders by obtaining resources (funding) and putting them to productive use by making sound investments.

21.5 WORKING CAPITAL MANAGEMENT

All companies require money for their short-term, day-to-day operations. This is also referred to as liquidity. Liquidity refers to a company's ability to meet its short-term obligations, like paying salaries, when they are due.

Companies have various types of assets and liabilities on their financial statements. These can be divided into long-term and short-term assets and liabilities. Current assets and liabilities are those assets and liabilities that will be converted into cash within 12 months and therefore have a short-term nature. Managing short-term or existing assets and liabilities is called working capital management.

> JERSIE manufactures and sells rugby jerseys to clubs and schools. As a result, JERSIE will need to consider the following as part of its working capital management:
>
> - How will they sell their jerseys, for cash or on credit?
> - How much stock should they keep on hand to have enough available when required?
> - Will they pay their suppliers immediately with cash or later on credit?

Cash is required for all daily transactions and to purchase stock. Inventory is necessary to conduct business, and customers that buy goods on credit become trade creditors. Luckily, the suppliers of goods that offer credit provide some relief to the short-term needs of a company as a trade creditor.

All the working capital management decisions ensure sufficient resources are available for the company to operate efficiently over the short term.

The day-to-day activities of any company will comprise converting assets into cash that will be used to purchase more assets that will be converted into cash again. There is a constant in-and outflow of money. Two important cycles can be calculated to help companies better understand their working capital management requirements: operating and cash conversion.

21.5.1 Cash Conversion Cycle

The cash conversion cycle refers to the time lapsed from the outflow of money to the inflow. A company's liquidity is better understood by calculating the cash conversion cycle.

The cash conversion cycle (CCC) consists of three components:

a) Average Age of Inventory (AAI)

A calculation of the days from when the inventory was purchased to when the stock was sold.

b) Average Collection Period (ACP)

The number of days that lapse between selling a product to a debtor (customer) and collecting the money from the debtor (customer).

c) Average Payment Period (APP)

The number of days that lapse between purchasing material from a creditor (supplier) and paying the creditor (supplier).

The cash conversion cycle is calculated as follows:

> CCC = AAI + ACP − APP
>
> Cash Conversion Cycle = Average Age of Inventory + Average Collection Period − Average Payment Period

The cash conversion cycle indicates the days that cash is invested in short-term assets like inventory or trade debtors and unavailable for day-to-day operations. It means the time the company needs to acquire another form of finance, e.g., bridging finance.

The cash conversion cycles of different companies will vary depending on the type of product or service and the industry in which they operate. The fast-food industry will, for example, have a short cash conversion cycle compared to a company with a long manufacturing process.

Effective working management will aim to shorten the period in which alternative sources of funding are required by shortening the cash conversion cycle.

21.5.2 Operating Cycle

The operating cycle (OC) determines the time that lapses from starting the manufacturing process until the final product is sold.

The operating cycle is calculated as follows:

> OC = AAI + ACP + APP
>
> Operating Cycle = Average Age of Inventory + Average Collection Period + Average Payment Period

Graphically it can be illustrated as follows:

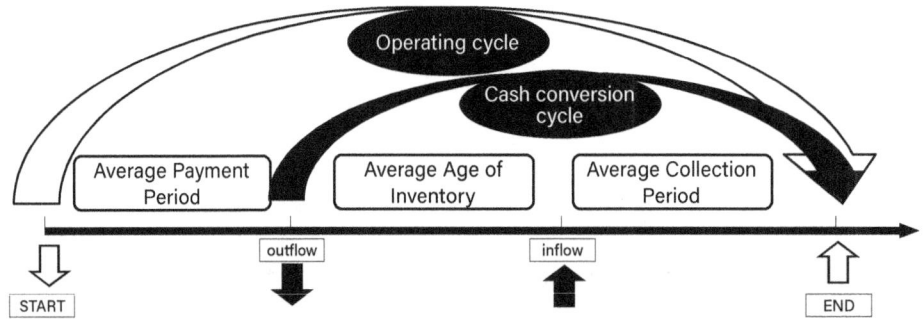

Figure 21.1: Graphical illustration of the operating and cash conversion cycles

Now that the short-term financing needs of a company have been considered, the longer-term financing options available will be investigated in the next section.

21.6 COST OF CAPITAL

Funding is required if a company wants to build a new factory or invest in a building like a new stadium. The financing will typically be needed for a extended period, in other words, more than 12 months.

There are various sources of funds available to a company. For example, it could use debt financing by applying for a long-term loan at a financial institution. Alternatively, equity financing could be obtained by issuing shares in the company. Typically, a combination of debt and equity funds is used to finance a company's investments. When different sources of funds are used to finance the longer-term operations of a company, the cost of capital needs to be determined.

Cost of capital refers to the combined cost of the different sources of funds.

The providers of the funds (or capital) require something in return for the money they invested. The return that the providers require will equal the cost for the company that receives the money.

Financial institutions like banks charge interest on outstanding loans, and shareholders require compensation in the form of dividends or capital growth in the share price.

The cost of capital can be summarised as follow:

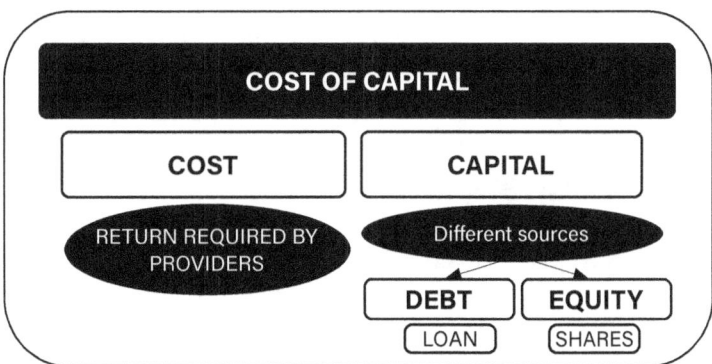

Figure 21.2: Graphical illustration of the cost of capital

the cost of capital is the combined cost of various sources of capital. When the cost of capital is calculated, the rate of return that must be earned to satisfy the capital providers is determined.

Green Courts, a local tennis club, is investigating an opportunity to build four new padel courts. The estimated return on this investment is 25%, however the capital required for this project is 18%. Green Courts should therefore invest in the new padel courts as the return on the project will be higher than the cost.

The cost of capital is therefore used as a long-term decision-making tool. The potential return on investment is compared to the cost of capital or the combined required return of the providers of capital. If the return on the investment will be higher than the cost, the project should be accepted. If not, it should be rejected. In this way, shareholders' wealth will be maximised.

21.7 BUDGETS

Superstars Football Club just secured a sponsorship deal for the following year. The club is also considering contracting a young talented player, but the club's coaching staff was promised a salary increase effective the next month. In addition, the lease for the training grounds has been renewed with a 15% increase. The team will play a training match in Cape Town next month, resulting in additional travelling costs. In this example, the football club may have more than enough money from the sponsorship deal to contract the new player, but do they have enough to contract the new player, pay the increased salaries and lease instalments and cover the additional travelling costs?

As much as the club would like to fulfil all its commitments, it needs to carefully consider the amount offered to the new player to ensure that there is money left for all the other expenses. This is budgeting.

The various activities within a company should be coordinated by preparing plans of action for future periods.

These detailed plans are referred to as budgets.

In other words, they are a road map that reveals a company's revenue streams and indicates where it intends to spend its money.

Budgets are tailored to the organisation's needs and can be prepared weekly, monthly or yearly. In addition, budgets can be prepared for the entire organisation's particular division or department according to the specific requirements.

21.7.1 Purpose of Budgets

Budgets are helpful for the following reasons:

1. It helps to anticipate the future and can be used as a strategic planning tool.

   Example: budgets indicate when additional revenue and expenditure are expected, like when revenue from a sponsorship deal is expected.

2. Indicates what resources are needed at what point in time.

   Example: when does a company need to purchase new machinery or do considerable maintenance work?

3. Identify where revenue shortfalls may occur.

   For example: if the revenue from stadium attendance is less than budgeted due to lousy weather, revenue will be shortfalls from the expected ticket sales stream.

4. Allows for better financial monitoring.

   Example: a soccer club can continuously monitor the amount spent on contracting players.

5. It helps communicate plans to various stakeholders and allows for a more precise measurement of financial performance.

Example: employees working in different departments of a company will understand the plan for their department by looking at the budget, e.g., will there be an expansion in the specific division?
6. All members of the business can use it to help make decisions.

Budgets are developed by examining business successes and failures, therefore they take time to develop. Initially, the first budget may need to be more specific and accurate, but it will be adjusted and improved over time.

A reasonable budget acts as a constraint on spending, provides a clear picture of the anticipated resource limitations, and predicts the future financial stability of a company.

21.7.2 Cost classification for Budgeting Purposes

To prepare a budget is essential to understand the different revenues and costs of the company. When considering costs, it is necessary to note that the term 'cost' can be interpreted differently. For budgeting purposes, a cost can be classified as fixed or variable.

21.7.2.1 Variable cost

A variable cost remains the same *per unit* but will change *in total* as the level of activity changes. If the number of spectators, clients or users increases, the total variable cost will increase, but per unit remains the same. A company that manufactures supporters' jerseys will purchase material to manufacture the jerseys. The material cost per jersey will remain unchanged regardless of the number of jerseys manufactured. The total material cost of the jerseys will increase if more jerseys are manufactured and decrease if fewer jerseys are manufactured.

21.7.2.2 Fixed cost

A fixed cost remains the same regardless of the total activity level. However, the fixed cost per unit will increase if the number of units decreases. The factory rental in which the supporter jerseys are manufactured is fixed. In total, the rental cost stays the same. The fixed cost allocated to the jerseys manufactured will increase per jersey if fewer jerseys are manufactured and decrease per unit if more jerseys if manufactured.

The activity level drives variable cost and can therefore be controlled to an extent. Fixed costs, on the other hand, remain unaffected by the level of activity. Thus, understanding the different cost classifications according to their behaviour to changing activity levels provides an opportunity to use the information for budgeting purposes.

21.7.3 Breakeven Analysis as a Budgeting Tool

Breakeven analysis is a valuable budgeting tool that is used to investigate the impact of revenue, cost and volume changes on profits. Therefore, breakeven analysis is also sometimes referred to as cost-volume-profit analysis.

The breakeven point in sales occurs when total revenue equals total cost. Sales below this point will result in losses and above this point in profits. This is a valuable decision-making and planning tool as it answers whether a sport event will succeed. The impact of changes in the ticket price, attendance numbers or membership numbers on profit or loss is reflected.

> Breakeven analysis is particularly applicable to event management and sport service delivery. First, it answers the question: what attendance level or usage rate is needed to ensure a viable event or operation? Next, it shows the changes in profits and losses resulting from changing attendance or usage patterns and price changes. As a result, it quickly indicates if an event or operation is likely to be a commercial success.
>
> There are several steps involved in identifying the break-even point. The first step consists of dividing costs into fixed and variable. For example, fixed costs remain constant for an event despite sales, membership and attendance changes. These include venue hire, rental, guest speakers, lights and power, insurance and the cost associated with core or permanent staff. Conversely, variable costs will vary directly with sales, membership and attendance changes. They include things like the use of casual staff, equipment, consumables, giveaways and catering. The second step is to estimate anticipated revenues for every level of sales, membership and attendance. Finally, the third step is to compare and contrast total revenue and total cost for every sales, membership and attendance level.[4]

21.8 FINANCIAL STATEMENT ANALYSIS

The evolution of sport from amateur to professional status has transformed the sport industry into a lucrative business. Therefore, from a financial perspective, effectively managing a sport organisation's financial affairs soundly and responsibly is essential to ensure financial viability.

Understanding the financial data provided in the financial records gives insight into the performance of the sport organisation from a monetary perspective. The different financial records of a company will be briefly discussed below to understand the information each contains.

Financial statements comprise of:

Income statement/Statement of comprehensive income:
- Displays a company's profitability over time.
- Shows the income and expenses.

Balance sheet/Statement of financial position:
- Displays the financial condition of the company at a point in time.
- Shows all assets and liabilities.

Statement of cash flows:
- Tracks the cash implications of transactions.

- Shows the flow of actual cash in and out of the business.

Notes to the financial statements

- Provides additional information regarding the various items (line items) on the income statement or balance sheet.

The main objective of financial statements is to provide valuable information to a wide range of users in making economic decisions. Analysis and interpretation of financial statements is the process of arranging, examining and comparing the results of an entity so that the users are equipped to make informed decisions.

Ratio analysis is a method of analysing financial statements. Ratios are calculated to determine a company's profitability, liquidity, long-term indebtedness and net worth.

The ratios can be categorised into the following categories:

Profitability

Has the business made a profit compared to its turnover, assets and capital employed?

Liquidity

Does the business have enough money to honour its short-term liabilities, pay wages or buy inventory?

Asset usage or activity

How effectively has the business used its fixed and current assets?

Debt/Solvency

Does the company have much debt, or is it financed mainly by equity?

Investor/Shareholder indicators

How does the market see this company?

The effective management of any sport organisation requires applying the key financial management concepts and a good understanding of the organisation's financial recording and reporting system. The financial ratios calculated from the information in the financial statements provide insight into the profitability, short-term financial stability, long-term financial stability, and finally, the level of wealth or net worth of the company.

The calculations of the different financial ratios fall outside the scope of this text.

21.9 CONCLUSION

Finance is a relevant topic with principles applicable to individuals or companies. Of course, companies and individuals differ, but finance principles remain the same and applicable to all, even sport organisations.

Financial management includes all the activities in a company that involves money. The focus of financial management is to create value for all stakeholders. Any sport organisation will thrive if the main objective of financial management is applied to all decisions, namely maximising shareholders' wealth.

Further reading

Fried, G., Shapiro, S. & Deschriver, T. 2008. *Sport Finance* (2nd ed.). Champaign, IL: Human Kinetics.
- Agency Problem and Cost, Fundamentals of Finance (Chapter 1)
- Working Capital Management, Fundamentals of Finance (Chapter 10)
- Cost of Capital, Fundamentals of Finance (Chapter 7)

Els, G., van Gaalen, R., Strydom, N.T. & Beekman, J. 2019. *Fundamentals of Finance* (7th ed.). Durban: Lexis.
- Budgets (Chapter 7).

SELF-ASSESSMENT

Complete the following questions by debating possible answers and selecting the most appropriate. Make sure that you are clear on why the answers indicated are correct.

Financial Management

1. The financial goal of any company is to ...
   a) avoid financial distress.
   b) optimise solvency.
   c) maximise shareholders' wealth.
   d) keep the amount of tax to be paid as low as possible.

2. Profit maximisation does not necessarily mean wealth maximisation, as it does not take...
   a) profit into account as profit is only an opinion.
   b) cash flow into account as cash flow is only an opinion.
   c) cash flow into account as cash flow is a fact.
   d) the financial objectives of a company into account.

3. State whether the following statement is TRUE or FALSE.

   The primary objective of a business is to grow funds that were invested by shareholders and maximise their wealth in the long term.

   True: The primary aim of a company is shareholder wealth maximisation

Agency problem

1. The agency problem refers to ...

   a) an inefficient marketing agency.

   b) industrial espionage.

   c) managers who do not focus on wealth creation as shareholders would.

   d) hiring the correct manager to represent the shareholders.

2. The agency problem arises when managers act in the company's owners' best interest rather than in their interest. First, identify which is not a solution to the agency problem.

   a) Measuring the performance of managers on a correct basis.

   b) Giving managers ownership in the form of shares.

   c) Bonuses linked to sales/revenue of the company.

   d) All of the above.

Working capital management

1. State whether the following statement is TRUE or FALSE.

   The operating cycle will *decrease* if a company implements a strategy only to sell its goods for cash.

   True – the operating cycle will decrease, accounts receivable period will be zero.

2. Quick Manufacturers has an average inventory period of 45 days, pays suppliers after 60 days and collects outstanding debtors' accounts after 80 days. Determine the cash conversion cycle of Quick Manufacturers.

   Cash conversion cycle = AAI+ACP - APP
   = 45 +60 – 80
   = 25 days

Cost of capital

1. Identify which of the following statements regarding the cost of capital is TRUE or FALSE.

   Cost of capital refers to the individual cost of different sources of capital invested in a company

   False – It is the collective charge of **all the providers of finance of a company**.

2. The cost of capital is the same as the required rate of return of investors.

   True – It is the return required by providers of capital.

Budgets

1. Identify which of the following statements regarding the cost of capital is TRUE or FALSE.

    Detailed plans of various activities within a company are coordinated by preparing plans of action for future periods.

    True

Analysing Financial Statements

1. A record that shows how profitable a company is, is a:

    a) Statement of Comprehensive Income

    b) Statement of Financial Position

    c) Statement of Cash Flows

2. What do liquidity ratios tell us about a company?

    a) Does the business have enough money to honour its short-term liabilities?

    b) Does the company have much debt and is it financed mainly by equity?

    c) How effectively has the company used its fixed and current assets?

    d) How does the market see this company?

SPORT FACILITY MANAGEMENT

Professor Marié EM Young, Phindile E Mahlalela and Dr Teneille Venter

> ## LEARNING OUTCOMES
>
> At the end of this chapter, you should be able to:
>
> 1. Outline the origins and evolution of sport facilities from past to present.
> 2. Identify different types of sports facilities.
> 3. Explain the planning and development of sports facilities in a South African context.
> 4. Define the main components of the operational management of sport facilities.

22.1 INTRODUCTION

A person's sport experience, whether as an athlete, participant at a health club or spectator at an event, most likely involves a sport facility. A sporting facility can be defined as an enclosed facility built and installed or a location (natural or man-made) where the sport is being played.[1] The management of these facilities keeping them in their optimal condition and ready for events, which are an enormous undertaking and can be complex.[2,3] A Sport Manager's important function requires thorough knowledge of the sport facility to ensure long-term operational success. It is also essential for the development of sport. Sport managers are faced with several tasks. Their work entails more than just planning, organising, managing people, keeping track of inventory, and controlling the daily processes of athletes, teams or events. Sport managers have several roles to fulfil, including the management of facilities. The sport facility industry can also provide various career opportunities to sport management students. It is therefore important to be adequately prepared to plan and manage sport facilities.

This chapter is devoted to providing a theoretical overview of the planning and management of sport facilities. It will provide an overview of the evolution of sport facilities, types of sport facilities, facility planning and design, and the operational duties of the sport Facility Manager. Practical examples of major sport facilities in South Africa, such as the Cape Town Stadium and the Moses Mabhida Stadium, will complement it. Focusing on major facilities provides all-inclusive knowledge of facility management that can be applied to smaller sport and recreation facilities.

22.2 THE EVOLUTION OF SPORT FACILITIES

Sports facilities have evolved significantly throughout history to meet the changing needs and demands of athletes, spectators and sport activities. Sport facilities have existed for almost three thousand years and were designed with striking elements of architecture being acknowledged as symbols of power.[4]

Here is a brief overview of the history of sports facilities:

22.2.1 Ancient Times

Between 8000 and 7000 BC, there was no organised sport. People prioritised self-sufficiency over building complex structures. However, ancient civilisations like the Greeks and Romans were important in developing sport facilities.

22.2.1.1 Ancient Greece

In Ancient Greece, the Greeks were the first to construct public sport facilities, including stadiums and swimming pools, between 800 and 600 BC. They had "Palaestras" in the 6th to 8th century BC, which were essentially open courts between columns and chambers where people could engage in various activities such as wrestling, boxing, playing ball sport and socialising. However, the most important activities were swimming and bathing.

In 776 BC, the first stadium was built in Greece, where 10,000 Greek residents gathered for the Olympic events.[5] The most famous of these stadiums is the Panathenaic Stadium in Athens. It was originally constructed in 331 BC and rebuilt in the 2nd century AD. Initially, stadiums were plain, flat, rectangular tracks sometimes built near existing hills to provide spectators with a clear view of the action.[6]

22.2.1.2 Ancient Rome

During ancient times, the Romans were known for their love of violent entertainment, which their rulers used as a tool to control the people for extended periods. Leaders constructed large facilities like the Colosseum and Circus Maximus to fulfil the needs of the sport. In the second century AD, the Romans improved their sport facilities by shifting from the initial rectangular design to a horseshoe shape. The facilities were adorned with opulent ornamentation and marble sculptures.[7] The Circus Maximus was constructed around the 6th century BC and was massive, with stone walls surrounding a sand-covered racetrack over 500 metres long. The Colosseum was smaller and could accommodate only around 50,000 people. The Colosseum was used until the 13th century, while the Circus Maximus remained in use until the 6th century.[8]

Between 300 and 100 BC, the Romans improved upon the Greek bathhouses by giving their baths and pools a pricey addition: heat! Ancient Romans could bathe and swim in warm water because of thermal springs and open fires heating the water. The Romans also constructed aqueducts, allowing for a more hygienic and healthy experience by continually circulating fresh water into the baths.[9] During this time, the largest pool constructed had a surface area of almost 900,000 square feet. In 43 AD, the Roman conquest of

Britain introduced their traditions of ceremonial bathing and recreational swimming. Romans constructed the vast Aquae Sulis "religious spa" around 75 AD, and it quickly became a popular location for worship, bathing, swimming and healing. Aquae Sulis was heated by thermal springs, making the water comfortable for swimming and worship.[10]

22.2.1.3 19th century

The Industrial Revolution brought significant changes in sport facilities. The emergence of organised sport and the growing popularity of spectator sport led to the construction of purpose-built stadiums and arenas. In 1871, the Rugby School in England formally established the Rugby Football Union and laid out the first set of standardised rules for the game.[11] This marked a turning point in the formalisation of sport and the need for dedicated sport facilities. There was an installation of undersoil heating beneath the football field in Goodson Park in 1958. A cable was installed beneath the ground to serve as a heating system to prevent the pitch from freezing, and it was more successful and efficient than before.[12] In 1960, the pitch was dug up and relayed with modern drainage systems since the outdated drainage system could not handle the new water floods.

After World War II, home swimming pools gained popularity in the United States. In Britain, swimming pools gained popularity in the middle of the 19th century. In London, England, there were six indoor swimming pools with diving boards as early as 1837. The first public indoor municipal swimming pool was built in England in 1828 and swimming became more widely available.[13] The British brought swimming pools and competitive swimming to southern Africa in the 19th century. Before indoor pools were constructed in Camps Bay (1905), Long Street and other city suburbs, the dry dock in Cape Town's harbour served as a location for aquatic carnivals. In 1898, Port Elizabeth constructed a saltwater pool at Humewood, while East London and Durban also built comparable structures. During the 1950s and 1960s, several cities constructed municipal Olympic-sized swimming pools, however few were heated, and none were covered.[14] It should be noted that while swimming pools gained popularity, amusement parks in America also increased.

Amusement parks grew in popularity in the 19th century. They became a new form of entertainment for the general public. Amusement parks, frequently found near cities, gave inhabitants a break from their obligations and labour. Coney Island in New York was the most well-known of the late 19th century amusement parks. However, others included Paragon Park and Revere Beach in Boston, later followed by Disneyland, which first appeared in 1955.[15] Amusement parks brought together a range of well-liked activities and attractions, all of which mirrored the era's cultural shift. The excitement of large groups of pleasure seekers to enjoy fun, innovative mechanical rides and exotic sideshows were what made the amusement park noteworthy.[16]

22.2.1.4 Early 20th century

The 20th century witnessed a rapid expansion in the construction of sports facilities, and the Olympic Games played a crucial role in shaping sports facilities. Multi-purpose stadiums, designed to host various sports and events, became prevalent. A ballpark was constructed in the United States for the first time in 1862 (Union Grounds) during the Early Modern period. Unfortunately, many of these early ballparks, constructed of wood, burnt down and had to be reconstructed multiple times.[17,18] From 1912 to 1930, several significant stadiums, including Fenway Park and the Yale and Yankee stadiums, were constructed. There are now collegiate sports facilities, including a football-only stadium. Franklin Field at the University of Pennsylvania was the first football stadium ever constructed for University -only sports. Subsequent editions prompted the construction of iconic venues like the Berlin Olympic Stadium (1936) and the Sydney Olympic Park (2000). The Berlin Olympic Stadium, which had a symmetrical oval shape and was constructed in the imposing Neoclassical style favoured by the Nazis, could accommodate 110,000 people. The field was around 40 feet (12 metres) below ground level due to the structure's partial digging into the earth. Its sheer size was supposed to astonish the globe and awe people, and it was successful in doing so.[19]

22.2.1.5 Late 20th century

The late 20th century saw a trend toward specialised sport facilities tailored to specific sport, such as baseball parks, football stadiums, and basketball arenas. The many purposes for which stadiums were created resulted in various stadium forms. Some were elliptical or U-shaped, while others were rectangular with rounded corners.[20] Shea Stadium in New York incorporated field seat sections that rotate around the stadium to enable conversion from a baseball to a football layout after Dodger Stadium in Los Angeles became the first tiered stadium to give column-free views from all seats in 1959.[21]

The Astrodome, the first important completely roofed stadium, was constructed in Houston, Texas, in 1965 and was a key milestone of the mid-20th century.[22] For the Olympics in 1960, the Roman sport complex was built, including the Palazzetto dello Sport with a ribbed-dome top. The New Orleans Superdome had a greater seating capacity and was constructed in 1975. Stadiums with retractable domes started to develop in the late 1980s, most notably Toronto's Rogers Centre.[23] A noteworthy advancement was using flexible steel wires to span huge roof dimensions. Cables significantly aided in accelerating construction, making the roof of covered stadiums lighter and lowering construction costs. In Minneapolis-St. Paul, Minnesota, a modern stadium, had this equipment installed.

22.2.1.6 Sport facilities today

Sustainability and eco-friendly designs have become increasingly important in modern sport facility construction, emphasising energy efficiency, waste reduction and renewable materials. The Union of European Football Associations (UEFA) and Fédération Internationale de Football Association (FIFA) launched quality control systems to develop artificial turf in 2001.[24] Thanks to it, they developed industry norms for its application in soccer. The International Football Association Board addressed the issue of grass in the 2004 *Laws of The Game*. Fourth-generation pitches, or 4G pitches, were introduced in 2010 and have gained popularity ever since.[25] The fields are made of artificial turf and real grass, making them extremely durable and long-lasting. Because they are not constantly illuminated or irrigated, these fields are simple to manage and groundskeepers can readily monitor them.

Stadiums have expanded exponentially and switched from standing to sitting after the Hillsborough tragedy in 1989. Before the 1994–95 season began, a rule required that all standing areas at Premier League grounds be changed to seating areas.[26] Several other nations, notably South Africa, have enacted the same restrictions. All seater stadiums are now required for all of FIFA and UEFA's championships. The emphasis on sustainability and energy efficiency has also been one of the main trends in pool design today. To lessen their influence on the environment, many pool owners are increasingly seeking pool designs that consume less energy and water and emit fewer emissions.[27] Nowadays, many swimming pools are equipped with energy-efficient filters and pumps, and a few even use solar panels to produce their electricity for heating purposes. These facilities are created to be highly functional.

22.3 SPORT FACILITY TYPES

Sport facilities come in various forms and sizes, catering to different sport and recreational activities. They can either be indoor or outdoor facilities depending on their purpose. Some facilities are presented in the following table.

Table 22.1: Examples of sport facilities

Stadiums	Large, enclosed structures primarily used for team sport like football (soccer), baseball, cricket or rugby. Stadiums often have seating capacity for thousands of spectators.
Arenas	Indoor venues designed for sport such as basketball, ice hockey, indoor soccer or concerts. They usually feature tiered seating and a central playing area.
Gymnasiums	Multi-purpose indoor facilities equipped for various sport and physical activities. Gymnasiums are commonly found in schools and community centres.
Athletic Fields	Open-air fields used for sport like football, rugby, field hockey, lacrosse, and track and field events. They may include features such as bleachers, lighting and scoreboard.
Tennis Courts	Dedicated areas for playing tennis, usually composed of a smooth playing surface surrounded by boundaries and a net in the middle.
Swimming Pools	Facilities designed for swimming and water-related activities. Pools can be indoor or outdoor and range from Olympic-sized to smaller community pools.
Golf Courses	Vast outdoor spaces with holes and fairways for playing golf. They can be designed as 9-hole, 18-hole, or even more extensive courses.
Skating Rinks	Ice rinks used for ice hockey, figure skating and recreational skating. They can also be converted into roller-skating or rollerblading rinks during warmer months.
Sports Halls	Large indoor venues that can accommodate multiple sports, including basketball, volleyball badminton, and indoor soccer.
Athletic Tracks	Synthetic or paved tracks used for running, sprinting and other track and field events. They often encircle a sport field.
Climbing Walls	Artificial structures designed for rock climbing and bouldering, providing climbers with various routes and difficulty levels.

Sports Centres	Comprehensive facilities that offer a range of sport amenities, including courts, pools, fitness areas and specialised spaces for specific sport or training.
Cycling Velodromes	Circular or oval-shaped tracks specifically designed for track cycling, featuring steeply banked curves.
Martial Arts Dojos	Training spaces for martial arts disciplines such as karate, judo, taekwondo or kung fu. They often have padded floors and mirrors.
Equestrian Centres	Facilities for horse-related activities, including riding arenas, stables and tracks for horse racing or show jumping.

These are just some examples of sport facilities; there are many more specialised venues and arenas for specific sports or activities depending on the region and cultural preferences.

22.4 SPORT FACILITY PLANNING AND DESIGN

Sport facilities planning and design in South Africa involve the process of developing and creating sport venues that cater to the needs of athletes, spectators and the community. Historically, the building of sport facilities was expensive due to the lack of technology and their maintenance were economically prohibitive.[28] Today this has changed as the focus has shifted to the sustainable design of multi-purpose facilities meeting the needs of many people. Here are some key considerations and examples of sport facilities planning and design in South Africa.

22.4.1 Facility Planning

Facility planning is the initial tasks that need to be completed in preparation for the course of action to be taken before designing the facility. The purpose is to provide sufficient information in order to make decisions.

22.4.2 Needs Assessment

The development of new facilities depends on the increased number, type, average, size and attendance of sport and entertainment events or opportunities for the growth of sport.[29] It is thus dependent on the needs of the community and sports organisations. This involves understanding the demand for different sports, identifying target user groups, and determining the required capacity and functionality of the facilities. In South Africa, the development of major sport facilities was driven by hosting the FIFA World Cup 2010. Many facilities were strategically planned and erected in different provinces as legacy projects, such as the Mbombela Stadium (Nelspruit), Nelson Mandela Bay Stadium (Port Elizabeth), Peter Mokaba Stadium (Polokwane), Moses Mabhida Stadium (Durban) and Cape Town Stadium (Cape Town). Other facilities underwent major upgrading to become world-class stadiums where games could be played, such as the Soccer City Stadium (the old FNB Stadium in Johannesburg), Ellis Park Stadium (Johannesburg), Loftus Versfeld Stadium (Pretoria), Royal Bafokeng Stadium (Rustenburg) and Free State Stadium (Bloemfontein).[30;31]

Facilities may also be developed to attract more tourists. For instance, the design of the Cape Town Stadium considered the location and environment being in Green Point at the foot of Signal Hill and the Atlantic Ocean, as well as the legacy it would leave.[32] Cape Town, as an existing tourist hub, was considered as it was said that the surroundings would be more attractive for spectators.[33] It was built in conjunction with Green Point Park Urban Park to attract more users to the area, and a walkway was created from the station through the city to the stadium.

22.4.2.1 Facility forecasting

Further to the above, it is important to conduct some forecasting of the growth and demand for a facility. The demand for a facility and the facility size is determined by the population or area of dominant influence (market) as determined by the local media.[34] Surveys can be used as a method to conduct forecasting of the growth and demand for facilities. It is also important that these facilities generate income from attendance which will only be possible with the community's support. With the evolution of technology, computer models can now be used to predict event range, numbers and attendance.

22.4.2.2 Facility feasibility

Once forecasting has been established, a feasibility study is conducted. A feasibility study is a comprehensive analysis of the potential project from a legal point of view on the ramifications, usage design, site, financial and administrative feasibility of the sports facility project.[35] In other words, it investigates how the facility can be transformed into a business entity.[36] It is used to determine the potential risks of building the sport facility and to determine if it is financially and practically feasible to continue with the project.[37] The feasibility study analyses the location, size and cost associated with the building of the sport facility and will further consider the economic and environmental impacts of the project. Many stadiums built for the 2010 FIFA World Cup (e.g., Moses Mabhida Stadium and Cape Town Stadium) ran severe financial losses after the World Cup because they were underutilised, experiencing profit loss and running the risk of becoming white elephants.[38] The City of Cape Town investigated how they could salvage the situation and conducted a feasibility study.[39] The City developed a business plan for the Cape Town Stadium and Green Point Park to make it more economically viable by lifting some restrictions and allowing more commercial activity in and around the stadium.[40] Feasibility studies include several components that are presented in the table below:

Table 22.2: Components of the Sports Facility Feasibility study[41]

Components	Explanation
Project Description	A general overview of the facility, including square footage, inclusions and amenities.
Site Selection	The location of the facility is crucial. Factors such as accessibility, available space, infrastructure and environmental considerations need to be considered. Facilities can be standalone or integrated within larger sports complexes. Additionally, there is a growing emphasis on incorporating sustainable design principles in sports facility planning. This involves energy-efficient lighting systems, water conservation measures, the use of eco-friendly materials and integration with the surrounding environment.
Scope of the Project	The processes required to define and control the work necessary to complete the project.
Constraints of the Project	Specific restrictions that may have an adverse effect on the scope of the project and related actions.
Needs Identification/ Assessment	The verification process as to whether the facility is essential. Includes identifying current and future trends, assessing similar facilities/ competition, evaluating the relevant social indicators, and determining demand/ usage potential.
Strategic Significance	The potential of having a positive, long-term impact based on the vision of the organisation.
Sport Impact	How the facility will have a direct effect on the development of sport in the locale.
Economic Impact	How the facility will directly stimulate the total amount of expenditures in the area.
Societal Impact	How the facility will directly affect the social fabric and well-being of the community.
Capital Costs	The expenses incurred for land, buildings, construction and equipment related to the management operation of the facility.
Revenue Projections	The forecasting of sales and other income sources to offset expenses and predict net profit or loss.
Timelines	The listing of specific benchmarks, deadlines and schedules related to effective and efficient management and operation.

22.4.3 Facility Design

Facility design is an important part of the planning and delivery process, as poorly designed facilities could alienate users rather than attract them. It could also create challenges for the Facility Manager and cause increased operational costs that should be attended to before the facility is built.[42] There are fundamental factors to consider when designing a sport facility. For example, what kind of sport will be played at the facility? These factors will affect the facility design and the spaces needed for the different sport types.[43]

22.4.3.1 Determine what sport activities will be hosted in the facility

Knowing which sport (amateur or professional), activities and services you want to accommodate will assist in the facility's architectural design.[44] The climate can also play a significant factor in your design in determining the materials and design of the facility.[45] Additionally, when hosting several sports in one facility, it must be designed to comply with the dimensions to cater to concurrent use by multiple sports. In South Africa, many sport facilities are designed to accommodate multiple sports and activities to maximise the utilisation and return on investment. These venues can host various events, including athletics, soccer, rugby, cricket and concerts. Although this chapter focuses on South African sport facilities, a good example of a well-designed multi-purpose sport facility is the Paralympic Training Centre in São Paulo, Brazil. The Training Centre can accommodate 15 Paralympic sports and has 86 athlete apartments, a medical centre, sport science and research facilities, and a hotel and convention centre.[46] It is also utilised for several national and international events and hosts international athletes for training camps.

22.4.3.2 Determine the needs of your athletes and spectators

Sport facilities must have proper infrastructure and amenities to cater for the basic needs of the athletes, spectators and officials. It is important to determine your users' needs and expectations. A good facility experience bolsters fan loyalty.[47] This includes playing fields, tracks, seating areas, locker rooms, medical facilities, media areas, concession stands and parking lots. Users also want to feel safe free of debris, holes, divots, depressions, ridges, lips and other potential safety hazards,[48] and expect the facility to be clean and comfortable and the atmosphere exciting.[49] To do so, reasonable expectations should be met in the facility's design. Accessibility for people with disabilities that is user-friendly should also be prioritised. The lack of accessibility for people with disabilities, or more so athletes with disabilities, could create barriers to sport participation.[50] Some standards refer to the rules and accessibility of sport facilities meeting the needs of persons with disabilities participating as athletes and spectators.[51] Some questions to consider in improving the user experience and meeting their needs are: Who will use this complex? What sport will be played here? Will there be membership fees? Are the facilities indoors or outdoors? Both? What will make an attendee's experience more enjoyable? How many fields/courts per sport should there be?

22.4.3.3 Legacy planning

Major sport events like the 2010 FIFA World Cup and the Olympic Games have prompted the development of state-of-the-art sport facilities in South Africa. Legacy planning involves considering the long-term use of the venues after the event, ensuring they can be repurposed or adapted for community use. Three prominent sport stadiums will be reflected on in this section.

Table 22.3: Prominent sport stadiums in South Africa

Stadium	Interesting Facts
 **Soccer City Stadium (FNB Stadium)**[52]	Soccer City Stadium, an award-winning stadium previously known as the FNB Stadium, is the largest stadium in South Africa and was revamped for the 2010 FIFA World Cup previously known as the FNB Stadium. It is located in Johannesburg. The design of the stadium was informed by the African craft traditions and mythology as well as to complement the aesthetic of the surrounding urban spaces and external concourses to complement the natural landscape and flora in the area. The stadium has a capacity of over 90,000 spectators. The new fabric roof, improved facilities and more corporate boxes were made for both players and spectators.[53]
 **Cape Town Stadium**[54]	Cape Town Stadium was originally constructed for the 2010 FIFA World Cup. It is situated in Cape Town and offers a picturesque backdrop of Table Mountain. It is an iconic landmark and provides excellent accessibility, facilities, staff and security. It hosts sport events as well as music and cultural events, and guided tours through the stadium are offered.[55] The stadium has a capacity of approximately 50,000 spectators and 2,000 underground parking bays. The Stadium was built in Green Point, which was seen as an undervalued and underutilised area in the city. It was also the only site with adequate development rights for such a big project. The location of the Stadium aimed to create a link between the city's commercial centre and existing sport facilities such as the Fort Wynyard artillery fort, Green Point cricket ground, and the golf club that was merged into the Green Point Park. The seating capacity for the World Cup was 68,000 with the inclusion of demountable temporary seats. The integration of the design to the surrounding landscape was of great importance. The Stadium has one of the most complex concrete and roof designs with supporting columns outside the berm of the stadium, resulting in the shape of a traditional hat worn by Venda woman.[56;57]
 **Moses Mabhida Stadium**[58]	The Moses Mabhida Stadium is located in the Durban sporting precinct on the shore of the Indian Ocean. This stadium was built for the 2010 FIFA World Cup but the design for a multi-functional stadium for up to 85,000 spectators was considered in order to host other big events such as the Olympic Games and the Commonwealth Games. Its iconic arch design and cable car ride offer panoramic views of the city and is interpreted as a unifying rainbow, From above, it provides the representation of the South African flag. The stadium can accommodate around 56,000 spectators.[59;60]

Other facilities to consider are the Loftus Versfeld stadium in Pretoria as one of the oldest sporting venues primarily used for rugby and soccer, as well as the Kingsmead Cricket Ground in Durban, which hosts international cricket matches.

These examples highlight the diverse range of sport facilities found in South Africa, catering to different sport and accommodating large numbers of spectators. The planning and design of such venues prioritise functionality, accessibility, safety and sustainability to create enjoyable experiences for athletes and fans alike.

22.4.4 Operational Management of Sport Facilities

The operational management of sport facilities involves overseeing a sport facility's day-to-day activities and functions to ensure its smooth operation. Operations of these sport facilities, which are used for public, private and non-profit purposes for sport, leisure and recreation, seek to maintain these facilities.[61] Furthermore, operations ensure the safe and secure production and distribution of sports events and related services. The operations manager must oversee other management team members and ensure cohesion for the smooth and effective running of the sports facility.[62] This can include various responsibilities such as facility maintenance, event management, staffing, customer service, financial management and marketing. Here are some key aspects to consider in the operational management of sports facilities:

22.4.4.1 *Facility maintenance*

Maintaining the facility is crucial to ensure a safe and functional environment for athletes and spectators. Infrastructural problems and damaged facilities and equipment are detrimental to the continuous operations of a sport facility[63;64] Any maintenance issues must be communicated to the facility maintenance manager. Maintenance includes regular inspections, repairs and upkeep of the premises, playing surfaces, seating areas, lighting, sound systems and other facilities within the sports venue. Besides maintaining the facility, part of facility maintenance includes equipment maintenance. All equipment that has been purchased and is available needs to be maintained and in such a condition that it supports the main purpose of facility[65] and its users. Equipment and facilities should be determined based on the programme's needs for the operations to run effectively. Furthermore, equipment must be acquired, properly accounted for, of good quality and maintained for future use.[66]

22.4.4.2 *Event management*

Sport events are linked to places they are hosted,[67] and sport facilities often host various events such as matches, tournaments, training sessions and recreational activities. Operational managers must coordinate and manage these events, including scheduling, booking, ticketing, security, crowd management and coordination with event organisers, teams and relevant stakeholders. High-quality venues and proper facility management are crucial for facilities to attract high-profile events. Each type of event that needs to be hosted has a long list of specific requirements; good event management will ensure the fulfilment of these requirements and, ultimately, the future success of the facility.

22.4.4.3 *Staffing*

Hiring, training and managing competent staff is essential for the smooth operation of a sport facility. This includes hiring and training personnel for facility management, maintenance, security, ticketing, concessions and other related roles. Staff should be well-versed in customer service, safety protocols and emergency response procedures. It is also important for all staff members working at sport facilities to have good communication skills and be well educated on the procedures and policies of the sports facility to ensure not only the smooth running of the facility, but to be competent to manage customer queries.[68;69]

22.4.4.4 Customer service

Providing excellent customer service is crucial to attract and retain patrons. Operational managers should ensure visitors have a positive experience at the facility, addressing their concerns, providing information, handling complaints, and ensuring a safe and enjoyable environment. Certain standards of conduct should focus on providing all users of the sport facility with the best possible experience.[70] Regarding customer service, the care, safety and welfare of all who enter the facility are paramount.[71]

22.4.4.5 Financial management

Sound financial management needs to underpin all successful facility management.[72] Managing the financial aspects of a sport facility involves budgeting, cost control, revenue generation and financial planning. This includes monitoring expenses, optimising revenue streams (e.g., ticket sales, concessions, sponsorships and rentals), negotiating contracts and maintaining financial records.

The different seasons of sporting events call for different financial management functions.[73] During the preseason, it is vital for the financial manager to obtain funds, prepare budgets as well as focus on the approval processes for any expenditures. It is important to determine who is responsible for certain financial duties such as securing funding, planning and preparing the budget, what systems need to be followed for expenses and what type of record keeping is needed. These functions must be done in the preseason phase to ensure everyone involved in financial management operations knows what is expected. During the in-season, the financial manager will need to make and/or approve certain purchases as they are needed, always remembering to keep within the budget and to keep records of payments. Post-season functions would include comparing the proposed income and expenses versus the actual income and expenses. It is important to have and analyse this information for the following year to make improvements, recommendations and highlight challenges that arose. One of the duties of financial management is to ensure all monies owed are paid into the facility, records and receipts are filed in an organised way, and reports for the financial year have been completed.

Sources of funding and raising money may also be a function of the financial manager. Financial managers will need to come up with ideas for crowd and other types of funding, networking to find suitable sponsors and sponsorships, and other types of funding which can include (but are not limited to), projects or events to raise funds, participation fees in workshops and coaching clinics, payments received for ticket sales and parking fees, advertising sales and donations.

22.4.4.6 Marketing and promotion

In essence, sport management is a business that acts on behalf of a sport property.[74] For this business to be successful, effective marketing and promotion are essential to attract visitors, teams and sponsors to the sports facility. Marketing and promotional ethics must be considered and focus on trending marketing strategies to get the best for the facility.[75] Operational managers should develop marketing strategies, create partnerships with local businesses, advertise events and leverage various channels such as social media, websites and traditional advertising to raise awareness and drive attendance.

22.4.4.7 Safety and security

The safety of a sport facility must be considered and be on the agenda of all sport staff.[76] In addition to the safety of all stakeholders of sport facilities, the security of a sport facility also needs attention. Security of sport facilities ranges from in-house staff to professional athletes and spectators. Ensuring the safety and security of athletes, spectators and staff is paramount. This involves implementing safety protocols, conducting risk assessments, maintaining emergency response plans, coordinating with local authorities and providing adequate security personnel and measures to prevent and manage potential risks or incidents. Regardless of the level of security required, a director of security should be appointed to be directly responsible for security and systems utilised by the facility.[77] The director of security should have a good liaison relationship with local law enforcement should any potential issues arise at the facility.[78] Employees of the sport facilities are essentially the eyes and ears and must report anything related to safety and security to the head of security. Responses can range from internal disciplinary actions for several offences to actions requiring the authority of local law enforcement.[79] Security personnel, as well as participants and spectators, need to be made aware of the rules of the organisation and the facility[80] to create an environment that is safe for all and serves its purpose.

22.4.4.8 Technology integration

Leveraging technology can enhance operational efficiency and the overall experience at sport facilities. This includes implementing ticketing systems, digital signage, access control systems, facility management software and other technologies to streamline operations, improve communication and enhance the overall visitor experience. Technological dimensions used in the management of sports facilities enhance the value of the facility.[81] Furthermore, integrating technology as a foundation for operational processes and interactions between people using the facilities has proven to enhance the smooth operations of the facilities.

In short, the operational management of sports facilities involves various aspects, from facility maintenance and event management to staffing, customer service, financial management and marketing. By effectively overseeing these areas, operational managers can ensure the smooth functioning and success of the sports facility.

22.5 CONCLUSION

This chapter highlights the complex role of a sports Facility Manager. Not only does the sports Facility Manager have to consider the operational management of sports facilities, but also the planning and design of the sports facility as a point of departure. The planning and design of a facility is essential to attract athletes and spectators. Also, with the evolution of sports facilities and the evolution of sport itself, new technology, features and the media must be considered. This chapter provided a theoretical overview of how sports facilities evolved over different eras, different kinds of sports facilities, the planning and development of these facilities, and the operational management functions of a sports Facility Manager. More importantly, the chapter focussed on sport stadiums in South Africa.

SELF-ASSESSMENT

1. Discuss how facilities evolved over the different eras.
2. Identify at least five different facility types and provide examples of each.
3. What are the main aspects to consider when planning and developing a sport facility?
4. Critically reflect on the management functions of a sports Facility Manager.

SPORT EVENT PLANNING AND MANAGEMENT

Dr Willien Fourie

LEARNING OUTCOMES

At the end of this chapter, you should be able to:

1. Describe, analyse and apply the planning principles of event management.
2. Identify and apply the four sub-systems forming the foundation of event planning.
3. Identify and use the 15 key steps of event planning.
4. Apply and link the four sub-systems with the 15 key steps.
5. Identify the 10 W questions and answer them in detail.
6. Plot the answers of the 10 W strategy in the four categories of the SWOT analysis.

23.1 INTRODUCTION TO SPORT EVENT MANAGEMENT

A well-planned event, based on event planning and management principles, brings to mind Brett Krafft's remark: *"Once you get to the actual event, it's a pretty amazing process to watch. All of the hard work you've put into planning the event goes into action when it's a success; it's beautiful".*

At present, a great number of athletes and coaches are full-time professionals and committed to international standards. Coaches and athletes (including at the school level) expect Sport Event Managers to be committed to meeting the international standards set out in an International Sport Federation's (ISF) rulebook and/or guidelines. Sport event managers, coaches and athletes need to form a collaborative team towards the success of the athletes and sport teams. Ekkart Arbeit, a renowned international athletics coach, emphasises that the scientific preparation of athletes includes athletes participating in well-organised events.[2]

As far back as 2002, at the South African Sports Conference, the then Minister of Sport and Recreation, Ngconde Balfour, referred to the professional era of sport and the challenges it held for the people involved in sport in South Africa. The Minister is quoted as saying: *"While the foundation of South African sport rests on voluntarism, sport is today a means of livelihood to many. By its very nature, it demands that we approach the management of sport differently".*[3] The Minister also referred to sport event management as a complex environment. During a live radio interview that Johann Russouw from Radio Sonder Grense (RSG) Sport, an Afrikaans radio station on the South African Broadcasting Corporation (SABC), had with the author on 14 February 2009, the telephone lines were opened for listeners to call in. The overwhelming majority of calls were from parents, grandparents and coaches complaining about events not starting on time, results that needed to be corrected or that were slow to be published on the notice boards, and new lane draws that had yet to be posted on the notice boards. This impacted the time athletes had to warm up properly for their events and other unprofessional conduct by technical officials, including poor decision-making, announcements, and unscheduled events.[4] This interview took place in 2009, but in 2023 we still have the same issues in individual and team sport events all over South Africa, as confirmed by the highly regarded athletic coach, Ans Botha, who has attended events in South Africa and abroad.

23.2 THE KEY TO SUCCESS

Elbert Hubbard[5] maintains that *"the best preparation for good work tomorrow is to do good work today",* while Stephen Covey concluded that one must *"apply the right principles, but be aware of staying focused on being successful".*[6] Sound planning is the fundamental key that assists event managers to stay focused on the essential aspects of an event. The more complex the event becomes, the more applicable the sentiments of Hubbard and Covey become.

The saying goes, *"Many people do not plan to fail; they fail to plan".*[7] Therefore, the focus on functional, more practical aspects with an emphasis on the planning function of event management and identifying critical steps imperative in organising and presenting a successful event, need to be understood and applied. Planning general lower-level sport events such as league events may not seem as complex as major or hallmark events such as the Diamond League or Olympic Games, but they are subject to similar standards to which event planners should adhere. Moreover, the standards set for athletes at these available sport events are not inferior to those required to achieve world or national records, or team events where players prepare or participate to be selected for higher honours.

John van Reenen's 64.46 metre discus throw (world and national record) on 14 March 1975 during a regular Stellenbosch University Championship and Frantz Kruger's national record of 69.75 metres in the discus throw at an ordinary throwers' event held at the Free State Stadium on 15 September 2000 serve as examples, as these throws could be added to the record books seeing that all the relevant rules and regulations were adhered to during the events.[8]

This clearly highlights the significance of the organisational skills required to execute an event successfully. Furthermore, it implies that event managers should exhibit high-level skills to meet specific event standards.[9]

23.3 THE FOUNDATION OF PLANNING AN EVENT

23.3.1 The Four-Pillar Foundation

Given the complexity and interrelatedness of all the elements contained in an integrated event management plan, a solid foundation is needed to build a successful event. Peter Senge's systems approach consists of four sub-systems, which need to be positioned in the planning phase and form the foundation of each event:[10]

1. Conducting an environmental analysis: There are different ways to do an environmental analysis of a sporting event; some are more formal, and others more operational.[11;12;13] In this chapter, a more operational active approach is followed, answering the 10 W questions of an environmental analysis.
2. Considering the intricacy of branding: Branding refers to the name or unique identifier of the event, the event itself, the quality of the organisation, and the quality of the athletes and their performances.[14]
3. Designing the event concept, logistics and coordination of technical aspects: The design of the ideas and the coordination of the various elements of an event are of utmost importance and require precise planning. This will form the foundation upon which the event operations will be built.[15]
4. Event close-down and debriefing: The event close-down needs to be planned as part of the planning process. A debriefing after the event assists with planning the next event. Event close-down, evaluation and debriefing are aspects of event management that need more attention. The temptation to pack up and leave as soon as possible after the last event/game could be a recipe for disaster, including accidents. As Shone and Parry observed referring to a mountain climber's approach: *"Accidents don't happen on the way up but on the way down"*.[16] Making this final effort, even when exhausted, will, in the long run, be time well spent.

For example, it has happened that a member of the local organising committee (LOC) responsible for a half marathon and 20 km racewalk requested at a meeting that the traffic department use a specific road for the races. Written confirmation from the traffic department was not requested, however, and the team managers were only informed the day before the 20 km racewalk that the road was unavailable. The significance of this particular event was that it served as part of the qualification for a major international event. The result of this miscommunication was that athletes could not qualify because the event took place on a track. Such incidents should be discussed at a debriefing meeting to ensure that they are avoided in future.

The four sub-systems form the foundation of the 15 key steps for a detailed plan, which a successful event is built on.[17;18] These steps provide a systematic process to develop an event plan.

23.3.2 15 Key steps

Step 1: Ask the initial event questions. Asking the initial questions is important in order to know what you are organising. The author formulated these questions into a 10 W strategy which is discussed in detail in section 4.

Step 2: Clarify and establish the event's aims and objectives. Each Local Organising Committee (LOC) member needs to define the objectives of the portfolio they are responsible for. For example, the media portfolio at the South African Track and Field Championships needs to identify objectives on how the results of the events should be distributed to the different media outlets. The outcomes should be benchmarked against the objectives identified in the 10 W questions.

Step 3: Conduct a feasibility study to evaluate the results, produce a written report, and briefly outline the areas where special requirements are necessary. Like at a National Track and Field Championship, this could refer to the equipment needed to meet the World Athletics standards for each event according to the World Athletics Rule Book and Organisational Handbook. Clear answers to the 10 W questions and a thorough strengths, weaknesses, opportunities and threats (SWOT) analysis will identify the feasibility of the event regarding not only the financial aspect, but the overall feasibility of the event. For example, the pole vault landing mat should be safe and secure for athletes jumping above six metres.

Step 4: Establish planning and implementation methodologies and draw up a schedule. A detailed checklist built on the aims and objectives of the event will assist in the quest to organise a successful event with a well-structured time management plan. For example, a detailed checklist of equipment required for the event, aligned with a schedule for obtaining these items, is imperative during the planning of an event. This should be monitored to establish the success of the process.

Step 5: Secure finance and any required approvals. Funding depends on the nature and extent of the event. The larger the sponsorship, the more complex it becomes, as the sponsor will have more requirements to satisfy. Many sponsors are very specific regarding what the sponsorship is for, like the programme and requirements related to VIP guests. This is essential when sponsors specify that the money cannot be used for anything other than what is agreed upon. It also refers to the budget and the amount of money available for each category that needs to be covered in the event. A league meeting, for example, will not have to budget for a full component of medical staff, unlike a national event where more medical staff will be required.

Step 6: Launch the event into the public arena. Media attention and media provision will vary substantially depending on the complexity, characteristics and the level of participation at the event. Live broadcasting will add to the complexity as it emphasises detailed time management, which also asks for very specific standards regarding, for example, floodlights at a stadium, especially during outdoor evening events. Adverse weather conditions could also cause major disruptions that must be considered in planning for live broadcasts.

Step 7: Establish operating structures and recruit key personnel. The complexity and characteristics of the event to be organised will impact the depth of skills required. It is suggested that a small core group be recruited initially and other members co-opted in as needed. When organising national championships, starting with the local management team of a club or province with a national representative of the National Sport Federation (NSF) would be advisable.

Step 8: Establish appropriate control systems. Continuous monitoring is embedded in good control systems. The checklist referred to in Step 4 for each aspect of the event that needs to be organised will assist and forms part of control systems.

Step 9: Achieve pre-event preparation through a trained, efficient workforce and a sound communication system. Efficient communication is at the core of an event's success. Meetings with all members working on a portfolio and/or short meetings on specific days with each portfolio as needed or as requested contribute positively to performance.

Step 10: Publicise the event. Marketing the event in the media (written, radio, social media and television) requires a team with the necessary knowledge of each media platform. The different kinds or levels of events will determine which media to use. For example, an ordinary league meeting will probably only use written and social media, while hosting a World Cup will use various media platforms, including national television, papers, etc.

Step 11: Complete a comprehensive and last-minute double-check of all arrangements. Checklists will allow a comprehensive final check of all aspects of an event. Peter Weiss, former Secretary General of the International Athletics Federation (IAAF) (now World Athletics), emphasised that event managers should have contingency strategies to activate when unforeseen situations arise during an event. For example, wind gauge readings are required to ratify jump distances for ranking purposes and international and national record-keeping purposes. At events in the past, no contingency plans were in place to address issues with faulty devices, thus issues such as these should be discussed at a debriefing meeting to ensure they do not occur in the future.

Step 12: Carry out the event as per the plan and contingency strategy. Due to the complexity and characteristics of a track and field event, or any other event unforeseen circumstances could occur and the LOC needs to have a contingency strategy (plan) in place. On 8 July 2011, at a Diamant League Athletics Meeting in Paris, France, the 200m race for men, in which the World Record holder, Usain Bolt, was in the line-up, the race was delayed for 10 minutes due to a technical problem at the start. Such an occurrence may have serious implications for athletes who are mentally prepared for the race and who may deal badly with such an example of negligence. The crisis situation could have been averted or minimised if unforeseen occurrences had been attended to in the planning phase by doing a thorough SWOT analysis of critical areas in the event. In this example, if the electronic starting blocks or starting system had a secure contingency plan in place, such an unforeseen situation would have had a minor effect on the race.

Step 13: Meet to review and evaluate the event after completion. It is essential that this meeting takes place soon after the event. A checklist of each portfolio and notes made during the event by the person or committee members responsible for the portfolio could assist at this meeting to discuss the negative and positive aspects thereof.

Step 14: Prepare a detailed report for appropriate personnel and future use. All positive and negative aspects of hosting the event should be captured in this report to enhance the delivery of future events. This could enable future local organising committees to host similar or other events.

Step 15: Consider the intricacy of the branding of the event. Event branding consists of three very important aspects that interlink with each other, namely:

1. The marketing of the event – how the event should/could be marketed.
2. The quality and standard of the event.
3. The quality of the athletes participating.[19]

These 15 key steps form the foundation of a successful event locally, nationally or internationally. To enable the sport event organiser and the LOC to translate the overall vision of an event into objectives, the LOC needs to find answers to the initial event questions, which have been formulated into 10 W questions by the author. Only then can the objectives and goals be understood and measured to meet the criteria set by the international and national standards of the specific sporting code and ensure a successful event.

23.4 THE 10 W STRATEGY[20]

An event 10 W strategy will assist organisers to establish "What" is to be organised and "Why" the event needs to be organised. This will also assist in establishing whether it will be feasible and what the "Cost?" of the event will be. The 10 W strategy will also answer the question of whether the coach or Sport Manager, for instance, at a school, will need to co-opt people to assist in the organising of the event and "What" checklists should be used to ensure that all that needs to be organised will be done to enable a successful event. When these 10 questions are answered, the key steps need to be addressed according to the level of the event. The answers to the 10 questions will guide the level of the event and what will be applicable regarding which checklists to use.

23.4.1 Question 1: Why?

The question "Why?" leads to answers that clarify the need to host an event and confirms the importance and viability of holding said event. Questions to consider when organising events include:

1. Will the event provide opportunities for athletes/players to qualify for subsequent events, such as provincial and national teams?
2. Will the event provide athletes/players and coaches opportunities to determine standards to adapt training programmes or for coaches to monitor athletes' progress?

The objective of the answers should be to organise an event that may contribute to providing the athlete/player with the environment to achieve the goals set by their coach and themselves, and a climate in which the international and national standards of sporting codes are met.

The "Why" question confirms the importance of an event. After understanding "Why" you are organising the event, you must determine "What" needs to be managed.

23.4.2 Question 2: What?

The "What" question relates to the type of event, such as a one-hour track event or a national hockey tournament to be presented over five days. This question is answered by matching the event with the needs, desires, wants and expectations of the participants, coaches and spectators. Therefore, LOCs and Sport Managers need to brainstorm the purpose of the event by asking the following questions:

1. How many hours or days will the event be?
2. What kind of event is being hosted? For example, a provincial championship, a more complex national championship or a league event?
3. No matter what level, the organisers must understand that international and national standards must be met at all events, from club and league to international level.
4. Will the event serve as a trial event for further qualification?

The more components added to the event to be organised, the longer and more complex it becomes. An athletics event could have journalists, live television and radio broadcasting, as well as athletes attempting to break records. This complexity will add to the planning and time management required to ensure that the event runs on time and according to the programme. Furthermore, the LOC and Sport Managers should consider whether the event is a morning, afternoon, evening or full-day event, as well as how many days it will last. This will also impact considerations related to catering for spectators. For example, a school athletics event could be expected to cater for grandparents, parents and children of all ages, adding to the complexity of the event. When the "What" has been fully considered, the cost to organise the event must be estimated by compiling a budget to ascertain whether sufficient funding is available to host a successful event.

23.4.3 Question 3: When?[21]

The question, "When?" elicits responses that have a bearing on much more than the date of an event. It emphasises the scheduling of the event far enough into the future to ensure that the event is organised successfully. This includes time management within the planning schedule and developing a realistic schedule to meet objectives. When a sponsor forms part of the financial assistance of the event, time management could become more complex as they often request to approve aspects that their name is associated with, such as the event programme. This could impact logistics regarding approval and having event programmes published and printed on time. The "When" question impacts, and is impacted by, the national and international calendar of events, especially when multimedia coverage is planned for the timely marketing of the event.

Sport event managers should be aware of what will occur around the prospective event date, which will influence the anticipated spectators. Scheduling a significant event in Stellenbosch or Potchefstroom during the recess period of the respective universities, for example, would be inappropriate, as a significant majority of the spectators come from the student communities. This will impact spectator numbers and income from entrance fees, and has implications for sponsors that expect to gain maximum exposure from capacity crowds. Furthermore, some events are influenced by school or university holidays. In such situations, a SWOT analysis of the event will allow the Sport Event Manager to analyse the event critically and develop innovative solutions to capitalise on the event. Ekkart Arbeit, world-renowned Olympic athletics coach, stated that the "When" question is most important when scheduled events are essential in planning athletes' training programmes.[22] Answers to the "When" question provide coaches with a planning framework to direct their athletes' scientific training programmes to a series of competitive events in preparation for a final event. The following factors may be considered when answering the "When" question.

23.4.3.1 The number of days

How many days or hours before the event will the LOC need to complete the planning and execution of tasks to ensure a well-organised event? Each aspect has a timeframe that must be organised according to checklists, especially when working with sponsors where certain documents and actions need approval. The LOC and Sport Manager also need to consider the kind of event to be organised by asking, "What?" Will it allow adequate time for the athletes/players to rest between contests? For example, when determining the number of days over which 400m heats, semi-finals and the final should be scheduled, consideration must be given to 400m athletes running in events such as the 200m and 800m.

23.4.3.2 Facilities

The LOC and Sport Manager need to look into the requirements of the event in order to meet the international and national standards of the specific sporting code, throughout all aspects of the event, including the stadium, venue or indoor facility. If the facilities or equipment do not meet the standards, will the budget be sufficient to carry the cost of buying or hiring adequate facilities? Determining whether the venue will be adequate to host the expected number of spectators is also essential. This could impact the selling of tickets and managing and monitoring ticket sales as part of risk management to avoid overcrowding the venue.

Other considerations include ensuring that floodlights comply with broadcasters' expectations, especially during evening events, providing designated parking for television broadcasting vans, and offering adequate facilities for commentators.

23.4.3.3 The convenience of the date

Sport event managers need to be aware of what other events are taking place before confirming a date for an event. When, for instance, major sport events in a country are scheduled, like the 2010 FIFA World Cup, a Grand Prix athletics event will not be viable to present on days when FIFA World Cup games are scheduled. Other situations could be that another sporting code could have a significant event on the same date as your event, impacting the number of spectators. This is an excellent time to negotiate a ticket package, especially if the times of the events are different. With adequate planning and preparation by using, for example, a SWOT analysis, events would not necessarily be negatively impacted by such clashes in the calendar.

23.4.3.4 Weather and weather predictions

Determining the weather at the "Where" and "When" phases is important. The weather may affect outdoor events regarding participation and spectator attendance, and the LOC should have a contingency plan in place to ensure maximum attendance. For example, an electric storm was experienced in the Free State during a Currie Cup rugby match and the 2023 USSA Athletics Championships. Both events were postponed for a few hours to let the storm and bad weather pass. In such cases, a Disaster Management Team consisting of the Sport Event Manager as director of the event and a medical doctor or any other person appointed before the event to assess the danger of participating during bad weather should convene to make informed decisions on whether the event should continue.

23.4.3.5 Time Management

The LOC and Sport Event Manager should determine the time required to organise the event. The higher the event level, the more time is usually required. For example, accommodation for VIP guests, teams and technical officials should be confirmed well before the event to enable the availability at the "Where" stage.

The LOC and event manager must assess whether enough time is available to meet the objectives set during the event's planning. It is advisable to schedule backwards, beginning with the event's start date and time and plot everything into time brackets to determine when to start the planning process. The implication for the LOC and Sport Event Manager is to arrange a schedule for the event, monitor the process and ensure that all objectives are met on time as planned. Besides answering the "What", "Why" and "When" questions, it is equally important to ask the "Where" question. The answer to this question needs to meet the international and national standards of the kind of event to be organised and "For whom?" (Standard of athletes, e.g., international, world record holders etc.) This also has a bearing on the capacity of the stadium and the standard of the sporting code, e.g., Astro, indoor facility and flooring.

23.4.4 Question 4: Where?

"Where?" refers to the city and the venue standard of the sport organisation (club, PSF, NSF) required to meet international and national standards. Based on the content applicable in the Safety at Sport and Recreation Events Act 2010,[23] the venue, event programme, safety and risk management, anti-doping facility and other aspects should be considered in the "Where" question.

23.4.4.1 Venue

Considerations must include whether the venue is appropriately equipped and if the playing surface meets international and national standards for the event level. One of the implications it could have for the LOC and Sport Event Manager is determining the budget for the necessary equipment and venue.

23.4.4.2 Programme

What takes place during the event is part of the event programme. In athletics, considerations could include whether different age groups are participating in the event and if males, females and athletes with disabilities are part of the programme. In rugby, if different matches are being played on different fields simultaneously and the main match after all other matches have been concluded, on which field or at which stadium the final will take place.

23.4.4.3 Safety and Risk Management

The LOC should ensure that all equipment and areas of participation are safe and secure. A safety and risk management plan should also be developed for the entire event, including the safety of all spectators. The programme must meet the standards and criteria of the Safety at Sport and Recreation Events Act 2010 (Act No 2 of 2010). An implication for the LOC and Sport Event Manager could be formulating a budget to meet the standards indicated in Act No 2 of 2010 to ensure that safety standards are met and risks are minimised.

23.4.4.4 In the Pavilion

If broadcasting, a media room should allow space for the press, radio and television (TV) broadcasters, with sufficient workspace. In addition, all other areas should be catered for as needed to perform the administrative functions of the event, including food for the technical officials and a separate room for VIPs. It is only sometimes possible for the media to leave their working station to go to a venue, for example, to have lunch. During an athletics event at the Belville stadium in Cape Town, no security was available to ensure that the expensive equipment of the media was safe, as the media's lunch was served in the VIP area away from their working station. This resulted in the media not having lunch. The LOC must ensure security at the venue or serve lunch at the working station.

23.4.4.5 Anti-Doping facility

SAIDS is the South African Institute for Drugfree Sport, commonly called Drugfree Sport. A member of the LOC needs to be appointed to liaise with SAIDS regarding their specific needs. The venue to be used for doping control at the event should provide at least the following:

1. A waiting area with sealed water in a cooler bag or fridge.
2. Chairs and an admin area to sign in.
3. A room set up with the doping control equipment with a table and two chairs.
4. A toilet facility adjacent to the room with a basin to wash hands if possible.
5. If the above is not available, a toilet facility with a door that can be locked exclusively for the use of the doping process.
6. An exit area that does not go through the waiting area.

The venues for sport codes could differ, which may impact the needs of the SAIDS officials. Therefore, a representative from the LOC must contact SAIDS to ensure that what is available will satisfy their needs.

23.4.5 Question 5: Who For?

Sport event managers at all levels in South Africa should join hands with coaches and NSFs to create an environment where athletes/players can perform to the best of their abilities.

Questions to consider when answering "Who for?" starts by determining the age group of participants:

23.4.5.1 The age group

Events in South Africa could occur under the auspices of a school's sporting body with its own rules and regulations regarding age groups.[24] The event itself should abide by the NSF's rules and regulations, however. The next level of participation falls under the University Student Sports Association (USSA). Student and senior competitions (including clubs) have standards to comply with. For example, in track and field, the athletes are licenced through the specific provincial sport federation (PSF) (where the athlete lives) to Athletics South Africa. That generally implies ensuring that there is a person at the event registration to attend to this matter. Enough tables, chairs, staff members and entry forms must be available, which will impact the administration of the event. The registration point should have a secure control system to verify age groups and entries. The staff working in this section need to know the rules and regulations of the competition and the national or provincial federation and, in some cases, the international laws and regulations of the competitions. The age groups of athletes/players participating will impact the accreditation process, the spectators attending, and the medical care provided at the event.

23.4.5.2 Accommodation

Accommodation for VIPs will impact the LOC's administration and planning of an event. Protocol plays a significant role, therefore a member of the LOC needs to be allocated to this portfolio. Some aspects that should be determined include security, the LOC's role regarding VIP transport and what medical services should be provided. Accreditation will impact the LOC as the accreditation of VIPs should be separate from the media, athletes and technical officials. This will apply to some national, continental or international events like hosting the World Cup Netball Tournament in 2023. The accreditation, for example, of the media and VIPs can take place at their respective accommodations.

Accommodation of the media must be separate from the athletes, technical officials and VIPs, therefore a member of the LOC should be appointed for this significant portfolio. Not all events will need accommodation, but accreditation separate from the athletes, technical officials and VIPs will be necessary. The following should be determined regarding the media:

1. Accommodation needs.
2. Registration process.
3. Transport needs.
4. Technical needs.
5. Medical care to be provided.

Accommodation for athletes/players and team management must be managed by a member of the LOC. Accommodation could be available on the event campus, which will be the LOC's responsibility.

Accommodation for technical officials is essential, especially when they travel from other provinces or countries. This will have an impact on the LOC not only in terms of logistics, but on the budget as well. A knowledgeable member of the LOC should be allocated to this significant portfolio. The budget must include technical officials' accommodation, transport, medical care and meals. The technical officials should be separate from the athletes, media and VIPs.

23.4.5.3 Medical care

Dr Louis Holtzhausen, who was responsible for medical care during the 2010 FIFA World Cup in the Free State in South Africa, compiled a useful tool (*Risk Score for Events*) to ensure that the event organisers had the necessary medical care for spectators. Medical care should be considered in conjunction with the rules and regulations of the specific sport. Most sports require separate medical teams for athletes, the public (spectators), technical officials and VIPs.

23.4.5.4 Equipment

When it comes to equipment, it is essential to consider the following: Does the venue meet the standard for the event to take place, taking into consideration the "What", "Where", "Why" and "Who for". The equipment should meet the international and national standards of the sport, thus the LOC member identified for this portfolio should know the standards required. Not complying with the expected standards could have significant consequences, such as in 1991 when pole vault athletes threatened to boycott an athletics meeting at the Pilditch Stadium in Pretoria unless the equipment was upgraded to comply with international standards. Their coach, Mr Andre Swart, described the equipment as "life-threatening".[25] Another important aspect to consider is whether athletes with disabilities will participate, and if they do, whether this will be in an individual format or in teams. A member of the LOC who is knowledgeable not only on sport for people with disabilities, but who understands the relevant technical standards and regulations, should be appointed.

Further, it is important to consider whether the event will be pitched on or set up on local, national or international level. Crucially, all equipment should be safe and appropriate for participation, such as the cages for discus at track and field events and the landing areas and mats in gymnastics.

23.4.5.5 Stadium/Venue

The LOC member allocated to work on this portfolio should appoint a working committee to attend to the following roles and responsibilities:

1. Security.
2. Crowd management (if applicable).
3. Medical team for the event.
4. Ticket sales.

The committee should determine the space required for seating for team management and athletes, VIPs, media, technical officials and spectators. In addition, it is essential to meet with the local Department of Disaster Management and the South African Police Department to decide on the level of risk management, crowd management and security management to adhere to Act No 2 of 2010. This interactions with these departments will be determined by the answers to "What", "Who will participate" and "Who will watch". The committee should also determine what facilities are needed for the medical teams; they could co-opt a medical representative onto the committee or the LOC to meet all their needs.

Furthermore, as recommended, enough ablution blocks (toilets) and entrance gates should be available according to spectator numbers. Finally, this committee should report to the LOC regarding the number of security members required to manage designated areas. Depending on the event and the number of spectators expected, the committee should also make recommendations on how much crowds should be managed.

23.4.5.6 Food and beverages

The LOC member responsible for this portfolio should oversee the appointment of stall owners if the stadium still needs to be equipped by contracted food providers. If not, the member must follow the rules and regulations of the host city or province. For example, refreshment stalls, the age spectrum of spectators, the number of hours per day and the number of days the event will take place should be considered. This will assist in determining the number of stalls and supplies required.

23.4.5.7 Risk management

The W questions that will inform the first step regarding the safety and capacity of the venue are: "Who will participate?", "Who will watch?" and "Where?" Before co-opting members to address aspects of risk, the LOC should have an informative meeting with the SAPD, security firm(s) where applicable, the local traffic department and the medical doctor on the LOC (where applicable) to determine risk management protocol.

23.4.5.8 Traffic management

The "Who for", "Who will watch" and "Where" questions, as well as the kind of event, will determine if specific aspects should be considered regarding traffic management. The following should be considered to guide the LOC:

1. The extent to which traffic officials are needed.
2. Whether a car watch company is needed.
3. The type of security assistance that is required.

For example, buses with athletes/teams and VIP vehicles might need to be escorted. International events will always involve the relevant traffic department, as the buses with athletes/teams should be accompanied for safety reasons and logistical considerations.

The LOC should ensure that designated parking areas are identified beforehand and appropriately staffed by security. The site for the medical team, especially the ambulance, requires an easily accessible entrance and exit route, and designated parking spaces for the media should also be prioritised.

23.4.5.9 Emergency vehicles and areas

The LOC should assign a member to coordinate emergency vehicles and allocate appropriate working areas as requested by the medical teams. The LOC should determine the following according to the criteria set by the specific sporting code and Act 2 of 2010, the level of event and type of event:

1. The level of medical services required.
2. The requirements demanded by the sporting code.
3. A risk score for the events tool (for spectators).
4. Whether the medical team for athletes should be distinct from the team for the spectators, media and VIPs.
5. If the venue allows line of sight on the competition area for the medical teams.
6. Whether there are clear notices in the designated areas.
7. If visiting teams require designated areas for their medical teams.

8. The number of medical personnel that need accreditation (in some cases, the LOC can limit the size of the medical teams).

23.4.5.10 Media involvement[26]

Concerning the media, the LOC should determine the following:

1. Will television and radio broadcasters be present and how many channels and stations will be represented?
2. How much space for the number of media stations is needed?
3. Will a press launch or conference take place?
4. Who will be responsible for press releases?

When an event takes place on a higher level, for example, a continental championship, the LOC needs to look into co-opting or assigning a LOC member to arrange a press launch.

23.4.5.11 Very important people (VIPs)

A member of the LOC should be designated to attend to the VIP portfolio. The level of the event and "Who" will participate should contribute to determining the following:

1. The number and kind of VIP guests who will attend the event.
2. The level of VIPs and the security that needs to be present.
3. The parking spaces that need to be available.
4. The time of arrival, according to protocol.
5. The need to book accommodation, taking protocol into consideration.
6. The level of VIPs.
7. The protocol attached to the status of VIP identified.
8. If transport will be required.
9. If accommodation is needed.
10. If a schedule for the arrival of VIP guests is applicable.

23.4.6 Question 6: Who watches?[27]

Once the "Who for" has been identified and the impact of the complexity of the event has been determined, the "Who watches?", referring to the spectators, becomes significant. The following areas need to be considered:

23.4.6.1 Expected crowd

It is essential to establish whether the number of seats in the stadium is enough for the expected crowd and teams. The following needs to be considered:

1. Monitoring sales to ensure communication to the media will indicate when the last tickets are sold. If there is more interest, fan parks can be erected.
2. Contingency plans regarding catering for crowds (food stalls).
3. Spectator access control through gates to the stadium.
4. Prohibited notices, such as indicating where there is no access allowed for spectators, for example warm-up areas for athletes.

23.4.6.2 Parking requirements

Secure parking for VIPs, technical officials, team busses, media and medical staff are important, however the most important aspect is to ensure that the public (spectators) have ample, safe parking. The LOC should consider the following:

1. Vehicle access control.
2. Easy and safe access to the stadium from where vehicles are parked.

23.4.6.3 Risk management

This area of responsibility is critical, as per Act No 2 of 2010. A well-organised risk management plan and programme should be established and communicated. The South African Police Department, Traffic Department, Medical staff and a Private Security Company are planning the risk management plan and programme. Each department needs to know its area of responsibility and have a member in the Joint Operation Centre (JOC). Co-opt identified members from the mentioned departments onto the LOC and assign a specific LOC member to this area of responsibility. The JOC should be established for the event and situated where they have a complete view of the event. In case of a risk issue, the JOC assists with the issue at the event and has a member who speaks to the media if necessary. On 12 April 2001, the newspapers in South Africa shared the following frontpage headings: "Ellis Park Stadium disaster in South Africa", "Spectators and medics trapped in chaos", "Stampede horror", and "Soccer's Day of tragedy". This is the biggest nightmare for any event manager, therefore the risk management plan should be a high priority in the planning phase of any event, no matter at what level. After this incident and before the 2010 FIFA World Cup, the governement put together the Safety at Sports and Recreational Events Act, 2010 (Act No 2 of 2010) to help risk management teams adhere to set criteria to prevent similar disasters.[28;29;30] Each Sport and Recreation Department in all provinces will assist with guidelines to adhere to the Act mentioned above.

23.4.6.4 Refreshment stalls

One of the success factors of an event is appropriate catering for all stakeholders. It is important, however, to adhere to the local provincial government's criteria and Act No 2 of 2010 regarding vendors. The composition of the spectators should also be taken into consideration. A member of the LOC should be assigned to manage this area of responsibility.

23.4.7 Question 7: Who Leads?[31]

Complex events will demand a higher level of operational and leadership skills backed by a comprehensive knowledge of the nature of the specific sporting event. Leadership also involves identifying the skills that require development in the event planning process. The leader should have the personality and skills to bring people together, provide strategic direction, communicate what is expected from each committee member, and motivate the team members. Leading is a management function that incorporates planning, organising, leading and controlling. Effective managers focus on setting a direction, determining the goals and objectives that will lead to achieving the envisaged outcomes, and implementing plans of action to achieve success. They are also effective at incorporating new members and monitoring and applying quality control measures in pursuit of organising a successful event.

23.4.8 Question 8: Who By?

This question deals with establishing a Local Organising Committee (LOC). The selection and appointment of LOC members should be aligned with the skills needed for the design and implementation of the event. Although the LOC is not always hand-picked, it often comprises elected executives, the teacher at a school assigned to the project, the Sport Manager and/or coaches at the school. The LOC's chairperson needs to know their committee members' skills and strengths and know when to co-opt. When appointing the LOC, the persons appointed should meet specific criteria, including knowledge of the event, area of responsibility and ability to adapt to new circumstances. In addition, they should be loyal to the event's purpose and willing to abide by the leader's leadership and direction.

The characteristics and the complexity of the event will furthermore dictate the composition of the committee. To establish the composition of the LOC, the different categories listed in the checklist could guide different portfolios. Once the LOC is selected and appointed, the chairperson should call a meeting and put the event into perspective for all portfolio holders. It will allow the chairperson to motivate the team to take the first steps in organising a successful event.

When the team has bought into and understands the importance of the event, and has formulated its objectives, the chairperson can activate the different areas of responsibility. The convenor needs commitment to the job required in each area of responsibility. Once the LOC is established, the committee must determine the event's financial impact by discussing two key questions, namely, "What will it cost?" and "Who will pay?"

23.4.9 Question 9: What Will it Cost?[32]

In drawing up budgeting objectives, "Who watches?" must be answered first. Projections regarding the number of spectators expected could lead to capacity crowds that may render substantial revenue for the event. Other factors that impact costs or income could be parking, the planned sales at refreshments stalls, specialised technical officials and the marketing budget. This significantly affects the marketing strategy that links to the question, "What will it cost?"

23.4.10 Question 10: Who Pays?

Having a sponsor for the event will lead to the question, "Who pays?", referring to who will take responsibility for which accounts. Therefore, with sponsors, it is necessary to identify the areas of responsibility and indicate who will take responsibility for different delivery sites, organisations and payments. The route to ratification of documentation and signing off goods, articles to be printed, etc., should be stated clearly.

After completing a session during which the 10 W questions are answered, plotting these answers in a SWOT analysis is worthwhile to verify the weaknesses and threats that could jeopardise the event's success and identify the strengths and opportunities that could enhance it.

23.5 CONCLUSION

Every event can be organised around four pillars: planning, applying, closing down and debriefing. Sound planning principles are the key to planning a successful event. The four pillars form the foundation on which the 15 key steps are determined to ensure a detail-oriented plan upon which a successful event is built. Step one took the reader to a newly developed 10 W question strategy developed by the author, which should enable the Local Organising Committee to obtain answers and plan in detail by plotting these answers in a SWOT analysis, thereby gauging challenges and formulating solutions. To assist with further planning, reference was made to checklists related to the planning and continuous control of documentation.

The checklists attached to the planning process serve the purpose of developing a planning document, setting agenda points for discussion at LOC meetings and ensuring that a quality control document is in place for the chairperson of the LOC. It also serves as a feedback document during close-down and debriefing.

Checklists, tables and figures are available (see email address below) to add more insight into the planning process discussed in this chapter. These documents cover the entire event management process based on a track and field event. They can be adjusted for any sporting code except the technical list and most figures. If Sport Event Managers use the reasoning behind the technical checklist, they can apply it to the sports event being organised. Time management, including a structured schedule, should be prioritised at all events. Finally, the chapter discussed the value of a thorough close-down and debriefing in order to determine whether the objectives were met and what lessons were learnt to carry over to subsequent events. Although the complete text (PhD) *The development of a track and field management manual for local organising committees in South Africa*, is based on a track and field event, it will give more in-depth discussions on the reason for planning in detail and what is expected to organise a successful event. Students who are interested in sport event management can request any document referred to in the chapter, as well as *Risk Scores for Events* (unpublished document) by Dr Louis Holtzhausen, from the author via email: **ironlady@mweb.co.za**.[33]

SELF-ASSESSMENT

1. Why is time management so critically important in event management?
2. What is the purpose of accreditation?
3. What is the purpose of plotting the answers of the 10 W questions in a SWOT analysis?
4. Will answers derived from the SWOT analysis assist in the planning process?
5. Complete the sentence: Sound ………….. principles are the fundamental …….to assist event managers to stay ………… on the ………aspects of the event.

MONITORING, EVALUATION AND IMPACT ASSESSMENT IN SPORT

Professor Wim Hollander & Professor Cora Burnett

LEARNING OUTCOMES

At the end of this chapter, you should be able to:

1. Explain the purpose of monitoring and evaluating a project or an event in the environment you are working or familiar with.
2. Distinguish between the concept's performance information, audit of performance information, monitoring, evaluation, impact assessment and learning within the Monitoring, Evaluation and Learning (MEL) process.
3. Identify and select indicators, establish benchmarks and apply data triangulation.
4. Be able to argue the relevance of the types of evaluation in sport programmes, projects and events, as well as able to apply them.
5. Debate the approaches to monitoring and evaluation.
6. Distinguish between indicators and benchmarks.
7. Explain the difference between qualitative and quantitative data or information and link them to monitoring and evaluation.
8. Explain and apply a theory of change to sport as a tool for development.
9. Explain the steps of monitoring and evaluating a sport programme.

24.1 INTRODUCTION

Monitoring and evaluation (M&E) represent a continuous process to establish progress towards obtaining the goals and objectives of organisations, programmes, events and projects. It is a management function that enables managers to establish and identify any intended and unintended programme or project effects or consequences to a strategic imperative, operational activities and the impact of organisations within and beyond the sport sector. It further provides managers with information on interventions' effectiveness and efficiency and helps identify challenges within these. Monitoring and evaluation, therefore, provide managers with opportunities to effectively use resources, supporting joint decision-making within organisations and between stakeholders. They further engage multiple people throughout the process towards refining the inputs (resources invested), outputs (directly related deliverables), outcomes (medium-term effects) and impact (longer-term effects) related to projects and interventions.

The questions asked are how and to what extent sport could contribute to aims and objectives through interventions such as programmes, events and competitions. A monitoring and evaluation process is required to answer this question, providing evidence of such. This process answers questions regarding the success or degree to which the programmes delivered the intended outcomes (aims and objectives), as well as lessons learnt. Consistent monitoring is necessary to ensure interventions are on track through gathering information needed to evaluate the programme.

In general, sport organisations such as sport clubs and others establish the success of their interventions by utilising measurements such as sales of tickets (attendance), availability of sufficient parking and security, beverage sales, access to ablution facilities, in-stadium programmes, and others. Similarly, national and international sport federations monitor the delivery of sport events such as the Olympic Games and Commonwealth Games, and Rugby, Netball, Cricket and Soccer World Cups.

24.2 DEFINITIONS AND CONCEPTS

Different concepts are utilised to describe and understand monitoring and evaluation, including its design and implementation as a management tool. Examples are performance information, indicators, benchmarks, monitoring, evaluation, impact assessment, indicators, benchmarks, data triangulation and performance information audits. These will be discussed in the following paragraphs.

24.2.1 Performance Information

Performance information in sport is data that describes the performance of interventions such as programmes, projects and events. It could refer to numbers (number of coaches trained), figures (60% of participants were male), descriptions (regular or monthly maintenance of facilities), explanations (vulnerable youth represent those who have dropped out of school), and statements (petty crime reduced by 20% among programme participants) that describe the performance of interventions, measured against defined outcomes and impact. Other examples include, for instance, the number of participants and spectators at a community sport event (400 school children attended), measured against the intended numbers (650 school children were invited); income generated through gate takings and sales of food and beverage (specific amounts); publicity obtained through the local newspaper or radio (news stories and interviews); and others. Performance information is typically captured in performance indicators.

24.2.2 Performance Indicators

Performance indicators are signals or gauges that provide information on the state of something. In the case of sport, indicators are mechanisms to monitor and evaluate aspects of the state of programmes, projects and events. To do this, performance indicators should comply with specific, measurable, achievable and relevant criteria which can be obtained within a set time frame.[1]

For instance, a performance indicator could read: "To have 40 men and 40 women qualified as level two coaches in Sport X within the next six months." Specificity refers to indicators being exact or specific in what should be evaluated, while measurability refers to performance indicators that can be measured that are also achievable through interventions. Apart from measurable and relevant indicators, they should be obtained within the set time frame.

In another example, the indicator states: On Saturday, 21 March 2023, 120 girls under 20 should participate in the annual Junior Netball festival at the University of Johannesburg. Netball facilities comply with all the criteria. The time frame is Saturday, 21 March 2023. The assessment is relevant to the event, being the number of u/20 netball participants, the indicator could be achieved as it is an annual event, it is measurable as the indicator refers to 120 players, and it is specific towards u/20 girls' netball at the University of Johannesburg.

A performance indicator could also be relevant on different levels. For example, it may state behaviour change for the individual (before and after the intervention or programme) or for a team or sport club. For instance, there should be a 10% increase in the number of girls taking part in the programme by next year, or there should be a decrease from the baseline (50 incidents reported in year X) of on-the-field violence (fighting or bullying) as reported by coaches and umpires during the competitive season of sport X. The source of reporting is also indicated to ensure the evidence is collected in the same way before and after an intervention (pre-post comparative design).

24.2.3 Benchmarks

Benchmarks are statements of the ideal as they present themselves in successful situations. In the case of sport, benchmarks are statements of standardised requirements of programmes, projects and events related to similar successful interventions. In other words, benchmarks are standardised and set requirements for similar interventions under similar circumstances. Although this could be a contentious issue in sport, benchmarks could be formulated and argued from the point of the strategic imperatives of organisations, programmes, projects and events. For example, a benchmark or target could be to have less than ten incidents of breaking a code of conduct (a reduced number from a previous baseline of 20 such incidences) during a competitive season across all age divisions in a specific sport.

24.2.4 Monitoring

Monitoring is establishing the progress or the quality of some aspect of the programme over a specific period. It reviews regularly to measure progress, compliance and implementation. For example, in sport, it could be on the plan of action and implementation of activities, progress towards achieving outcomes and impact of programmes.[2] Monitoring data and information should be collected regularly to measure change over time and establish to what extent changes should be made to implementation. Data obtained during the monitoring process could be used to evaluate progress and success against set performance indicators.

24.2.5 Evaluation

Evaluation is a process of judging collected information or data from the monitoring process. Judgements relate to ratings such as sound, adequate, poor, ahead of schedule, on or behind schedule. These ratings are compared with set benchmarks or outcomes such as percentages, numbers, periods, etc.[3] Evaluation is a value statement based on information gathered during the monitoring processes about set performance indicators.

24.2.6 Impact Assessment

Most significant changes (MSC) are measured over time as they may directly or indirectly relate to observable changes caused by a specific intervention or programme. The impact is a change that manifests at a broader or societal level and happens in the longer term. For example, a programme may have an envisaged impact to create youth employment in or through sport that would meaningfully contribute to the survival of impoverished households.[4] Schulenkorf, Sugden and Sugden[5] refer to the ripple effect of change – from the individual and inter-personal (micro-level), spreading to the household or school (social institution) (meso-level) and eventually demonstrating 'manifested change' or 'impact' at the community level (between schools and different social institutions). An example is to develop active citizenship through an observable or measurable value or figure, such as an increase in the number of volunteers within a club in a specific time frame.

The theory of change (ToC) shows the process from input to impact that could be traced over time as one level of change leads to another and eventually brings about system change.

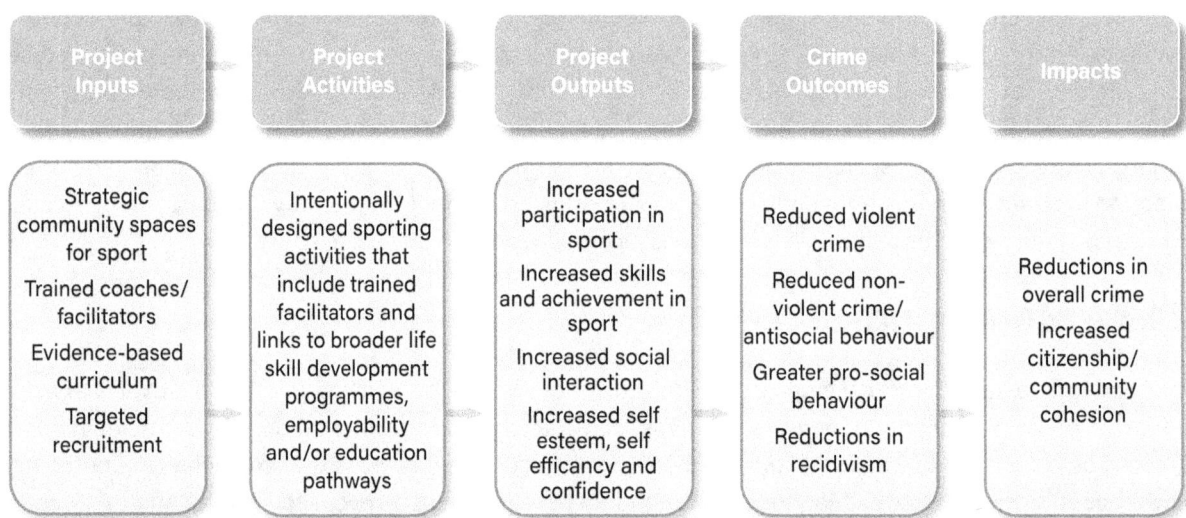

Figure 24.1: Example results chain – social cohesion and crime reduction policy rationale for increasing participation in sport[6]

24.2.7 Triangulation of Data

Triangulation is the corroboration of data and information from different data sources to support statements and results. For example, information obtained from interviews with athletes on experiences during training sessions could be corroborated with similar information obtained from interviews with coaches and administrators on the same topic. In other words, data and information obtained through different research instruments such as interviews, focus groups and questionnaires are compared to establish to what extent certain information gathered are the same. Such data and information would be considered valid, as different sources provided similar information. This is called the triangulation of data or information.

Triangulation of data and information provides an opportunity for managers of sport to not only validate or audit information, but also to establish the validity and reliability of such. Triangulation may also 'triangulate' different methods used during monitoring and evaluation, such as a questionnaire and interviews. Multiple perspectives and voices ensure the information gathered is valid, reliable and trustworthy.

24.2.8 Audit of Performance Information

The audit of performance information is a process to validate data and information. This process is to secure the authenticity of data and information to be declared valid, reliable and trustworthy. Audited information and data provide managers with performance information that could be utilised during the evaluation and other planning processes of future similar interventions. Therefore, validated performance information is essential for managers of sport.

24.3 TYPES OF EVALUATION

Five types of evaluation, as part of the development and implementation pathway of sport interventions, are evident: diagnostic, design, implementation, impact and economic evaluations. Each is described depending on the intervention stage or focus of evaluation on the programme, project and event pathway.

Diagnostic evaluation refers to analysing and evaluating the overall context of planned interventions. This is seen as the first stage of evaluation, where the general contextual information of potential projects is gathered, analysed and evaluated.[7] Examples are establishing the need of community members to participate in a planned event, availability of potential sponsors, appropriate time of year for events, duration of events, interested clubs from other regions, availability of facilities and equipment, and various other aspects to stage events. Therefore, the diagnostic evaluation is a situation analysis that provides managers with relevant information to decide whether to continue with planned sport interventions.

Design evaluation is a comprehensive assessment of the organisational processes and procedures that includes project mechanisms such as the input of resources, output activities, envisaged outcomes and impact of interventions.[8] This supposes that the design of interventions is evaluated to ensure that programmes and projects are delivered successfully. This evaluation provides information on the detailed design of interventions, such as strategy, structure, operational aspects and others, to ensure flawless implementation.

Implementation evaluation determines the assessment of the extent to which the envisaged design of interventions is being, and has been, implemented. This evaluation secures evidence of the implementation, including the distribution and use of resources such as finances, facilities, equipment, people and information, marketing, and delivery of interventions.[9] Examples are how finances and human resources are utilised, marketing undertaken, participants recruited, and activities scheduled and delivered. This is to secure the delivery of interventions and the economic viability thereof. Therefore, implementation evaluation should occur during and after interventions are delivered.

Economic evaluation requires an assessment of the economic viability of interventions to assure the financial sustainability of both the interventions and the sport organisation. This includes securing sources of income, monitoring expenditures against budgets, and the overall financial viability of interventions. It is called the bottom line of interventions and organisations in some environments. Economic evaluation forms the core of the planning and delivery of interventions such as programmes, projects and events.

Lastly, **impact evaluation** refers to the social, economic and environmental effects or changes interventions cause. Social changes mainly refer to the impact on participants, coaches, supporters and community members where interventions reside.[10] Impact could be seen as the value-add of interventions that goes beyond its economic viability, but also the impact on people, organisations, community and the environment.[11]

24.4 APPROACHES TO MONITORING AND EVALUATION

Three monitoring and evaluation approaches are reported in mainstream literature: result-oriented or result-based, constructivist and reflexive. Each has its own aim and instruments towards monitoring and evaluation.

The result-oriented or result-based monitoring and evaluation approach focuses on evaluating predefined programme processes and procedures linked to objectives, outcomes and results. It allocates accountability to designers and implementers to obtain agreed-upon results that mainly ask the 'what' question of programmes. Examples of monitoring and evaluation instruments utilising this approach are LogFrames, Logic Charts and the Theory of Change.[12]

The paradigm of the constructivist approach to monitoring and evaluation presupposes that reality is constructed through interaction and negotiation between people. The main objective is to learn from each other during modifying processes of programmes based on the negotiation of meanings and values. This approach aspires to answer the 'how' of programme implementation and delivery through bargaining. Examples of instruments are Learning Histories, Responsive Evaluation and Most Significant Change.[13]

The reflexive monitoring and evaluation approach presupposes that existing practices and institutional settings are incorrect and should be questioned. This requires that learning occurs during reconstruction to develop a new reality. Within the context of sport, it refers to the members of sport organisations questioning the current ways of delivering programmes, projects and events.[14] Examples of methods that support this approach to monitoring and evaluation are Reflexive Monitoring in Action, Reflexive Process Monitoring and the Interactive Learning Approach.

It should be noted that although the approaches to monitoring and evaluation discussed above are defined as separate entities, they could be applied within a mixed-methods approach. Although the review implemented could be one of these approaches, it does not necessarily exclude elements of other approaches in the same assessment.[15] For example, utilising the Theory of Change, which is a result-oriented approach, to evaluate, amongst others, the outcomes of programme management and delivery, such as the input of resources about the number of participants in programmes, age and gender distribution, and others. This could be combined with Most Significant Change, which utilises a paradigm of constructivist evaluation to establish the impact of interventions on people participating in these.

24.5 THE MONITORING AND EVALUATION PROCESS

Monitoring and evaluation are continuous management functions to assess progress in achieving expected results, from programme design to the maturation phase. It supposes periodic repeated monitoring and evaluation, starting with baseline measurements providing data on entry situations of programmes and insights on their required future growth.[16] This approach to monitoring and evaluation further provides an opportunity to measure progress regularly. In addition, it allows managers to adjust programme processes and procedures as and when required.

To be able to do this, managers should understand the monitoring and evaluation process within each period. This includes quality performance information, data collection instruments, data capturing, validation and management, data interpretation and reporting. Each will be discussed in more detail.

24.5.1 Quality Performance Indicators

Quality performance information in monitoring and evaluation refers to data or information that describes performance. Within the context of sport, it relates to data and information that describe effective and efficient interventions that obtain outcomes and desired impacts. This implies that performance information is utilised as indicators to monitor and evaluate the effectiveness and efficiency of programmes against set targets (indicators) and standards (benchmarks). Indicators and benchmarks should be placed in a framework of programme requirements.

Initially, LogFrames were, and currently the Theory of Change is, used as a framework to guide managers of sport in developing and implementing sport interventions, aligned with indicators and benchmarks for monitoring and evaluation purposes.[17] The Theory of Change is a planning process for sport organisations that works backwards from desired impact and outcomes and establishes required output, activities and resources to accomplish these.[18] This theory mainly focuses on envisioning the required change as the impact of interventions related to programme management and delivery. Although the original design of the Theory of Change focuses mainly on programme design, it could also be utilised for monitoring, evaluation and impact assessment purposes by formulating indicators and benchmarks for each component.

24.5.1.1 Input indicators

Input indicators refer to the indicator fields of human, physical, financial and information resources for effective programme delivery. Human resources indicators include the required number of coaches, administrators, technical officials and others to deliver effective and efficient sport projects and events with the desired impact.[19] It also supposes the required human resources experience, knowledge, competencies and skills to deliver activities such as coaching, training, competitions and others.

The physical resources input indicator field refers to the required facilities and equipment to deliver effective and efficient sport interventions. The availability of facilities such as the number and condition of sports grounds, fields, turf, change rooms, offices, storerooms, cleaning and maintenance are examples of indicator areas of physical resources. In addition, required sports equipment such as balls, bats, whistles, attire, maintenance, repair, storage and others should also be included as indicators for monitoring and evaluation purposes of sport interventions.[20] To access these, sufficient finances should be available to fund sport initiatives.

Finances as an indicator field refer to acquiring finances through sponsorships, naming and television rights, ticket sales, and sales of memorabilia and beverages. Financial indicators should not only focus on expenditure, but also on income targets, processes and procedures. Financial indicators allow managers of sport to monitor and evaluate the extent that finances are, and will be, available and what is spent on funding sport interventions.[21] It further provides an opportunity to monitor and evaluate expenditures comparatively to budgets.

Information as an input indicator field includes a variety of types of information. Examples are the required types and levels of publicity of events; local, regional, national and international marketing requirements; and communication requirements with clubs, sponsors, players, supporters and others. In addition, data acquisition of players, supporters, sponsors and activities could further form part of the information input indicator field.

24.5.1.2 Activity indicators

The activity indicator field includes information on activities that constitute sport interventions, such as programmes, projects and events.[22] Examples are practice sessions presented per week and month at the club, duration of practice sessions, number of matches organised and played, number of events staged at the club and others. These indicators should be formulated to establish deliverables against planned output indicators.

24.5.1.3 Output indicators

The output indicator field captures output data or information about activities and activity indicators. Output indicators refer to the output of activities and should therefore relate to activity indicators.[23] An example is that compliance with the activity indicator of several training sessions per week would impact the output indicator of the number of participants that attended practice sessions per week. Examples of output indicators in this field are u/13, u/15, u/17 and u/18 boys and girls attended sport practices, attendance of supporters and spectators at events, and others.

24.5.1.4 Outcome indicators

As demonstrated in Figure 24.1, outcome indicators refer to those that register a 'most significant change' (MSC) measured in observable or reported change. For example, if a value-based educational programme focuses on changing the behaviours of participants to be more 'pro-social' on the one end or 'less anti-social', managers of sport could determine that by having a questionnaire (self-reported) reporting on (less destructive) coping mechanisms such as excessive alcohol use or improved social relationships with a coach, team members or household members. The latter refers to the possible behaviour transfer from the sport to everyday living. Lag indicators refer to tracing an outcome (result) as an after-the-event/programme measurement to chart progress.

24.5.1.5 Impact indicators

As previously stated, there should be a link (causality) between the input-output, output-outcome, and outcome-impact indicators. The Commonwealth Secretariat developed the SDG (Sustainable Development Goal) aligned Model Indicator Bank and Toolkit (v4.0) with lead indicators.[24] These indicators relate to impact (manifested change over time) at the global, regional, national, sub-national or local levels. Most national and local organisations or entities rely on context-SDG-specific indicators to guide the measurement of social change (including socio-economic, socio-political and community-level changes). These changes may include increased employment (sport-for-employment), reduction in anti-social behaviours (e.g., gender-based violence), social integration (e.g., inclusion and nation-building), and addressing inequalities in and through sport, such as gender inequality. Programmatic indicators (Category 3) guide project-level interventions that prioritise local outcomes linked to local needs that may be linked to prioritised SDGs and targets.[25]

24.5.2 Data and Information Collection Instruments

Two types of data and information present themselves in monitoring, evaluation and impact assessment: quantitative and qualitative. Quantitative data are numerical information that can be counted, measured or expressed using numbers.[26] Examples are the number of participants and their age and gender distribution in an athletic programme, the envisaged financial income sponsorship could generate and the number of sports grounds per type at a sports facility.

Qualitative data is information that cannot be counted and presents itself as what people say, written in text, recordings and observations. Examples are child participants indicating that, "We enjoyed visiting 'other' schools during our rugby tour" or teachers indicating that they experience that learners participating in sport do better in their schoolwork.

Quantitative data is mainly collected through completing data sheets, financial and other statistical reports, and questionnaires where numbers and figures form the core of answers to questions. Qualitative information, on the other hand, is mainly collected using interviews, focus groups, observations, written reports and questionnaires, where information is written down.

Managers must use applicable and appropriate data collection instruments to obtain indicator-related data and information on sport interventions. These instruments are aligned with the type of data or information (quantitative or qualitative) to be obtained. Figure 24.2 shows the different methods for capturing qualitative and quantitative data. The more open-ended qualitative methods are on the left, while the more quantitative ones are on the right of the continuum. Approaches may differ according to the topic or thematic area being assessed.

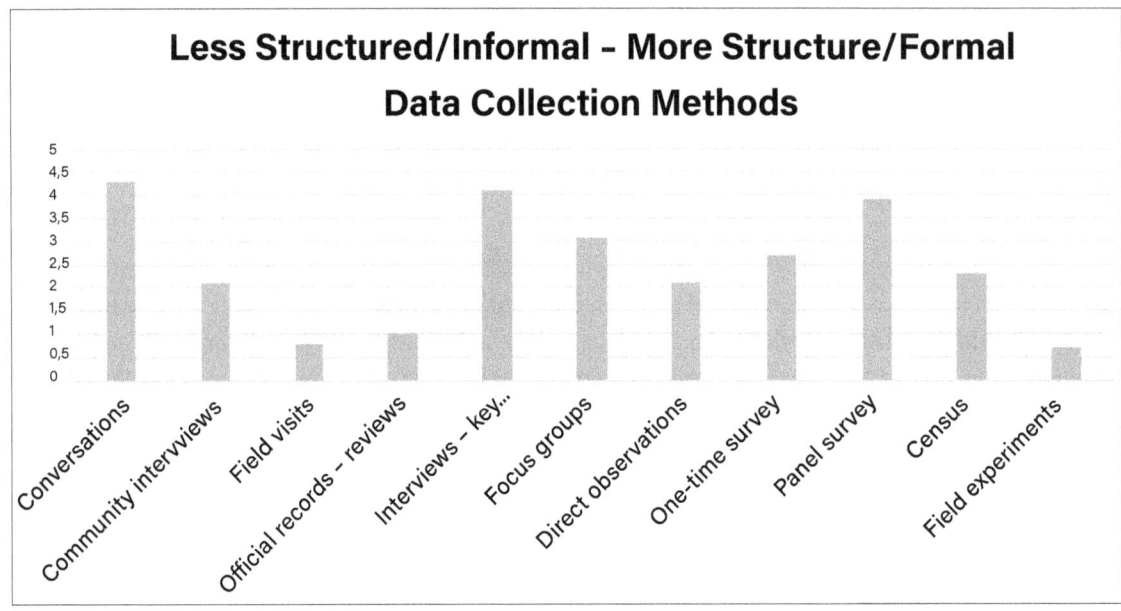

Figure 24.2: A continuum of data collection ranging from informal to formal methods

24.5.3 Data Capturing, Validation and Management

The capturing of quantitative data is relatively easy as it can be done through online surveys or quantifiable data obtained by capturing numeral information from data sheets (e.g., attendance registers and annual reports). The verification of such data lies in the triangulation of different sources to ensure the correctness of the information. For instance, if a record shows that 120 grassroots-level coaches were trained, of which 28% were female, different documents should have the same numbers. If there is a discrepancy, interviews should be conducted to verify the numbers. The same goes for qualitative data, but in this case, the evaluator should know that other research participants capture different perspectives.

If the topic concerns 'safeguarding' in sport, women and girls will have different views and experiences than their male counterparts. Also, coaches will have different opinions and understandings based on their experiences, views and mandates. Qualitative data is then coded – first, the evaluators will read through the texts and ensure that precise units of meaning are grouped before cross-referencing to semantically related information. This way, the units are collapsed into sub-themes and further integrated into themes. Once this is done, the data sets are ready to be combined and data can be meaningfully interpreted.

24.5.4 Data Interpretation

The evaluator would be guided by deductive concepts and themes for interpretation that derive from the envisaged outcomes, such as 'gender equality'. Literature and documents such as strategic plans and envisaged outcomes will inform those themes of relevance that link to programme outcomes and impact. For instance, if 'gender equality' is to be unpacked and broken down into measurable units, it may entail equality of input in terms of allocation of facilities (type and number), scheduling of events (weekdays and weekends, during off and competitive seasons), earnings of coaches and players (e.g., prize money, endorsements and salaries) and leadership (male: female ratios in executive boards, head coach positions and levels of qualifications in different sports).

Data sets will have different types of information. In some cases, the quantified information (numbers and frequencies) could be reported as trends, whilst the qualitative data obtained from interviews and focus groups could add information about the context. If players indicate that they are dissatisfied with the quality of the facilities, the descriptive or narrative accounts will more fully explain 'why'. It may be that young mothers are disappointed because they do not have a childcare facility or service, safety may be an issue, or the quality of the fields may be due to poor maintenance. In strategic research, the challenges encountered should be accompanied by suggestions or recommendations for change. Again, the recommendations may be specific to stakeholders, such as the clubs' management, coaches, participants, community leaders and parents.

24.5.5 Reporting

The report should be in easily understandable language (user-friendly), emphasising learnings or lessons regarding intended and unintended outcomes and impact. In addition, it should mention ethical issues, conduct, and clear demarcation and scope of the primary literature linked to the findings. Usually, there is a preliminary report where the results and 'sense-making' is presented to management and the critical stakeholders for their final input – mainly to be guided by the availability of resources, strategic direction and stakeholder relations. Once the last feedback has been obtained, the report could be finalised and disseminated in collaboration with interested groups in the sport club or organisation and funder/s who may require different types of reporting (e.g., social media reporting, a blog, a PowerPoint presentation, case studies or another format).

Different stakeholders, such as the management of a sport club, coaches, administrators or participants, may require other formats of reporting, and in some cases they may provide an example or templates. However, a standardised reporting format would usually include the following sections:

1. Acknowledgement
2. List of acronyms/abbreviations
3. Executive summary
4. Table of contents
5. List of figures
6. List of tables

7. The main body of the report
   - 7.1 Introduction/Background
   - 7.2 The evaluation or impact assessment (outcomes, assessment tools, results)
   - 7.3 The main findings - linked to challenges and good practices
   - 7.4 Recommendations for different stakeholders
   - 7.5 Conclusion
8. List of references
9. Appendices

24.6 CONCLUSION

This chapter addressed monitoring and evaluation as a management instrument for Sport Managers. First, various concepts in monitoring and evaluation were addressed, followed by a discussion and explanation of the types of evaluation, approaches and the six steps of monitoring and evaluation. These steps are quality performance information, data collection instruments, data capturing, validation and management, data interpretation and reporting.

SELF-ASSESSMENT

1. Explain the purpose of monitoring and evaluating any project or event in your working environment.
2. Distinguish between the concepts of performance information, audit of performance information, monitoring, evaluation, impact assessment and learning within the Monitoring, Evaluation and Learning (MEL) process.
3. Identify and select indicators, establish benchmarks and apply data triangulation.
4. Argue the relevance of the types of evaluation in sport programmes, projects and events and apply them in a monitoring and evaluation process.
5. Debate the approaches to monitoring and evaluation.
6. Distinguish between indicators and benchmarks.
7. Explain the difference between qualitative and quantitative data or information and link them to monitoring and evaluation.
8. Explain and apply a theory of change to sport as a monitoring, evaluation and impact assessment tool.
9. Explain the steps of monitoring and evaluation of a sport programme.
10. Apply the monitoring and evaluation process in any sport club.

PART III

CONTEMPORARY ISSUES AND THE MANAGEMENT OF SPORT

ENTREPRENEURSHIP AND THE MANAGEMENT OF SPORT

Dr Louis Nolte

LEARNING OUTCOMES

At the end of this chapter, you should be able to:

1. Define entrepreneurship.
2. Describe different theoretical frameworks of entrepreneurship and demonstrate how they relate to sport.
3. Identify the principles of entrepreneurship and apply them to sport.
4. Describe the entrepreneurship ecosystem in the context of sport.
5. Identify different types of sport-related entrepreneurship in South Africa.

25.1 INTRODUCTION

Many countries dedicate their economies to entrepreneurship through innovation and job creation. For example, governments in the United Kingdom and mainland Europe have emphasised enterprise, innovation and entrepreneurship as key ingredients for a healthy economy. Similarly, the personal orientations of individuals to engage in entrepreneurial ventures (entrepreneurial intentions) significantly impact the economies of developing countries such as the BRICS (Brazil, Russia, India, China and South Africa) countries.[1] In these countries, micro, small and medium enterprises (SMEs) are generally businesses developed as a result of the entrepreneurial activities of individuals. In South Africa, SMEs account for at least 40% of gross value added (GVA).[2] SMEs in countries with developed economies usually have fewer than 500 employees. In contrast, countries with developing economies, like South Africa, generally have lower thresholds of 1 to 200 employees.[3] This chapter discusses entrepreneurship, theories, principles and types of entrepreneurship in sport and how they apply to the South African sport context.

25.2 ENTREPRENEURSHIP IN SPORT

From the perspective of Schumpeter's economic development theory, entrepreneurs act as agents of change that disrupt by introducing new products (or methods of production), creating out new organisations, revising methods of production, or opening new markets.[4] In essence, these entrepreneurial acts are performed to exploit gaps in the market and generate income. It is evident from discussions in this textbook that sport occurs in a dynamic, multi-faceted and fast-changing environment, and within diverse contexts. The sport industry is increasingly becoming fertile ground for investment and conducting business as the industry takes on characteristics of becoming a branch of local, national and international economies.[5] Therefore, sport forms part of an innovative and entrepreneurial industry within the SME sector. In South Africa, the sport SME sector displays similar characteristics, presenting as a heterogenous marketplace that is highly segmented and cuts across various other industries such as tourism (sport tourism), media (sport media), medicine (sport medicine), education (sport education), manufacturing and retail.[6] For example, during the 2010 FIFA World Cup in South Africa, a shop that sells local merchandise to tourists might have promoted local and national culture while expecting increased sales and higher profits. However, systemic challenges such as trade restrictions during these major sport events could adversely affect SMEs. Similarly, the media could use images that capitalise on Cape Town's popularity among tourists to promote sport events. In contrast, universities might capitalise on local sport events to promote their sports education programmes.

Whilst the initial focus of entrepreneurship was on the individualistic, personality-based behaviour of the individual, there has been an increasing shift towards understanding the community's role in carrying out entrepreneurial activities, including social, cultural and economic factors.[7] Therefore, while Schumpeter argued from the perspective of a theory of economic growth that entrepreneurs are the key drivers through innovation,[8] others have emphasised that innovation, uncertainty and the ability to recognise business opportunities are closely related to entrepreneurs, the act of entrepreneurship and an enabling environment that provides access to resources. The trends of professionalisation and commercialisation of the sport industry (see Chapter 2) provides access to a potentially enabling context by enhancing the ability of entrepreneurs to gain access to financial, human and other related resources. For example, hosting highly commercialised sport events such as the FIFA, Rugby and Cricket World Cups, Sevens Rugby tournaments, Formula 1 motorsport events and the Summer and Winter Olympic Games are often associated with perceived immediate and long-term benefits for local and national economies by boosting tourism and sales, as well as promoting new business opportunities related to these events.

Considering that the country's context could also play a significant role in entrepreneurship, the national culture, for example, could impact entrepreneurship. In turn, entrepreneurs could display the dominant characteristics of their national cultures.[9] Hofstede Insights evaluated South African culture from the lens of a six-dimensional model, which included **power distance** (the extent to which people accept that there is unequal power distribution in societies, institutions and organisations); **individualism** (the degree to which there is interdependence among people in a society); **masculinity** (the extent to which people in a society prioritise striving for success or liking what they do); **uncertainty avoidance** (the extent to which members of a culture feel threatened by uncertain or ambiguous situations and have created beliefs or institutions that avoid these); **long-term orientation** (how societies prioritise dealing with their past whilst confronting present challenges); and **indulgence** (the extent to which people attempt to control their impulses and desires based on how they were raised). In this context, South Africa displays characteristics of an individualist society that expects individuals to care for themselves and their direct families only.[10] In line with this, the most popular form of entrepreneurship in South Africa is a sole proprietorship (a business that is owned and operated by one individual).[11]

In addition, entrepreneurship relates to numerous aspects such as the economy and generating profit, introducing creative ideas and practices in management, establishing businesses or organisations, and displaying the ability to analyse and capitalise on gaps in the industry. These contextual characteristics have resulted in multiple attempts to define entrepreneurs and entrepreneurship from various perspectives, such as economics, management, business, psychology and sociology.[12] However, a lack of definitional clarity persists. For this reason, Prince et al.[13] defined entrepreneurship at a more fundamental level, describing it as, *"the act of generating and developing an idea for validation".* This definition is informed by common entrepreneurship principles, including **uncertainty**, **business creation**, **innovation**, **opportunity** and **value creation**, prevalent in the work of prominent authors in the field, such as Hull et al.,[14] Knight,[15] Brockhaus,[16] Schumpeter[17] and others.

As a result of the complexities in defining entrepreneurship, multiple theoretical perspectives have emerged that consider the entrepreneurial ecosystem about the systems theory and the application to sport (sport-based entrepreneurship). These are discussed in the following section.

25.2.1 Theories of Entrepreneurship in Sport

There is growing recognition that entrepreneurs operate in collaboration. From this perspective, the commercialisation of entrepreneurial ventures is constrained and facilitated by the collective effort of a network of entrepreneurs in the public and private sectors. These entrepreneurs create social and economic conditions that could enable access to key resources (e.g., finances and facilities); markets (e.g., the professional sport market or sport participation market); business functions (e.g., companies that contribute to the production of goods); and institutions (e.g., local and national sport organisations) to form an entrepreneurial ecosystem that considers geographical, spatial, temporal, social, organisational and market contexts (see Figure 25.1).[18] These ecosystems vary in terms of the complexity of the relationships that shape the context in which SMEs operate. For example, an entrepreneur in South Africa may recognise a demand in the local market for supplying sport kit to schools. To do so, they would need the appropriate knowledge and skills to analyse the market to ascertain the level of competition in the market; understand laws and policies to register and manage the business and source the kit (possibly by importing the kit from another country) to secure the lowest possible costs; establish an effective supply chain; negotiate and collaborate with schools; market the business effectively; gain access to funding; and many others. Stam and Van de Ven[19] proposed an ecosystem based on a systems theory approach (see Chapter 9 for more on the Systems Theory) as displayed in Figure 25.1. In this ecosystem, the first component is institutional arrangements, the second component is resource endowments, and new value creation is captured in the third component (productive entrepreneurship).

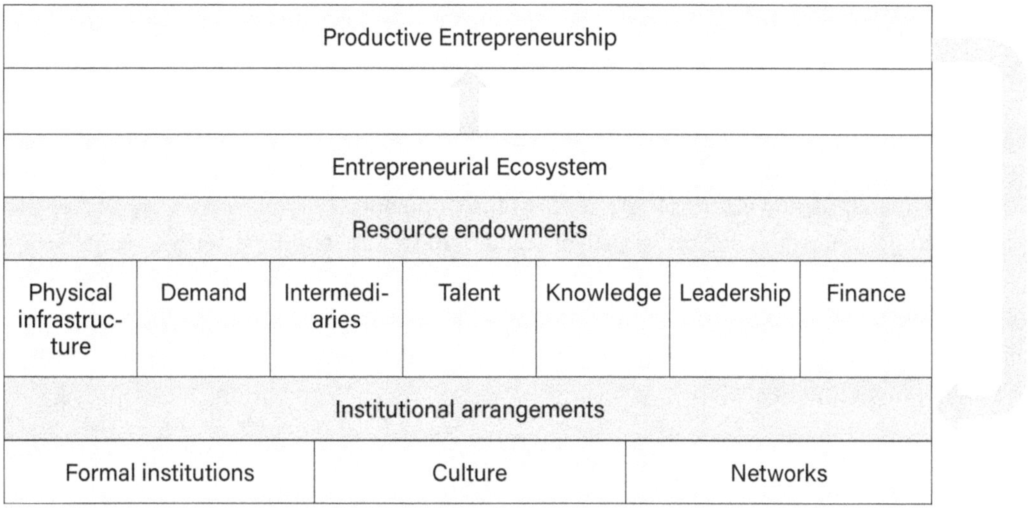

Productive Entrepreneurship						
Entrepreneurial Ecosystem						
Resource endowments						
Physical infrastructure	Demand	Intermediaries	Talent	Knowledge	Leadership	Finance
Institutional arrangements						
Formal institutions		Culture			Networks	

Figure 25.1: Entrepreneurship ecosystem

The World Economic Forum (WEF) projected that South Africa would have the highest unemployment rate in the world by 2023.[20] Considering SMEs' role in the country's economy, the potential for addressing unemployment is substantial. However, significant inhibiting factors in the country constrain the growth of this sector, including competition from large firms, inadequate (access to) technology and equipment, a lack of skills due to a failing education system, the high prevalence of crime, the cost of labour and the prevailing economic conditions locally and nationally.[21] In addition, excessive bureaucracy and inefficient decision-making in the regulatory and government policy environment result in, among others, cumbersome legal, tax, administrative and business registration processes.[22] Against this backdrop, it is estimated that approximately 70% of SMEs in South Africa fail within the first year of business.

Ratten[23] considers innovation, being proactive and being willing to take risks as key characteristics of entrepreneurship in profit and non-profit sport organisations when theorising about sport-based entrepreneurship. She defined sport-based entrepreneurship as *"when an entity in sport acts collectively to respond to an opportunity to create value"*. Informed by this theoretical perspective, Ratten identified the dynamic aspects of sport-based entrepreneurship that impact management, such as business strategy, crisis management, new sport development, performance management, product innovation, promotional strategies, social issues, sustainability concerns and technological developments. Theoretical frameworks on entrepreneurship have resulted in the identification of, and are informed by, different types and principles of entrepreneurship.

25.3 TYPES OF ENTREPRENEURSHIP

Various types of entrepreneurship exist that incorporate these principles to different extents. In this context, Ratten[24] identified several sport-based types of entrepreneurship that are discussed accordingly.

25.3.1 Community-based Entrepreneurship

Community-based entrepreneurship could occur when sport teams, organisations or athletes from the community partner with the community to achieve specific goals. Community-based entrepreneurship is an alternative model of social enterprise that incorporates the use of business logic in novel, entrepreneurial ways to address the needs and issues of segments of the population.[25] In essence, they address the needs of individuals and groups within society to deliver sustainable short- and long-term benefits. For example, a local judo club could partner with schools in the community to present self-defence courses to address crime-related issues. This type of entrepreneurship could also be seen as the judo club adding value to the community through service delivery by utilising their resources, including expertise (also see Chapter 5 on Sport for Development and Peace).

25.3.2 Corporate Entrepreneurship

This type of entrepreneurship occurs when businesses are involved in the community, delivering products or services. For example, Dell Technologies is involved in innovation to deliver real-time data analytics for national rugby teams in South Africa. Through this entrepreneurship, the brand and product of Dell are sponsored, providing viability to the brand and product range of Dell Technologies. This normally relates to sponsorship and/or the provision of products to sport organisations (see Chapter 20 on Sport Marketing).

25.3.3 Ethnic Entrepreneurship

Ethnic entrepreneurship is business ownership by ethnic group members, which generally promote ethnic mobility. Some of the most significant examples in South Africa are Siya Kolisi (the first Black South African to captain South Africa and win a Rugby World Cup) and the symbolic gesture of Nelson Mandela's appearance in a Springbok jersey to congratulate Francois Pienaar on winning the 1995 Rugby World Cup, signifying unity in a nation previously segregated by race. Another example is the International Judo Federation's refugee programme, which enables refugees in countries worldwide (including South Africa) to participate in judo free from discrimination. These forms of ethnic entrepreneurship are significant drivers of social change.

25.3.4 Institutional Entrepreneurship

Sport organisations could pursue efforts to make institutional changes to how they are structured or operate. Whilst not without controversy, one example of such entrepreneurship was how Dr Louis Luyt (former President of the South African Rugby Football Union) was instrumental in introducing the 'chequebook' professional era of rugby in South Africa during the 1980s. One of Dr Luyt's key contributions was negotiating SANZAR's (South Africa, New Zealand and Australian Rugby) first television broadcast deal to the value of US$555 million and ensuring that South Africa received the majority stake of this money. Another was successfully hosting the 1995 Rugby World Cup in South Africa.[26] This profoundly impacted rugby's transition from amateur to professional following the isolation experienced during the Apartheid era.

25.3.5 International Entrepreneurship

International entrepreneurship refers to initiatives where organisations engage in international business operations. In sport, these organisations could tap into international markets. In the context of commercialisation, the recognition of larger television audiences combined with more accommodating time zones resulted in SA Rugby's decision to pursue gaining access to the European rugby market by including the Cell C Sharks, DHL Stormers, Emirates Lions and Vodacom Bulls in the United Rugby Championships. At an individual level, golfers such as Gary Player and Ernie Els continue to play a significant role in promoting golf in South Africa as an international destination. They do this by using their significant fame and following to maintain a South African presence on the world tour, design golf courses in South Africa and globally, and capitalise on their international presence to establish charities that support global causes, such as the Gary and Vivienne Player Foundation to support underprivileged children and the Els for Autism Foundation to support individuals with autism.

25.3.6 Technology Entrepreneurship

This type of entrepreneurship refers to entrepreneurship within the context of promoting and using technology. Technology played a significant role in sport over the past decade (see Chapter 26). Young football players often need help accessing the scouting and recruitment market, which is essential to secure professional careers. In recognition of the gap between young footballers, clubs, and agents, the South African footballers Brighton Mhlongo and Oupa Manyisa have become entrepreneurs by establishing an application called 'My Football CV'. This application provides a platform for young players to bridge the gap by completing their profiles in partnership with agents.

25.3.7 Women's Entrepreneurship

Hegemonic masculinity has played a significant role in sport, particularly due to the emphasis on winning.[27] This is no different in South Africa, where sports like football have often contributed to reinforcing messages of male dominance over females.[28] In this context, women's entrepreneurship in instituting change has become prominent through women's sport teams and athletes advocating for the involvement and participation of female athletes. Examples include the success of the Banyana Banyana team that won the Women's Africa Cup of Nations, multiple winners of the Sportswoman with a Disability award, tennis player Kgothatso Montjane and Olympic gold medallist swimmer Tatjana Schoenmaker, who use their success on the international stage as a platform to advocate for gender equality. Women's entrepreneurship, therefore, refers to women involved in and accelerating the business or sport environment.

25.4 PRINCIPLES OF ENTREPRENEURSHIP

The principles of entrepreneurship discussed in this chapter are based on Prince et al.'s definition of entrepreneurship discussed previously. These principles relate closely to the main characteristics of entrepreneurship, including innovation, proactiveness and risk.

25.4.1 Business Creation

Business creation is often regarded as a rational decision-making process that incorporates aspects of economics and business management, whereby individuals assess whether they have the necessary skills and knowledge to establish a new company.[29] In this process, individuals often attempt to avoid unknown and uncertain situations. However, not all acts of entrepreneurship involve business creation, although the principle of validating an idea remains consistent among all entrepreneurial activities. For example, Oliver Power, Lee Hartman and Andrew Smith established a small South African comic book business in 2001, which was responsible for producing the football comic book, *Supa Strika*. The comic book is based on a pan-African team, 'the World's Greatest', that continually adapts to compete against a range of innovative opponents. The concept addressed a gap in the market that consumers have validated to the extent that this small entrepreneurial venture has since grown into an internationally recognised company.[30] In another context, an individual or a team in a company might convince the Board of Directors of a sport organisation to adopt a new unique technology that revolutionises the broadcasting of live events. Although this does not represent a form of business creation, the concept might create enabling conditions that could be validated by increased spectatorship and higher recruitment of sponsors.

25.4.2 Innovation

Innovation, or introducing new ideas, processes, products or changes to processes and products that add value to products and/or services, is a necessary quality of entrepreneurial activities. Therefore, innovation could take the form of an idea, concept or act performed by an entrepreneur. Innovation in sport can occur at the organisational, team or individual level and has largely been driven by the rapid development of technology (see Chapter 26). For example, Cricket South Africa (CSA) recently introduced the SA20, a shortened version of cricket that offers a local league based on the franchise model of the world-leading Indian Premier League (IPL). The IPL represents a groundbreaking form of innovation that introduced a new way of playing and managing the game of cricket. In the case of the SA20, despite some similarities there are also unique aspects, such as how the final playing teams are announced, indicating some acts of innovation.

At the team level, Rassie Erasmus, the Director of Rugby at the South African Rugby Union (SARU), was renowned for introducing innovative team selections and strategies, resulting in a 2019 Rugby World Cup victory for the Springboks. The paralympic bilateral above-knee athlete Ntando Mahlangu used innovative prosthetic technology to win two gold medals at the 2020 Tokyo Paralympic Games.[31]

25.4.3 Opportunity

Entrepreneurs exploit opportunities (a gap in the market based on their creativity and innovation), mainly to generate profit. They could do this by using their position, personal knowledge and network in the industry, for example, Gary Player and Ernie Els have capitalised on opportunities with the expansion of golf in previously underdeveloped markets to design golf courses in places such as China and North Africa. Others include Nneile Nkohlise, a well-known entrepreneur and technologist in South Africa, who has applied her knowledge and skills to develop software (3DIMO) that addresses a gap in the sport market by assisting sport coaches with biomechanical data to prevent injuries from occurring.[32]

25.4.4 Value Creation

Value creation (the process of utilising labour and resources to meet the demands of others)[33] is regarded as an essential component in the process of validation, however the meaning of the concept of 'value' in entrepreneurship is not always clear. Lackéus[34] positioned value within a value framework that describes five different types of value, namely economic (delivering what others need to create value for oneself); enjoyment (being entrepreneurial purely for enjoyment); social (making others happy or relieving their suffering); harmony (values that make more sense as a collective, such as common good values and culture); and influence (increasing personal influence, value and position of power). One of the most significant forms of value creation in the modern sport context is through social media platforms. The process of value creation could take the form of companies marketing products through social media platforms such as Instagram, Facebook and others. These social media platforms offer users the ability to share posts, make comments, provide feedback on products and express opinions. It is interesting that in this process, consumers take on the role of producers and consumers of value.

25.4.5 Uncertainty

In essence, the extent of validation determines the success of entrepreneurial ventures. Inherent in all instances of validation is the uncertainty associated with the validation process. Therefore, the decisions, activities and processes that entrepreneurs engage in incorporate a degree of uncertainty, implying that there is risk involved. For example, sport organisations can engage in risk-taking behaviour when investing significant amounts of resources in the hosting of major sport events, despite the uncertainty of the return on investment.

25.5 CONCLUSION

This chapter has provided insight into some theoretical perspectives that have been adopted in the process of positioning and defining entrepreneurship within various contexts. Economics, management, business, psychology and sociology are examples of fields of study that have taken an interest in this process. Despite the relative lack of clarity in defining entrepreneurship, certain principles have emerged including business creation, innovation, uncertainty, opportunity and value creation. In sport, these principles translate into various types of entrepreneurships that can be applied to a South African sport context, including, among others, community-based, technology and women's entrepreneurship.

Informed by these principles, one of the main characteristics among sport entrepreneurs in the profit and non-profit sector is innovation, which could occur at the individual, team and/or organisational levels. Another key characteristic of sport entrepreneurs is that they are proactive in their entrepreneurial pursuits, implying that they can analyse the market accurately, identify gaps and capitalise on opportunities that exist. Finally, the process of validation in the development of entrepreneurial ideas implies a degree of uncertainty. Regardless, sport entrepreneurs are prepared to invest resources, implying a willingness to take risks.

SELF-ASSESSMENT

1. Define entrepreneurship.
2. Describe different theoretical frameworks of entrepreneurship and demonstrate how they relate to sport.
3. Identify the principles of entrepreneurship and apply them to sport.
4. Describe the entrepreneurship ecosystem in the context of sport.
5. Identify different types of sport-related entrepreneurship in South Africa.

TECHNOLOGICAL INNOVATION IN SPORT

Dr Louis Nolte

LEARNING OUTCOMES

At the end of this chapter, you should be able to:

1. Define the concepts of sport technology, digital technology and digital literacy skills.
2. Understand technological innovation in and through sport in the context of the Industrial Revolution.
3. Critically analyse technological innovation in South African sport within an appropriate framework.
4. Apply the concepts of sport technology, digital technology, digital literacy skills and technological innovation to sport in South Africa.

26.1 INDUSTRIAL REVOLUTION AND TECHNOLOGICAL INNOVATION IN SPORT

Strategic sport management occurs in a dynamic environment (see Chapter 9). Innovation also thrives in these dynamic environments, leading to the emergence of new sport, social impact and technological development. This increasing presence, strategic use and innovative application of technology in various sporting contexts have profoundly changed the sport industry globally. In this context, sport technology refers to *"human-made means to reach human interests and goals in or related to sport"*.[1] At the same time, innovation is defined as *"a process of introduction and application of new ideas, processes or procedures, designed to significantly benefit the individual, group, organisation or wider society"*.[2] Digital technology is the range of technologies, tools, services and applications that make use of a variety of soft- and hardware such as personal computers, mobile phones, radio, digital television and robots. In contrast, digital literacy skills are required to navigate the industry.

In this sense, significant technological development and innovation could be understood in the context of the industrial revolution, which began in the 18th century. The first industrial revolution is recognised as having occurred in Great Britain between approximately 1760 and 1850, and profoundly impacted the United

States of America and Western Europe. During this time, the British Empire established itself in South Africa through the Cape Colony (in 1815) and Natal (in 1843).[3] The most significant advances made in this period were the rise of the factory industry, how work was organised to separate labour according to task specialisation, and the associated increase in productivity due to innovation and machine manufacturing. Some significant technological changes during this time included using iron and steel and generating energy through coal and steam. The first industrial revolution resulted in long working hours and little free time, however by the middle of the 19th century, higher factory output resulted in more free time for employees. Capitalist employees were increasingly concerned for the welfare of their workers during this free time, resulting in the banning of many blood sports to avoid injuries, and restrictions were placed on alcohol consumption to prevent days missed at work. This coincided with the enhanced recognition and utilisation of sport to promote healthier societies, while higher wages and discretionary income provided opportunities for spectators to enjoy sport. This led to the first codified and commercialised opportunities to participate in and consume sport events.[4]

The second industrial revolution took place from 1870 to 1914.[5] It continued to enhance productivity, with some of the significant contributions being the introduction of the assembly line by Ford Motor Company, the improvement of the telecommunications industry with inventions such as the telephone, the rapid expansion of the transportation industry through rail and air, and the invention of the automobile. However, one of the most significant impacts on the sport industry was the revolution of transport, which reduced travel time for athletes and teams and enabled them to compete abroad. Major international sporting events in South Africa were predominantly influenced by the presence of British soldiers stationed in the country. These included the first official international men's rugby match between the British and Irish Lions and the Springboks in 1891, the English football club Corinthians toured South Africa for the first time in 1897, and the first South African Open for golf was hosted in 1903. Similarly, the first international cricket test match in South Africa occurred between England and South Africa in 1889.

The third industrial revolution began in 1969 and could be recognised as a time when the development and use of electronics, telecommunications and the rapid development of computing power transformed how people generate, process and share information.[6] While the start date is still debated, the fourth phase of the industrial revolution is regarded as coinciding with the increasing use of the internet and the development of virtual reality worlds and artificial intelligence. In sport, technological innovations such as artificial intelligence have impacted coaching in areas such as gene sequencing and quantum computing. At the same time, ordinary citizens have become sport consumers under the control of franchised sport conglomerates and corporate sponsors through streaming devices and television, rather than being producers of values.[7]

When considering the development of technological innovations in sport over time, it is evident that technological innovation has influenced a range of aspects, from enhancing the performance of individual athletes to improving the governance of sport organisations.

26.2 CATEGORIES OF TECHNOLOGICAL INNOVATION IN SPORT

Marques and Biscaia[8] categorised technological advancement into product, service and process (e.g., introducing new products to the market or ways of improving systems to deliver effective and efficient services); and managerial, management and governance-related innovations (e.g., enhancing communication between staff members and departments or adopting innovative financial solutions).

26.2.1 Product, Service and Process Innovation

Product and service innovation refers to new products or services invented or introduced. It could also be unique and innovative ways to offer these services and products. Process innovation refers to the backstage of a product or service that could enhance access and contribute to sport logistics. In South Africa, this could be as simple as offering books on sport in eBook format, of which various already exist. Internet-based product and service innovation could also include streaming services based on enhanced internet access. In South Africa, approximately 68% of the population (about 41 million) were using the Internet by January 2022.[9] Additionally, subscription-based video-on-demand streaming services are projected to grow from 7.61 million in 2023 to 9.83 million users in 2027, with Netflix being the most popular (3.68 million users in 2022[10]). Increased access to internet-based streaming services in South Africa makes Netflix programmes such as *Bad Sport* more accessible. This sport-based programme examines true crimes in sport, such as the match-fixing scandal involving the former Protea men's cricket team captain, Hansie Cronje. Another significant development in product and service innovation is the electronic sports (Esports) industry.

26.2.1.1 Esports

The Esports industry has grown exponentially to attract more than 500 million people globally. The origins of Esports can be traced back to the 1970s with the introduction of arcade machines, game consoles and the first Esports tournament at Stanford University in the USA in 1972. The Esports industry has subsequently developed and, since the 2000s, diversified to incorporate, among others, structures, organisations, prizes, sponsorships and multiple sectors of society, including government agencies, specialist gaming companies and the media. Increased commercialisation and professionalisation of the Esports industry have also resulted in the contracting of Esports players, team transfers and online broadcasting of events. The online broadcasting of events creates opportunities for spectators to attend in person and via streaming platforms, and provides Esports with a unique opportunity to increase spectatorship using technology. Esports are uniquely embedded in the technology industry. Their events offer unique opportunities for companies to develop their hardware and software infrastructure, while relying on technological advancements to enhance participants' experiences. These companies are often sponsors of Esports events, such as Intel. While Esports were traditionally regarded as competitive gaming, such as the League of Legends, there is an increasing trend of International Sport Federations (ISFs) of 'traditional' sports embracing electronic versions of their sport in the form of highly structured and organised competitive events. Some examples include football, with events such as the FIFA World Cup; cycling, with events such as the UCI Cycling Esports World Championships; and motorsport, with the FIA Motorsport Games.

Some developments concerning Esports in South Africa align with these global trends. South Africa is home to the largest Esports market in Africa, with Esports players and teams able to participate in local events and regularly participating in international events hosted locally and internationally. Sailing South Africa, for example, presents opportunities to participate in online events such as virtual regattas. University Sport South Africa (USSA) and the Africa Electronic Sport Association (AESA) are examples of national and continental governing bodies of Esports, and some of these events form part of the Esports Entertainment Association (ESEA) League that offers prize money. Promising South African Esports players have also been recruited to play in internationally based teams. In contrast, South African-based teams such as Goliath Gaming have partnered with numerous companies, including Acer, which specialise in digital technology.

An additional benefit of Esports was experienced during the height of the Covid-19 lockdowns in South Africa. For example, the Cinetic Club, part of Western Cape Cycling, hosted a range of online competitions on the Zwift platform to enable cyclists to continue training and competing, despite being unable to leave their homes.[11] Besides Esports, product and service innovation in mainstream sports such as swimming, athletics, cricket and golf are increasingly visible due to the recognition of technological innovation's potential positive impact on performance from athletes to events.[12]

26.2.1.2 Mainstream sport

Sport and science are often the same, with the goal of scientific advancement through technological innovation to transcend the boundaries of athletic performance.[13] One example is the impact of the development of Fastskin swimsuits. These full-body swimsuits were designed to use biomimetic material and were based on shark skin scales to reduce drag in the water. In addition, Speedo developed an LZR swimsuit in collaboration with NASA, using computational fluid dynamics to produce revolutionary bonding material, thus removing stitching from these swimsuits (to further reduce drag) and trap air between the swimmer's body and the water (to improve buoyancy). The result was that a vast number of international races won and records broken belonged to swimmers using this technology. Ultimately, a debate was raised about possible technological doping in swimming, and FINA eventually moved to ban full-body swimsuits.

In 2019, Eliud Kipchoge became the first person to run a marathon in under two hours in Vienna, Austria. This was primarily attributed to the technological and scientific development of Nike's Vaporfly running shoes. Product, service and process innovation could also enhance amateur and professional athlete experiences. For example, South African golfer Ernie Els recently invested in the 18Birdies golf app, which rewards golfers with various prizes based on the number of times they play golf, regardless of the quality of their performances.

Various innovations have also been applied to the sport sector from a coaching perspective. For example, video technology provides access to a relatively inexpensive tool for coaches to provide visual feedback to athletes and teams, analyse game performances, and analyse and develop technical skills. Real-time recording software also offers vital insight into the movement analysis of athletes. In 2014, the South African Rugby Union's (SARU) High-Performance Department embraced technology by adopting the computer-based programmes Footprint and Stratus. The purpose of the former was to maintain a player database and record vital information and statistics on talented players from as young as 13 years of age, whilst the latter combined with Footprint to monitor on-field performance. SARU also launched a High-Performance

Mobi-Unit to deploy expert coaches at the provincial and national levels. Similar types of innovation occur at the club level, such as the Mamelodi Sundowns Football Club's partnership with the University of Pretoria. In this partnership, knowledge exchange between coaches and athletes in the Club with experts at the University is recognised as the key to advancing scientific and medical knowledge and innovative technology that strategically positions the Mamelodi Sundowns and the University of Pretoria as global leaders in their respective industries.

Another significant product, service and process innovation in traditional sport relates to the spectator experience. As the mainstream sport sector has increasingly shifted to the entertainment industry, various innovative developments have focused on enhancing sports fans' experience using technology. In South Africa, this has evolved from attending events with manual flip scoreboards and being limited to watching only real-time play, to digital scoreboards and watching replays on big screens during events. Cricket fans can also follow umpire reviews live. One of the most significant recent technological innovations to enhance spectator experiences is the development of virtual reality experiences. SARU has partnered with Dell to provide fans with immersive virtual reality experiences in pursuit of its digital transformation goals. This technology also provides athletes and coaches with instant access to valuable analytical tools regardless of location. At the provincial level, Vodacom has partnered with the Blue Bulls Rugby Union (BBRU) to offer stable internet connectivity during matches to enhance spectator experiences during live events. In cricket, the Indian Premier League has used holograms to incorporate commentators from other countries in live broadcasts, such as the Australian Steve Smith.

Besides the fan experience at events, social media platforms have resulted in public sports domains at interpersonal, intercultural and international levels for sport coverage. The *2022 BCW* (Burson, Cohn and Wolfe) *International Sports Federations Social Media Rankings* report[14] provides insight into the social media footprint of ISFs. It emphasises that managers of sport should capitalise on the opportunities that these platforms offer. From this report, the International Cricket Council (1st), FIFA (3rd), World Athletics (6th), World Rugby (7th) and the International Cycling Union (9th) are among the top ten globally for the highest number of followers on Facebook. Cricket South Africa makes strategic use of Facebook to communicate openly with fans about various cricket activities and events, and their success is demonstrated by their significant following of more than four million followers.

26.2.2 Managerial and Management Innovation

Managerial innovation mainly refers to internal information-sharing processes and collaboration among workers. In contrast, management innovation could refer to changes and experimentation at, among others, strategic, financial, organisational design and leadership levels. The workers in sport organisations could refer to staff, volunteers, athletes and clients. Together with the increasing integration of technology in organisations globally, the Knowledge-Based Economy (KBE) has taken priority. In this context, the free flow of information in sport organisations is regarded as one of their most essential resources. In contrast, the extent to which information and communication technology are effectively applied and utilised could provide a strategic competitive advantage.[15] One example is cloud-based management solutions that could assist with various functions such as workflow automation, task monitoring and asset inventory management.

The South African Football Association (SAFA) has a clear communication strategy that utilises a range of technological innovations to communicate internally and distribute critical information to external stakeholders. Core to this strategy is an internal management system that uses information distribution technology and electronic devices such as emails, cellular phones, media interfaces such as media briefings, and intuitive tools such as computers. SAFA's central server also provides staff access to essential documents such as key policies and strategic documents. In addition, using a website and social media platforms such as Facebook, Twitter/X, YouTube and Instagram provides instant communication of aspects such as the organisation's vision, mission and values. Furthermore, recognising the importance of developing volunteers as officials, Sailing South Africa offers unique and innovative opportunities such as Long-Term Official Development, which includes the development of language, mathematical and writing skills to prepare volunteers adequately. Besides internal organisational innovation related to the management of sport organisations, innovative ways of utilising technology at the local, provincial and national levels exist that contribute to the governance of sport organisations.

26.2.3 Governance Innovation

The Institute of Directors[16] identified four characteristics that organisations should incorporate to establish optimal conditions for innovative governance. These include:

1. a board-level appreciation of the relevance of innovation to the company's strategy and business model;
2. undertaking innovation to achieve identified objectives or outcomes;
3. integrating innovation appropriately into the company's processes and activities; and
4. a culture that encourages innovation.

In South Africa, various National Sport Federations (NSFs), such as SARU, SAFA and Netball South Africa (NSA), explicitly recognise the value of innovation. According to SARU, innovation is an essential characteristic captured in their policies at youth and junior levels to grow the sport at the school level. The recognition of the benefits of innovation in this context demonstrates SARU's willingness to embrace a culture of innovation in governance. Similarly, SAFA recognises that the innovative use of technology could address previous mistakes, such as the need for maintaining a player database at the under-17 level. They recently launched an interprovincial tournament for players under 15 years of age and monitored the progress of these athletes using appropriate information systems. In NSA's case, their President recognised that a partnership with Discovery Health would provide an innovative way to promote female sport participation and health.[17]

At the provincial level, the BBRU have partnered with Luno, a global cryptocurrency company founded by South Africans. Strategically, they have aligned with Luno by indicating that the cryptocurrency market is volatile and unpredictable, like rugby. However, the BBRU agreement also explicitly recognises the value of such innovative partnerships to modernise rugby.[18] In a similar fashion, Kaizer Chiefs Football Club has partnered with PinkCodrs. This initiative promotes the empowerment of female software developers with a focus on the Fourth Industrial Revolution, cloud development, machine learning and Artificial Intelligence.[19] Whilst empowering females and developing employability skills through digital technology is a core focus of this programme, Kaizer Chiefs also benefit from gaming development and brand promotion by positioning the organisation as a supporter of female empowerment. In addition, Kaizer Chiefs have incorporated the position of Head of Digital in their organisational structure, indicating that they are striving to embed the use and development of digital technology to benefit the club.

Some examples of the role that technology could play in sport transcend the range of innovations discussed above. In the province of KwaZulu-Natal, various challenges exist in developing digital literacy skills in rural areas due to a lack of access and infrastructure development. The South African Local Government Association (SALGA) Games, in partnership with the KwaZulu-Natal Department of Sport, Arts and Culture, introduced a new initiative called the SALGA Tech Games, with students competing in technological gaming areas, ranging from application development to computer coding. These Games are hosted to identify talent and alleviate poverty by developing employment skills.[20]

26.3 CONCLUSION

Technological innovation could empower managers of sport in South Africa, enabling them to overcome geographical and other challenges, as well as address issues such as unemployment. Consensus exists that South African sport organisations from club to national level could benefit from technological innovation, and the development of digital technology and literacy. These benefits could range from improved managerial processes and governance to coaching and the identification and development of talented athletes from a scientific perspective. Furthermore, spectator value could be enhanced through immersive experiences such as virtual reality. However, these come with challenges. For instance, in South Africa, constant power supply issues due to ageing infrastructure and allegations of rampant corruption and mismanagement at the national electricity supplier (ESKOM) stand in stark contrast to the ideals of developing digital technologies and literacy, related skill development and growing a knowledge-based economy. Failing to address these issues in the immediate and long term could reduce the contribution that sport could make to the South African economy, as well as cause more significant disparities at a societal level due to the lack of access to digital technology, which will inevitably be reflected in and through sport organisations at the local, provincial and national levels.

SELF-ASSESSMENT

1. Define the concepts of sport technology, digital technology and digital literacy skills.
2. Describe technological innovation in and through sport in the context of the Industrial Revolution.
3. Critically analyse the development of technology in South African sport within a framework of technological innovation.
4. Apply the concepts of sport technology, digital technology and digital literacy skills to sport in South Africa.

CORRIDORS OF UNCERTAINTY: CRICKET AND MANAGING THE RACE TO TRANSFORM

Professor Ashwin Desai

LEARNING OUTCOMES

At the end of this chapter, you should be able to:

1. Describe the historical context in which transformation is located.
2. Explain the impact of the political transition to democracy on sport.
3. Debate the broad transformational areas of race, gender and class.
4. Argue the broader context of socio-economic conditions, especially schooling, on transformation in sport.
5. Explain challenges, especially that of racial quotas.

27.1 INTRODUCTION

One of the most arresting moments in post-Apartheid South African sport came when Nelson Mandela wore a Springbok jersey while holding the Webb Ellis Cup aloft in 1995. The Springbok captain, Francois Pienaar, stood alongside him as the newly liberated nation basked in the glow of their new moniker, the 'Rainbow Nation'. While sceptics at the time pointed to the enduring legacy of Apartheid, the African National Congress (ANC) government noted that it was embarking on a journey to redress racial inequities and that this vision included sport. It was a time of 'Madiba Magic', and little attention was given to how a programme to level the country's playing fields would gradually unfold. The nitty-gritty of this transformation would fall to the game administrators, who were batting on changing wickets. This would involve several challenges. One of the most stark, especially in cricket and rugby, was the racial composition of the provincial and national teams. Women's cricket, rugby and soccer (football) had also been historically marginalised, as had sport for those with disabilities (see Chapter 8). All this was happening in the context of the growing commercialisation of sport; in the case of cricket, the Indian Premier League (IPL) allowed private ownership to enter the game, and South African rugby became professional after the 1995 Rugby World Cup.

In cricket, from a base of racially segregated structures, administrators were tasked with managing a series of cross-cutting, often contradictory, demands in an environment where their work was immediately up for public scrutiny. This chapter assesses the challenges of managing transformation in South African sport, with particular emphasis on cricket, where the national team (the Proteas), at the onset of entering foreign fields in the early 1990s, was dominated by White players.

27.2 UNDERSTANDING THE FIELD

This history of sport in South Africa is a history of separate and unequal development. Sport facilities for the White population were on par with those of Northern Hemisphere countries, and a single White school could have more sport fields than an entire Black township.[1;2]

In 1990, as Nelson Mandela strode out of prison, the two worlds of sport edged closer together. In 1991 they united at the top in the form of the South African National Sport Council (NSC), and international recognition quickly beckoned. A debate emerged in the South African sport movement, however, with a strong lobby from those schooled in the anti-Apartheid struggle for international competition to be embargoed until there was a commitment to level the playing fields. The ANC, on the other hand, leaned towards an immediate return.

The politics of transition and the 'unity' of sport organisations have received attention in many publications (also see Chapter 4).[3;4] The push for an immediate lifting of the international sport boycott was leveraged on the basis that it would garner much-needed funds for the development of cricket in underprivileged areas and play a decisive role in levelling the playing fields.[5]

Of course, this debate was linked to a rapidly changing political climate. The ANC wanted to "normalise" South African society after many years of "ungovernability", which was encapsulated by their slogan, *'Ready to Govern'*. Part of this process included South Africa's acceptance into existing global organisations, whether the World Bank through funding or the International Olympic Committee (IOC) resubmitting South Africa to participate in the Olympic Games.

On 29 June 1991, the United Cricket Board of South Africa (UCBSA) was formed, uniting the South African Cricket Union (SACU) and the South African Cricket Board of Control (SACBOC). The founding statements promised much, with the new Board committing to: "formulate strategies to redress urgent imbalances regarding separate educational systems, sponsorships and facilities and contribute, through cricket, to creating a just society in South Africa where everybody democratically has a common say and a common destiny".[6]

Cricket made a strong commitment to transforming the game from White dominance into one that was inclusive, and increasingly began to reflect the country's demographics. Very little was said about how this transformation agenda would be managed, however. Policies were often adopted on the hop, and implementation was ad hoc. This pressured those tasked with managing the game post-1991.

27.2.1 Managing the Transition

The ANC placed much store in its Reconstruction and Development Programme (RDP) of 1994, which promised a heady mix of measures to address the expectations of the majority of South Africans.[7] The RDP specifically addressed the disparity in sport and recreation, referring to it as *"[o]ne of the cruellest legacies of Apartheid"* and signalling an emphasis on the *"provision of facilities at schools and in communities where there are large concentrations of unemployed youth"*. As with the RDP, the document tempered this commitment by recognising that *"sport is played at different levels of competence and… there are different specific needs at different levels"*.[8]

After the 1995 Rugby World Cup, South Africa appeared to be heading towards parity on increasingly level playing fields. However, as the transition unfolded, the challenges of redress and change would see the sport become an arena of intense engagement, contestation and dreams both broken and realised.

In discussions and debates around policy formulation for the 'new' South Africa, two approaches that could broadly be labelled 'reformative' and 'transformative' emerged. The transformative programme sought to transform society fundamentally; its economic emphasis was best captured in the popular slogan, 'Growth through redistribution'. In sport, this would mean a bottom-up, mass-based approach. On the other hand, the reformative approach prioritised reconciliation and cooperative governance in the interests of economic growth and acceptance into a neoliberal world order. In this scenario, conditions best suited to facilitate an environment for doing business in South Africa would be created. The logic underlying this paradigm was that the benefits of economic growth would 'naturally' trickle down to the poorest members of society. This argument was encapsulated in the adage 'Redistribution through growth'. In this model, state intervention would be key in de-racialising the uppermost reaches of class hierarchy through pursuing Black Economic Empowerment (BEE). In sport, this would be seen in the emphasis on high-performance centres for developing and preparing national athletes and the racial composition of national teams. Billions of rands would also be pumped into mega sport events, such as football's FIFA World Cup in 2010.

At the onset, there appeared to be a merging of the transformative and reformative approaches. The Minister of Sport and Recreation, Makhenkesi Stofile, promised in 2004 that:

> *"Our focus will be to build the right attitude and skills from below. The starting place to achieve this is to get the basics right. Community sport clubs must be developed, and our children in townships and village schools must be assisted in doing sport. There is no shortcut to this… schools sport is the nursery for participants in senior competition…. We strongly argue for focused attention on the schools and community clubs in building a broad base for talent scouting, developing and nurturing. This is the mass that will transform society and de-racialise it. We must go back to Wednesday afternoons as school sports days. But this cannot happen by chance."*[9]

Ultimately, it was the reformative programme that came to dominate. A tremendous amount of resources were thrown into mega stadiums and the professionalisation of sport, with the theory being that the largesse from these developments would trickle downwards and begin to redress historical inequalities. Administrators had to be Janus-faced; they had to ensure that their teams were internationally competitive while at the same time finding resources to begin to take the game into Black townships through development programmes. In terms of the latter, they were tasked with redressing a state of affairs that had separated South Africa into two worlds: in the established White schools there would be four or five fields, floodlights, Olympic-size swimming pools and highly qualified coaches; in the Black townships, the sporting fields consisted of sandpits that passed for football pitches, a lack of even rudimentary equipment, and the erosion of organised school sport.

Not too long into the transition to democracy, it was becoming increasingly clear that despite the speech-making and high-sounding programmes, the ANC-led government did not have a sustained plan to nurture sport in previously disadvantaged areas. However, this did not mean that the government realised its culpability in the degeneration of township sport. Rather, it began to attack CSA for the Protea's lack of racial transformation. The UCBSA's (later Cricket South Africa [CSA]) approach that their township development programmes needed government support was brushed off with continuing attacks. The custodians of CSA decided that they would fast-track gifted young Black cricketers by offering them scholarships to attend formerly White schools. While this began to bear results, it had a downside; township school cricket began to be neglected as development became a racial numbers game in the national team. It was a justified quick fix, and the results were palpable. It was the all-round development of players that was crucial. Siya Kolisi, the current Springbok rugby captain, succinctly noted: *"Imagine if I hadn't gone to an English school. I wouldn't have eaten properly, I wouldn't have grown properly and I wouldn't have had the preparation that the other boys did"*.[10]

27.2.2 New Racial Categories for New Times

South Africa was at once dealing with the historical legacy of Apartheid while struggling to develop a new national ethos. In this fluid environment, the management challenges were a moving target. As the Mandela and Thabo Mbeki eras passed, there were rumblings about a narrower-based African nationalism. From the outset of unity in cricket, Black was seen as encompassing African, Coloured and Indian, but the lack of Black African players in the international team came under scrutiny. CSA was called out for not producing enough Black African players at the national level some 20 years after the unity process, and once again, the administrators were in the firing line. Haroon Lorgat, CEO of CSA from 2012 to 2017, attempted to respond by pointing out that producing international standard African cricketers was a complex process:

One must understand why the talent is not coming through or even entering the system. Are the talented players doing something else? Are they being blocked off or lost somewhere in the system? If I were to venture a guess, I'd think that the lack of facilities, development and coaching is the root cause of them not coming through. And particularly with batsmen, you know, bowling is more physical; you can practice independently, whereas, on the batting side, you need skilled coaches to work almost every day with you. That may be a deficiency.

And there could be social reasons for the need for African players. There could be greater social demands on Black (African) people, including the need to work to bring essentials home. You go to school, and then you've got to have time to practice and earn money by working. One of the three things will fall away. A White kid can go to school and play cricket simultaneously. So there's a better synergy between those two demands, and that kid has got little or no demands at home, whereas it is expected from a Black (African) kid to do some work, to bring money to put food on the table or pay for some bare necessities. Something fails out of those three demands in that kid's life. I think someone like (Kagiso) Rabada is an example of a 'White' kid even though he is African, having gone to a school where you could have educated yourself and played the game. And he didn't have to worry about home as his parents are professionals, so his potential was nurtured, and he came through.[11]

Lorgat was referring here to the importance of class and underscoring how multi-faceted the issue of transformation is. When Whites controlled cricket, it was easy to blame their racism for the shortage of Black talent, but Black administrators faced similar development challenges. When Lorgat stated that Rabada, an African fast bowler, was an example of a "White kid", he meant that he is from a middle-class urban background and attended an elite private school with outstanding sport facilities. The majority of African children, in contrast, do not have facilities at school and also have to face poverty, making bare survival their main priority in life. However, in blithely referring to Rabada as 'White', he wrote out the whole historical legacy of Apartheid with its role models and networks and the prejudice that someone who is Black will face at school and in the dressing room because of the colour of their skin.

Whatever one's take is on Lorgat's response, it points out how sometimes managing race at one level reveals new contradictions that must be addressed.

As the debates over the transformation in sport have unfolded in cricket, the category 'Black', which had included Africans, Coloureds and Indians, was disaggregated so that the transformation remit mutated into a focus on upping the numbers of Black Africans, a strategy that occluded broader questions of class privilege.[12] The racial targets introduced by CSA stipulated that each provincial team of 11 had to field six players of colour, including three Black Africans. It was hoped that this would increase the pool of Black African players available for the national team. The target for the national team was four players of colour, including at least one Black African.[13] While most Whites abhor quotas, Merrett, Tatz and Adair have pointed out that: *"Racial quotas have always shaped South African identity; that is, divisions, assignments, allowances and allocations based on socially created ideas of race and difference."*[14]

While racial quotas are strictly enforced at the provincial level, the situation is more flexible at the national level, where the Proteas are required to field a minimum of six players of colour, including two Black Africans, but this is averaged over a season. It is alleged that the team is usually loaded with Black players against weaker opposition to meet these targets, although this has lessened as Black players with top global rankings have come through. However, the situation is topsy-turvy. Selectors find it challenging to meet selection targets when leading African players, like batsman Temba Bavuma or bowlers like Kagiso Rabada and Lungi Ngidi, are injured or out of form, especially because Black players like Hashim Amla, Vernon Philander and J.P. Duminy, who were regular members of the team, have retired.[15]

Moonda captured the complexity of race when she wrote:

> *"The rainbow nation is not without shades of grey. There is a difference in this country between Black and Black Africans; it is both problematic and necessary. While all Black people were affected by the evils of the Apartheid regime, the Black African population were the most severely marginalised and mistreated. They are also, by far, the biggest majority. Redressing the wrongs committed against them is non-negotiable, but where does that leave other Black people, those who are Coloured, mixed-race or of Indian descent?"*[16]

Cricket administrators face many challenges that often take work to balance. For example, demands are made to produce more Black (African) cricketers, but the ANC government, which makes this demand, still needs to nurture the game in township schools. When CSA plucks talented Black players and places them in formerly White schools, they are accused of reinforcing and not confronting old divisions. When CSA puts resources into townships, they come up against a culture that privileges soccer over cricket. Meanwhile, resources dwindle as sponsors want a winning national team and see limited mileage in putting money into developmental projects that fly under the media's radar.

27.2.3 Race and Class Apartheid

Given the failure to produce Black African cricketers by the late 1990s and still lacking facilities in townships, cricket administrators placed talented Black cricketers in elite former White Model C (government) or private (independent) schools. Most Black players from these elite schools, when they had access to a privileged education, excellent diet, outstanding facilities and high-level coaching, were selected to meet 'race' quotas and were exhibited as proof of cricket's transformation.

Race and class remain at the forefront of discussions about cricket and rugby in South Africa, however. If the status quo remains, the transformation will be viewed as a race issue. Only when facilities are extended into the townships and the base of cricket, rugby and other sports is expanded will the gap between the haves and have-nots narrow. Meanwhile, this class bias is overridden by an almost messianic drive enveloping some cricket administrators to 'Africanise' the game. Still, in the absence of massive spending on school sport and townships, the pool of African players will continue to come from the elite strata of society and schools. While quotas have facilitated the emergence of African players, this development needs to address the workings of class and privilege in sporting achievement. To effect real change, macro-economic structural change that leads to a more equitable redistribution of resources and equality of opportunity is required.

The roads into national teams for Black players have been almost exclusively through ex-Model C or private schools. The downside of this transformation model is that it removes the imperative to develop a cricket culture in the townships.

Class Apartheid can be witnessed in the very geography of South African cities and is reinforced by a bountifully endowed private and semi-private school system, versus township schools that struggle with huge numbers and largely non-existent sporting facilities.

But this is not to discount the heart-warming changes that have taken place. The complexion of the national teams has changed, and Black stars have not only emerged, but have led their teams onto the field of play.

Yet few saw the hidden impact of transformation. What went on inside the changerooms? This was brought into the public domain when Cricket South Africa sponsored the Social Justice and Nation-Building Initiative (SJN).

27.2.4 The Changeroom

The SJN hearings were designed to hear allegations of racism in cricket and the evidence was haunting. Some of South Africa's most beloved cricketers, like Paul Adams, spoke about their experiences. Ashwell Prince, the usually quietly spoken Proteas' batsman, spoke about the pain and labelling he endured. Prince exposed the reception he received when he entered the Proteas dressing room:

> "There was no welcome from the coach. There was no (sense of) let's make this guy comfortable. It was a lonely place. A person knows when they are welcome, and you know when you are unwelcome. You can understand whether people want you here or don't want you here. It would have been nice for people to back you. You saw it happening to other guys your age, your peers. You saw it happening to a new player if he was White but it wasn't happening if the player wasn't White."[17]

In an earlier interview, Prince reflected:

> "Transformation has been a topic for as long as I can remember. From the day I made my first-class debut in 1995 to the day I retired in 2015, I heard every kind of abuse you could think of under the sun. The message is all very much the same, just varying in expletives, but basically trying to tell me that I'm not good enough, that I will never be good enough, and that I'm only there because of my skin colour. The difficulty we face in South Africa is that the influential people, i.e., captains, coaches and selectors, until recently, have predominantly been White. The fact that those people are/were predominantly White shouldn't necessarily be a negative for a non-White player provided those people have transformed hearts and minds. Unfortunately, in my experience as a player, that did not seem to be the case. White coaches and captains seemed to prefer to stick to 'what they know'; in other words, their kind, because that is what they feel they can trust."[18]

The retired much-lauded Proteas fast bowler, Makhaya Ntini, also spoke about loneliness.

> "I would go to the driver of the bus early in the morning and I would give him my bag. I would say to him, 'I will meet you at the ground'. I would put on my running shoes and run to the cricket ground. On my way back, I would give the bus driver my dirty clothes and say, 'I'll see you at the hotel'. I would run back to the hotel. I was running away from the loneliness of driving back to the hotel. If I sit at the back, the rest are at the front. I was forever lonely. Being lonely is not having someone knock on your door and say, 'Let's go for dinner'. You'll watch friends calling each other, making plans right before you, and then you'll be skipped. They will have dinner, lunch and breakfast at the same time. If I was the first one in the breakfast room, the next guy would never come to sit next to me."[19]

While race was the seeming focus of the SJN, class was not far away, however. The SJN hearings heard evidence of the perilous state of schools' cricket in township schools. Rajan Moodley from the Eastern Province gave the following testimony:

> "In June of last year (2022), the Minister of Sport was presented with a report from persons known as the Eminent Persons Group and in that report, it highlighted the fact that less than 10% of the 25,000 schools that we have participated in sport [own emphasis]: ...If you look at - and again, these are horrible terms, but let's use them - in Black African cricket in your Proteas setup at the moment,

which schools do they come from? And I am not blaming these kids. I take my hat off because they've achieved what is due to them, but where do they come from? St Stithians, Hilton College, SACS Cape Town, Marist Brothers, Joburg... You need to ask yourself: When are we going to get people coming from Langa, Gugulethu (own emphasis)... I conducted a study of township schools in Eastern Province Cricket from 2009 to 2019... for that entire period, the average representation of township schools in all those age-group teams is also less than 10%. So while we are meeting the required quotas because it says 50% of those teams must be players of colour, the question is, where are they coming from? They are coming from affluent or elite schools, but they're not coming from township schools (own emphasis).[20]

Beyond the school system, the dire position of cricket in Black townships was brought to the fore by Geoffrey Toyana, a highly successful Black Gauteng coach. According to Toyana:

"The main challenge that we have in every township in South Africa is something that breaks me. I come from Soweto. It's quite sad that the Soweto Cricket Oval has not improved since I last played. I mean, I was involved in Soweto Cricket in the late '90s and early 2000s, for me to see that there's no change and no improvement in that facility and other facilities as well as all over South Africa. I know CSA has hubs to try to close gaps at the moment, but I don't think that's how you need to close gaps. It will be a shock for me to see a Black African kid coming from the township without any private education go play franchise cricket.... Do all coaches understand this? Are they taught about this? Or are they just given a piece of paper telling them they must put in three Black Africans per game without any explanation?"[21]

Toyana, amidst several haunting points, also raised how bean counting has become how transformation in sport is assessed.

27.2.5 Number Crunching

A typical example of this bean counting was set out in the June 2020 Report on Transformation in Sport compiled by the Eminent Persons Group (EPG). In his foreword, the then Minister of Sport, Arts and Culture, Nathi Mthethwa, conceded that:

"The impact of increasing levels of poverty and inequality is dividing the sports system in two – one for those who can afford to play, and another for those who cannot afford to play. It is, therefore, crystal clear that if we fail to administer tough reforms and find reliable partners in implementing the transformation agenda, we will be failing our society and future generations."[22]

The central approach of these transformation efforts is to closely monitor the organisations running sport, demanding that they provide minute details of ensuring progressive moves towards demographic representation at all levels of the organisation. The emphasis is on self-policing and numbers. In the words of the Minister:

"Transformation status is established by measuring actual federation performance in 18 categories (defined by the Charter) against two sets of targets in scorecard format. The one scorecard is based on the achievement of the prescribed and one-size-fits-all targets of the Charter and the other, the

'Barometer' (introduced in 2016/2017), is based on the achievement of a National Sport Federation's (NSFs) own or self-set and forward-projected targets. Both measures are milestones directing an NSF's transformation journey towards 'an accessible, equitable, sustainable, demographically representative and competitive sport system'. As the adage goes, 'You can't improve what you don't measure'. Therefore, the quality of data collected and submitted by NSFs becomes integral to the audit process. Though there has been some improvement in the data submitted, more still needs to be done... With all the barometer forecasts reviewed and changed where required, penalties will be rigorously applied in 2020. Four pilot federations, namely rugby, cricket, football and netball, achieved their self-set barometer targets in 2018/19."[23]

Sport administrators are thus reduced to filling in forms and providing 'progress' reports on racial representation. Growing the game, building township facilities and progressively amalgamating the two sport systems are not the priorities. Administrators are there to meet targets, not to be thinking, imaginative human beings who are responding to local nuance and changing global dynamics.

27.2.6 Managing an Uncertain Corridor

To manage cricket is to be at once local and global. The coming of the IPL has been a game-changer in several ways. It has accelerated the privatisation of the game while affording players lucrative contracts, and players can increasingly de-link from national teams and local cricket commitments. With the IPL set to offer longer contracts and the 20/20 expanding globally, cricket administrators of the national set-up and provincial franchises are scrambling for resources. International tours, once the pinnacle of finance and allied sponsorship, are more difficult to secure.

Meanwhile, there are pressures to broaden the game by throwing more resources into grassroots cricket. School cricket in previously disadvantaged areas gets zero government support, yet the government berates the cricket authorities for not meeting targets. One is constantly batting in the proverbial uncertain corridor, and no management textbook or MBA will provide a model answer.

27.3 CONCLUSION

The game that begins as it ends

To be a cricket administrator in South Africa is not only to ensure that the fundamentals are in place so that the game can be played, but also to have the ability to deal with a range of issues beyond the boundary. As this chapter shows, one of the vital areas to address is transformation in terms of race; one cannot simply ignore this with the refrain that one is administering sport and nothing else matters. In South Africa, with its particular history and need for nation-building, one has to consider broader issues. Of course, one almost feels like a high-jumper. As one flies over the bar, it is set even higher. This job has no set formula; it is as fluid as a river in full flow. But by understanding our histories, taking hope from the Mandela Moment, and learning from the national team's victories on the field of play, one gets a sense of how we get it more right than wrong. Transformation is not a 20/20 game; it is a test match where the game ebbs and flows, and a new day brings new challenges.

SELF-ASSESSMENT

1. Explain why Mandela's attendance at the 1995 Rugby World Cup Final was important in South African history and sport?
2. Why is transformation a buzzword in sport in South Africa?
3. While there are several areas of transformation (gender, disability, class and race), argue why race is considered a vital area.
4. Explain the pros and cons of racial quotas in national sport teams.
5. Why are issues beyond the boundary of the actual playing of sport important for Sport Managers?

SAFEGUARDING AND PROTECTION: THE MANAGEMENT OF SAFE AND INCLUSIVE SPORT

Anneline Lewies & Dr Elizabeth Smith

LEARNING OUTCOMES

At the end of this chapter, you should be able to:

1. Demonstrate understanding of the legislative and regulatory framework for safeguarding and protection protocols.
2. Recognise stakeholders and role players in safeguarding sport and implementing policy and the STEP Model within the safeguarding and protection context in sport.
3. Understand the purpose of safeguarding and protection, the principles of management by coaches and other sport entities, and the ability to establish a local working group and reporting structures.
4. Understand the role and responsibilities of the coach, parent/guardian, manager, National Federations, SASCOC, SASCA and athlete commissions in safeguarding and protecting children and vulnerable persons.
5. Evaluate the legal responsibility in dealing with abuse within sport (why, who, when) and the reporting procedures.

28.1 INTRODUCTION

Sport coaches of children and young persons with disabilities act in *loco parentis* (in the place of parents). While these youth are in their care, they fulfil a broader role than merely imparting technical skills; every coach is a confidante, mentor, carer, watchdog and protector of the young/vulnerable person. For this reason, the coach is responsible for creating an environment of care, patience, understanding and encouragement.

Furthermore, each young athlete has legal rights, and coaches are legally responsible for protecting every child in their care from abuse and discrimination. It is well-known that experiencing violence in childhood impacts lifelong health and well-being. Violence is traumatic, *"evoking toxic responses to stress that cause both immediate and long-term physiological and psychological damage ... that poses a real risk for the onset and persistence of mental health conditions".*[1]

Legally, coaches should ensure that children and vulnerable persons receive equal opportunities and treatment, regardless of ability, age, gender, sexual orientation, race, language, religion or culture. For example, the United Nations Convention on the Rights of the Child enshrines children's rights.[2] In addition, the United Nations Convention on the Rights of Persons with Disabilities reinforces the need to protect the rights of children and adults with disabilities and to ensure their full and equal participation in society.[3,4]

At the 2014 Beyond Sport Summit, a group of organisations formed the International Safeguarding Children in Sport Working Group, detailing eight elements that should be put in place for any organisation working with children in sport:

1. Developing your Policy
2. Procedures for Responding to Safeguarding Concerns
3. Advice and Support
4. Minimising Risks to Children
5. Guidelines for Behaviour
6. Recruiting, Training and Communicating
7. Working with Partners
8. Monitoring and Evaluation

At the 2016 Beyond Sport Summit, the team developed this further with the launch of an implementation guide, which helps organisations work toward applying these safeguards. Since its launch in 2014, more than 80 organisations have confirmed their commitment to working towards the safeguards, ensuring that sport fulfils their duty to protect children participating in sport and providing a significant opportunity to understand their rights and feel safe outside sport.[5] In South Africa, SASCOC and United Through Sport South Africa are signatories to this workgroup.

The World Health Organisation (WHO)[6] estimates that globally, up to one billion children aged 2–17 years have experienced physical, sexual or emotional violence or neglect in the past year. Children with disabilities are almost four times more likely to experience violence than non-disabled children; 3.7 times more likely than non-disabled children to be victims of violence; 3.6 times more likely to be victims of physical violence; and 2.9 times more likely to be victims of sexual violence. Children with mental or intellectual impairments appear among the most vulnerable, with 4.6 times the risk of sexual violence than their non-disabled peers.[7]

Similarly, adults with disabilities are 1.5 times more likely to be victims of violence than those without a disability. At the same time, those with mental health conditions are at nearly four times the risk of experiencing violence. A further complication is that people with disabilities who suffer from communication impairments are hampered in their ability to disclose abusive experiences.[8]

Child abuse and neglect are defined as the physical or mental injury, sexual abuse or exploitation, negligent treatment or maltreatment of:

1. a child under the age of 18, except in the case of sexual abuse, when the age is specified in criminal and child protection legislation;
2. by an adult person (including any caregiver or person who has control over the child) or anyone who is physically, intellectually, emotionally and sexually more mature than the child victim;
3. in circumstances that indicate the child's health or well-being is harmed or threatened.[9]

28.2 LEGISLATIVE AND REGULATORY FRAMEWORK

The legal environment and legislation form part of the external sport management environment. Regarding safeguarding, effective management refers to informed decision-making. The parameters set by law can be disastrous to the success of sport should the obligations imposed on sports people through legislation need more control to enable management of this aspect.[10]

The legislation clearly defines the legal responsibility of various persons in reporting child abuse cases. The relevant legislation will be referred to and then explained below. It is important to remember that all the Acts must be considered one body of information. One acts as an informed sport person when reporting an incident, belief or suspicion.

South African legislation, global regulations and guidelines form the framework relevant to South African safeguarding protocols for sport. A comprehensive list is included in Annexure A. In addition, some key focus areas are explained below.

28.2.1 Key Focus Areas

28.2.1.1 Criminal Law (Sexual Offences and Related Matters) Amendment Act 32 of 2007

This Act specifies that individuals are obliged to report abuse where they reasonably suspect or believe it has occurred, whether towards a child or a person with a disability. Not reporting such abuse is considered a criminal offence. Legislated reporting procedures are explained in Paragraph 8. This legislation shows that there is an onus on individuals to report abuse where they reasonably suspect or believe it has occurred, and failure to report is an offence.

28.2.1.2 Children's Act 38 of 2005 as amended by Children's Amendment Act 17 of 2022

This Act confirms the duty of sport coaches to report any suspected sexual abuse, deliberate neglect and physical injury. The Act clearly defines maltreatment, abuse, neglect and degrading of a child by a parent or a caregiver (a coach fulfils this responsibility whilst having the child in his/her care at a school, club or recreation facility), or behaviour that harms the physical, mental or social well-being of a child, labour practices and child trafficking. Trafficking refers to the recruitment, sale, supply, transportation, transfer, harbouring or receipt of children within or across the borders of the Republic of South Africa. It also refers to any means, including the use of threat, force or other forms of coercion, abduction, fraud, deception, abuse of power or the giving or receiving of payments or benefits to achieve the consent of a person having control of a child or due to a child in a position of vulnerability, for exploitation.[11] To this extent, it is important to consider the recruitment of children by schools, clubs and recreation facilities by offering bursaries, accommodation and monetary benefits with the parents' consent as an act or form of trafficking. The Act also describes people considered unsuitable to work with children in any social environment, education environment, clubs or public recreation centres.

It is an offence not to report suspected cases of child abuse when one has knowledge, reasonable belief or suspicion that a person with a mental disability is being abused. Reasonable belief or suspicion is required and is gained from knowing what constitutes child abuse and what signs and symptoms could be present in abused children or the mentally challenged. The person reporting the abuse is protected if it is done without ulterior motives, and persons making the report cannot be criminally charged or sued if they request an investigation according to the law. It is not the role of a sports coach to investigate the suspicion or do more than ask the child if anything is wrong, and handle the subsequent disclosure and referral to the correct authorities as determined by the Act.

28.2.1.3 Films and Publication Act 65 of 1996

It is illegal to have any involvement in child pornography, and it is a criminal offence not to report child pornography. The question then arises: How is this Act relevant to coaching; how does it impact you as a coach? Implications are that no minor athletes (younger than 18 years of age) may be photographed, videoed or otherwise represented in any media without the signed consent of a parent/guardian. Should athletes be older than 18, they must personally sign the consent form, agreeing to the photographing/videoing.

28.2.1.4 Disaster Management Act (Act No 57 of 2002)

During any pandemic, the Disaster Management Act and resultant regulations by the President's office of South Africa supersede all other legislation. In the case of the Covid-19 pandemic, this Act regulated which places were closed to the public in the interests of public health: "any place or premises where … sporting … activities may occur: public parks, swimming pools, beaches etcetera."[12]

Further regulations resulting from this Act, which impacted the practicing of sport, were passed on 7 October 2020.[13] These measures were specifically formulated during 2020 and 2021 to prevent and combat the spread of Covid-19 in sport, arts and culture:

1. All spectators are allowed at fitness centres or on sports grounds once the President declares all danger of Covid-19 has passed. Swimming pools and sports grounds can operate at 50% of their capacity during competitions or events. Only players and essential personnel are allowed in the venue/on the field.
2. At all events, registers must be kept to comply with quarantine and isolation regulations.

3. Strict compliance must be adhered to concerning all protocols and social distancing.
4. All temperatures are to be taken before relevant persons are allowed to enter venues.
5. Sanitising protocols of venues must be strictly enforced.
6. Notices should be prominently displayed at all venues concerning wearing face masks and other protocols.
7. Only pre-packed meals and drinks in disposable drinking bottles may be on offer.
8. Adequate ventilation must be in place. In addition, air filters must be regularly replaced as per prescriptions.
9. Each venue is to have a designated isolation area to isolate suspected cases/persons with raised temperatures until they can be removed from the premises.
10. Compliance officers must be appointed and on duty.
11. Personal protective equipment must be available for all employees.
12. No childcare facilities may be open.

It is always advisable to remember the above measures for any possible disaster, especially during a pandemic, and to advise participants to always maintain sanitising and hand-washing protocols. Other diseases such as chickenpox, diphtheria, H1N1 flu (swine flu), cholera and many others may also present a need for disaster measures.

28.2.2 Role Players in Safeguarding Sport

The following are some of the sport, governmental and non-governmental departments, agencies, organisations, institutions, federations and individuals in South Africa which, under their role and commitment to children, are bound by safeguarding protocols: SASCA (South African Sports Coaching Association – professional body for coaches), SASCOC (South African Sport Confederations and Olympic Committee),[14] sport confederations and federations and coaches; legal and judicial system professionals; law enforcement / South African Police Services (SAPS); health care professionals; welfare professionals; parents, primary caregivers and guardians; mental health professionals; educators and coaches; and community service providers such as church groups, places of safety, recreation facilities and government institutions.

To protect children and other vulnerable persons from abuse, sporting associations or recreational bodies are responsible for providing a safe environment that protects against unsuitable persons.

28.3 SAFETY REQUIREMENTS FOR SPORT ORGANISATIONS

The International Olympic Commission demands that all sporting codes abide by international standards and have a Safeguarding Policy for children and the vulnerable in sport. Safety requirements for organisations comprise having the following in place: policies, correct reporting procedures and formulated safety measures. Detailed sport-specific information regarding safety is available from national and international sporting federations, SASCOC, SASCA, SAPS, Courts of Law and Ministerial Offices. The following information will guide policy, correct reporting procedures and formulated safety measures.

28.3.1 Policy

All organisations (e.g., sport's governing bodies, local authorities, clubs and schools) must have formulated safeguarding policies, procedures and guidelines on their websites. At SASCA, all coaches must sign the Coaching Charter (Code of Conduct)[15] as part of this policy. SASCOC is the multi-sport organisation that monitors and evaluates the implementation of such policies and embeds safeguarding in their partnerships. Since the 2022 Constitution of SASCOC was accepted, SASCOC has suspended at least eight confederations and federations for non-compliance. They should be able to resolve this situation through negotiation, building capacity or ending the partnerships. Safeguarding in sport can also be followed internationally on Athelet365. This initiative is the official community for elite athletes and Olympians and provides relevant advice, tools and services to support athletes.[16]

28.3.1.1 Scope and purpose

a) The Safeguarding Policy should apply to all individuals, entities and organisations in the Republic of South Africa governed by the Department of Sport, Arts and Culture South Africa, SASCOC, SASCA and the national federations and confederations. These include the following:

   1. Permanent, maximum term and casual staff
   2. Individual contractors and consultants
   3. Volunteers
   4. Board members
   5. Partners that have a formal/contractual relationship with sport members
   6. Interns
   7. Work experience students

b) For others engaged by sporting bodies (known as 'representatives') having contact with children for a period of one day or longer, including the following:

   1. Journalists and media personnel
   2. Photographers
   3. Donors
   4. Supporters
   5. Guest presenters
   6. Entertainers
   7. Visitors, including spouses/partners, family members, personnel and associates

The policy does not need to be signed by people engaged by sporting staff for less than one day and/or who will have no contact with children. These people must be aware of the policy and the child protection standards and be supervised by staff members at all times.

This policy regulates the protection of children against abuse, violence, neglect and exploitation. It is an obligation shared by many role players, including various government departments, public society agencies, communities and families. Considering the Human Rights and Business Principles and the Convention on the Rights of the Child, as well as the African Charter on the Rights and Welfare of the Child and the Children's Act, 38/2005 and Regulations, protecting children is recognised as the responsibility of the private sector – in this instance sporting bodies and national federations.[17]

28.3.2 Safety Measures for Sport: The Step Model – Coaches Must Sign a Code

STEP is an acronym denoting Space, Task, Equipment and People. It was developed by the Youth Sport Trust to assist teachers, coaches and community sport deliverers to ensure that participants with varying abilities can be included in physical activities. Changes in how training is delivered for inclusion can occur in one or more STEP areas. Several factors must be considered when reviewing safety requirements and measures for any sporting event. Black and Williamson's STEP model provides a helpful guide for systematically reviewing factors which could offer potential hazards.[18]

28.3.2.1 The STEP Model: Space

Ensure well-lit venues that are free of unnecessary obstacles and persons. Facilities, sporting equipment and protective equipment should meet the standard safety requirements for all sports and be regularly inspected. The risk of infection increases when young people:

1. live and train in close contact with others, thus increasing cross-infection;
2. train in environments where germs breed (e.g., change rooms);
3. share contaminated items (e.g., drink bottles);
4. are exposed to new environments when travelling to compete;
5. damage the skin allowing the transfer of germs; and
6. come in contact with other people's blood or other bodily fluids.

Disability inclusion requires the coach to adapt the space to allow for inclusion. Examples include increasing or decreasing the size of the playing area; varying the distances to be covered in practices to suit different abilities or mobility levels; and using zoning, for example, where players are matched by knowledge and therefore have more opportunity to participate.

28.3.2.2 The STEP Model: Task

Coaches should ensure that every person responsible for the arrangements for the session has been allocated specific tasks and that these have been carried out according to sport-specific requirements. Leave nothing to chance: check personally or delegate a suitable person/compliance officer. The coach should properly supervise all participants during sessions and enforce safety rules (ensure that all participants are visible at all times to prevent injuries or harm due to incorrect space allocated for an activity). This will afford young people the opportunity to experience and enjoy fun and success, with less likelihood of injury.

It is also necessary to ensure that no unnecessary people or objects are on site, and allow no shoddy artistry. The people appointed at a session should follow protocol rather than just another body that may create an opportunity for error, block admission or exits of sites through unnecessary furniture or obstacles. Cancel matches or training sessions if an inspection indicates that playing surfaces and/or equipment are unsafe, or the facility or venue poses a risk. Take photos and file a report.

28.3.2.3 The STEP model: Environment and Equipment

In managing risk, consideration must be given to environmental factors and their impact on participants.

a) Weather conditions

Regions/districts in South Africa vary in their definitions of 'extreme' weather conditions due to specific acclimatisation issues within local environments. Sometimes extreme weather conditions (e.g., heat, cold, rain or wind) make it best to postpone training and competitions.

b) Sun protection

Organisers of sport competitions and events are responsible for protecting young people, to the greatest extent practical, from the dangers of sun exposure. Young people should be encouraged to wear appropriate protective clothing and use the correct sunscreen on exposed skin. Sport organisers should also maximise shade and shaded areas at venues and events.

c) Equipment: installation and maintenance

Safety gear, uniforms and footwear should be sport-specific and fit correctly. All equipment must be fit for purpose, such as post padding (hockey, netball, rugby, basketball); correctly installed; in good working order; and regularly inspected and maintained. The dimensions of playing equipment must be suitable for the participants' size and physical abilities, for example, in ball games (netball, football, tennis, bulletjie rugby), increase or decrease the size of the ball to suit the ability or age range of the players, or depending on the skill being practiced, provide options that enable athletes to send or receive a ball in different ways. Match players of similar ability in small-sided activities and balance team numbers according to the group's overall ability. It may be preferable to play with teams of unequal numbers to facilitate the inclusion of some players and maximise the participation of others.[19]

28.3.2.4 The STEP model: People

a) General guidelines for coaching

Sports coaches are in a position of trust, thus they must be aware of their legal responsibilities, especially concerning the advice they give their athletes and how they manage and supervise sports participation. Coaches have a legal responsibility to their athletes and should give appropriate advice and guidance; they should only offer advice within their level of qualification.

Coaches are responsible for the health and safety of the athletes in their charge, therefore they should have access to first aid facilities and know how to contact emergency services. The importance of coaches knowing health aspects and first aid procedures cannot be negotiated; a coach could be liable if evidence can show that normal standards and practices were not followed.

Coaches have a responsibility to protect children from all forms of abuse. All coaches should be able to recognise indicators that may signify abuse and take appropriate action if concerned. There are four main forms of abuse, and as outlined above, there are other forms of abuse as per South African legislation:

1. Neglect (providing inadequate food).
2. Emotional abuse (being threatened or taunted or not given equal opportunity).
3. Sexual abuse (grooming, sexual exploitation, being shown pornographic material).
4. Physical abuse (hitting, over-training).

To ensure non-discrimination, ensure that all players have equal opportunities to participate, and provide an adequate opportunity to practice skills or components individually or with a partner before including them in small-sided team games.

Direct discrimination occurs when children or young people are:

1. treated less favourably, for instance, given less access to training or selection in teams because of an attribute or characteristic such as their gender, race, disability or sexual orientation; or
2. refused or provided membership on less favourable terms and conditions than other members because of an attribute or characteristic.

Indirect discrimination is a practice imposed that does not appear to be discriminatory, but which impacts one young person more than another because of a personal attribute or characteristic. The attributes or characteristics of discrimination differ, but generally include age, disability, physical features, race, religious belief/activity and gender.[20]

Coaches may favour some players and, due to participants needing to be at the same level of development, afford more opportunities to those children who have already reached their developmental milestones in certain areas.

b) Physiological and health guidelines

Ensure you have all the necessary documentation on each child/vulnerable person. For example, it is an excellent policy to insist on a physical examination report by a medical practitioner or a signed form from the parent absolving you from any liability in cases of injury.

Specific warm-up and cool-down exercises should accompany all sport activities. Every effort should be made to eliminate unsafe skills practices so young people do not sustain injuries due to these techniques. Young people should play in various positions and not over-train in particular skills. The age and stage appropriateness concept of coaching children should always set the standard for activities to develop skills and ensure learning for all participants. The 5Cs of coaching children are Character, Competence, Caring, Confidence and Connection, and should be applied during all sporting activities presented to young people and children.[21]

- Body temperature regulation

Young people have a larger skin surface-to-body mass ratio than adults and their sweat glands are immature, making them more susceptible to heat loss and heat gain. In extreme temperature and humidity conditions, the duration of sport sessions should be shortened or cancelled. Uniforms should also be suitable for the climate. Young people who are most at risk of heat-related decreases in performance lack cardio-vascular fitness, have a high body-mass index (BMI), are poorly acclimatised or are in poor health.

- Fluid balance

Fluid balance is always essential but requires more attention in certain weather conditions. Therefore, in adverse weather conditions, specific fluid practices should be followed:

1. Young people should be reminded to drink water before, during and after training and competing.
2. Drink about one cup of water (or sports drinks) every 15 to 20 minutes to avoid stomach cramps from drinking large amounts of fluids at once. Discourage drinking carbonated beverages or caffeine.
3. The coach must be alert for signs of possible dehydration and act accordingly: extreme thirst, weakness, headache or dizziness, dark-coloured urine and slight weight loss. If you suspect dehydration, ensure the athlete takes fluids immediately, followed by a snack. Always consult a healthcare professional for a diagnosis since symptoms may denote other medical problems.

- Nutrition

The nutritional needs of junior sport participants are affected by their activity levels. For this reason, a balanced diet with adequate caloric intake, including iron and calcium, which provides them with all the essential elements, should be encouraged.

- Diseases

The risk of infection increases in certain conditions and environments and has been discussed in an earlier section.

The risk of contracting illnesses such as Covid-19, hepatitis, skin infections and upper respiratory tract infections (URTI) increases under some sports conditions. Therefore, parents and coaches should take every precaution to eliminate these dangers.

28.4 ROLES, RESPONSIBILITIES AND RELATIONSHIPS

The typical and often expected range of behaviours and practices that follow the coach's interpretation of their part in a set of circumstances to achieve improved or sustained performance from the participants for the purpose of sport coaching is conceptualised as the 'role' of the coach. The coach's role should be considered in the context of the organisational dimension, any 'essential' element and contributions of other relevant individuals involved in the sport coaching. It is also important to consider the domain expectations and boundary markers for defining or delimiting the role that could possibly impact role behaviours.[22]

28.4.1 The Role of the Coach

Sport coaches are in a position of trust, thus they must be aware of their legal responsibilities, especially concerning guidance given to athletes and how they manage and supervise sports participation. Furthermore, coaches have a legal obligation towards the health and safety of the athletes in charge. A coach could be held legally liable if evidence can show that usual standards and practices were not followed in cases of injury. All coaches must be familiar with all health aspects, first aid procedures and how to access emergency medical care.

The role of the coach as a trustworthy person includes attitudes, behaviour and responsibility to the coach self in coaching as an occupational grouping. The role of the coach is the expected scope of behaviour in particular circumstances to achieve the purpose of sport coaching. The coach needs to review the expectations to perform because of his/her position. There are core expectations of the role of the coach and the individual can bring additional elements beyond that role with situational and personal qualities. It is important that individuals learn about their roles in social life or become socialized into their roles. Therefore, understanding the coach's practice and the effect of the organisational and social factors on the coach's role.[23]

28.4.1.1 Coaches' responsibilities towards others

Social structures, social trends and power relationships shape sport coaching structures. It is important to discuss the coach's responsibility to protect participants from abuse and use of prohibited substances in sport.

a) Protection against abuse

The coach is responsible for protecting children from all forms of abuse. Coaches should be able to recognise indicators that may signify abuse and take appropriate action. The following diagram details signs of abuse.

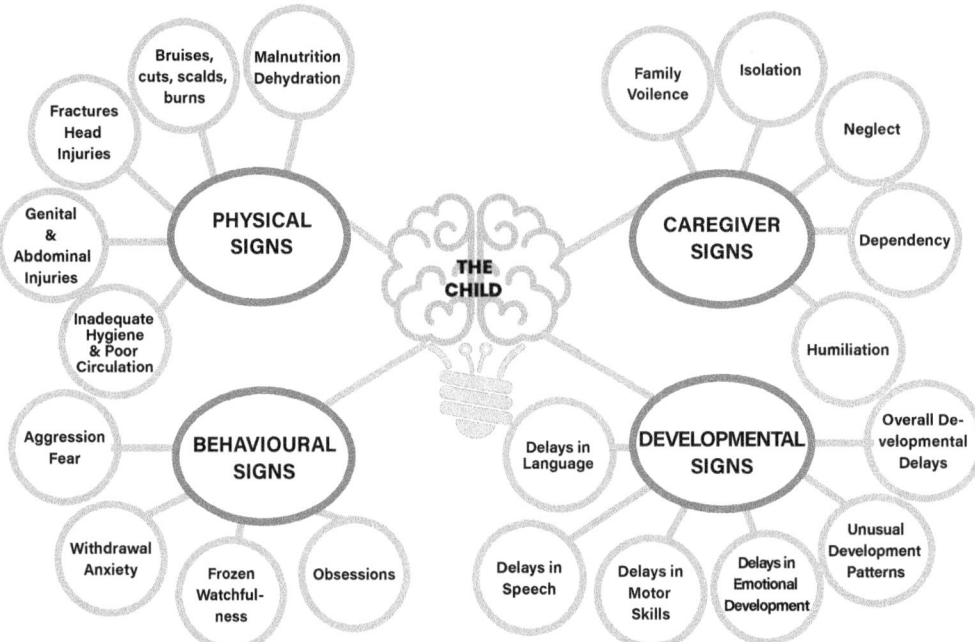

Figure 28.1: Signs of abuse

The coach should apply the principles of good practice and sub-discipline knowledge. The diagram presents knowledge of the signs of abuse to be attentive to. Coaches in training with participants often see burns, scalds, cuts and bruises, and must be able to identify malnutrition and dehydration. Should a pattern be observed, it is necessary to record such injuries for reporting purposes. Signs of sexual and sometimes physical abuse are not visible, however a coach may observe behavioural signs that indicate trauma or anxiety. The coach's role is vast and often incorporates being a nurse, social worker, psychologist and counsellor, so they need to know the participant he/she is coaching. This includes knowledge of the child's background and history and identifying children in difficult circumstances, thus forming the basis for, and knowledge of, caregiver signs. Lastly, coaches should know didactics; the domains such as cognitive, psychomotor, physical, social and effective; as well as the variables for entry for the participant, which are intelligence, motivation, various developmental delays and age and stage-appropriate competencies (e.g., what should a 12 year old be able to do compared to other 12 years olds?).[24]

b) Responsibility towards drug abuse and supplement use

Coaches have an ethical and legal responsibility to educate their athletes about drug (supplement) use and abuse, and provide general and appropriate nutritional advice.

Partners with specific knowledge concerning drugs, such as the South African Institute for Drug-free Sport (SAIDS) and the World Anti-Doping Agency (WADA), and nutrition (registered dieticians) should be consulted to assist in the education of athletes. This aspect is discussed in detail in another chapter.

**NO SUPPLEMENTS ARE RECOMMENDED FOR USE BY ANYONE AND
SPECIFICALLY NOT FOR
ANYONE UNDER THE AGE OF 18**

28.4.1.2 Coaches' attitudes and behaviours

Coaches should maintain a professional yet warm and approachable relationship with athletes in their care. They should:

1. be professional in their dealings with parents and colleagues;
2. make it a policy to always maintain privacy and confidentiality; and
3. be flexible, reliable and consistent.

When working with children and vulnerable persons, additional input is required to:

1. recognise the basic psychological needs of security, status, achievement and independence;
2. recognise the need to communicate, to express feelings and the difficulty in communication resulting from speech impediments or other disabilities;
3. respond to children and vulnerable persons in a professional yet age-appropriate manner;
4. remain objective yet display warmth and understanding;
5. respond to verbal and non-verbal cues;
6. control feelings;
7. remain sensitive to the feelings of another person;
8. not condone socially inappropriate behaviour or discrimination; and
9. act if aware of any cases of bullying, racism or sexual abuse.

28.4.1.3 Coaches' responsibility towards self

The coach, whether employed or a volunteer, fulfils an occupational role. Role-related terminology is considered to be applied to all complex occupational activities. The role can be divided into subsidiary parts such as *"direct intervention, intervention support, constraints management and strategic coordination".*[25] The subsidiary parts have consequences within the occupational role, therefore the coach needs to anticipate obstacles, identify these obstacles and search for solutions.[26] The discussion below about insurance, transportation of participants and sufficient information provide some solutions to the occupational role of the coach.

a) Insurance

Coaches should ensure appropriate insurance covering public liability and personal accidents. Public liability insurance is protection against claims made by a third party. These claims can be based on damage, injury or death due to operations within the sporting environment. In addition, many governing bodies include insurance as part of their affiliation fees. An example of a liability is Joe Lorenco (former national gymnastics coach), who sexually abused several of his male gymnastics athletes over a period of time. He was found guilty and had to pay damages towards counselling services for these victims before he committed suicide.

b) Transportation

Coaches should refrain from using their vehicles to transport athletes to and from venues. Coaches should be correctly licensed (PDP) and insured if they use their cars. With young athletes, coaches should seek the assistance of parents/guardians.

c) Sufficient information

To safeguard oneself and be better informed, coaches should request that parents/guardians complete a pre-participation screening questionnaire dealing with any special needs and implications for the child/vulnerable person's sports participation. Sport providers must then ensure that relevant personnel within the organisation know the information in the pre-participation screening questionnaire and that the data is used appropriately, such as in an emergency. A failure by the sport provider to use the information may result in legal liability.

An additional safeguard is to obtain a declaration from the parent/guardian that the child/vulnerable person is medically and physically sufficiently fit and able to participate in sport activities, and that the parent/guardian will immediately notify the sport provider in writing of any change to medical condition, fitness or ability to participate. This option places the onus on the parent/guardian to ensure that the child/vulnerable person is medically and physically fit and able to participate.

28.4.2 Role of Parents/Guardians

Parent-coach teamwork contributes significantly to a child's happy participation in sport. The aim is to create a safe and fun environment where a child-centred approach puts the participants at the centre of all activities. To this end, parents are the legal guardians of children and have decision-making powers regarding the well-being of their children. However, it is important to note that parents may not always make informed decisions in the best interests of their children, which is why legislation to protect children exists. Communication with parents and involving them in the sport organisation assists in a safe and positive experience for children.

28.4.2.1 Rights of parents/guardians

A parent/guardian has the right to:

1. be assured that their child is safeguarded during their participation in sport;
2. be informed of problems or concerns relating to their children;
3. be notified if their child is injured;
4. give consent for issues such as trips, making videos or taking photos;

5. contribute to decisions within the club;
6. have any concerns about their child's welfare be heard and responded to;
7. carry out background checks on the coaches of their children;
8. request to see the sport provider's safeguarding policies; and
9. view safeguarding processes, especially in cases where talent pathway sports remove young people from the relatively safe club structure.

28.4.2.2 The sports responsibility of parents/guardians

The sport physical rights and responsibilities of parents/guardians is to ensure that their children are physically fit to participate in a particular sport. Reports from physicians can reveal physical strengths and weaknesses and can help determine an appropriate sport, especially in disability inclusion programmes. Updated reports should be shared with the child's coach. As stated above, the onus is on the parent/guardian that the child/vulnerable person is medically and physically fit and able to participate.

28.4.2.3 When are children ready to participate in sport?

Starting a child in sport participation too young may not benefit the child physically. Children can start playing team sports when they express a strong interest and parents believe they can handle the sporting environment. Also, consider the child's ability to understand the concept of rules and teamwork. Base decisions on whether to allow the child to participate in a particular sport on age, weight, build, physical development, emotional development and interest in the sport. The professional knowledge of the coach, especially regarding didactics, will complement the coach's decisions for the child's participation.[27] The American Academy of Paediatrics recommends that late-developing teens should not participate in contact sports until their bodies have developmentally "caught up" with their peers. Readiness to participate in sport is a considered safeguarding option when applying the principles of good practice and understanding the signs of developmental child abuse.

28.4.3 Athletes and Abuse

Athletes can receive age-appropriate information on reporting abuse or concerns regarding possible threats, harassment or discrimination. They should not fear disclosing any form of abuse within the sport environment.

28.4.3.1 Adults at risk

Athletes and professional sportspeople often work under intense pressure and in close relationships with their personal coaches and support teams. As a result, safeguarding issues can arise "... when someone is in a team or on a pathway ... vulnerability inevitably increases, as so much is taken out of their control".[28]

Grey-Thompson points out that safeguarding support is not as well-developed internationally for adults in sport as for people younger than 18. This is true, particularly around young people "*transitioning into the 18-25 year age group, ... for disabled participants, who tend to be more at risk ... (and)... vulnerable adults* from minority groups such as women, ethnic minorities and Lesbian, Gay, Bisexual and Transgender (LGBT) persons".[29]

28.4.3.2 Vulnerable persons

A vulnerable person is defined as someone whose survival, care, protection or development may be compromised due to a particular condition, situation or circumstance which prevents the fulfilment of his or her rights.[30]

28.4.4 Sensitive Issues in Sport and Sport Relationships

Some of the sensitive issues surrounding coaching will be discussed in this section, including touch versus harassment, discrimination, disability inclusion and parent-coach teamwork for special needs children.

28.4.4.1 Touch vs. harassment

Touch as a form of communication can be a powerful tool, especially in practicing sport. However, those working in sport should be particularly conscious of maintaining clear boundaries when touching. Below are some guidelines:

1. Ensure that any touch results in clear messages.
2. Ensure it does not become an instrument of control, harassment or abuse. Discretion is needed to determine where and when not to use touch in professional coaching relationships.
3. Be mindful of the responsibility to protect the welfare and rights of those under your protection.

Harassment is defined as a single incident or pattern of behaviour where the purpose or effect is to create a hostile, offensive or intimidating environment, such as physical or emotional abuse; public defamation of another's good name; racial insults; derogatory ethnic slurs; unwelcome sexual advances or touching; sexual jokes or sexual comments; requests for sexual favours; or the display of lewd or offensive materials. Ensure that physical action towards those in your care cannot be seen as harassment.

28.4.4.2 Discrimination

Sporting organisations, schools and club teams should adopt zero tolerance for discriminatory language and behaviour by athletes, parents, fans, coaches and support staff. Coaches, teachers and officials in direct contact with athletes should undergo mandatory training to best support athletes from various backgrounds, protected categories, personalities and varying cognitive abilities. In addition, sporting bodies should publicly take a strong stand against discrimination, and explicitly specify that all forms of discrimination are counter to the values of their sport.

Inclusion should lead to increased participation by people with disabilities in socially expected life roles and activities, such as using public resources, moving about within communities, receiving adequate health care, having relationships and enjoying other activities, including sports participation.

28.4.4.3 Disability inclusion: facilities and equipment

The WHO defines disability as:

> "... an umbrella term covering impairments, activity limitations and participation restrictions... An impairment is a problem in body function or structure; an activity limitation is a difficulty encountered by an individual in executing a task or action; while a participation restriction is a problem experienced by an individual in involvement in life situations."[31]

The United Nations Convention on the Rights of Persons with Disabilities explains disability as:

> "Disability is imposed by society when a person with a physical, psychosocial, intellectual, neurological and sensory impairment is denied access to full participation in all aspects of life and when society fails to uphold the rights and specific needs of individuals with impairments."[32]

In sport, the view embedded in the UN's Article 30.5, *'to enable persons with disabilities to participate on an equal basis with others'* allows for segregated contexts in which persons with disabilities can be physically active together with their peers and competitors with similar functioning levels.[33]

For this reason, it is essential to provide barrier-free, appropriate, effective, efficient and coordinated service delivery to persons with disabilities. Event owners have a legal responsibility regarding disability inclusion, but it is also imperative to ensure inclusion by providing a welcoming environment. This should examine how people with disabilities can participate, rather than focusing on barriers.

Organisers must ensure that an application for event approval is made timeously and complies with additional safety procedures, for example, specific to wheelchairs. Maralack recommends inviting key stakeholders (e.g., the Western Province Sport Association for Physically Disabled [WPSAPD] in Cape Town) to assist with expert-led decision-making, guidance, monitoring and feedback for improvement. In road races, for example, current policies promote disabled (including wheelchair) participation, but the guidelines for safe implementation and accommodation are left to the event organisers.[34]

Welcoming people with disabilities to everyday activities, including encouraging them to have roles like their disability-free peers, is termed 'disability inclusion'. This involves much more than merely encouraging active participation in society and sports; it requires ensuring that adequate policies and practices are in effect in communities or organisations.

28.4.4.4 Parent-coach teamwork for special needs children

Special needs children, including those with a disability or chronic health problems, are sometimes not encouraged to exercise, however parents of special needs children should encourage participation in sport and physical activity.

Ensure that coaches understand the child's disability. Coaches must know how a disability might affect the child who plays, participates or takes instructions. They must know the correct way to talk to and work with children to make sports participation a positive, safe and healthy experience. Parents are the best resource here – schedule an introductory session with them.

Some young people have chronic medical conditions which affect their participation in sport. In addition, particular care must be taken for long-term conditions such as asthma and other respiratory infections, diabetes, epilepsy, heart or lung disease, hepatitis and HIV.

In all cases, a medical opinion should be sought when the fitness or performance of any young person is questionable and when recovering from illness or injury is in doubt.

28.5 SPORT INJURIES AND PREVENTION

Children are at greater risk of sport injuries than adults because their bodies are growing and their coordination is still developing. Many children aged 14 and younger are treated for sports-related injuries each year. Many of these injuries can be prevented with the proper use of safety gear, such as head and face shields in hockey, shin pads in soccer, and changes to the playing environment, such as conducive playing surfaces. Adherence to sport rules is a significant factor in preventing injuries.

Poorly conditioned players are at risk of sports injuries, thus the onus is on coaches to remain vigilant during sessions to prevent unnecessary injuries. During training, coaches should carefully observe the movement of players and act immediately if abnormalities occur. If any injury occurs during exercise or playing, the activity should be stopped and communicated with the player/s. Once it has been established that there is no danger to players' lives, first aid should be applied and the relevant medical officers contacted.

28.6 ROLES AND RESPONSIBILITIES OF MANAGERS AND ADMINISTRATORS

Sport organisations have a strategic and delivery role concerning children, youth and vulnerable people. Where organisational partnerships, membership, funding or commissioning relationships are in place with other agencies, the organisation should use its influence to promote the implementation of safeguarding measures by providing or signposting support and resources. Safeguarding guidance is provided by the eight International Safeguards for Children in Sport, which can be found online.

Sport providers, managers and administrators are, among other things, responsible for the following aspects of safety:

1. Fulfilling their legal duty of care to protect the welfare of young and vulnerable people to ensure they are not exposed to risk in any aspect of sport delivery.
2. Ensuring the safety and physical well-being of all people playing, supporting, officiating and watching sport.
3. Ensuring that policies are in place to:
    a) identify the underlying legal issues relevant to the provision of sport;
    b) identify safety concerns, such as personal abuse, environmental conditions, medical conditions, facilities, equipment, infectious diseases, drugs and dealing with emergencies;

c) establish that each federation/association/club has a Member Protection Regulation (MPR) in place to deal with screening potential staff;
d) safeguard that clear and adequate processes are in place for dealing with harassment or abuse complaints;
e) certify that schools' policies for member protection (available from national or provincial education departments) are in place;
f) establish that occupational or workplace health and safety (OHS) regulations are followed to the letter. The OHS legislation may apply to workers, volunteers, students or club members; and
g) safeguard that a risk management procedure is in place to cope with any problems regarding exposure to health and safety risks.

The Welsh Sport Association identifies a further possible manager role as one where a coach may have to combine their role of Team Manager with that of welfare officer for their club or sports organisation. Therefore, coaches must be aware of their organisation's good practice guidelines for working with children and ensure that they are acting safely and appropriately, e.g., being approachable and remaining neutral.

28.7 THE SPORT COACHING CHARTER

SASCOC initially compiled the Sport Coaching Charter to protect South African coaches, coach developers and athletes. All coaches/coach developers must sign the Charter as a pre-requisite to becoming a South African professional coaching body member with the South African Sports Coaching Association (SASCA), as recognised by the South African Qualifications Authority (SAQA). Notwithstanding that a sports coach may range from being voluntary to being partly or wholly dependent and/or employed as a sports coach or coach developer in their professional career, they will constantly apply their best endeavours to deliver professional standards that ensure the best interests of the athlete are addressed for their well-being, development and performance.

The key principles and focus of the Sports Coaching Charter and integrated Code of Conduct are competence, continuous professional development (CPD), confidentiality, trustworthiness, respect, caring, integrity, fairness, responsibility and diligence. Should a sports coach/sports coach developer transgress this Code of Conduct, the matter will be referred to a disciplinary committee appointed by the Professional Body for Sports Coaching (SASCA) and referred to the disciplinary board of the SASCA. The public is encouraged to contact the Professional Body for Sports Coaching SA (SASCA) at www.sasca-pb.co.za.

28.8 DEALING WITH ABUSE

28.8.1 Legal Responsibility

Legislation such as the Children's Act, 38/2005 as Amended and the Sexual Offences and Related Matters Amendment Act, 32/2007, clearly defines the legal responsibility of various persons in reporting child abuse cases. If coaches suspect abuse, it must be reported to the proper authorities. Failure to do so is considered a criminal offence.[35]

28.8.1.1 The first step: interaction with the victim (How?)

When dealing with a suspected case of abuse, coaches/caretakers should:

1. listen to the child or vulnerable person;
2. show and tell them that you are taking what they say seriously;
3. reassure them and stress that they are not to blame;
4. keep questioning to a minimum and be careful not to put words into their mouth;
5. stay calm and do not rush into actions that may be inappropriate – ensure the child or vulnerable person is safe and feels safe;
6. call someone else to help with the situation;
7. make notes about what they said as soon as possible after the event (see below);
8. involve parents, carers or guardians where appropriate;
9. maintain confidentiality as far as possible – only tell others who can assist in protecting the victim;
10. not take sole responsibility – consult someone else (the designated welfare officer at the club or organisation) to protect the victim and yourself; and
11. follow the guidelines or procedures laid down by the organisation.

Remember that the role of coaches is not that of investigating officers or deciding whether or not the child is being abused. It is, however, their responsibility to act if they have any concerns by discussing it confidentially with the organisation's designated safeguarding officer, social services or the police.

28.8.1.2 The person reporting (Who?)

As discussed earlier, The Sexual Offences Act (32 of 2007) compels all citizens (i.e., all persons living in South Africa entitled to the rights promised by the Constitution in terms of Section 3) who are aware of the sexual exploitation of children to report the offence to the police.

To whom must they report? Section 110(1) of the Children's Act 38 of 2005 as Amended stipulates that suspected child abuse must be reported to child protection organisations, the provincial Department of Social Development or the South African Police Service (SAPS). A child protection organisation is defined in the Act as *"any welfare organisation designated in terms of section 107, to render child protection services".*[36] Some provincial websites, notably that of the Western Cape, contain lists of organisations registered under section 107. All reports (even those made to SAPS) must be referred to the provincial Department of Social Development. The provincial department is tasked with investigating the allegation of abuse and taking appropriate measures to ensure the child's safety. The department must also follow legal processes if its investigation reveals cause for legal action.

Furthermore, in section 54(b) of the Sexual Offences and Related Matters Act, 32 of 2007, failure to report sexual abuse or exploitation of children and mentally disabled persons is deemed an offence punishable with a fine or imprisonment of up to five years if the perpetrator is found guilty.[37]

The person reporting the abuse is legally protected if it is done without ulterior motives. The person making the report cannot be criminally charged or sued if they request an investigation according to the law.

28.8.1.3 Reporting suspected abuse (When?)

While the law does not define how likely abuse must be before it is required to be reported, a rule of thumb is that it should be reported whenever there is suspicion of abuse/neglect.

Section 110 of the Children's Amendment Act (and the reporting Form 22) implies that reporting the suspicion of abuse must be done as soon as the fear is formed on reasonable grounds. The purpose of reporting is ultimately to ensure the safety and protection of the child in question. Reporting a sexual offence must be done 'immediately' according to Section 54(1) (a) of the Sexual Offences Act, 32/2007. 'Immediately' can be interpreted as becoming aware of the sexual abuse or when there is a reasonable suspicion of abuse of a sexual nature.

A coach must maintain confidentiality throughout the process and keep the child/vulnerable person informed. If the victim is a child, the coach should explain what they will do in age appropriate language and why.

28.8.1.4 Reporting procedures

The abuse must be reported on either Form 22 or Form 25, depending on the form of abuse. The report may be made to the Provincial Dept of Social Development, a designated Child Protection organisation, a SAPS official or a Clerk of the Children's Court.

If a coach finds that a child needs care and protection, they must report this to a social worker, who will decide on the best way forward. From the side of the reporting person, the following steps can help prepare for the report:

1. Gather all the information you can about the suspected incident or incidents and write it up in factual and behavioural terminology (this means no opinions, interpretations, assumptions or guesses, just factual observations or information, i.e., The child said...; I directly observed...; There were black and blue marks on their legs... etc.).
2. Do not under any circumstances photograph injuries if you are alone with the child or not accompanied by a designated person dealing with the case.
3. In cases of suspected rape, do not allow the victim to wash or bath. All clothing must be kept as evidence.
4. Notify your direct senior/administrator/manager of the information you have that caused you to suspect abuse or neglect. Here again, verbalise only facts.
5. The administrator may call SAPS, the Department of Social Development or Childline.
6. Once you have a counsellor on the phone, immediately ask for their name and note the time and date of your call.
7. Inform the counsellor that you believe you have a suspected abuse or neglect case. Report only facts and direct observations.

8. Have the following information available: the victim's full name and address, birth date, the parent's/guardian's first and last names, the child's telephone number, the parent's/guardian's work number if known, other siblings in the house and their ages, the grade of the child and the school and school district of the child. They may assign a case number, so be prepared to jot this down.
9. Ask the counsellor if they feel the child can go home or if the school/club/SAPS should retain them until the case worker appears. The school has this right if the child's health or safety will be compromised by returning home after school.

28.9 CONCLUSION

This chapter has provided guidelines enabling those involved in sport to safeguard children and vulnerable persons by examining the inter-sectoral roles of sport, health and welfare, safety and security, justice and education. Furthermore, it offers guidelines which will assist sport coaches/event organisers to ensure inclusion in sport where relevant.

The key points in this discussion:

1. provided a background to some of the current issues surrounding safety and inclusion in sport;
2. supplied valuable information for safeguarding athletes, especially children, athletes with disabilities and vulnerable adults from minority groups (women, ethnic minorities and Lesbian, Gay, Bisexual and Transgender (LGBT) persons);
3. offered guidance applicable to all sports, including how to apply the guidelines provided here to a specific sport; and
4. described reporting procedures for suspected abuse.

In recent decades, national and international sporting bodies have done much work on this subject, and more information is available on the Internet than can be provided in this introductory module. Coaches are advised to read widely on this subject to provide the best possible care and protection for the vulnerable athletes in their care.

SELF-ASSESSMENT

1. Describe the importance of safeguarding and protecting knowledge and protocols, subject to the legislative and regulatory framework within the South African context of safe and inclusive sport management. Summarise the application in one to two paragraphs.
2. Identify all stakeholders (show and describe your brainstorming ideas/processes) and briefly describe each stakeholder.

3. The balance of responsibilities regarding safeguarding will differ according to the various role players and stakeholders. What is the balance of roles for these role players?
4. Debate your understanding of the role and responsibilities of the coach, parent/guardian, manager, national federations, SASCOC, SASCA and athlete commissions in safeguarding and protecting children and vulnerable persons. Give examples of each role and responsibility.
5. Describe the legal responsibilities in dealing with abuse in sport, children and vulnerable persons, and reporting procedures to be followed.

ANNEXURE A

- Amendment of Directions issued in terms of Regulation 4 (10) of the regulations made under section 27(2) of the Disaster Management Act 2002 (Act 57 of 2002): Measures to prevent and combat the spread of Covid-19: Sport, Arts and Culture
- Constitution of the Republic of South Africa
- The Children's Act, Act 38 of 2005 and Regulations
- Children's Amendment Act, Act 41 of 2007
- Child Justice Act, Act 75 of 2008
- The Convention on the Rights of the Child
- The Prevention of Family Violence Act, Act 33 of 1983
- Disaster Management Act 57 of 2002
- Domestic Violence Act 116 of 1998
- The Criminal Procedure Amendment Act, Act 9 of 2012
- The Criminal Law Amendment Act, Act 135 of 1991
- The Criminal Procedures Act, Act 51 of 1977
- The Sexual Offences Act, Act 32 of 1957 (as amended)
- The Sexual Offences and Related Matter Amendment Act, Act 32 of 2007
- Prevention and Treatment of Drug Dependency Act, Act 20 of 1992
- Promotion of Equality and prevention of unfair discrimination Act, Act 52 of 2002
- Promotion of Administrative Justice Act, Act 3 of 2000
- The Labour Relations Act and Amendments, Act 66 of 1995
- The Basic Conditions of Employment Act
- National Sport and Recreation Act as amended 2007
- South African Institute of Drug-Free Sport Act, Act 14 of 1997

- South African Schools Act of 1996
- South African Sport Commission Act, Act 110 of 1998
- Safety and Sport and Recreation Events Act, Act 2 of 2010
- White Paper on the Rights of Persons with Disabilities: Official Publication (09 March 2016)
- Policy on Disability Department of Social Development (no date)
- Vulnerable Groups Policy (Policy Number 12399a)
- Other documentation and legislation relevant and supplementary to the Protocol as it applies specifically to sport coaches:
- SASCOC and SASCA Sport Coaching Charter (Nov 2018)
- SA Coaching Framework, Transformation Charter, White Paper on Sport and Recreation, SASCOC and National Federations' Constitutions; Intergovernmental Relations Framework Act; Film and Publications Act; Medical and Dental Act; Tobacco and Alcohol Act; Occupational Health and Safety Act; The Health Act (63 of 1977 as amended); Chapter 2 of The Bill of Rights (Section on Children).

DOPING IN SPORT

Professor Heather Morris-Eyton and Dr Amanda Claassen-Smithers

> **LEARNING OUTCOMES**
>
> At the end of this chapter, you should be able to:
>
> 1. Identify the different role players within the anti-doping space.
> 2. Discuss the prevalence and types of anti-doping rule violations.
> 3. Explain the role of Sport Managers in the anti-doping domain.
> 4. Understanding the anti-doping rules and the role Sport Managers play in calling attention to the risks of anti-doping rule violations.

29.1 INTRODUCTION

Sport management provides opportunities through its unique position within the sport landscape; it pivots between management, policy formulation and implementation, and is the conduit between athletes, coaches and policymakers. Whether or not this positionality functions optimally within sport can be debated according to current and contextual issues and associated sport management practices. However, it is through the lens of constructive debate, delivering insight into the complex phenomena of sport, as well as being ideally situated to provide possible solutions to the many challenges confronting sport, that Sport Managers are significant contributors.[1] Furthermore, due to the interdependency within sport, sport management as a discipline is well positioned to understand the complexity of the drivers at the epicentre of doping practices, aiding in the prevention of doping and putting in place various preventive strategies to assist in the fight against doping.[2] For this reason, a chapter examining doping in sport is included as a contemporary issue within the sport management space.

Doping in sport is a global issue and has become important in South Africa, where a relatively large proportion of athletes are serving bans for anti-doping rule violations (ADRVs). In the 2019 World Anti-Doping Agency (WADA) annual report, South Africa was ranked 14th globally for total ADRVs.[3] This is significant for South African sport as it provides a microcosmic view of decision-making that permeates a 'dopogenic' environment. This type of environment considers two pillars of influence:[4] 1) local factors, where sports teams and clubs are important drivers; and 2) structural factors, such as the sport structures at the national and international levels, including government policies, social values, belief systems and education and health systems. It is within the pillars of influence that interact between and within the sports clubs and teams as well as the sport federations and structures governing sport, that decisions are made which define the lines upon which an anti-doping rule violation is actioned or not. Considering these mighty pillars of influence, individual ethics and morality are sidelined, and the interactions between athletes' social networks and their structural sport systems intersect at the point of decision-making regarding doping or anti-doping practices.[5]

This chapter explores these issues and makes practical recommendations for sports managers working with teams and athletes in South Africa. This will include explaining the global and national drivers of anti-doping, considering the prevalence of doping and the challenges within the South African context. The use of supplements within an unregulated market will also be examined. Lastly, Sport Managers' role in the anti-doping environment will be discussed.

29.2 THE "WHO'S WHO" IN THE FIGHT AGAINST DOPING

Globally, two 'movements' are at the core of the fight against doping: the World Anti-Doping Agency (WADA) and the UNESCO International Convention Against Doping in Sport. WADA, established in 1999 as an independent international agency, is responsible for developing, standardising, coordinating and monitoring the effective implementation of anti-doping rules and policies across all sports and countries. WADA actively drives and supports scientific and social science research in its continued efforts to eliminate doping and create a play-true sporting environment. The rules and policies are contained within the World Anti-Doping Code (Code),[6] the core document that standardises the implementation of anti-doping programmes within sport organisations and among public authorities worldwide. The Code works in conjunction with eight International Standards (IS) that are aimed at fostering consistency among anti-doping organisations with regards to testing and investigations (ISTI), handling and analysis of samples by laboratories (ISL), therapeutic use exemptions (ISTUE), prohibited list (the List), results management (ISRM), education (ISE), protection of privacy and private information (ISPPPI) and code compliance by signatories (ISCCS). Four of these, the List, ISTUE, ISRM and ISE, are discussed in more detail later.

According to WADA, approximately 700 sport organisations have accepted the Code to date, including the International Olympic and Paralympic Committees (IOC and IPC), International Sport Federations (ISFs, including all IOC-recognised ISFs), National Olympic and Paralympic Committees, and National and Regional Anti-Doping Organisations (NADOs and RADOs). The South African government is a signatory to the Code and the UNESCO Convention (Figure 29.1). The South African Institute for Drug-Free Sport (SAIDS) was established as the country's NADO by an Act of Parliament (Act 14 of 1997, as amended 24 of 2006),[7] and was tasked with the implementation and enforcement of the Code (and related international standards) within South Africa. The Act recognises SAIDS' jurisdiction and independence in conducting its operations in compliance with the Code (and UNESCO Convention); its application within South African law and context is contained within SAIDS' Anti-Doping Rules.[8]

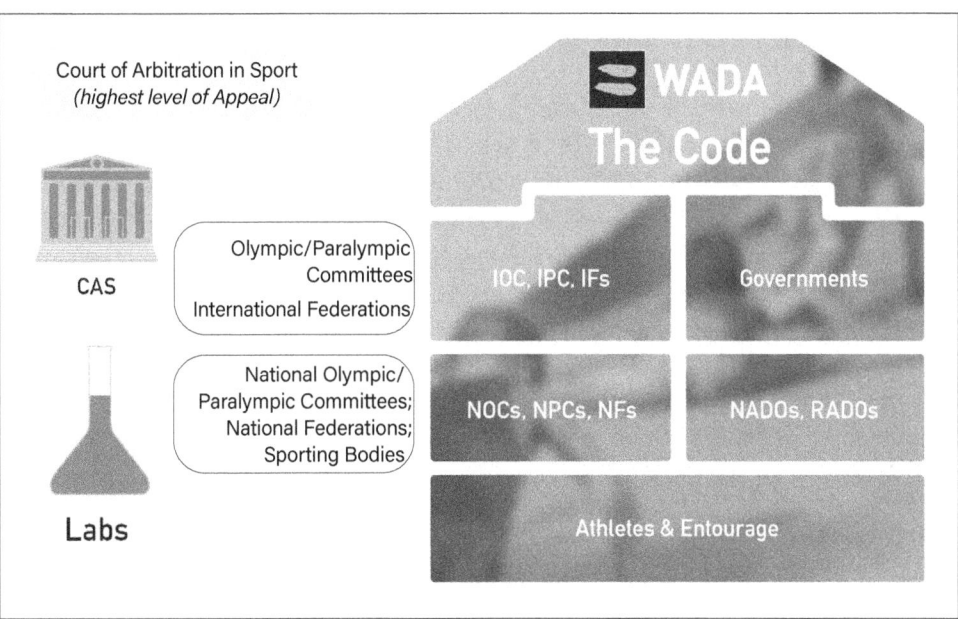

Figure 29.1: Roleplayers in the fight against doping[9]

As the United Nations' lead agency for physical education and sport, UNESCO promotes the educational, cultural and social dimensions of sport and physical education. It further supports the fight against doping in sport through two fundamental principles – the protection of the physical and mental health of both amateurs and professionals involved in sport, and the preservation of sport ethics and values, or the 'spirit of sport'. UNESCO recognises that in a highly competitive sporting environment, athletes and their support personnel are under increasing pressure to win and, as such, may be tempted to use prohibited substances and methods. The temptation is not limited to elite athletes only; it extends to young people and amateur sports enthusiasts alike. As such, doping has become a public health concern, along with its impact on degrading sport's values, ethics and integrity. The UNESCO International Convention against Doping in Sport (the Convention) was adopted in 2005. It came into force in 2007, becoming the most successful convention in the history of UNESCO regarding the pace of ratification after adoption. The Convention is now the second most ratified of all UNESCO treaties, with 191 signatories. The Convention represents the commitment from governments worldwide to apply the force of international law to anti-doping in sport. The Code and the International Standards guide the Convention to provide all athletes a fair and equitable playing environment. Whereas the Code is a non-governmental document that applies only to sports organisations, the Convention provides the legal framework under which governments can address anti-doping in sport.

As a signatory to the Convention, governments commit to: a) encouraging international cooperation to protect athletes and the ethics of sport; b) limiting the availability of prohibited substances and methods by combating trafficking; c) facilitating doping controls and supporting national testing programmes; d) encouraging producers and distributors of dietary supplements to establish 'best practice' in the labelling, marketing and distribution of products that might contain prohibited substances; e) supporting the implementation of anti-doping education programmes; and f) promoting anti-doping research.

29.3 PREVALENCE OF DOPING

According to WADA's latest available Anti-Doping Rule Violation (ADRV) statistics report, from a total of 278,047 samples collected and analysed, 2,701 samples (1%) were reported as "adverse analytical findings" (AAFs, commonly known as 'positives'). Of these, 1,537 samples (57%) were confirmed as ADRVs resulting in a sanction (the majority for the use of anabolic steroids, followed by stimulants); 297 samples (11%) were dismissed due to a valid medical reason; 274 samples (10%) were categorised as case closed for a valid reason other than medical reasons; 49 samples (2%) resulted in the athlete being exonerated; and 544 samples (20%) were still pending (data from 2019, report published 2021).[10]

Table 29.1 provides a breakdown of the number of ADRVs relating to the other non-AAF Anti-Doping Rules or Articles as contained in the 2015 Code and the number of Athlete Support Personnel (ASP) involved in committing ADRVs.

Table 29.1: Type of non-AAF ADRV based on the Code Articles[11]

	Occurrences:	
	Atletes	ASP
Article 2.2: Use or attempted use	178	1
Article 2.3: Refusing, failing without compelling justification or evading	106	N/A
Article 2.4: Whereabouts violations	23	N/A
Article 2.5: Tampering or attempted tampering	22	7
Article 2.6: Possession	94	3
Article 2.7: Trafficking or attempted trafficking	14	3
Article 2.8: Administration, attempted administration or assisting.	10	13
Article 2.9: Complicity (encouraging, aiding, abetting, covering up, etc.)	11	12
Article 2.10: Prohibited association	8	N/A

*Note: With the updated Code that came into effect January 2021, Article 2.11 – Whistleblower Protection – was added.

The top five sports with the highest number of ADRVs globally are bodybuilding (22%), athletics (18%), cycling (14%), weightlifting (13%) and powerlifting (9%). The Russian Federation (19%), Italy (18%) and India (17%) are top of the list for the number of ADRVs, however the prevalence of doping in sport has yet to be discovered. Prevalence models have reported rates of 10%-60% depending on the country, sport and level of participation. These models are consistently higher than those reported by WADA (1%-2%).[12]

A point of concern for national federations and the South African sporting fraternity is that in 2019, South Africa occupied the 14th position globally, with 42 ADRVs.[13] Of these, the top three sports contributing the most were rugby union (15), bodybuilding (12) and athletics (5). South African rugby also has the highest number of ADRVs globally.

Even more concerning is the number of ADRVs committed by youth, notably in the sport of rugby, but increasingly seen in other sports, e.g., athletics.[14] The SAIDS performs doping control (testing) at the annual Craven Week Rugby Tournament, organised by South African Rugby (national federation) for under 18-year-old school boys (on average 20 teams with 23 players each, and ~120-140 doping control tests performed per tournament). Testing typically results in approximately six ADRVs, nearly half of the total number of ADRVs seen in South African rugby annually. When adding ADRVs from U/20 and Varsity Cup tournaments, the average increases to approximately 60% of SA Rugby ADRVs. The majority relates to the use of anabolic steroids from Class 1.1 of the Prohibited List, as well as Class 1.2, which contain anabolic agents deemed unfit for human use, unapproved drugs including SARMs (selective androgen receptor modulators), and substances commonly found in 'dietary' supplements.[15] Many ADRVs are related to dietary supplements (locally and globally) and are discussed in more detail later.

The susceptibility of the youth to engage in doping behaviour has also been highlighted in various research surveys. For example, a study examining the attitudes, beliefs and knowledge of doping among competitive South African high school athletes found that 4% admitted to using a prohibited performance-enhancing drug (PED), and more than 14% of the athletes would consider using a PED if they would not get caught.[16] Coaches may also be unaware of any ADRVs their athletes engage in.[17]

The SA Institute for Drug-Free Sport has a dedicated education and testing programme for schools, whereby individual schools can sign up voluntarily and at no cost. Testing is done within the ambit of the SA Schools Act. In 2018/19, the 'SAIDS Clean School Sport Policy' was extended to include testing at prominent school sports tournaments. The awareness and uptake of the programme remain challenging: 15-30 education sessions are done annually across South Africa; there are ~60 sport-focused public high schools (excluding sport academies)[18] and ~24,000 schools (of which ~6,200 high schools) in total in South Africa.[19] It remains an initiative that all should encourage, as the earlier athletes can be empowered with anti-doping 'know-how', the better.[20]

29.4 POSITIONING SPORT MANAGERS WITHIN THE ANTI-DOPING DOMAIN

Sport managers and those working within sport need to know their positionality within the context of anti-doping. This is important as team managers increasingly become an intimate part of the athlete's (or team's) support personnel. This responsibility becomes heightened when examining the role of athlete support personnel (ASP) in the fight against doping. ASP are becoming more accountable for anti-doping rule violations, which requires making informed decisions regarding an athlete's well-being, nutrition and whereabouts. If more than two members of a team test positive for an ADRV, the possibility is that the whole team could face a ban, which reflects negatively on the team and its brand. An investigation into ASP is usually undertaken to examine what role, if any, they played (complicity).

Article 21 of the SAIDS Anti-Doping Rules provides the "Additional Roles and Responsibilities of Athlete Support Personnel"[21] as follows:

1. To be knowledgeable of and comply with the anti-doping rules.
2. To cooperate with the athlete testing programme.
3. To use their influence on athlete values and behaviour to foster anti-doping attitudes.
4. To disclose to the SAIDS and their international federation any decision by a non-signatory finding that they committed an anti-doping rule violation within the previous 10 years.
5. To cooperate with anti-doping organisations investigating anti-doping rule violations. Failure by any ASP to cooperate in full with anti-doping organisations investigating anti-doping rule violations may result in a charge of misconduct under their national federation or sporting code's disciplinary rules/code of conduct.
6. Athlete support personnel shall not use or possess any prohibited substance or prohibited method without valid justification. Any such use or possession may result in a charge of misconduct under their national federation or sporting code's disciplinary rules/code of conduct.
7. Offensive conduct towards a doping control official or other person involved in doping control by ASP, which does not otherwise constitute tampering, may result in a charge of misconduct under their national federation or sporting code's disciplinary rules/code of conduct.

Anti-doping rules govern the conditions under which sport is played. These programmes conducted by the SAIDS within sport federations, schools and at major events are embedded within the intrinsic values of sport and Olympism.[22] These values include:

1. protecting the health of athletes;
2. ensuring ethical conduct, fair play, honesty, and integrity whilst participating in sport;
3. providing an enabling environment for performance excellence;
4. having fun whilst participating;
5. teamwork and developing skills to be an effective team player;
6. commitment and dedication;
7. respecting the rules of the game, including opponents, the technical officials, teammates, coaches and athlete support personnel, as well as respecting oneself;
8. showing courage during adversity; and
9. developing a sense of community and solidarity.

In its continued focus on using education to assist in keeping sport clean, WADA uses its Anti-doping Education and Learning platform.[23] This global platform provides free educational resources and online courses for those involved in sport who need to know about anti-doping. In addition, values-based education has become an increasingly important part of education, aiming to instill the fundamental values of sport, i.e., respect, equality and inclusion. Courses are aimed at children (Sport Values Online) and teachers (Sport Values in Every Classroom) and are embedded within the coach education curriculum.

29.4.1 A Brief Overview of the Anti-Doping Rules (Articles 2.1 to 2.11, 2021 WADC, in Force)

For athlete support personnel to comply with their role of supporting athletes and teams, the anti-doping rule violations (ADRV) must be understood and regularly discussed with athletes and their support teams.

Anti-doping rule violations are not just about doping or the presence of a prohibited substance in an athlete's sample. Rather, they encompass a range of activities that violate the values of true sportsmanship that is embedded within sport:

1. *Presence of a prohibited substance in an athlete's sample, including metabolites or markers.* WADA updates the banned list on the 1st of January every year, therefore athletes and ASP must check and re-check all medication they use against the new list. Tools and phone applications are available to assist, for example, the SAIDS medication check tool and app to check medicines registered within South Africa, or the GlobalDro tool to check for medications from various other counties.[24]
2. *Use or attempted use of a prohibited substance.* This includes using prohibited methods (as per the Prohibited List).
3. *Refusing to submit a sample after notification has been given.* This includes deliberately evading the sample collection process.
4. *Failure to file athlete whereabouts information and missing tests.* This rule pertains to athletes who have been notified for inclusion in a Registered Testing Pool (RTP), either through their international federation (or testing authority) or through their national anti-doping organisation (e.g., SAIDS). These are typically top-level athletes who compete internationally. RTP athletes need to provide their 'whereabouts,' i.e., where they stay, train and compete, at any time to be located for regular, 'no-notice,' out-of-competition testing. Any combination of three filing failures or missed tests within 12 months can result in an ADRV.
5. *Tampering with any part of the doping control process.* This includes trying to evade the doping control process or team, tampering with testing equipment (or any part of the testing process) and bribing a doping control officer.
6. *Possession of a prohibited substance or method by an athlete or athlete support personnel.* This includes in and out of competition. Athlete support personnel may not have a banned substance or method in connection with an athlete in or out of competition unless an acceptable justification warrants such.
7. *Trafficking in a prohibited substance or method.* This would include handling, transporting, selling or attempting to sell banned substances.
8. *Administering or attempting to help give a prohibited substance or method to an athlete in or out of competition.*
9. *Complicity in an anti-doping rule violation.* This includes assisting, encouraging, aiding, abetting, conspiring, covering up, turning a blind eye, etc. A sanction of two years to a lifetime ban could be levied against athletes, coaches, medical staff, etc.
10. *Prohibited association with a sanctioned ASP or athlete.*

11. *Intimidating a whistleblower.* Introduced with the 2021 Code, a sanction of two years could be levied against anyone trying to frighten, threaten or obstruct a person trying to report doping, or carrying out an act of revenge against the whistleblower. It aims to provide protected spaces for whistleblowers to assist in combatting ADRVs.

29.4.2 Harsher penalties for Athlete Support Personnel (ASP; 2021 Code)

The Code (and SAIDS Rules) consider that ASP and other persons involved in 'doping' athletes or covering up doping should receive harsher sanctions than the athletes themselves. Since the authority of sport organisations is generally limited to ineligibility for accreditation, membership and other sport benefits, reporting ASP to competent authorities is essential in deterring doping. For violations of Rules 7 and 8 (or Articles 2.7 or 2.8 of the Code), a sanction of a minimum of four years up to life can be given, depending on the seriousness of the violation.

Violations involving a 'Protected Person' (see the International Standard for Results Management section for the definition) are considered particularly serious and may result in a lifetime ban from sport if committed by any ASP. In addition, significant violations of Articles 2.7 or 2.8, which may also violate non-sporting laws and regulations, shall be reported to the administrative, professional or judicial authorities (SAIDS Rules).

29.4.3 A brief overview of the International Standards Accompanying the 2021 Code

We focus on four of the International Standards (two newly introduced in 2021) to highlight key points of information and insight for Sport Managers.

29.4.3.1 *International Standard Prohibited List (the List)*

The List is updated on an annual basis; it typically becomes available in October each year to allow the opportunity to get familiarised with the changes, which then come into effect on the 1st of January annually. The List contains prohibited substances and methods, some of which are always prohibited (e.g., anabolic agents, peptide hormones and growth factors, hormone and metabolic modulators, Beta-2 agonists, diuretics and masking agents), and some of which are prohibited in-competition only (e.g., stimulants, narcotics, cannabinoids and glucocorticoids). The in-competition period typically starts at 11:59 pm the night before (when doping control testing can commence) and ends after the competition and doping control process have been concluded. There may be competitions where the start of the in-competition period differs, such as certain multi-day events (e.g., the Olympic Games). Any prohibited substance present in an athlete's sample taken during the in-competition period may result in an adverse analytical finding (or ultimately an ADRV), regardless of when the substance was taken (pre- or in-competition). Prohibited methods include chemical and physical manipulation of samples (including IV infusions above a specified amount), manipulation of blood and blood components, and gene and cell doping.

29.4.3.2 Substances of abuse

These are what we know as 'illicit drugs', which are frequently abused in society outside of the context of sport, e.g., cocaine, heroin, ecstasy and tetrahydrocannabinol (THC, 'dagga'). The 2021 Code has given special consideration in support of athletes addressing illicit drug abuse by offering a reduction in sanction if a recognised drug rehabilitation programme is completed.

29.4.3.3 International Standard for Therapeutic Use Exemptions (ISTUE)

The ISTUE provides the specific criteria and process to be followed should an athlete need to use a prohibited substance or method for valid medical reasons. The requirements on who needs to apply in advance versus retrospectively, the four criteria for all TUE applications, the checklists for various medical conditions, and the application form can be obtained from the SAIDS website (drugfreesport.org.za/tue). A particular note of caution is given for those athletes who must have their TUE in place 'in advance'. If the TUE has not been granted and they test positive, an ADRV and sanction may result, regardless of a valid medical reason (i.e., they cannot apply retroactively after testing positive).

29.4.3.4 International Standard for Results Management (ISRM)

The ISRM (newly introduced with the 2021 Code) provides more rigorous standards for the process, principles and obligations of the various parties, notably the anti-doping organisations, that come into play when evidence of an ADRV has been found. It sets out the core obligations applicable to the various phases of the 'Results Management' process, from the initial review and notification of potential anti-doping rule violations, through provisional suspensions, the assertion of ADRVs and the proposal of consequences (individuals versus teams*), the hearing process until the issuance and notification of the decision, and appeal.

Additional Code Articles (not mentioned above) contained within the Results Management process include what constitutes proof of doping (Article 3), right to a fair hearing (Article 8), confidentiality and reporting (Article 14) and implementation of decisions and additional roles and responsibilities of Code signatories and WADA (Article 20).

If more than two members of a team are found to have committed an ADRV during an event, the whole team may be sanctioned (e.g., loss of points, disqualification or other sanction) in addition to any consequences imposed upon the individuals who committed the ADRV. The ruling body for an event also has the right to impose even stricter punishments for the event, e.g., the International Olympic Committee could establish rules that would require the disqualification of a team from the Olympic Games based on a lesser number of anti-doping rule violations during the period of the Games (SAIDS Rules).

29.4.3.5 Results management agreements

The 2021 Code has considered 'enticing' athletes and ASP to own up to committing an ADRV, thereby reducing time and resources being spent unnecessarily by all parties, as well as implicating others involved in doping. A 4-year sanction could be reduced by one year for admitting guilt within 20 days of being notified of the ADRV, and a reduction can be negotiated if substantial assistance, i.e., sufficient information, is provided to implicate others involved in doping, a criminal offence and breaching of professional or sports rules. WADA can also agree to not publicly disclose an ADRV in exchange for substantial assistance.

29.4.3.6 'Protected Persons' and recreational athletes

A 'protected person' is defined as an athlete or other natural person who, at the time of the ADRV, (i) is under 16 years old; (ii) is under 18 years old and is not included in any Registered Testing Pool and has never competed in any international event in an open category; or (iii) for reasons other than age has been determined to lack legal capacity under applicable national legislation.

The Code treats Protected Persons differently in certain circumstances based on the understanding that, below a certain age or intellectual capacity, the athlete or person may not have the mental ability to understand and appreciate the conditions in the Code. This would include, for example, a paralympic athlete with a documented lack of legal capacity due to intellectual impairment. The term "open category" is meant to exclude competition limited to junior or age group categories.

Where a protected person (as defined in the SAIDS Rules) or recreational athlete commits an anti-doping rule violation, and they can establish no significant fault or negligence, then the sanction can be, at a minimum, a reprimand up to a maximum of two years (i.e., less than the typical 4-year sanction), depending on the protected person or recreational athlete's degree of fault. Mandatory public disclosure (Article 14.3.2) is not required for a minor (under the age of 18 years), a protected person or a recreational athlete. Any optional public disclosure shall be proportionate to the facts and circumstances of a case.

29.4.3.7 International Standard for Education (ISE)

Although the importance of education has always been highlighted in the Code, in 2021 it was formalised and standardised as one of the mandatory international standards accompanying the Code. The ISE 2021 provides set roles, responsibilities and obligations for all signatories to the Code, including athletes and ASP. The ISE requires, at a minimum, that athletes and ASP at national and international levels be educated before participating in significant events, including athletes in a registered testing pool. Sanctioned athletes (and their ASP) must also be educated before returning to sport. Where resources permit, education activities should be extended to athletes and ASP along the athlete development pathway to foster the values and know-how to compete 'cleanly' and limit the risk of inadvertent doping.

We wish to highlight the responsibility of national (and international) federations to work with their NADO and SAIDS to actively promote, plan and implement anti-doping education activities (e.g., talks, workshops, webinars, information booths at sports events, e-Learning) within their structures (members, affiliates, clubs etc.). Again, the view is that the sooner and younger anti-doping education can start, and the more members of the athlete's support team can be included, the better the chances of addressing the dopogenic environment.[25]

29.4.4 Minimising The Risk of Inadvertent Doping: The Role of Unregulated Medicines and Products within The SA Sports Context

29.4.4.1 Dietary Supplements

Due to a rise in doping cases related to supplement use over the years, WADA and all anti-doping organisations (including the SAIDS) are cautioning athletes against the indiscriminate use of dietary supplements. This is echoed in the UNESCO Convention Against Doping, where governments are called upon to improve the regulation of the supplement market and improve the quality, safety, efficacy, labelling and ethical marketing of these products.[26] Education on the risks posed by dietary supplements is also specified in the International Standard for Education as one of the critical topics that athletes and athlete support personnel need to familiarise themselves with.

The consensus from leading authorities, including the IOC expert panel on sport nutrition, is that supplements should only be considered: a) after a comprehensive nutrition assessment has been conducted; b) when the risks for adverse health events and testing positive for a prohibitive substance are low; and c) a health and physical performance benefit is likely.[27]

Most nutritional products sold locally (and abroad) have yet to undergo the credible and sound testing required to sufficiently answer questions of safety and efficacy. This starkly contrasts with their advertising claims, where 'evidence' is often misrepresented, exaggerated or fabricated by supplement manufacturers or those profiting from selling the products, enticing an ever-increasing consumer base to believe in and use them without applying a risk-benefit analysis.

Of particular concern is the growing number of consumers (including youth) reporting adverse side-effects and athletes testing positive for prohibited substances linked to supplements.[28] Also, pharmaceutical-grade ingredients such as anabolic steroids, stimulants and other potentially harmful components (some deemed unfit for human use) found in supplements are often not listed on the product labels.[29] 'Proprietary' blends/formulations, where the exact ingredients and amounts are kept a trade secret, are a further contributing factor. Supplements claimed to have muscle building, weight loss, fat burning, energy-boosting effects, 'pre-workouts' and 'SARMs' (selective androgen receptor modulators) pose the highest risk of containing banned substances.[30]

The extent of the poor quality of ingredients and lack of trust in product labels have been highlighted in many research studies globally and locally.[31;32;33] In a study by the Clean Label Project (a non-profit organisation in the USA), 134 top-selling protein supplements were laboratory tested for 130 toxins.[34] Many contained heavy metals such as lead, arsenic, cadmium, mercury, bisphenol-A (BPA) and other contaminants with links to cancer and other health conditions. Some toxins were present in significant quantities. In a study by the University of Cape Town, 138 protein supplements available on the South African market were laboratory tested for melamine.[35] Of the products manufactured in South Africa, 82% tested positive for melamine, and 58% of those imported into SA. Although the melamine was within the safety limits, the concern arises with dosage and frequency of use (particularly in children and adolescents, for which melamine poses more significant risks) and when more than one product is used. A study from the University of KZN revealed that nine of the 15 popular whey protein supplements analysed were non-compliant with labelling regulations, deliberately manipulating and overstating products' protein and amino acid content.[36]

The IOC expert panel devised a practical flow diagram (Figure 29.2) to guide consumers through a supplement-use risk-benefit analysis.[37] Notably, the IOC decision tree starts with the critical question of whether the athlete is at an appropriate age, level of maturation and experience to warrant the use of supplements.

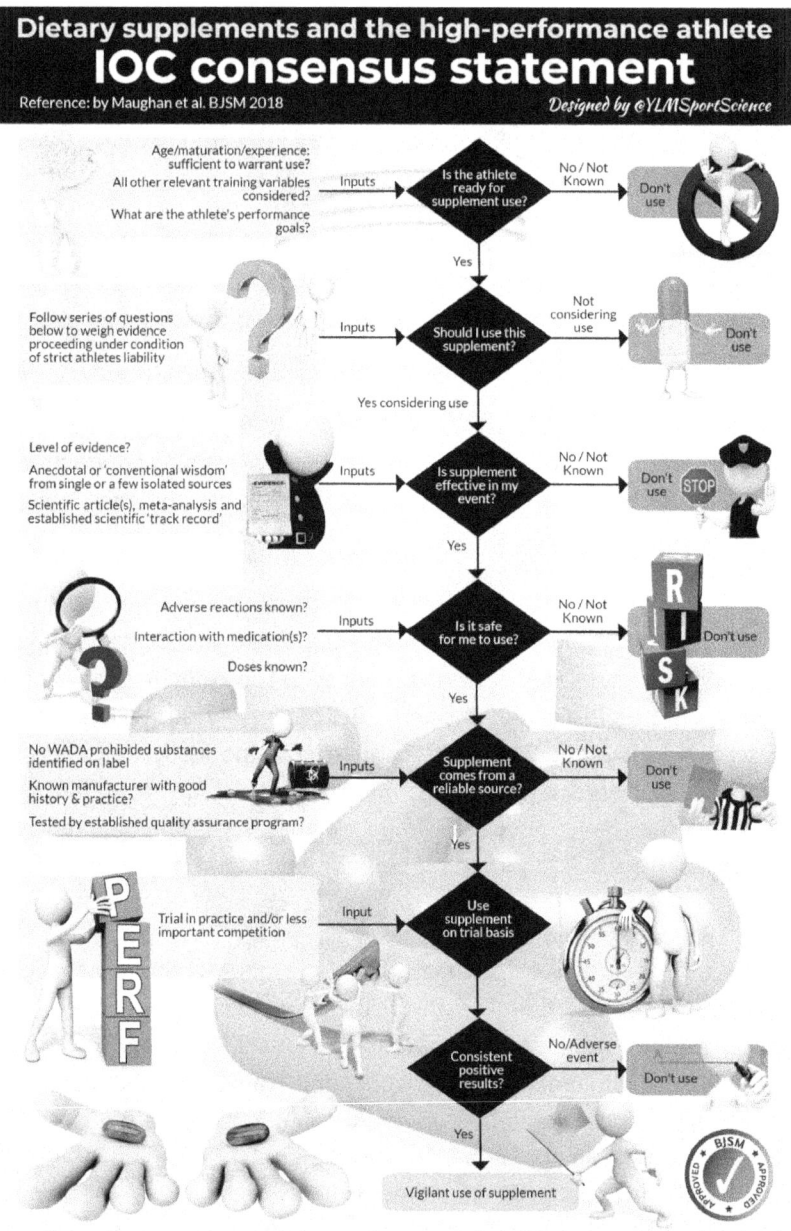

Figure 29.2: IOC consensus statement regarding dietary supplements and high-performance athletes[38]

Leading sporting and health organisations call for caution when encouraging supplements to enhance performance in young athletes.[39] Their concerns are related to the potential to negatively affect aspects of health, growth and development, exacerbated by the risks posed by an unregulated market and questionable products.[40]

There are also concerns related to encouraging supplement use from a young age or supplement use by children/adolescents, given the potential for causing an unhealthy fixation on supplements, 'pills and potions', fueled by aggressive marketing of supplement use to youth and schools. Messaging often pitches supplements as the quick fix, a 'must-have' or superior to what can be achieved through sound nutritional (and training) strategies alone. Products claiming to be 'uniquely formulated for youth' are not necessarily superior in quality nor specifically tested to substantiate any safety or efficacy claims.

During adolescence, eating behaviour is heavily influenced by the environment and 'important others', e.g., peers, teammates, professional athletes, coaches and management teams, celebrities and the media.[41] Unhealthy behaviours and nutrition misinformation (including supplement advertising and messaging) can set a young athlete on a path that could undermine athletic performance, contribute to sports injuries, and result in serious health consequences. Vulnerability to nutritional risk can include restrictive eating, disordered eating, misuse of nutritional supplements, "uninformed" vegetarianism and various unhealthy weight loss practices (including weight loss supplements) that can sabotage athletic performance, growth, development and maturation.[42] Nutrition advice should ideally come from trained professionals (without a vested interest in supplement sales) and should be food-based, practical, achievable and personally relevant.

In summary, athletes use supplements under the condition and principle of strict liability, meaning the athlete is ultimately responsible for the prohibited substance(s) found in their sample, regardless of how it got there and whether its ingestion was intentional or inadvertent (e.g., through the use of unregulated products such as a supplement, traditional or homoeopathic medicine where the ingredient was not made explicit on the label or otherwise).[43] A manager or ASP advising an athlete should keep a record of their guidance (education) provided to the athlete, especially where youth athletes are concerned. This could help in cases where their role (complicity) in an ADRV can be defended and prove that they are fulfilling their role and responsibility as defined in the Code. Protection of the athlete's health and awareness of potential harm must be paramount. Although there may be a few nutrients that have the necessary scientific backing to show possible performance-enhancing effects in certain types of sports, there is no guarantee as to whether the formulation within the final product has been adulterated (prohibited substances willfully added), contaminated (poor manufacturing standards and control, or contaminated base ingredients), and that the label is accurate (the product contains what it says, in the correct dosage).

29.4.4.2 How to reduce the risk of supplements?

It stands to reason that with the risks to health and sporting careers on the line, the aim would always be to optimise nutrition, training and rest strategies, only considering supplements after a risk-benefit analysis warrants it. A registered dietitian specialising in sports nutrition can work with an athlete to benefit from the latest evidence-based performance nutrition strategies tailored to individual circumstances, needs and goals for training and competition and, where appropriate, help devise a low-risk supplement-use plan.

Supplements independently batch-tested for a list of prohibited substances can lower some risks (e.g., Informed Sport testing or certification programme). When a product is advertised as 'tested', it is essential to check what the certification means or does not mean. Each batch is not tested with the Informed Choice programme, which increases the risk. Furthermore, while batch-testing reduces the risk, it does not eliminate it; products may still contain other harmful ingredients that are not being tested for or are not yet on the list of prohibited substances. Other safety aspects are also not tested for, such as whether the product contains what is said on the label (ingredients, dosage), its efficacy and other such claims. Product batch testing also comes at an additional expense for supplement manufacturers, which means not many products on the market (in SA in particular) are part of an independent batch-testing programme. Those that typically test only one or two of their products may advertise such testing across their product range, so it is always good to double-check the product and batch number on the independent testing provider's website.[44] Lastly, no dietary supplement tested to date can compensate for poor nutrition, training and rest strategies, which, independently and combined, have a far more significant impact on optimal health and performance and should be the primary focus.

29.4.4.3 Over-the-counter medicines

Although there is some regulation, there is limited enforcement of over-the-counter medicines. Many of these products have not been evaluated by the South African Health Products Regulatory Authority (SAHPRA) and, as such, may pose a risk to the ingestion of prohibited substances. Check the label or package insert; if it says it has not been evaluated by SAHPRA, use it cautiously. Such products will also not appear on the SAIDS medication check tool, as the actual contents of the products cannot be verified with certainty.

29.4.4.4 Homoeopathic and herbal medicines

The medicinal formulations used in homeopathy are not regulated, therefore the actual contents are largely unknown. Claims that products contain 'natural' or 'herbal' ingredients do not necessarily mean 'safe' or 'harmless'. Some herbal ingredients can result in a positive doping test or have detrimental health effects if misused.

Examples of herbals that naturally produce substances that are prohibited in sport include: cannabis sativa, which produces THC and many other cannabinoids that are prohibited in competition; ephedra (multiple species), which produces ephedrine and pseudoephedrine; citrus aurantium (orange peel or bitter orange), which naturally produces octopamine which is prohibited in-competition; and tinospora cripsa and other plants are known to produce higenamine, a beta-2 agonist that is prohibited at all times.[45]

29.4.4.5 Cannabis (Marijuana or 'Dagga')

Athletes and ASP need to note that, regardless of its legal status for personal medicinal use, cannabis remains on the list of prohibited substances in sport. Consumers should also heed the health risks associated with using cannabis, particularly in youth. The Substance Abuse and Mental Health Services Administration (SAMSA) website details the detrimental effects on brain and mental health, the respiratory system and sporting performance.[46]

29.4.4.6 Status of 'CBD' products

Synthetic cannabidiol (or CBD) is permitted in sport, however CBD extracted from cannabis plants may contain varying amounts of THC, which is prohibited in-competition. As with dietary supplements, CBD products are unregulated and product labels (actual ingredients, dosage, etc.) and claims are not verified by health or other regulatory authorities. Not knowing what is in the products poses a risk of an inadvertent ADRV.

29.4.4.7 African herbal and traditional medicines

African traditional medicine and rituals are an essential part of the culture and traditions of African people.[47] The main component of traditional medicine is herbal medicine, which in South Africa accounts for 5.6% of the national health budget.[48] Medicinal plants are used for remedies to treat medical conditions or within symbolic social and cultural practices.[49] The World Health Organisation has suggested that as much as 80% of the population in Africa is dependent on traditional medicine for their primary health care.[50] It is within the realm of herbal medicine that traditional health care practitioners (THPs) become critical players in providing primary health care and inadvertent doping practices within sport. Of particular concern are the methods and preparation of remedies where safety, efficacy and quality control still need to be established.

A South African study found that a small cohort of professional soccer players had used some form of traditional medicine for their soccer-related performances.[51] This included treatment of physical ailments, enhancing performance and as part of mandatory team rituals. The taking of traditional medicine and partaking in team rituals is shrouded in secrecy, and team managers were identified as the key personnel who organised the sangoma (diviner) and muthi (medicine usually made from bark, roots, seawater, leaves, herbs or animal parts) for the team.[52]

29.5 ADAPTING AND IMPLEMENTING PROCESSES FOR CHANGE

Within the South African sporting landscape, implementing the following social and structural resources could provide significant inroads to assisting with anti-doping awareness and practices:[53]

1. Improving access to qualified and knowledgeable coaching and athlete support personnel (including Sport Managers and medical professionals) at all levels of sport participation to participate in the SAIDS anti-doping awareness and education campaigns and promote evidence-informed, practical, and cost-effective alternatives to doping.
2. Examine and address the 'quick fix' strategies for enhancing and improving performance, including managing the attitudes and perceptions of athletes, parents and ASP regarding doping.
3. Critically examine the sporting calendar at all levels of participation, particularly as athletes move through the athlete development system to break through into the high-performance echelons of professional sport. The provision of sufficient recovery, monitoring competition load and being mindful of long-term athlete development could assist in decreasing the need for prohibited substances used for recovery and decreasing the time required for return to play after injury.

4. Changing the sport culture from winning at the expense of athlete welfare, across the athlete development pathway. This includes athletes participating at all levels, from school to club, district, university, provincial and national structures. In addition, safeguarding athletes from potential abuse or neglect must be prioritised across all levels of participation.
5. Implementing a regulated system for the nutritional supplement industry would prevent inadvertent doping and accessibility to unregulated products, which continue to pose significant risks to athletes and athlete support personnel giving unintentional nutritional advice.

29.6 CONCLUSIONS

As sports managers are an integral part of the athlete support personnel, especially in team events and at the professional level where managers are employed as part of the support system, awareness and compliance with the WADA code is essential to avoid an ADRV and possible sanctions.

SELF-ASSESSMENT

1. List four different role players within the anti-doping space.
2. How many anti-doping rule violations are there? Briefly explain each of them.
3. Explain the role Sport Managers play in averting the risks of doping.
4. Identify and explain the main rules of anti-doping.

THE FUTURE OF SPORT GOVERNANCE IN SOUTH AFRICA

Ilhaam Groenewald and Dr Nana Adom-Aboagye

LEARNING OUTCOMES

At the end of this chapter, you should be able to:

1. Understand the South African sport governance landscape.
2. Be informed on suggested governance principles and guidelines designed to counter failures in governance.
3. Understand the international context that influences the South African sport governance landscape.
4. Identify the future agenda for the South African sport governance landscape.

30.1 SOUTH AFRICAN SPORT GOVERNANCE LANDSCAPE

Considering the history, legislation, policies and structures of sport in South Africa, the country has a well-defined governance system, with stakeholders' areas of jurisdiction and responsibilities identified (see Chapter 4, 10 and 11). However, challenges have and may continue to arise when it comes to the application of good governance procedures. This chapter provides insights that can strengthen sport governance for South Africa and sport organisations in general.

Corporate governance principles and their relevance to the sport industry have been debated extensively in the literature.[1;2] South Africa's legacy of Apartheid and the country's history of racial segregation significantly impacted sport governance. In recent years, there has been a growing recognition of the importance of good governance in sport in South Africa and worldwide. Corporate sponsors and donors have also begun to emphasise good governance in sport, recognising its role in building sustainable sporting organisations. Many corporate sponsors now require sport organisations to adhere to strict governance standards as a condition of sponsorship.[3] Corporate governance principles and their relevance to the sport industry have been debated extensively in the literature.[4;5;6;7]

In recent years, the issue of good governance has climbed to the top of the sport/political agenda, highlighted by several international and national sport governing bodies being beset with corruption scandals.[8] In addition, cases of outright failure to govern have led to calls for the better governance of sport organisations from both governments and independent agencies.[9;10;11] This call has led to a range of suggested governance principles and guidelines being designed to counter failures in governance:

1. Democratic structures/democracy: ensuring sporting organisations have democratic structures allowing fair and transparent decision-making processes.
2. Equity: promoting fairness and equal treatment for all individuals involved in the sporting organisation, regardless of their background or status.
3. Accountability: ensuring those responsible for making decisions within the sporting organisation are held accountable for their actions.
4. Transparency: ensuring that the decision-making processes and outcomes of the sporting organisation are transparent and easily accessible to all stakeholders.
5. Equality: promoting equality and non-discrimination within the sporting organisation.
6. Term limits and age: setting term limits and age restrictions for board members to promote turnover and prevent stagnation.
7. Board skills vs. only representation: ensuring those on the board have the necessary skills and expertise to govern the sporting organisation effectively.
8. Separation of board chair and CEO roles: separating the roles of board chair and CEO to prevent conflicts of interest and promote effective governance.
9. Codes of ethics and conflicts of interest: developing codes of ethics and policies to prevent conflicts of interest and promote ethical behaviour within the sporting organisation.
10. Athlete involvement/representation: including athletes in the decision-making processes of the sporting organisation to ensure that their perspectives and interests are considered.
11. Stakeholder participation/representation: ensuring that all stakeholders, including fans, sponsors and community members, are represented in the decision-making processes of the sporting organisation.
12. Anti-bribery/corruption codes: developing policies and procedures to prevent bribery and corruption within the sporting organisation.
13. Autonomy/independence: ensuring that the sporting organisation has the freedom and independence to make decisions without external influences.
14. Board evaluation through board charters: evaluate the board's performance regularly to identify improvement areas and ensure effective governance.
15. Access and timely disclosure of information: ensure stakeholders have access to all relevant information about the sporting organisation and that this information is disclosed promptly.[12;13]

Not only have cases of poor sport governance drawn worldwide public and political attention, but there is also a growing awareness that the failures of sport governance are long-lasting and systemic.[14] Similarly, the governance of sport in South Africa since 1994 has been plagued by bad decisions. There have been numerous scandals, power struggles, financial impropriety, corruption, doping, match-fixing and boardroom challenges involving managers and directors at various levels of the sporting hierarchy. These issues have tarnished the reputation of sport and placed the very integrity and sustainability of sport at risk.[15]

Corporate governance is primarily concerned with economic prosperity and the survival of organisations within the formal business sector. As the sport industry has moved into this sector, it has become imperative that sport organisations are aware of, and can comply with, the principles of good governance. The importance, relevance and global context of sport governance make it clear that integrity in playing and managing sport is a critical issue facing the international sports community and its governance. This issue highlights the vital role of policymakers and managers in sport, especially in South Africa, to ensure the professional management of sport organisations for the betterment of those involved.[16]

30.1.1 International Context That Influences and Impacts The South African Sport Governance Landscape

The ongoing spate of high-profile corruption scandals within major international sport organisations (ISOs) has increased calls for greater public scrutiny and for sport organisations to take steps towards improved corporate governance. The public calls have also noted the growing need for sport to restore public trust and reduce the risk of poor governance to improve business integrity.

30.1.1.1 IOC governance model

The IOC was a pioneer in establishing an independent Ethics Commission in 1999. The Commission was tasked with creating a Code of Ethics to address violations of ethical principles, analysing complaints and recommending sanctions. In addition, the Commission also advises the IOC on implementing ethical principles.[17] Following this process, the IOC further strengthened its corporate governance, resulting in a comprehensive governance model.

The IOC's risk and assurance governance model aims to help the organisation reduce potential risks and follow the internationally recognised 'Three Lines Model' for risk management under the authority of the IOC President, the Ethics Commission and the Audit Committee. This model distinguishes three groups with different roles and responsibilities, and consists of (1) operational functions that own and manage risks; (2) managerial functions that help build and/or monitor the first-line controls and serve as an oversight function, ensuring that controls, frameworks, policies and procedures are implemented; and (3) an independent function that assures the IOC's governing bodies, which is critical to ensuring objectivity.[18] This can be viewed in Figure 30.1 below.

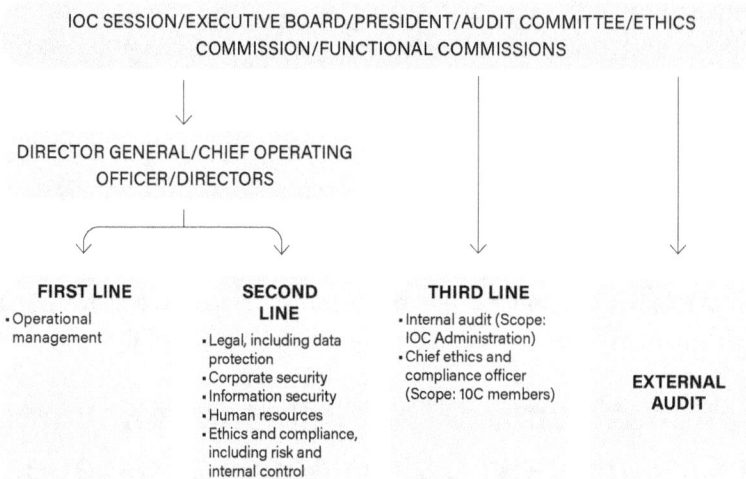

Figure 30.1: The IOC's Risk and Assurance Governance Model

30.1.1.2 UNESCO

In 2013, the United Nations Educational, Scientific and Cultural Organisation (UNESCO) issued the *Declaration of Berlin*[19] following a conference to generate a global consensus on orientations and principles for promoting sport and physical education. The Declaration, which was adopted by all 121 sport ministers and officials in attendance, including South Africa, stressed the need for public authorities and other stakeholders to combat threats to the integrity of sport through doping, corruption and manipulating sport competitions. In addition, weight was given to promoting sport organisations' efforts to achieve good governance. To achieve this objective, the focus should be on strengthening democratic structures, increasing transparency and improving financial management.[20]

30.1.1.3 *King Corporate Governance Principles*

Locally, the King Committee on Corporate Governance was established in 1992 by the Institute of Directors in Southern Africa to provide thought leadership and promote corporate governance. The first King Report was published in 1994, and subsequent reports have been released with updates and revisions, with the latest being the King IV Report in 2016. The King Reports provide guidelines and recommendations for effective corporate governance practices in South African companies, focusing on ethical leadership, transparency, accountability and stakeholder engagement. The reports also emphasise the role of boards of directors in overseeing and guiding a company's strategic direction, risk management and performance.[21] The King Reports have significantly impacted corporate governance practices in South Africa, with many companies adopting their recommendations and principles, including sport organisations such as SASCOC, SARU and Cricket South Africa (CSA). The reports have also influenced corporate governance developments in other countries, particularly in the African region.[22]

30.2 THE FUTURE AGENDA TO ADVANCE SPORT GOVERNANCE IN SOUTH AFRICA

The heightened interest in sport shown by participants, fans, politicians, legislators, sponsors, donors and government has increased the demand for long-term sustainability and compliance with best-practice corporate governance principles. Adequate evidence exists of problems with corruption and system and process breakdowns, which require an ethical and moral organisational culture, both internationally and in South Africa. Thus, this chapter focuses on the future agenda to advance sport governance in South Africa, raising questions as to whether the governance models adopted by many sports bodies are suited for their role and the environment in which they operate.

It is acknowledged that new challenges have presented themselves to sport, including the emergence of new stakeholders that pose new questions for governance, democracy and the representation of interests within the sport movement. The governance challenges facing sporting bodies are, in some ways, the same as other sectors. However, because of the history of sport in South African society and its unique role, existing governance in sport is to be challenged to suit the needs of society today. It should be about the needs of stakeholders and ensuring a governance system that builds confidence for the present and future. Identifying critical issues for current and future sport governance agendas is also important.

30.2.1 Critical Issues for Current and Future Sport Governance Agendas

Research conducted by Parent and Hoye[23] highlights some of the critical issues for current and future sport governance agendas, namely: (1) the impact of gender quotas for board composition on governance outcomes; (2) the impact of external forces, including government policy on governance practices; (3) seeking to explain governance performance; (4) the role and structure of boards; and (5) the extent of the adoption of specific governance principles by sport organisations.

In addition, the following ongoing global developments will remain critical agenda items for all three types of sport organisations within South Africa, namely: (1) governing bodies (either at the international, national or state levels); (2) amateur sport organisations; and (3) professional sport organisations.

30.2.1.1 Globalisation

While globalisation has benefited many sport stakeholders, such as media companies, professional teams and leagues, it is essential to acknowledge and address the negative consequences it brings. These include athlete migration, environmental concerns, the impact of global media and the need for the sustainability efforts. Developing effective governance policies that examine the interrelationships between all stakeholders involved in globalisation is crucial.

30.2.1.2 Board size, diversity and skills

Sport organisations should explore how adopting specific governance principles impacts actual governance outcomes or the performance of sport organisations. This has been considered in South Africa through the recent adoption of a draft Board Charter by SASCOC.[24]

30.2.1.3 Sport and gender

In South Africa, addressing gender in sports governance has become an increasingly critical agenda item. Historically, sports in South Africa have been male-dominated, with limited opportunities for women's participation and leadership. The South African government has taken several steps to address gender inequality in sports, including the introduction of gender quotas for sports teams and boards, and the development of policies aimed at promoting women's participation in sports. Despite these efforts, significant challenges still need to be addressed, including inadequate funding for women's sports and a need for more female representation in sports leadership positions. By prioritising gender in sports governance, South Africa can work towards creating a more inclusive and equitable sports sector that benefits all athletes, regardless of gender.

30.2.1.4 The decision-makers

Amidst growing athlete activism, exemplified by movements such as #BlackLivesMatter and the Cricket South Africa investigation into systemic racism, decision-makers must heed athletes' voices. It is time for sports leaders to show the same courage as athletes and undertake much-needed sports governance and law reforms.[25]

30.2.1.5 Safeguarding

To strengthen its commitment to the principles of safe sport and good governance, SASCOC developed a policy to prevent harassment and abuse within sport. The policy requires each SASCOC member to adopt and implement suitable safeguarding policies and procedures independently or in partnership with SASCOC or a relevant government organisation.[26]

30.2.1.6 Anti-doping

South African National Anti-Doping Rules, certified as code compliant by the World Anti-Doping Agency (WADA), apply to all National Sport Federations (NSFs) recognised by SASCOC. Although NSF members of SASCOC are automatically subject to these rules, their consistent application still needs to be improved, as evidenced by several recent cases.[27]

30.3 **CONCLUSION**

Sport governance scholarship has evolved in tandem with the commercialisation and professionalisation of the sport industry.[28] Researchers have focused mainly on sport organisations in Western countries, particularly Australia, Canada and England.[29;30] Recent research has also begun to explore sport governance in more diverse contexts, such as in India,[31] however, what needs to be improved is sufficient research in developing contexts, especially research aimed at generating impact and driving progress within the South African sports industry. To enhance sport governance, South Africa needs to focus on three main types of sport organisations, namely: (1) governing bodies (either at the international, national or state levels); (2) amateur sport organisations; and (3) professional sport organisations. A key focus should be on developing an understanding of good governance in these three contexts, as well as defining and assessing principles of good governance, specifically in sport.[32]

Recent governance changes implemented by SASCOC[33] specifically focused on the board of directors as the unit of analysis and defining the strategic role and capability of the board (independence, skills and expertise requirements), along with a list of by-laws to manage nominations, membership recognition and compliance, conflicts and board performance.

Establishing generally accepted policy frameworks for sport governance, adopted by public and private sports bodies, is crucial in creating consensus on a limited number of core principles. This minimalist approach should focus on a transparent operationalisation process that adapts indicators to sport organisations' cultural and structural specificities. Doing so can generate more explicit expectations, ensure autonomy and enhance the impact of reforms by renewing trust among stakeholders in sport. Implementing this approach will require strong leadership, trained and motivated staff, introducing new control mechanisms and bodies, monitoring the reform process, and communicating expectations. It may also entail amending statutes to align them with the new policies.[34;35]

SELF-ASSESSMENT

1. Identify the major developments that influenced and shaped the South African sport governance landscape.
2. Outline the governance principles and guidelines designed to counter failures in governance.
3. Unpack the international context and specific governance structures and policies that influence the South African sport governance landscape.
4. Identify key issues that will inform the future agenda of the South African sport governance landscape.

ABBREVIATIONS

Advent Sport Entertainment and Media (ASEM)
Africa Electronic Sport Association (AESA)
African National Congress (ANC)
African Paralympic Committee (APC)
African Sports Confederation of Disabled (ASCOD)
African Union Sports Council (AUSC)
Annual General Meeting (AGM)
Anti-Doping Rule Violations (ADRVs)
Athlete Support Personnel (ASP)
Athletics South Africa (ASA)
Australian Institute of Sport (AIS)
Australian Sports Commission (ASC)
Average Age of Inventory (AAI)
Average Collection Period (ACP)
Balanced Scorecards (BSCs)
Basketball South Africa (BSA)
Black Economic Empowerment (BEE)
Blue Bulls Rugby Union (BBRU)
Body-Mass Index (BMI)
Cash Conversion Cycle (CCC)
Children of the Dawn (COTD)
Commonwealth Games Associations (CGAs)
Commonwealth Games Federation (CGF)
Communist Party (CP)
Comrades Marathon Association (CMA)
Confederation of African Deaf Sports (CADS)
Continuous Professional Development (CPD)
Council for Adult and Experiential Learning (CAEL)
Cricket South Africa (CSA)
Critical Success Factors (CSFs)
Department of Basic Education (DBE)
Department of Sport and Recreation (DSR)
Department of Sport, Arts and Culture (DSAC)
Disability Sport South Africa (DISSA)
Eminent Persons Group (EPG)
Esports Entertainment Association (ESEA)
Federation Equestre Internationale (FEI)
Fédération Internationale de Basketball (FIBA)
Fédération Internationale de Football Association (FIFA)
Fédération Internationale de Natation (FINA)
General Counsel (GC)
Gross Value Added (GVA)
Gymnastics South Africa (GSA)
High Performance (HP)
Hout Bay United FC (HBUFC)
Indian Premier League (IPL)
Integrated National Disability Strategy (INDS)
International Amateur Athletics Federation (IAAF)

International Blind Sports Association (IBSA)
International Cricket Council (ICC)
International Day of Sport for Development and Peace (IDSDP)
International Olympic Committee (IOC)
International Paralympic Committee (IPC)
International Sport Federation (ISF)
International Sport Organisations (ISOs)
International Sports Organisation of Disabled (ISOD)
International Standard for Education (ISE)
International Standard for Results Management (ISRM)
International Standard for Therapeutic Use Exemptions (ISTUE)
International Stoke Mandeville Wheelchair Sports Federation (ISMWSF)
International Year of Sport and Physical Education (IYSPE)
Japan Sport Council (JSC)
Joint Operation Centre (JOC)
Judo South Africa (JSA)
Kazan Action Plan (KAP)
Key Result Indicators (KRIs)
Knowledge-Based Economy (KBE)
Leg Before Wicket (LBW)
Lesbian, Gay, Bisexual and Transgender (LGBT)
Local Organising Committee (LOC)
Long-Term Athlete Development (LTAD)
Long-Term Coach Development (LTCD)
Long-Term Participant Development (LTPD)
Member Protection Regulation (MPR)
Members Council (MC)
Memorandum of Understanding (MoU)
Ministerial Task Team (MTT)
Monitoring Evaluation and Learning (MEL)
Most Significant Changes (MSc)
Motorsport South Africa (MSA)
Mzansi Super League (MSL)
National Football League (NFL)
National Lotteries Commission (NLC)
National Olympic Committee of South Africa (NOCSA)
National Olympic Committee (NOC)
National Paralympic Committee (NPC)
National Paralympic Committee of South Africa (NAPCOSA)
National Party (NP)
National Qualifications Framework (NQF)
National Sport and Recreation Act (NSRA)
National Sport and Recreation Plan (NSRP)

National Sports Council (NSC)
National Sports Federations (NSFs)
Netball South Africa (NSA)
Non-Governmental Organisations (NGOs)
Operating Cycle (OC)
Pacific Netball Partnership (PNP)
Pan African Congress (PAC)
Performance-Enhancing Drug (PED)
Physical Education (PE)
Political, Economic, Social, Technological, Environmental and Legal (PESTEL)
Post Graduate Teachers Diploma (PGTD)
Premier Soccer League (PSL)
Presidential Employment Stimulus (PES)
Pure Tone Average (PTA)
Qualify Physical Education (QPE)
Reconstruction and Development Programme (RDP)
Registered Testing Pool (RTP)
Resource Dependence Theory (RDT)
SA Sport Coach (SASCA)
SA Sports Association for Physically Disabled (SASAPD)
Safety at Sports and Recreation Events Act (SASREA)
School Governing Bodies (SGBs)
Self-Determination Theory (SDT)
Soccer Football Association (SAFA)
South African Broadcasting Corporation (SABC)
South African Council of Sports (SACOS)
South African Cricket Board of Control (SACBOC)
South African Cricket Union (SACU)
South African Cricketers Association (SACA)
South African Deaf Sports Federation (SADSF)
South African Equestrian Federation (SAEF)
South African Health Products Regulatory Authority (SAHPRA)
South African Institute for Drug-free Sport (SAIDS)
South African National Olympic Committee (SANOC)
South African Qualifications Authority (SAQA)
South African Rugby Players Association (SARPA)
South African Rugby Union (SARU)
South African Sport Confederation and Olympic Committee (SASCOC)
South African Sports Association (SASA)
South African Sports Association for Severely Mentally Handicapped (SASASMH)
South African Sports Commission (SASC)
South African Student Sports Union (SASSU)
Southern African Legal Information Institute (SAFLII)
Special Olympics South Africa (SOSA)
Sport and Recreation South Africa (SRSA)
Sport for Development and Peace (SDP)

Sport for Social Change Network Africa (SSCNA)
Sport for the Intellectually Disabled South Africa (SIDSA)
Sport-in-Development Assessment Tool (SDIAT)
Substance Abuse and Mental Health Services Administration (SAMHSA)
Sustainable Development Goals (SDGs)
Theory of Change (ToC)
Union of European Football Associations (UEFA)
Union of Soviet Socialist Republics (USSR)
Unique Selling Point (USP)
United Nations Educational, Scientific and Cultural Organisation (UNESCO)
United Nations Office for Sport for Development and Peace (UNOSDP)
University Sport South Africa (USSA)
Upper Respiratory Tract Infections (URTI)
Venue Operations Centre (VOC)
World Anti-Doping Agency (WADA)
World Economic Forum (WEF)
World Health Organisation (WHO)

ENDNOTES

Chapter 1

1. Gammelseater, H. 2020. Sport is not industry: Bringing back to sport management. *European Sport management Quarterly*, March 2022: 257-279. https://doi.org/10.1080/16184742.2020.1741013.
2. Sage, G.H. 1987. Pursuit of Knowledge in Sociology of Sport: Issues and Prospects. *Quest*, 39: 255-281.
3. Brohm, J. 1978. *Sport: a Prison of Measured Time.* London: Ink Links.
4. Dunning, E. & Rojek C. 1992. *Sport and leisure in the civilizing process: Critique and Counter Critique.* Toronto: University of Toronto Press.
5. Burnett, C. 1998. *The Symbiotic Relationship between Sport and Society: Discourse and Debate.* Johannesburg: Rand Afrikaans University. (Inaugural Lecture as Professor in Sport and Movement Studies, 20 May 1998).
6. Frey, J.H. & Eitzen, D.S. 1991. Sport and Society. Annual Reviews. *Sociology of Sport,* 17: 503-522.
7. Coakley, J. & Pike, E. 1998. *Sport in Society: Issues and Controversies* (6th ed.). New York: Irwin McGraw-Hill.
8. Ibid.
9. Anderson, B. 1991. *Imaged Communities: Reflections on the Origin and Spread of Nationalism.* New York: Verso.
10. Anon, 1995. *The Story of the Rugby World Cup South Africa.* Cape Town: Royston Lamond International. p. 1.
11. Coakley & Pike, 1998.
12. Coakley & Pike, 1998.
13. Cashmore, E. 1990. *Making Sense of Sport.* London: Routledge.
14. Coakley & Pike, 1998.
15. Rojek, C. 1995. *Decentring Leisure: Rethinking Leisure Theory.* London: Sage Publications.
16. Morgan, W.J. 1997. Yet Another Critical Look at Hegemony Theory: A Response to Ingram and Beamish. *Sociology of Sport Journal,* 14: 187-195.
17. Lapchick, R.E. 1995. *Sport in Society: Equal Opportunity or Business as usual?* London: Sage Publications; Shropshire, K. 1997. *In Black and White: Race and Sports in America.* New York: New York University Press.
18. Morgan, W.J. 1997. Yet Another Critical Look at Hegemony Theory: A Response to Ingram and Beamish. *Sociology of Sport Journal,* 14: 187-195.
19. Coakley, J. & Pike, E. 1994. *Sport in Society: Issues and Controversies* (5th ed.). Chicago: Mosby.
20. Silk, M. 1999. Local/Global flows and Altered Production Practices. *International Review for the Sociology of Sport,* 34(2): 113-123.
21. Burnett, C. 1998. *The Symbiotic Relationship between Sport and Society: Discourse and Debate.* Johannesburg: Rand Afrikaans University. (Inaugural Lecture as Professor in Sport and Movement Studies, 20 May 1998).
22. Schots, H. 1999. Die ekonomiese magtigste man in die wêreld. *Die Beeld,* 16 August: 16.
23. Coakley & Pike, 1998.
24. Frey & Eitzen, 1991.
25. Williams, R. 1977. *Marxism and Literature.* New York: Oxford University Press.
26. Morgan, 1997.
27. Dunning, E. 1994. *Aspects of the Relationship Between History and Sociology: Notes on the Work of EH, Carr, EH, Abrams, P and Elias, R. with Special Reference to Sociology of Sport.* Leicester: The Centre for Research into Sport and Society in association with the Sir Norman Chester Centre for Football Research.
28. Murphy, P. 1994. *Introduction to Figurational Sociology.* Leicester: The Centre for Research into Sport and Society, Leicester University.

Chapter 2

1. Hollander, W.J. 2017. *Can you fly this space ship, Captain Kirk?* Unpublished inauguration speech, University of Johannesburg.
2. Miller, P. 1991. *Transformation agenda in sport. London Times,* March 25: 4: p. 265.

3   Hollander, W.J. 2000. *Beroepgeorienteerde bestuursopleiding vir die Suid Afrikaanse Sport Industrie.* Unpublished thesis, University of Johannesburg.
4   Ibid.
5   Anon, 1995. *The Story of the Rugby World Cup South Africa.* Cape Town: Royston Lamond International.
6   Department of Basic Education. 2011. *Curriculum and Assessment Policy Statement. Life Orientation, Senior Phase 7 – 9.* Pretoria: Government Printing Works. Available at https://www.education.gov.za/Portals/0/CD/National%20Curriculum%20Statements%20and%20Vocational/CAPS%20FET%20_%20LIFE%20ORIENTATION%20_%20GR%2010-12%20_%20WEB_E6B3.pdf?ver=2015-01-27-154251-017
7   Siegfried, N., Schlesinger, T., Bayle, E. & Giauque, D. 2015. Professionalisation of sport federations – a multi-level framework for analysing forms, causes and consequences. *European Sport Management Quarterly*, 15(4): 407-433.
8   Bayle, E. & Robinson, L. 2007. A framework for understanding the performance of national governing bodies of sport. *European Sport Management Quarterly*, 7: 249–268.
9   Shilbury, D. & Ferkins, L. 2011. Professionalisation, sport governance and strategic capability. *Managing Leisure*, 16: 108-127.
10 Shor, E. & Galily, Y. 2012. Globalization and Glocalization in the Development of Israeli Basketball. *Sociology of Sport Journal,* 29: 526-545.
11 Ryan, G. (Ed.). 2008. *The changing face of Rugby: The Union game and professionalism since 1995.* Newcastle: Cambridge Scholars Publishing; Collins, T. 2005. Australian nationalism and working-class Britishness: The case of Rugby League football. *History Compass, 3:* 1-19.
12 Hollander, 2017.
13 York, R., Gastin, P. & Dawson, A. 2014. What About Us? We Have Careers Too! The Career Experiences of Australian Sport Scientists. *International Journal of Sports Science & Coaching,* 9(6): 1437-1456.
14 Hollander, 2000.
15 Donnely, P. 1997. Child Labour, Sport Labour: Applying Child Labour Laws to Sport. *International Review for the Sociology of Sport*, 32(4): 389-406.
16 York, Gastin & Dawson, 2014.
17 Amusa, L.O. & Toriola, A.L. 2012. Professionalisation of Physical Education and Sport Science in Africa. *African Journal for Physical, Health Education, Recreation and Dance*, 18(3): 628-642.
18 Coakley, J.J. 1998. *Sport in Society: Issues and Controversies* (6th ed.). New York: Irwin McGraw-Hill.
19 Ryne, S.B. & Mallett, C.J. 2012. Understanding the work and learning of high performance coaches. *Physical Education and Sport Pedagogy,* (17)5: 507-523.
20 De Knop, P. & Standeven, J. 1998. Sport Tourism: a New Area of Sport Management. *European Journal for Sport Management*, 5(1): 30-45.
21 Hollander, 2017.
22 Ibid.
23 Smith, E. & Hattery, A. 2011. Race Relations Theories: Implications for Sport Management. *Journal of Sport Management*, 25: 107-117.
24 FIFA. 2014. *Committee for Women's Football and the FIFA Women's World Cup™*. Available at http://www.fifa.com/aboutfifa/organisation/bodies/standingcommittees/committee=1882028.html; Legg, D. & Steadward, R. 2011. The Paralympic Games and 60 years of change (1948–2008): Unification and restructuring from a disability and medical model to sport-based competition. *Sport in Society*, 14(9): 1099-1115.
25 Hollander, 2000.
26 Ellis, M.J. 1988. The Business of Physical Education. In: J.D. Masengale (ed.). *Trends Toward the Future in Physical Education*. Champaign, IL: Human Kinetic Books, pp. 69-84.

Chapter 3

1   Chelladurai, P. 1992. A Classification of Sport and Physical Activity Services: Implications for Sport Management. *Journal of Sport Management*, 6(1): 38-51.

2. Cuskelly, G. & Ault, C.J. 1991. Perceived Importance of Selected Job Responsibilities of Sport and Recreation Managers: An Australian Perspective. *Journal of Sport Management,* 1(5): 34-46.
3. De Sensi, J.T. 1994. Multiculturalism as an Issue in Sport Management. *Journal of Sport Management,* 8(1): 63-74.
4. Kjeldsen, E. 1990. Sport Management Careers: A Descriptive Analysis. *Journal of Sport Management,* 2(4): 121-132.
5. Hollander, W.J. 2000. *Beroepgeorienteerde Bestuursopleiding vir die Suid Afrikaanse Sport Industrie.* Unpublished thesis, University of Johannesburg.
6. Parks, J.B., Zanger, B.R.K. & Quarterman, J. 1998. *Contemporary Sport Management.* Champaign, IL: Human Kinetics.
7. Mullin, B. 1985. Marketing Management: Characteristics of Sport Marketing. In: G. Lewis and H. Appenzeller (eds.). Charlottesville, VA: The Michie Company, pp. 101-123.
8. Hollander, 2000.
9. Ibid.
10. Burnett, C. & Hollander, W.J. 1999. Sport Development and the United Kingdom – South Africa Sports Initiative: A Pre-evaluation Report. *Journal of Sport Management,* 13(3): 237-251.
11. Hollander, 2000.
12. Gouws, J.S. 1997. *Sport Management: Theory and Practice.* Randburg: Knowledge Resources.
13. Mullin, 1985.
14. Lli, M. 1993. Job satisfaction and Performance of Coaches of the Spare-Time Sport Schools in China. *Journal of Sport Management,* 7(2): 132-140.
15. Hollander, 2000.
16. Cousens, L. 1997. From Diamonds to Dollars: The Dynamic of Change in AAA Baseball Franchise. *Journal of Sport Management,* 11(4): 316-334.
17. Hollander, 2000.
18. Department of Basic Education. 1995. Government Gazette No. 1521 of 1995. *South African Qualifications Authority Act,* No. 58 of 1995. Pretoria: Government Printing.
19. Hollander, 2000.

Chapter 4

1. Corrigall, M. 1971. *International Boycott of Apartheid Sport by Mary Corrigall.* Paper prepared for the United Nations Unit on Apartheid in 1971. Available at: https://www.sahistory.org.za/archive/international-boycott-Apartheid-sport-mary-corrigall
2. Guttmann, A. 1992. Chariot races, tournaments and the civilizing process. In E. Dunning & C. Rojeck (eds.). *Sport and Leisure in the Civilizing Process: Critique and Counter-Critique.* Toronto: University of Toronto Press, pp. 137-160.
3. The Newsroom. 2016. *Remembering rebel All Blacks tour of Apartheid South Africa. The Scotsman.* Available at: https://www.scotsman.com/sport/remembering-rebel-all-blacks-tour-Apartheid-south-africa-1477708
4. Linnell, G. & Humphries, D. 2019. *From the Archives. 1985: Rebel cricketers banned for tours of South Africa.* Available at: https://www.smh.com.au/sport/cricket/from-the-archives-1985-rebel-cricketers-banned-for-tours-of-south-africa-20190726-p52b6l.html
5. Barnes, C. 2008. *International isolation and pressure for change in South Africa.* Available at: https://www.c-r.org/accord/incentives-sanctions-and-conditionality/international-isolation-and-pressure-change-south
6. Keech, M. 2000. At the centre of the web: The role of Sam Ramsamy in South Africa's readmission to international sport. *Culture, Sport Society,* 3(3): 41-62.
7. The Commonwealth. 2017. *From the Archive: Sanctions agreed against Apartheid-era South Africa.* Available at: https://thecommonwealth.org/news/archive-sanctions-agreed-against-Apartheid-era-south-africa
8. Bose, M. 1994. *Sporting colours: Sport and politics in South Africa.* London: Robson Books Limited.
9. Guelke, A. 1993. Sport and the End of Apartheid. In L. Allison (ed.). *The changing politics of sport,* 151-170. Manchester: Manchester University Press.
10. Merrett, C. 2003. Sport and nationalism in post-liberation South Africa in the 1990s: Transcendental euphoria or nation building? *Sport History Review,* 34(1): 33-59.

11 Booth, D. 1997. The South African Council on Sport and the political antinomies of the sports boycott. *Journal of Southern African Studies*, 23(1): 51-66.
12 Booth, D. 1998. *The race game: Sport and politics in South Africa.* Abingdon, Oxon: Frank Cass Publishers.
13 Guelke, 1993.
14 Burnett, C. 2010. The role of the state in sport for development: South African scenario management and marketing. *African Journal for Physical Health Education, Recreation and Dance*, 16(1): 44-55.
15 Steenveld, L. & Strelitz, L. 1998. The 1995 Rugby World Cup and the politics of nation-building in South Africa. *Media, Culture & Society*, 20(4): 609-629.
16 Burnett, C. 2011. Local agency as a strategic imperative in sport for development. *African Journal for Physical Health Education, Recreation and Dance*, 17(si-2): 917-926.
17 Green, M. & Oakley, B. 2001. Elite sport development systems and playing to win: uniformity and diversity in international approaches. *Leisure studies*, 20(4): 247-267.
18 De Bosscher, V., Shilbury, D., Theeboom, M., Van Hoecke, J. & De Knop, P. 2011. Effectiveness of national elite sport policies: A multidimensional approach applied to the case of Flanders. *European Sport Management Quarterly*, 11(2): 115-141.
19 Gulbin, J. & Weissensteiner, J. 2013. Functional sport expertise systems. In D. Farrow, J. Baker & C. MacMahon (eds.). *Developing Sport Expertise: Researchers and coaches put theory into practice*. Abingdon, Oxon: Routledge, pp. 45-67.
20 Republic of South Africa. 1998a. *South African Sports Commission Act 1998*. Available at: https://www.gov.za/sites/default/files/gcis_document/201409/a109-98.pdf
21 Republic of South Africa. 1998b. *National Sports and Recreation Act 1998*. Available at: https://www.gov.za/sites/default/files/gcis_document/201409/a110-98.pdf
22 Burnett, 2011.
23 Ministerial Task Team on Sport. 2002. *Ministerial Task Team on Sport: A High-Performance Sports System for South Africa*. Available at: https://www.gov.za/sites/default/files/gcis_document/201409/sport1.pdf
24 Sport and Recreation South Africa (SRSA). 2009. *Draft strategy for delivery of integrated support services for priority sport codes in advance of 2012 and beyond*. Unpublished document. Pretoria: Sport and Recreation South Africa.
25 Sport and Recreation South Africa (SRSA). 2012b. *The White Paper on Sport and Recreation for the Republic of South Africa*. Available at: https://www.gov.za/sites/default/files/gcis_document/201409/white-paper-sport-and-recreation-june-201110.pdf
26 Sport and Recreation South Africa (SRSA). 2012a. *National Sport and Recreation Plan*. Available at: https://www.gov.za/sites/default/files/gcis_document/201409/nasional-sport-and-recretion-plan-draft-200.pdf
27 Sport and Recreation South Africa (SRSA). 2012c. *Transformation Charter for South African Sport*. Available at: https://www.westerncape.gov.za/text/2011/8/transformation_charter_with_scorecard_-_draft_7_11_july_2011.pdf
28 Sport and Recreation South Africa (SRSA), 2012b.
29 Ferkins, L. & Shilbury, D. 2012. Good boards are strategic: What does that mean for sport governance? *Journal of Sport Management*, 26(1): 67-80.
30 Zulman Commission. 2018. *Final Report of The Ministerial Committee Appointed to Investigate Alleged Irregularities or Malpractices in the Governance and Management of the South African Sports Confederation and Olympic Committee (SASCOC)*. Available at: https://static.pmg.org.za/190212SASCOCReport.pdf
31 Ibid.
32 SASCOC. 2022. *SASCOC Constitution*. Available at: https://www.teamsa.co.za/constitution/
33 Sport and Recreation South Africa (SRSA). 2020. *National Sport and Recreation Amendment Bill, 2020*. Available at: https://www.gov.za/sites/default/files/gcis_document/201912/bill-b-2020.pdf
34 Sport and Recreation South Africa (SRSA), 2009.
35 Sport and Recreation South Africa (SRSA), 2012a.
36 Sport and Recreation South Africa (SRSA). 2007. *Vote 18: Sport and Recreation South Africa*. Available at: https://www.treasury.gov.za/documents/national%20budget/2007/ene/18%20sport.pdf
37 Ibid.

38 Ibid.
39 Burnett, 2010.
40 Sport and Recreation South Africa (SRSA), 2007
41 Labuschagne, P. 2008. The impact of sport on nation building: A critical analysis of South Africa and the 2010 FIFA World Cup. *Africa Insight*, 38(3): 3-14.
42 Burnett, 2010.
43 University Sport South Africa (USSA). 2017. *The History of a Unified Student Sport Movement in South Africa*. Available at: http://ussa.org.za/1history.php
44 Ministerial Task Team on Sport, 2002.
45 Department of Sport and Recreation. 2009. *Sport and Recreation White Paper*, 2009.
46 Sport and Recreation South Africa (SRSA), 2009.
47 Burnett, 2010.
48 SASCOC, 2022.
49 National Government of South Africa. 2023. *South African Local Government Association (SALGA)*. Available at: https://nationalgovernment.co.za/units/view/171/south-african-local-government-association-salga#:~:text=SALGA%20aims%20to%20ensure%20that,of%20space%2C%20economies%20and%20people.
50 Department of Basic Education (DBE). 2011. *Draft School Sport Policy for schools in South Africa*. Available at: https://www.gov.za/sites/default/files/gcis_document/201409/34830gon1025.pdf
51 Sport and Recreation South Africa (SRSA), 2012a
52 Department of Basic Education & Sport and Recreation South Africa. 2011. *Memorandum of Understanding between the Department of Basic Education and Sport and Recreation South Africa*. Available at: https://www.education.gov.za/Portals/0/Media/Parliamentary%20Questions/NA%201466%20MOU%20SRSA%20and%20DBE%202011.pdf?ver=2015-02-01-105825-940
53 Burnett, C. 2020. Key findings of a national study on school sport and physical education in South African public schools. *South African Journal for Research in Sport, Physical Education and Recreation*, 42(3): 43-60.

Chapter 5

1 Beutler, I. 2008. Sport serving development and peace: Achieving the goals of the United Nations through sport. *Sport in Society*, 11(4): 359-369. Doi: 10.1080/17430430802019227
2 Lindsey, I., Chapman, T. & Dudfield, O. 2020. Configuring relationships between state and non-state actors: A new conceptual approach for sport and development. *International Journal of Sport Policy and Politics*, 12(1): 127-146. Doi: 1080/19406940.2019
3 Sport for Development & Peace (SDP) IWG. 2008. *Harnessing the Power of Sport for Development and Peace: Recommendations to Governments*. Available at: https://www.sportanddev.org/sites/default/files/downloads/rtp_sdp_iwg_harnessing_the_power_of_sport_for_development_and_peace.pdf
4 Hayhurst, L.M. 2009. The power to shape policy: Charting sport for development and peace policy discourses. *International Journal of Sport Policy and Politics*, 1(2): 203-227. Doi: 10.1080/19406940902950739
See adoption of resolution. Available at: https://www.icsspe.org/system/files/UN%20%28A-RES-63-135%29%20Sport%20as%20a%20means%20to%20promote%20education%2C%20health%2C%20development%20and%20peace.pdf
5 Lindsey et al., 2020.
6 See overarching focused strategy of the IOC aiming to connecting people to Olympic values - everywhere, everyday. Available at: https://olympics.com/ioc/news/olympism-365-from-strategy-to-implementation
7 The author was involved in the development and presentation of the UN SDP Toolkit.
8 See National Sport and Recreation Plan https://www.gov.za/sites/default/files/gcis_document/201409/nasional-sport-and-recretion-plan-draft-200.pdf
9 Sport and Recreation South Africa (SRSA). 2013. *National Sport and Recreation Plan*. Pretoria: Sport and Recreation South Africa.

10 Burnett, C. & Hollander, W.J. 2006. *The impact of the Mass Participation Project of Sport and Recreation South Africa (Siyadlala) 2004/5*. Pretoria: Sport and Recreation South Africa.
11 Burnett, C. & Hollander, W.J. 2008. *The pre-impact assessment of the School Sport Mass Participation Project*. Johannesburg: University of Johannesburg, Department of Sport and Movement Studies.
12 Burnett, C. 2013. GIZ/YDF and youth as drivers of sport for development in the African context. *Journal of Sport for Development*, 1(1): 4-15. https://jsfd.files.wordpress.com/2020/08/burnett.giz_.ydf_.sfd_.in_.africa.pdf
13 MOU between DSAC and DBE as a revised document in 2017 after the initial MOU signed in 2012 https://www.gov.za/speeches/school-sports-30-may-2018-0000.
14 Sport and Recreation South Africa, 2013.
15 Caputo, E.L. & Reichert, F.F. 2020. Studies of physical activity and Covid-19 during the pandemic: a scoping review. *Journal of Physical Activity and Health*, 17(12): 1275-1284. Doi: 10.1123/jpah.2020-0406
16 Teare, G. & Taks, M. 2021. Exploring the impact of the Covid-19 pandemic on youth sport and physical activity participation trends. *Sustainability*, 13(4): 1744. Doi: 10.3390/su13041744.
17 Burnett, C. 2020. From policy to practice for school sport: Lessons from South Africa. *Journal of Physical Education and Sport*, 20(4): 1754-1761. Doi: 10.7752/jpes.2020.04238; Burnett, C. 2021. A national study on the state and status of physical education in South African public schools. *Physical Education and Sport Pedagogy*, 26(2): 179-196. Doi: 10.1080/17408989.2020.1792869
18 Collison, H. & Marchesseault, D. 2018. Finding the missing voices of Sport for Development and Peace (SDP): using a 'Participatory Social Interaction Research methodology and anthropological perspectives within African developing countries. *Sport in Society*, 21(2): 226-242. Doi: 10.1080/17430437.2016.1179732
19 Greco, G., Andriani, O., D'Arcangelo, E. & de Ronzi, R. 2022. Sports activities as primary prevention of youth deviant behaviours: an educational intervention research. *Journal of Physical Education and Sport*, *22*(2), 479-488. Doi: 10.7752/jpes.2022.02060
20 Coalter, F. & Taylor, J. 2010. *Sport-for-development impact study: A research initiative funded by Comic Relief and UK Sport and managed by International Development through Sport.* Stirling, UK: University of Stirling, p.1.
21 See listed documents that informed the definition as indicated in the text. Available at: http://www.sport-for-development.com/essentials?id=1#cat1
22 Coalter & Taylor 2010, p. 1.
23 Sherry, E., Schulenkorf, N., Seal, E., Nicholson, M. & Hoye, R. 2017. Sport-for-development in the South Pacific region: Macro-, meso-, and micro-perspectives. *Sociology of Sport Journal*, 34(4): 303-316. Doi: 10.1123/ssj.2017-0022
24 Sugden, J. & Tomlinson, A. 2017. *Sport and peace-building in divided societies: Playing with enemies*. London: Routledge.
25 Donnelly, P. 2008. Sport and human rights. *Sport in Society*, 11(4): 381-394. DOI: 10.1080/17430430802019326
26 Schulenkorf, N. & Spaaij, R. 2016. Commentary: Reflections on theory building in sport for development and peace. *International Journal for Sport Management and Marketing*, 16(1/2): 71-77. https://opus.lib.uts.edu.a
27 Coalter, F. 2013. *Sport for development: What game are we playing?* London: Routledge.
28 UNOSDP. 2014. *Sport for Development and Peace International Working Group*, Available at: https://www.un.org/sport/content/un-players/me/ (accessed 20 January 2023).
29 Sportanddev.org. 2023. United Nations Perspective on Sport and Development. Available from: http://www.sportanddev.org/sport-and-development/uns-perspective-sport-and-development
30 Front page of the SRSA 2011 National Sport Plan. Available at: https://www.globalgoals.org/news/sport-for-development-and-peace/
31 See Report on the International Year for Sport and Physical Education – Sport for a Better World (IYSPE). Available at: http://www.sportanddev.org/research-and-learning/resource-library/report-international-year-sport-and-physical-education-iyspe
32 See Report from SDP IWG. Available at: https://www.sportanddev.org/sites/default/files/downloads/rtp_sdp_iwg_harnessing_the_power_of_sport_for_development_and_peace.pdf
33 See TAFISA's Mission 2030 – Sport for a better world through sport for all. Available at: http://tafisa.org/sites/default/files/pdf/2018/TAFISA_Mission2030.pdf

34. Kidd, B. 2008. A new social movement: Sport for development and peace. *Sport in Society*, 11(4): 370-380. Doi: 10.1080/17430430802019268.
35. Kidd, B. 2011. Cautions, questions and opportunities in sport for development and peace. *Third World Quarterly*, 32(3): 161. Doi: 10.1080/01436597.2011.573948
36. Japan Sport Council (JSC). 2022. *Bridging the Divide in Sport and Sustainable Development: A guide for translating policy into practice and effective programme management.* Available at: https://www.iir.jpnsport.go.jp/en/sdgs/#page=1 and various relevant sections on the sportanddev.org platform, pp. 30 & 31.
37. MINEPS VI, the sixth International Conference of Ministers and Senior Officials Responsible for Physical Education and Sport (MINEPS VI) - Kazan, Russian Federation - 13-15 July 2017. Available at: https://en.unesco.org/mineps6
38. Japan Sport Council (JSC) & International Platform on Sport and Development (sportanddev). 2022. *Bridging the Divide in Sport and Sustainable Development.* Available at: https://www.iir.jpnsport.go.jp/en/sdgs/#page=1 and various relevant sections on the sportanddev.org platform, pp. 30 & 31.
39. See UNGA. 2018. *Strengthening the Global Framework for Leveraging Sport for Development and Peace. Report of the Secretary-General*, A/73/325. Available at: https://undocs.org/A/73/325
40. Commonwealth Secretariat Indicator Bank and Toolkit Available at: https://production-new-commonwealth-files.s3.eu-west-
41. World Health Organization (WHO). 2018. *Global Action Plan on Physical Activity 2018-2030*. Available at: https://apps.who.int/iris/bitstream/handle/10665/272722/9789241514187-eng.pdf
42. See information about GBEM programme and guidebook from UNICEF South Africa. Available at: https://www.unicef.org/southafrica/reports/i-am-my-sisters-brothers-keeper. Also see link to Fit4Life programme from UNESCO. Available at: https://www.unesco.org/en/fit4life
43. Nols, Z., Haudenhuyse, R., Spaaij, R. & Theeboom, M. 2019. Social change through an urban sport for development initiative? Investigating critical pedagogy through the voices of young people. *Sport, Education and Society,* 24(7): 727-741. Doi: 10.1080/13573322.2018.1459536
44. Darnell, S.C., Chawansky, M., Marchesseault, D., Holmes, M. & Hayhurst, L. 2018. The state of play: Critical sociological insights into recent sport for development and peace research. *International Review for the Sociology of Sport*, 53(2): 133-151. Doi: 10.1177/1012690216646
45. Coalter, 2013.
46. Schulenkorf, N., Sugden, J. & Burdsey, D. 2014. Sport for development and peace as contested terrain: Place, community, ownership. *International Journal of Sport Policy and Politics*, 6(3): 371-387. Doi: 10.1080/19406940.2013.825875
47. Sherry et al., 2017.
48. Burnett, C. 2023. Issues of gender in sport leadership: reflections from Sub-Saharan Africa. *Third World Quarterly*, 44(1): 1-21. Doi: 10.1080/01436597.2022.2121694
49. Burnett, C. 2022. Employability pathways in a sport-for-development programme for girls in a Sub-Saharan impoverished setting. *Journal of Physical Education and Sport*, 22(4): 863-869. Doi: 10.7752/jpes.2022.04109
50. Mxekezo-Lallie, K.B. & Burnett, C. 2022. The value of volunteering in pursuit of improved employability in the sport for development sector: a case study in sub-Saharan Africa. *South African Journal for Research in Sport, Physical Education & Recreation*, 44(2): 53-62. Doi: 10.36386/sajrsper.v44i2
51. Guest, A.M. 2009. The diffusion of development-through-sport: Analysing the history and practice of the Olympic Movement's grassroots outreach to Africa. *Sport in Society*, 12(10): 1336-1352. Doi: 10.1080/17430430903204868
52. Coalter, 2013.
53. Darnell et al., 2018.
54. Laureus Sport for good Foundation South Africa. 2019. *Sport for development in South Africa: A systematic review of the field.* Available at: http://www.sportanddev.org/sites/default/files/downloads/systematic_review_final.pdf
55. Langer, L. 2015. Sport for development–a systematic map of evidence from Africa, *South African Review of Sociology*, 46(1): 66-86. Doi: 10.1080/21528586.2014.989665
56. Swanson, S., Collison, H., Burnett, C., Skinner, J. & Meeks, V. 2021. *Sport for Development and Olympic Movement Stakeholders: A Social Network Analysis.* Report for the IOC Olympic Studies Centre Advanced Olympic Research Grant Programme 2019/2020 Award.

57 Giulianotti, R. 2011. Sport, peace-making and conflict resolution: a contextual analysis and modelling of the sport, development and peace sector. *Ethnic and Racial Studies*, 34(2): 207-228. Doi: 10.1080/01419870.2010.522245
58 Lindsey et al., 2020.
59 Kidd, 2008.
60 Laureus Sport for Good - South Africa. 2023. *Laureus Fast Facts: Statement about the organisation*. Available at: https://www.laureus.co.za
61 See Annual Report of Laureus South Africa where 28 organisations feature and benefited through their partnership with Laureus Sport for Good South Africa. Available: https://www.laureus.com/sport-for-good/south-africa
62 See website for more information. Available at: http://www.sscn.co.za
63 National Youth Service. 2021. A Programme of the Presidential Youth Employment Intervention led by the National Youth Development Agency (NYDA). Request for Proposals. Unpublished document, p. 2.

Chapter 6

1 Barcelona, R., Wells, M. & Arthur-Banning, S. 2015. *Recreational sport: program design, delivery, and management*. Champaign, IL: Human Kinetics.
2 Mull, R., Bayless, K., Ross, C. & Jamieson, L. 1997. *Recreational Sport Management*. Champaign, IL: Human Kinetics.
3 Kelly, J.R. 2012. *Leisure*. Urbana, IL: Sagamore Publishing.
4 Leitner, M.J. & Leitner, S.F. 2012. *Leisure enhancement*. Urbana, IL: Sagamore Publishing.
5 Lewis, 2003.
6 McLean, D. & Hurd, A. 2011. *Kraus' Recreation and Leisure in Modern Society*. Burlington, MA: Jones and Bartlett Publishers.
7 Rossman, J.R. & Schlatter, B.E. 2008. *Recreation programming: designing leisure experiences* (5th ed.). Champaign, IL: Sagamore Publishing.
8 Parr, M.G. & Lashua, B.D. 2004. What is leisure? The perceptions of recreation practitioners and others. *Leisure Sciences*, 26(1): 1-17.
9 Edginton, C.R. & Chen, P. 2008. *Leisure as transformation*. Champaign, IL: Sagamore Publishing.
10 Floyd, M.F. & Mowatt, R.A. 2014. Leisure among African Americans. In M. Stodolska, K. Shinew, M. Floyd and G. Walker (eds.). *Race, ethnicity, and leisure*. Champaign, IL: Human Kinetics, pp. 53-75.
11 Fox, K., McAvoy, L., Wang, X. & Henhawk, D.A. 2014. Leisure among Alaskan Natives, American Indians, First Nations, Inuit, Métis, Native Hawaiians, and Other Pacific Islanders. In M. Stodolska, K. Shinew, M. Floyd and G. Walker (eds.). *Race, ethnicity, and leisure*. Champaign, IL: Human Kinetics, pp. 111-128.
12 Heintzman, P. & Stodolska, M. 2014. Leisure among Religious Minorities. In M. Stodolska, K. Shinew, M. Floyd, and G. Walker (eds.). *Race, ethnicity, and leisure*. Champaign, IL: Human Kinetics, pp. 129-150.
13 Stodolska, M. & Shinew, K.J. 2014. Leisure among Latino Americans. In M. Stodolska, K. Shinew, M. Floyd, and G. Walker (eds.). *Race, ethnicity, and leisure*. Champaign, IL: Human Kinetics, pp. 75-96.
14 Walker, G.L. & Deng, J. 2014. Leisure among Asian North Americans. In M. Stodolska, K. Shinew, M. Floyd, and G. Walker (eds.). *Race, ethnicity, and leisure*. Champaign, IL: Human Kinetics, pp. 97-109.
15 Chick, G. 1998. Leisure and culture: issues for an anthropology of leisure. *Leisure Sciences*, 20: 111-133.
16 Edginton, C.R., Hanson, C.J., Edginton, S. & Hudson, S.D. 2004. *Leisure programming: a service-centred and benefits approach* (4th ed.). New York: McGraw-Hill.
17 Veal, A.J. 1992. Definitions of leisure and recreation. *Australian Journal of Leisure and Recreation*, 2(4): 44-48, 52. Republished by School of Leisure, Sport and Tourism, University of Technology, Sydney, as Working Paper No. 4, http://www.business.uts.edu.au/lst/research. Date of access: 29 April, 2023.
18 Chick, 1998.
19 Clawson, M. & Knetsch, J.L. 2013. *Economics of Outdoor Recreation* (2nd ed.). New York, NY: Routledge.
20 Goodin, R.E., Rice, J.M., Bittman, M. & Saunders, P. 2005. The time-pressure illusion: discretionary time vs. free time. *Social Indicators Research*, 73(1): 43-70.

21 Henderson, K.A. 2010. Importance of Leisure to individuals and society. In Human Kinetics (eds.). *Dimensions of leisure for life*. Champaign, IL: Human Kinetics, pp. 3-26.
22 Kelly, 2012.
23 Lewis, 2003.
24 Kelly, 2012.
25 Kelly, J.R. & Freysinger, V.J. 2000. *21st Century Leisure: Current Issues*. Boston, MA: Allyn and Bacon.
26 Lewis, 2003.
27 Csikszentmihalyi, M. 1975. *Beyond boredom and anxiety*. San Francisco, CA: Jossey Bass.
28 Peterson, 2004.
29 Recours, R.A., Souville, M. & Griffet, J. 2004. Expressed motives for informal and club/association-based sports participation. *Journal of Leisure Research*, 36(1): 1-22.
30 Ryan, R.M. & Deci, E.L. 2000. Self-determination theory and the facilitation of intrinsic motivation, social development, and well-being. *American Psychologist*, 55(1): 68-78..
31 Ntoumanis, N., Pensgaard, A.-M., Martin, C. & Pipe, K. 2004. An idiographic analysis of amotivation in compulsory school physical education. *Journal of Sport and Exercise Psychology*, 26(2): 197-214.
32 Rossman & Schlatter, 2008.
33 Barcelona, Wells & Arthur-Banning, 2015.
34 Edginton, Hanson, Edginton & Hudson, 2004.
35 Russell, R.V. & Jamieson, L.M. 2008. *Leisure program planning and delivery*. Champaign, IL: Human Kinetics.
36 Ibid.
37 Edginton, Hanson, Edginton & Hudson, 2004.
38 Schneider, I.E. & Kivel, B.D. 2016. *Diversity and inclusion in the recreation profession: organizational perspectives* (3rd ed.). Champaign, IL: Sagamore Publishing.
39 Woods, R.B. 2011. *Social issues in sport* (2nd ed.). Champaign, IL: Human Kinetics.
40 Barcelona, Wells & Arthur-Banning, 2015.
41 Ibid.
42 Ibid.
43 Edginton, Hanson, Edginton & Hudson, 2004.
44 Driver, B.L. & Bruns, D.H. 1999. Concepts and uses of the benefits approach to leisure. In E.L. Jackson and T.L. Burton (eds.). *Leisure studies: Prospects for the twenty-first century*. State College, PA: Venture Publishing, pp. 349-369.
45 Bocarro, J.N. & Kanters, M.A. 2010. Leisure, health, and physical activity. In *Human Kinetics. Dimensions of leisure for life*. Champaign, IL: Human Kinetics, pp. 67-87.
46 Kanters, M.A. 2000. Recreational sport participation as a moderator of college stress. *Recreational Sports Journal*, 24(2): 11-24.
47 Belch, H.A., Gebel, M. & Maas, G.M. 2001. Relationship between student recreation complex use, academic performance, and persistence of first-time freshmen. *NASPA Journal*, 38(2): 254-268.
48 Caldwell, L.L. 2005. Leisure and health: why is leisure therapeutic? *British Journal of Guidance & Counselling*, 33(1): 7-26.
49 Morton, S., Mergler, A. & Boman, P. 2014. Managing the transition: the role of optimism and self-efficacy for first-year Australian university students. *Journal of Psychologists and Counsellors in Schools*, 24(1): 90-108..
50 Villatte, A., Marcotte, D. & Potvin, A. 2017. Correlates of depression in first-year college students. *Canadian Journal of Higher Education*, 47(1): 114-136.
51 Edginton, Hanson, Edginton & Hudson, 2004.
52 Ibid.
53 Crawford, D.W. & Godbey, G. 1987. Reconceptualizing barriers to family leisure. *Leisure Sciences*, 9(2): 119-127.
54 Crawford, D.W., Jackson, E.L. & Godbey, G. 1991. A hierarchical model of leisure constraints. *Leisure Sciences*, 13(4): 309-320.
55 Jackson, E.L. 1993. Recognizing patterns of leisure constraints: Results from alternative analyses. *Journal of Leisure Research*, 25(2): 129-129.
56 Jackson, 1993.

Chapter 7

1. Van den Berg, L, Jonck, P & Surujlal, J. 2021. Investigating the Youth Sports Development Pathway Within a South African Context. *Frontiers in Psychology*, 12. Available from: https://www.frontiersin.org/articles/10.3389/fpsyg.2021.694548/full
2. Burnett, C. 2021. Trends in sport participation at South African universities. *African Journal for Physical Activity and Health Science*, 4(12), 12–24. http://dx.doi.org/10.4314/ajpherd.v16i4.64259
3. Hollings, S.C. 2013. *The Transition from Elite Junior Athlete to Successful Senior Athlete - Implications for Athletics High-Performance Programmes.* Doctoral thesis. Auckland: Auckland University of Technology.
4. Hardell, E. 2017. *Youth Sport Development Pathways and Experiences of NCAA Division I Women's College Soccer Players.* Ph.D. thesis. San Jose, CA: San Jose State University.
5. Cohen, L., Manion, L. & Morrison, K. 2018. *Research Methods in Education* (8th ed.). London: Routledge. https://doi.org/10.4324/9781315456539
6. Schlossberg, N.K. 2011. The challenge of change: the transition model and its applications. *Journal of Employment Counseling*, 48(4): 159. Available at: https://go.gale.com/ps/i.do?id=GALE%7CA275850105&sid=googleScholar&v=2.1&it=r&linkaccess=abs&issn=00220787&p=AONE&sw=w&userGroupName=anon%7Ec391e-67b&aty=open+web+entry
7. Balyi, I. & Way, R. 1998. 'Long-term Planning for Athlete Development: the training to train phase', *Faster, Higher, Stronger*, 1: pp. 8–11.
8. Department of Sport, Arts and Culture. 2022. Home Page. Available from: http://www.dac.gov.za/
9. van den Berg, L., Jonck, P. & Surujlal, J. 2021. Investigating the Youth Sports Development Pathway Within a South African Context. *Frontiers in Psychology*, 12: 694548. https://doi.org/10.3389/fpsyg.2021.694548
10. Balyi, Way & Hicks, 1998.
11. Balyi, Way & Hicks, 1998.
12. Van Zyl, L.J. 2018. *Challenges of transitioning from school to senior level athletics in South Africa.* Unpublished MEd dissertation, University of Pretoria.
13. Sabato, T.M., Walch, T.J. & Caine, D.J. 2016. The elite young athlete: strategies to ensure physical and emotional health. *Journal of Sports Medicine*, 7: 99-113.
14. Sabato, Walch & Caine, 2016: p. 76.
15. van den Berg, Jonck & Surujlal, 2021.

Chapter 8

1. World Health Organisation. 2002. *Towards a Common Language for Functioning, Disability and Health ICF*, p. 2. Available at: https://www.who.int/standards/classifications/international-classification-of-functioning-disability-and-health
2. World Health Organisation. 2001. *International Classification of Functioning, Disability and Health*. Geneva. Available at: https://www.who.int/standards/classifications/international-classification-of-functioning-disability-and-health
3. World Health Organisation, 2002: 8.
4. Ibid, 9.
5. Ibid, 11.
6. GT Independence. 2020. *A Quick History of Disability Rights*. Available at: https://gtindependence.com/a-quick-history-of-disability-treat-ment/#:~:text=The%20first%20recorded%20reference%20to,with%20disabilities%20were%20publicly%20persecuted
7. Office of the Deputy President. 1997. *Integrated National Disability Strategy White Paper.* Available at: https://www.gov.za/sites/default/files/gcis_document/201409/disability2.pdf
8. Human Rights Commission. 2022. *Disability*. Available at: https://www.sahrc.org.za/index.php/focus-areas/disability-older-persons/disability

9 Integrated National Disability Strategy, 1997: 55.
10 Ibid, 36.
11 Collins Dictionary. 2023. *Definition of "Amakrokokroko"*. Available at: https://www.collinsdictionary.com/dictionary/english/amakrokokroko#:~:text=Amakrokokroko%20in%20British%20English,Collins%20English%20Dictionary
12 Craigieburn Secondary College. n.d. *Comparative essay Years 7 – 9: Compare the Ancient and Modern Olympics*. Available at: https://lms.craigieburnsc.vic.edu.au/pluginfile.php/8497/mod_resource/content/0/Comparative%20essay%20Yrs%207%20-%20%209.pdf
13 Burchell, A., Jarvis, P., Legg, D. & Sainsbury, T. 2008. The Athletic Ability Debate: Have we reached a tipping point? *Palaestra 25*(1): 19-25.
14 Deaflympics, 2023a. *About the ICSD*. Available at: https://www.deaflympics.com/icsd
15 Deaflympics. 2023c. *Timeline*. Available at: https://www.deaflympics.com/icsd/time-line
16 Ibid.
17 National Paralympic Heritage Trust. n.d. *Professor Sir Ludwig Guttman*. Available at: https://www.paralympicheritage.org.uk/professor-sir-ludwig-guttmann
18 World Abilitysport. 2023. *History*. Available at: https://iwasf.com/about/who-we-are/history/ and https://worldabilitysport.org/about/who-we-are/history/
19 International Paralympic Committee. n.d. *Paralympics History*. Available at: https://www.paralympic.org/ipc/history#:~:text=On%2029%20July%201948%2C%20the,who%20took%20part%20in%20archery
20 Special Olympics. 2023a. *History*. Available at: https://www.specialolympics.org/about/history/the-beginning-of-a-worldwide-movement?locale=en
21 Special Olympics. 2023b. *Sports Partnerships: International Olympic Committee and others*. Available at: https://www.specialolympics.org/get-involved/sports-partnerships/international-olympic-committee#:~:text=In%20a%20Protocol%20Agreement%20signed,individuals%20with%20an%20intellectual%20disability
22 World Abilitysport, 2023.
23 International Blind Sports Federation. n.d. *History*. Available at: https://ibsasport.org/about/who-we-are/history/
24 Virtus. n.d. *We are Sports*. Available at: https://www.virtus.sport/about-virtus
25 Deaflympics. 2023b. *The World Games for the Deaf and the Paralympic Games*. Available at: http://www.ciss.org/the-world-games-for-the-deaf-and-the-paralympic-games
26 Inside the Games. 2023a. *World Abilitysport formed after IWAS and CPISRA merger*. Available at: https://www.insidethegames.biz/articles/1135951/world-abilitysport-iwas-cpisra
27 Union of International Associations. 2022a. *Global Civil Society Database: International Wheelchair Tennis Federation*. Available at: https://uia.org/s/or/en/1100045054
28 International Olympic Committee. 2021. *New Structures for IPC*. Available at: https://olympics.com/ioc/news/new-structures-for-ipc
29 World Archery. 2023. *Disciplines: Para Archery*. Available at: https://www.worldarchery.sport/sport/disciplines/para-archery#:~:text=World%20Archery%20organises%20a%20para,world%20ranking%20of%20para%20archers
30 Cycling South Africa. 2021. *Para-Cycling*. Available at: https://www.cyclingsa.com/para-cycling/
31 Fédération Équestre Internationale. 2023. *Welcome to Para Dressage: History of Para-Equestrian within the FEI*. Available at: https://inside.fei.org/fei/disc/para-dressage#:~:text=Born%20from%20the%20desire%20to,disciplines%20regulated%20by%20the%20FEI
32 IInternational Canoe Federation. n.d. *Paracanoe*. Available at: https://www.canoeicf.com/disciplines/paracanoe
33 World Rowing. 2020. *A Short History of Para-Rowing*. Available at: https://worldrowing.com/wp-content/uploads/2020/12/AShortHistoryofPara-Rowing.pdf
34 World Taekwondo. n.d. *International Paralympic Committee*. Available at: http://www.worldtaekwondo.org/para-wt/para_about.html#:~:text=World%20Taekwondo%20PARA&text=In%202005%20the%20World%20Taekwondo,to%20athletes%20of%20all%20disabilities
35 World Triathlon. n.d. *About Para Triathlon*. Available at: https://triathlon.org/paratriathlon/about
36 World Boccia. 2014. *BISFed becomes the first international federation client of Sport*. Available at: https://www.worldboccia.com/2014/02/03/bisfed-become-first-international-federation-client-of-sport80/

37 International Federation of CP Football. 2023. *About IFCPF*. Available at: https://www.ifcpf.com/about-ifcpf
38 FIBA basketball. n.d. *FIBA Family: Wheelchair Basketball (IWBF)*. Available at: https://www.fiba.basketball/organisation/fiba-family/wheelchair-basketball
39 International Paralympic Committee. n.d. *History of Para-Badminton*. Available at: https://www.paralympic.org/badminton/about
40 Inside the Games. 2021a. *IPC to cease acting as an international federation for ten sports by the end of 2026*. Available at: https://www.insidethegames.biz/articles/1116688/paralympic-order-ipc-general-assembly
41 International Committee of Sports for the Deaf. 2023a. *South Africa*. Available at: http://www.ciss.org/countries/rsa
42 International Committee of Sports for the Deaf. 2023b. *Constitution*. Available at: http://www.ciss.org/icsd/constitution
43 South African Sports Association of Physically Disabled. n.d. *History*. Available at: https://www.sasapd.org.za/history/
44 Coetzee, G.J. 1989. *Betrokkenheid van Suid-Afrika by die Internasionale Stoke Mandeville-Spele (1962-1985)*. Unpublished dissertation, Stellenbosch: University of Stellenbosch, pp. 46–51.
45 Ibid, 46–51.
46 The Commonwealth Secretariat. 2023. *From the Archive: Gleneagles Agreement on Sport*. Available at: https://thecommonwealth.org/news/archive-gleneagles-agreement-sport
47 Tennis South Africa. 2017. *Wheelchair Tennis*. Available at: https://www.tennissa.co.za/w/wheelchair-tennis
48 Western Cape Government. 2013. Intellectually Impaired Sports Team Makes Western Cape Proud. Available at: https://www.westerncape.gov.za/news/intellectually-impaired-sports-team-makes-western-cape-proud
49 Special Olympics South Africa. n.d. *South Africa Fact Sheet*. Available at: https://media.specialolympics.org/resources/leading-a-program/program-profiles/SOA/South-Africa-FactSheet-2017.pdf?_ga=2.65140014.1635433565.1678515833-1035721515.1677388866
50 Special Olympics. 2023. *Special Olympics World Games Berlin Opening Ceremony Kicks Off World's Largest Sporting and Humanitarian Event in 2023*. Available at: https://www.specialolympics.org/about/press-releases/special-olympics-world-games-berlin-opening-ceremony-kicks-off-worlds-largest-sporting-and-humanitarian-event-in-2023?locale=en
51 Ibid.
52 Special Olympics South Africa. 2017. *South Africa Fact Sheet*. Available at: https://media.specialolympics.org/resources/leading-a-program/program-profiles/SOA/South-Africa-FactSheet-2017.pdf?_ga=2.65140014.1635433565.1678515833-1035721515.1677388866
53 Parliamentary Monitoring Group. 2003. *Presentation to the Portfolio Committee on Sport and Recreation*. Available at: https://pmg.org.za/docs/2003/appendices/030610dissa1.ppt
54 South African Sports Association of Physically Disabled, n.d.
55 ABC News. 2020. *Sydney Paralympians relive Spanish basketball cheating scandal*. Available at: https://www.abc.net.au/news/2020-10-27/sydney-2000-paralympics-spanish-basketball-cheating-scandal/12749156
56 International Paralympic Committee. 2007. *Annual Report*. Available at: https://www.paralympic.org/sites/default/files/document/120201081823082_2006_Annual_Report.pdf
57 Inside the Games. 2023b. *SASCOC hold a workshop to discuss Para sport inclusion in National Federations*. Available at: https://www.insidethegames.biz/articles/1133215/sascoc-para-sport-inclusion
58 Union of International Associations. 2022b. *Global Civil Society Database: African Paralympic Committee*. Available at: https://uia.org/s/or/en/1100021261
59 Novak, A. 2014. Disability Sport in Sub-Saharan Africa: From Economic Underdevelopment to Uneven Empowerment. *Disability and the Global South*, 1(1): 44-63. Available at: https://disabilityglobalsouth.files.wordpress.com/2012/06/dgs-01-01-04.pdf
60 Sport and Recreation South Africa. 2002. *Ministerial Task Team on Sport: A High-Performance Sports System for South Africa*. Available at: https://www.gov.za/sites/default/files/gcis_document/201409/sport1.pdf
61 International Paralympic Committee n.d.
62 The Presidency. n.d. *Zanele Situ*. Available at: https://www.thepresidency.gov.za/national-orders/recipient/zanele-situ-1971

63. EWN News. 2021. *Chasing medals with Ernst van Dyk.* Available at: https://ewn.co.za/2021/10/12/chasing-medals-with-ernst-van-dyk
64. Team South Africa. n.d. *Ernst van Dyk.* Available at: https://www.teamsa.co.za/ernst-van-dyk/
65. Bleacher Report. 2012. *Blade Runner Oscar Pistorius a Symbol of Spirit Worldwide.* Available at: https://bleacherreport.com/articles/1195225-blade-runner-oscar-pistorius-a-symbol-of-spirit-worldwide
66. Players' Bio. 2022. *12 Tallest Basketball Players in the World.* Available at: https://playersbio.com/tallest-basketball-players/#:~:text=on%20the%20court.-,1.,Cleveland%20Cavaliers%20in%20the%20NBA
67. Coetzee, 1989: 46–51.
68. Roussow, C.C. 1974-1988. unpublished notes, Annual General Meetings documents of SASAPD from 1974 to 1988, class notes including "Die storie van hoe dit alles gebeur het……."
69. Ibid.
70. Ibid.
71. International Paralympic Committee. 2015. *IPC Athlete Classification Code: Rules, Policies and Procedures for Athlete Classification.* Available at: https://www.paralympic.org/sites/default/files/document/150813212311788_Classification+Code_1.pdf
72. International Paralympic Committee. n.d. *IPC Classification: what is classification?* Available at: https://www.paralympic.org/classification
73. Ibid.
74. International Paralympic Committee n.d. *Eligible Impairment Types in the Paralympic Movement.* Available at: https://www.paralympic.org/classification
75. Virtus. 2023. *Athlete Eligibility Application Guidance Notes.* Available at: https://www.virtus.sport/wp-content/uploads/2022/01/Guidance-Notes-v12-JAN23.pdf
76. World Para Athletics. 2018. *Classification Rules and Regulations: 146.* Available at: https://www.paralympic.org/sites/default/files/document/180305152713114_2017_12_20++WPA+Classification+Rules+and+Regulations_Edition+2018+online+version+.pdf
77. Ibid.
78. Special Olympics. n.d. *Division - Fact Sheet.* Available at: https://media.specialolympics.org/resources/sports-essentials/divisioning/Divisioning-Fact-Sheet.pdf?_ga=2.132813838.1635433565.1678515833-1035721515.1677388866
79. International Committee of Sports for the Deaf. 2018. Audiogram regulations. Available at: http://www.deaflympics.com/pdf/AudiogramRegulations.pdf
80. International Paralympic Committee. n.d. *IPC highlights from the first 25 years.* Available at: https://www.paralympic.org/ipc-25-year-anniversary/history
81. International Olympic Committee. 2018. *IOC and IPC to partner until 2032.* Available at: https://olympics.com/ioc/news/ioc-and-ipc-to-partner-until-2032
82. Mallon, W. 2000. The Olympic Bribery Scandal. *Journal of Olympic History,* 8(2): 11-27. Available at: http://isoh.org/wp-content/uploads/2015/04/93.pdf May 2000
83. Inside the Games. 2021b. *Saudi Arabia's NOC and NPC merge to form Saudi Olympic and Paralympic Committee.* Available at: https://www.insidethegames.biz/articles/1117069/saudi-arabia-noc-npc
84. Special Olympics. 2023. *Sports Partnerships.* Available at: https://www.specialolympics.org/get-involved/sports-partnerships?locale=en
85. International Olympic Committee. 2023. *Tokyo 2020.* Available at: https://olympics.com/en/olympic-games/tokyo-2020
86. Commonwealth Games Federation. 2023. *Para Sports.* Available at: https://www.commonwealthsport.com/about/para-sports

Chapter 9

1. Doherty, A. 2013. Investing in sport management: The value of good theory. *Sport Management Review,* 16(1): 5-11.
2. Chelladurai, P. 1987. Multidimensionality and Multiple Perspectives of Organizational Effectiveness. *Journal of Sport Management,* 1(1): 37-47.
3. Trenberth, L. & Hassan, D. 2013. *Managing Sport Business: An Introduction* (1st ed.). Oxon: Routledge.
4. Nienhüser, W. 2008. Resource dependence theory: How well does it explain behavior of organizations? *Management Revue,* 19(1-2): 9-32.
5. PMG. 2021. *Parliamentary Monitoring Group.* Available at: https://pmg.org.za/committee-meeting/32324/ [Accessed 24 March 2023].
6. Sam, M. 2009. The public management of sport: Wicked problems, challenges and dilemmas. *Public Management Review,* 11(4): 499-514.
7. Parent, M. & O'Brien, D. 2018. Organisation theory and sport management. In: D. Hassan, ed. *Managing Sport Business: An introduction.* London: Routledge, p. 179.
8. O'Brien, D., Parent, M.M., Ferkins, L. & Gowthorp, L. 2019. *Strategic Management in Sport,* (1st ed.). London: Taylor & Francis.
9. O'Brien, D. & Gowthorp, L., 2017. Organizational structure. In: R. Hoye & M. M. Parent, eds. *Handbook of sport management.* London: SAGE, pp. 39-61.
10. Motorsport South Africa. 2023. *About Motorsport South Africa.* Available at: https://eolstoragewe.blob.core.windows.net/wm-553616-cmsimages/MSAOrganogram01.02.2019.pdf [Accessed 21 March 2023].
11. Daft, R.L. 2008. *Organization Theory & Design* (10th ed.). Mason: Cengage Learning.
12. Gravity Media. 2023. *Production Facilities For ICC Cricket World Cup.* Available at: https://www.gravitymedia.com/projects/icc-cricket-world-cup/ [Accessed 31 March 2023].
13. Shaban, A.R.A. 2018. *South Africa football violence: Major facts of Kaizer Chiefs stadium riot.* Available at: https://www.africanews.com/2018/04/25/south-africa-football-violence-major-facts-of-kaizer-chiefs-stadium-riot// [Accessed 12 April 2023].
14. O'Brien, et al., 2019: 4.
15. Clegg, S.R., Pitelis, C., Schweitzer, J. & Whittle, A. 2020. *Strategy: Theory and Practice* (3rd ed.). London: SAGE.
16. SA Rugby. n.d.. *Strategic Transformation Charter 2030.* Available at: https://www.sarugby.co.za/media/q03hxfmw/strategic-transformation-development-plan-2030-cycle-1.pdf [Accessed 23 February 2023].
17. Ibid.
18. eNCA. 2013. *Puma drops Safa partnership.* Available at: https://www.enca.com/sport-soccer/puma-drops-safa-partnership [Accessed 13 February 2023].
19. UK Sport. 2023. *A Code for Sports Governance.* Available at: https://www.uksport.gov.uk/resources/a-code-for-sports-governance [Accessed 19 March 2023].
20. De Aragao, M.M. 2015. *ScholarWorks at WMU.* Available at: https://scholarworks.wmich.edu/cgi/viewcontent.cgi?article=3609&context=honors_theses [Accessed 16 May 2023].
21. SA Rugby, n.d.
22. Liu, Y. & Yin, J. 2020. Stakeholder Relationships and Organizational Resilience. *Management and Organization Review,* 16(5): 986-990.
23. Sotiriadou, P. 2009. The Australian sport system and its stakeholders: Development of cooperative relationships. *Sport in Society,* 12(7): 842-860.
24. Leidecker, J.K. & Bruno, A.V. 1984. Identifying and using Critical Success Factors. *Long Range Planning,* 17(1): 23-32.
25. Parmenter, D. 2019. *Key Performance Indicators: Developing, Implementing, and Using Winning KPIs* (4th ed.). Hoboken: Wiley & Sons.
26. Ibid, 10-11.

Chapter 10

1. Delport, P. 2016. *Henochsberg on the Companies Act 71 of 2008.* Durban: LexisNexis.
2. Cloete, R. (ed). 2005. *Introduction to Sports Law in South Africa.* Durban: LexisNexis.
3. Gardiner, S. 2012. *Sports Law* (4th ed.). London: Routledge.
4. Cloete, R. (ed). 2005. *Introduction to Sports Law in South Africa.* Durban: LexisNexis.
5. Ibid.
6. Ibid; Gardiner, 2012.
7. Gardiner, 2012.
8. Institute of Directors South Africa. 2016. *King IV Report™ and the Code™.* Available at: https://www.iodsa.co.za/page/king-iv
9. Cloete, 2005.
10. Louw, A.M. 2010. *Sports Law in South Africa.* Alphen aan den Rijn Wolters Kluwer.
11. Ibid.
12. Basson, J.A.A. & Loubser, M.M. 2000. *Sports and the Law in South Africa.* Durban: LexisNexis.
13. Cloete, 2005.
14. Ibid.
15. Davis, D. (ed). 2013. *Companies and other Business Structures in South Africa.* Cape Town Oxford University Press.
16. Institute of Directors South Africa. 2016.
17. South African Government. 2008. *Companies Act 71 of 2008.* Available at: https://www.gov.za/documents/companies-act
18. Delport, 2016.
19. Ibid.
20. Ibid.
21. Louw, 2010.
22. Ibid.
23. Ibid.
24. Basson & Loubser, 2000.
25. Southern African Legal Information Institute (SAFLII). 2018. *Ndoro and Another v South African Football Association and Others* [2018] 3 All SA 277 (GJ) 282 par 26. Available at: http://www.saflii.org/za/cases/ZAGPJHC/2018/74.html
26. Gardiner, 2012.
27. Louw, 2010.
28. South African Government. 2010. *Safety at Sports and Recreational Events Act 2 of 2010.* Available from: https://www.gov.za/documents/safety-sports-and-recreational-events-act
29. Blackshaw, I. 2013. Match fixing in sport: a top priority and ongoing challenge for sports governing bodies. *De Jure,* 46(4): 945.
30. South African Government. *South African Institute for Drug-Free Sport Act 14 of 1997.* Available from: https://www.gov.za/documents/south-african-institute-drug-free-sport-act#:~:text=to%20promote%20the%20participation%20in,and%20well%2Dbeing%20of%20sportspersons%3B
31. Cloete, 2005.
32. Ibid.
33. Botha, M.M. 2008. Can whistle-blowing be an effective good governance tool? *THRHR Journal of Contemporary Roman-Dutch Law,* 71: 482.
34. Landman, A. 2001. Charter for whistle blowers – a note on the Protected Disclosure Act 26 of 2000. *Industrial Law Journal,* 22 /Lj: 37.
35. South African Government. 2013. *Protection of Personal Information Act 4 of 2013.* Available at: https://www.gov.za/documents/protection-personal-information-act#:~:text=to%20provide%20for%20the%20issuing,provide%20for%20matters%20connected%20therewith.
36. Cloete, 2005.

Chapter 11

1. Hutchinson, D. & Pretorius, C. 2022. *The Law of Contract in South Africa.* Cape Town: Oxford University Press, p. 21.
2. Moodie, G. 2010. Stricter regulations loom for SA sports broadcast rights. *Moneyweb.* Available at: http://www.moneyweb.co.za/moneyweb-soapbox/stricter-regulations-loom-for-sa-sports-broadcast
3. Klopper, H. & Van der Spuy, P. 2012. *Law of Intellectual Property.* Pretoria: AbeBooks.
4. Bruce, S. & McConnel, C. 2014. *Essentials of Economics.* Sydney: McGraw-Hill Education.
5. Ibid, 62.
6. Ibid, 62.
7. Miller, C. 2020. Scalping isn't scamming. In N.G. Mankew. *Principles of Macroeconomics.* Boston: Cengage Learning, p. 146.
8. Preuss, H. 2004. *The Economics of Staging the Olympics: A Comparison of the Games, 1972-2008.* Cheltenham: Edward Elgar Publishing, p. 232.
9. Healy, D. 2010. *Sport and the Law.* Sydney: UNSW Press, p. 143.
10. Neethling, J., Potgieter, J. & Knobel, J.C. 2021. *Law of Delict.* Durban: LexisNexis, p. 369 *ff.*
11. Epstein, M.A. & Politano, F.L. 2002. *Drafting Licence Agreements.* Aspen: Wolters Kluwer, p. 1-3.
12. Cloete, R. 2005. *Introduction to Sports Law in South Africa.* Durban: LexisNexis.
13. Nafziger, J. 2004. *International Sports Law.* Leiden: Brill, p. 172.
14. Schwartz, E.C. & Hunter, J.D. 2017. *Advanced Theory and Practice in Sports Marketing.* London: Taylor & Francis, p. 253.
15. Epstein, A. 2003. *Sports Law.* Boston: Cengage Learning, p. 252.
16. Schwartz & Hunter 2017:253.
17. Ferrand, A., Torrigiani, L. & Camps, A. 2006. *Routledge Handbook of Sports Sponsorship: Successful Strategies.* London: Routledge, p. 38.
18. Neethling, Potgieter & Knobel 2021:89.
19. Neethling, J. Pothieter, J. & Roos, A. 2019. *Neethling on Personality.* Durban: LexisNexis, p. 315.
20. Neethling, Potgieter & Knobel 2021:108.
21. Neethling, Potgieter & Roos 2019:110.
22. Ibid, 109-110.
23. Ibid, 109-110.
24. Cloete 2005:69 *ff.*
25. Neethling, Potgieter & Roos 2019:112.
26. Rubinkam, M. 2014. NFL to Remove $675 Million Cap on Concussion Damages. *Huffington Post.* Available at: http://www.huffingtonpost.com/2014/06/25/nfl-concussion-damages-remove-cap_n_5529916.html
27. Ibid.
28. Ibid.
29. Neethling, Potgieter & Roos 2019:112.
30. Ibid, 113.

Chapter 12

1. Burnett, C. 2019. Value of Sport in Post-Apartheid South Africa, *South African Journal for Research in Sport, Physical Education and Recreation,* 41(2): 11 - 27.
2. Davies, S.E.H. 2022. A Comparative Analysis of Financial and Employment Indicators at Volunteer Supported Events in the Western Cape Province, South Africa. *African Journal of Hospitality, Tourism and Leisure,* 11(4): 1301-1316. DOI: https://doi.org/10.46222/ajhtl.19770720.292.
3. Van den Berg, I., Cuskelly, G. & Auld, C. 2015. A comparative study between Australian and South African university sport students' volunteer motives and constraints. *African Journal for Physical, Health Education, Recreation and Dance,* November 2015 (Supplement 1): 127-141.

4   Compion, S., Cnaan, R.A., Brudney, J.L., Jeong, B.G., Chao Zhang, C. & Haski-Leventhal, D. 2021. 'Young, Fun, and Free:' Episodic Volunteers in Ghana, South Africa and Tanzania. *International Society for Third-Sector Research, Voluntas*. Available at: https://doi.org/10.1007/s11266-021-00324-y.
5   Davies, 2022.
6   Ibid.
7   Maralack, D., Jurgens, D. 2018. South Africa. In: Hallmann, K., Fairley, S. (eds) Sports Volunteers Around the Globe. *Sports Economics, Management and Policy*, vol 15. Cham: Springer. https://doi.org/10.1007/978-3-030-02354-6_19.
8   Cape Town Cycle Tour. 2021. *2021 Cape Town Cycle Tour*. Available at https://www.capetowncycletour.com/
9   Cape Epic. 2021. *ABSA Cape Epic*. Available at https://www.cape-epic.com/riders/new-riders/about-the-race.
10 Two Oceans Marathon. 2021. *Total Sports Two Oceans Marathon*. Available at https://www.twooceansmarathon.org.za/about-two-oceans/history/
11 Khoo, S.H., Surujlal, J. & Engelhorn, R. 2011. Motivation of volunteers at disability sports events: A comparative study of volunteers in Malaysia, South Africa and the United States. *African Journal for Physical, Health Education, Recreation and Dance,* 16(3): 447-461.
12 Davies, 2022.
13 Maralack & Jurgens, 2018.
14 Burnett, 2019.
15 Ibid.
16 Maralack & Jurgens, 2018
17 Compion et al., 2021.
18 Ibid.
19 Ibid.
20 Ibid.
21 Ibid.
22 Van den Berg, Cuskelly & Auld, 2015.
23 Khoo, Surujlal & Engelhorn, 2011.
24 Compion et al., 2021.
25 Ibid.
26 Van den Berg, Cuskelly & Auld, 2015.
27 Van der Klashorst, E. 2010. Exploring the economic, social and cultural rights of youth leaders working in Sport for Development initiatives at the grassroots level in South Africa. *Leisure Studies*, DOI: 10.1080/02614367.2017.1383504.
28 Burnett, 2019.
29 Maralack & Jurgens, 2018
30 Van den Berg, Cuskelly & Auld, 2015.
31 Compion et al., 2021.
32 Ibid.
33 Ibid.
34 Volunteering Barnet (VB). 2022. *The Future of Volunteering*. Available at: https://volunteeringbarnet.org.uk/the-future-of-volunteering/
35 Burnett, 2019.
36 Van den Berg, Cuskelly & Auld, 2015.
37 Ibid.
38 Maralack & Jurgens, 2018.
39 Republic of South Africa. 2012. *Sport and Recreation South Africa: National sport and recreation plan*. Pretoria: Government Printers.
40 Maralack & Jurgens, 2018.
41 Davies, 2022.
42 Krajňáková, E., Šimkus, A., Pilinkiene, V. & Grabowska, M. 2018. Analysis of barriers in sports volunteering. *Journal of International Studies,* 11(4): 254-269. doi:10.14254/2071-8330.2018/11-4/18.

43 Davies, 2022
44 Krajňáková et al., 2018.
45 Maralack & Jurgens 2018.
46 Van den Berg, Cuskelly & Auld, 2015.
47 Van der Klashorst, 2017;
48 Compion et al., 2021.
49 Compion et al., 2021.
50 Davies, 2022.
51 Van der Klashorst, 2017.
52 Burnett, 2019.

Chapter 13

1 South African Rugby. 2019. *Strategic Transformation Development Plan 2030*. Available at: https://www.sarugby.co.za/media/q03hxfmw/strategic-transformation-development-plan-2030-cycle-1.pdf.
2 Hoye, R., Smith, A.C., Nicholson, M. & Stewart, B. 2015. *Sport Management: Principles and Applications* (4th ed.). London: Routledge.
3 The South African Sports Confederation and Olympic Committee (SASCOC). 2019. *About us*. Available at: https://www.teamsa.co.za/about-us/#:~:text=SASCOC%20is%20South%20Africa's%20national,Games%20and%20Zone%20VI%20Games [Accessed 2023-05-30]
4 Sotiriadou, P. & De Bosscher, V. 2018. Managing high-performance sport: introduction to past, present and future considerations. *European Sport Management Quarterly*, 18(1): 1-7.
5 Ibid.
6 Department of Sports, Arts and Culture. 2020. *Strategic Plan 2020 – 2025*. Available at: http://www.dac.gov.za/sites/default/files/DSAC%20Strategic%20Plan%202020%20-%202025%20Final.pdf
7 The South African Sports Confederation and Olympic Committee (SASCOC). 2023. *SASCOC's operation excellence: The facts*. Available at: https://www.teamsa.co.za/sascocs-operation-excellence-the-facts/
8 Rudansky-Kloppers, S. 2015. *Principles of Sport Management*. Cape Town: Oxford University Press.
9 Hoye, Smith, Nicholson & Steward, 2015.
10 Rudansky-Kloppers, 2015.
11 Bill, K. (ed.). 2009. *Sport management. Learning Matters*. Available at: https://b-ok.africa/book/1125939/9959e0
12 Masteralexis, L.P., Barr, C.A. & Hums, A. 2019. *Principles and practice of sport management* (6th ed.). Louisville, Kentucky: Jones & Bartlett Learning.
13 Lussier, R.N. & Kimball, D.C. 2009. *Applied sport management skills*. Champaign, IL: Human Kinetics.
14 Bill, 2009.
15 Hoye, Smith, Nicholson & Steward, 2015.
16 Rudansky-Kloppers, 2015.

Chapter 14

1 SASCOC. 2011. *South African Coaching Framework*. Available at: https://www.teamsa.co.za/sa-coaching-framework/
2 South African National Planning Commission. 2013. *National Development Plan 2030*. Available at: https://www.gov.za/issues/national-development-plan-2030#:~:text=The%20NDP%20aims%20to%20eliminate,leadership%20and%20partnerships%20throughout%20society
3 Cassidy, T., Jones, R. & Potrac, P. 2009. *Understanding Sports Coaching. The Social, Cultural and Pedagogical Foundations of Coaching Practice* (2nd ed.). London: Routledge.
4 South African Football Association (SAFA). 2023. Latest Coaching News. Available at: http://www.safa.net/coaching-education/

5. SASCOC, 2011.
6. SASCOC. 2020. *The South African Coaching Framework*. Johannesburg: SASCOC. Available at: https://sasca-pb.co.za/wp-content/uploads/2020/04/SACF-Book-1.pdff
7. SASCOC, 2011.
8. Ibid.
9. SASCOC. 2012a. *South African Model for long-term coach development*, p. 14. Available at: https://sasca-pb.co.za/wp-content/uploads/2020/04/SA-Long-Term-Coach-Development.pdf
10. Ibid.
11. Ibid.
12. SASCOC, 2012b.
13. SASCOC, 2011.
14. Edwards, L.C., Bryant, A.S., Keegan, R.J., Morgan, K. & Jones, A.M. 2017. Definitions, foundations and associations of physical literacy: a systematic review. *Sports Medicine*, 47: 113-126.
15. SASCOC, 2012b.
16. Kubayi, A., Coopoo, Y. & Morris-Eyton, H. 2017. Work-related constraints in sports coaching: Perceptions of South African female coaches. *International Journal of Sports Science & Coaching*, 12(1): 03-108.
17. Kubayi, et al., 2015a.
18. Kubayi, et al., 2015b.
19. Whitley, A., Gould, D., Missy Wright, E. & Hayden, L. 2018. Barriers to holistic coaching for positive youth development in South Africa. *Sports Coaching Review*, 7(2): 171-189.

Chapter 15

1. Sport New Zealand. 2014. *Roles of Officials*. Available at https://sportnz.org.nz/resources/roles-of-officials/#:~:text=A%20sports%20official%20must%20have,the%20responsibility%20without%20being%20overbeariNG
2. van Bokhorst, L.G., Knapová, L., Majoranc, K., Szebeni, Z.K., Táborský, A., Tomić, D. & Cañadas, E. 2016. It's Always the Judge's Fault: Attention, Emotion Recognition, and Expertise in Rhythmic Gymnastics Assessment. *National Library of Medicine, 7*: 1008. Doi: 10.3389/fpsyg.2016.01008.
3. Heiniger, S. and Mercier, H. 2021. Judging the judges: evaluating the accuracy and national bias of international gymnastics judes. *Journal of Quantitative Analysis in Sports*. Available at: https://doi.org/10.1515/jqas - 2019 - 0013.
4. Flessas, K., Mylonas, D., Panagiotaropoulou, G., Tsopani, D., Korda, A., Siettos, C., Di Cagno, A., Evdokimidis, I. & Smyrnis, N. 2015. Judging the judges' performance in rhythmic gymnastics. *Medicine & Science in Sports & Exercise, 47*(3): 640-648. Doi: 10.1249/MSS.0000000000000425.
5. Starkes, J.L. & Ericsson, K.A. 2003. *Expert Performance in Sports: Advances in Research on Sport Expertise*. Champaign, IL: Human Kinetics.
6. Sacchi, A. 2022. *Technology in Sport: Learn the benefits, Trends and 4 Examples*. Available at https://master.org.br/en/news/technology-sport/
7. International Chess Federation (FIDE). 2020. *FIDE Arbiters' Manual: Regulations for the Titles of Arbiters (B06)* (4th ed.). Lausanne: Fide Arbiters' Commission.
8. International Rugby Board. 2015. *Rugby Refereeing in Practice: A Guide for Rugby Referees* (2nd ed.). Dublin: publisher.
9. Sheehan, M. 2011. *Top-10 Technological Innovations in Sports*. Available at https://bleacherreport.com
10. Lakhotia, N.K. 2017. *Scoring in Cricket is a Technical Art*, p. 9. Available at https://cricketgraph.com
11. Spitz, J., Wagemans, J., Memmert, D., Williams, A.M. & Helsen, W.F. 2020. Video assistant referees (VAR): The impact of technology on decision-making in association soccer referees. *Journal of Sport Sciences, 39*: 147-143.
12. Masters Swimming Australia. 2008. *Technical Course Modules – Support Material*. 4.2.8 General Principles of Officiating Part A: Module 1 Self-Management Candidates Notes.
13. South African Sport Confederation and Olympic Committee. 2022. *Constitution of the South African Sports Confederation and Olympic Committee*. Johannesburg: Olympic House.

14. Department of Sport and Recreation. 1998. *National Sport and Recreation Act, 1998 amended 2007*. Government Gazette. RSA, Cape Town.
15. Department of Sport and Recreation. 2010. *Safety at Sport and Recreational Events Act, 2010*. Government Gazette. RSA, Cape Town.
16. Department of Sport and Recreation. 2011. *Sport and Recreation White Paper, 2011*.
17. International Weightlifting Federation. 2011. *Technical Official's Guidebook* (2nd ed.). Hungary: International Weightlifting Federation.
18. International Rugby Board, 2015.
19. Sport New Zealand, 2014: 1.
20. International Netball Federation. 2020. *Rules of Netball*. Salford UK: World Netball.
21. International Rugby Board, 2015.
22. Ibid.
23. International Olympic Committee (IOC). 2021. IOC Principles. Available at: https://olympics.com/ioc/principles#:~:text=The%20three%20values%20of%20Olympism,to%20building%20a%20better%20world.
24. Côté, J. & Gilbert, W. 2009. An Integrative definition of coaching effectiveness and expertise. *International Journal of Sports Science & Coaching*, 4(3): 307-323.
25. Munyai, O. 2022. S*AFA suspends referees and clubs for match-fixing*. Available at https://farpost.co.za/2022/10/25/safa-suspend-referees-and-clubs-for-match-fixing.

Chapter 16

1. FIFA. 2022. *Football Agent Regulations*. Available at: https://digitalhub.fifa.com/m/1e7b741fa0fae779/original/FIFA-Football-Agent-Regulations.pdf
2. SA Rugby. 2021. *The South African Rugby Player's Agents Regulations*. Available at: https://www.sarugby.co.za/media/ihwpfjmr/player-agent-regulations-dec21.pdf
3. World Rugby. 2023. *Regulations*. Available at: https://www.world.rugby/organisation/governance/regulations/reg-1
4. UCI. 2021. *Regulations.* Available at: https://www.uci.org/regulations/3MyLDDrwJCJJ0BGGOFzOat

Chapter 17

1. Department of Sport and Recreation. *South African Sports and Recreation Act 110 of 1998*. Available at https://www.gov.za/documents/national-sport-and-recreation-act
2. Cloete, R. 2011. *Introduction to Sports Law*. Durban: Lexis Nexus.
3. Hellriegel, D., Slocum, J.W., Jackson, S.E., Louw, L., Saude, G., Amos, T., Klopper, H.B., Louw, M., Oosthuizen, T., Perks, S. & Zindiye S. 2017. *Management*. Cape Town: Oxford University Press.
4. Demirtas, O. & Karaca, M.A. 2020. *Handbook of Leadership Styles*. New Castle: Cambridge Scholars Publishing.
5. Uslu, O. 2019. The general overview to leadership theories from a critical perspective. *Marketing and Management of Innovation, 1*(2019): 161-172. Available at https://www.researchgate.net/publication/332106314_General_Overview_to_Leadership_Theories_from_a_Critical_Perspective
6. Uslo, 2019.
7. Hollander, W. 2016. Sports leadership. In T.H. Veldsman & A.J. Johnson. 2016. *Leadership Perspectives from the front line*, pp. 249-260. Randburg: KR Publishing.
8. Ibid.
9. Indian Express. 2021. *ICC CEO Manu Sawhney resigns amid inquiry over conduct*. Available at: https://indianexpress.com/article/sports/cricket/icc-ceo-manu-sawhney-resigns-amid-inquiry-over-conduct-7395560/
10. Ko, C., Ma, J., Bartnik, R., Haney, M.H. & Kang, M. 2018. Ethical leadership: An integrative review and future research agenda. *Ethics & Behavior, 28*(2): 104-132..
11. Ibid.

12 Brenner, S.N. 1995. Stakeholder Theory of the Firm: Its Consistency with Current Management Techniques. In J. Näsi (ed.). *Understanding Stakeholder Thinking.* Helsinki: LSR-Julkaisut Oy, pp. 75-96.
13 Getz, D. 1997. *Event Management and Event Tourism.* New York, NY: Cognizant.
14 Ibid.
15 Koehn, N. 2022. Real leaders are forged in crises. *Harvard Business Review.* Available at https://hbr.org/2020/04/real-leaders-are-forged-in-crisis

Chapter 18

1 Mele, A. 1995. Motivation: Essentially Motivation-Constituting Attitudes. *The Philosophical Review,* 104(3): 387-423.
2 Hamilton, A. 2023. *Motivation in Sports Psychology.* Available at: https://www.sportsperformancebulletin.com/psychology/motivation-in-sports-psychology.
3 Kazdin, A.E. 2000. *Encyclopedia of Psychology.* Oxford: Oxford University Press.
4 Ryan, R.M. & Deci, E.L. 2000. Self-Determination Theory and the Facilitation of Intrinsic Motivation, Social Development, and Well-Being. *American Psychologist,* 55(1): 68-78.
5 Karageorghis, C. 2023. *Motivation in Sports Psychology: Coping with emotions.* Available at: https://www.sportsperformancebulletin.com/psychology/coping-with-emotions/motivation-in-sports-psychology.
6 Wasserman, T. & Wasserman, L. 2020. *Motivation, Effort, and the Neural Network Model.* Cham: Springer.
7 Pardee, R.L. 1990. *Motivation Theories of Maslow, Herzberg, McGregor & McClelland. A Literature Review of Selected Theories Dealing with Job Satisfaction and Motivation.* Washington, D.C.: ERIC Clearinghouse.
8 Crandall, A., Powell, E.A., Bradford, G.C., Magnusson, B.M., Hanson, C.L., Barnes, M.D., Lelinneth, M., Novilla, B. & Bean, R.A. 2020. Maslow's Hierarchy of Needs as a Framework for Understanding Adolescent Depressive Symptoms Over Time. *Journal of Child and Family Studies,* 29(2): 273-281.
9 Otundo, J.O. & Garn, A.C. 2020. Testing an Integrated Model of Interest Theory and Self-Determination Theory in University Physical Activity Classes. *The Physical Educator,* 70(3): 575-594.
10 Radel, R., Pjevac, D., Davranche, K., D'Arripe-Longueville, F., Colson, S.S., Lapole, T., et al. 2016. Does intrinsic motivation enhance motor cortex excitability? Intrinsic motivation and corticospinal excitability. *Psychophysiology,* 53(11): 1732-1738.
11 Ryan & Deci, 2000.
12 Ibid.
13 Dewani, V. 2013. *Motivation.* Available at: https://www.slideshare.net/vijaydewani7/motivation-15959567
14 Cherry, K. 2022. *What Is Self-Determination Theory?* Available at: https://www.verywellmind.com/what-is-self-determination-theory-2795387.
15 Crandall, Powell, Bradford, Magnusson, Hanson, Barnes, Lelinneth, Novilla & Bean, 2020.
16 Cherry, 2022.
17 University of Rochester Medical Center. 2023. *Our Approach: Self-Determination Theory.* Available at: https://www.urmc.rochester.edu/community-health/patient-care/self-determination-theory
18 University of North Carolina at Chapel Hill. 2023. *Motivation.* Available at: https://learningcenter.unc.edu/tips-and-tools/motivation/
19 Bar-Eli, M., Tenenbaum, G., Pie, JS., Btesh, Y. & Almog, A. 1997. Effect of goal difficulty, goal specificity and duration of practice time intervals on muscular endurance performance. *Journal of Sports Sciences,* 15(2): 125-135.
20 Davis, W. E., Kelley, N. J., Kim, J., Tang, D. & Hicks, J. A. 2016. Motivating the academic mind: High-level construal of academic goals enhances goal meaningfulness, motivation, and self-concordance. *Motivation and Emotion,* 40(2): 193-202.
21 Steinmetz, L.L. 1983. *Nice Guys Finish Last: Management Myths and Reality.* Boulder: Horizon Publications.

Chapter 19

1. Larkin, M. & Thompson, A. 2011. Interpretative phenomenological analysis. In D.H. & A.R. Thompson (eds.). In *Qualitative Research Methods in Mental Health and Psychotherapy: A Guide for Students and Practitioners* (1st ed.). Hoboken, New Jersey: John Wiley & Sons, Ltd, pp. 99-116. https://doi.org/10.1002/9781119973249
2. Devers, K.J. & Frankel, R.M. 2000. Study design in qualitative research-2: Sampling and data collection strategies. *Education for Health*, 13(2): 263–271.
3. Ritchie, J., Lewis, J. & Elam, G. 2003. *Designing and selecting samples*. Thousand Oaks, CA: SAGE Publications.
4. Tracy, S.J. 2010. Qualitative quality: Eight "big-tent" criteria for excellent qualitative research. *Qualitative Inquiry*, 16(10): 837-851.
5. Denzin, N. & Lincoln, Y. 2011. *The Sage handbook of qualitative research*. Thousand Oaks, CA: SAGE Publications.
6. Smith, H.J., Chen, J. & Liu, X. 2008. Language and rigour in qualitative research. *BMC Medical Research Methodology*, 8(1): 44.
7. Pietkiewicz, I. Smith, J.A. 2014. A practical guide to using Interpretative Phenomenological Analysis in qualitative research psychology. *Social Sciences & Humanities*, 20(1): 7-14. https://doi.org/10.14691/CPPJ.20.1.7
8. Cushion, C. 2006. Mentoring : Harnessing the power of experience. In R.L. Jones (ed.). *The Sports Coach as Educator: Re-Conceptualising Sports Coaching* (1st ed.). London: Routledge.

Chapter 20

1. Mandela, N. 2000. *Speech by Nelson Mandela at the Inaugural Laureus Lifetime Achievement Award, Monaco 2000*. Monte Carlo, 25 May.
2. Mullin, J., Hardy, S. & Sutton, W. 2014. *Sport Marketing* (4th ed.). Champaign, IL: Human Kinetics, p. 50.
3. Ibid, 385.
4. Kotler, P., Saunders, J., Armstrong, G.J. & Wong, V. 1999. *Principles of Marketing* (2nd ed.). London: Prentice Hall, p. 106.
5. Ibid, 399.
6. Ibid, 434.
7. IEG. 2017. *IEG's guide to sponsorship*. Chicago: IEG, p. 5.
8. Shankly, B. 1981. *Quote by Bill Shankly in an interview on Granada TV's afternoon chat show*. Granada TV, UK.
9. Skildum-Reid, K. 2003-2015. Last Generation Sponsorship, p. 9. Available at: https://powersponsorship.com/sponsorship-white-papers-templates/ [Accessed 18 May 2023]
10. IEG, 2017.
11. Media Update. 2013. *Willowton Group claims gold at 2013 PRISM Awards*. Available at: https://mediaupdate.co.za/publicity/53055/willowton-grooup-claims-gold-at-2013-prism-awards
12. IEG, 2017.
13. Ogilvy South Africa. n.d. *SAB Carling Black Label Be the Coach Case Study*. Available at: https://vimeo.com/31145219
14. Meta. 2020. *#MarketingMasterminds: How Carling Black Label Changed the Game*. Available at: https://www.bizcommunity.com/Article/196/860/202342.html
15. IEG, 2017.
16. Ibid.
17. Skildum-Reid, 2023.
18. IEG, 2017.
19. Skildum-Reid, 2023.
20. Skildum-Reid, 2003-2015:5-6.

Chapter 21

1. Beech, J. & Chadwick, S. 2004. *The Business of Sport Management.* Harlow: Prentice Hall - Financial Times.
2. Fried, G., Shapiro, S. & DeSchriver, T. 2008. *Sport Finance* (2nd ed.). Champaign, IL: Human Kinetics.
3. Els, G., van Gaalen, R., Strydom, N.T. & Beekman, E. 2019. *Fundamentals of Finance* (7th ed.). Durban: Lexis Nexis.
4. Stewart, B. 2007. *Sport Funding and Finance.* Oxford: Butterworth-Heinemann.

Chapter 22

1. Russo, F. 2020. History and future of sport and public assembly facilities, in Fried, G. & Kastel, M. (eds.). *Managing Sports Facilities.* Illinois: Human Kinetics, pp. 3-36.
2. BibLlus, 2022. *What is sport facility management?* Available at: https://biblus.accasoftware.com/en/what-is-sport-facility-management/
3. Christiansen, B. 2023. Taking Sports Facility Management to the Next Level. Available at: from: https://limblecmms.com/blog/sports-facility-management/
4. Ainbinder, R. 2020. *Why we need Sports Facilities? Sports, Tech, Biz.* Available at: https://www.sportstechbiz.com/p/why-we-need-sports-facilities
5. Karikari, B. 2017. *Sports Stadiums Past and Present. Allsite structure rentals.* Available at: https://allsitestructures.com/history-sports-stadiums/
6. Cartwright, M. 2012. Stadium. *World History, Encyclopedia.* Available at: https://www.worldhistory.org/Stadium/
7. Ward, C. 2019. *Circus Maximus – Rome's Original Stadium.* Available at: from: https://www.sightseeingtoursitaly.com/tips-articles/circus-maximus-romes-original-stadium/
8. Upton, E. 2013. *While the Roman Colosseum is more famous today, its predecessor, the Circus Maximus, could hold about 3 to 6 times more people.* Today I Find Out, Feed your brain. Available at: https://www.todayifoundout.com/index.php/2013/10/colosseum-wasnt-finished-80-ad-games-held-circus-maximus/
9. Kilbane, B. 2022. *Want to Visit a Bathhouse? Here's All You Need to Know.* Allure. Available at: https://www.allure.com/story/bathhouses-history-rules
10. The City of Bath World Heritage Site Management Plan. 2010. *Post Consultation Draft.* Available at: from https://democracy.bathnes.gov.uk/documents/s3084/World%20Heritage%20Site%20Draft%20Management%20Plan.pdf
11. Allé, H.D. 2022. History of rugby, DTU exiles rugby. Available at: https://exiles.dk/default.aspx
12. Nassar, E. 2021. *History of sport arenas from originality to modern arenas.* Issuu. Available at: https://issuu.com/elionassar/docs/ice_hockey_arena_milano_thesis_book_issuu.1/s/23617860
13. International Military Sports Council, 2023. *History of swimming.* CISM Europe. Available at: from https://www.cismeurope.org/history-swimming/
14. Rhodesia, B. 2022. *Swimming Pools in South Africa.* Available at: https://swimhistory.co.za/index.php/pools-and-places/swimming-pools
15. Shenoda, M. 2022. *History of New York City.* A TLTC blog. Available at: https://blogs.shu.edu/nyc-history/coney_island/
16. Gulliver, K. 2021. *The Evolution of Fun. City Journal.* Available at: https://www.city-journal.org/article/the-evolution-of-fun
17. Centerfield, M. 2016. *Brooklyn's First Ball Park: The Union Grounds (1862-1883).* Available at: http://www.centerfieldmaz.com/2016/02/brooklyns-first-ball-park-union-grounds.html
18. Goldberg-Strassler, J. 2014. *Fifth Third fire brings back memories of past ballpark blazes.* Available at: https://ballparkdigest.com/201401176982/minor-league-baseball/features/fifth-third-fire-brings-back-memories-of-past-ballpark-blazes
19. Gilbert, A. 2023. *Berlin Olympic Stadium. Encyclopaedia Britannica.* Available at: https://www.britannica.com/topic/Berlin-Olympic-Stadium

20 Zetlin, L. 2023. *Stadium*. Encyclopedia Britannica. Available at: https://www.britannica.com/technology/stadium

21 David, H. Tonja, J. & Sag, M. 2013. *League Structure & Stadium Rent Seeking the Antitrust Role Reconsidered*. Loyola University Chicago, School of Law. Available at: https://lawecommons.luc.edu/cgi/viewcontent.cgi?article=1205&context=facpubs

22 Trumpbour, R. 2023. *Astrodome (Houston, TX)*. Society for American football research. Retrieved June Retrieved June 30, 2023, from 30, 2023, from https://sabr.org/bioproj/park/astrodome-houston-tx/

23 Tikkanen, A. 2023. *Design innovations*. Encyclopedia Britannica. Retrieved June 30, 2023, from https://www.britannica.com/technology/stadium/Design-innovations

24 Fédération Internationale de Football Association (FIFA). 2015. *FIFA Quality Programme for Football Turf*. Retrieved June 30, 2023, from: https://www.uefa.com/MultimediaFiles/Download/uefaorg/Stadium&Security/02/54/11/96/2541196_DOWNLOAD.pdf

25 Jordan, A. 2010. *Artificial Pitches and Football: A History*. Retrieved June 30, 2023, from: https://bleacherreport.com/articles/449490-artificial-pitches-and-football-a-history

26 Rigg, D. 2019. Time to take a stand? The law on all-seated stadiums in England and Wales and the case for change. *International Sports Law Journal 18*, 210–218. Retrieved June 30, 2023, from: https://doi.org/10.1007/s40318-018-0136-9

27 Pote, B. 2023. *Ecological impact of a private pool*. Available at: https://bonpote.com/en/ecological-impact-of-an-private-pool/

28 Milica I., Miomir V., Dragan K., Vuk M. & Nikola C. 2014. *Sports facilities sustainable design*. In Engineering: integration of science and practice: proceedings of the international scientific conference. Moscow, Russia, 26-28 November, 2014 (p. 96).

29 Farmer, PJ., Mulrooney, AL. & Ammon Jr, R. 1996. *Sport Facility Planning and Management*. Sport Management Library. Fitness Information Technology, Incorporated.

30 SA-Venues.com, 2010. *South Africa 2010 Stadiums*. Available at: https://www.sa-venues.com/2010/2010-stadium.htm

31 The Stadium Guide, 2017. *FIFA World Cup 2010 Stadiums - South Africa*. Retrieved June 30, 2023, from https://www.stadiumguide.com/tournaments/fifa-world-cup-2010/

32 AECOM. 2023. *Cape Town Stadium: Cape Town, South Africa*. Available at: https://aecom.com/projects/cape-town-stadium/

33 Alegi, P. 2008. 'A Nation To Be Reckoned With.' The Politics of World Cup Stadium Construction in Cape Town and Durban, South Africa. *African Studies, 67*(3):397-422.

34 Farmer, Mulrooney & Ammon, 1996.

35 Ibid.

36 Schwarz, E. C., Hall, S. A. & Shibli, S. 2015. *Sport facility operations management: A global perspective*. Routledge, p.53.

37 Lyberger, M., Yim, B. H. & Mccarthy, L. M. 2020. Sport Facility Feasibility Study: Assessment, Value and Demand. *Asia Pacific Journal of Applied Sport Sciences, 1*(1), 35-51.

38 Ngxongo, N.A. & Chili, N.S. 2018. The strategic marketing analysis of Moses Mabhida stadium as a major tourism destination in Kwazulu-Natal: an action research. *African Journal of Hospitality, Tourism & Leisure, 7*(8), 1-21.

39 City of Cape Town. 2012. *Business plan for Cape Town Stadium and Green Point Park: A public information summary and report*. Cape Town: Tandym Print.

40 Ibid.

41 Schwarz, Hall & Shibli, 2015: 53.

42 Government of South Australia, 2018. *Recreation and Sport Facility Design Guide*. Retrieved June 30, 2023, from https://www.orsr.sa.gov.au/places-and-spaces/documents/FACILITY_DESIGN_GUIDE.pdf

43 USAShade. 2021. *What To Consider When Designing a Sports Complex? Tips for Designing Sports Complexes*. Retrieved June 30, 2023, from https://www.usa-shade.com/resources/articles/tips-for-designing-sports-complexes

44 Ibid.

45 Build Magazine. 2021. *What Climate Factors are Important Considerations for Building Projects?* Available at: https://www.build-review.com/what-climate-factors-are-important-considerations-for-building-projects/

46   Armacell. 2018. *Paralympic Training Center, São Paulo, Brazil: Armaflex Insulation Given Opportunity to Perform at New Brazilian Paralympic Centre in São Paulo*. Available at: https://www.armacell.us/resources/case-studies/paralympic-training-center-sao-paulo-brazil/
47   Giorgio, P., Reichheld, A., Deweese, C. & Ebb, S. 2018. *The Stadium Experience: Keeping sports fans engaged – and loyal*. Retrieved June 30, 2023, from https://www2.deloitte.com/content/dam/Deloitte/us/Documents/technology-media-telecommunications/us-tmt-stadium-experience-keeping-sports-fans-engaged-loyal.pdf
48   National Interscholastic Athletic Administrators Association. 2013. *NIAAA's guide to interscholastic athletic administration*. Champaign, IL: Human Kinetics.
49   Giorio et al., 2018.
50   DePauw, K.P. & Gavron, S.J. 2005. *Disability Sport*. Champaign, IL: Human Kinetics.
51   Fitri, M., Zainal Abidin, N.E., Novan, N.A, Kumalasari, I., Haris, F., Mulyana, B., Khoo, S. & Yaacob, N. 2022. Accessibility of Inclusive Sports Facilities for Training and Competition in Indonesia and Malaysia. *Sustainability, 14*(21), 14083. https://doi.org/10.3390/su142114083
52   The Stadium Guide, 2017.
53   Populous. 2023. *Soccer City*. https://populous.com/project/soccer-city
54   AECOM, 2023.
55   Cape Town Green Map. 2023. *Welcome to the Cape Town Green Map*. Available at: https://www.capetowngreenmap.co.za/
56   City of Cape Town, 2012.
57   AECOM, 2023.
58   Davids, 2018.
59   Jordana, S. 2010. *South Africa World Cup 2010: Moses Mabhida Stadium / gmp architekten*. Available at: https://www.archdaily.com/44595/south-africa-world-cup-2010-moses-mabhida-stadium-gmp-architekten
60   Davids, K. 2018. *Moses Mabhida Stadium. SA Stadiums*. Available at: https://sastadiums.com/moses-mabhida-stadium/
61   Wondemagnegn, A. & Zemikael, G. 2022. A Qualitative Report of Sport Facilities Management. *Study of Management, Economic and Business*. Vol 1(4): 134 – 138.
62   Schwarz, Hall & Shibli, 2015: 53
63   Ibid, 53
64   Schwarz, E.C., Westerbeek, H., Liu, D., Emery, P. & Turner, P. 2016. Managing sport facilities and major events (2nd Ed). Taylor & Francis.
65   Adiele, D. & Gundani, D.P.M. 2018. Assessing Management Practises of Sport Facilities and Equipment by the Municipality Council. *International Journal of Science and Healthcare Research*, 3(2): 44 – 49.
66   Adiele & Gundani, 2018.
67   Schwarz et al., 2016
68   Ibid.
69   Adiele & Gundani, 2018
70   Schwarz, E. C., Hall, S., & Shibli, S. 2010. *Sport Facilities Operation Management. A global perspective*. Oxford: Elsevier.
71   Ibid.
72   Ibid.
73   Martens, R. 2004. *Successful Coaching*. Third Edition. Champaign, IL. Human Kinetics, pp. 432–433.
74   Schwarz *et al.*, 2016.
75   Ibid.
76   Adiele & Gundani, 2018.
77   Schwarz, Hall & Shibli, 2015.
78   Ibid.
79   Ibid.
80   Adiele & Gundani, 2018.
81   Ibid.

Chapter 23

1. Fourie, W. 2013. *The development of a Track and Field Management Manual for local organising committees in South Africa.* Thesis (PhD). Central University of Technology, Free State, Bloemfontein, p. 1.
2. Ibid, 1.
3. Fourie, W. 2008. *The development of a Track and Field Management framework for local organizing committees in South Africa.* Thesis (M Ed). Central University of Technology, Free State, Bloemfontein, p. 2.
4. Fourie, 2013:3.
5. Watt, D.C. 1998. *Event Management in Leisure and Tourism.* London: Addison Wesley Longman Ltd, p. 8.
6. Covey, S.R. 1999. *First Things First.* London: Simon & Schuster, p. 36.
7. Horine, L. & Sotlar, D. 2004. *Administration of Physical Education and Sport Programs.* New York: McGraw-Hill, p. 16.
8. Botha, L. 2000. *Kruger reg vir bestes: Afrika-rekord met diskus (Kruger ready for the best: African record with discus).* Volksblad, 16 September, p. 14.
9. Capriello, A. & Rotterham, I.D. 2011. Building a preliminary model of Event Management for rural communities. *Journal of Hospitality Marketing & Management*, 20(3/4), p. 246.
10. Senge, P.M. (ed.). 1994. *The Fifth Discipline Field Book: Strategies and Tools for Building a Learning Organization.* London: Nicholas Brealey Publishing, p. 90.
11. Watt, D.C. 2003. *Sports Management and Administration* (2nd ed.). London: Routledge.
12. Goldblatt, J.J. 2002. *Special Events* (3rd ed.). New York: John Wiley & Sons.
13. Shone, A. & Parry, B. 2001. *Successful Event Management: A Practical Handbook.* London: Continuum.
14. Fourie, 2013:28.
15. Ibid, 28.
16. Shone & Parry, 2001:256.
17. Fourie, 2013:28-29.
18. Watt 2003:4.
19. Fourie, 2013:28-56
20. Ibid, 71-111.
21. Ibid, 74-79.
22. Ibid, 76.
23. South African Government. 2010. Safety at Sports and Recreational Events Act 2 of 2010. Available at: https://www.gov.za/documents/safety-sports-and-recreational-events-act
24. Fourie, W. 2009. *Event Management: Planning framework for successful track and field events.* Köln, Germany: Lambert Academic Publishing AG & Co, pp. 75-76.
25. Lombaard, H. 1991. *Paalspringer kan Pilditch boikot (Pole vaulters can boycott Pilditch).* Beeld, 15 April, p. 14.
26. Fourie, 2013: 148.
27. Ibid, 33
28. Cooper, B., Sepotokele, T. & Rantoa, R. 2001. *Stampede horror.* Star, 12 April, p. 1-2.
29. Cape Argus Editorial. 2001. *Soccer's Day of tragedy.* Cape Argus, 12 April, p. 17
30. Sunday Times Editorial. 2001. *When will we learn our lesson?* Sunday Times, 15 April: p. 16
31. Fourie, 2009: 102.
32. Fourie, 2013:111; Fourie, 2009: 94-95.
33. To find the two Acts referred to in the chapter, go to https://www.gov.za Act 2 of 2010 & https://www.gov Act 57 of 2002.

Chapter 24

1. Jeanes, R. & Lindsey, I. 2014. Where's the "evidence"? Reflecting on monitoring and evaluation within sport-for-development. In K. Young and C. Okada (eds.). *Sport, Social Development and Peace*. Bingly, UK: Emerald Group Publishing.
2. Engelhardt, J. 2019. SDP, monitoring and evaluation. In H. Collison, S.C. Darnell, R. Giulianotti and P.D. Howe (eds.). *Routledge Handbook of Sport for Development and Peace* (pp. 128-140). London and New York: Routledge.
3. Ibid.
4. Burnett, C. 2022. Employability pathways in a sport-for-development programme for girls in a Sub-Saharan impoverished setting. *Journal of Physical Education and Sport*, 22(4): 863-869. Doi: 10.7752/jpes.2022.04109.
5. Schulenkorf, N., Sugden, J. & Sugden, J. 2016. Sport for conflict resolution and peace building. In AUTHORS *Managing Sport Development*. Oxon: Routledge, pp. 147-158.
6. Commonwealth Secretariat (ComSec). 2020. *'Sport and SDG Toolkit Version 4' and Indicator Bank*. Available at: https://thecommonwealth.org/sites/default/files/inline/Sport%20and%20SDG%20Cat1%20indicators%20%28v4.0%29.pdf
7. Department of Culture, Sport and Recreation, Mpumalanga. 2015. *DCSR: Monitoring and Evaluation Framework*. Available at: https://dcsr.mpg.gov.za/Policies/DCSR%20Monitoring%20and%20Evaluation%20Framework.pdf.
8. DCSR, 2015.
9. Hollander, W.J. 2015. Monitoring and evaluation as a management tool for programme effectiveness: "Just do it". *African Journal for Physical, Health Education, Recreation and Dance (AJPHERD)*, March 2015: 12-22
10. Burnett, C. & Hollander, W.J. 2007. The Sport-in-Development Assessment Tool (SDIAT). *African Journal for Physical, Health Education, Recreation and Dance (AJPHERD)*, 10 (2):1: 123-135.
11. Kay, T. 2009. Developing through sport: Evidencing sport impacts on young people. *Sport in Society*, 12(9): 1177-1191. Doi: 10.1080/17430430903137837.
12. Martinek, T. 2017. Enhancing youth development programs through logic model assessment. [Aumentar los programas de desarrollo juvenil a través de la evaluación del modelo lógico]. *RICYDE. Revista Internacional de Ciencias del Deporte*, 13(49): 302-316. Doi: 10.5232/ricyde.
13. Burnett & Hollander, 2007
14. Kay, T. 2012. Accounting for legacy: Monitoring and evaluation in sport in development relationships. *Sport in Society*, 15(6): 888-904. Doi: 10.1080/17430437.2012.708289.
15. Popp, J., Grüne, E., Carl, J., Semrau, J. & Pfeifer, K. 2021. Co-creating physical activity interventions: A mixed methods evaluation approach. *Health Research Policy and Systems*, 19(1): 1-9. Doi: 10.1186/s12961-021-00699-w.
16. Cloete, F., Rabie, B. & De Coning, C. 2014. *Evaluation Management in South Africa and Africa*. Stellenbosch: Sun Media.
17. Blamey, A. & Mackenzie, M. 2007. Theories of change and realistic evaluation: peas in a pod or apples and oranges? *Evaluation*, 13(4): 439-55. Doi: 10.1177/1356389007082129.
18. Coalter, F., Theeboom, M., Taylor, J., Commers, T. & Derom, I. 2021. *Sport and Employability: A Monitoring and Evaluation Manual*. Brussels: Vrije University, Sport & Society.
19. Hollander, W. 2007. A facility audit for Siyadlala: A mass participation programme of Sport and Recreation South Africa. *African Journal for Physical, Health Education, Recreation and Dance (AJPHERD)*, Special Edition, June: 31-44.
20. Hollander, 2007.
21. Burnett & Hollander, 2007.
22. Devine, A., Carrol, A., Naivalu, S., Seru, S., Baker, C., Bayak-Bush, B. & Marella, M. 2017. They don't see my disability anymore–The outcomes of sport for development programmes in the lives of people in the Pacific. *Journal of Sport for Development*, 5(8): 4-18.
23. Burnett & Hollander, 2007.
24. ComSec, 2020.
25. Ibid.

26 Burnett, C. & Hollander, W.J. 2000. Pre-evaluation Report of the United Kingdom-South Africa Sports Initiative. In: L.O. Amusa, A.L. Toriola and M. Wekesa (eds.). *Proceedings of the Third Scientific Congress of the Africa 11 Association for Health, Physical Education, Recreation, Sport and Dance (AFAHPER-SD).* 11th – 15th September 1997, Nairobi, Kenya.

Chapter 25

1 Gaba, A.K. & Gaba, N. 2022. Entrepreneurial Activity and Economic Growth of BRICS Countries: Retrospect and Prospects. *The Journal of Entrepreneurship,* 31(2): pp. 402-424 doi: https://doi.org/10.1177/09713557221097160
2 OECD. 2022. South Africa. In *Financing SMEs and Entrepreneurs 2022: An OECD Scoreboard.* Paris: OECD Publishing. https://doi.org/10.1787/4bada6a3-en
3 Heere, B., van der Manden, P. & van Hemert, P. 2015. The South Africa World Cup: The ability of small and medium firms to profit from increased tourism surrounding mega-events. *Tourism Analysis,* 20: 39-52.
4 Schumpeter, J. 1911. *The Theory of Economic Development.* Cambridge: Harvard University Press.
5 Nikolaeva, I., Shikhovtsov, Y., Nikolaev, P. & Levchenko, A. 2020. *Entrepreneurship in the sports industry: Role in the country's economy.* London, European Publisher, pp. 1-1004.
6 Mothilall, K. 2012. *An analysis of opportunities and trends in the sport business industry with a focus on entrepreneurship and small, medium, micro enterprises,* Johannesburg: University of Johannesburg.
7 Stam, E. & van de Ven, A. 2019. Entrepreneurial ecosystem elements. *Small Business Economics,* 56: 809-832.
8 Tülüce, N.S. & Yurtkur, A.K. 2015. Term of Strategic Entrepreneurship and Schumpeter's Creative Destruction Theory. *Procedia - Social and Behavioral Sciences,* 207: 720-728.
9 Thomas, A. & Mueller, S. 2000. A case for comparative entrepreneurship: Assessing the relevance of culture. *Journal of International Business Studies,* 31(2): 287-299.
10 Hofstede Insights. 2023. *Country Comparison Tool.* Available at: https://www.hofstede-insights.com/country-comparison-tool?countries=south+africa#:~:text=Uncertainty%20Avoidance&text=South%20Africa%20scores%2049%20on%20this%20dimension%20and%20thus%20has,norm%20is%20more%20easily%20tolerated.
11 Kotze, C. 2020. *5 types of business enterprises in South Africa: A comprehensive guide.* Available at: https://www.gawieleroux.co.za/blog/5-types-business-enterprises-south-africa-comprehensive-guide#:~:text=A%20sole%20proprietorship%20is%20the,business%20enterprise%20in%20South%20Africa
12 Prince, S., Chapman, S. & Cassey, P. 2021. The definition of entrepreneurship: is it less complex than we think?. *International Journal of Entrepreneurial Behavior & Research,* 27(9): 26-47.
13 Ibid, 29.
14 Hull, D.L., Bosley, J.J. & Udell, G.G. 1980. Renewing the hunt for the Heffalump: Identifying potential entrepreneurs by personality characteristics. *Journal of Small Business Management (pre-1986),* 18: 11-18.
15 Knight, F. 1921. *Risk, Uncertainty and Profit.* New York: The Riverside Press Cambridge.
16 Brockhaus, R. 1980. Risk taking propensity of entrepreneurs. *Academy of Management Journal,* 23(3): 509-520.
17 Schumpeter, 1911.
18 Stam & van de Ven, 2019.
19 Ibid.
20 World Economic Forum. 2023. *Mapped: Unemployment Forecasts by Country in 2023.* Available at: https://www.weforum.org/agenda/2023/02/unemployment-forecast-work-country/.
21 Adspace Audio. 2022. *The essential role of SMEs in the economy.* Available at: https://www.news24.com/fin24/partnercontent/the-essential-role-of-smes-in-the-economy-20220510.
22 Herrington, M., Kew, J. & Kew, P. 2010. *Tracking Entrepreneurship in South Africa: A GEM perspective.* Cape Town: Graduate School of Business, University of Cape Town.
23 Ratten, V. 2011. Sport-based entrepreneurship: Towards a new theory of entrepreneurship and sport management. *International Entrepreneurship and Management Journal,* 7: 57-69.
24 Rahman, A. 2019. *What is 3DIMO? Sport tech start-up using AI to predict injuries when athletes train.* Available at: https://www.nsmedicaldevices.com/news/3dimo-startup-predict-injuries-athletes/

25 Saebi, T., Foss, N.J. & Linder, S. 2018. Social Entrepreneurship Research: Past Achievements and Future Promises. *Journal of Management,* 45(1): 70-95.
26 Nell, S. 2013. *Luyt leaves a sizeable legacy.* Available at: http://en.espn.co.uk/timeline/rugby/story/176434.html
27 English, C. 2017. Toward sport reform: hegemonic masculinity and reconceptualizing competition. *Journal of the Philosophy of Sport,* 44(2): 183-198.
28 Mcghee, S.T. 2012. *Masculinity, Sexuality, and Soccer: An Exploration of Three Grassroots Sport-for-Social-Change Organizations in South Africa.* PhD thesis, University of South Florida.
29 Martínez, C.N. & Bañón, A.R. 2023. The Business Creation Process and Latin American Entrepreneurs. *Latin American Research Review,* 58: 90-109.
30 Herrington, et al., 2010.
31 Jumping Kids. 2023. *Tokyo Paralympics A Triumph For IceXpress Progressive Prosthetics And Jumping Kids Associates.* Available at: https://www.jumpingkids.org.za/news/tokyo-paralympics-a-triumph-for-icexpress-progressive-prosthetics-and-jumping-kids-associates/
32 Rahman, 2019.
33 Dieffenbacher, S.F. 2022. *Value Creation Definition, Model, Principles, Importance & Steps.* Available at: https://digitalleadership.com/blog/value-creation/
34 Lackéus, M. 2018. "What is Value?" – A Framework for Analyzing and Facilitating Entrepreneurial Value Creation. *ÅRGANG,* 41(1): 10-28.

Chapter 26

1 Loland, S. 2002. Technology in sport: Three ideal-typical views and their implications. *European Journal of Sport Science,* 2(1): 1-11. doi: 10.1080/17461390200072105.
2 Cabrilo, S. & Dahms, S. 2018. How strategic knowledge management drives intellectual capital to superior innovation and market performance. *Journal of Knowledge Management,* 22(4): 621-648. doi: 10.1108/JKM-07-2017-0309.
3 UK Parliament. 2023. *The settler colonies: South Africa.* Available at: https://www.parliament.uk/about/living-heritage/evolutionofparliament/legislativescrutiny/parliament-and-empire/parliament-and-the-american-colonies-before-1765/the-settler-colonies-south-africa/
4 Vamplew, W. 2016. Sport, industry and industrial sport in Britain before 1914: review and revision. *Sport in Society,* 19(3): 340-355.
5 Mokyr, J. 1998. *The Second Industrial Revolution, 1870-1914.* Available at: https://faculty.wcas.northwestern.edu/jmokyr/castronovo.pdf [Accessed 24 March 2023].
6 Davis, N. 2016. *What is the fourth industrial revolution?* Available at: https://www.weforum.org/agenda/2016/01/what-is-the-fourth-industrial-revolution/
7 Cleophas, F. 2019. *The fourth industrial revolution and sport: why we need to be vigilant.* Available at: https://theconversation.com/the-fourth-industrial-revolution-and-sport-why-we-need-to-be-vigilant-110380
8 Marques, L. & Biscaia, M.S.P. 2019. Leisure and innovation: exploring boundaries. *World Leisure Journal,* 61(3): 162-169.
9 Kemp, S. 2022. *Digital 2022: South Africa.* Available at: https://datareportal.com/reports/digital-2022-south-africa
10 Statista. 2023. *Video Streaming (SVoD) - South Africa.* Available at: https://www.statista.com/outlook/dmo/digital-media/video-on-demand/video-streaming-svod/south-africa
11 WCPSC. n.d. *Innovation order of day for WC Cycling.* Available at: https://wcpsc.co.za/innovation-order-of-day-for-wc-cycling/
12 Ratten, V. 2020. Sport technology: A commentary. *The Journal of High Technology Management Research,* 31(1): 100383. doi: 10.1016/j.hitech.2020.100383.
13 Trabal, P. 2008. Resistance to technological innovation in elite sport. *International Review for the Sociology of Sport,* 43(3): 313-330.
14 BCW. 2022. *2022 International Sports Federations Social Media Ranking.* Lausanne: BCW Sports.
15 Chelladurai, P. & Kerwin, S. 2017. *Human Resource Management in Sport and Recreation* (3rd ed.). Champaign, IL: Human Kinetics.

16 Institute of Directors. 2023. *IoD identifies links between governance and innovation.* Available at: https://www.iod.com/news/governance/iod-identifies-links-between-governance-and-innovation/
17 Discovery. 2023. *Discovery teams up with Netball SA as Official Wellness Partner to the SPAR Proteas and announces Vitality's title sponsorship of the Netball World Cup 2023.* Available at: https://www.mynewsdesk.com/za/discovery-holdings-ltd/pressreleases/discovery-teams-up-with-netball-sa-as-official-wellness-partner-to-the-spar-proteas-and-announces-vitalitys-title-sponsorship-of-the-netball-world-cup-2023-3232680
18 Vodacom Bulls. 2023. *Bulls Rugby.* Available at: https://bullsrugby.co.za/vodacom-bulls-welcome-luno-to-the-capital/#:~:text=The%20Vodacom%20Bulls%20are%20happy,performance%20incentives%20for%20the%20team
19 Kaizer Chiefs Football Club. 2019. *Kaizer Chiefs and PinkCodrs join forces.* Available at: https://www.kaizerchiefs.com/news/kaizer-chiefs-pinkcodrs-join-forces
20 Makhanya, S. 2022. *Sporting enthusiasts will converge on the Amajuba District in Newcastle for the South African Local Government Association (Salga) games.* Available at: https://www.iol.co.za/dailynews/news/salga-empowers-youth-through-sport-0ad68af5-80c7-49ae-8e10-95ee2e7f2b77

Chapter 27

1 Nauright, J. 1998. *Sports, identities and cultures in South Africa.* London: Philip.
2 Booth, D. 1998. *The race game: Sport and politics in South Africa.* London: Frank Cass Publishers.
3 Ramsamy, S. (with E. Griffiths). 2004. *Reflections on a life in sport.* Cape Town: Greenhouse.
4 Desai, A. (Ed.). 2010. Introduction: Long run to freedom? In Ashwin Desai (ed). *Race to transform: Sport in post-Apartheid South Africa.* Pretoria: HSRC Press, pp. 1-13.
5 Nauright, 1998:157-8.
6 Gemmell, J. & Hamill, J. 2005. No-one in Dolly's class at present? In S. Wagg (ed.). *Cricket and national identity in the postcolonial age.* London: Routledge, pp. 48-74.
7 African National Congress (ANC). 2012. *Organizational renewal: Building the ANC as a movement of power.* Available at: http://www.anc.org.za/docs/discus/2012/organizational renewalf.pdf
8 ANC, 2012.
9 Stofile, M. 2004. *Minster of Sport and Recreation Speech.* Available at: www.info.gov.za/speeches/2004/04061511451004.htm
10 Mjo, O. 2019. Siya Kolisi catches heat on twitter after transformation comments. *Times Live,* Jan 8. Available at: https://www.timeslive.co.za/sport/rugby/2019-01-08-siya-kolisi-catches-heat-on-twitter-for-transformation-comments/
11 Vahed, G. 2020. Negotiating the (uncertain) corridors of power in post-Apartheid South African cricket. *South African Historical Journal,* 72(3): 495-519.
12 Desai, A. 2019. The race chase: The colour of cricket transformation in South Africa. *Africa Review* 11(2): 132. https://doi.org/10.1080/09744053.2019.1631079
13 Moonda, F. 2016. CSA confirms guideline on selection quota. *ESPN Cricinfo,* April 18. Available at: https://www.espncricinfo.com/story/_/id/21176431/csa-confirms-guideline-selection-quota.
14 Merrett, C., Tatz, C. & Adair, D. 2011. History and its racial legacies: Quotas in South African rugby and cricket. *Sport in Society,* 14(6): 754.
15 Moonda, F. 2020. Black lives matter: South African cricketers mull fresh expression for 3TC game. *Cricinfo,* July 8. Available at: https://www.espncricinfo.com/story/_/id/29429297/south-african-cricketers-mull-fresh-expression-3tc-game
16 Moonda, 2020.
17 Vahed, G. & Desai, A. 2021. Inside the cricket change room: Undressing whiteness in South Africa. *Journal of Contemporary African Studies,* 39(2): 199-213.
18 SA Cricket Magazine. 2017. P*rince slams quota critics.* Available at: https://www.sacricketmag.com/prince-slams-quota-critics/

19 Ephraim, A. 2020. Makhaya Ntini reveals his loneliness and isolation in Proteas team. *Eyewitness News*, July 17. Available at: https://ewn.co.za/2020/07/17/makhaya-ntini-shares-painful-experience-of-racism-in-cricket
20 Social Justice and Nation Building Project (SJN). 2021. *Independent enquiry into the causes, nature and extent of racial discrimination and lack of transformation in cricket structures since unification.* Pretoria: Cricket South Africa.
21 Gcwabe, O. 2020. Being black in South African cricket. *Cricket Fanatics Magazine*, June 4. Available at: https://cricketfanaticsmag.com/being-black-in-sa-cricket/
22 Sports and Recreation SA. 2020. *Sport and Recreation South Africa, EPG Comparative Sport Federation Transformation Status Dashboard*, p. 5. Available at: https://www.srsa.gov.za/sites/default/files/Transformation%20Status%20Report%20-%202016-2017%20EPG%20-FINAL.pdf
23 Sports and Recreation SA, 2020:5.

Chapter 28

1 United Nations (UN). 2020. *Hidden scars: how violence harms the mental health of children.* New York: United Nations Publications, p. 9.
2 United Nations (UN). 1989. *Human Rights: Convention on the Rights of the Child.* New York: United Nations Publications.
3 United Nations (UN). 2008. *United Nations Convention on the Rights of Persons with Disabilities Equality and Diversity (NCPRD).* New York: United Nations Publishers.
4 South African Government. 2016. *White Paper on the Rights of Persons with Disabilities.* Cape Town: Government Gazette.
5 Social Development Direct. 2016. *Beyond Sport Summit 2016: International Safeguarding Children in Sport Working Group: A Guide for Organizations who Work with Children.* London: International Safeguarding Children in Sport.
6 World Health Organization (WHO). 2012. *Violence against Children* (February 2012). New York: United Nations Foundation.
7 Hillis, S., Mercy, A., Amobi, A. & Kress, H. 2016. *Global prevalence of past-year violence against children: a systemic review and minimum estimates.* Washington, D.C.: World Health Organization.
8 World Health Organization (WHO). 2012. *Violence against children.* (July 2012). New York: United Nations Foundation.
9 Republic of South Africa. 2005. *Children's Act 38 of 2005 as amended by Children's Amendment Act 41 of 2007 and Amendment Act, 17 of 2022.* Cape Town: Government Gazette.
10 Müller, C. 2008. *Legal Issues in Managing a Business.* In L.J.R. van Rensburg (ed.). *Business Management: An Introduction* (2nd ed.). Pretoria. Van Schaik Publishers.
11 Republic of South Africa. 2005.
12 Republic of South Africa. 2002. *Disaster Management Act 57 of 2002.* Cape Town: Government Gazette.
13 Amendment of Directions issued in terms of regulation 4 (10) of the rules made under section 27 (2) of the Disaster Management Act 2002 (Act No 57 of 2002).
14 SASCOC. 2012. The South African Model for Long-Term Coaches Development (LTCD). Johannesburg: SASCOC House.
15 SASCA. 2019. The *Sports Coaching Charter.* Johannesburg: Sports Coaching South Africa.
16 International Olympic Commission (IOC). 2023. *Who we are.* Available at: IOC Athletes' Commission - Athlete365 - Who We Are (olympics.com)
17 Lewies, A. 2015. *Learner Guide. Child Safeguarding and Protection.* Johannesburg: SASCOC House.
18 Black, K. & D. Williamson. 2011. Designing Inclusive Physical Activities and Games. *Design for Sport Milton.* Park Oxfordshre: Routledge, pp. 212-213.
19 Ibid, 213.
20 Lewies, 2015.
21 SASCOC, 2011. *The South Africa Model for Long-Term Participant Development (LTPD).* Johannesburg: SASCOC House.

22 Lyle, J. & Cushion, C. 2017. *Sport Coaching Concepts*. 2nd Edition. New York: Routledge.
23 Ibid.
24 Roux, C.J. 2012. *Didactics in Sport: Netball.* Presentation for beginner coaches at Netball Coaching Indaba, Potchefstroom. University of Johannesburg.
25 Lyle & Cushion, 2017:79-92.
26 Meintjes, A.J. 2008. Establishment issues of the New Business. In L.J.R. van Rensburg (ed.). *Business Management: An Introduction* (2nd ed.). Pretoria. Van Schaik Publishers.
27 Roux, 2012.
28 Grey-Thompson, B.T. 2017. *Duty of Care in Sport: Independent Report to Government*. London: National Society for the Prevention of Cruelty to Children, Weston House, London EC2A 3NH. Incorporated by Royal Charter, p. 20.
29 Ibid, 20.
30 United Nations. (UN). 2006. *Vulnerable Groups Policy, Art 30.5. Policy Number (12399A) Revised and Approved: 04 December 2013 C24/12/13.* New York: United Nations Publishers.
31 World Health Organisation (WHO), 2012.
32 United Nations (UN), 1989.
33 United Nations (UN), 2006.
34 Maralack, D. 2016. *Enabling disabled participation in sport: Roadrunning.* PhD: School of Management Studies, University of Cape Town, South Africa.
35 Republic of South Africa, 2005.
36 Ibid.
37 Republic of South Africa. 2017. *Criminal Law (Sexual Offences and Related Matters) Amendment Act, 32 of 2007.* Cape Town: Government Gazette.

Chapter 29

1 Engelberg, T. & Skinner, J. 2016. Doping in Sport: Whose problem is it? *Sport Management Review*, 19(1): 1-5. https://doi.org/10.1016/j.smr.2015.12.001.
2 Ibid.
3 World Anti-Doping Agency. 2019. *2019 Annual Report: Towards a World of Clean Sport: Celebrating 20 Years of Progress in Anti-doping*. Available at: https://www.wada-ama.org/sites/default/files/resources/files/ar2019_single_08102020_digital.pdf
4 Backhouse, S., Whitaker, L., Patterson, L., Erickson, K. & McKenna, J. 2016. *Social Psychology of Doping in Sport: A Mixed Studies Narrative Synthesis*. Project Report. World Anti-Doping Agency, Montreal, Canada: Available at: https://eprints.leedsbeckett.ac.uk/id/eprint/3433/
5 Backhouse, S., Griffiths, C. & McKenna, J. 2017. Tackling doping in sport: a call to take action on the dopogenic environment. *British Journal of Sports Medicine*, 52: 1485-1486. https://doi.org/10.1136/bjsports-2016-097169
6 World Anti-Doping Agency. 2021. *World Anti-Doping Code 2021*. Available at: https://www.wada-ama.org/sites/default/files/resources/files/2021_wada_code.pdf
7 South African Institute for Drug-Free Sport (SAIDS). n.d. *About Us*. Available at: https://drugfreesport.org.za/about-us/
8 South African Institute for Drug-Free Sport. 2021. *Anti-Doping Rules*. Available at: https://drugfreesport.org.za/wp-content/uploads/2020/12/SAIDS-ANTI-DOPING-RULES-2021.pdf
9 Qvarfordt, A., Hoff, D., sa Bäckström, Å. & Ahmadi, N. 2019. *Performance Enhancement & Health, 7*(1-2). Available at: https://www.sciencedirect.com/science/article/pii/S2211266919300234
10 World Anti-Doping Annecy. 2021. *Anti-Doping Statistics*. Available from: https://www.wada-ama.org/en/data-research/anti-doping-statistics
11 World Anti-Doping Agency. 2019. *Anti-Doping Rule Violations (ADRVs) Report*, p. 31. Available at: https://www.wada-ama.org/sites/default/files/2022-01/2019_adrv_report_external_final_12_december_2021_0_0.pdf
12 de Hon, O., Kuipers, H. & van Bottenburg, M. 2015. Prevalence of Doping Use in Elite Sports: A Review of Numbers and Methods. *Sports Medicine,* 45: 57-69. https://doi.org/10.1007/s40279-014-0247-x

13 World Anti-Doping Agency (WADA), 2019.
14 South African Institute for Drug-Free Sport, 2021.
15 Van Wagoner, R.M., Eichner, A., Bhasin, S., Deuster, P.A. & Eichner, D. 2017. Chemical composition and labelling of substances marketed as selective androgen receptor modulators and sold via the internet. *Jama*, 318(20): 2004-2010. https://doi.org/10.1001/jama.2017.17069
16 Nolte, K., Steyn, B., Krüger, P. & Fletcher, L. 2014. Doping in sport: Attitudes, beliefs and knowledge of competitive high school athletes in Gauteng Province. *African Journal of Sports Medicine,* 26(3): 81-86. DOI: https://doi.org/10.7196/SAJSM.542.
17 Kisten, T. & Naidoo, R. 2019. The perspectives of amateur soccer players and their coaches on the use of performance enhancing substances. *Global Journal Health Science*, 11(7): 154-163. https://doi.org/10.5539/gjhs.v11n7p154.
18 Department: Government Communication and Information System. 2019. *South Africa Yearbook 2018/19: Sports and Recreation*. Available at: https://www.gcis.gov.za/sites/default/files/docs/resourcecentre/yearbook/yb1919-21-Sport-and-Recreation.pdf
19 Basic Education Department. 2022. *2021 School Realities*. Available at: https://www.education.gov.za/Portals/0/Documents/Reports/School%20Realities%202021.pdf?ver=2022-02-07-094832-243
20 SAIDS, 2021.
21 Ibid.
22 Ibid.
23 ADEL. n.d. *Welcome to ADEL!* Available at: https://adel.wada-ama.org/learn/external-ecommerce;view=none;redirectURL=
24 SA Institute for Drug-Free Sport. 2023. *Medication Check*. Available at: https://drugfreesport.org.za/online-medication-check/
25 Backhouse, et a., 2017.
26 UNESCO. n.d. *International Convention against Doping in Sport*. Available at: https://en.unesco.org/themes/sport-and-anti-doping/convention
27 Maughan, R., Burke, L., Dvorak, J., Larson-Meyer, D., Peeling, P., Phillips, S., Rawson, E., Walsh, N., Garthe, I., Geyer, H. & Meeusen, R. 2018. IOC consensus statement: dietary supplements and the high-performance athlete. *International Journal of Sport Nutrition and Exercise Metabolism*, 28(2): 104-125. https://doi.org/10.1123/ijsnem.2018-0020.
28 UNESCO, n.d.
29 Siddique, A., Siddique, O., Einstein, M., Urtasun-Sotil, E. & Ligato, S. 2020. Drug and herbal/dietary supplements-induced liver injury: A tertiary care center experience. *World Journal of Hepatology*, 12(5): 207-219. https://doi.org/10.4254/wjh.v12.i5.207.
30 Van Wagoner et al., 2017.
31 Gabriels, G., Lambert, M., Smith, P., Wiesner, L. & Hiss, D. 2015. Melamine contamination in nutritional supplements--Is it an alarm bell for the general consumer, athletes, and 'Weekend Warriors'? *Nutrition Journal*, 17(14): 69. https://doi.org/10.1186/s12937-015-0055-7
32 Ibid, 69.
33 Naidoo, K., Naidoo, R. & Bangalee, V. 2018. Regulating the South African sport supplement industry: 'Whey' overdue. *South African Medical Journal*, 27108(3): 166-167. https://doi.org/10.7196/SAMJ.2018.v108i3.12961
34 Harvard Health Publishing. 2022. *The hidden dangers of protein powders*. Available at: https://www.health.harvard.edu/staying-healthy/the-hidden-dangers-of-protein-powders
35 Ibid.
36 Naidoo et al., 2018.
37 Maughan et al., 2018.
38 Ibid.
39 Australian Institute of Sport (AIS). 2022. *Supplements and Sports Foods in High Performance Sport*. Available at: https://www.ais.gov.au/__data/assets/pdf_file/0014/1000841/Position-Statement-Supplements-and-Sports-Foods.pdf
40 Or, F., Yongioo, K., Simms, J. & Austin, B. 2019. Taking stock of dietary supplements' harmful effects on children, adolescents and young adults. *Journal of Adolescent Health, 65*(4), p. 455-461. https://doi.org/10.1016/j.jadohealth.2019.03.005.

41. Bingham, M., Borkan, M. & Quatromoni, P. 2015. Sports nutrition advice for adolescent athletes: A time to focus on food. *American Journal of Lifestyle Medicine*, 9(6): 398-402. https://doi.org/10.1177/1559827615598530.
42. Ibid.
43. World Anti-Doping Code, 2022.
44. LGC. n.d. *Every Batch. Tested*. Available at: https://sport.wetestyoutrust.com/
45. USADA. 2021. *Natural Products Derived from Plants and Animals*. Available at: https://www.usada.org/spirit-of-sport/natural-products-derived-plants-animals/
46. Substance Abuse and Mental Health Services Administration (SAMHSA). 2023. *Learn about Marijuana Risks*. Available at: https://www.samhsa.gov/marijuana
47. Mulungwa, C., Holtzhausen, L., Joubert, G. & Mofolo, N. 2018. Exploring the use of African traditional medicines and rituals in South African Professional football. *Indilinga – African Journal of Indigenous Knowledge Systems*, 17(2): 219-233.
48. Tsele-Tebakang, T. 2022. *Disclosure between patients and primary healthcare providers relating to herbal medicine use: A framework to develop a patient empowerment programme to avoid herb-drug intervention*. Unpublished doctoral thesis. University of Johannesburg, Auckland Park.
49. Ibid.
50. World Health Organisation. 2013. *WHO Traditional Medicine Strategy 2014-2023*. Available at: http://www.who.int/medicines/publications/traditional/trm_strategy14_23/en/
51. Mulungwa et al., 2018.
52. Ibid.
53. Backhouse et al., 2017.

Chapter 30

1. Segaert, B., Theeboom, M., Timmerman, C. & Vanreusel, B. (eds.). 2012. *Sports governance, development and corporate responsibility*. New York/London: Routledge.
2. Malagila, J.K., Zalata, A.M., Ntim, C.G. & Elamer, A.A. 2021. Corporate governance and performance in sports organisations: The case of UK premier leagues. *International Journal of Finance & Economics*, 26(2): 2517-2537.
3. Burger, S. 2004. *Compliance with best practice governance systems by National Sports Federations of South Africa* (Unpublished Doctoral dissertation). University of Pretoria.
4. Ibid.
5. Institute of Directors in Southern Africa. 2002. *King II: Report on Corporate Governance for South Africa 2002*. Available at: https://cdn.ymaws.com/www.iodsa.co.za/resource/collection/94445006-4F18-4335-B7FB-7F5A8B23FB3F/IoDSA_King_II_web_version.pdf
6. Kilmister, T. 1999. *Governing Sport: The Role of the Board and CEO*. Belconnen: Australian Sports Commission.
7. Governance in Sport Working Group. 2001. *"The Rules of the Game": Europe's first conference on the Governance of Sport* (Brussels, 26 & 27 February 2001). Available at: https://www.fia.com/sites/default/files/basicpage/file/governance_sport.pdf
8. Hoye, R. 2017. Sport governance. In R. Hoye and M.M. Parent (eds.). *Handbook of Sport Management*. London: Sage, pp. 9-23.
9. Zulman Commission. 2018. *Final Report of The Ministerial Committee Appointed to Investigate Alleged Irregularities or Malpractices in the Governance and Management of the South African Sports Confederation and Olympic Committee (SASCOC)*. Available at: https://static.pmg.org.za/190212SASCOCReport.pdf
10. Australian Sports Commission. 2015. *Mandatory Sports Governance Principles: June 2015*. Available at: https://www.clearinghouseforsport.gov.au/__data/assets/pdf_file/0011/867692/Mandatory_Sports_Governance_Principles_June_2015.pdf
11. Geeraert, A. 2018. *National Sports Governance Observer. Indicators and instructions for assessing good governance in national sports federations*. Aarhus: Play the Game / Danish Institute for Sports Studies.
12. Chappelet, J.L. & Mrkonjic, M. 2019. Assessing sport governance principles and indicators. In Mathieu Winand & Christos Anagnostopoulos. *Research Handbook on Sport Governance*. Cheltenham, UK: Edward Elgar Publishing, pp. 10-28.

13   Zulman Commission, 2018.
14   Geeraert, 2018.
15   Zulman Commission, 2018.
16   Burger, 2004.
17   International Olympic Committee (IOC). 2020. *IOC governance model to ensure integrity.* Available at: https://olympics.com/ioc/integrity/ioc-governance-model-to-ensure-organisational-integrity#:~:text=The%20IOC%20Risk%20and%20Assurance,of%20its%20missions%20and%20objectives.
18   Ibid.
19   United Nations Educational, Scientific and Cultural Organisation (UNESCO). 2013. *Declaration of Berlin.* Available at: https://unesdoc.unesco.org/ark:/48223/pf0000221114
20   Ibid.
21   Institute of Directors in Southern Africa. 2016. *King IV: Report on Corporate Governance for South Africa 2016.* Available at: https://cdn.ymaws.com/www.iodsa.co.za/resource/collection/684B68A7-B768-465C-8214-E3A007F15A5A/IoDSA_King_IV_Report_-_WebVersion.pdf
22   Institute of Directors in Southern Africa, 2002.
23   Parent, M.M. & Hoye, R. 2018. The impact of governance principles on sport organisations' governance practices and performance: A systematic review. *Cogent Social Sciences*, 4(1): 1-24.
24   SASCOC. 2022. *SASCOC Constitution.* Available at: https://www.teamsa.co.za/constitution/
25   Schwab, B. 2021. *Embedding athlete rights - not censorship and scripting - the only way forward for the Olympic Movement.* Available at: https://www.insidethegames.biz/articles/1107314/brendan-schwab-guest-blog
26   SASCOC. 2019. *Safeguarding policy against harassment and abuse in all sport.* Available at: https://www.teamsa.co.za/wp-content/uploads/2021/03/SAFEGUARDING-POLICY-SOUTH-AFRICAN-SPORTS-CONFEDERATION-AND-OLYMPIC-COMMITTEE-Final.pdf
27   Theunissen, G. 2020. *The rise of doping in SA sports.* Available at: https://www.businesslive.co.za/fm/features/2020-02-27-bad-medicine/#:~:text=There%20is%20a%20burgeoning%20culture,a%20poorly%20regulated%20supplements%20sector&text=As%20South%20Africans%20bask%20in,a%20reputation%20for%20sports%20doping.
28   Shilbury, D. & Ferkins, L. 2011. Professionalisation, sport governance and strategic capability. *Managing Leisure*, 16(2): 108-127.
29   Parent, M.M., Naraine, M.L. & Hoye, R. 2018. A new era for governance structures and processes in Canadian national sport organizations. *Journal of Sport Management*, 32(6): 555-566.
30   Parent, M.M., Hoye, R., Taks, M., Thompson, A., Naraine, M.L., Lachance, E.L. & Séguin, B. 2021. National sport organization governance design archetypes for the twenty-first century. *European Sport Management Quarterly*, (1)21: p. 1115-1135.
31   McLeod, J., Star, S. & Shilbury, D. 2021. Board composition in national sport federations: a comparative cross-country analysis of diversity and board size. *Managing Sport and Leisure*, 0(0): 1-18.
32   Chappelet, J.L. 2018. Beyond governance: The need to improve the regulation of international sport. *Sport in Society*, 21(5): 724–734
33   SASCOC, 2022.
34   Burger, S. & Goslin, A.E. 2005. Best practice governance principles in the sports industry: An overview. *South African Journal for Research in Sport, Physical Education and Recreation*, 27(2): 1-13.
35   Chappelet, 2018.

INDEX

A

activity indicators, 330
adapting and implementing processes for change, 401
adults at risk, 377
advance sport governance, 407
Advent Sport Entertainment and Media (ASEM), 110–111
Africa Electronic Sport Association (AESA), 348
African herbal and traditional medicines, 401
African National Congress (ANC), 12, 31, 353
African Paralympic Committee (APC), 93
African Sports Confederation of Disabled (ASCOD), 93
agency and sport agents, 208
agency cost, 277, 279
agency problem, 277, 279, 288–289
ambush marketing, 148–151, 156, 267
anti-doping, 67, 75, 96, 133, 141, 313–314, 374, 387–393, 395–397, 401–402, 408
anti-doping domain, 387, 391
anti-doping facility, 313–314
anti-doping rules, 133, 387–388, 390, 392–393, 408
anti-doping structures, 75
approaches to monitoring and evaluation, 323, 328–329, 334
athlete development, 67–75, 78, 117, 178, 187, 189–190, 249, 396, 401–402
athlete development support structures, 69–70
athlete exploitation and abuse, 133
athlete performance pathways, 67, 69, 74–75, 79
athlete practices in sport, 177, 182–183
athlete success, 182
Athlete Support Personnel (ASP), 390
athletes and abuse, 377
Athletics South Africa (ASA), 70, 125
attracting athletes, 179–180
audit of performance information, 323, 327, 334
Australian Sports Commission (ASC), 43
Average Age of Inventory (AAI), 281
Average Collection Period (ACP), 281

B

Balanced Scorecards (BSCs), 122
basketball, 36, 42, 50, 62, 85, 87–88, 90–91, 93, 95, 214, 294–295
Basketball South Africa (BSA), 214
best practices in sport governance, 136–137
Black Economic Empowerment (BEE), 355
Blue Bulls Rugby Union (BBRU), 349
board size, diversity and skills, 408
bonus scandal, 134
brand and communication, 228
branding and merchandising, 149
breakeven analysis as a budgeting tool, 286
Broadcasting Rights and Commercialisation, 131
build brand awareness and visibility, 269
build brand stature, salience and image, 269–270

C

Cannabis (Marijuana or 'Dagga'), 400
career advancement, 250
cash conversion cycle, 277, 281–282, 289
challenges coaches face, 190
challenges in the high-performance phase, 67, 77, 79
challenges with performance pathways, 75
changeroom, 359
characteristics of a sport agent, 209
Children of the Dawn (COTD), 51
civil liability, 139, 153
classification of athletes with intellectual impairment, 99
club or other affiliation, 146
coach education and development, 74
coaches' attitudes and behaviours, 375
coaches' practices, 185
coaches' responsibilities towards others, 373
coaches' responsibility towards self, 375
commercial aspects of sport, 148
commercial rights matrix, 264
Commonwealth Games Associations (CGAs), 102
Commonwealth Games Federation (CGF), 30
Communist Party (CP), 31
community-based entrepreneurship, 340
competition director, 192, 194, 201–202
Comrades Marathon Association (CMA), 268
Confederation of African Deaf Sports (CADS), 88
contemporary issues and the management of sport, 335
corporate entrepreneurship, 340
Corporate Governance, 127, 406
corridors of uncertainty, 353
corruption and bribery, 132
cost classification for budgeting purposes, 285
cost of capital, 283–284, 288–290
cricket and managing, 353
Cricket South Africa, 106–107, 116, 118, 125, 134, 221, 224–225, 261, 267, 356, 358, 406, 408

Cricket South Africa (CSA), 106–107, 116, 118, 125, 134, 221, 225, 261, 267, 342, 406
criminal law, 365, 385
crisis management, 219, 227, 339
Critical Success Factors (CSFs), 121
current and future sport governance, 407
cycling, 14, 86, 88, 90, 93, 95, 216, 296, 347–349, 390

D

data and information collection instruments, 331
data capturing, validation and management, 329, 332, 334
data collection, 51, 329, 332, 334
data interpretation, 329, 333–334
dealing with abuse, 363, 381, 385
decision-makers, 81, 408
deficit perspective, 48, 52
definition of governance in sport, 126
delivery of contractual rights, 266, 274
democratic elections and impact on sport governance, 31
Department of Basic Education (DBE), 38–39
Department of Sport, Arts and Culture (DSAC), 34, 69
Department of Sport and Recreation (DSR), 23, 92
developing athletes, 77, 91, 177–179, 181, 188
dietary supplements, 389, 391, 397–398, 401
dietary supplements and high-performance athletes, 398
differences in sport for persons with disability, 95
disability in sport, 84
Disability inclusion, 369, 379
disability sport, 81, 83–84, 86, 88–89, 91–94, 101–103
Disability Sport South Africa (DISSA), 89, 91
disaster management, 142, 312, 316, 366, 385
disciplinary hearings, 146–147
discrimination, 30, 33, 46, 83, 131, 133, 135, 137, 141, 143, 371, 375, 377–378
diverse coaching and training plans, 75–76
divisional design, 110–111
doping in sport, 133, 141, 387–390
drive brand loyalty, 269–270
drug use and anti-doping, 133
duties and responsibilities of sport agents, 212

E

education and training sector, 26
effective sport leadership, 224
eligible impairment types and description, 97
elite athlete development, resources and support, 178
embracing failure, 240
emergency vehicles and areas, 317
emerging sports technologies, 133
Eminent Persons Group (EPG), 360
empowering mentorship, 243, 246, 257
entrepreneurship ecosystem, 336, 339, 344
entrepreneurship in sport, 336–338
Esports Entertainment Association (ESEA), 348
ethical considerations in mentorship, 255
ethical issues and challenges in sport governance, 132
ethical leadership, 225, 406
ethics and morality, 225, 388
ethnic entrepreneurship, 340
event and facilities management, 226
event management, 16, 26, 159, 227, 286, 301, 303, 305–307, 321–322
event planning and management, 305
events and facility sector, 26
evidence and knowledge production, 49
evolution of sport facilities, 291–292
experiential learning, 248
extrinsic motivators, 232–234

F

facilities and equipment, 25, 62, 107, 119, 221, 301, 327, 330, 379
facilities for elite athletes, 74
facility design, 299
facility feasibility, 297–298
facility forecasting, 297
facility planning, 291, 296, 298
Fédération Internationale de Football Association (FIFA), 212, 260, 267, 294
Fédération Internationale de Natation (FINA), 133
figurative or process theory, 2, 8, 10
financial management, 125–126, 136–137, 277–280, 287–288, 301–303, 406
financial statement analysis, 286
financial support to build the right infrastructure, 74
fitness and health sector, 27
flexibility and adaptability, 254
food and beverages, 316
formal preventative measures, 175
foundation of planning an event, 307
four-pillar foundation, 307
frameworks of analysis, 118, 123
functional design, 109, 111
functional theory, 3–5, 9–10, 14

future generation athletes and coaches, 256
future of sport governance, 403

G

gambling and match-fixing, 143
goal of financial management, 278
good governance in sport, 125–126, 403
governance in sport, 33, 125–126, 138, 403, 407
governance innovation, 350
governance of technical officials, 195
governance structures, 29, 33–34, 36–37, 39, 67, 125, 129, 131, 136, 138, 409
grassroots sports development, 261
Gymnastics South Africa (GSA), 105

H

High Performance (HP), 107
historical perspective, 4, 8, 11, 19, 84
history of classification, 96
homoeopathic and herbal medicines, 400
Hout Bay United FC (HBUFC), 51
human resource management process, 177, 179, 183
human resource practices, 157, 182–183
human resources and athlete management process, 179–180
human resources planning phase, 180

I

impact assessment, 49, 323–324, 326, 329, 331, 334
impact indicators, 331
imperative through volunteerism, 173
inadequate support system, 76
inadvertent doping, 396–397, 401–402
inclusivity and diversity, 126–127, 136
increased scrutiny and accountability, 130
Indian Premier League (IPL), 134, 275, 342, 354
Influence of Global Sporting Events on Governance, 130
Infrastructure Development and Governance Reforms, 131
institutional entrepreneurship, 340
integrity in sport, 139, 143
interaction with the victim, 382
Internal Structure of Motorsport, 110
International Amateur Athletics Federation (IAAF), 30
international and South African properties and their rights holders, 267
International Cricket Council (ICC), 13, 36, 125, 267

International Day of Sport for Development and Peace (IDSDP), 46
international entrepreneurship, 341
International Olympic Committee (IOC), 30, 36, 42, 84, 130, 201, 267, 354
International Paralympic Committee (IPC), 85
international reputation, 31, 131
International Sports Organisation of Disabled (ISOD), 85
International Standard for Education (ISE), 396
International Standard for Results Management (ISRM), 395
International Standard for Therapeutic Use Exemptions (ISTUE), 395
International Standard Prohibited List, 394
International Standards, 388–389, 394
International Stoke Mandeville Wheelchair Sports Federation (ISMWSF), 85
international training centres, 74
International Year of Sport and Physical Education (IYSPE), 45
interpersonal compatibility and coordination, 65
interpersonal constraints, 64–65
intrinsic motivators, 233
investment decisions, 280
inviting volunteers, 171
IOC Governance Model, 405
IOCs Risk and Assurance Governance Model, 406

J

Joint Operation Centre (JOC), 319
Judges, Referees, Umpires and Arbiters, 192
Judo South Africa (JSA), 116

K

Kazan Action Plan (KAP), 46
key components of strategy, 115
key focus areas, 93, 365
Key Performance Indicators (KPIs), 122
Key Result Indicators (KRIs), 121
King Corporate Governance Principles, 406
King IV™ Report on Corporate Governance, 127
Knowledge-Based Economy (KBE), 349

L

leadership in other sporting structures, 221
leadership in sport, 219–220
leadership positions/structures in sport, 220

leadership power, 221, 224
leadership power and styles, 221
leadership styles, 219, 221–224, 229
leadership theories, 223
legacy and sustainability, 131
legacy planning, 131, 299
legal responsibility, 363, 365, 370, 374, 379, 381
legislative and regulatory framework, 363, 365, 384
legislative governance framework, 32
leisure constraints, 55, 64–66
Lesbian, Gay, Bisexual and Transgender (LGBT), 378, 384
lifelong learning process, 250
Local Organising Committee (LOC), 308, 320
Long-Term Athlete Development (LTAD), 69
long-term athlete development framework, 70, 72
long-term coach development, 187–188
Long-Term Coach Development (LTCD), 187
Long-term coach development model, 187
Long-Term Participant Development (LTPD), 188

M

macro, meso and micro levels of sport governance, 35
macro-environment of sport, 117, 119
mainstream sport, 348–349
management of sport, 3–4, 7–8, 11–12, 19, 55, 104–106, 121, 123, 291, 301, 306, 335–336
manager of sport, 8–10
managerial and management innovation, 349
managerial context of sport, 1
managing the transition, 355
manipulation, 7, 9, 12–14, 96, 394
market (meso-level) environment of sport, 117
marketing and promotion, 163, 302
match-fixing, 118, 132, 137, 139, 143, 145, 156, 204, 347, 404
match-fixing and betting, 132
matrix design, 111–112
Medals won by South Africa at Paralympic Games, 94
media accreditation, 135
media involvement, 318
media rights, 110, 112, 148, 151, 225
medical care, 82, 315, 373
Member Protection Regulation (MPR), 381
Members Council (MC), 135
Memorandum of Understanding (MoU), 39
mentorship in advancing coaching, 245, 248
mentorship in coach development, 244
mentorship in sport, 243
mentorship programmes, 225, 243, 246, 248, 250, 252, 256

meso-level of sport governance, 36
micro-environment in sport, 118
micro-level of sport governance, 37
Ministerial Task Team (MTT), 32, 36
monitoring, evaluation and impact assessment in sport, 323
monitoring and evaluation process, 324, 329, 334
motivation in sport, 231
Motorsport South Africa (MSA), 109
Mzansi Super League (MSL), 135

N

national and provincial legislative governance, 32
National Football League (NFL), 155, 259
National Lotteries Commission (NLC), 108
National Olympic Committee of South Africa (NOCSA), 23
National Olympic Committee (NOC), 102
national paralympic committee, 89, 91
National Paralympic Committee (NPC), 91
National Paralympic Committee of South Africa (NAPCOSA), 89
National Party (NP), 30
National Qualifications Framework (NQF), 26
National Sport and Recreation Act, 32, 34, 140, 196, 385
National Sports Council (NSC), 23, 34
National Sports Federations (NSFs), 34
needs analysis for different sports codes, 74
needs of your athletes and spectators, 299
negotiation model, 65
Netball South Africa (NSA), 24, 116, 125, 268, 350
netball world cup, 24, 26, 159, 168–169, 275
network design, 112–113
nurturing and maintaining motivation, 236

O

olympic gold, 231–233, 237–241, 341
olympic gold medal, 232, 238–239
operating and cash conversion cycles, 282
operational management of sport facilities, 291, 301
organisation theory, 106, 108, 123
organisational structures in sport, 105, 109
overcoming mental barriers, 240
over-the-counter medicines, 400

P

Pacific Netball Partnership (PNP), 48

Pan African Congress (PAC), 31
parent-coach teamwork, 376, 378–379
partnerships and collaboration, 74
penalties for athlete support personnel, 394
performance indicators, 121–122, 324–326, 329
performance measurement, 121, 123
performance pathway theoretical framework, 68
perspectives on disability, 81
phases of SDP at the global level, 45
policy and regulatory reforms, 131
Political, Economic, Social, Technological, Environmental and Legal (PESTEL), 119
political leadership in sport, 220
post-olympic gold, 241
potential mentors/mentees, 252
power of motivation, 231, 240
power-interest matrix, 120
Premier Soccer League (PSL), 260, 268
Presidential Employment Stimulus (PES), 51
principal and agent relationship, 208
principles of entrepreneurship, 336, 339, 341, 344
professional team management, 228
property's strategic marketing plan, 261, 274
provincial and club leadership, 220
Provincial sport organisations, 195, 220

Q

qualification standards and expectations, 75–76
qualifications of sport agents, 211
quality performance indicators, 329

R

race and class apartheid, 358
race to transform, 353
racial categories for new times, 356
rationale for increasing participation in sport, 326
Reconstruction and Development Programme (RDP), 12, 355
recreation and sport tourism sector, 26
recreational athletes, 396
recruitment, selection and promotion of technical officials, 200
regulating sport agents, 212–213
reporting procedures, 363, 365, 367–368, 383–385
reporting suspected abuse, 383
Resource Dependence Theory (RDT), 107
resourcing of athlete performance pathways, 74
results management agreements, 395
retaining athletes, 179, 181–182
rewarding volunteers, 169
rights of parents/guardians, 376
risk of supplements, 399
role of sponsorship, 268
role of the coach, 373, 375
role of the financial manager, 279–280
role players in safeguarding sport, 363, 367
roles, responsibilities and relationships, 372
roles and domains within which coaches operate, 187
Rugby, 4–6, 16–17, 24–25, 31, 38, 87, 116, 125, 215, 222, 267, 293, 337, 340–342, 348–349, 354–355, 391

S

SA Sports Association for Physically Disabled (SASAPD), 88
safeguarding and protection, 197, 363
safeguarding volunteers, 174
safety and risk management, 313
Safety at Sports and Recreation Events Act, 142
safety measures for sport, 369
safety requirements for sport organisations, 367
School Governing Bodies (SGBs), 39
school sport, 13, 22, 35, 38–39, 43, 94, 186, 195, 220, 356, 358
segments and sectors of the sport industry, 21–22, 28
self-confidence and improvement in coaching, 248
setbacks and failures in the motivational process, 231, 237
setting goals and staying focused, 238–239
sexual offences and related matters, 365, 381–382
signs of abuse, 373–374
skills for sport agents, 210
Soccer Football Association (SAFA), 12
social cohesion and crime reduction policy, 326
social justice and nation building, 135
social perspective on sport, 2, 11
social theories and sport, 3
social theories and value, 9
South African athlete development support structures, 69
South African Boxing Act, 143
South African Broadcasting Corporation (SABC), 306
South African Coaching Framework, 186
South African Council of Sports (SACOS), 12
South African Cricket Board of Control (SACBOC), 354
South African Cricket Union (SACU), 354
South African Cricketers Association (SACA), 135
South African Deaf Sports Federation (SADSF), 88

South African Health Products Regulatory Authority (SAHPRA), 400
South African Institute for Drug-free Sport (SAIDS), 141, 374
South African Institute for Drug-free Sport Act, 141
South African long-term athlete development framework, 70
South African National Olympic Committee (SANOC), 30
South African Qualifications Authority (SAQA), 27, 381
South African Rugby Players Association (SARPA), 215
South African Rugby Union (SARU), 24, 38, 116, 125, 177, 226, 261, 267, 342
South African Sport Confederation and Olympic Committee (SASCOC), 23, 27, 69, 108, 129, 185, 220
South African sport system, 190
South African Sports Association (SASA), 12
South African Sports Association for Severely Mentally Handicapped (SASASMH), 92
South African Sports Commission (SASC), 32
South African Student Sports Union (SASSU), 36
special needs children, 378-379
Special Olympics South Africa (SOSA), 51, 91
sponsors, 16-17, 23-25, 92-93, 101-102, 105-106, 117-118, 120-121, 133-134, 211-212, 225-226, 259-262, 264, 266-268, 270-273, 302, 308, 311-312, 330, 346-347, 403-404
sponsorship leverage, 272-274
sponsorship measurement, 259, 273-274
sponsorship sales, 264, 274
sport activities, 15, 58, 62, 66, 159, 292, 299, 371, 376
sport and gender, 408
Sport and Recreation South Africa (SRSA), 32, 36, 140, 168
sport and the law, 139
sport as a tool and social movement, 46
sport coaching charter, 381, 386
Sport Entertainment and Media, 110-111
sport facilities, 15, 25-26, 164, 221, 291-296, 299-301, 303, 354, 357
sport facilities today, 294
sport facility planning and design, 296
sport facility types, 295
sport finance, 277-278, 288
sport for development, 41-44, 46, 53, 340
Sport for Development and Peace (SDP), 41, 44
Sport for Social Change Network Africa (SSCNA), 51
Sport for the Intellectually Disabled South Africa (SIDSA), 91

sport governance, 31-37, 40, 125, 132-133, 136-138, 196, 403-405, 407, 409
sport governance changes, 33
sport governance structures, 33-34, 125, 138
sport independence, 86
sport industry, 11, 16, 21-28, 106, 277, 286, 337, 345-346, 403, 405, 409
sport injuries and prevention, 380
sport management environments, 116
sport marketing, 27-28, 259-260, 340
sport participation and performance segment, 23-25, 28
sport promotion segment, 22-23, 27-28
sport sciences support, 75, 179
sport stadiums in South Africa, 304
Sports Facility Feasibility study, 298
sports governing bodies, 129, 132, 134
sports responsibility of parents/guardians, 377
stakeholder analysis, 120
stakeholder management, 127, 130, 225, 229
stakeholder types, 49, 52
strategic management in sport, 114
strategic management of sport, 105, 121, 123
strategic sponsorship selection criteria, 271, 274
strategic sport management process, 114
substances of abuse, 395
successful mentor and mentee relationship, 243, 251, 257
support structures in South Africa, 69

T

talent identification structures, 75
team and athlete leadership, 221
TechBank's sponsorship leverage tactics, 274
technical officials, 30-31, 92, 107, 117-118, 191-193, 195-203, 205, 306, 313-316, 319-320, 330
technical officiating in sport, 191
technological innovation in sport, 345, 347
technology entrepreneurship, 341
technology integration, 303
Tennis, 86, 90, 93, 215, 295
touch judges and assistant referees, 193
touch vs. harassment, 378
toxic leadership, 219, 224-225, 229
transformation, 6-7, 29, 33, 35, 116-117, 121, 123, 141, 185, 188, 190, 224, 226, 353-354, 356-362
transparency, accountability and responsibility, 126
trends impacting the management of sport, 11
types of entrepreneurship, 336, 339

U

unequal power relations, 47
Union of European Football Associations (UEFA), 294
Union of Soviet Socialist Republics (USSR), 15
United Nations Educational, Scientific and Cultural Organisation (UNESCO), 406
United Nations Office for Sport for Development and Peace (UNOSDP), 42
University Sport South Africa (USSA), 36, 348
unregulated medicines and products, 397

V

Venue Operations Centre (VOC), 142
video assistant referee and digital technology, 194
volunteering and the 'youth trap', 48
volunteering functions, 163
volunteerism in sport, 158
volunteers, 15, 23, 35, 38, 48, 117, 120, 122, 158–175, 197–198, 349–350

W

whistleblower protection, 390
working capital management, 277, 280–281, 288–289
World Anti-Doping Agency (WADA), 133, 374, 387–388, 408
World Economic Forum (WEF), 339
World Health Organisation (WHO), 46, 81

Y

youth employment project, 51

www.ingramcontent.com/pod-product-compliance
Lightning Source LLC
Chambersburg PA
CBHW081413230426
43668CB00016B/2222